Geopolitics and Strategic Management in the Global Economy

Angelo Presenza
University of Molise, Italy

Lorn R. Sheehan
Dalhousie University, Canada

A volume in the Advances in Business Strategy
and Competitive Advantage (ABSCA) Book Series

Published in the United States of America by
> IGI Global
> Business Science Reference (an imprint of IGI Global)
> 701 E. Chocolate Avenue
> Hershey PA, USA 17033
> Tel: 717-533-8845
> Fax: 717-533-8661
> E-mail: cust@igi-global.com
> Web site: http://www.igi-global.com

Library of Congress Cataloging-in-Publication Data

Names: Presenza, Angelo, 1975- editor. | Sheehan, Lorn R., 1964- editor.
Title: Geopolitics and strategic management in the global economy / Angelo
  Presenza and Lorn R. Sheehan, editors.
Description: Hershey, PA : Business Science Reference, [2018] | Includes
  bibliographical references and index.
Identifiers: LCCN 2017008229| ISBN 9781522526735 (hardcover) | ISBN
  9781522526742 (ebook)
Subjects: LCSH: Strategic planning. | International business
  enterprises--Management.
Classification: LCC HD30.28 .G45 2018 | DDC 658.4/012--dc23 LC record available at https://lccn.loc.gov/2017008229

This book is published in the IGI Global book series Advances in Business Strategy and Competitive Advantage (ABSCA) (ISSN: 2327-3429; eISSN: 2327-3437)

British Cataloguing in Publication Data
A Cataloguing in Publication record for this book is available from the British Library.

For electronic access to this publication, please contact: eresources@igi-global.com.

Advances in Business Strategy and Competitive Advantage (ABSCA) Book Series

Patricia Ordóñez de Pablos
Universidad de Oviedo, Spain

ISSN:2327-3429
EISSN:2327-3437

MISSION

Business entities are constantly seeking new ways through which to gain advantage over their competitors and strengthen their position within the business environment. With competition at an all-time high due to technological advancements allowing for competition on a global scale, firms continue to seek new ways through which to improve and strengthen their business processes, procedures, and profitability.

The **Advances in Business Strategy and Competitive Advantage (ABSCA) Book Series** is a timely series responding to the high demand for state-of-the-art research on how business strategies are created, implemented and re-designed to meet the demands of globalized competitive markets. With a focus on local and global challenges, business opportunities and the needs of society, the **ABSCA** encourages scientific discourse on doing business and managing information technologies for the creation of sustainable competitive advantage.

COVERAGE

- Customer-Orientation Strategy
- Innovation Strategy
- Entrepreneurship & Innovation
- Value Chain
- Adaptive Enterprise
- Strategic alliances
- Business Models
- Competitive Strategy
- Strategy Performance Management
- Outsourcing

IGI Global is currently accepting manuscripts for publication within this series. To submit a proposal for a volume in this series, please contact our Acquisition Editors at Acquisitions@igi-global.com or visit: http://www.igi-global.com/publish/.

Titles in this Series

For a list of additional titles in this series, please visit: www.igi-global.com/book-series

Driving Agribusiness With Technology Innovations
Theodore Tarnanidis (University of Macedonia, Greece) Maro Vlachopoulou (University of Macedonia, Greece)
and Jason Papathanasiou (University of Macedonia, Greece)
Business Science Reference • copyright 2017 • 384pp • H/C (ISBN: 9781522521075) • US $205.00 (our price)

Transcontinental Strategies for Industrial Development and Economic Growth
Bryan Christiansen (PryMarke LLC, USA) and Gulsah Koc (Yildiz Technical University, Turkey)
Business Science Reference • copyright 2017 • 346pp • H/C (ISBN: 9781522521600) • US $205.00 (our price)

Risk Management Strategies in Public-Private Partnerships
Peter Adoko Obicci (POA-Kittim Consultants, Uganda)
Business Science Reference • copyright 2017 • 363pp • H/C (ISBN: 9781522525035) • US $215.00 (our price)

Handbook of Research on Small and Medium Enterprises in Developing Countries
Noor Hazlina Ahmad (Universiti Sains Malaysia, Malaysia) T. Ramayah (Universiti Sains Malaysia, Malaysia)
Hasliza Abdul Halim (Universiti Sains Malaysia, Malaysia) and Syed Abidur Rahman (Universiti Utara Malaysia,
Malaysia)
Business Science Reference • copyright 2017 • 479pp • H/C (ISBN: 9781522521655) • US $255.00 (our price)

Technology-Driven Productivity Improvements and the Future of Work Emerging Research and Opportunities
Göran Roos (University of Adelaide, Australia)
Business Science Reference • copyright 2017 • 255pp • H/C (ISBN: 9781522521792) • US $175.00 (our price)

Entrepreneurship and Business Innovation in the Middle East
Philippe W. Zgheib (Lebanese American University, Lebanon)
Business Science Reference • copyright 2017 • 357pp • H/C (ISBN: 9781522520665) • US $190.00 (our price)

Comprehensive Problem-Solving and Skill Development for Next-Generation Leaders
Ronald A. Styron, Jr. (University of South Alabama, USA) and Jennifer L. Styron (University of South Alabama,
USA)
Business Science Reference • copyright 2017 • 389pp • H/C (ISBN: 9781522519683) • US $205.00 (our price)

Diasporas and Transnational Entrepreneurship in Global Contexts
Sanya Ojo (University of East London, UK)
Business Science Reference • copyright 2017 • 334pp • H/C (ISBN: 9781522519911) • US $200.00 (our price)

701 East Chocolate Avenue, Hershey, PA 17033, USA
Tel: 717-533-8845 x100 • Fax: 717-533-8661
E-Mail: cust@igi-global.com • www.igi-global.com

Editorial Advisory Board

Table of Contents

Detailed Table of Contents

Chapter 1

    James P. Murphy, Dalhousie University, Canada
    Carolan McLarney, Dalhousie University, Canada

Regionalism and the Multilateral Trading System: The Role of Regional Trade Agreements is a discussion about the new reality and the evolution of the reduction of international barriers to freer trade under the World Trade Organization (WTO) formerly the General Agreement on Trade and Tariffs (GATT). The chapter devotes time to the two largest regional trade agreements (RTAs), the European Union (EU) with 28 countries and North American Trading Agreement (NAFTA) with three countries account for half of all world trade. The US set a course post World War II as the proponent of globalization and freer trade. RTAs at that time were failing or inconsequential. In response to the EU trading block, the US committed to a (Free Trade Area) FTA with Canada and subsequently the NAFTA with Canada and Mexico the rest of the world began to become concerned about being shut out of a preferential trade deal. The main theme of the chapter is that trade liberalization is moving forward because of Regional Trading agreements, not the WTO which is stalled and may never restart in its current form.

Chapter 2

    Oleksiy Osiyevskyy, University of Calgary, Canada & Northeastern University, USA
    Milena Troshkova, Northeastern University, USA
    Yongjian Bao, University of Lethbridge, Canada

A firm's business model is an essential mechanism determining how an organization creates value for its stakeholders and captures part of the created value as profit for its owners. Global enterprises secure their market positions through properly functioning business models that are globally scalable. Once a globally scalable business model is successfully designed and validated in one location, it becomes a non-location-bound firm-specific advantage, promoting the firm's international expansion. This chapter addresses the following research questions: (1) What is the role of a business model in the success of global enterprises? (2) Which common attributes do business models of successful global companies possess? and (3) How to make a business model more suitable for global expansion? The theoretical analysis of these questions yields a conceptual framework for examining the global companies through the business model lens. The developed conceptual framework is illustrated and corroborated with the mini-cases of global companies.

Chapter 3

With the convergence of information, communication and technology and global collaboration drives in modern management, it becomes imperative and crucial to understand the critical success factors (CSFs) for executives. In this globalized scenario, the internet has a dramatic impact on every kind of organization. It forms completely new challenges on the one hand but on the other hand it offers entirely new facilities. Additionally, spatiotemporal borders disappear. Totally new business models are being developed and companies have discovered completely new strategies to gain competitive advantage in this information age. Further, the advancements in society and technology, coupled with accelerations in globalization, competitive environments and changing customer's preferences have created new challenges as well as opportunities for executives. There is need to leverage on this vicissitude. To do so, it is essential to identify and understand the critical success factors (CSFs) fundamental to the success of executives and that is the core objective of this chapter.

Chapter 4

This study is focused on the role, importance and practice of Business Continuity Management (BCM) in relation with Strategic Planning (SP) and Cultural Context (CC) by offering a holistic framework for short-term and long-term strategic business analysis. The purpose is to create a unique structured plan for understanding the organizational failure willingness and to create a culture of readiness, feedback and risk management. The methodology used is quantitative with questionnaire for collection data. The study sample includes 50 organizations from four different sectors: banking, services, industrial and insurance in Shkoder (Albania). The research findings show a positive correlation between SP and BCM (0.54%), with a significant positive impact of SP on BCM. A positive correlation is founded between SP and CC (0.588%). The study suggests that placing the BCM in the Corporate Culture may be entitled as another manner of integrating BCM and SP in one structure. Between culture and strategy there is a huge number of characteristics and similarities they have in common with each other.

Fatma Gülruh Gürbüz, Marmara University, Turkey
Hande Sinem Ergun, Marmara University, Turkey
Seray Begum Samur-Teraman, Marmara University, Turkey

Strategy as Practice (hereafter S-As-P) is referred as a research topic concerning with the doing of strategy; who does it, what they do, how they do it, what they use and what implications this has for shaping strategy. The developing field has taken the concern of "humanize management" seriously by bringing human actors to the center of the strategy. This study aims to furnish insights into the S-as-P approach. In this sense, it considers extended mainstream strategy research and focuses on light practices that have largely passed and unnoticed. Furthermore, its reflections on businesses operating in global economy are discussed.

Serkan Gürsoy, Beykoz University, Turkey
Murat Yücelen, Yeditepe University, Turkey

This chapter deals with the evolution of communities of practice by considering two key components which facilitate knowledge sharing: Organizational Learning and Social Capital. Dualities and intersections between the building blocks of these two components are investigated by discussing organizational learning in its explorative and exploitative forms, while considering social capital in its bridging and bonding forms. As a critical contemporary step of evolution, information and communication technologies are also elaborated in order to examine the impact of constant and instant tools on these facilitators of knowledge sharing. The study aims to derive proxies among these components of organizational learning and social capital in order to design an integrated framework that reflects the nature of online communities of practice.

Tindara Abbate, University of Messina, Italy
Angelo Presenza, University of Molise, Italy
Lorn Sheehan, Dalhousie University, Canada

Social entrepreneurship and social innovation are attracting increasing attention from policy makers, practitioners, as well as academics. They represent different ways of thinking and addressing social issues often overlooked by public/private organizations and also provide a viable means of responding to multiple social, economic and environmental crises. With this in mind, this chapter leads to a better understanding of social entrepreneurship and social innovation in the non-profit sector, using one specific case followed by a more generalized discussion. The case of "Banca Prossima" illustrates engagement in social problems and trying to find and apply new solutions that simultaneously meet a social need while also leading to new or improved capabilities and relationships and a better use of assets and resources.

    Rossella Canestrino, Parthenope University of Naples, Italy
    Pierpaolo Magliocca, University of Foggia, Italy

The aim of this chapter is to explore the how international players, acting at global level, may overcome a "moral gap" when it arises. In doing this, the linkage between culture and Business Ethics was examined in order to highlight the way values and believes differently affect a) the assumption about what is right or wrong, b) the individual/organizational moral reasoning, and c) the consistency between individual/ organizational behaviour and the moral standards that prevail in a given context. Relevant issues were investigated referring to all the levels – individual, corporate and systemic – within which a "moral gap" may arise. Accordingly, "Bridging" diversities was identified as a good solution to solve a "moral gap" at all the mentioned levels. Cross-cultural sensitivity and cross-cultural negotiation were finally claimed as necessary to look for a trade-off between universal norms and local particularism, as well as to finally identify new common standards respectful of the opposite positions.

    Mirko Perano, Reald University of Vlore (ASAR), Albania
    Bice Della Piana, University of Salerno, Italy
    Gian Luca Casali, Queensland University of Technology, Australia

Project management is one of the possible ways to improve the organizational reputation and create value. The control achievable on each project' constrains (time, cost and quality) and the actions consequent by assessment process can represent in theory a guarantee for the success of a project. In practical, there are many risks capable of upsetting the project dynamics leading to failures. Risk management, or the specific area of knowledge of Project Risk Management, are useful to prevent this possible occurrence. The global dimension of organizations' networks that use PM, moves this quality to the project that this organizations do. A definition of global project is provided as well as also the consequent considerations about the cross-cultural aspect within the peoples involved in this type of project. It is framed and proposed a new category of risk related to management of global project: cultural risk analysis.

    Ninel Ivanova Nesheva-Kiosseva, New Bulgarian University, Bulgaria

This chapter presents the issue of the risks associated with the increase of the price (tariffs) of water, which are, and promise to be, a growing challenge for the sustainable management of the companies. At the beginning of the chapter the term risk is operationalized and water-related risks are classified. The reasons and their specific characteristics for the raising of water prices and the objective risks they create for the companies have been identified in the main part of the chapter. This part informs the company management about the possible causes of unjustified increase in the price of the water used in their activities. Several informational and analytical solutions and guidelines for the management have been marked in the end. These can prove useful in preventing and reducing the abovementioned risks and in aiding the sustainable management of the companies.

This chapter calls for understanding the perspective of multinational enterprises (MNEs) on international differences in income inequality. The authors set a research agenda on how national differences in income inequality influence MNE expansion strategies. Applying a transaction cost framework, both negative and positive economic outcomes of income inequality, from the MNE's perspective, are identified. Low levels of income inequality may deter foreign investment, as MNEs prefer countries where they incur lower levels of transaction costs arising from interactions with various market and non-market actors. However, the positive effect of income inequality on location attractiveness will likely diminish at higher levels of inequality when benefits are increasingly offset by additional monitoring, bargaining and security costs owing to instability and conflict. The chapter further explores the implications for level of MNE equity applied in the choice of entry mode under different levels of income inequality.

We explore how income differences influence heterogeneous entrepreneurial responses to the institutional environment in Brazil shapes low-income entrepreneurs' propensity to exploit the informal rather than the formal economy. Drawing on the Brazilian Global Entrepreneurship Monitor (GEM) data, entrepreneurship discourse and institutional theory, we discuss the influence of inadequate preparedness and barriers to institutional support influencing entrepreneurs' abilities to engage in productive economic activities. We contribute to the entrepreneurship discourse by suggesting that concepts developed within the context of relatively prosperous settings do not adequately reflect how low-income entrepreneurs respond to institutional settings.

The aim of this study is to identify the determinants of US Dollar/Turkish Lira currency exchange rate for strategic decision making in the global economy. Within this scope, quarterly data for the period between 1988:1 and 2016:2 was used in this study. In addition to this aspect, 10 explanatory variables were considered in order to determine the leading indicators of US Dollar/Turkish Lira currency exchange rate. Moreover, Multivariate Adaptive Regression Splines (MARS) method was used so as to achieve this objective. According to the results of this analysis, it was defined that two different variables affect this exchange rate in Turkey. First of all, it was identified that there is a negative relationship between current account balance and the value of US Dollar/Turkish Lira currency exchange rate. This result shows that in case of current account deficit problem, Turkish Lira experiences depreciation. Furthermore, it was also concluded that when there is an economic growth in Turkey, Turkish Lira increases in comparison with US Dollar. While taking into the consideration of these results, it could be generalized that emerging economies such as Turkey have to decrease current account deficit and investors should focus on higher economic growth in order to prevent the depreciation of the money in the strategic investment decision.

This chapter is intended to analyze the advantages to associate with a developing country like México from the perspective of the theories of the Agency, Institutional, Resource-based Theory and the Theory of Transaction Costs. Generally, FDI contributes to capital formation, expansion and diversification of exports, increasing competition, provide access to top technology and improving management systems. Mexico is of the largest FDI recipients within the developing countries. Japan, on the other hand, is one of the largest sources of FDI worldwide, and is gaining a larger share in the Mexican FDI context since the onset of the Economic Partnership Agreement. In this paper, factors that might lead to the depletion of productive spillovers from Japanese manufacturing companies are reviewed from a qualitative perspective. The analysis suggests that inefficiencies in endogenous companies; and Japanese companies being part of firm networks (keiretsu), might lead to productive spillovers depletion.

The recent development of Chinese cities has witnessed an increasing number of foreign nationals working in China. Foreign nationals tied up with MNEs are one of the powerful drivers for urban transformation in the post-reform era. However, little attention has been paid to their socio-economics characteristics. This chapter, therefore, is to analyse characteristics of foreign nationals in socio-economic, demographic and spatial aspects. This chapter focuses on a globalising Chinese second tier-city, Suzhou as a case study.

Chapter 16
Cooperation and Competition Among Regions: The Umbrella Brand as a Tool for Tourism
Competitiveness 315

Arminda Almeida Santana, Universidad de Las Palmas de Gran Canaria, Spain
Sergio Moreno Gil, Universidad de Las Palmas de Gran Canaria, Spain

Many brands exist within the tourism industry. Territorial brands exist at local, regional, national, and supranational level where they overlap and are interrelated. Therefore, it is necessary that tourist destinations develop and manage their brands to obtain a strong differentiated position in the competitive market. This study analyzed relationships between destinations in the new global scenario. It aimed to improve brand architecture and increase tourist loyalty. A comprehensive analysis considering 6,964 tourists from 17 countries was applied. The study offered recommendations to destinations in order to expand the design of marketing activities, improve coopetition strategies, and advance competitiveness. The results confirmed that the destinations must adapt their promotional strategies to the new global landscape of interconnected business. In addition, they need to develop strategies for horizontal loyalty between destinations.

Foreword

Strategic Management is a discipline that evolved from a world of business where managers felt that doing things right was not enough: it became also necessary to do the right things. In fact, Strategic Management has been defined as a discipline oriented to help managers to do the right things, which goes beyond the operations of management, which is limited to do things right. Business survival and success require both: doing the right things right. Moreover, the two components need to be pursued in sequential manner. We must first observe whether what we have decided to do is the right thing (for example, launching a new product focused on a certain segment of the international market); and then carry it out rightly (efficiently, with the desired quality level, etc.). Strategy, thus, affects both the overall well-being of the organization and society.

Although constantly evolving, strategy and the strategic management process were originally conceived as tasks of the top/general managers, identifying the content of the strategy with an explanation the company's success (the 'flamboyant' discipline of business success). Sometimes such reasons were found in external factors -the competitive structure of the industry- and in other occasions in internal factors -the core resources and capacities of the organization. Hence, over time and depending on the circumstances, strategy has placed its emphasis on one or another type of factors, which might aptly be likened to the swing of a pendulum. This also alludes to its evolution as a scientific discipline, through the succession of theoretical approaches intending to shed some more light on how strategies are formulated and put into practice, as well as on their outcomes.

Strategy has brought to management science a conceptual tool to facilitate the alignment or fit between the company and its environment. Increasingly the environment evidences higher levels of volatility, uncertainty, complexity and ambiguity. A very significant part of that environment is the shift from national or regional economies, to one global or world economy.

Consequently, we now live in a truly global, digital and hyper-connected world, driven substantially by technological developments, which, as an ongoing process, is having an enormous impact on business strategies. Today we can easily recognize companies that are born global, and Internationalization strategies (in its diverse typologies) are pursued not by big multinationals only, but more and more often by small and medium enterprises as well. New business models are replacing others misfit to this new economy. Technology revolution (rather than evolution) is causing severe impacts because of the tremendous progress in artificial intelligence, automation, and the like.

Meanwhile, within this framework shaped by an apparently unstoppable trend, a new scenario has emerged as a result of geopolitical uncertainties caused by growing controversial reactions against globalization in some parts of the world. The actions of nationalist (named as populists by some) political parties and governments have created tensions caused by restrictions to immigration, protectionist trade policies, the outright rejection of the status of free trade areas, and currency wars. Both the UK's withdrawal from the European Union (Brexit) and Donald Trump's election to the Presidency of the United States are obvious recent examples of this trend. This is a call for organizations to rethink the current system and status quo. We are at the precipice of a new era, in which the old mould is being demolished and the new one is still unknown. All the while, not knowing whether it is for the better or for worse for our world.

For all these reasons, a collective book like this edited by Angela Presenza and Lorn Sheehan is absolutely necessary, as is other work under the same core topic. "Geopolitics and Strategic Management in the Global Economy" is a wide and fascinating theme that no single book can tackle given all its perspectives, dimensions and nuances. In addition, the timing for its launch is ideal, given its present relevance.

This book provides valuable insight to a cadre of areas related to Global Strategic Management, with their corresponding challenges and opportunities, such as: cross-cultural issues, business ethics, strategy as a practice in global environments, the trade-off between cooperation and competition, strategic partnerships, learning organizations and the knowledge sharing process driven by ICTs, social entrepreneurship and innovation, global business models, key success factors for executives in the global economy, regional free trade agreements, etc. Its approach is diverse and versatile: in some occasions the focus is on cities, in others on regions or countries, and, of course, in companies and other organizations.

Obviously, its contents don't exhaust the theme, but they make a valuable contribution for those interested in gaining a better understanding of the changing nature of strategic management against the backdrop of the current economy and its intimate connection to rapidly evolving geopolitical forces. Hopefully this foreword serves as a kind invitation to dive into its reading, with the spirit of a strategist, ready to think through and live out new approaches to strategy.

Alfonso Vargas-Sánchez
University of Huelva, Spain

Preface

The world has evolved and as result the concept of globalization remains a focus of investigation by scholars and practitioners across disciplines and industries. Almost every country's economy is either dependent on or heavily influenced by global markets, factors of production and technology, especially those categorized as "Emerging Economies". It is within this framework that global managers face significant and highly dynamic geopolitical issues. These challenges encompass geopolitical and economic risks, foreign country expansion, foreign currency wars, country of origin and brand recognition as a result of frauds and falsification, data breach, etc. In addition, forces of change in the political, economic, social, technological, legal, and environmental realms significantly affect the global business landscape.

There is a need for the global manager to stay informed and constantly vigilant of the threatening and potentially catastrophic events that may negatively affect global operations. As a result, scholars engage in conducting research with the aim of understanding and mediating the potentially negative impact caused by the ever-changing external environment. In turn, managers can apply the findings to their operations to improve productivity, profits, and return on investment. Successful managers can identify trends that lead to opportunities or threats, direct resources innovation, enhance employee motivation and productivity, and reduce employee turnover, all of which have a direct effect on the sustainable profitability and longevity of the firm.

The purpose of this book is to contribute to the body of knowledge and research on global strategic management. It takes a global view of the challenges and opportunities organizations face in the global market place. The topics cover several industries as well as several countries. The contributing authors have addressed issues such as: multinational enterprises strategies, global risk management and resilience, global ethics in the digital world, critical success factors and strategy making, global entrepreneurship, social entrepreneurship, comparative management, issues in globalization, centralization, and decentralization of firms.

In sum, the book on *Geopolitics and Strategic Management in the Global Economy* is for a wide audience including scholars in higher education, graduate students, managers across industries, consultants, and government agencies.

ORGANIZATION OF THE BOOK

The book is divided into 16 chapters which are designed as standalone readings. However, they are presented in an order that takes the reader from the broad to the specific. In this regard, the book begins with chapters that frame the topic with an understanding of how global trade has evolved, how organizations have responded with global business models as well as strategy-making in a global context, and the types of success factors required by leaders of these organizations.

From there, several topics germane to understanding the socio-cultural dimensions of strategic management in a global context are introduced, including social capital, social innovation, cultural diversity, cross-cultural risks, and cultural context. The remainder of the book chapters delve into specific issues ranging from the effect of income inequality on MNE location choice to the impact of specific country trade relationships – all of which have geopolitical implications for strategic management. The following is a brief summary of each chapter.

Chapter 1: Regionalism and the Multilateral Trading System – The Role of Regional Trade Agreements

This chapter discusses the new reality and the evolution of the reduction of international barriers to freer trade under the World Trade Organization (WTO). With the 2008 collapse of Doha, the latest round of the WTO trade negotiations, some question whether or not the WTO will ever be as relevant to trade liberalization. More recent trade liberalization has largely moved forward because of regional trade agreements (RTAs). The two largest RTAs, the European Union (EU), and North American Trading Agreement (NAFTA) along with three countries accounted for half of all world trade in 2013. However, even the future of RTAs is uncertain given recent developments such as the UK's exit from the EU (Brexit) and a new United States president taking office in 2017.

Chapter 2: What Makes a Global Business Model?

A firm's business model is an essential mechanism determining how an organization creates value for its stakeholders and captures part of the value as profit for its owners. Global enterprises secure their market positions through properly functioning business models that are globally scalable. Once a globally scalable business model is successfully designed and validated in one location, it becomes a non-location-bound firm-specific advantage, promoting the firm's international expansion. This chapter addresses the following research questions: (1) what is the role of a business model in the success of global enterprises? (2) which common attributes do business models of successful global companies possess? and (3) how can a business model be made more suitable for global expansion? The theoretical analysis of these questions yields a conceptual framework for examining global companies through the business model lens. The developed conceptual framework is illustrated and corroborated with several mini-cases of global companies.

Chapter 3: Critical Success Factors for Executives in the Global Economy

The global economy has been fueled by a convergence of information, communication and technology and collaboration as organizations search for lower costs, differentiation, and new markets. The new challenges and opportunities created by the internet have had a dramatic impact on every kind of organization. As a result, spatiotemporal borders are disappearing, new business models are being developed, and companies have discovered completely new strategies to gain competitive advantage. The resulting societal and technological changes, coupled with accelerating globalization, competitive environments and changing customer's preferences require responses from executives. This chapter identifies and explains the critical success factors fundamental to the success of executives in the global economy.

Chapter 4: Strategic Planning, Cultural Context, and Business Continuity Management – Business Cases in the City of Shkoder

Crises, risk, and destruction all threaten the survival of organizations. This chapter examines the role, importance and practice of business continuity management in relation to strategic planning and cultural context and offers a holistic framework for short-term and long-term strategic business analysis. The purpose is to create a unique plan for understanding the antecedents to organizational failure and to create a culture of readiness, feedback, and risk management. The findings, based on a quantitative study of 50 organizations from four different sectors, suggest that embedding business continuity management in the corporate culture may be seen as another way of integrating business continuity management and strategic planning.

Chapter 5: A Proposition of Strategy Making in Global Firms – Reflections From Strategy as Practice

This chapter provides insights into the Strategy-as-Practice approach. In this sense, it considers the extant mainstream strategy research and focuses on practices that have largely gone unnoticed yet are highly relevant to operating in the global economy. Consistent with an approach to strategy that "humanizes management", they advocate bringing human actors to the center of the strategy to pose questions around the doing of strategy – Who does it? What do they do? How do they do it? What do they use? And what are the implications for shaping strategy?

Chapter 6: Efficacy of Organizational Learning and Social Capital in Online Communities of Practice – Dualities and Intersections

This chapter deals with the evolution of communities of practice by considering two key components which facilitate knowledge sharing: organizational learning and social capital. Dualities and intersections between the building blocks of these two components are investigated by discussing organizational learning in its explorative and exploitative forms, while considering social capital in its bridging and bonding forms. As a critical contemporary step of evolution, information and communication technologies are also elaborated in order to examine the impact of constant and instant tools on these facilitators of knowledge sharing. The chapter outlines proxies among these components of organizational learning and social capital in order to design an integrated framework that reflects the nature of online communities of practice.

Chapter 7: Social Innovation in the For-Profit Organization – The Case of Banca Prossima

Social entrepreneurship and social innovation are attracting increasing attention from policy makers, practitioners, as well as academics. They represent different ways of thinking and addressing social issues often overlooked by public/private organizations and also provide a viable means of responding to multiple social, economic and environmental crises. With this in mind, this chapter leads to a better understanding of social entrepreneurship and social innovation in the non-profit sector, using one specific case followed by a more generalized discussion. The case of "Banca Prossima", illustrates engagement in social problems and an attempt to find and apply new solutions that simultaneously meet a social need and lead to new or improved capabilities and relationships and a better use of assets and resources.

Chapter 8: Managing Business Ethics in a Global Environment – The Impact of Cultural Diversities

This chapter explores how international players, acting at the global level, may overcome a "moral gap" when it arises. In doing this, the linkage between culture and business ethics is examined in order to highlight the way values and beliefs differently affect: a) the assumption about what is right or wrong; b) the individual/organizational moral reasoning; and c) the consistency between individual/organizational behaviour and the moral standards in a given context. Relevant issues are investigated at three levels – individual, corporate and systemic – within which a "moral gap" may arise. Accordingly, "bridging" diversities are identified as a good solution to solve a "moral gap" at all levels. Cross-cultural sensitivity and cross-cultural negotiation are seen as necessary to find a trade-off between universal norms and local particularism, as well as to identify new common standards respectful of the opposite positions.

Chapter 9: Project and Risk Management in a Global Context – The Importance of Cultural Risk

This chapter describes how project risk management can be used to improve organizational reputation and create value. The control achievable on each project's constraints (time, cost and quality) and the actions that result from assessment processes can, at least in theory, guarantee the success of a project. However, in practice, there are many risks capable of upsetting the project dynamics which ultimately lead to failure. Risk management, or more specifically, the knowledge of project risk management, is useful to prevent this possible occurrence. The global dimension of organizations' networks requires that the knowledge of project risk management also be applied to its global projects. A definition of a global project is provided as well as the consequent cross cultural considerations related to the people involved in a global project. A new risk management framework is advanced. The framework proposes "*cultural risk analysis*" as a new category of risk related to management of global project.

Chapter 10: Water-Related Price Risks – Implications for Firm Competitiveness

This chapter presents the risks associated with an increase of the price (tariffs) of water, which are, and promise to continue to be, a growing challenge for the sustainable management of companies. The term risk is operationalized and water-related risks are classified. The reasons and their specific characteristics for the raising of water prices and the objective risks they create for the companies are identified. This informs management about the possible causes of unjustified increases in the price of water used in their activities. Several informational and analytical solutions and guidelines for management can prove useful in preventing or reducing the identified risks and in aiding the sustainable management of companies.

Chapter 11: National Income Inequality, Society, and Multinational Enterprises

This chapter calls for understanding the perspective of multinational enterprises (MNEs) on international differences in income inequality. This chapter sets an agenda for research on how differences in national income inequality influence MNE expansion strategies, focusing on both questions of where (i.e. location choice) and how (i.e. equity vs. non-equity investment). Applying a transaction cost framework, it is argued that there are both negative and positive economic outcomes of income inequality from the MNE's perspective, which influence its financial performance, and hence preferences towards level of national income inequality. Low levels of income inequality may deter foreign investment, as MNEs prefer countries where they incur lower levels of transaction costs arising from interactions with various market and non-market actors. However, the positive effect of income inequality on location attractiveness will likely diminish at higher levels of inequality when benefits are increasingly offset by additional monitoring, bargaining and security costs owing to instability and conflict. Thus, it is argued that inequality has a positive but diminishing impact on investment location attractiveness. The chapter further explores the implications for level of MNE equity applied in the choice of entry mode under different levels of income inequality. It is suggested that MNEs will prefer to enter moderate inequality markets with higher equity modes such as wholly owned subsidiaries or majority joint ventures, while preferring a smaller stake in the highest inequality countries.

Chapter 12: Low vs. High Income Entrepreneurial Households – Heterogeneous Response to Common Institution Environment in Developing Countries

We explore how income differences influence heterogeneous entrepreneurial responses to the institutional environment in Brazil and shape the low-income population's propensity to exploit the informal rather than the formal economy. Drawing from the Brazilian Global Entrepreneurship Monitor data, entrepreneurship discourse, and institutional theory, we discuss the influence of lack of preparedness and barriers to institutional support on entrepreneurs' limitations to engage in productive economic activities. As expected, the data shows that low-income start-up entrepreneurs are mostly older, more likely to be female, less educated, have less confidence in their skills and know fewer entrepreneurs than high-income entrepreneurs. We found that low-income entrepreneurs lacking formal education were as alert as their highly educated and high-income counterparts. We contribute to the entrepreneurship discourse by suggesting that concepts and theories developed within the context of relatively prosperous settings do not adequately reflect how low-income entrepreneurs will respond to institutional settings, and provide insights on why lower income entrepreneurs often prefer to exploit opportunities within the informal economy.

Chapter 13: Determining Influencing Factors of Currency Exchange Rate for Strategic Decision Making in the Global Economy Using the MARS Method

This chapter presents the results of a study to identify the determinants of US Dollar/Turkish Lira currency exchange rate for strategic decision making in the global economy. Using quarterly data for the period 1988 to 2016, this study considered 10 explanatory variables to determine the leading indicators of the US Dollar/Turkish Lira currency exchange rate. Results indicate that two different variables affect the exchange rate. First, there is a negative relationship between the current account balance and the value of US Dollar/Turkish Lira currency exchange rate whereby a current account deficit leads to depreciation of the Turkish Lira. Second, when there is economic growth in Turkey, the Turkish Lira increases relative to the US Dollar. Overall, all other things being equal, emerging economies seeking to stabilize or strengthen their currency, should consider efforts to decrease their current account deficit and increase investment that leads to economic growth.

Chapter 14: Economic Partnership Agreement Mexico-Japan and Its Impact on Foreign Direct Investment – A Strategic Analysis

This chapter analyzes the advantages of partnering with a developing country like México from several theoretical perspectives, including Agency Theory, Institutional Theory, Resource-based Theory, and the Theory of Transaction Costs. Generally, foreign direct investment (FDI) contributes to capital formation, expansion and diversification of exports, increasing competition, provides access to leading technology and improves management systems. Mexico is of the largest FDI recipients among the developing countries. Japan, on the other hand, is one of the largest sources of FDI worldwide, and is gaining a larger share in the Mexican FDI context since the onset of the Economic Partnership Agreement. This chapter reviews factors that might lead to the depletion of productive spillovers from Japanese manufacturing companies. The analysis used suggests that inefficiencies in endogenous companies, and Japanese companies being part of firm networks (keiretsu), might lead to productive spillover depletion.

Chapter 15: A Profile of Foreign Nationals in a Globalising Second-Tier City, Suzhou

This chapter analyzes the characteristics of foreign nationals from socio-economic, demographic and spatial perspectives. Foreign nationals linked to multinational enterprises (MNEs) are one of the powerful drivers for urban transformation in the post-reform era. However, little attention has been paid to their socio-economics characteristics. This chapter focuses on a globalizing Chinese second tier-city, Suzhou as a case study. The recent development of Chinese cities has witnessed an increasing number of foreign nationals working in China due to a wide range of driving forces including MNEs.

Chapter 16: Cooperation and Competition Among Regions – The Umbrella Brand as a Tool for Tourism Competitiveness

The tourism industry may be characterized as a competitive multi-brand environment in which territorial brands at local, regional, national and supranational levels are overlapping and interrelated. In this context, it is necessary for tourism destinations to develop and manage their brands in order to achieve a clearly differentiated position. This chapter analyzes the relations between destinations in the new global economy, with the aim of improving brand architecture and increased levels of tourist loyalty. Based the analysis of 6964 tourists from 17 countries, the study results confirm that destinations must adapt their promotion strategies to the new global landscape of interconnected business, as well as the development of strategies for horizontal loyalty between destinations.

In summary, this book presents insights to the complex and rapidly evolving landscape of geopolitics and strategic management in the global economy. There are many relevant perspectives on the topic to be sure. We have chosen several that we believe are reflective of the breadth and diversity that are relevant to practitioners and researchers. The practitioner will likely seek more breadth and comprehensive coverage of issues and views, while the researcher will likely seek more depth with theoretical and empirical rigor. We understand that we may not have served either as well as we might have had we chosen to focus on one or the other. However, it is our contention that we must do as much as we can to bring practitioners (the doers) and researchers (the dreamers) together in discourse. From this, both groups and society broadly speaking, will benefit – we hope.

Angelo Presenza
University of Molise, Italy

Lorn Sheehan
Dalhousie University, Canada

Acknowledgment

We would like to acknowledge the help of all the people involved in this project. More specifically, we sincerely thank the chapter authors and reviewers for contributing their intellectual efforts and for patiently working with us in making the necessary revisions following the double-blind review process. Without their support, this book would not have become a reality. We thank everyone at IGI Global but especially Marianne Caesar, for her incredible patience and guidance she has given us during the last stages of the manuscript completion process.

We would also like to thank Prof. Angelo A. Camillo for his support. Our sincere gratitude goes to him for his time and expertise that he so kindly gave to us.

Angelo Presenza
University of Molise, Italy

Lorn Sheehan
Dalhousie University, Canada

Chapter 1

Regionalism and the Multilateral Trading System:
The Role of Regional Trade Agreements

James P. Murphy
Dalhousie University, Canada

Carolan McLarney
Dalhousie University, Canada

ABSTRACT

Regionalism and the Multilateral Trading System: The Role of Regional Trade Agreements is a discussion about the new reality and the evolution of the reduction of international barriers to freer trade under the World Trade Organization (WTO) formerly the General Agreement on Trade and Tariffs (GATT). The chapter devotes time to the two largest regional trade agreements (RTAs), the European Union (EU) with 28 countries and North American Trading Agreement (NAFTA) with three countries account for half of all world trade (WTO, 2017a). The US set a course post World War II as the proponent of globalization and freer trade. RTAs at that time were failing or inconsequential. In response to the EU trading block, the US committed to a (Free Trade Area) FTA with Canada and subsequently the NAFTA with Canada and Mexico the rest of the world began to become concerned about being shut out of a preferential trade deal. The main theme of the chapter is that trade liberalization is moving forward because of Regional Trading agreements, not the WTO which is stalled and may never restart in its current form.

INTRODUCTION

The topic "Regionalism and the Multilateral Trading System: The Role of Regional Trade Agreements" is as much about the multilateral trading systems successes and failures as it is about the role of the regionalism in the mix. One, (multilateral) gave birth to the other (regional) after meeting with little success, initially. The paper traces out the evolution of the systems by focusing on the most significant regional and multilateral systems and expands on the evolution of free trade moving forward.

DOI: 10.4018/978-1-5225-2673-5.ch001

The chapter is broken down into sections, covering the current systems of international trade: What gives rise to regionalism? Why does regionalism work so well? The North American Free Trade Agreement (NAFTA) and the European Union; Comparison of Regionalism to the World Trade Organization (WTO) and the multilateral system; Other trade factors and concluding with an expectation for the next phase of trade development.

The first section discusses the systems of international trade and provides an overview of the worldwide trade in goods today: Where the main participating countries and regions are located; Defines the benefits of increased trade; Where does the WTO fits in to the multilateral system; What the regional trading system is and the institutions of the WTO.

The next two sections discuss how multilateral trade agreements spur on regionalism, a brief history of the multilateral trading system, the General Agreement on Tariffs and Trade (GATT)/WTO and the benefits, the obstacles and the implementation challenges. The next sections elaborate on regionalism and the measured benefits, statistics on the main regional agreements (the NAFTA and the EU) and an overview of other regional agreements in Table 1. The next sections look at the EU and the NAFTA in greater detail followed by a comparison of RTAs, how they fill the multilateral trade agreement void and some of the inherent problems of RTAs. Finally, the paper looks at other factors effecting trade including social, political and environmental issues and the way they are addressed in RTAs and multilateral agreements.

BACKGROUND

Systems of International Trade

World trade in 2014, from all the WTO countries, in goods represented $19.0 trillion dollars up from $2.3 trillion in 2010. It was no doubt spurred on by the worldwide growth in trade after WWII and the backward protectionist "beggar thy neighbour policies" of the 1930s (WTO, 2017b). Here one country attempts to make corrections in its economy and in doing so they trigger negative economic consequences to its "neighbour". To encourage trade and take advantage of the benefits of increased trade, governments worked together to create organizations to spur on trade. The predominant one is GATT/WTO, a multilateral trade agreement to reduce the tariff barriers between countries levied against imported goods.

Benefits and Definitions

There are many kinds of free trade agreements, designed to create increased trade between nations with 354 such agreements currently in force according to the WTO. The WTO states (2017a) that free trade benefits include: growth in income; greater peace; easy dispute resolution; order and rules; lower cost of living; more consumer choice; greater overall income; growth; efficiencies; less government interference and pressure from internal special interests through the reduction of barriers to trade (WTO, 2017b). The argument for freer trade is pervasive where everyone is required to play by the same rules under the WTO. Many products and services are difficult to agree on and so are not covered by the free trade agreements such as agricultural subsidies or reductions, non-trade barriers, services, customs procedures, anti-dumping and the environment to name a few.

Free trade areas can be bilateral (between two countries), regional such as the NAFTA or more broadly based multilateral trade agreements the largest being the GATT. According to the WTO "the GATT became the only multilateral instrument governing international trade from 1948 until the World Trade Organization (WTO) was established in 1995." (WTO, 2017b: 1) There are currently 164 member countries in the WTO (WTO, 2017c). The GATT and the WTO have basic principles of reciprocity and non-discrimination with WTO having power to enforce the non-compliance of the agreement. Regional or preferential trading agreements do not have the same enforcement mechanisms (Bagwell & Staiger, 1998).

Bhagwati (1992: 535) broadly defines regionalism "as preferential trade agreements among a subset of nations". According to Bagwell and Staiger (1998) regional trade agreements have the added benefit in that they can facilitate multilateral liberalization when multilateral trading systems are not working well and the enforcement mechanisms are unworkable as has been seen with the latest round of the WTO. The trade discussion has shifted from the WTO to more focused trade deals as the Economist states, "Regional deals are the only game in town." (The Economist, Dec 2012). Bilateral trade agreements comprise the majority of trade agreements put into force since the year 2000. Approximately 130 bilateral agreements, many of which include the European Union and other nations and 11 regional trading agreements, are in force according to the WTO (WTO, 2017e). Regional trading agreements (RTAs) have taken off since 1990. With the failure of the Doha Round at the WTO, agreements rose from 70 in 1990 to over 300. More than 354 RTAs are in force (WTO, 2017d). Regional trading agreements are liberalizing trade worldwide and according to The Economist (2012) could be greatly advanced by a deal between the US and the EU. Regional Trade agreements lower barriers to trade specifically tariffs and subsidies (The Economist, 2012).

Who is Involved in the Multilateral Trading System?

The WTO is a multilateral trading system that administers trade agreements among all its 164 members, settles trade disputes, seeks to expand world trade further, assists governments in negotiating trade agreements and administers the rulings. The GATT created many of the foundation pieces for the WTO (WTO 2017g). The institutions of the WTO are located in Geneva Switzerland and are made up of a Ministerial Conference, a General Council and meet as both the Trade Policy Review Body and the Dispute Settlement Body. Additionally, there are also the Goods Council, Services Council and the TRIPs the Intellectual Property Council (WTO 2017g). Scholars argued whether Customs Unions (CUs) and Free Trade Areas (FTAs) are beneficial to the countries involved or for the world (Bhagwati, 1992). These arguments will be explored further because they are contrary to the principles of the WTO.

WHAT IS IT ABOUT THE MULTILATERAL TRADING SYSTEM THAT GIVES RISE TO REGIONALISM?

History

The GATT, signed in 1947, granted Most Favoured Nation (MFN) status to its members and non-discrimination over the flow of goods among the 23 parties to the agreement. It does give approval under section XXIV to Customs Unions and Free Trade Areas within the group as long as substantially all trade is covered by the agreement (Bhagwati, 1992). Post WWII, the United States was more interested in pro multilateral trade than it was in preferential economic unions such as The European Community (EC). The EC, including six countries, came into being in 1958. In the 1960s, even developing countries hoped to speed along their industrialization by signing preferential bilateral agreements in order to access neighbouring markets. The developed countries did so as well. For both, the experience was less than ideal. Regional agreements just did not have the appeal they have today. In the 1960s the North Atlantic Trading Area, Pacific Free Trade Area and The Latin American Free Trade Area failed. Only the EC and the European Free Trade Association (EFTA) managed to survive the decade. Bhagwati (1992) attributes the newfound interest in the regional agreements worldwide to the United States new focus on its own self-interest.

When the US was faced with a new trading block in Europe they decided to craft their own deals. The shift happened with the change in the US when they negotiated a free trade agreement with Israel followed by an agreement with Canada and later with Mexico. The US changed its position from being an advocate of multilateral trade to one of regional trade, which represented a significant shift as the US was the main proponent of multilateral trade during the post war period.

Multilateral Trading Agreements are Worthwhile but Difficult to Implement

Worthwhile

Merchandise trade (exports) in the WTO countries has grown from $5.8 trillion to $16.7 trillion per year from 2001 to 2011 an increase of 188% (WTO, 2017i). Worldwide exports of Commercial Services have grown equally as fast from $1.5 trillion worldwide to $4.2 trillion over the same period (WTO, 2017i).

Comparative advantage, according to the economist David Ricardo, suggests that trade between two countries is beneficial to both (WTO, 2017i). Freer trade (the reduction of barriers to trade) should make them even better off. The WTO advocates freer trade through negotiations, Most Favoured Nation (MFN) status, and non-discrimination among trading partners, meaning that any special trade deals are offered to all. The WTO has the legal ability to enforce those agreements (WTO, 2017).

World trade growth stagnated through the 1930s and 1940s. The GATT resuscitated world trade. For 25 years after WWII, while world GDP growth was averaging 5% per year, world trade grew even faster at 8% per year (WTO, 2017i). Even as recently as 2015 world merchandise exports have grown 75% faster than GDP from 2005-2011 according to the WTO (WTO, 2017i). The increased trade objective of the WTO amongst member countries appears to be working even in the absence of a new agreement.

Difficult to Implement

Multilateral trade agreements such as GATT and the WTO take decades to negotiate and involve well over hundreds of national governments and agencies, whereas the regional trading agreements can involve as little as two national governments or agencies by comparison. The health of the GATT and later the WTO was not affected by the GATT itself but by other events happening in the world of trade agreements, specifically the EU in Europe and NAFTA in North America (Baldwin, 1993). There is little doubt the benefits of liberalized trade worldwide are many according to the WTO, it just takes a long time to gain consensus. The Uruguay Round of GATT that formed the WTO took eight years and the WTO Doha Round started in 2001 has not yet concluded (WTO, 2017h). According to Baldwin (1993) negotiations have been long, slow and difficult. Most countries that are part of the WTO are also involved in a bilateral free trade agreement, likely because they are losing patience (Whalley, 1998).

WHY DOES REGIONALISM WORK SO WELL?

Econometrically Speaking

Regional agreements allow the partners to the agreement to negotiate a broader range of issues than would otherwise be possible with GATT or the WTO. (Ethier, 1998) Baier & Bergstrand (2007) discovered that bilateral agreements improve countries trade with each other by 100 percent on average after 10 years.

They focused on the econometrics of free trade in their evaluation of the impact. They also suggest that the successful gains of the GATT and the WTO are attributed to the reduction in tariff barriers to trade post WWII and that the more difficult barriers to negotiate are causing the discussions to stall such as "deeper integration" issues, which can be answered with regional agreements (Baier & Bergstrand, 2007: 78). The deeper integration issues are more difficult to negotiate.

They have also concluded that the main equation, the gravity equation, for evaluating the impact on the benefit of regional free trade areas (FTAs) does not lead them to conclude that the FTAs do have an undeniable impact on trade despite the increase in the number of FTAs over the from 1992-2007. Further study is warranted. They tried to answer the question "Do free trade agreements actually increase members' international trade?" The found, using other measurement techniques, the FTA is an endogenous variable in the calculation versus an exogenous variable (Baier & Bergstrand, 2007: 78).

Statistics on Regional Agreements

A sampling of regional agreements including the NAFTA and EFTA and EU provides some insights into the success of some regional agreements and their impact over a 10-year period from 2001 to 2011. Over that time frame world trade (exports) in goods increased 195%, going from $6.2 trillion to $18.3 trillion according to the WTO, of which countries in the WTO accounted for 90% (2013a). The major regional trading partners NAFTA, EFTA and the EU saw their increase account for nine percent, two percent and 30 percent respectively. Both NAFTA and the EU have seen their relative importance diminish over the same 10-year period. NAFTA trade in 2001 represented 19 percent of all world exports down to nine percent in 2011 while EU exports shrunk from 40 percent to 30 percent over the same time period. In dollar terms trade grew for both the EU and NAFTA still accounting for 46% of world exports in goods. The other largest increases came from the Middle East and Asia at 16 percent.

Major Regional Trading Regions and Agreements

While the major regional trading agreements of the EU and NAFTA export volumes shrunk in their relative importance down from 61% to 48% they still grew over the 10-year period more than doubling trading volumes from $3.8 trillion to $8.7 trillion per year up $4.9 trillion. The WTO countries maintained 92 percent of export volume down from 94 percent in 2001. The South and Central America regional trade agreements, African and Middle Eastern RTAs grew rapidly over the 10 years at almost double the pace of the North American and Europe exports. (WTO, 2013b) RTAs accounted for 68% of world trade in 2011 (Table 1).

It would appear from the evidence and numbers that the RTAs do in fact help to increase trade, more significantly the growth in trade among the smaller RTAs is quite dramatic over the 10-year period.

Table 1. Major regional trading regions and agreements

Regional Trade Agreements (Initial Enforce Year)	Percentage of world Trade (exports) 2011	RTAs Primary Countries (2011)
North America & Europe	48%	
EFTA (1960)	2%	European Free Trade Association: Iceland, Liechtenstein, Norway, Switzerland
European Union (1958)	33%	Austria, Belgium, Bulgaria, Croatia, Cyprus Czech Republic, Denmark, Estonia, Finland, France, Germany, Greece, Hungary, Ireland, Italy, Latvia, Lithuania, Luxembourg, Malta, Netherlands, Poland, Portugal, Romania, Slovak Republic, Slovenia, Spain; Sweden, United Kingdom
NAFTA (1994)	13%	Canada, Mexico, USA
South & Central America	3%	
Andean Community (1988)	1%	Bolivia, Colombia, Ecuador, Peru
MERCOSUR (1991)	2%	Southern Common Market: Argentina, Brazil, Paraguay, Uruguay
Africa	4%	
COMESA (1994)	1%	Common Market for Eastern and South Africa: Angola, Burundi, Comoros, Eritrea, Ethiopia, Kenya, Lesotho, Malawi, Mauritius, Rwanda, Sudan, Swaziland, Tanzania, Uganda, Zambia, Zimbabwe
ECCAS	1%	Economic Community of Central African States: n/a
ECOWAS (1993)	1%	Economic Community of West African States: Benin; Burkina Faso, Cape Verde, Cote d'Ivoire, Ghana, Guinea, Guinea-Bissau, Liberia, Mali, Niger, Nigeria, Senegal, Sierra Leone, Gambia, Togo
SADC (2000)	1%	South African Development Community: Angola, Botswana, Lesotho, Malawi, Mauritius, Mozambique, Namibia, South Africa, Swaziland, Tanzania, Zambia, Zimbabwe
Middle East and Asia		
ASEAN Free Trade Area (1992)	7%	Association of Southeast Asian Nations: Brunei, Cambodia, Indonesia, Laos, Malaysia, Myanmar, the Philippines, Singapore, Thailand, Vietnam
GCC (2003)	6%	Gulf Cooperation Council: UAE, Bahrain, Saudi Arabia, Oman, Qatar, Kuwait
SAPTA (1995)	3%	South Asian Preferential Trading Arrangement: Bangladesh, Bhutan, India, Maldives, Pakistan, Nepal and Sri Lanka.

Source: *(WTO, 2013a-c)*

NAFTA AND THE EUROPEAN UNION

The most significant regional trading agreements are the NAFTA and the EU. Combined they account for 46 percent of the world's trade in goods (Table 2). The NAFTA came into force in 1994 and the EU in 1958 (WTO, 2013c). At the leading edge, the environmental rules of the NAFTA and the EU are considerably further ahead of the WTO because WTO has so many diverse economic systems that make it very difficult to agree on any issues (Steinberg 1997).

NAFTA

NAFTA, a regional trade agreement amongst three governments of the United States, Canada and Mexico. It is designed to facilitate the barrier free movement of goods and services between individual countries with most favoured nation status for each. NAFTA was negotiated with the intention of lowering tariffs on goods and services. NAFTA, section 102, states that the agreement was to remove barriers to trade in goods and services, improve opportunities for investment, protect intellectual property rights, and create procedures to settle disputes (NAFTA 2013). The study by Mehanna & Shamsub (2002) shows that NAFTA has created more trade in all three countries with the largest impact from a GDP perspective on Canada's economy with the US benefiting with the most trade created. NAFTA created more trade up 200% from 1993-2006 and increased direct foreign investment (FDI), increased economic integration in all three countries (Schott & Hufbauer, 2007).

NAFTA History

The political discussions in the late 1980s were about the Canada-US FTA. In 1987 Canada and the USA agreed to an FTA (CUSFTA) covering tariffs and non-tariff barriers and trade in services. The US was going to negotiate a bilateral trade agreement with Mexico. Canada at the time was concerned about the impact of being on the outside. The CUSFTA was replaced by NAFTA, which included Mexico. (Foreign Affairs, 2017). Ironically, NAFTA, which had been the leading opponents to NAFTA while they were in opposition (Schwartz 1998). NAFTA entered into force in 1994 (WTO, 2013c).

Strengths and Weaknesses

There are a few areas of strengths and weaknesses to be highlighted in the NAFTA (Table 3).

European Union

The EU is now made up of 28 countries (Table 4). Candidate counties include Iceland, Montenegro, Serbia, Macedonia, Turkey and potential candidates: Albania, Bosnia and Herzegovina and Kosovo (EU, 2017a). The institutions of the EU include, The European Council which sets the political agenda, The European Parliament, elected by the people, along with Council of the European Union made up of government representatives and the European Commission and is responsible for making laws governing the EU (EU, 2017c). The deal goes deeper than a free trade agreement.

Table 2. Merchandise trade by selected groups of economies, 2001-2011

	2001	2002	2003	2004	2005	2006	2007	2008	2009	2010	2011	Growth 2001-2011	Average Grwoth Factor	Dollar Growth 2001-2011	Trade Percent 2001	Trade Percent 2011
EXPORTS																
World	6191	6492	7586	9218	10495	12120	14012	16140	12542	15274	18255	195%	1.9	1064	100%	100%
North Amercia and Europe																
EFTA	143	154	176	208	238	274	313	378	291	331	399	178%	1.8	256	2%	2%
EU	2469	2638	3149	3762	4065	4591	5347	5923	4595	5157	6039	145%	1.4	3569	40%	33%
NAFTA	1148	1106	1163	1320	1476	1664	1841	2035	1602	1964	2282	99%	1.0	1135	19%	13%
Total	**3760**	**3897**	**4487**	**5290**	**5779**	**6529**	**7501**	**8336**	**6489**	**7452**	**8770**	**132%**	**1.3**	**4960**	**61%**	**48%**
South and Central Amercia																
Andean Pact	25	26	30	39	51	65	77	94	79	99	134	430%	4.3	109	0%	1%
CACM	14	17	18	20	22	24	27	30	26	30	36	148%	1.5	21	0%	0%
CARICOM	8	7	9	11	15	20	20	26	15	18	22	180%	1.8	14	0%	0%
MERCOSUR	88	89	106	136	164	190	224	278	217	281	353	302%	3.0	266	1%	2%
Total	**135**	**139**	**163**	**206**	**252**	**299**	**348**	**428**	**337**	**428**	**545**	**303%**	**3.0**	**409**	**2%**	**3%**
Africa																
CEMAC	8	9	12	17	23	27	30	43	27	35	45	440%	4.4	37	0%	0%
COMESA	28	29	37	49	66	83	99	127	93	118	97	246%	2.5	69	0%	1%
ECCAS	16	19	23	32	50	62	78	111	72	92	118	641%	6.4	102	0%	1%
ECOWAS	28	29	37	54	67	78	87	112	83	113	154	456%	4.6	126	0%	1%
SADC	49	52	62	80	98	117	144	178	131	170	210	331%	3.3	161	1%	1%
WAEMU	7	9	10	12	13	14	15	19	19	19	22	222%	2.2	15	0%	0%
Total	**136**	**146**	**180**	**243**	**317**	**381**	**454**	**589**	**425**	**547**	**646**	**377%**	**3.8**	**510**	**2%**	**4%**
Middle East and Asia																
ASEAN	388	407	475	569	656	770	865	990	814	1052	1242	220%	2.2	855	6%	7%
GCC	160	168	213	285	398	481	555	762	519	665	934	483%	4.8	774	3%	5%
SAPTA	64	71	84	105	133	159	190	241	206	277	367	469%	4.7	302	1%	2%
Total	**612**	**646**	**771**	**969**	**1186**	**1409**	**1610**	**1993**	**1539**	**1994**	**2543**	**315%**	**3.2**	**1931**	**10%**	**14%**
Memorandum																
ACP	107	112	137	181	227	270	317	399	288	379	479	346%	3.0	371	2%	3%
LDCs	36	40	46	60	82	103	128	168	127	162	203	463%	5.0	167	1%	1%
WTO Members	**5801**	**6084**	**7097**	**8595**	**9714**	**11175**	**12911**	**14757**	**11558**	**14020**	**16714**	**188%**	**2.0**	**10913**	**94%**	**92%**

Source: *(WTO, 2013b)*

Table 3. NAFTA: Strengths and weaknesses

Strengths	Weaknesses
• Economies are better off with greater three-way trade. • Canada has the resources, US has the education system and Mexico has the young labour (Sirkin 2012) • The countries share common borders and already have significant cross border trade with each other.	• Detractors say that jobs have gone to Mexico from the US. • Needs better integration to take advantage of the education system of the US compared to Mexico and to better utilize the under educated and under employed people of Mexico. (Sirkin, 2012) • The environmental standards and not well defined. ("Alphabetti", 1998)

Table 4. European Union Members

Austria, Belgium, Bulgaria, Croatia, Cyprus, Czech Republic, Denmark, Estonia Finland	France, Germany, Greece, Hungary, Ireland, Italy, Latvia, Lithuania, Luxemburg, Malta	Netherlands, Poland, Portugal, Romania, Slovakia, Slovenia, Spain, Sweden, United Kingdom

Source: (EU, 2017a)

EU History

The European Union (EU) started in 1956 with Belgium, France, Italy Luxemburg and the Netherlands after the Coal and Steel community in 1950 began to link country's economies. The treaty of Rome in 1957 formed the European Economic Community (EEC), which grew into a larger common market over the subsequent decades with its own currency and open borders. Later the EU was to let members live anywhere in the EU, soldiers to be under one leadership, central bankers no longer answering to their own governments and finance ministers no longer permitted to set their own deficit amounts ("What's in a deal", 1991). The EU is a much deeper integration than NAFTA in that covers even more economic issues (Ethier, 1998). The Maastricht Treaty covers economic, monetary union as well as political union with common foreign policies ("What's in a deal", 1991).

Monetary Union

For individual countries to ride out any demand shocks to their economies, the union needs to be able to account for any impact. Spain and Germany's economies are quite different. With a single currency, any disruption (sudden and dramatic rise in interest rates globally) that will lower investment and consumer spending could have a greater negative impact on one economy versus the next within the EU. The individual governments' fiscally and monetary policies are severely restricted with spending and interest rates managed centrally. Feldstein (1997) recommends: flexibility in wages and prices, labour mobility where displaced workers can move to areas where employment opportunities are greater, and fiscal transfers where the central government can transfer monies to those areas negatively affected by the changes.

Strengths and Weaknesses

The EU is also about a common market and currency. Some of its strengths and weaknesses are found in Table 5.

COMPARISON OF REGIONAL AGREEMENTS TO THE WTO

The NAFTA and the EU and other regional agreements are very different when compared to the GATT and the WTO. Issues including EU agricultural subsidies and political unwillingness to let up on anti-dumping legislation and immigration reform in the US and current account deficits in both regions and

Table 5. EU: Strengths and weaknesses

Strengths	Weaknesses
• The EU's sheer size is strength. It has more people than the NAFTA countries. • Its currency is a strength. • The increased trade internally is a strength.	• Some countries institutions need further development first to fit in. ("Keeping Up", 2013) • The many languages of the countries in the EU limit the mobility of its labour force. • Agriculture subsidies distort trade. (Bergsten, 2005) • The region may be becoming too large to function properly with 28 members. (EU, 2017b) • Countries entering the EU after the Maastricht treaty will find that their controls over their economies both domestically and internationally will no longer be theirs. (Feldstein, 1999)

"growing anti-globalization sentiment on both sides of the Atlantic" make the WTO even more difficult to implement (Bergsten, 2005: 4). Many RTAs are very different as they are negotiated to accomplish different goals. The EU was negotiated in the 1950s in order to give the parties more bargaining power with the US in multilateral negotiations (Whalley, 1998). Exporters benefit from the additional business and are more willing to lobby for joining a regional trade agreement (Baldwin, 1993).

NAFTA is a trade agreement with benefits for the three parties involved which reduced the barriers to trade in those countries involved. The environmental and labour standards of the NAFTA were greater in scope of the standards of the GATT/WTO at the time. The CUSFTA also negotiated trade in services that was not covered by the GATT/WTO (Whalley, 1998). The NAFTA agreement focused of services, environment, labour standards, countervailing duties on the auto and textiles whereas the EU was more focused on agriculture and steel, regional social transfers (Whalley, 1998). The NAFTA could go further in the integration and the EU may be reaching its limits for country involvement.

The EU involves 28 parties. The EU is very integrated with increased trade, lower barriers to the mobility of its citizens and established a common currency (EU Enlargement, 2013). The WTO on the other hand has made little progress since 2001 when the DOHA Round began. The agenda of the WTO is huge and the number of countries involved is enormous. While the WTO has stalled, the EU is making progress and many other regional trade agreements are lowering the barriers to trade. The concessions that countries were not willing to make at the WTO are made to join the EU. The EFTA members joined the EU for fear of being left out.

Bilateral Agreements

Many bilateral agreements have been signed for the same reason, countries were scrambling to join the EU. A smaller economy needs to have access to the larger economy to avoid being shut out. Many of the bilateral RTAs signed since the WTO Doha Round stalled, have been signed by countries aligning themselves with a significant trading partner such as the EU, US, China, Japan, EFTA, ASEAN, Central America or instances of countries such as Russia Turkey and Georgia aligning themselves with neighbouring countries bilaterally (WTO, 2017e).

The NAFTA came about because the FTA Canada signed was threat to Canada when the US was considering a FTA with Mexico. Two bilateral agreements became one larger regional agreement. Regional trading agreements succeed because many of the countries are already have substantial trade already and are in close geographic proximity with low barriers to trade already, so in the end the step to a bilateral agreement is less disruptive to cross border traffic (Fernández & Portes, 1998).

Foreign investment is a significant impetus for less developed countries to sign RTAs as well, even though they will be suffering with lost revenue for import tariffs (Fernández & Portes, 1998). Another reason for the success for the RTAs is the superior enforcement mechanisms, through direct retaliation if an industry is given preferential treatment by the government, causing governments to cease from acting in this manner. GATT was not as strong and the enforcement was not as direct (Fernández & Portes, 1998).

Regional Trade Agreements Promote Further Multilateral Trade Negotiations

The Doha Round of the WTO negotiations stalled as have the previous rounds of the WTO. The WTO needs to continue moving to further trade liberalization and avoid moving toward "bilateralism and protectionism" to remain relevant. Previous talks stalled in the WTO Uruguay Round because of the EU agricultural subsidies. The US negotiated NAFTA, and threatened to create a trade pact with the Pacific area countries with the APEC Summit. The EU changed its stance one month later. Sometimes regional agreements, or the threat of them, helps to get multilateral deals moving forward (Bergsten, 2005).

Problems with RTAs

One of the problems with RTAs is that regional trade patterns are more dictated by GDP of a country or the distance between it and a trading partner than anything else (Ethier, 1998). The "beggar-thy-neighbour effect" can also make RTAs an attractive proposition for potential members, for goods can be substituted within the RTA away from goods that are imported with tariffs attached to them. The third party, the low-cost producer is shut out of the game. With the low-cost producer outside the region "Trade diverting" occurs, when a regional block is formed and the external tariffs remain high resulting in the direction of trade to a higher cost country in the block from a lower cost country outside the block.

This distortion on trade leaves everyone worse off. Some argue the negative trade diverting effect has implications because the EU has subsidies and tariffs countries in the union pay too much for many agricultural products (Fernández & Portes, 1998). Another problem is RTAs do not reform monetary or fiscal policies of the national governments, rather they tempt governments to manipulate them (Fernández & Portes, 1998).

RTAs That Failed

The new regionalism of the 1960s and the old regionalism in the 1980s differ in that we saw that it was every country for itself. Under the old regionalism, the US did not want to have any part of any regional trade agreement. The bureaucratic entanglement in negotiations for the less developed countries derailed any attempt at negotiating FTAs, as these countries desperately needed the economies of scale of industrialization. Since, there has been an outbreak of new deals (Bhagwati, 1992). For example, the 1998 the Asia-Pacific Economic Cooperation (APEC) forum has a target date for 2020 for a new major regional trade deal ("Aphagetti" 1998).

OTHER FACTORS EFFECTING RTAS AND MULTILATERAL AGREEMENTS

Politics of RTAs

RTA tend to provide increased trade protection in many areas resulting in trade diversion and an economically inefficient situation. To make the agreement work and gain acceptance by politically motivated special interest groups, total social welfare will be reduced. With the exclusion of some sectors the political opposition to the agreement is lessened. Producers benefit and consumers lose out. Grossman (1993) also suggested that there should be a mechanism by which exporters who are made better off in one country compensate the importer competitors who are made worse off, however, this is unlikely to ever happen (Grossman, 1993). Exporters can win if they can lobby the government. There is an incentive for countries, as in the case of Mexico, to negotiate from a position of weakness to grant concessions to leverage domestic reforms that were otherwise not possible (Whalley, 1998). It is a strange political outcome; a trade deal that can impose domestic reforms.

Social or Environmental Focus of WTO and RTAs

The greener, wealthier nations have forced their environmental standards on the poorer nations. As trade becomes more integrated, the environmental considerations of trade become more relevant. Trade liberalization increases the threat to health and safety standards, lowers standards for goods produced in the countries with lower standards of toxins, can create environmental degradation in border regions, and creates trade institutions that monitor and resolve environmental issues (Steinberg, 1997). Trade liberalization is therefore good for the environment.

Steinberg (1997) suggests that more trade friendly environmental rules are the result of more extensive trade liberalization. Labour and environmental language was been incorporated into NAFTA after its inception (Schott, J. & Hufbauer, 2007). The WTO in the Doha Round negotiated for the freer movement of environmental goods and consistency with environmental rules (WTO, 2017f). Environmental rules around trade are more developed in the EU and the NAFTA than the WTO. The countries in the EU and the countries in the NAFTA each in their own way share similarities of geography and business dealings. Environmental rules can be more easily developed in the EU and the NAFTA than the WTO who has many diverse and developing countries which are less concerned with environmental issues than the more developed countries of the EU and NAFTA.

Special Interest Groups

As previously mentioned, special interest groups include exporters and importers (Baldwin, 1993). Ethier (1998) states that protectionist special interest groups are the norm for the integrated RTAs of today. The EU has established an Economic and Social Committee that listens to input from employers, employees and other interested groups such as farmers and consumer groups (EU, 2017d). Agricultural issues have been an integral part of trade negotiations both with the WTO and the NAFTA discussions (Ogden, 1996). The NAFTA lobbies for commodities are very strong in Mexico and the US. Supporters of trade liberalization included corn growers, livestock processors, and detractors include the farmer's union, wheat producers and fruit and vegetable producers to name a few. "In 1990 GATT was deadlocked on agriculture" as well (Orden, 1996: 74).

Impact on RTAs

Governments are lobbied to increase tariffs but when a FTA is agreed upon, not only are the tariffs inside the group reduced but it impacts the external tariffs as well, reducing them, which is an unexpected outcome (Ornelas, 2005). Looking at the reasons for implementing a FTA, Ornelas (2005) suggests that the political stock of governments from lobby group contributions and the tariff tax revenues losses need to be balanced against the consumer benefits of the reduced costs and the access to other export markets for the producers and choice for consumers.

Impact on Multilateral Trading System

The WTO claims rightly that special interest groups do not have a significant impact on the WTO. In their literature, they speak of the limited effect of lobby groups on the multilateral trading system. Unfortunately talks have not progressed in any substantial way for the latest round to reduce tariffs, quotas or subsidies (WTO, 2017f). According to Ornelas (2005), as governments move toward multilateral trade the political contributions disappear and total welfare becomes more important than special interests. Special interest groups have little influence on something that does not work, the WTO.

SOLUTIONS AND RECOMMENDATIONS

Regionalism is not the answer but it may be the only answer with the stalled WTO Doha Round of talks on such a broad array of topics that it is unlikely that any consensus will ever be built. Bhagwati (1992) who claims that "multilateral free trade for all" is the goal but in the face of all the regional trade agreements since the 1980s it may be undermined. He thinks its revival is unfortunate. Ethier (1998) states that the close proximity of trading partners will lead to greater trade and the fewer number of partners to the agreement the greater number of terms can be agreed upon and then it will be easier to reach an agreement. Countries seek bilateral agreements because it provides them with benefits that could not be obtained either by going alone or just by only being part of the WTO (Table 6).

Agriculture represents a small percentage of GDP for most developed countries (Ogden 1996) yet developing countries that can produce goods much cheaper are effectively shut out because of the agriculture support structures (subsidies and quota guaranteed prices) in many developed countries (WTO, 2017f). RTAs are the future. Governments lower their tariffs after joining a RTAs and so improve their welfare resulting in trade flow increases both internally and externally. All countries gain from the RTAs. The RTAs can help "to pave the way" toward multilateral freer trade benefiting "the world trading system" (Ornelas, 2005: 491).

FUTURE RESEARCH DIRECTIONS

If we were to look into the future fifty years from now what will we see in terms of trade agreements. Will there be none? If there are none does that mean we will have true free global trade or will there be islands of protectionism where there is little or no trade between nations. We feel that somewhere between full globalization and pure isolationism our future will exist. Brown (2016) puts forth the idea that we

Table 6. Assessing the importance of country objectives for particular regional agreements

COUNTRY OBJECTIVES	REGIONAL TRADE AGREEMENT			
	EC	NAFTA	Canada-US	Mercosur
Traditional Trade Gains	W			W
Strengthening Domestic Policy Reform		S (Mexico)		
Increased Multi-Lateral Bargaining Power	W			W (Bargaining in NAFTA)
Access Guarantees		W	S (Canada)	
Strategic Linkage	S			
Multi-Lateral and Regional Interplay		W (US)	W (Canada, US)	S

(Notes: S = strong objective; W = weaker objectives)
Source: *(Whalley, 1998, p. 75)*

might be moving into the era of mega-regional agreements. This is where we feel the next generation of research needs to be focused. These mega-regional agreements appear to be on the rise due to two forces: global supply chains and China. Future research into the role of fully integrated global supply chains, as are seen in the automotive industry need to be understood as mega-agreements on their own. In terms of China, its rise has caused ripples of geo-political uncertainty and a shift in trade negotiations toward Asia Pacific. Future research needs to focus on agreements like the Trans Pacific Partnership (TPP).

CONCLUSION

The evolution of multilateral trading system and the importance of GATT/WTO cannot be underestimated as a means to open up world trade by lowering barriers to trade. Very little cross border trade took place in the 1930s where there was a dramatic beggar thy neighbour attitude with protectionist tariffs. It is less likely now to have a country invade another when many foreign direct investments and significant bilateral trade takes place. Europe has been fairly peaceful for over 60 years now. The GATT/WTO had a great impact on the growth in trade for a few years with 164 members currently.

Regional Trading Agreements now represent the largest blocks of trade in goods after the WTO with the EU and NAFTA dominating the scene after the WTO. With the 500 million people in the EU and the 400 million in NAFTA representing 46% of world trade in goods, the regional blocks are most formidable and in some cases, more responsive and in all cases growing (WTO, 2017j).

The WTO is struggling to maintain its mandate. National policies that increase market access by foreign companies are not the concern of national governments focused on domestic social issues, politics, culture and economic concerns over increased trade (Patterson, 2010). Governments are not likely to give up their control over the next group of changes coming from the WTO, whose Doha Round talks were suspended in 2008 (Patterson, 2010).

The chapter has discussed the current systems of international trade: regional trade agreements and international trade institutions. It has explored the questions "What gives rise to regionalism? And Why does regionalism work so well"? It specifically looked at The North American Free Trade Agreement (NAFTA) and the European Union and compared Regionalism to the World Trade Organization (WTO). Finally, it concluded with an expectation for the next phase of trade development.

REFERENCES

Affairs, F., & the Trade and Development Canada. (2017). *Canada-United States Free Trade Agreement (FTA)*. Retrieved February, 13, 2017, from http://www.international.gc.ca/trade-agreements-accords-commerciaux/agr-acc/us-eu.aspx?lang=eng

Alphabetti spaghetti: Are regional trade agreements a good idea? (1998). *The Economist*. Retrieved February, 12, 2017, from http://www.economist.com/node/605199

Bagwell, K., & Staiger, R. W. (1998). Will Preferential Agreements Undermine the Multilateral Trading System. *The Economic Journal*, *108*(July), 1162–1182. doi:10.1111/1468-0297.00336

Baier, S. L., & Bergstrand, J. H. (2007). Do Free Trade Agreements Actually Increase Members International Trade? *Journal of International Economics*, *71*(1), 72–95. doi:10.1016/j.jinteco.2006.02.005

Baldwin, R. (1993). *A Domino Theory of Regionalism*. National Bureau of Economic Research Working Paper Series, 4665. Retrieved September, 9, 2013 from http://www.nber.org/papers/w4465.pdf

Bergsten, F. (2005). Rescuing the Doha Round. *Foreign Affairs*. Retrieved October, 23, 2016, from http://s06.middlebury.edu/ECON0340A/Rescuing%20the%20Doha%20Round.pdf

Bhagwati, J. (1992). Regionalism versus Multilateralism. *World Economy*, *15*(5), 535–556. doi:10.1111/j.1467-9701.1992.tb00536.x

Building blocks: Regional deals are the only game in town for supporters of free trade. Are they any good? (2012). *The Economist*. Retrieved August, 12, 2016, from http://www.economist.com/news/finance-and-economics/21568717-regional-deals-are-only-game-town-supporters-free-trade-are-they-any

Ethier, W. J. (1998). The New Regionalism. *The Economic Journal*, *108*(July), 1149–1161. doi:10.1111/1468-0297.00335

European Union. (2017a). *The history of the European union*. Retrieved February, 4, 2017, from http://europa.eu/about-eu/eu-history/index_en.htm

European Union. (2017b). *How the EU Works: Countries*. Retrieved February, 4, 2017, from http://europa.eu/about-eu/countries/index_en.htm

European Union. (2017c). *How the EU Works: EU Institutions and other bodies* Retrieved February, 4, 2017, from http://europa.eu/about-eu/institutions-bodies/index_en.htm

European Union. (2017d). *How the EU Works: European Economic and Social Committee*. Retrieved February, 4, 2017, from http://europa.eu/about-eu/institutions-bodies/ecosoc/index_en.htm

European Union Enlargement. Keeping up with the Croats. (2013). *The Economist*. Retrieved February, 1, 2017, from http://www.economist.com/news/leaders/21580145-after-croatias-accession-europe-should-be-ready-admit-more-new-members-keeping-up

Feldstein, M. (1997). *The political economy of the Europe economic and monetary union: Political sources of an economic liability.* National Bureau of Economic Research. Retrieved February, 12, 2017, from http://www.nber.org/papers/w6150.pdf

Fernández, R., & Jonathan Portes, J. (1998). Returns to Regionalism: An Analysis of Nontraditional Gains from Regional Trade Agreements. *The World Bank Economic Review, 12*(2), 197–220. doi:10.1093/wber/12.2.197

Grossman, G. M., & Helpman, E. (1995). The Politics of Free Trade Agreements. *The American Economic Review, 85*, 667–690.

Mehanna, R. A., & Shamsub, H. (2002). Who is benefitting the most from NAFTA? An intervention time series analysis. *Journal of Economic Development, 27*(2), 69–79.

NAFTA Secretariat. (1994). *North American Free Trade Agreement.* Retrieved January, 30, 2017, from http://www.nafta-sec-alena.org/en/view.aspx?conID=590&mtpiID=ALL

Orden, D. (1996). *Agricultural Interest Group Bargaining over the North American Free Trade Agreement.* The Political Economy of Trade Protection.

Ornelas, E. (2005). Endogenous Free Trade Agreements and the Multilateral Trading System. *Journal of International Economics, 67*(2), 471–497. doi:10.1016/j.jinteco.2004.11.004

Patterson, E. (2010). What's Wrong with the WTO: Rethinking the Institutional Design. *Global Policy Journal.* Retrieved February, 3, 2017, from http://www.globalpolicyjournal.com/articles/world-economy-trade-and-finance/what%C3%A2%E2%82%AC%E2%84%A2s-wrong-wto-rethinking-institutional-design

Schott, J., & Hufbauer, G. (2007). NAFTA Revisited. *Policy Options.* Retrieved February, 17, 2017, from http://archive.irpp.org.ezproxy.library.dal.ca/po/archive/oct07/schott.pdf

Schwartz, M. A. (1998). NAFTA and the Fragmentation of Canada. *The American Review of Canadian Studies, 28*(1-2), 1–2, 11–28. doi:10.1080/02722019809481561

Sirkin, H. L. (2012). Nafta: After 20 Years, We're Not There Yet. *Bloomberg BusinessWeek.* Retrieved February, 14, 2017, from http://www.businessweek.com/articles/2012-08-01/nafta-20-years-and-not-there-yet

Steinberg, R. H. (1997). Trade-Environment Negotiations in the EU, NAFTA, and WTO: Regional Trajectories of Rule Development. *The American Journal of International Law, 91*(2), 231–267. doi:10.2307/2954211

The deal is done. (1999). *The Economist.* Retrieved February, 7, 2017, from http://www.economist.com/node/8765752?zid=307&ah=5e80419d1bc9821ebe173f4f0f060a07

Whalley, J. (1998). *Why Do Countries Seek Regional Trade Agreements?* National Bureau of Economic Research. Retrieved February, 14, 2017, from Google Scholar http://www.nber.org/chapters/c7820

World Trade Organization. (2013a) *Key developments in 2011 a snapshot Table 1.1 [Excel spreadsheet].* Retrieved October, 30, 2017, from http://www.wto.org/english/res_e/statis_e/its2012_e/its12_world_trade_dev_e.htm

World Trade Organization. (2013b). *Merchandise trade by a selected group of economies 2001-2011 Table A4* [Excel spreadsheet]. Retrieved October, 30, 2017, from http://www.wto.org/english/res_e/statis_e/its2012_e/its12_appendix_e.htm

World Trade Organization. (2013c). *Regional Trade Agreements-RTA Database.* Retrieved October, 30, 2017, from http://rtais.wto.org/UI/PublicAllRTAList.aspx

World Trade Organization. (2017a). *Understanding the WTO: Basics The GATT years: from Havana to Marrakesh.* Retrieved February, 2, 2017, from http://www.wto.org/english/thewto_e/whatis_e/tif_e/fact4_e.htm

World Trade Organization. (2017b). *10 benefits of the WTO trading system.* Retrieved February, 2, 2017 from http://www.wto.org/english/thewto_e/whatis_e/10ben_e/10b00_e.htm

World Trade Organization. (2017c). *Understanding the WTO: Members and Observers.* Retrieved February, 2, 2017, from http://www.wto.org/english/thewto_e/whatis_e/tif_e/org6_e.htm

World Trade Organization. (2017d). *Regional Trade Agreements.* Retrieved February, 2, 2017, from http://www.wto.org/english/tratop_e/region_e/region_e.htm

World Trade Organization. (2017e). *RTA Database Free Trade Agreements* [Excel Spreadsheet]. Retrieved February, 2, 2017, from http://rtais.wto.org/UI/PublicSearchByCrResult.aspx

World Trade Organization. (2017f). *Doha Round: What are they negotiating?* Retrieved February, 7, 2017, from http://www.wto.org/english/tratop_e/dda_e/update_e.htm

World Trade Organization. (2017g). *Understanding the WTO: Who we are.* Retrieved February, 2, 2017, from http://www.wto.org/english/thewto_e/whatis_e/who_we_are_e.htm

World Trade Organization. (2017h). *World Trade Organization...In Brief.* Retrieved February, 2, 2017, from http://www.wto.org/english/res_e/doload_e/inbr_e.pdf

World Trade Organization. (2017i). *Understanding the WTO.* Retrieved February, 2. 2017, from http://www.wto.org/english/thewto_e/whatis_e/tif_e/understanding_e.pdf

World Trade Organization. (2017m). *Statistics Database: Trade Profiles.* Retrieved February, 2, 2017, from http://stat.wto.org/CountryProfile/WSDBCountryPFReporter.aspx?Language=E

KEY TERMS AND DEFINITIONS

Common Market: A form of regional economic integration where all barriers to trade are removed, a common external trade policy is adopted, and factors of production are given mobility.

Customs Union: A form of regional economic integration where all barriers to trade are removed and a common external trade policy is adopted.

Economic Union: A form of regional economic integration where all barriers to trade are removed, common external trade policy is adopted, factors of production are given mobility, common currency is established, tax rates are harmonized, and there is a common monetary and fiscal policy.

Free Trade Area: A form of regional economic integration where all barriers to trade are removed and each member determines its own trade policy.

Maastricht Treaty: Is an international agreement signed in maastricht, netherlands by all eec member states on february 7, 1992. It established the european union (eu).

Regional Trade Agreements: Agreements among countries in a geographic region to reduce, and ultimately remove, tariff and nontariff barriers to the free flow of goods, services and factors of production among each other.

Trade Diversion: Occurs when trade is diverted from a more efficient exporter towards a less efficient as a consequence of a regional trade agreement.

Treaty of Rome: Is an international agreement, signed in Rome, Italy on march 25, 1957, by Belgium, France, the Federal Republic of Germany (then West Germany), Italy, Luxembourg, and the Netherlands. it established the European Economic Community (EEC) and created a common market and customs union amongst its members.

Chapter 2
What Makes a Global Business Model?

Oleksiy Osiyevskyy
University of Calgary, Canada & Northeastern University, USA

Milena Troshkova
Northeastern University, USA

Yongjian Bao
University of Lethbridge, Canada

ABSTRACT

A firm's business model is an essential mechanism determining how an organization creates value for its stakeholders and captures part of the created value as profit for its owners. Global enterprises secure their market positions through properly functioning business models that are globally scalable. Once a globally scalable business model is successfully designed and validated in one location, it becomes a non-location-bound firm-specific advantage, promoting the firm's international expansion. This chapter addresses the following research questions: (1) What is the role of a business model in the success of global enterprises? (2) Which common attributes do business models of successful global companies possess? and (3) How to make a business model more suitable for global expansion? The theoretical analysis of these questions yields a conceptual framework for examining the global companies through the business model lens. The developed conceptual framework is illustrated and corroborated with the mini-cases of global companies.

INTRODUCTION

The keystone of any global enterprise lies in its non-location-bound (NLB) firm-specific advantages (FSAs), which, once developed in one location, can be executed in other locations with marginal benefits exceeding marginal costs, by this means creating the incentives for global expansion (Rugman & Verbeke, 1992; Rugman & Almodóvar, 2011; Verbeke & Yuan, 2010; Grøgaard & Verbeke, 2012; Verbeke, 2013; Verbeke, Zargarzadeh, & Osiyevskyy, 2014). Traditionally, non-location-bound firm-specific advantages

DOI: 10.4018/978-1-5225-2673-5.ch002

were considered to be originating from the R&D or marketing activities through creation of intangible assets (such as new products, globally recognized brand name or reputation) that can be profitably leveraged on a global scale (Verbeke et al., 2014). In this chapter we suggest that these sources of FSAs have to be supplemented by one more essential factor, the firm's business model, which – once successfully developed and validated – becomes a firm-specific advantage itself (Osiyevskyy & Zargarzadeh, 2015), simultaneously becoming a critical determinant of the possibility of leveraging other non-location-bound firm-specific advantages in other markets (Hennart, 2014).

A firm's business model is the organizational meta-routine serving two basic purposes: (1) value creation for the firm stakeholders, and (2) value appropriation for firm owners (Osiyevskyy & Dewald, 2015a; Osiyevskyy & Zargarzadeh, 2015). Value creation is achieved through providing attractive value propositions to key stakeholders, while value appropriation is determined by the firm's ability to sustain the economic rents thanks to superior bargaining power vis-à-vis essential resource providers and customers. Importantly, it is only the combination of high value creation and appropriation that leads to a sustainable, "Winner" business model; whereas superior results in only one of these dimensions lead to inherently unsustainable positions of a "Giver trap" [having happy stakeholders yet unhappy shareholders] or a "Taker trap" [companies that enjoy temporarily high profits unsupported by superior stakeholder value] (Biloshapka et al., 2016).

The "routine" conceptualization of the business model allows proper anchoring of this still contentious construct (Zott et al., 2011) within the traditional evolutionary economic theory terms (Nelson & Winter, 1982), defined as intentional, repetitive patterns of activity within the organization (Osiyevskyy & Zargarzadeh, 2015).

An interest in the business model concept has dramatically increased over the 15-year period between 1995 and 2010 (Zott et al., 2011). Scholars claim that this resulted largely from the advent of the Internet (e.g., Amit & Zott, 2001), rapid growth in emerging markets (Prahalad & Hart, 2002; Seelos & Mair, 2007; Thompson & MacMillan, 2010), and the expanding industries and organizations dependent on post-industrial technologies (Perkmann & Spicer, 2010). These trends led to business model becoming a new unit of analysis that is distinct from the product, firm, industry, or network; even though it is based on a focal firm, its boundaries expand further than those of the firm (Zott et al., 2011; Zott & Amit, 2013). Firms do not execute their business models in a competitive vacuum, but rather compete through their business models that serve as a potential source of competitive advantage (Osiyevskyy, 2014) and superior value creation (Morris et al., 2005). Importantly, as any routine, a business model acts as a mechanism of organizational memory (Nelson & Winter, 1982), accumulating the knowledge about a successful way of generating and capturing economic value, particularly in a global context.

Similarly to other types of commercial organizations in a free market economy, global enterprises secure their market positions and profit through properly functioning business models (Osiyevskyy & Zargarzadeh, 2015; Hennart, 2014). The business models of such enterprises are globally scalable, allowing profitable international expansion.

As we are showing in this study, the globally scalable business models have essential peculiarities that make them suitable for international expansion. Yet, despite the crucial importance of specific features of globally scalable business models, this topic received insufficient attention in prior literature. This sets the motivation for the current chapter, which intends to examine the global companies through the business model lens, addressing the following formal questions: (i) what is the role of a business model in the success of a global enterprise? (ii) which common attributes do business models of successful global companies possess? and (iii) how to make a business model more suitable for global expansion?

This chapter is divided into three sections. First, we introduce an original framework for systematic analysis and comparison of business models. Second, we conceptually examine the characteristics of business models of global companies, including International New Ventures (INVs) and Multinational Enterprises (MNEs). Third, we offer practical managerial advice on how to make a business model more suitable for global expansion. The discussed theoretical concepts are illustrated and corroborated with the mini-cases of global enterprises, demonstrating the applicability of the developed deductively framework to real-world situations (Siggelkow, 2007).

BUSINESS MODEL CHARACTERISTICS: AN ANALYTIC FRAMEWORK

Four-Dimensional Business Model Structure

For the purposes of our comparative analysis, it is convenient to analyze a firm's business model through the four-dimensional theoretical lens. It summarizes and integrates in a coherent way the proposed in prior literature approaches towards structuring the business models, most importantly the three-dimensional business model view [value, transactive and resource dimensions: see George & Bock (2011), Osiyevskyy & Dewald, (2015b)], or the widely adopted in practice '9 Building Blocks' of a business model canvas (Osterwalder & Pigneur, 2010).

The proposed in this paper framework emphasizes four essential areas that allow analyzing a firm's business model and comparing business models of different firms with each other. The underlying reasoning behind the proposed analytical framework is that a business model is defined by four broad characteristics: the target industry, the stakeholder value proposition, the design of activity system, and the resources for the business model (see Table 1).

Target Industry

An industry can be broadly defined as a group of firms that produce products or services that serve the same general purpose (Meyer & Crane, 2014). The target industry sets the stage for choosing, designing, and supporting a business model, and hence should be analyzed as an essential part of a business model (Biloshapka et al., 2016). An industry is comprised of segments (a set of competitors addressing

Table 1. Business model analysis framework

Target Industry	Stakeholder Value Proposition
• Broad industry definition • Customer segments/niches (initial target, expansion plans)	• Key stakeholders: end users (consumers), channel partners, suppliers, government… • Value proposition to each stakeholder: problem solved, solution's differentiating factors
Design of Activity System	**Resources for the Business Model**
• Revenue model • Go-To-Market model • Production model • Product/service development model	• Investment capital • Human capital • Partnerships • Tangible assets • Intangible assets

particular customer groups), and niche markets. Whereas large established companies usually dominate a set of segments within a particular industry (e.g., Google having substantive position in the segments of automated web search and e-mail within the broader Internet industry), the entrepreneurs founding new ventures most often focus on creating winning products for a niche market before expanding (e.g., Amazon in 1994-1997 concentrating on on-line book selling niche, before expanding to other segments/ niches within the e-commerce industry). This is due to a niche market holding a specific pocket for opportunity within a segment. There are a number of factors to be evaluated when determining an attractive industry/segment/niche (Meyer & Crane, 2014): a) its current size and growth rates of customer demand, b) major trends sweeping across the industry, c) the competition in the industry and the evidence of successful business models, d) the activity level of new companies, venture deals, and M&A transactions, e) the technology life cycle stage of the industry overall, f) the channels of distribution within an industry, g) reasonably priced and widely available key components, technologies, and ingredients needed for the production and delivery of a product or service, and h) the absence of existing barriers to entry.

Stakeholder Value Proposition

The ultimate driving forces of any commercial enterprise in a market economy is in resolving stakeholders' problems in an industry by introducing a product/service developed with the use of proper technology. The role of the stakeholders is essential here, as they provide the firm with resources needed for its functioning. In addition to winning the customers' support, most business models require to attract at least one more crucial stakeholder, e.g.: the beverage producers need to establish the relationship with distributors; or the web search companies need to secure the buy-in form advertisers. In general, the list of key stakeholders to consider within the business model analysis and design process includes end-users, buyers, sales channel partners, suppliers, government, employees, investors, and local communities the company operates in. In order to win their support, a business model needs to provide an attractive value proposition: the problem being solved (what exactly the pain point is that the business model solves or the passion it satisfies), the proposed solution (i.e., how exactly the business model does it), and the differentiation from the existing alternatives on the market (e.g., advanced accessibility, price for customer, multi-functionality, privacy, and user control). Moreover, the design of a business model usually has to successfully manage the conflicting expectation of stakeholders by providing a balanced solution (Falkenberg & Osiyevskyy, 2014).

Design of Activity System

The design of an activity system reflects the transactive part of the business model (George & Bock, 2011; Zott & Amit, 2010), determining "the way operations (business processes) are organized to utilize available resources toward delivering value to stakeholders" (Osiyevskyy & Dewald, 2015b, p.1012). In particular, the design of an activity system of a business model comprises its revenue model, go-to-market model, production model, and product/service development model (Meyer & Crane, 2014; Biloshapka et al., 2016).

The revenue model describes the way a firm charges its customers, including the revenue type (one-time sale fee / subscription / usage fee / brokerage commission) and pricing. Obviously, a company can have more than one revenue stream: e.g., the audiobook seller Audible (now part of Amazon) charges its customers both a monthly subscription fee and one-time sale fee for additional audiobooks.

The go-to-market model determines the way a business model interacts with customers: the sales channels (e.g., direct sales, web-site, distribution network), promotion and branding approach, and the economics of customer acquisition within the business model (customer lifetime value versus the cost of customer acquisition).

The production model determines the system of processes that deliver on the stakeholder value proposition: i.e., how exactly the company makes and delivers its products or provides its services (manufacturing, logistics, supply chain management, after-sales support processes), the effectiveness and efficiency of this configuration.

Finally, the product/service development model describes the approach of a business model towards R&D (e.g., internal or outsourced) and protection of intellectual property.

Resources for the Business Model

The resources for the business model dimension determines the essential assets and capabilities needed for deploying and sustaining the business model (Osiyevskyy & Dewald, 2015b): e.g., investment capital, human capital, partnerships, tangible and intangible assets.

An example of applying the proposed business model analysis framework to the case of Facebook is presented in Table 2.

In the next section we will apply the suggested analytical framework for determining the peculiarities of the globally scalable business models.

CHARACTERISTICS OF GLOBAL COMPANIES' BUSINESS MODELS

International New Ventures (INVs) and Multinational Enterprises (MNEs)

Multinational Enterprise is traditionally defined as an enterprise that has its facilities and other assets in at least one country other than its home country (Dunning, 2012). International new venture (INV)

Table 2. Facebook, Inc: Business model analysis framework

Target Industry		Stakeholder Value Proposition	
• Broad industry definition: *Internet* • Key customer segment: *Social Network Users*		• Key stakeholders: *end-users (social network users), advertisers* • Value proposition to end-users: *satisfies the need for communication through a free social network with the broadest global user base* • Value proposition to advertisers: *allows to reach the target audience (of social network users) with precise, targeted, highly effective advertising messages*	
Design of Activity System		Resources for the Business Model	
• Revenue model: *free for end-users, advertising fee for advertisers* • Go-To-Market model: *key channel: web-site* • Production model: *key processes (user support, advertiser support) are organized internally* • Product/service development model: *(1) internal R&D processes; (2) acquiring startups with promising technologies*		*Key resources needed to maintain the business model:* • *Large customer base (of social network users), to attract advertisers* • *Unique social network technologies* • *Brand recognition*	

is "a business organization that, from inception, seeks to derive significant competitive advantage from the use of resources and the sale of outputs in multiple countries" (Oviatt & McDougall, 1994, p.49). In other words, INVs are firms that internationalize from the outset, or soon afterward, and eventually sell a high share of their output abroad (Hennart, 2014; Verbeke et al., 2014).

Both INVs and MNEs are global enterprises that create and appropriate value globally through their business models (Osiyevskyy & Zargarzadeh, 2015). Moreover, both INVs and MNEs are able to expand by leveraging their non-location-bound (NLB) firm specific advantages (FSAs) (Rugman & Verbeke, 1992; Rugman & Almodóvar, 2011; Verbeke & Yuan, 2010; Verbeke, 2013; Verbeke et al., 2014). In line with the internationalization theory, the foundation for a successful global expansion in terms of value creation and appropriation is built on ownership, control and/or a superior combination of not fully utilized resources, their distribution and coordination abroad, in addition to the choice of the comparatively most efficient foreign operating mode (Verbeke, 2013; Grøgaard, & Verbeke, 2012). Thus, any form of global expansion in terms of scale, entry mode or location and its timing is controlled by FSAs, both existing and developing (Verbeke et al., 2014).

The Role of a Business Model in the Success of Global Enterprises

Similarly to other types of for-profit firms in a free market economy, global enterprises secure their market positions and rents through properly functioning business models (Osiyevskyy & Zargarzadeh, 2015; Hennart, 2014). The business models of such enterprises are globally scalable, allowing profitable international expansion. Once a globally scalable business model is successfully designed and validated in one location, it becomes a non-location-bound firm-specific advantage, promoting the firm's international expansion through replication of the value creation and appropriation routine in other parts of the world. Replicating a business model in foreign markets allows global enterprises to exploit their resource (Penrosian) advantage by leveraging the unique, valuable and inimitable capabilities; to achieve the Bainian market power by improving the firm's bargaining position; and to secure the innovator's quasi-rents (of Schumpeterian type) by coming up with business model innovations in one context and then scaling them up to the global context (Osiyevskyy & Zargarzadeh, 2015). Predictably, the replication of local market routines, including the key organizational routine – its business model, without innovative modifications often faces unpredictable issues in foreign markets (Osiyevskyy & Zargarzadeh, 2015).

Globally Scalable Business Models: Common Attributes

Globally scalable business models have a set of distinct characteristics (see Table 3) that ensure successful global expansion of an enterprise, either MNE (Osiyevskyy & Zargarzadeh, 2015) or INV (Hennart, 2014). Obviously, not all of these characteristics must be present in each global business model; yet, each of them increases a firm's chances of successful internationalization, with the benefits of this process exceeding the costs.

In terms of target industry, the globally scalable business models usually originate from countries with a small home market for their product or service – the environment that forces the companies to consider internationalizing from day one (e.g., consider the Israeli start-ups: Senor & Singer (2009)). Obviously, the countries with large home markets (e.g., the U.S. or China) also host numerous successful MNEs,

Table 3. Distinctive common features of global business models

Target Industry	Stakeholder Value Proposition
• Based in a country with a small home market for their product or service • Distinctive niche products and services	• Key stakeholders: internationally dispersed *expert* customers • Customers have homogenous tastes • Value proposition flexible to local peculiarities
Design of Activity System	**Resources for the Business Model**
• Go-To-Market model: *avoiding international marketing mix adaptations; low-cost means of communication and delivery* • Production model: *services or low weight, non-perishable products; production processes located in low-cost countries; minimal after-sales support* • Product/service development model: *R&D aimed at innovations applicable outside home market*	• Non-location-bound firm-specific advantages: • *Founding entrepreneurs' characteristics (education, experience, international connections)* • *Globally recognized brand/reputation* • *Innovative product portfolio / technology* • *Unique valuable knowledge*

but in such circumstances the global expansion is preceded by a long process of establishing the market position in a home market, and the chances of internationalization for such firms are much lower. Second, globally scalable business models are more likely to be developed around distinctive niche products and services demanded by internationally dispersed expert customers (Hennart, 2014). This enables INVs to reach customers through low cost means (since the buyers will be actively searching for a solution), as less time is spent on market research, advertising, and sales promotion.

A firm is more likely to expand globally if consumers have homogenous tastes – a condition that allows an internationalizing company to minimize or avoid international marketing mix adaptations for its products and services (Hennart, 2014). For example, a business model deploying a proven cancer drug (Verbeke et al., 2014) is very likely to be suitable for global scaling. Thus, globally scalable business models are likely to be designed around low-cost means of communication (e.g., Internet advertising and word-of-mouth).

In terms of production model, global business models usually rely on delivery of low weight, non-perishable products (Hennart, 2014): e.g., luxury watch brand is more suitable for global expansion, comparing to luxury food provider. Successful MNEs also make a full use of locating the production in countries with relatively low cost levels. The R&D processes at global companies are usually aimed at innovations applicable outside their home markets.

Finally, the key resources underpinning globally scalable business models are non-location-bound firm-specific advantages, serving as the basis for international expansion: e.g., the globally recognized brand/reputation, social network ties, or globally applicable technology. These FSAs are either developed within the firm over time through investments into R&D and marketing (the Uppsala model of MNE expansion), or are embedded with the funding team of INV (Verbeke et al., 2014). Corroborating the latter point, the INVs studies demonstrate that the founding entrepreneurs' pre-launch experience, managerial capacity, and international business networks are fundamental to new venture success (Autio et al., 2000; Zahra 2005; Cressy, 2006; Verbeke et al., 2014). Given the above, founder-entrepreneurs with higher education levels are more likely to internationalize in the early years of a new venture (Verbeke et al., 2014). New ventures with immigrant founding entrepreneurs are also more likely to expand to foreign markets in the early years of operation.

GLOBALLY SCALABLE BUSINESS MODELS: CASE EXAMPLES

Jacob Jensen Design (JJD): Success of Interwoven IP Elements

The outstanding success of Jacob Jensen Design's global endeavor can be explained by our business model framework, particularly when the four areas are interwoven together around an IP (intellectual property right) protecting JJD branding capability as its core competence.

JJD was a creation of Jacob Jensen more than fifty years ago. His design is on the CNN top 12 list of "Best Designs in the last 100 Years". The studio has been famous for its commissioned works for Bang & Olufsen, Bosch, Siemens, GE, Lego, Toshiba and Volvo. Companies from different countries loved JJD's design as well as appreciated the simple and pure lifestyle of Scandinavian countries.

When his son, Tim Jacob Jensen, took the helm of the studio, he decided to leverage the reputation of JJD's design competence for a global brand that offers "affordable design" to a mass market. He changed the corporate strategy, re-organized the structure, and staged local presence in China, Thailand, and South Africa first. In a decade, JJD oriented toward a global network of regional branch offices that distribute brand products and design services for clients in four continents – Europe, Asia, Africa, and South America.

From a design studio to a global emporium of "affordable designs", JJD has made substantial progress over the past ten years. This venture's future is promising because all four areas identified by our framework are naturally interwoven together and centered on JJD's strong IP-based branding power. Table 4 summarizes how these four criteria are complementary to each other.

JJD used to be a strong player in a small niche market of industrial design in Denmark. Having learned from painful experiences of IP encroaching before, JJD tried to fuse design services with JJD brand products. The changing of market positioning was perfectly timed with global endearment of Scandinavian life style and Danish design. So, JJD chose to target the market in emerging economies with "affordable designs" from Denmark, which included both design service and brand products.

Table 4. JJD business model of interwoven IP elements

Target Industry	Stakeholder Value Proposition
• Home country with a small market: *Denmark* • Affordable Danish design for the world • Industrial design service and JJD brand products for emerging markets	• Manufacturers: *face-lifting industrial design by famous JJD Studio* • Interns: *apprenticeship, royalty from winning designs, employment opportunity* • Franchisees: *association with JJD, distribute brand products* • Value proposition flexible to local peculiarities: *design education for local government and universities, inclusive vernacular designs*
Design of Activity System	**Resources for the Business Model**
• Multiple revenues: *commission, sales, royalty, franchise fee* • Marketing via design campaign: *partnership with government, trade associations and educational institutions.* • Local sourcing production: *resident designers, internship student designers, local franchisees* • Product/service development model: *Total design solution. Corporate infrastructure support on design, business dealing, and administration*	• Non-location-bound firm-specific advantages: *legendary reputation of the founders, organizing capability of the CEO, relationship with Danish government, carefully selected local partners* • Founding entrepreneurs' characteristics: *not too much formal education, street smart, extensive international experiences, risk taking personality* • Globally recognized brand/reputation: *Jacob Janssen is credited the father of modern industrial design, has works exhibited in many museums including MOMA in New York*

To better serve its stakeholders, JJD re-organized its activity system for efficiency and exclusiveness. Relying on government enthusiasm on industrial design education, JJD worked with Danish government for promotion of national events overseas. It also formed strategic alliances with local government and education institutions in Thailand and China for design education. JJD set up a design academy and used educational events to promote its brand and raise awareness of its services among local clients. This design of marketing saved JJD a lot of costs.

JJD also focused on non-location bounded portion of production. It offered industrial designs, marketing strategy, and franchise arrangement. For the physical production of brand products, JJD relied on OEM, manufacturing clients, franchised distributors and branch stores to carry out tangible aspects of production. This mode of production allowed JJD to scale up from one country to another easily.

To influence as well as serve local partners, JJD continued to work on R&D, design form language, design procedure framework, and other meta-languages of design at the corporate level. It also has a consolidated business platform at the corporate level which is user-friendly even at a local level. Its R&D activities continue to strengthen the know-how, and transfer capabilities to divisions and branch levels when needed.

Jacob Jensen has five areas of income: 1) indirect sale of brand products to branch offices which then sell the brand products directly to retailers; 2) royalties that branch offices receive from their clients for the design solutions; 3) royalties from brand products designed by Jacob Jensen for its Licensing Partners; 4) commission on all time and material invoiced clients for design solutions by branch offices; 5) franchise fees that each branch office pays Jacob Jensen for the right to run a regional/local Jacob Jensen business. The above organization of activity system enables JJD to offer three key stakeholders unique values.

Under the general value proposition as "affordable design", JJD tailored specifics for different JJD stakeholders. For manufacture clients, JJD enables them to face-lift their old products with new industrial designs. For business customers (boutiques, retail chains, department stores), JJD provides high quality, brand products that are affordable. For partner education institutions, JJD facilitates industrial design education and furnishes internship for students. JJD owns the brand, manages product portfolio, controls design form and framework, while products are co-designed with students and manufactured by partner companies locally.

JJD would not be able to offer total design solution with brand products, had it not owned a set of firm-specific resources, which contributed to its firm-specific advantages. Free or low marketing resources came from JJD's leveraged reputation and brand attraction. Its leading designers often conducted interviews and newspaper featured articles. It also enjoyed free promotion from participating in local design festivals and news events.

JJD also developed a network of designers, clients and local partners. It allowed the firm to acquire low cost office space, resident designers and local staff. JJD strategically develops its brand power of attracting production partners step by step. As a result of forming alliances with foreign universities and business enterprises, JJD established its presence in local markets with heavy subsidies from partners. Once JJD built up its branch offices and business network, it attracted international experts to be their resident designers. Meanwhile, local students upon graduation have joined the JJD workforce in many branch offices. So for design studio, the production is organized both internationally for resident designers and locally for low-level assistants.

The founder's internationally well-known reputation turns out to be the most valuable resources for JJD. The founder has several works exhibited in MOMA New York. He was ranked among the top modern influential industrial designers.

Under the leadership of Tim Jacob Jensen, JJD strategically converted reputed intangible resources into brand power in foreign countries. Tim Jensen worked closely with the Danish Embassy on various events to promote Denmark, meanwhile bringing the attention to JJD. By participating in design education in China and Thailand, JJD acquired business venues and operational supports with minimum costs in those locations.

Another critical resource JJD possesses is the designers network initiated by Tim Jensen. It brought internationally dispersed resident designers into local studios of JJD. In addition, JJD has also enjoyed the benefit of bringing up quality staff from students who had an internship experience there. This network guaranteed JJD the most efficient and capable human resources.

Within seven years, JJD grew from a highly reputed local design studio in Denmark into a global network of brand products and industrial design. Its initial success reflected strategic utilization of all four areas of our business model framework.

Shanghai Green Court Investment Group (Green Court): Success of Interconnected Social Capital

Listed in Shanghai Stock Exchange with both class A and B shares, Green Court was formed in 1985, and had its first IPO in 1993. The company had been making poultry and processed food products for nearly three decades until 2014. It first branched into private equity investment in China, then ventured into the U.S. market for global asset management.

The sharp turn confused investors at the beginning. After two years of transformation, the market has started to respond positively to its new international venture. Our business model framework (Table 5) provides a concise explanation of its initial success during the transition. Green Court took advantage of its interconnected social capital out of three areas of the framework, which allowed the company to target a thick market opportunity with concentrated demands from customers. Green Court targeted a special segment in the financial industry: private equity and global asset management. It is a compara-

Table 5. Green Court business model, advantage out of interconnected social capital

Target Industry	Stakeholder Value Proposition
• Real estate based asset management • Securitized financial products for Chinese investors who need global assets management portfolio	• Rich global investors from China: *preferred real estate based financial products with controllable risks* • China financial retailers: *unique and attractive products for local customers* • Value proposition flexible to local peculiarities: *real estate, global asset allocation, U.S. market, currency exchange rate hedging, country risk hedging*
Design of Activity System	**Resources for the Business Model**
• Revenues: *commission, sales, capital appreciation* • Marketing based on social capital: *endorsement of local business leaders, perceived prestige with leading university, alumni referral, research reports from opinion leaders* • Mezzanine Style Production: *intermediate fund management team, joint venture of Mezzanine funds, alliance with retailers and distributors* • Product/service development model: *internal team supervised the execution and provided on-call advisory to partners*	• Non-location-bound firm-specific advantages: *funds from transformed IPO companies, social connections and knowledge of both U.S. and China markets* • Founding entrepreneurs' characteristics: *expatriates, successful entrepreneurs, circle of alumni* • Globally recognized reputation: *community leader of the founder, previous success in real estate and food industries*

tively mature segment in the United States. However, Green Court identified a unique niche of "global asset portfolio allocation" for rich Chinese investors who have been concerned about Chinese currency depreciation and looking for real estate assets in the United States. Green Court's financial products allow investors to capture growth opportunity in the United States and hedge against risks of market correction in China simultaneously. But setting up the architecture for cross-country trading and reaching clients across cultures was not easy. Green Court did it because it leveraged social capital in the two markets for advantage-building.

The niche market for Green Court is built upon several major changes in the Chinese economic environment. Derived from 30 years of rapid economic growth, China produced the largest number of multi-millionaires next to the United States. However, the economic trend is turning downward, and the currency of Chinese RMB is doomed to depreciate in the long term. This created an incentive for the rich Chinese to diversify their assets globally. The U.S. market has been considered the primary choice for global asset relocation. Green Court sensed the emerging market opportunity and the lack of professional firms who would be able to conduct trans-pacific portfolio management for the Chinese clients.

To take advantage of a new market opportunity, Green Court developed a Mezzanine fund structure that offers a unique value to clients in China: 1) they can participate in real estate projects; 2) they can purchase financial products that are investments in real estate projects; 3) they are able to buy while in China with Chinese Yuan; 4) the assets would be denominated in U.S. dollars. This structure has allowed the Chinese investors to benefit from real estate projects and to hedge against volatility of currency exchange rates.

Global asset portfolio allocation is a very specialized area that usually requires many years of experience and a market record in order to acquire licenses in any operating countries. Adding to these difficulties would be the recruitment of clients who have large amounts of disposable income for investment. In other words, the costs, both time and financial, of expanding to a global market and building capabilities up would scare away many potential entrants.

What Green Court has been doing is quite firm specific. First, instead of constructing the production line from scratch, it has formed a strategic alliance with West Group, an established real estate investment entity in the United States. The joint venture immediately provided Green Court the needed credentials in the United States as well as initial portfolio of financial products. The initial portfolio included Moynihan Station Project, Dulles Metrorail, World Trade Center Re-development, and UNCF Headquarters projects. In order to expand into the Chinese market, Green Court leveraged its social network and business relationships with banks and financial retail companies to promote its products without directly interacting with end customers. The alliance for sales strategy speeded up the expansion process.

To further assist partners on both sides, China and the United States, Green Court has organized a small cohort of professionals within the firm, as well as a research institute with a well-known university in Shanghai, Fudan University. Both designs facilitate Green Court's capability in product and service development.

The internal cohort are experienced professionals, and they have received new training from Green Court on how to "raise, manage, govern, and exit" the funds. They act like "pit boss" or fund leader for self-selected funds, in which individual managers are also invested proportionally, so they have "skin in the game" and are self-motivated to perform. Fund leaders are actively involved in the entire process of the development and capitalization of financial products. With the incentive alignment, their professional capability and in-depth involvement effectively guides the growth of the funds.

In addition to close involvement of fund leaders, partner institutions who distribute the products in China also receive knowledge-based advice from research reports out of Green Court Research Institute. Since the products and services are novel for Chinese investors, the continuous support of information and know-how help to educate business partners and facilitate the sales at their ends.

The unique way of organizing the activity system allows Green Court to directly contribute to Green Court attracting a valuable base of stakeholders: rich Chinese investors who need to diversify their assets, and business partners who distribute their products in the large Chinese market. For investors, an asset portfolio based on real estate is more substantial and realistic than other financial products. Investors, the Chinese investors in particular, have perceptual preferences to real estate. Projects in hot areas in the United States made the value proposition easy to apprehend. As for the financial retailers, banks and fund management firms, Green Court has provided a new product tailored to the passion of their clients, growing with a mature market in a mature industry.

The Chair of Green Court, Ms. N.F. Yu, organized firm's resources effectively. She strategically mobilized social capital in both markets, China and the United States, that made a significant difference in creating the firm's core competence. The Chair of Green Court has been a socially active entrepreneur in Shanghai and Washington. She was a community leader while growing up in Shanghai, which allowed her to access financial and education resources quicker than others. While she studied and worked in the Bay area, Chair Yu built up a network with high tech and real estate businesses. Her active participation in professional organizations in Shanghai and Washington helped the formation of strategic alliances with key partners in both countries. It also expedited the formation of a professional team within Green Court. Currently, all key members of the management team have shared experiences from colleagues or previous workplaces. That is strong evidence of the role of connectivity and social capital accounting for a rapid transition of Green Court into the global market.

Other firm-specific resources include the credibility of an IPO company in Shanghai. Green Court has a long history in the Shanghai Stock Exchange, which reinforced its social legitimacy when promoting funds to the public. Its direct association with Green Court Research Institute in a well-known university also created positive halo effects for its products. Together with the internal professional team and members' performance records, Green Court successfully constructed a new core competence out of interconnected social capital and human resources.

Detao Masters Academy: Failure by Intermingled Execution

On January 2016, Detao Masters Academy (DTMA) was accredited as the "Platform Provider" by the Council for Higher Education Accreditation (CHEA/CIQG). DTMA turned out to be the first certified for-profit education institution in Asia by CHEA. It was designed as a super channel for creative knowledge production. The design was so novel that the admirers were from around the world, including MBA students from Europe and America.

DTMA's business model consists of three pillars: recruiting the leading experts in industry around the world; setting up a "master studio" for the experts in China; and integrating apprenticeship and business venturing (Table 6). The design aimed to be a "super channel for creative knowledge education and production." However, after 6 years and more than 50 million-dollars of investment, the entity is hobbling towards an uncertain future. Our business model framework identified a vulnerability of DTMA's strategy, and its fatal weakness in its activity system: the intermingled execution suffocated its strategic potential.

Table 6. DTMA global business model of intermingled execution

Intermingled Target Industry	Diffused Stakeholder Value Proposition
• Super channel for creative knowledge education and production • Master Studios for apprenticeship and product development	• Experts: *free entry into China market, subsidy on commercial projects* • Apprentices who want personal mentoring: *internationally well-known masters provide direct coaching and mentoring* • Businesses that aspire for transformative advisory: *consulting and partnership* • Universities demand for industrial experts: *co-delivery of courses*
Intermingled Activity System	**Non-Sustainable Resources Management**
• Traditional marketing: *billboard, online, and news media* • Expensive production model: *international experts on call, translation of speeches, advisory team, paid publication of books* • Replicated services: *simple replication of existing services from masters' home country* • Revenues: *tuition, royalty, capital gain, service sales*	• Key resources are location-bound: *foreign experts cannot stay in China too long* • No firm-specific advantages • Experts also collaborated with others, hard to maintain the exclusiveness • Lack of middle level adopters: *foreign expertise often was lost in translation* • Lack of means to capitalize the experts' reputation and brands

From the beginning, DTMA endeavored to create a new market place by combining global education resources and domestic business opportunities in China. But the market is too novel to be exploited in the short term, and the four areas of DTMA business model happened to have high cost items that were not sustainable for long term success. Among all the issues, the high cost and intermingled execution prevented effective value appropriation. In the past 6 years, DTMA brought many social benefits to its stakeholders, but it hasn't achieved its revenue target. We will use our global business model framework to highlight potential value of DTMA and where it fumbled.

In China, education is an ever-green business. Chinese families are famous in the world for preparing their children for life starting from kindergarten. For example, according to the Ministry of Education of China, more than 50,000 Chinese students went abroad to pursue higher education in 2015 alone. Among all paths of growth, being mentored by celebrity educators has always been perceived as a powerful recipe for career development. In this cultural context, DTMA tried to offer a turbo-charged solution: taking apprenticeship with world leading experts, being mentored by the experts in their studios, and having opportunities to work with the experts for commercial projects.

This value proposition suits the interests of four key stakeholders. For experts (DTMA called them masters), free entry into the Chinese market via DTMA Studios provides benefits from cheap labor of apprentices for their commercial projects. For prospective students, the benefits include mentorship, working opportunity, and seed funding for qualified venture projects. For partner universities and local governments, they could access talent pools from overseas for educational courses. For domestic companies, they would receive cost-effective consultation from internationally well-known experts invited by DTMA.

To create the super knowledge channel for the above stakeholders, DTMA recruited more than 500 industrial experts from 23 countries. These experts were selected by their award-winning achievements and high reputations in their field. Some of these experts were the founder of Frog Design, Hartmut Esslinger, scientist Jay Lee, and Sir John Daniel who was president of Open University in U.K. and officer of UNESCO. Together, the 500 recruited experts won more than 2000 awards in 57 fields. None of any education entity in Asia has ever housed so many experts with rich industrial experiences.

After the recruitment, DTMA started the first 15 Master Studios on trendy businesses, such as industrial design, animation, and fashion design. DTMA's model has been widely reported by news media, and attracted visitors from the United States and Europe. But the issues with value appropriation and the activity system continued to haunt the company. Their lack of global management capability posed a direct challenge to the future of DTMA. Valuable but not appropriable value proposition was a result of several weaknesses in the four areas of DTMA's business model.

DTMA planned to have multiple revenue sources: tuition for apprenticeship, royalty payment by clients, capital gains from invested ventures by the experts, and sales of knowledge services to university and government agencies. DTMA's expert resources have been highly valued by local stakeholders, such as local universities. It formed a strategic alliance with highly reputed universities in China, such as Beijing University and Shanghai Visual Arts Institution. They have built up model classes with more than 400 participants in the past three years. However, the partner universities considered the programs charity and donation from DTMA, instead of business collaboration. With the large investment from DTMA in building up the studio, experts are supposed to bring up at least 5 cohorts of apprentices each year in order to make the ends meet. However, it would be hard to achieve such goal with the current activity system and resource configuration.

The entire process of the activity system made it too luxurious to be profitable. Master Studios is the first education project of DTMA. With no history, DTMA used financial incentives to attract the leading figures in industry to sign contracts. Industrial experts from foreign countries were invited with round-trip business class tickets and benefits for spouses. Master Studios in Shanghai and Beijing were fully financed by DTMA equipped with a team of supportive staff for business operation. International experts were chauffeured around to visit potential business partners as well as sightseeing attractions. When all the costs were added up, Master Studios expected to bring in apprentices and businesses quickly in order to make the ends meet. Unfortunately, this goal has not been achieved.

Another example of insufficient planning of operational process is related to the scheduling difficulties and language obstacles with the international experts. All of them have their established lines of business in home countries. This led them to often treat the Chinese studio as a side deal or even a working vacation from their busy schedules back home. With a very limited stay in China, studios had hard time planning for apprenticeship programs. Additionally, international experts from 23 different countries often communicated in their native languages. For apprentices and business partners, the language and culture barriers were substantial and realistic. Very often, the Chinese would find themselves being lost in translation, which also caused problems in communication between experts and top management team.

Since the business model is quite novel and the value proposition inapprehensible by the first look, DTMA has been struggling in marketing messages and go-to-market choices. It tried university channel by hosting free seminars in partner institutions, explored airport advertising board, and promoted via trade magazines. None of them hit the targeted customers effectively. People often have three separate perceived values of international experts, apprenticeship, and co-venturing business between apprentices and their mentors. None of the messages delivered an integrated value proposition to targeted customers.

A gap between resources and capabilities engulfed the tremendous potential of DTMA's business model. The super channel of creative knowhow is new not only in China but everywhere in the world. DTMA tried successfully to put a variety of international experts and domestic education partners together in its platform. However, integrating the resources and delivering the products required a business-specific capability.

The capability must include the following elements, which DTMA failed to build up. First, staff with domain knowledge, so they can communicate with experts from 57 fields without problem. DTMA has a large team of administrative assistants, but failed to train and equip them with required domain knowledge. Second, coordinating routine between staff and experts to generate suitable products and services in China. DTMA relied heavily on foreign experts to develop projects in China alone. The experts lacked local market knowledge and could not flip their practices into marketable services in China. Third, Chinese customers had a general tendency to appreciate tangible aspects of services and discounted the value of intellectual property rights. To be successful, studios need to develop hybrid of service and product for the market. That has been missing in the process of development.

In conclusion, with the tremendous and valuable resources DTMA hoarded, it failed to demonstrate the capabilities to convert the intangible resources of international experts into tangible services and products. Our framework highlighted the weaknesses in four areas of DTMA's model, and revealed the problem of intermingled execution.

Wanhua Industrial Group Inc.: A Success Story of Integrated Production

Polyurethane raw materials (MDI, TDI) are chemical materials that are used in almost all consumer products. However, its production had been monopolized by a few leading companies, such as BASF, Covestro (former Bayer), Huntsman (acquired ICI), Dow, NPU, Mitsuichem, until Wanhua Industrial Group Inc. (Wanhua hereafter) came to the market. Wanhua overcame technological barriers in the 1990s and grew into a conglomerate including Wanhua Chemical, its largest subsidiary that issued its first IPO in Shanghai Stock Exchange in 2001. By 2015, Wanhua had grown into a global enterprise with 40% of its 3.3 billion USD revenue from the overseas market.

Wanhua's successful globalization was exemplified by its acquisition of BorsodChem Zrt in 2011, a Hungarian isocyanate producer. The acquisition that was worth 12.6 billion EUR made Wanhua the third largest isocyanate producer in the world. Our global business model framework shows how Wanhua succeeded in its strategic expansion into Europe (Table 7).

Wanhua's success has been firmly rooted in a Niche Market. Wanhua targeted the upstream raw materials production (MDI, TDI, ADI), because they have extensive applications in almost all consumer products, cars, shoes, cloths, as well as medical suppliers. The segment used to be monopolized by the

Table 7. Wanhua Group business model of integrated production

Target Industry	Stakeholder Value Proposition
• General purpose chemical raw materials • MCI, TCI, ACI and their derivative products	• Industrial customers all consumer products market • New material manufacturers • Derivative products for special purpose manufacturing, such as healthcare devices
Design of Activity System	**Resources for the Business Model**
• Go-To-Market model: *closeness to industrial customers, customized delivery by sizes and purity* • Production model: *low cost production of MCI/TCI/ACI, critical ingredients that require no after sale services* • Product/service development model: *R&D aimed at high margin new applications of the chemical ingredients* • Revenue: *sales of raw materials*	• Production knowhow and risk management capability are not bounded by locations, can be applied in different locations internationally, such as plant in Hungary. • Globally recognized reputation of reliable production and risk control, as well as low labor costs

top 6 chemical companies in the world. It created a high return due to the concentration of producers. The demand of its products is general, consistent, and significant, the suppliers are limited, and the return is high.

Wanhua concentrated its business in the niche market for another reason. Due the capital requirement, high regulation on risk management, and complexity of industrial knowhow, this niche market has high barriers to any prospective entrants.

A non-substitutable value proposition guaranteed sustainability of its model. Users of MDI and TDI are from all industries of consumer goods as well as industrial goods, such as medical devices. The chemical materials of MDI and TDI have extensive applications and are used in almost every part of our life. The market is universal, no cultural or national differences. The needs of business customers are homogenous, except for requests for customized sizes and degrees of purity.

Advantages also came from the integrated activity system and global resource allocation. Wanhua's management team focused on three factors for strengthening its advantages: the degree of integration of the production system, the global production facility and the research capability of derivative products determine an advantageous position.

The production process demands many other industrial chemicals from coal, oil and gas. A high degree of integration helps to reduce costs as well as improve purity. The global production facility will reduce the risks and costs of transportation. It can also improve business status when negotiating with competitors for distribution cooperation and countertrade. Due to the costs and risks of transportation, competitors often involve countertrade with each other, and distribute the purchase on behalf of competitors.

A third factor is that research and development capabilities affect the product portfolio of the company. MDI has many derivative products, but the company must have high R&D capability to extract the derivatives to satisfy particular needs from customers from different industries. For example, a pharmaceutical company may request a special catalyst from MDI. It is usually a small amount but with high margin.

Wanhua benefited from all three factors. It has successfully constructed an industrial eco-system to integrate inputs and production within its system. The production of all related inputs are either done internally or by joint venture partners. The high degree of integration guaranteed Wanhua a reliable supply chain.

In summary, the potent sources of competitiveness are from the intangible resources of Wanhua's talents. Wanhua set up research centers in Beijing, Shanghai, and America. It also built up a sales network in 40 countries. The local offices continued to feed market intelligence back to research centers. With half of the overhead costs of the industry average, Wanhua employed more than 1000 highly trained technicians and researchers to study market trends and develop premium products rapidly.

With the consolidation of the four areas of its business model, Wanhua was able to take advantage of the 2008 crisis to acquire BorsodChem Zrt, a production facility in Hungary. This strategic move allowed Wanhua a primary position in the European market. It also improved its strategic flexibility in the global market, since it could easily adjust the production and distribution schedule to counter-act rival's moves. After the acquisition, the Financial Times praised the timing of Wanhua's entry into the European market. Our analysis showed steadfast build-up in all four areas of its model before Wanhua took the opportunity to strike a good deal in the tough market of Europe. In this case both process and timing are two phenomena that were successful to the business model.

DISCUSSION

In this study we concentrated on answering the following research questions: (1) what is the role of a business model in the success of global enterprises? (2) which common attributes do business models of successful global companies possess? and (3) how to make a business model more suitable for global expansion? Relying on prior literature for deductive development of the presented conceptual argument, we demonstrated the importance of a firm's business model for global expansion, as well as the particular attributes of business models that increase the chances of a firm's successful internationalization. From a theoretical perspective, we demonstrate that the business models framework is instrumental in explaining the process of expansion and growth of MNEs. Once a successful business model is designed in any location, it becomes the FSA, and then the further expansion of the firm happens largely through successfully replicating it in other contexts. The provided case material is used to demonstrate the applicability of the deductively developed framework, rather than as means to inductive theory building (Siggelkow, 2007).

The prior conceptual argument and case examples discuss the common characteristics of globally scalable business models. Although not all of these characteristics must be present for successful internationalization, each of the factors listed in Table 3 increases the chances of successful global scaling.

The management of established companies or founding teams of potential international ventures should devote sufficient attention to proper initial segment choice (for INVs) or proper positioning within the available industry (for MNEs), to reach the internationally dispersed expert customers with relatively homogenous tastes, in the active search for solutions to their real problems. This would allow the companies to reach their customers through low-cost means, spending less time and resources on market research, advertising, and sales promotion. The globally scalable business models are usually designed using low-cost means of communication (e.g., Internet advertising and word-of-mouth). Yet, despite the best efforts to select the homogenous customer group, in most cases there will be the need of adjusting the value proposition for satisfying stakeholders beyond the home country. For this reason the benefits of global scope will be fully utilized only if the business model's activity system is designed for efficient business model operation worldwide. In terms of production model, the global business models usually rely on delivery of low weight, non-perishable products. The successful MNEs also make full use of locating production in the countries with relative low cost levels. The R&D process in global companies should be aimed at innovations applicable outside their home markets.

Finally, the key resources underpinning the globally scalable business models must be based on non-location-bound firm-specific advantages, serving the basis for international expansion: e.g., the globally recognized brand/reputation, social network ties, or globally applicable technology. These FSAs are either developed within the firm over time through investments into R&D and marketing (the Uppsala model of MNE expansion), or are embedded with the funding team of INV.

An essential note has to be added regarding the process of international expansion. Local autonomy, leading to decentralization, creates the conditions for the emergence of the organizational innovation capability. This, in turn, facilitates changes in organizational products, processes and administrative systems - essential components of the business model - during global expansion (Osiyevskyy & Zargarzadeh, 2015). Diversity and unpredictability of decision-making outcomes resulting from the involvement of a high number of employees in the process stimulate organizational innovation capability (Osiyevskyy & Zargarzadeh, 2015). Thus, employee autonomy is one of the key enablers of routines and behaviours fundamental to MNE innovation capability.

Furthermore, recombination of resources is an essential factor in the successful alteration of an MNE's business model to be suitable for global expansion (Verbeke, 2013; Grøgaard et al., 2011). In the international context, MNEs should find innovative ways to change their host country business models and craft novel ways of combining internal and external resources as a response to perceived opportunities (Osiyevskyy & Zargarzadeh, 2015).

Future Research Directions

The findings presented in this study open a set of avenues for further research. *First*, although not a part of the "globally scalable business model" concept, an important tactical decision of any MNE is the mode of foreign expansion (e.g., exporting, licensing, franchising, contract manufacturing, offshoring, service sector outsourcing, turnkey operations, management contracts, international joint ventures, wholly owned subsidiaries). Of course, the selection of the optimal mode of entry to a foreign market is endogenous with respect to a firm's business model and host country characteristics, such as political and economic environment. We strongly encourage further papers investigating the link between the attributes of the globally scalable business models and models of foreign expansion.

Second, we encourage future deductive, theory-testing studies that would corroborate and refine the conceptual framework presented in this chapter regarding the peculiarities of the globally scalable business models (such as Verbeke et al., 2014, testing a limited set of characteristics of business models of INVs).

CONCLUSION

As a general conclusion, our argument suggests that a business model framework is instrumental in explaining the process of expansion and growth of global businesses (INVs and MNEs). Once a successful business model is designed in any location, it becomes the core FSA, and the subsequent further expansion of the firm happens largely through successfully replicating it in other contexts, with appropriate modifications. As such, the construct of a globally scalable business model becomes essential for the field of international business studies.

REFERENCES

Amit, R., & Zott, C. (2001). Value creation in e-business. *Strategic Management Journal, 22*(6-7), 493–520. doi:10.1002/smj.187

Autio, E., Sapienza, H. J., & Almeida, J. G. (2000). Effects of age at entry, knowledge intensity, and imitability on international growth. *Academy of Management Journal, 43*(5), 909–924. doi:10.2307/1556419

Biloshapka, V., Osiyevskyy, O., & Meyer, M. H. (2016). The value matrix: A tool for assessing the future of a business model. *Strategy and Leadership, 44*(4), 41–48. doi:10.1108/SL-04-2016-0026

Cressy, R. (2006). Why do most firms die young? *Small Business Economics, 26*(2), 103–116. doi:10.1007/s11187-004-7813-9

Dunning, J. H. (2012). *International Production and the Multinational Enterprise (RLE International Business)* (Vol. 12). Routledge.

Falkenberg, L., & Osiyevskyy, O. (2014). Managing conflicting stakeholder expectations in the publishing industry. In J. Bishop (Ed.), *Gamification for Human Factors Integration: Social, Educational, and Psychological Issues* (pp. 52–79). IGI Global. doi:10.4018/978-1-4666-5071-8.ch004

George, G., & Bock, A. J. (2011). The business model in practice and its implications for entrepreneurship research. *Entrepreneurship Theory and Practice*, *35*(1), 83–111. doi:10.1111/j.1540-6520.2010.00424.x

Grøgaard, B., & Verbeke, A. (2012). Twenty key hypotheses that make internalization theory the general theory of international strategic management. Handbook of Research in International Strategic Management, 7-30.

Grøgaard, B., Verbeke, A., & Zargarzadeh, M. A. (2011). Entrepreneurial Deficits in the Global Firm. *Entrepreneurship in the Global Firm*, *6*, 117–137. doi:10.1108/S1745-8862(2011)0000006009

Hennart, J. F. (2014). The accidental internationalists: A theory of born globals. *Entrepreneurship Theory and Practice*, *38*(1), 117–135. doi:10.1111/etap.12076

Meyer, M. H., & Crane, F. G. (2014). *New Venture Creation*. SAGE Publications.

Morris, M., Schindehutte, M., & Allen, J. (2005). The entrepreneurs business model: Toward a unified perspective. *Journal of Business Research*, *58*(6), 726–735. doi:10.1016/j.jbusres.2003.11.001

Nelson, R. R., & Winter, S. G. (1982). *An Evolutionary Theory of Economic Change*. Cambridge, UK: Belknap.

Osiyevskyy, O. (2014). *Established Firms' Strategic Decision Making when Faced with Low-End Disruptive Innovation* (Doctoral dissertation). University of Calgary. Available from: http://theses.ucalgary.ca/jspui/handle/11023/1412

Osiyevskyy, O., & Dewald, J. (2015a). Explorative versus exploitative business model change: The cognitive antecedents of firm-level responses to disruptive innovation. *Strategic Entrepreneurship Journal*, *9*(1), 58–78. doi:10.1002/sej.1192

Osiyevskyy, O., & Dewald, J. (2015b). Inducements, impediments, and immediacy: Exploring the cognitive drivers of small business managers intentions to adopt business model change. *Journal of Small Business Management*, *53*(4), 1011–1032. doi:10.1111/jsbm.12113

Osiyevskyy, O., & Zargarzadeh, M. A. (2015). Business model design and innovation in the process of expansion and growth of global enterprises. In A. A. Camillo (Ed.), *Global Enterprise Management: New Perspectives on Challenges and Future Development* (Vol. 1, pp. 115–133). New York, NY: Palgrave McMillan. doi:10.1057/9781137429599.0011

Osterwalder, A., & Pigneur, Y. (2010). *Business Model Generation: A Handbook for Visionaries, Game Changers, and Challengers*. John Wiley & Sons.

Perkmann, M., & Spicer, A. (2010). What are business models? Developing a theory of performative representations. *Research in the Sociology of Organizations, 29,* 269–279. doi:10.1108/S0733-558X(2010)0000029020

Prahalad, C. K., & Hart, S. L. (2002). The fortune at the bottom of the pyramid. *Strategy+Business, 26*(First Quarter), 2-14.

Rugman, A. M., & Almodovar, P. (2011). The born global illusion and the regional nature of international business. The future of foreign direct investment and the multinational enterprise (pp. 251-269). London: Emerald Group Publishing.

Rugman, A. M., & Verbeke, A. (1992). A note on the transnational solution and the transaction cost theory of multinational strategic management. *Journal of International Business Studies, 23*(4), 761–771. doi:10.1057/palgrave.jibs.8490287

Seelos, C., & Mair, J. (2007). Profitable business models and market creation in the context of deep poverty: A strategic view. *The Academy of Management Perspectives, 21*(4), 49–63. doi:10.5465/AMP.2007.27895339

Senor, D., & Singer, S. (2009). *Start-up nation: The story of Israel's economic miracle.* McClelland & Stewart.

Siggelkow, N. (2007). Persuasion with case studies. *Academy of Management Journal, 50*(1), 20–24. doi:10.5465/AMJ.2007.24160882

Thompson, J. D., & MacMillan, I. C. (2010). Business models: Creating new markets and societal wealth. *Long Range Planning, 43*(2), 291–307. doi:10.1016/j.lrp.2009.11.002

Verbeke, A. (2013). *International Business Strategy.* Cambridge University Press. doi:10.1017/CBO9781139227162

Verbeke, A., & Yuan, W. (2010). A strategic management analysis of ownership advantages in the eclectic paradigm. *Multinational Business Review, 18*(2), 89–108. doi:10.1108/1525383X201000012

Verbeke, A., Zargarzadeh, A., & Osiyevskyy, O. (2014). Internationalization theory, entrepreneurship and international new ventures. *Multinational Business Review, 22*(3), 246–269. doi:10.1108/MBR-06-2014-0023

Zahra, S. A. (2005). A theory of international new ventures: A decade of research. *Journal of International Business Studies, 36*(1), 20–28. doi:10.1057/palgrave.jibs.8400118

Zott, C., & Amit, R. (2010). Business model design: An activity system perspective. *Long Range Planning, 43*(2), 216–226. doi:10.1016/j.lrp.2009.07.004

Zott, C., & Amit, R. (2013). The business model: A theoretically anchored robust construct for strategic analysis. *Strategic Organization, 11*(4), 403–411. doi:10.1177/1476127013510466

Zott, C., Amit, R., & Massa, L. (2011). The business model: Recent developments and future research. *Journal of Management, 37*(4), 1019–1042. doi:10.1177/0149206311406265

KEY TERMS AND DEFINITIONS

Business Model: The key organizational routine serving two purposes: (a) creating value for firm stakeholders (most important: customers); (b) capturing part of the created value for firm shareholders.

Globally Scalable Business Model: An organizational routine of value creation and appropriation that allows profitable international expansion. Once a globally scalable business model is successfully designed and validated in one location, it becomes a non-location-bound firm-specific advantage, promoting the firm's international expansion through replication of the value creation and appropriation routine in other locations.

International New Venture (INV): A new venture that internationalizes from the outset or soon afterward, and eventually sells a high share of its output outside its home country.

Multinational Enterprise (MNE): An enterprise that has its facilities and other assets in at least one country other than its home country.

Chapter 3
Critical Success Factors for Executives in Global Economy

Neeta Baporikar
Namibia University of Science and Technology, Namibia & University of Pune, India

ABSTRACT

With the convergence of information, communication and technology and global collaboration drives in modern management, it becomes imperative and crucial to understand the critical success factors (CSFs) for executives. In this globalized scenario, the internet has a dramatic impact on every kind of organization. It forms completely new challenges on the one hand but on the other hand it offers entirely new facilities. Additionally, spatiotemporal borders disappear. Totally new business models are being developed and companies have discovered completely new strategies to gain competitive advantage in this information age. Further, the advancements in society and technology, coupled with accelerations in globalization, competitive environments and changing customer's preferences have created new challenges as well as opportunities for executives. There is need to leverage on this vicissitude. To do so, it is essential to identify and understand the critical success factors (CSFs) fundamental to the success of executives and that is the core objective of this chapter.

INTRODUCTION

Critical Success Factor refers to an element of organizational activity which is central to its future success. Critical success factors may change over time, and may include items such as product quality, employee attitudes, manufacturing flexibility, and brand awareness. This can enable analysis. Critical Success Factor can also be any of the aspects of a business that are identified as vital for successful targets to be reached and maintained. Critical success factors are normally identified in such areas as production processes, employee and organization skills, functions, techniques, and technologies. The identification and strengthening of such factors may be similar. Thus, Critical Success Factor (CSF) or Critical Success Factors is a business term for an element which is necessary for an organization or project to achieve its mission? For example, a CSF for a successful Information Technology (IT) project is user involvement. The importance of CSFs in management first gained widespread attention following publication

DOI: 10.4018/978-1-5225-2673-5.ch003

of an article by Rockart (1979). It showed the need among top executives for certain critical elements of information, not provided by the management information systems (MIS) or the data analysis systems available. Rockart (1979) defined CSFs as: …the limited number of areas in which results, if they are satisfactory, will ensure successful competitive performance for the organization. They are the few key areas where things must go right for the business to flourish. If results in these areas are not adequate, the organization's efforts for the period will be less than desired. He further described them as "areas of activity that should receive constant and careful attention from management." Thus the core aim of this chapter is to identify, understand and evaluate the critical success factors for executives in developing global markets. In doing so, the objectives are: to understand the relevance of executives in building excellent organizations, identify the critical success factors for executives and evaluate the identified critical factors.

The chapter consists of the following parts: following a brief introduction, is the background giving the general perspective of the globalized environment, economy, business, expected role of executives and broad definitions of the terms including literature review and the objectives of the chapter. Followed by that is the identification of the critical success factors for executives along with the discussion therein. Next there are the recommendations, followed by future areas for further research and finally the conclusion is given.

BACKGROUND

The objective of management, especially in global economy is repetitive success. This is also the expectation from executives. Hence, it does little good if executives are considered successful but do not know why they were successful and do not know how to repeat their successes. Success that is the result of luck is not really success. Hence there is a need to identify and understand the factors which are critical in making the executives successful repeatedly. But, with phrases like Critical Success Factors and Executives having 'common usage' within technical environments it is difficult to identify the true history in the context of business, management and human resources. Spencer (1955) asks the question: "What are the essential factors that produce success in my company?" which for 1955 is getting close to the beginnings of CSFs – so for those interested in the early beginnings is worth a look. Predating these pieces is a short entry by Lebreton (1957, p. 103) "the factors which seem to be paramount in determining success in this industry" this is by far the earliest mention of what is today known as "Critical Success factors". Ronald (1961), does not use the term CSF or even the phrase Critical Success factors, but does discuss critical elements and non-critical elements of a business leading to "controlling competitive success". He also uses the term "success factors" in the context that we would understand today. One test for originality is the use of the TLA (Three Letter Acronym) of CSF (Rockart, 1979). To our mind the first published work of this approach is by Rockart.

There are four basic types of *critical success factors* (CSF's). They are:

1. Industry critical success factors (CSF's) resulting from specific industry characteristics;
2. Strategy critical success factors (CSF's) resulting from the chosen competitive strategy of the business;
3. Environmental critical success factors (CSF's) resulting from economic or technological changes; and

4. Temporal critical success factors (CSF's) resulting from internal organizational needs and changes.

Things that are measured get done more often than things that are not measured. Thus, each critical success factors (CSF's) should be measurable and associated with a target goal. You don't need exact measures to manage. Primary measures that should be listed include critical success levels (such as number of transactions per month) or, in cases where specific measurements are more difficult, general goals should be specified (such as moving up in an industry customer service survey).

CRITICAL SUCCESS FACTORS

Identifying and managing CSFs, and tracking them separately from the ever increasing amount of data to which executives are subjected, has been the focus of significant private sector research. Some of the research has limited the study to those activities over which the program manager has direct control (Cleland and King, 1988); the majority of researchers have broadened the focus to include elements beyond the direct control of a project manager, but still within the sphere of things that either he could manage, or that could exert significant influence on his activities. Bullen (Bullen and Rockart, 1981) has suggested that CSF identification be focused on whether CSFs fall into one or more of several key areas. These key areas, plus one (effectiveness of executives) we have added, are:

*   **Global or Industry Related:** These are activities essential to project success that would be true of any project or company operating in the particular environment (industry or business area).
*   **External Influences:** These CSFs are governed by external factors that can significantly influence the success of your endeavor.
*   **Internal Influences:** These are determined by internal factors that can significantly influence project success.
*   **Current and Future:** Included here are time-driven CSFs that are essential to project success. Current CSFs are activities that must be done in the near future. Future CSFs are those which are long range. Planning for the success of future CSFs may be an activity that requires immediate attention.
*   **Temporal and Enduring:** These are significant influences that either have a short-term duration or are present through most or all of a project.
*   **Risk Abatement:** Some activities are necessary in order to avoid significant identified risks to project success.
*   **Performance:** These are identifiable levels of performance or achievement that must be realized for the project to be successful.
*   **Special Monitoring:** These activities or events require special monitoring, protection, or contingency planning in order to assure project success.
*   **Quality:** Quality requirements, if not met, will mean the failure of the project.
*   **Effectiveness of Executives:** Some activities or conditions that currently exist or are currently planned will, if not managed appropriately, by and through effectiveness of executives, will lead to failure.

Most research has been focused on the identification of CSFs for executive level managers in specific industries, or heads of specific kinds of departments, principally MIS departments. There has also been some minimal research focused on the diversity of applications of CSFs. One fairly common problem with much of the reported research is that many of the identified CSFs have not been stated in the form of an activity, as was clear in the original group of definitions given by Rockart and noted above. This led to the identification of CSFs that were ambiguous and hard to measure. One of the early research studies that demonstrated this problem was conducted by Boynton and Zmud (1984). This research focused on the use of CSF, and showed that CSF analysis can be used successfully to identify key concerns of senior MIS management, can be used in developing strategic plans, and can help identify critical implementation issues. CSFs can also be used to help managers achieve high performance and establish guidelines for monitoring a corporation's activities. They also noted that CSF analysis demonstrated certain weaknesses. Boynton and Zmud (1984) conclude that the weaknesses attributed to CSFs can be overcome through careful application of the method, while CSF strength as a structured design process for eliciting both MIS plans and managerial information needs would be a key to its success. In another significant study, "Variation of Critical Success Factors over Stages in the Project Life Cycle" (Pinto and Prescott, 1988), the authors hypothesized a set of CSFs, and then conducted a validation study based on empirical evidence. Zahedi (1987) developed an evaluation of reliability of an information system as a measure of the system's success based on CSFs. This research addressed the issue of the difference between behavioural and perceived measures of IS effectiveness resulting from a lack of conceptual foundation to guide proper measurement development, and the absence of a rigorous program of measurement validation.

It identified the need to define CSFs and identify how they are interconnected. This was another look at a question similar to that investigated by Pinto and Prescott (1988), but looking at the set of CSFs from a reliability viewpoint. In each case the CSFs were not treated as isolated objects but rather activities that are interrelated. In "The Multiple Uses of CSFs" (Leidecker and Bruno, 1984), the authors stress the applicability of CSFs for strategic planning and business strategy development, identification of threats and opportunities, and identifying a criterion for strengths and weaknesses assessment. Walsh and Kanter (1988) stress the importance of using the CSF identification process to identify major causes of project failure and then ranking these major causes by relative value, so that such problems can be avoided in future programs. One of the few comparative studies done (Chung, 1987) concluded that if the inquirer wants to know what management is, then the process view should be studied. However if one wants to know why selected organizations are successful in highly competitive environments, then one must study the three critical success factors of corporate strategies, human resources, and operational systems. His conclusion is that the truly successful companies deal with these three CSFs differently from the way they are treated in other companies. More recently, the research has continued with the same commercial emphasis as described above, but applied to current business trends. One group studied critical success factors as they apply to establishing strategic alliances (Rai, Borah, and Ramaprasad, 1996). A further study of CSFs in business alliances, this time with a process focus in the oil and gas industry, was reported in the trade press (Seven Critical Success Factors, 1996). CSF analysis has also been used for community improvement. This is closer to the public sector than most studies, and is an example of the analysis being applied to a fairly narrow focus area (VanDeusen, 1996). The researcher gleaned six factors from 14 community scale future search conferences conducted between 1993 and 1995. These CSFs are leadership, scope, participation, structure, results, and strong conference management.

One can again note the ambiguity and the problem when CSFs are not specified in terms of activities. It is very difficult to measure something like "structure" or "scope" or even "leadership," especially when something like leadership can be defined and measured in so many different ways. Business processes for new product development have not escaped the application of CSF analysis. A benchmarking research study of 161 business units (Cooper and Kleinschmidt, 1996) identified the CSFs for new product performance at the business unit level. The researchers found that the CSFs fell into major categories. Two key performance dimensions—profitability and impact—were identified. Four key drivers were identified: a high-quality new product process, the new product strategy for the business unit, resource availability, and research and development spending levels. Merely having a formal new product process had no impact. CSF analysis has also been applied directly to people, to measure productivity. Christine Bullen, one of the leaders in the application of CSF analysis, completed a research study of knowledge worker productivity (Bullen, 1995). She found that the context-specific nature of personal productivity demands an understanding of the processes by which knowledge workers achieve their goals and objectives. Once the nature of personal productivity is understood, measurement becomes a much simpler task and the measures have real meaning. These studies all show how CSF analysis is applicable to a wide variety of industries and subsets of industries.

CSF analysis has also been effectively applied to individual process areas within a corporation, such as strategic planning and information technology implementation; although it is not routinely found as a part of strategic management and the use of critical success factors (CSFs) in the management of corporations has been the subject of several published studies. Research on the application of CSFs to executives and in particular to executives in global economy is lacking. Research on evaluating the true criticality of identified CSFs is lacking in global environment be it for government or private sector. There is an implied assumption in much of the research to date that managers are relatively equal in their ability to identify CSFs that truly are critical to success. This is easier said than done especially in the light of complexities and the globe becoming boundary less. Moreover, due to the pressures of globalization and competition, the quality of executives has come under great scrutiny as questions are being raised worldwide regarding the ability of executives and leaders to articulate and deliver a vision commanding the broad support of investors, customers, employees, and other stakeholders that is be innovative (Baporikar, 2014d). Most large companies acknowledge the need to be more responsive to shifting societal expectations, to be better able to establish trusting relationships with stakeholders, and to become more open and accountable. And yet those same companies often struggle to translate good intentions into good practice. In no small way this is due to the lack of any serious, practical guidance addressing the outmoded way in which their executives/leaders tend to be selected and developed.

BUT WHAT CONSTITUTES 'EXECUTIVE'

Senior management, executive management, or management team is generally a team of individuals at the highest level of organizational management who have the day-to-day responsibilities of managing a company or corporation. They hold specific executive powers conferred onto them with and by authority of the board of directors and/or the shareholders. An executive management team is directly responsible for managing the day-to-day operations profitably for a company. Positions that are commonly considered to be part of that team include the following: Chief executive Officer (CEO), Chief Financial Officer (CFO), Chief Security Officer (CSO)/Chief Information Security Officer (CISO), Chief Information

Officer (CIO), Legal Advisor, Chief Operations Officer (COO), Chief Procurement Officer (CPO), Chief Technology Officer (CTO), Chief Human Resources Officer (CHRO). Of late with knowledge society and knowledge management becoming a competitive advantage, the organizations are supposed to be embedded with learning mechanisms so Chief Learning Officer (CLO) is a new addition to management teams. Thus, the executive management typically consists of the heads of the firm's product and/ or geographic units and of functional executives such as the chief financial officer, the chief operating officer, and the chief strategy officer (Menz, 2012)

However, the terms "manager" and "executive" are sometimes used interchangeably. Although the two functions have similarities and frequently overlap in the business world, distinct differences exist in the roles that managers and executives play within a company. These differences often have specific legal implications on workplace issues, specifically where work schedules and overtime pay are involved. Hence, manager is one who oversees specific operations within a company, such as a division or section. Managers often have one or more employees that report directly to them, either connected to a particular project, or assigned to a specific division. While managers can be an essential element in making a company work, in many instances, managers do not direct the policy or mission of the company. On the other hand, executives guide the general policy and the overall mission of a company and are commonly assigned to the highest levels of the organizational ladder (Drucker, 1967). Executives often have broad latitude and authority to make decisions that affect large segments of a company, if not the entire company (Mintzberg, 1973). Without getting into the nuisances of the nomenclature we review the roles which executives have to play before identifying the CSFs. According to Mintzberg (1975), they can be grouped into three major types:

- Decisional roles require managers to plan strategy and utilize resources.
- Interpersonal roles require managers to direct and supervise employees and the organization.
- Informational roles are those in which managers obtain and transmit information.

For these roles to be played effectively there are essentials skills required. According to Menz, 2012, these are five critical skills:

- Technical skill involves understanding and demonstrating proficiency in a particular workplace activity.
- Interpersonal skill involves human relations, or the manager's ability to interact effectively with organizational members.
- Conceptual skill is a manager's ability to see the organization as a whole, as a complete entity.
- Diagnostic skill is used to investigate problems, decide on a remedy, and implement a solution.
- Political skill involves obtaining power and preventing other employees from taking away one's power.

To these, in the current scenario of globalization, we would like to add the following:

- Geopoltical skill involving the abilities to understand how nations interact for different reasons based on geography and political alignment.
- Knowledge broking skill involving the abilities to leverage and use knowledge as a basis for negotiations (Baporikar, 2014c).

- Ethical and value skill involves the abilities to distinguish right from wrong and credible versus non-credible.
- Sustainability skills involve the competencies and abilities to endure and hold on for long term success including the inclusive approach to be adopted (Baporikar, 2016b).

However, in today's environment industry consolidation—creating huge global corporations through joint ventures, mergers, alliances, and other kinds of interorganizational cooperative efforts—has become increasingly important (Hansen and Nohria, 2004). Among organizations of all sizes, concepts such as agile manufacturing, just-in-time inventory management, and ambidextrous organizations are impacting managers' thinking about their organizational structure (O'Reilly and Tushman, 2004). Indeed, few organization and executives are likely to blindly implement the traditional hierarchical structure common in the first half of the century (Mintzberg, 1980). The first half of the twentieth century was dominated by the one-size-fits-all traditional structure. The early twenty-first century has been dominated by the thinking that changing organizational structures, while still a monumental managerial challenge, can be a necessary condition for competitive success (Brews and Tucci, 2004). Moreover, every knowledge worker in a modern organization is an "executive" if, by virtue of his position or knowledge, he or she is responsible for a contribution that materially affects the capacity of the organization to perform and to obtain results. For the authority of knowledge is surely as legitimate as the authority of position (Drucker, 1967).

LEADERSHIP DEFINED

Discussing executives without the concept of leadership may leave the discussion incomplete. Moreover, executives are in leading position and one of their important tasks is to lead and motivate people for achieving the objectives of the organizations. Leadership may be seen as the action of leading a group of people or an organization, or the ability to do this. Leadership style is the way the executive/manager behaves in his or her role. The behaviour differs from individual to individual, nature of work, and place of work. Leadership is defined as "exercising of command and direction in a skilful and responsible fashion" (Rosenberg, 1983). However, there are various types of leadership which are classified and based on the style and functions. Some of the important ones are briefly discussed below:

- Transformational Leadership: a leader develops "creative self-efficacy (CSE) and employee creativity to do things in a better way and develops knowledge sharing in employee for high performance" (Swati and Lochan, 2015:894).
- Shared Leadership: a leader concentrates in getting team cohesion to keep all employees (subordinates) together rather than aiming for performance (Mathieu, Kukenberger, D'Innocenzo, Reilly, 2015).
- Behavioural Leadership: is where "politics" play a major part in decision making ignoring the values. The "silo" mental outlook of the leader results in poor alignment of resources with goals. It is correctly stated that "Too many leaders are ill-equipped to lead in the current climate, as they are not in possession of the behavioural science knowledge and skills required of leaders to be successful in today's academic health enterprise. A shift in orientation from knowing to doing is a critical leadership competency" (Grigsby, 2015 p. 123).

- Servant Leadership: is a modern leadership approach where the leadership encompasses the elements such as love, humility, altruism, vision, trust, empowerment and service (Lokman and Sitki, 2014).

- Situational Leadership: the leader uses his/her faculty in understanding the situation (problem) and takes appropriate decision, but there are flaws in this leadership such as frequent changes of decisions due to lack of continuity and conformity (Baporikar, 2017b).

- Transactional Leadership: will be created where there is short term relationship between the leader and the follower. In this case it is to be found often that both transactional and transformational behaviour are applied (Baporikar, 2017a).

- Entrepreneurial Leadership: the leader takes risk in the running of an organization to improve the organization's performance. If the leader imposes modern practices the staff may have temporary negative perceptions. In the long run, there will be improved perceptions by staff when it is established that there is significant correlation between entrepreneurial leadership and improving the results and quality (Akmaliah, Afsaneh and Soaib, 2014).

- Women Leadership: the main thrust is to develop women to become leaders by offering 'women only training, an equality and diversity board and women's network (Kate, 2013). Parker and Welch (2013, p. 332) observed that: "women are more likely to be in discipline leadership positions and less likely to be a leader of a research center or have an administrative university leadership position [and] having more women in the network reduces the likelihood of holding discipline leadership positions and less likely to be a leader of a research center or have an administrative university leadership position... having more women in the network reduces the likelihood of holding discipline or center leadership positions".

- Ethical Leadership: is mainly seen as being based on the characteristics of the leader, as Moses sheds a light on the formative experiences of an ethical leader (from a Christian perspective) and his actions demonstrate how such a leader can act under challenging circumstances (Shlomo and Karsten, 2012, p. 962).

Parker and Welch (2013) also suggested the creation of a common leadership language. Work load factors, succession planning and orientation have an impact in leadership development (Ladyshewsky and Flavell, 2012). To become effective executives, particularly corporate global executives, certain ingredients are required such as; education, training, experience, career management, family influence, networking, sponsorship and organizational support (Sexton, Lemak, Wainio, 2014).

Leadership Theories Effect on Executive Behaviour

Early leadership studies focused on the "great man" theory: leaders are born (mostly as white males), not developed, and have almost mythical qualities that ensure a bevy of followers (Gallagher, 2012). Modern leadership theory first emerged in the 1940s, following the machine-like principles of scientific management (Rost, 1997). This "rational man" model is implemented via command-and-control structures and a strict hierarchical division of labor (Dugan and Komives, 2010). In the 1950s, the transactional leadership theory emerged with the recognition that workers perform better when attention is paid to motivation. While still mechanistic and linear in its approach, transactional leadership emphasizes the role of workers in the success of an organization and a leader by offering rewards for better performance. Transformational leadership, popularized in the late 1970s and still the dominant leadership model taught in higher education (Hunt 1999) and the popular literature, takes this evolution one step further. Charismatic "transformational" leaders transform entire organizations toward a "higher ethical purpose" through their skills in visioning, communication and building trust and loyalty (Bass and Steidlmeier, 1999). Environmental leadership as a subset of modern leadership theory is in the early developmental phase in the literature and in practice. Early environmental leaders tended to be naturalists and intellectuals (e.g., William Bartram and Ralph Waldo Emerson) or key figures in the civic reform movements of the early 20th Century (Andrews, 2012). Leadership arose organically, based on local concerns (e.g., sanitation or the protection of a particular area), often with a charismatic figure as the public voice.

IDENTIFIED CSFS FOR EXECUTIVES

Graf (2008) discussed two types of CSFs in the context of strategic management: administrative CSFs and operational CSFs, which addressed the resources and competencies of the organization. It can be seen, that CSFs vary from organization to organization, and even among the managers within the same organization (Geller, 1985). Different organizations have different priorities in terms of strategies and different perceived critical success factors which would have a snow ball effect on critical success factors for executives (Baporikar, 2013). Though, the critical areas are unique to individual companies-reflecting industry position, age, competitive strategy, environmental factors, management style, financial strength, and so on (Geller, 1985), the identified CSFs for factors for executives are:

1. **Understanding the Wider Picture:** Organizations today are part of a wider picture of a world with new challenges that business has to address. The current agenda includes a complex mixture of geo-political uncertainty caused by the fall in the oil price and speculation about its future, and regional unrest in Ukraine, parts of the Middle East and the South China Sea. On the face of it, the fall in the oil price has been good for business. It is part of what one CEO delegate calls a 'double shot in the arm' for businesses. The other part is quantitative easing by the banking and financial institutions world over. With these two reductions in input prices, organizations need to do some of the structural reforms that it has so far resisted. If it misses this window of opportunity, they may end up less competitive. But the oil price fall could prove a mixed blessing, as it brings down the cost of oil commodities which helps industries that use them, but it may discourage investment in future exploration. Moreover, businesses want and need stability so they can plan for the future. But the present global environment has created a climate of uncertainty. The lack of a clear vision about what either 'in' or 'out' looks like and the blurring of geographical boundaries in business, meaning that stability may be some way off. There is also a wider picture to consider. The fall in the oil price has delivered a benefit to most companies, but there are signs that labour rates are beginning to rise and that stagnation has led to a misalignment of salaries and skills. Global executives will be at the heart of all these debates.

2. **Tax Versus Incentives:** Tax has become a major issue on the public agenda, but also subject to major misunderstanding – sometimes what are seen by business as legitimate incentives are interpreted by broader public opinion as aggressive tax avoidance. It is clear that executives and their companies cannot avoid the connection between paying tax and their reputation as good corporate citizens. 'Reputational economics' has become a new issue on boardroom agendas.

3. **Leadership in the Digital Age:** Because customers increasingly do business with brands they trust, managing corporate reputation is becoming more important. But in the age of social media and increased scrutiny, this involves more than simple compliance and reliance upon regulation – it requires a new kind of 'moral courage' and judgement that must be led from the top and embedded among managers at all levels. The need to embrace new technologies is becoming increasingly critical but many organisations are not exploiting the digital development that could transform performance and labour costs. Executives and other leaders must tackle these issues in a world where there is a growing 'spectrum of uncertainty'. There is now a link between ethics and value creation which raises two key questions: How is that link to be managed? Another points out that this means organisations working in a different kind of way – less hierarchical. 'You can no longer rely on hierarchy alone to provide you with solutions you thought you had before.' That is because in the Digital Age, when a problem needs attention, there is a premium on taking a decision before the issue escalates through social media. Leadership has two key roles in the technology debate for the Digital Age. First, leaders must articulate the need for governments, business organisations and others to provide the digital skills that are currently in short supply. Second, they need to tackle the fear factor which paralyses too many organisations into inaction when they come to consider technology issues. Certainly, there are challenging issues to tackle – building future-proof systems, strengthening cyber security and others – but it is leadership from the top that will spur an organisation to tackle them. As one executive notes: 'It takes a lot of courage to manage that change process. It takes a brave person to say, "We must go forward. We can't just fossilise".'

4. **People, Pay, and Performance:** Expressed concerns about the difficulties of recruiting accountancy professionals with the right experience for demanding roles, and the pay pressures which seem to be mounting both in the profession and the wider labour market. An executive who is a board member in a public sector organisation sees recruitment in the present climate as 'a real challenge'. The lesson for global organizations - is that skills planning require a long-term horizon (Baporikar, 2016).

5. **Business Horizon:** It is rightly remarked that 'spectrum of uncertainty' clouds the business horizon. The world exists in an endless process of ever faster change (Baporikar, 2015). The minimum task for business executives and leaders is to prevent their organisations falling behind. Whether it's thinking through the implications of Britain inside or outside the EU, the future of the oil price, or which new digital technologies to back, executive team and professionals have a growing role. But, if they are to play that role effectively, they will need to draw not only on their traditional skills, but on new leadership qualities. Moreover, it is true that 'Leaders are not necessarily managers and good managers do not necessarily make leaders.' Thus one of the core qualities of a leader is to be able to see through the complexity to what is important at that moment – and deal with it.

6. **Working as One:** The establishment of the ASEAN Economic Community (AEC) provides an impetus for South East Asian countries to develop trade within the region and integrate their economies. But while South East Asia is a cohesive geographical region, it contains a wide range of cultures which may hinder integration. One approach for multinational businesses is to develop common policies designed to build trust between participants from different countries. Trust building begins by respecting the cultural and business diversity within the region. In developing an integrated regional economy, one of the key issues that will need to be tackled is corruption.

There is currently insufficient emphasis on governance issues. Businesses and government will need to place governance and ethics at centre stage in the future if the region is to build a series of integrated economies with global standards. The starting point for building that trust, is respecting the cultural and business diversity within the region. Not every country is as developed as, for example, Singapore. But it's wrong to impose ideas. It's much more effective to give people space to learn. The aim is for a cohesive global economy – but that doesn't mean every economy has to be the same. Cohesion is about finding ways to work together rather than creating a set of identikit economies.

7. **Building Honest Economies:** One of the big issues for global executives – is corporate governance. Hanging over the question of governance is the spectre of corruption, which remains ingrained in business culture in many. Hence necessary training and development to provide with both the skills and the 'moral compass' to be in the front row of the fight against corruption is required. Hence, a fresh view of governance is much needed. Governance raises a host of difficult questions, such as ethics, diversity and sustainability, which today's businesses need to answer. As the public perception of what is the right thing to do changes, it is not easy to chart a course through a moral minefield.

8. **Leading the Change:** Growing economies are banking on local talent to achieve growth. However, if the latent talent is to be used to best effect, local and international businesses will need to develop policies designed to train and develop local people, ensuring a balance of expertise. The traditional hierarchical societies have created a culture where it has been difficult for new talent to emerge. Leaders of the future will come from the millennial generation which has a more international approach and is less constrained by traditional culture.

9. **Branding the Profession:** Professionally trained executives need to be valued at par, but this is not so and the value placed is different in different parts of the world. This needs to change if the profession is to make a fuller contribution to the development of the region. But where the profession is able to engage the enthusiasm of the best young talent, it will nurture the leaders of the future and also accelerate the pace of change.

10. **Growth Challenge:** Despite doubts about the world economy, growth in the US economy remains strong. But there are concerns that over-heating financial markets could cause problems similar to the credit crunch. The US has a combination of unique strengths – a can-do business culture, access to capital markets and world-leading innovative technologies – which will enable it to continue to grow. There are concerns, however, that the level of corporate taxes in the US may encourage some companies to expand overseas rather than at home. Innovative technologies may also pose a challenge. There are few traditional business models that will not be disrupted by technology in the years ahead. Executives will find their work changes as new technologies take over, enabling them to focus more on future risks than past performance.

11. **Hunt for Talent:** The ability to link talent and technology is a critical success factor in modern business. The young are a source of new talent – and can also provide fresh insights into how to use new technologies most effectively. But the 'millennial generation' have a different attitude to work and careers. Millennials are more likely to be excited about working on a succession of projects in tune with their own values and aspirations than in developing a traditional linear career in one organisation.

SOLUTIONS AND RECOMMENDATIONS

Based on the identified CSFs and the role of executives discussed above recommendations are given below:

- Educate managers and their staff in the CSF identification process. The failure to explicitly identify CSFs for a particular function or role will invariably result in the continued focus on cost and schedule after they become problems, will inhibit the development and use of effective life cycle measures, and will prevent the development of a truly effective organization. Cost and schedule problems are generally effects, not causes. They are the results of conditions that should be identified and managed much earlier than the time when a cost and schedule variance first appears. It is also essential to educate the functional managers and their staff in development of information networks consistent with the critical success factors and establishing oversight reporting mechanisms consistent with critical success factors so that critical information is reported when it is needed.
- It is recommended that organizations, when planning and developing their information strategies, should take into account the perceived or anticipated management information needs of heads of departments to a much greater extent than it is usually done (Baporikar, 2014b).
- It is recommended that organizations should consider ways in which they might provide more effectively structured training not only for newly appointed executives and managers but also for those wishing to refresh or update their managerial skills (Baporikar, 2014a).
- It is recommended that top management or board of directors, in conjunction with other members of the organizations senior management team re-examine the relevance of the financial information they supply to executives, the form and manner in which such information is communicated and the frequency with which it is communicated. Unless this is streamlined and efficient many executives with limited financial management skills or have considerable difficulty in understanding or interpreting the financial information provided to them, or both, will not be able to make better decisions with better impact even if CSFs are well identified.
- It is recommended that the conditions and manner of appointment of individuals to the post of executives should be more closely examined and rationalized and that, in particular, the potential value of providing formal longer periods in office should be considered.
- It is recommended that organizations should consider the balance between the work-life of their executives as it is evident their growing managerial responsibilities, not least the need to meet the growing demands made upon them by their organizations substantially encroach on time which many of them would otherwise devote to self-development and learning.

FUTURE RESEARCH DIRECTIONS

Research to reflect whether there are any changes to the CSFs as reported by managers need to be on a continuous basis. Change in the strategies, new market development, new products or service introduced will bring a change in the CSFs which need to be well predicted. Continued research is also required to produce a model for evaluation of actual criticality of reported CSFs. It is anticipated that the development of such models will provide a means to alleviate the need to assume that all executives are equally skilled in their ability to identify CSFs and engage in effective strategic thinking. Even industry – firm comparison of CSFs would be interesting areas of research which will enable benchmarking for efficiency and productivity.

CONCLUSION

Executive and leadership debates are increasingly about corporate themes of governance, ethics and values – all issues critical to future business success. Leadership is not demonstrated when someone from the C-suite issues a set of specific edicts, but rather when those individuals develop objectives, strategies, and a disciplined plan that both guide and respond to the best people and ideas across an increasingly diverse portfolio of markets and business functions. This has implications for senior managers as well as for those who hold executive roles in other parts of the organization. It is notable that many of the "leading company" are characterized by decentralized authority and decision-making. More companies are extending this approach to include key external stakeholders who, until recently, were not considered critical players in corporate decisions. Furthermore, as companies look to attract and develop their next generation of leaders, they will need different skill sets to be able to manage the increasingly complex sustainability factors impacting companies (Deshpande and Baporikar, 2014a). Thus, effective corporate executive ship, at all levels of an organization - from front-line change agents to senior management - will increasingly depend on a sophisticated ability to identify, engage, and incorporate the needs and interests of a diverse range of internal and external stakeholders.

Some of the most difficult decisions which executives must make are about how to balance growth against sustainability criteria. With a global outlook, executives must be in a well placed to provide a significant contribution to this debate. It is rightly said: "executives of tomorrow need to have the ability to step back and define the problem they are trying to address and to assess the resources they need to solve the problem. Increasingly, those resources will be about quality of knowledge, skills and innovation and how you put all that to work." The ability to think strategically should lie at the heart of the executive mind set. The problem-solving training which most executives receive should enable them to analyse situations and bring a global perspective to their solutions. Successful executives of the future will need the ability to bring together not only talent and technology to create new ways of doing business but also to lay their hands and mind on the CSFs in relation to their businesses and organizations. Finally, the world and the business models are disruptive; hence to be winners, the executives will be those who disrupt rather than those who are disrupted.

REFERENCES

Akmaliah, P. P., Afsaneh, B., & Soaib, A. (2014). School Leadership and Innovative Principals: Implications for Enhancing Principals' Leadership Knowledge and Practice. *Proceedings of the European Conference on Management, Leadership & Governance*, 162-167.

Andrews, R. N. (2012). History of environmental leadership. In D. R. Gallagher (Ed.), *Environmental leadership: A reference handbook* (Vol. 1, pp. 17–28). Los Angeles, CA: SAGE Publications. doi:10.4135/9781452218601.n3

Baporikar, N. (2013). CSF Approach for IT Strategic Planning. *International Journal of Strategic Information Technology and Applications*, *4*(2), 35–47. doi:10.4018/jsita.2013040103

Baporikar, N. (2014a). Effective E-Learning Strategies for a Borderless World. In J. Pelet (Ed.), *E-Learning 2.0 Technologies and Web Applications in Higher Education* (pp. 22–44). Hershey, PA: Information Science Reference. doi:10.4018/978-1-4666-4876-0.ch002

Baporikar, N. (2014b). Information Strategy as Enabler of Competitive Advantage. *International Journal of Strategic Information Technology and Applications*, *5*(1), 30–41. doi:10.4018/ijsita.2014010103

Baporikar, N. (2014c). Organizational Barriers and Facilitators in Embedding Knowledge Strategy. In M. Chilton & J. Bloodgood (Eds.), *Knowledge Management and Competitive Advantage: Issues and Potential Solutions* (pp. 149–173). Hershey, PA: Information Science Reference. doi:10.4018/978-1-4666-4679-7.ch009

Baporikar, N. (2014d). Innovation in the 21st Century Organization. In B. Christiansen, S. Yildiz, & E. Yildiz (Eds.), *Transcultural Marketing for Incremental and Radical Innovation* (pp. 339–365). Hershey, PA. doi:10.4018/978-1-4666-4749-7.ch016

Baporikar, N. (2015). *Innovation Knowledge Management Nexus. Innovation Management* (pp. 85–110). Berlin: De Gruyter.

Baporikar, N. (2016a). Talent Management Integrated Approach for Organizational Development. In A. Casademunt (Ed.), *Strategic Labor Relations Management in Modern Organizations* (pp. 22–48). Hershey, PA: Business Science Reference. doi:10.4018/978-1-5225-0356-9.ch002

Baporikar, N. (2016b). Strategies for Enhancing the Competitiveness of MNEs. In M. Khan (Ed.), *Multinational Enterprise Management Strategies in Developing Countries* (pp. 50–71). Hershey, PA: Business Science Reference. doi:10.4018/978-1-5225-0276-0.ch003

Baporikar, N. (2017a). Corporate Leadership and Sustainability. In Z. Fields (Ed.), *Collective Creativity for Responsible and Sustainable Business Practice* (pp. 160–179). Hershey, PA: IGI Global; doi:10.4018/978-1-5225-1823-5.ch009

Baporikar, N. (2017b). Imperatives in Leading Institutions of Higher Learning: Focus B-School. *International Journal of Technology and Educational Marketing*, *7*(1), 38–51. doi:10.4018/IJTEM.2017010104

Bass, B. M., & Steidlmeier, P. (1999). Ethics, character, and authentic transformational leadership behavior. *The Leadership Quarterly*, *10*(2), 181–217. doi:10.1016/S1048-9843(99)00016-8

Boynton, A. C., & Zmud, R. W. (1984). An Assessment of Critical Success Factors. *Sloan Management Review*, *25*, 17–27.

Brews, J., & Tucci, C. L. (2004). Exploring the Structural Effects of Internetworking. *Strategic Management Journal*, *25*(5), 429–452. doi:10.1002/smj.386

Bullen, C. V. (1995). Productivity CSFs for knowledge workers. *Information Strategy: The Executive's Journal*, *12*(1), 14–20.

Bullen, C. V., & Rockart, J. F. (1981). *A Primer on Critical Success Factors*. Center for Information Systems Research, Sloan School of Management, Massachusetts Institute of Technology.

Chung, K. H. (1987). *Management: Critical success factors*. Newton, MA: Allyn and Bacon, Inc.

Cooper, R. G., & Kleinschmidt, E. J. (1996). Winning businesses in product development: The critical success factors. *Research-Technology Management, 39*(4), 18–29.

(1988). Critical success factors in effective project implementation. InCleland, D. I., & King, W. R. (Eds.), *Project management handbook* (2nd ed., pp. 479–512). New York: Van Nostrand Reinhold.

Deshpande, M., & Baporikar, N. (2014). Excellence in a Borderless World: Evidence from Pune Auto-Components SMEs. *Journal of Shinawatra University, 1*(2), 182–196.

Drucker, P. F. (1967). *The Effective Executive*. Harper Business.

Dugan, J. P., & Komives, S. R. (2010). Influence on college students capacities for socially responsible leadership. *Journal of College Student Development, 51*(5), 525–549. doi:10.1353/csd.2010.0009

Gallagher, D. R. (2012). Why environmental leadership? In D. R. Gallagher (Ed.), *Environmental leadership: A reference handbook* (Vol. 1, pp. 3–10). Los Angeles, CA: SAGE Publications. doi:10.4135/9781452218601.n1

Geller, N. (1985). Tracking the Critical Success Factors for Hotel Companies. *The Cornell Hotel and Restaurant Administration Quarterly, 25*(4), 76–81. doi:10.1177/001088048502500414

Graf, N. S. (2008). Industry critical success factors and their importance in strategy. In Olsen & Zhao (Eds.), Handbook of Hospitality Strategic Management. Elsevier. doi:10.1016/B978-0-08-045079-7.00004-1

Grigsby, R. K. (2015). Enhancing the Behavioral Science Knowledge and Skills of 21st-Century Leaders in Academic Medicine and Science. *Journal of Organizational Behavior Management, 35*(1/2), 123–134. doi:10.1080/01608061.2015.1031428

Hansen, M. T., & Nohria, N. (2004). How to Build Collaborative Advantage, *MIT. Sloan Management Review, 46*(1), 22–31.

Hunt, J. G. (1999). Transformational/charismatic leaderships transformation of the field: An historical essay. *The Leadership Quarterly, 10*(2), 129–144. doi:10.1016/S1048-9843(99)00015-6

Ksenia, Z. (2014). Leadership in organizational practice: Closing the knowing-doing gap. *Strategic HR Review, 13*(2), 69–74. doi:10.1108/SHR-10-2013-0093

Ladyshewsky, R. K., & Flavell, H. (2012). Transfer of Training in an Academic leadership Development Program for Program Coordinators. *Educational Management Administration & Leadership, 40*(1), 127–147. doi:10.1177/1741143211420615

Lebreton, P. P. (1957). The Case Study Method and the Establishment of Standards of Efficiency. Academy of Management Proceedings, 103.

Leidecker, J. K., & Bruno, A. V. (1984). Identifying and using critical success factors. *Long Range Planning, 17*(1), 23–32. doi:10.1016/0024-6301(84)90163-8

Lokman, D., & Sitki, C. (2014). The Relationship between Servant Leadership Behaviors and Leader-Member Exchange: A research on a State University. *Suleyman Demirel University Journal of Faculty of Economics & Administrative Sciences, 19*(4), 287–310.

Mathieu, J. E., Kukenberger, M. R., DInnocenzo, L., & Reilly, G. (2015). Modeling reciprocal team cohesion–performance relationships, as impacted by shared leadership and members competence. *The Journal of Applied Psychology, 100*(3), 713–734. doi:10.1037/a0038898 PMID:25751749

Menz, M. (2012). Functional Top Management Team Members: A Review, Synthesis, and Research Agenda. *Journal of Management, 38*(1), 45–80. doi:10.1177/0149206311421830

Mintzberg, H. (1973). *The Nature of Managerial Work*. New York: Harper & Row.

Mintzberg, H. (1975). The Manager's Job: Folklore and Fact. *Harvard Business Review*, 56–62.

Mintzberg, H. (1980). Structure in 5's: A Synthesis of the Research on Organization Design. *Management Science, 26*(3), 322–341. doi:10.1287/mnsc.26.3.322

O'Reilly, C. A., & Tushman, M. L. (2004). The Ambidextrous Organization. *Harvard Business Review, 82*(4), 74–82. PMID:15077368

Parker, M., & Welch, E. W. (2013). Professional networks, science ability and gender determinants of three types of leadership in academic science and engineering. *The Leadership Quarterly, 24*(2), 332–348. doi:10.1016/j.leaqua.2013.01.001

Pinto, J. K., & Prescott, J. E. (1988). Variations in critical success factors over the stages in the project life cycle. *Journal of Management, 14*(1), 5–18. doi:10.1177/014920638801400102

Rai, A., Borah, S., & Ramaprasad, A. (1996). Critical success factors for strategic alliances in the information technology industry: An empirical study. *Decision Sciences, 7*(1), 141–155. doi:10.1111/j.1540-5915.1996.tb00848.x

Report, C. P. (2011). *Best Buy Children's Foundation Youth Grants*. Academic Press.

Rockart, J. F. (1979). Chief executives define their own data needs. *Harvard Business Review, 57*(2), 81–93. PMID:10297607

Ronald, D. D. (1961). Management Information Crisis. *Harvard Business Review, 39*(5), 111–121.

Rosenberg, J. M. (1983). Dictionary of Business and Management (2nd ed.). A Wiley-Inderscience Publication.

Rost, J. C. (1997). Moving from individual to relationship: A post-industrial paradigm of leadership. *The Journal of Leadership Studies, 4*(4), 3–16. doi:10.1177/107179199700400402

Rost, J. C. (1997). Moving from individual to relationship: A post-industrial paradigm of leadership. *The Journal of Leadership Studies, 4*(4), 3–16. doi:10.1177/107179199700400402

Sexton, D. W., Lemak, C. H., & Wainio, J. A. (2014). Career inflection points of women who successfully achieved the hospital CEO position. *Journal of Healthcare Management, 59*(5), 367–383. PMID:25647957

Shlamao, B., & Karsten, J. (2012). Ethical Leadership: Lessons from Moses. *Journal of Management Development, 31*(9), 962–973. doi:10.1108/02621711211259901

Spencer, L. M. (1955). 10 problems that worry presidents. Harvard Business Review, 33(6), 75-83.

Swati, M., & Lochan, D. R. (2015). Transformational leadership and employee creativity. *Management Decision, 53*(5), 894–910. doi:10.1108/MD-07-2014-0464

VanDeusen, J. (1996). Honing an effective tool for community improvement. *Journal for Quality and Participation, 19*(5), 54–63.

Walsh, J. J., & Kanter, J. (1988). Toward more successful project management. *Journal of Systems Management,* 16–21.

Zahedi, F. (1987). Reliability of information systems based on the critical success factors—Formulation. *Management Information Systems Quarterly, 11*(2), 187–203. doi:10.2307/249362

KEY TERMS AND DEFINITIONS

Barrier: An external condition or organizational (internal) weakness that hinders an organization's ability to accomplish a goal or objective.

Critical Success Factors (CSFs): The handful of key areas where an organization must perform well on a consistent basis to achieve its mission.

Enabler: An external condition or organizational strength that facilitates an organization's ability to accomplish its goals or objectives.

Executive Performance Measure: Performance targets relevant to each executive versus objective.

Executive: A person with senior managerial responsibility in a business.

Information Technology (IT): The hardware, software, and telecommunications that facilitate the acquisition, processing, storage, delivery, and sharing of information and other digital content in an organization.

Operational Planning: The process of making decisions about the allocation of organizational resources (capital and staff) to pursue a strategy.

Strategic Goal: A primary goal of an organization or enterprise that implies a particular strategy or set of strategies.

Strategic Planning: A process for defining an organization's strategy, or direction, and making decisions about how to allocate its resources to pursue this strategy, including its capital and people.

Strategy: A derived approach to achieving the mission, goals, and objectives of an organization. It supports the organizational vision, takes into account organizational enablers and barriers.

Chapter 4
Strategic Planning, Cultural Context, and Business Continuity Management:
Business Cases in the City of Shkoder

Mirko Perano
Reald University of Vlore (ASAR), Albania

Xhimi Hysa
Epoka University, Albania

Mario Calabrese
Sapienza University of Rome, Italy

ABSTRACT

This study is focused on the role, importance and practice of Business Continuity Management (BCM) in relation with Strategic Planning (SP) and Cultural Context (CC) by offering a holistic framework for short-term and long-term strategic business analysis. The purpose is to create a unique structured plan for understanding the organizational failure willingness and to create a culture of readiness, feedback and risk management. The methodology used is quantitative with questionnaire for collection data. The study sample includes 50 organizations from four different sectors: banking, services, industrial and insurance in Shkoder (Albania). The research findings show a positive correlation between SP and BCM (0.54%), with a significant positive impact of SP on BCM. A positive correlation is founded between SP and CC (0.588%). The study suggests that placing the BCM in the Corporate Culture may be entitled as another manner of integrating BCM and SP in one structure. Between culture and strategy there is a huge number of characteristics and similarities they have in common with each other.

DOI: 10.4018/978-1-5225-2673-5.ch004

INTRODUCTION

Even though crises, risk, and destruction intimidate the short/long-term survival of some business organizations, and regardless the risk has the most important impact in organizational dynamics in front of this hastily changing business world, still strategic management scholars continue to demonstrate limited and partial awareness in the organizational risk. It also must be considered that the effect of geopolitical actions impact on the globalization and the organizations can react differently depending on cultural context and on interest markets. Overall, the studies about the relationship between organizational risk and strategy are limited. Such limits have their consequences in these studies which are constrained to be divided and to change the face of organizational risk from application and responsibility (Wiseman, 1999; Ruefli et al., 1999).

According to Ritchie (2003), for making a strategic plan it is needed to make some additional research and experimental work and also some enlargements of the conceptual model linked to crises operation, risk and destruction. It also required expanding the meaning of the implementation of crises operation, risk and destruction by usage of further fields and regulations, by giving attention to the disciplinary-action of the organizational crises, which appeal for an integrative approach of crises operation, risk and destruction (Sheaffer & Mano-Negrin, 2003).

Referring to Graham and Kaye (2006), the organization should firstly inspect the business and figure out the risk in order to determine and to fulfill a valuable program for business continuity management and finally to fulfill effectively the business continuity program.

According to Selden and Perks (2007), failing to plan is planning to fail. It means that businesses must know to manage the urgent situation they may face in any time. The greatest plan is to be done before the incident and not after it. It has been pointed out by the author also the importance about the integration of Business Continuity Management (BCM) with Strategic Planning (SP) in one structure which is in the same line with this study's research aim.

The aim of this study is to underline the role, importance, and the practice of Business Continuity Management (BCM), Strategic Planning (SP), and the relation between them in short and long-term. In addition, the study focuses on integrating in one holistic framework that includes BCM with SP by analyzing the factors that are likely to influence the integration of BCM with SP by analyzing the factors that are likely to influence the integration of BCM with SP in one structure.

By studying the relation between BCM and SP, particular attention has been given to the intervention of Cultural Context (CC) as a moderating variable, especially by defining the timeframe orientation (long term or short term). Also, the research work is centered on the key components of Business Continuity Planning which provide an obvious plan for organizational failure willingness. It means paying more interest in practical strategies and having a total approach to construct general ability in the urgent willingness and feedback as well as to have risk elimination.

Herbane et al. (2004) mentioned that more research and practical studies centered on the strategic role of BCM about integrating BCM and SP in one structure are needed since the field of the study so far is without revealing. In addition, literature shows that ample research in the field of BCM is strongly connected with CC. Cultural context is a unique factor that directs regulation and ultimately the planning success, because every organization has a special plan, and because it does not exist in any manual solution design in business continuity management.

The Business Continuity Institute's Good Practice Guide for several years has supported "Integrating BCM in the Organization's culture" as the only one of the management practices. Regardless of this practice or maybe the reason of it, there are a lot of cultural obstacles such as "it will never be happening this to us" syndrome situation. This happens because of confusing the increasing responsiveness and skills training with the cultural transformation. To transform the CC, it requires more knowledge than the procedure of what includes the BCM. It needs to study a wider level of the management understanding and to be organized with further management control inside the business. Notably it is necessary to insert knowledge of the CC within the practices and apply this knowledge in order to increase the attraction and importance of the BCM in organizations. In case it is difficult to understand the importance of culture within organizations, or in case the management supra-structure enforces cultural transformation, then there is the risk of "conformity". It must work in group with strategic managers and with leadership of the Human Recourses Department in order to have a control or change the culture and then to form a culture of continuity or flexibility (Simpson, 2013). In addition, to better understand there are developed three steps just to improve some skills, capabilities to get connected with other cultures and to identify the necessities of the cultural change in organizations. These steps are: first one, it is difficult to go beyond the common culture of the BCM; secondly, understanding how to integrate culture into organizations in one structure; and thirdly, understanding the culture of the BCM and finally prove to support the others to make some transformations. As a result, this research puts an emphasis in identifying some of the Business Continuity Management (BCM) researchers who have underlined the importance of increasing a better perception about the relation between SP, CC and BCM in order to find out about the business activities in long and short-term period. Other emphasis is on the BCM practice and the impact of integrating BCM with SP in one structure and to reach an integrated strategic structure for BCM and SP which aims to give to the business a broad potential of flexibility beside powerful organizational crises, risk and destruction. The benefits from this integration can be considered as part of competitive advantage in general for the organizations that operate in globalizations markets, but in particular for the Albanian firms participating in the survey, which, with the next entry in the European Union, they will face more problems arising from the geopolitical actions. The correct integration between SP, CC and BCM and their integration in the organizations' culture can represent a way to facilitate the competitiveness not only in the European but also in the global economy.

THEORETICAL BACKGROUND

Strategic Planning (SP)

The survival of each organization depend on its capability to reach the specific goals and maintain a high adapting capability to the dynamic markets, especially for the organizations operating in internationalized markets and more in the context of emerging economy. These goals can have similarity between organizations in the same sector, but they have specificity for each organization. The way that can help to reach each goal depend on the ability of the management to read the environment and anticipate the competitors' actions by building an adequate strategic planning system and select (from strategic decision making) the better strategy for that moment and that organization. Among these (planning and strategies) there is a relation (Mintzberg, 1994a) that impact, for organizations, on the capability of value creation for survive; but definitely "strategic planning is not strategic thinking". Strategic thinking is a "synthesis" and "involves intuition and creativity" (Mintzberg, 1994b). This synthesis can be realized by using appropriate analytical techniques for understand and develop strategy (Porter, 1987). From literature on strategic management field, this rational and analytical approach (Ansoff, 1991; Goold, 1992) was often considered as synonymous with strategic planning (Camillus, 1986; Goold and Quinn, 1993; Lorange et al., 1986; Porter, 1980; Richards, 1986). Henry Mintzberg (1973) defined Planning and adaptive strategy making like different approaches to strategy formulation.

The strategic planning is a method that shifts the educational organization throughout the steps about understanding the differences in external environment, evaluating strengths and weaknesses, expanding the vision of the desired future about the organization and several methods to attain the mission (Brown, 1987). The role of strategic planners is to "[…] support strategy making by aiding and encouraging managers to think strategically".

For having greatest outcomes, the strategic planning needs to collect efficient information, enlarging and looking for strategic options, and also highlighting the future suggestions for the existing choices (Bryson, 1995). In addition, it recognizes the appropriate operations in the environment, evaluates the powerful suggestions, and develops united strategy to conduct the future actions in front of uncertainty (Cooper, 2003). The better benefit in having a good strategic planning as mechanism for improving the strategic decision is "[…] coordinating strategic decision making and (for) driving performance improvement" (Grant, 2003).

Strategic planning in its potential structure begins with the society as the principal client and receiver and continues to determine the allocation of the organizations. This technique comforts the relation between the organizations creation, applying, distribution and the external outcomes (Kaufman, 1996).

The strategic planning process permits community groups to predict reasonable options for future that help to obtain proper strategic purposes by using the right information about linking movement and increasing the collection along the method of the environmental examination.

The key purpose of the strategic planning is saving the organization from being a "hostage" of uncertainty, having alternatives and performing to build the future, and changing activity for being a motivated and dynamic member in order to be flexible by adjusting itself when unexpected change happens (Romney, 1996). In addition, it illustrates both the opinion of the people and offers to the stakeholders a chance to have optimism about the future of the institutions and pay attention to the most important problems by dealing with them in advance.

The strategic planning process involves a thoughtful methodology to have a wide understanding about the feelings and performance of the stakeholders' activity. It is recommended to apply numerous data collection methods by involving document gathering, monitoring and informal interviews (Bishop, Hines, and Collins, 2007).

Culture Context (CC)

Culture is the concept of producing different perceptions where people understand their knowledge and direct the activity. Also the culture is a directed structure of definitions and symbols where it obtains social relations (Tharp, 2010).

Culture aspect emerge from interactions and relations between organizations and its stakeholders in a specific ecosystem. From a quality and cultural orientation of this relations can depend the survival of each component of ecosystems (Pellicano, Perano, Casali, 2016).

The organizational aspect in culture context is seen as a key aspect for having business success, sometimes more than strategy and structure. The characteristics of organizational culture are norms, values, beliefs and regulations and the methods of behavior, which are implemented between people in any organization. It is implied that the managers' capability is affected from organizational culture for developing information and applying tactics during the decision-making methods (Hofstede et al., 2010).

In order to get things completed, the structure of norms, values, attitudes, principles, assumptions and beliefs might be unwritten actions and this gives a special illustration to the organizational structure. The goal of the culture is to get together the correct people for accomplishing the organizational objectives. It results that the team orientation that is a trait of the organizational culture is related with the attainment-oriented culture. According to Brown (1998), basic sources of organizational culture are: general cultures, climate investigation, the human resource management and organizational structure.

Business Continuity Management (BCM)

The BCM recognizes the main important part in the organization where it is difficult to manage loses, as well as the information, stock, properties, and the personnel, and also to make plans to avoid the unpredictable crises and risks (Protiviti, 2013). Furthermore, BCM enlarges the strategies, plans and activities which ensure the defense and the different methods for the function of these actions or for the business development, but in case these become discontinuous then the organizations will face large and important loses outcomes.

The BCM commits the prediction of incidents, which will involve the mission of significant task and development of the organization, and be ready to any unpleasant incident in a premeditated and prepared method.

It is compulsory for the organization to have a "secret" plan and to use it in case of any incident in order to ensure organizational survivor with little and small damages (Gallagher, 2003). BCM is not only a topic referred to plans.

A positive side of the BCM is about to make sure that actions are established to decrease the chances of the problems and to include basics of the flexibility and eventuality into the business which also includes formation of the proper BCM culture aspects. BCM improves the ability of avoiding, organizing, reacting, managing and improving from the influence of critical incidents (Gallagher, 2003). In addition, it builds more resilient organizations.

The Relation and Integration Between SP, CC and BCM

It is highlighted the significance of placing BCM in the culture of the organization through a continuing program of testing, preservation, training and improving the on-going plans (Dawes, 2004; Savage, 2002; Wojcik, 2002; Kippenberger, 1999). Placing the Business Continuity Management in the corporate culture may be entitled as another manner of integrating BCM and SP in one structure.

In relation with the cultural context (CC), the SP and CC can be replaceable with each other, particularly when the community culture is dissimilar and constrains the organizations to make extra plans (Weick, 1987). On the other side, BCM aims to expand the organizational culture flexibility and every employee is required to take part, cooperate and respond to failures and crises with a planned strategy.

BCM is related with the way of thinking, answering and behaving in front of unpredicted events and incidents. Furthermore, it is not sufficient only to identify the BCM as an applied and implemented plan. According to Alesi (2008), the BCM can be seen as an advanced learning in every day activity which highlights the flexibility, portability and technological combination and have to be implanted in the culture of the organization. In a culture of flexibility there is a free environment for announcing and concentrate on trouble solutions and in the organizational threats and risks (Elliot et al., 2010). According to Starr (2002) the flexible organizations are able to resist disruptions and discontinuity because they are adaptable in a changing environment.

The successful cultural changes are accomplished with training (Self et al., 2007). Therefore, integrating BCM in the organizational culture might be accomplished as a result of creating continuity participatory plans by inviting every employee in the BCM, by forming plans which are flexible and understandable, and by inspirational leadership (Alesi, 2008; Elliot et al., 2010; Schraeder et al., 2005). BCM can be embedded in the organization's culture through continuous training, testing, maintenance and updating of the BCM plans, including the business continuity plan and the disaster recovery plan (Low, 2010; Gibb and Buchanan, 2006).

Performing such activities (which are also referred to as BCM program management) on regular basis creates and preserves continuity culture and encourages all the employees to participate actively in BCM.

Throughout the years 1970s and 1980s it was a decrease of the SP reputation but several researchers mentioned that SP continues to be useful and the traditional SP methods continue to be helpful (Glaister, 1999). However, strategic planning must be changed for holding stability and combining it with the external environment, as it is known the business environment is changing rapidly (Proctor, 1997)

According to (Kash & Darling, 1998; Preble, 1997; Camillus, 1996), even though SP assists to predict the future, still planning practices in business are missing when it comes to manage crisis, risk, and destruction. By integrating BCM with SP in one structure it is likely to establish the organizational strategic potential flexibility (Herbane et al, 2004).

BCM as a concept has been coined in 2000s and consequently is a new qualified practice (Borodzicz, 2005). Thus, few studies are done on the topic of integrating BCM with SP in one structure (Herbane et al., 2004; Malone, 198; Wong, 2009)

Integrating BCM with SP in one structure helps the organizations to recover from the crises with a slight collision to the environment competitiveness (Wong, 2009). According to a study of 12 North American organizations it was suggested to form BCM within strategy because it will assist to have long term goals, build up protective capability, develop the Strategic Planning and form a flexibility culture (Foster & Karen, 2005).

According to Malone (1989) and Collins & Porras (1996) it exist a positive correlation between SP and BCM where this last has the capability to accomplish business vision because it is evaluated as the element of the strategic planning and also can predict the future continuity. This signifies the integration of BCM with SP in one structure by connecting with the business vision. Actually, the new ISO 22301 resilience standard has implied that BCM program plan should be more strategic supporter (Potter, 2014).

Finally, several factors related with organizational responsibility, future crises and destruction forecast, and the importance of increasing the strategic level of the business continuity management have been studied (Herbane et al., 2004; Hurley-Hanson, 2006; Ritchie, 2003; Roberts & Stephens, 2009; Hiles, 2004; Kash & Darling, 1998; Smith, 2002, 2013). The main factors of the external business environment are: the business concerns for defending the clients, concerns about the economic threat, about technological threat, about environmental threat (global warming), about political threat, about social and cultural threat, concerns for globalization threat, and the necessity to fulfill international and legal rules/regulations. The business environment is affected even from some internal factors, such as: human skills, risks that affect corporate services, individuals and structures, concerns for supporting competitive improvements and also the validity of the infrastructure, time and the budget.

METHODOLOGY AND ANALYSIS

The research done in this work is a quantitative one based on the descriptive design and exploratory under positivism philosophy for validate our research hypothesis. From the positivism it is illustrated the deductive approach. For the strategy it was applied the survey method.

Concretely, the research is focused on the relationship between some variables that the authors have called as SP (strategic planning), CC (cultural context) and BCM (business continuity management). Therefore, the research questions aroused are:

- What is the relationship between Strategic Planning and Cultural Context?
- What is the relationship between Strategic Planning and Business Continuity Management?

The verification of the proposed model is structured into the following phases:

1. Research Design.
2. Survey and Data Collection.
3. Data Analysis and Research Findings.

Data are gathered through the instrument of questionnaire and analyzed statistically through the EViews software. Research setting refers to the ancient city of Shkoder, located in the northern part of Albania and populated by different business categories.

Research Design

The theme of the Strategic Planning has been addressed almost entirely to the performance of organizations (Ong'ayo, 2012; Arasa & K'obonyo, 2012). According to us, no research has instead focused on the relationship between SP and CC and relationship between SP and BCM. Consequently, it was considered to test exploratory purposes, and the model shown in reference to this context. To test hypotheses, mentioned above, the authors thought to focus on the identification of the relationships (Robinson, 2003). According to Mugenda and Mugenda (2008), social phenomena (that depend on human behavior) are best explained using qualitative and quantitative research.

Survey and Data Collection

The data used in this study are primary data sources, collected by questionnaires. The main tool for collecting data in this study was questionnaires. According to Patton (2002), the quality of the data obtained through this type of collection for art, is largely dependent on the skills of the researcher conducting the analysis. By coding the answers in the order of sequential associations you can get a rough measure of their relative strength (Hutchinson, 1983). Unlike the vast majority of existing studies in the literature, performed using a composite sample of university students, our choice was to focus on the interviews of 50 organizations in a developing country from four different sectors: banking, services, industrial and insurance in different businesses in Shkoder (Albania). Considering the exploratory nature of the analysis and the Albanian geographical dimension (and numerosity of organizations of each sector investigated), the sample collected can be considered suitable.

According to Knight (2001), the questionnaire contains all the necessary elements to get the answers. To use a questionnaire within a survey study it permits the researcher to get the data through people's thoughts, judgments and activities. Moreover it helps the researcher to gather information's regarding the people's awareness about the risk, culture and experiences and for the future prospects (Neuman, 2000). In addition, by analyzing the literature review it was revealed that the questionnaire was the most frequent data collection instrument applied on BCM research (Chow, 2000; Woodman, 2008; Pitt & Goyal, 2004), confirming with this the research setting.

Accordingly, the organizations in the city of Shkoder are very sensitive in sharing their information regarding BCM, organizational culture and SP, because they consider it as confidential. In addition, to have straight entrance through BCM, organizational culture and SP it might be somehow difficult and might take times. Moreover, using a questionnaire method in these studies it will permit the researcher to gather additional responses and maybe to ask private questions since the questions are prepared to be in a confidential way (Knight, 2001). For these reasons mentioned above in this research study it is used a questionnaire method.

The questionnaires are divided in two different types, such as: self-administered and interviewer administered, according to (Saunders et al., 2015). The self-administered questionnaires are fulfilled by respondents itself; in contrast, the interviewer administered questionnaires are fulfilled by interviewer regarding the answers of respondents. Furthermore, the self-administered questionnaires involve three different ways of collecting the answers, through: online, e-mail and distribution and gathering the questionnaires. Moreover, the interviewer administered questionnaires involve two ways for gathering the answers, through: structured interviews and phone questionnaire. In this work are used both types of questionnaires but mostly it is centered into interviewer-administered questionnaire, except the fact this kind of questionnaire waste the time and is expensive for researchers (Knight, 2001).

In this study it was selected the structured interview type of interviewer administered questionnaire. The questionnaire was a bit long because intends to examine the role, importance and practice of the BCM and SP, and the relation between SP, CC and BCM (long/short-term period). In addition, it was aimed the integration of BCM with SP in one structure and the analysis of the several factors that are likely to influence the integration of BCM with SP in one structure. It is suggested that long question-naires are performed as structured interviews (Saunders et al., 2015).

Regarding the sample, 50 organizations from different sectors were chosen randomly from Albanian Shkoder city area. The demographic sample characteristics are shown in table 1.

Data Analysis and Research Findings

Data analysis is the process that begins with the collection phase and ends with the stage for the preparation and data interpretation (Kothari, 2004). For the data analysis it is used the EViews software. In table 2 it is shown the correlation analysis between SP and CC based on the answers given by the responders in consideration to the administered questionnaire.

According to the correlation test mainly the correlation of the question is positive but not very strong. The highest correlation is found between question 6 of SP and question 3 of CC at a value of 0.62%. Thus, scanning the business environment is highly correlated with implementing continuously new methods in the business in order to improve it.

However there are also some very low negative correlation between question 2 of SP ("Motivating innovation and creation") and question 9 of CC ("People understands what needs to be done for us to

Table 1. The Demographic Sample Characteristics

	Frequency	%
EMPLOYEES		
Less than 10	34	65%
10-49	13	26%
50-249	2	4%
More than 250	1	2%
YEARS IN SP		
Less than 1 year	3	6%
1-5 years	12	24%
6-15 years	24	48%
More than 15 years	11	22%
CATEGORIES OF THE ORGANIZATIONS INDUSTRY		
Industrial	5	10%
Banking	7	14%
Insurance	2	4%
Service	3	64%
Other	4	8%
TYPES OF SHAREHOLDERS OF THE ORGANIZATIONS OWNERSHIP		
Private Organizations	49	98%
Governments	1	2%
RISK LEVEL		
Very Low	6	12%
Low	21	42%
Medium	23	46%

Table 2. Analyzing the relationship between Strategic Planning (SP) and Cultural Context (CC)

	SP1	SP2	SP3	SP4	SP5	SP6	SP7	SP8
CC1	0.350512	0.096457	0.100721	0.525296	0.108722	0.35484	0.370568	0.199246
CC10	0.312359	0.168127	0.165888	0.460301	0.173203	0.329515	0.178011	0.17856
CC11	0.263943	0.16218	0.246117	0.430117	0.008981	0.298443	0.043111	0.189817
CC12	0.324969	0.170847	0.319459	0.422611	0.098863	0.267761	0.240894	0.268326
CC13	0.410525	0.103792	0.141629	0.363481	0.117882	0.211366	0.130886	0.135662
CC14	0.153651	0.211387	0.159078	0.018795	0.265708	0.224869	-0.02779	0.104205
CC2	0.111883	0.242351	0.208664	0.312284	-0.03381	0.273261	0.377256	0.473676
CC3	0.460224	0.544062	0.465434	0.431147	0.062392	0.621395	0.522399	0.387153
CC4	0.327408	0.160394	0.00905	0.379439	0.281595	0.288164	0.549056	0.075735
CC5	0.498356	0.339898	0.10743	0.467717	0.122882	0.384437	0.527476	0.365846
CC6	0.322877	0.19241	0.307861	0.488759	-0.05417	0.420381	0.159833	0.092443
CC7	0.377304	0.227582	0.23857	0.482943	-0.02571	0.336161	0.228911	0.066573
CC8	0.334957	0.445215	0.513168	0.339683	-0.01195	0.482066	0.326283	0.429363
CC9	0.167459	-0.00038	0.120502	0.322382	0.274543	0.333865	0.216529	0.081354

succeed in the long-run"), between question 5 of SP ("Identifying various types of risks facing the organization") and question 2, 6, 7, and 8 of CC ("We respond well to competitors and other changes in the business environment", "There is a purpose and long-term direction", "There is a clear strategy for the future", and "Leaders set goals that are ambitious, but realistic"), and between question 7 of SP ("Ensuring the existence of proactive business continuity planning") and 14 of CC ("We are able to cope with short-term requirements without compromising our long-term vision"). The correlation of the total point of SP and CC is positive at the amount of 0.588%, as declared in table 3.

Table 4 reflects the analysis of the impact of each CC question on the total SP point taken for each company. Accordingly, the questions 3 and 7 of CC have the highest impact on SP, and respectively question 3 has a positive impact of 3.4 points and question 7 a negative impact of 4.6 point. In addition, these two questions are the only questions that have significant impact on SP. Thus, continuously adopted new ways and improved to do the work have a significant positive impact on SP of the company while having a fixed strategy for the future affects negatively in SP of the company.

In table 5 it is analyzed the impact of the question of CC divided on three groups: analysis, motivation and long term, on the average point taken for each company in SP. Accordingly the group of strategy and motivation have the highest impact on SP, where motivation is significant at significance level of 0.1 and the other two groups have insignificant impact on SP.

Accordingly, CC has a significant positive impact in SP (Table 6).

In table 7 it is shown the correlation analysis between the questions of SP and BCM.

According to the correlation test mainly the correlation of the question is positive but not very strong. The highest correlation is found between question 1 of SP and question 17 of BCM and question 7 of SP and 11 of BCM, respectively at a value of 0.64% and 61%. Thus, achieving sustainable competitive advantage and ensuring the existence of proactive business continuity planning are respectively highly correlated with concerns about maintaining customers and the need to recover effectively from disasters. However there are also some very low negative correlations between question 1 of SP ("Accomplishing sustainable competitive advantages") and question 7 of BCM ("Compliance to legal acts"), between question 4 of SP ("Ensuring ongoing growth and success") and questions 6, 7, 8, and 18 of BCM ("Concerns about natural risk", "Compliance to legal acts", "Concerns about the forces of globalization", and "Concerns about social risk") and between question 5 of SP ("Identifying various types of risks facing the organization") and 7 of BCM ("Compliance to legal acts"), between question 6 of SP ("Scanning business environment") and question 8 and 12 of BCM ("Concerns about the forces of globalization" and "Concerns about biological risk"). The correlation of the total points of SP and BCM is positive at the amount of 0.54%, as it is evidenced in table 8.

The following table 9 reflects the impact of each SP question on the total BCM point taken for each company. Accordingly, the highest impact on BCM comes from the questions 4 and 7 of SP; respectively,

Table 3. The correlation of the SP and CC

	SPTOT	**CCTOT**
SPTOT	1.000000	0.588149
CCTOT	0.588149	1.000000

Table 4. Analysis of the impact of each CC question on the total SP point for each company

Dependent Variable: SPTOT Method: Least Squares Date: 05/23/15 Time: 15:56 Sample (adjusted): 1 49 Included observations: 49 after adjustments				
Variable	**Coefficient**	**Std. Error**	**t-Statistic**	**Prob.**
CC1	1.841633	1.096939	1.678884	0.1023
CC2	-0.131055	0.814166	-0.160968	0.8731
CC3	3.402335	0.913611	3.724054	0.0007
CC4	0.394849	1.015793	0.388710	0.6999
CC5	0.190874	0.804928	0.237131	0.8140
CC6	2.133705	1.469129	1.452360	0.1556
CC7	-4.680808	1.825084	-2.564708	0.0149
CC8	0.492434	0.880205	0.559453	0.5795
CC9	0.061900	0.500618	0.123648	0.9023
CC10	0.330115	1.059017	0.311718	0.7572
CC11	-0.348709	1.164959	-0.299331	0.7665
CC12	0.861957	0.673924	1.279012	0.2096
CC13	-0.307906	0.821033	-0.375022	0.7100
CC14	-0.506759	0.784056	-0.646330	0.5224
C	18.30073	5.641218	3.244110	0.0026
R-squared	0.619428	Mean dependent var		32.93878
Adjusted R-squared	0.462721	S.D. dependent var		4.875142
S.E. of regression	3.573445	Akaike info criterion		5.631722
Sum squared resid	434.1633	Schwarz criterion		6.210851
Log likelihood	-122.9772	Hannan-Quinn criter.		5.851443
F-statistic	3.952793	Durbin-Watson stat		2.031593
Prob(F-statistic)	0.000522			

question 4 has a negative impact of 4.7 points and question 7 a positive impact of 3.8 point. Moreover, the questions that have a significant impact on BCM are 3, 4, 5 and 7. Thus, "Implementing productive action plans", "Identifying various types of risks facing the organization", and "Ensuring the existence of proactive business continuity planning" have a significant positive impact of BCM while "Ensuring ongoing growth and success" has a significant negative impact of BCM.

Moreover, SP questions are divided in three groups: analyzing, management and success. In the tables below (10 and 11) it is analyzed the impact of these three groups on BCM where the highest impact and the only significant impact is resulted by management group.

Furthermore, in Tables 10 and 11, the significant positive impact of SP on BCM is shown.

Table 5. CC impact divided on three groups: analysis, motivation and long term

Dependent Variable: TOTAL_AVG_POINT_SP
Method: Least Squares
Date: 05/23/15 Time: 15:35
Sample: 1 50
Included observations: 50

Variable	Coefficient	Std. Error	t-Statistic	Prob.
STRATEGY	0.230857	0.181441	1.272352	0.2096
MOTIVATION	0.241703	0.143254	1.687230	0.0983
LONG_TERM	0.011185	0.175791	0.063629	0.9495
C	2.196665	0.444333	4.943732	0.0000
R-squared	0.364353	Mean dependent var		4.105556
Adjusted R-squared	0.322898	S.D. dependent var		0.599009
S.E. of regression	0.492902	Akaike info criterion		1.499606
Sum squared resid	11.17581	Schwarz criterion		1.652568
Log likelihood	-33.49015	Hannan-Quinn criter.		1.557855
F-statistic	8.789069	Durbin-Watson stat		1.999105
Prob(F-statistic)	0.000102			

Table 6. Analysis of the total impact of CC on SP

Dependent Variable: SPTOT
Method: Least Squares
Date: 05/23/15 Time: 16:20
Sample (adjusted): 1 49
Included observations: 49 after adjustments

Variable	Coefficient	Std. Error	t-Statistic	Prob.
CCTOT	0.302101	0.060594	4.985638	0.0000
C	16.19374	3.406548	4.753708	0.0000
R-squared	0.345919	Mean dependent var		32.93878
Adjusted R-squared	0.332003	S.D. dependent var		4.875142
S.E. of regression	3.984507	Akaike info criterion		5.642664
Sum squared resid	746.1858	Schwarz criterion		5.719881
Log likelihood	-136.2453	Hannan-Quinn criter.		5.671960
F-statistic	24.85659	Durbin-Watson stat		2.007240
Prob(F-statistic)	0.000009			

FUTURE RESEARCH

Strategic aspect in managing organization is an old but even new topic on which scholars and practitioners give attention. Strategic Planning, as mentioned, is not strategic management, but it can be considered as a relevant process in searching of competitive advantages. Do SP requires knowledge

Table 7. Analyzing the relationship between Strategic Planning (SP) and BCM

	SP1	SP2	SP3	SP4	SP5	SP6	SP7	SP8
B1	0.437785	0.260959	0.178526	0.446596	0.17635	0.322675	0.359476	0.134657
B2	0.360711	0.199278	0.350314	0.400026	0.196706	0.400605	0.290497	0.02755
B3	0.438315	0.232394	0.016339	0.240954	0.50605	0.113247	0.295615	0.111792
B4	0.230267	0.407794	0.517768	0.209422	0.167923	0.424925	0.427345	0.284363
B5	0.077469	0.04785	0.220099	0.073115	0.179059	0.197597	0.110144	0.228062
B6	0.07325	0.120181	0.153596	-0.03716	0.012408	0.25644	0.081192	0.22087
B7	-0.1567	0.139332	0.366006	-0.24661	-0.05585	0.12276	-0.01843	0.177287
B8	0.11698	0.06914	0.121984	-0.24083	0.233691	-0.16168	-0.0128	0.006624
B9	0.171831	0.255804	0.362838	0.08593	0.019131	0.148505	0.355648	0.32518
B10	0.436284	0.413458	0.380762	0.282959	0.328251	0.387087	0.562679	0.568066
B11	0.404058	0.368752	0.42064	0.326927	0.336741	0.304058	0.608423	0.371527
B12	0.231595	0.154659	0.23574	0.07599	0.37872	-0.08501	0.289981	0.10654
B13	0.382444	0.391391	0.326336	0.053907	0.342048	0.186848	0.345953	0.261722
B14	0.026876	0.368369	0.404494	0.027345	0.294179	0.256546	0.329333	0.237032
B15	0.125411	0.45641	0.282468	0.085728	0.283876	0.437846	0.491335	0.445312
B16	0.222953	0.075424	0.180594	0.517991	0.226214	0.087752	0.401229	0.038723
B17	0.639693	0.270122	0.235192	0.360293	0.309767	0.191511	0.329211	0.262607
B18	0.226446	0.387904	0.340742	-0.03726	0.326388	0.039056	0.345041	0.213078

Table 8. The correlation of SP and BCM

	BTOT	SPTOT
BTOT	1.000000	0.546348
SPTOT	0.546348	1.000000

(not only technical), but also related to cultural context and continuity management. Starting from this consideration and from the results obtained, the next step of this research can be extend the sample and achieve a statistical representativeness at least for Albanian territory. Achieved this second goal, it will be possible to further extend the sample with other territories, or countries and realize a comparative analysis to highlight possible other aspect related to CC and BCM and SP.

CONCLUSION

This study has shown both theoretically and empirically that in the field of SP it is very significant to accomplish some organizational principles such as: accomplishing sustainable competitive advantages, motivating the innovation and foundation, applying a helpful action plan, and make sure the continuing development and achievement of the organization. The SP was furthermore significant to attain

Table 9. Analysis the impact of each SP question of the total BCM point for each company

Dependent Variable: BTOT
Method: Least Squares
Date: 05/23/15 Time: 16:27
Sample: 1 50
Included observations: 50

Variable	Coefficient	Std. Error	t-Statistic	Prob.
SP1	1.743729	1.564079	1.114860	0.2714
SP2	-0.339848	1.614279	-0.210526	0.8343
SP3	3.601028	1.407586	2.558300	0.0143
SP4	-4.740229	2.094604	-2.263067	0.0290
SP5	2.502456	1.197059	2.090503	0.0428
SP6	-0.114161	1.466163	-0.077864	0.9383
SP7	3.868924	1.639608	2.359665	0.0231
SP8	0.487715	1.396402	0.349265	0.7287
C	15.02779	8.590402	1.749370	0.0877
R-squared	0.475521	Mean dependent var		42.08000
Adjusted R-squared	0.373184	S.D. dependent var		9.271065
S.E. of regression	7.340063	Akaike info criterion		6.986121
Sum squared resid	2208.938	Schwarz criterion		7.330285
Log likelihood	-165.6530	Hannan-Quinn criter.		7.117181
F-statistic	4.646602	Durbin-Watson stat		2.268235
Prob(F-statistic)	0.000428			

Table 10. Impact analysis of SP questions divided on three groups: analyzing, management and success

Dependent Variable: TOTAL_AVG_POINT_BCM
Method: Least Squares
Date: 05/23/15 Time: 16:37
Sample: 1 50
Included observations: 50

Variable	Coefficient	Std. Error	t-Statistic	Prob.
ANALYSIS	0.040835	0.184256	0.221621	0.8256
MANAGEMENT	0.331496	0.131422	2.522372	0.0152
SUCCESS	0.237535	0.132007	1.799403	0.0785
C	0.965779	0.538685	1.792844	0.0796
R-squared	0.392446	Mean dependent var		3.443333
Adjusted R-squared	0.352823	S.D. dependent var		0.634175
S.E. of regression	0.510177	Akaike info criterion		1.568501
Sum squared resid	11.97291	Schwarz criterion		1.721462
Log likelihood	-35.21251	Hannan-Quinn criter.		1.626749
F-statistic	9.904463	Durbin-Watson stat		1.859328
Prob(F-statistic)	0.000037			

Table 11. Analysis the SP impact of BCM

Dependent Variable: BTOT Method: Least Squares Date: 05/23/15 Time: 16:38 Sample: 1 50 Included observations: 50				
Variable	**Coefficient**	**Std. Error**	**t-Statistic**	**Prob.**
SPTOT	1.049250	0.232169	4.519338	0.0000
C	7.496707	7.732309	0.969530	0.3371
R-squared	0.298496	Mean dependent var		42.08000
Adjusted R-squared	0.283881	S.D. dependent var		9.271065
S.E. of regression	7.845527	Akaike info criterion		6.996942
Sum squared resid	2954.510	Schwarz criterion		7.073423
Log likelihood	-172.9236	Hannan-Quinn criter.		7.026067
F-statistic	20.42442	Durbin-Watson stat		2.059281
Prob(F-statistic)	0.000041			

the organizational principles linked with BCM through: recognizing different kind of risks faced by the organization, analyzing the business environment, providing the continuation of proactive business continuity planning, and showing resilient capabilities after a failure or a disaster. Furthermore, it shows the unionization of BCM and SP through the empirical results given.

According to the correlation test mainly the correlation of the questions is positive but not very strong. The correlation of the total point of SP and BCM is positive at the amount of 0.54%. Accordingly, the highest impact on BCM has the questions 4 and 7 of SP; respectively, question 4 has a negative impact of 4.7 points and question 7 a positive impact of 3.8 point. Additionally, SP has a significant positive impact on BCM. Therefore, in the same time the correlation of the total point of SP and CC is positive at the amount of 0.588%; it is positive but not very strong. The highest correlation is found between question 6 of SP and question 3 of Culture Context at a value of 0.62%. Thus, scanning the business environment is highly correlated with implementing continuously new methods in the business in order to improve it. However, there are also some very low negative correlation between question 2 of SP and question 9 of CC, between question 5 of SP and question 2, 6, 7, and 8 of CC and between question 7 of SP and 14 of CC. The study suggests that placing the Business Continuity Management in the Corporate Culture may be entitled as another manner of integrating BCM and SP in one structure. Sometimes, strategy and culture together overlap and have common characteristics with many topics in the organization, which some consider strategy and some others consider culture. Furthermore, between culture and strategy exists a huge number of common characteristics and similarities.

Regarding the need to integrate holistically in one structure the BCM within business organizations located in Shkoder, along permanent testing, training and renewing the plans, the method of BCM implemented in Shkoder city has the possibility to help in realizing and attaining the integration of BCM with SP in one structure. The previous analysis shows also that in some businesses there are several disadvantages and barriers for the integration of the proposed framework, like: lack of experienced human resources, concerns about the economic risk, concerns about technological risk, concern of cultural change, natural disasters, concerns about keeping clients, and concerns about the globalization. In contrast, there are also some accelerating factors which advantage the businesses in Shkoder in order to integrate the BCM with SP in one structure, such as: to make sure the long term continuance of the organizations, availability of time, to reduce risk, to recognize the business environment, compliance with corporate governance, availability of organizational infrastructure and concerns about internal organizational risks.

Despite the contribution of the present study, some limitations are to be mentioned. For instance, this research relies on a survey research strategy and exploratory approach. While the methodology used in this research has accomplished some of the weaknesses in the past literature, however it could not find deep details of some sectors linked with BCM, of the impact related with the integration BCM with SP in one structure, and of the significance of culture context relation between the two.

Another problematic encountered during data gathering regards the respondents' feelings and skepticism about the confidentiality of answers. The respondents demonstrate doubtful willingness to answer the questions and, in some cases, they perceive their information as personal. Therefore, some respondents did not answer some of the questions.

The preferred target of respondents was that of senior managers since the authors deal with strategic issues, but it was hard and complicated to realize this for every business in Shkoder. Even some senior managers could not fulfill and answer all the questions for their personal purposes and motives. In the absence of the senior managers in those organizations, it was the possibility to contact with the other experts who had the right background to answer the questions.

Finally, it seems physiological after this research to offer some recommendations for future inquires. According to the findings of this research, it is recommended for businesses in Shkoder that it is needed to pay more attention to the topics, which facilitates the extension of the business continuity management into a strategic field, and to sustain the CC within BCM and SP. The businesses of Shkoder must raise their understanding of the importance of these topics and subjects for accomplishing the integration of BCM with SP in one structure, also to align themselves with the geopolitical new trends in order to seize all the opportunities emerging from global economy.

There is no necessity to follow any training of actions in view of the fact that the businesses are not likely to display and uncover the imported risk cases. It is recommended that every organization must make further endeavors within the vulnerability analysis and evaluation with the reason to understand the weak points because it will encourage and improve extra actions for integrating BCM in one structure with SP.

REFERENCES

Alesi, P. (2008). Building enterprise-wide resilience by integrating business continuity capability into day-to-day business culture and technology. *Journal of Business Continuity & Emergency Planning*, 2(3), 214–220. PMID:21339108

Ansoff, H. I. (1991). Critique of Henry Mintzbergs. The design school: Reconsidering the basic premises of strategic management. *Strategic Management Journal*, 12(6), 449–462. doi:10.1002/smj.4250120605

Arasa, R., & K'obonyo, P. (2012). The relationship between strategic planning and firm performance. *International Journal of Humanities and Social Science*, 2(22), 201–213.

Bishop, P., Hines, A., & Collins, T. (2007). The Current State of Scenario Development: An Overview of Techniques. *Foresight, 9*(1), 5–25. doi:10.1108/14636680710727516

Borodzicz, E. P. (2005). *Risk, Crisis and Security Management.* Chichester, UK: John Wiley & Sons.

Camillus, J. C. (1986). *Strategic Planning and Management Control: Systems for Survival and Success.* Lexington, MA: Lexington Books.

Camillus, J. C. (1996). Reinventing Strategic Planning. *Strategy and Leadership, 24*(3), 6–12. doi:10.1108/eb054552

Chow, W. S. (2000). Success factors for IS disaster recovery planning in Hong Kong. *Information Management & Computer Security, 8*(2), 80–87. doi:10.1108/09685220010321326

Collins, J. C., & Porras, J. I. (1996). Building your company's vision. *Harvard Business Review, 74*(5), 65–77.

Dawes, T. (2004). Crisis planning. *British Journal of Administrative Management, 42*(Aug/Sep), 26–27.

Elliot, D., Swartz, E., & Herbane, B. (2010). *Business Continuity Management: A Crisis Management Approach* (2nd ed.). London, UK: Rutledge.

Foster, S. P., & Karen, D. (2005). Building continuity into strategy. *Journal of Corporate Real Estate, 7*(2), 105–119. doi:10.1108/14630010510812530

Gallagher, M. (2003). *Business Continuity Management: How to protect your company from danger.* London, UK: Financial Times Management.

Gibb, F., & Buchanan, S. (2006). A framework for business continuity management. *International Journal of Information Management, 26*(2), 128–141. doi:10.1016/j.ijinfomgt.2005.11.008

Glaister, K., & Falshaw, R. (1999). Strategic planning: Still going strong? *Long Range Planning, 32*(1), 107–116. doi:10.1016/S0024-6301(98)00131-9

Goold, M. (1992). Design, learning and planning: A further observations on the design school debate. *Strategic Management Journal, 13*(2), 169–170. doi:10.1002/smj.4250130208

Goold, M., & Quinn, J. J. (1993). *Strategic Control: Establishing Milestones for Long-term Performance.* Reading, MA: Addison-Wesley.

Graham, J., & Kaye, D. (2006). *A Risk Management Approach to Business Continuity: Aligning Business Continuity with Corporate Governance.* Rothstein Associates Inc.

Grant, R. M. (2003). Strategic Planning in a Turbolent Environment: Evidence from the Oil Majors. *Strategic Management Journal, 24*(6), 491–517. doi:10.1002/smj.314

Herbane, B., Elliott, D., & Swartz, E. (2004). Business Continuity Management: Time for a Strategic Role? *Long Range Planning, 37*(5), 435–457. doi:10.1016/j.lrp.2004.07.011

Hiles, A. (2004). *Business Continuity Management: Global Best Practices* (4th ed.). Rothstein Publishing.

Hofstede, G., Hofstede, G. J., & Minkov, M. (2010). *Cultures and Organizations: Software of the Mind* (3rd ed.). New York: McGraw-Hill.

Hurley-Hanson, A. E. (2006). Organizational responses and adaptations after 9-11. *Management Research News*, *29*(8), 480–494. doi:10.1108/01409170610692806

Hutchinson, J. W. (1983). Expertise and the structure of free recall. In R. P. Bagozzi & A. M. Tybout (Eds.), *Advances in consumer research* (Vol. 10, pp. 585–589). Ann Arbor, MI: Association for Consumer Research.

Kash, T. J., & Darling, J. R. (1998). Crisis management: Prevention, diagnosis and intervention. *Leadership and Organization Development Journal*, *19*(4), 179–186. doi:10.1108/01437739810217151

Kippenberger, T. (1999). Reducing the Impact of the Unexpected. *Management Research*, *4*(3), 28–31.

Knight, P. (2001). *Small-Scale Research: Pragmatic Inquiry in Social Science and the Caring Professions*. London, UK: SAGE Publications.

Kothari, C. R. (2004). *Research methodology: methods and techniques*. New Delhi, India: Age International.

Lorange, P., & Vancil, R. F. (1995). How to design a strategic planning system. In P. Lorange (Ed.), *Strategic Planning and Control: Issues in the Strategy Process*. Cambridge, MA: Blackwell.

Low, S. P., Liu, J., & Sio, S. (2010). Business continuity management in large construction companies in Singapore. *Disaster Prevention and Management*, *19*(2), 219–232. doi:10.1108/09653561011038011

Malone, S. (1989). Selected correlates of business continuity planning in the family business. *Family Business Review*, *2*(4), 341–353. doi:10.1111/j.1741-6248.1989.tb00003.x

Mintzberg, H. (1973). Strategy making in three modes. *Management Review*, *16*(2), 44–53.

Mintzberg, H. (1994a). *The Rise and Fall of Strategic Management*. Hemel Hempstead, UK: Prentice-Hall.

Mintzberg, H. (1994b). The Rise and Fall of Strategic Management. *Harvard Business Review*, *72*(1), 107–114.

Mugenda, O. M., & Mugenda, A. G. (2008). *Research methods*. Nairobi, Kenya: Nairobi Press.

Neuman, W. L. (2010). *Social Research Methods: Qualitative and Quantitative Approaches* (4th ed.). Pearson Education.

Ong'ayo, E. (2012). *Employee perception of the influence of strategic planning on organization performance at the ministry of Foreign affairs, Kenya* (Unpublished MBA thesis). University of Nairobi, Nairobi, Kenya.

Patton, M. Q. (2002). *Qualitative research*. London, UK: John Wiley and Sons Limited.

Pellicano, M., Perano, M., & Casali, G. L. (2016). The Enterprise Relational View (ERV): Exploring future in Strategic Management. In *Book of Abstract of fourth B.S. Lab International Symposium on Governing Business Systems, Theories and Challenges for Systems Thinking in Practice* (pp. 105-109). Vilnius, Lithuania: Mykolas Romeris University, B.S. Lab.

Pitt, M., & Goyal, S. (2004). Business continuity planning as a facilities management tool. *Facilities, 22*(3/4), 87–99. doi:10.1108/02632770410527824

Porter, M. (1987). The State of Strategic Thinking. *Economist,* (May): 23.

Porter, M. E. (1980). *Competitive Strategy.* New York: Free Press.

Potter, P. (2014). *Building a Stronger, More Strategic BCM Program.* Retrieved March 10, 2016, from https://www.continuityinsights.com/article/2014/02/building-stronger-more-strategic-bcm-program

Preble, J. (1997). Integrating the Crisis Management Perspective into the Strategic Management Process. *Journal of Management Studies, 34*(5), 769–791. doi:10.1111/1467-6486.00071

Proctor, T. (1997). Establishing a strategic direction: A review. *Management Decision, 35*(2), 143–154. doi:10.1108/00251749710160304

Protiviti. (2013). *Guide to Business Continuity Management* (3rd ed.). Retrieved April 15, 2016, from https://www.protiviti.com/en-US/Documents/Resource-Guides/Guide-to-BCM-Third-Edition-Protiviti.pdf

Richards, M. D. (1986). *Setting Strategic Goals and Objectives* (2nd ed.). St. Paul, MN: West Publishing.

Ritchie, B. W. (2004). Chaos, Crises and Disasters: A strategic Approach to Crisis Management in the Tourism Industry. *Tourism Management, 25*(6), 669–683. doi:10.1016/j.tourman.2003.09.004

Roberts, P. W. F., & Stephens, M. (2009). Implementing Business Continuity Management in a Distributed Organisation. *The Business Continuity Journal, 3*(4), 16–26.

Robinson, D. T. (2003). Strategic alliances and the boundaries of the firm. *Review of Financial Studies, 21*(2), 649–681. doi:10.1093/rfs/hhm084

Ruefli, T. W., Collins, J. M., & Lacugna, J. R. (1999). Risk measures in strategic management research: Auld lang syne? *Strategic Management Journal, 20*(2), 167–194. doi:10.1002/(SICI)1097-0266(199902)20:2<167::AID-SMJ9>3.0.CO;2-Q

Saunders, M., Lewis, P., & Thornhill, A. (2015). *Research Methods for Business Students* (7th ed.). Essex, UK: Pearson.

Savage, M. (2002). Business continuity planning. *Work Study, 51*(5), 254–261. doi:10.1108/00438020210437277

Schraeder, M., Tears, R., & Jordan, M. (2005). Organizational Culture in Public Sector Organization: Promoting Change through Training and Leading by Example. *Leadership and Organization Development Journal, 26*(6), 492–502. doi:10.1108/01437730510617681

Selden, S., & Perks, S. (2007). How a structured BIA aligned business continuity management with Gallaher's strategic objectives. *Journal of Business Continuity & Emergency Planning, 1*(4), 348–355.

Self, D. R., Armenakis, A. A., & Schraeder, M. (2007). Organizational change content, process, and context: A simultaneous analysis of employee reactions. *Journal of Change Management, 7*(2), 211–229. doi:10.1080/14697010701461129

Sheaffer, Z., & Mano-Negrin, R. (2003). Executives Orientations as Indicators of Crisis Management Policies and Practices. *Journal of Management Studies, 40*(2), 573–606. doi:10.1111/1467-6486.00351

Simpson, K. (2013). *Embedding Culture Into BCM*. Retrieved April 10, 2016, from: http://www.conti-nuityinsights.com/arti cles/2013/03/embedding-culture-bcm

Smith, D. J. (2002). *Business Continuity Management: Good Practices Guidelines*. London, UK: The Business Continuity Institute.

Smith, D. J. (2013). Organisational Resilience and BCM. *Institute of Business Continuity Management*, 1-33. Retrieved April 03, 2016, from: https://www.continuitycentral.com/organisational resilienceandBCM.pdf

Starr, R., Newfrock, J., & Delurey, M. (2003). Enterprise Resilience: Managing Risk in the Networked Economy. *Booz & Company, 30*. Retrieved April 07, 2016, from: http://www.strategy-business.com/article/8375?gko=1c92d

Tharp, B. M. (2009). *Defining "Culture" and "Organizational Culture": From Anthropology to the Office*. Haworth. Retrieved from: http://www.haworth.com/en-us/knowledge/workplace-library/documents/defining-culture-and-organizationa-culture_5.pd

Weick, K. E. (1987). Organizational Culture as a Source of High Reliability. *California Management Review, 29*(2), 112–127. doi:10.2307/41165243

Wiseman, R., & Gomez-Mejia, L. R. (1998). A behavioral agency model of risk taking. *Academy of Management Review, 23*(1), 133–153.

Wojcik, J. (2002). Continuity Management Requires Commitment. *Business Insurance, 36*(17), 18.

Wong, W. (2009). The Strategic Skills of Business Continuity Manager: Putting Business Continuity Management into Corporate Long-term Planning. *Journal of Business Continuity & Emergency Planning, 4*(1), 62–68. PMID:20378494

Woodman, P. (2008, March). Business Continuity Management. Chartered Management Institute, 1-17.

KEY TERMS AND DEFINITIONS

Business Continuity Management: The BCM recognizes the main important part in the organization where it is difficult to manage loses, as well as the information, stock, properties, and the personnel, and to make plans to avoid the unpredictable crises and risks.

Business Ecosystem: A social-economic community in which peoples and organizations interacts. In this community organization produces good and services that may have value for the ecosystem members. The members can be suppliers, lead producers, competitors and other stakeholders.

Business Environment: Environment in which it generates demand and supply of goods and service. When the exchange generate monetary (but not only) flows, it can generate competitive dynamics.

Cultural Context: Culture is the concept of producing different perceptions where people understand their knowledge and direct the activity. In addition, the culture is a directed structure of definitions and symbols where it obtains social relations depending by the context in which this culture was acquired.

Risk Management: Is the activities, or part of more complex process, useful to identify, assess, and prioritize of risks. These activities are followed by coordinated and economical by a professional figures (generally called "risk manager") with the objective of minimize, monitor, and control the probability of occurrence of negative events or to evaluate and maximize the occurring opportunities.

Shkoder: Albanian city.

Strategic Planning: Is a method that shifts the educational organization throughout the steps about understanding the differences in external environment, evaluating strengths and weaknesses, expanding the vision of the desired future about the organization and several methods to attain the mission.

Chapter 5
A Proposition of Strategy Making in Global Firms:
Reflections from Strategy as Practice (S–As–P)

Fatma Gülruh Gürbüz
Marmara University, Turkey

Hande Sinem Ergun
Marmara University, Turkey

Seray Begum Samur-Teraman
Marmara University, Turkey

ABSTRACT

Strategy as Practice (hereafter S-As-P) is referred as a research topic concerning with the doing of strategy; who does it, what they do, how they do it, what they use and what implications this has for shaping strategy. The developing field has taken the concern of "humanize management" seriously by bringing human actors to the center of the strategy (Jarzabkowski & Spee, 2009). This study aims to furnish insights into the S-as-P approach. In this sense, it considers extended mainstream strategy research and focuses on light practices that have largely passed and unnoticed (Vaara & Whittington, 2012). Furthermore, its reflections on businesses operating in global economy are discussed.

INTRODUCTION

Managers are dealing with complicated issues that are both regional and global in nature. Among those issues, wider intra and/or extra organizational constituents have a role in shaping the future of the organization. This situation has also changed the way of looking at the strategy. Strategy is an important issue, because it sets direction for an organization in line with an agreed upon vision. There is a tendency to offer one simple definition of strategy, but Mintzberg, Ahlstrand and Lampel (1998) argue that a number

DOI: 10.4018/978-1-5225-2673-5.ch005

of definitions are required to adequately capture its nature. They explain strategy within a framework of five definitions as follows:

1. Strategy is plan, a direction, a guide and course of action into the future, a path to get from here to there.
2. Strategy is a pattern, that is consistency in behavior over time.
3. Strategy is a position, locating of particular products in particular markets.
4. Strategy is a perspective not only looking inside the organization but also looking at the grand vision of an enterprise.
5. Strategy is a ploy that is a specific maneuver intended to outwit an opponent or competitor.

Although these definitions give us a way to visualize and understand the nature of strategy, throughout the evolution of strategic thinking different perceptions of strategy and ways of strategy making have been developed (Varyani and Khammar, 2010). The field of strategic management can be traced back to 1960s with Alfred Chandler, Igor Ansoff and Kenneth Andrews's works with their more contingent views where organizations need to adapt to their external environment. During the 1970's transition began towards more realistic conceptions of process with Quinn's "logical incrementalism", Mintzberg and Waters' emergent strategy" views. Through this period, Micheal Porter made valuable contributions to the field with his proposed framework to understand the structure of an industry. This was a useful tool for assessing an industry's attractiveness and facilitating competitor analysis. The main focus of these works was on the relationship between the environment and the firm. From the 1980's onwards, the focus changed to the understanding of firms' internal structure, resources and capabilities. Transaction cost economics and agency theory emerged as two streams of research in the field. Transaction cost economics mainly dealt with structural forms of organizations and their effects on performance. Agency theory also tried to explain separation of ownership and control.

Other views that gave direction to the strategic management field were the resource-based view, dynamic capabilities and knowledge based approach. The main proposition of these theories were that a firm could be conceptualized as a bundle of productive resources and that these could be strength or weakness (Furrer, Thomas and Goussevskia, 2008; Varyani and Khammar, 2010). During this transition strategy thinking evolved mainly under the framework of two approaches: the prescriptive approach and the emergent approach. The prescriptive approach is also named as deliberate, rational and intended way of strategy making. Under this approach it is assumed that strategic analysis, strategic development and strategic implementation occurs sequentially. The strategy makers first do the analysis, then develop the strategy and then implement the strategy (Lynch, 2009). Igor Ansoff, a seminal scholar of this approach, proposes that strategy makers should systematically analyze the external environment and develop strategies that align the organization with these challenges. Michael Porter, another important contributor of the prescriptive approach, bases his view on economics. According to his view, environmental scanning and industry analysis are vital for strategy development.

Although the mainstream strategic management field is dominated by the prescriptive approach, in recent years this point of view has attracted criticism from scholars, academicians and practitioners in the field. First of all, this approach considers strategy making as a linear process (Shah et al., 2015). However, in practice linearity is highly debatable due to the difficultly of separating the formulation of strategy from its implementation due to environmental uncertainty (Hart, 1992). Another critique of the prescriptive approach is the lack of "human" element in strategy making. In addition, the top down approach that is embedded in this approach has also lost its popularity (Shah et al., 2015). There are several problems that this traditional view of strategic management faces. Consider, for example, the case of small and entrepreneurial businesses, which are the result of innovative solutions, that lie outside of the guidelines of traditional strategic management. Such companies, by their very nature, are concerned more with what is actually done than with what has been planned. This is also true for other businesses at other scales. In other words, rational decision making assumptions and comparing what has been done with what actually occurs, as a common way of defining strategy making is losing its validity.

Due to the afore-mentioned fallacies and pitfalls of the traditional strategic management perspective, new alternative approaches have emerged. The emergent approach, also termed the non-rational or realized strategy, is the opposite view of prescriptive strategy. This view argues that strategic analysis, strategic development, and strategic implementation do not follow a sequential path. Rather, strategy evolves during the course of its existence at the same time as it is being implemented. The main assumption of the emergent view is that the environment is so uncertain and unpredictable that it is impossible and ineffective for organizations to develop strategies (Lynch, 2009). The pioneer of emergent approach, Mintzberg, argues that "a strategy is not a fixed plane, nor does it change systematically at a pre-arranged time solely at the will of management" (Mintzberg, 1978).

The emergent approach focuses on strategic learning (Mintzberg and Water, 1985). Rather than planning, organizations should develop capabilities that enable them to adapt to the environment and learn continuously. Therefore, strategy making is an experimental process rather than pre-determined steps (Lynch, 2009). In other words, for the emergent approach strategy is a process rather than an ultimate outcome. In this strategy making process the main actors are the organizational members. This assumption puts the "human" element at the core of strategy and differentiates the two approaches from each other. According to the scholars of this approach, behavioral and political processes are extremely influential in decision-making processes of organizational spaces (Fahey, 1981; Mintzberg 1978).

Both prescriptive and emergent strategy approaches are still used by many organizations and both of these approaches have advantages and disadvantages. Today researchers and strategists are moving towards an emergent approach due to environmental uncertainty. A company may employ a prescribed approach to strategy making but have an emergent process view of strategy that improves its strategy making processes. As stated above, prescriptive models and frameworks in strategy research have created concern especially with the way the strategy research has developed over the last three decades (Jarzabkwoski, Balogun and Seidl, 2007). The dominant theories of strategy assume that strategy is something that organizations possess. However, over the last decade a shift has occurred.

This new movement focuses on "practice" approaches in strategy making and how strategy work is actually done within organizational spaces (Varyani and Khammar, 2010). This practice view of strategy is called Strategy as Practice (hereafter S-as-P). S-as-P refers to a process approach in the study and understanding of organizational strategy making. S-as-P feeds on ideas of Weick and Mintzberg. It is said to share the same skepticism about the rational accounts of strategy (Clegg, Carter, Kornberger and Schweitzer, 2011). The term S-as-P is first used by Richard Whittington in 1996 in his article. In the 2000's, the need for more research and focus on practice oriented strategy making was heavily emphasized by scholars in the field (Johnson, Melin, & Whittington, 2003). Since then, S-as-P has gathered attention from scholars in the field. S-as-P offers an alternative way to strategizing through the lenses of strategy praxis, practitioners, practices and strategy texts that go beyond a purely organizational agenda (Fenton and Langley, 2008; Jarzabkowski et al. 2007; Jarzabkowski and Whittington, 2008; Whittington, 2006). It also takes into account the process which is mostly ignored while making plans for future.

S-as-P refers to a research methodology concerned with the doing of strategy; who does it, what they do, how they do it, what they use and what implications this has for shaping strategy. It offers a new perspective for strategic management. From this mostly sociological perspective, strategy is defined as something linking the interior world of the organization to the exterior worlds of the environments in which it operates (Clegg, Carter, & Kornberger, 2004).

The field has taken seriously the call to "humanize management" by bringing human actors to the center of the strategy (Jarzabkowski and Spee, 2009). Thus, the aim of this chapter is to introduce a S-as-P tool for scholars and practitioners in the field which enable them to identify the emergent nature of their strategies and the actual activities constituting strategy making (Sithole, 2011). Based on these, this chapter tries to furnish insights into the S-as-P approach and how managers can use this approach in their strategic decision making process. The first contribution of this chapter is to provide a conceptual framework for understanding how strategic thinking has evolved towards S-as-P research and what kind of innovative thinking has accompanied it. Second, introducing this research agenda and its premises provides practitioners with a valuable tool for better understanding what they are doing and why they are doing it (Downs, 2014).

Next, the conceptual framework with its main assumptions is provided. Managerial implications are also discussed in order to reveal the dynamics of international business management and how to overcome difficulties coming from an ever-changing internal and external environment.

BACKGROUND

Introducing the Strategy as Practice (S-as-P) Perspective: What Do We Mean by S-as-P?"

This part introduces the S-as-P perspective approach and reveals the distinctive features of S-as-P from the traditional view of strategy making.

S-as-P mainly considers the making and doing of strategy and strategic change in organizations. In this sense, S-as-P scholars deal with the processes and practices constituting the everyday activities of organizational life and relating to strategic outcomes (Carter, Clegg and Kornberger, 2008). S-as-P is essentially concerned with strategy as an activity in organizations and mainly considers the strategy as an interaction of people, rather than as the property of organizations (Johnson, Langley, Melin and Whittington, 2007). In this sense, S-as-P is defined by Johnson and his colleagues as a concern over what people do in relation to strategy and how this is influenced by and influences their organizational and institutional context (Johnson, et al 2007). It is something linking the interior world of the organization to the exterior worlds of the environments in which it operates (Clegg, Carter, Kornberger, 2004).

As for distinctive features of this approach, instead of assuming that strategy is something organizations have, where strategy is conceived as a property of organizations (Johnson et al 2007), S-as-P research is more concerned with the inside of the organization. This view primarily draws on sociological theories of practice rather than economic theories (Vaara and Whittington, 2012). It also concerns itself with a range of outcomes, such as the political consequences of particular strategizing episodes, or the effects of strategy tools, or the involvement of particular types of practitioners. S-as-P adds to conventional research in strategic management by extending the range of outcomes, particularly by broadening the understanding of performance to more than just economic ones. Additionally, S-as-P is argued to significantly extend the sectorial scope of the strategic management field to not only deal with profit seeking organizations but also not-for-profit ones. This extends the economic environments, which were previously more narrowly defined (Vaara and Whittington, 2012).

From a practice perspective the actors of strategy are seen as a part of larger social groups. This renders obsolete the notion that only the upper levels of management are relevant as the strategy makers. Rather, it recognizes that people from all levels, different social environments, and newly emerged professions form part of larger picture that play an important role in the process with implications going far beyond particular organizations (Chia and MacKay, 2007; Scott 2000 cited in Whittington, 2006; Vaara and Whittington, 2012). On the other hand, this research stream has created a substantial methodological shift from preferred statistical techniques with ever increasing sample sizes to qualitative methods especially case contexts in single organizations. Researchers adopting such a view have been trying to get closer to their subjects (Vaara and Whittington, 2012) and tend to reflect their experiences in the field. Since each case researcher and subjects have different interactions, this yields new research experiences for which generalizability will become meaningless.

Based on a practice perspective, it is such common practices that become the units of analysis, and it is their performance, rather than that of particular organizations, that needs to be explained (Whittington, 2006). Strategy practice research thus becomes concerned with both the internal and external dissemination of strategy practices and avoids the micro/macro distinction so intimately tied to the social sciences in general and to strategy research in particular (Chia and MacKay, 2007; Scott 2000 cited in Whittington, 2006; Vaara and Whittington, 2012). Certainly both the extra-organizational and the intra-organizational level constituents could attain better understanding of strategy. At the broadest sense, this means effective participation of a particular management team in strategy practice. Approaching strategy as something people do or social practice is said to add an extra dimension to the discipline's traditional concern for endowing particular organizations with winning strategies or efficient processes (Whittington, 2001; 2006). Traditional abstraction often approaches the issues of managing strategies at only a superficial level whereas S-as-P can get to grips with concrete details.

This new post-modern approach assumes that "Strategy" is always a work in process and a piece of social construction. Social construction because it is not the idiosyncratic product of a particular corporate culture, but part of a major societal change, with effects extending far beyond single organizations (Whittington, 2006). Accordingly, analyzing strategy is said not to be merely reporting activity comparing the expectations and actual outcomes. It is not only about what it is done but also about what is not done that is not practiced, that is not said, using external stakeholder articulations as signs of what might be but is not (Carter et al 2008; Clegg et al., 2004). It is not enough simply to 'make a decision', or even to make a decision and announce it. A decision takes its meaning from the social practice and discourse within which it is located, and for an announcement to be effective, it must take account of that context (Hendry, 2000).

In conclusion, this approach directs our attention towards several processes in which many actors have a role in strategy making. It is also worth mentioning that strategy is not only a master plan or prescription designed for achieving a mission and objectives. In other words, strategy is not a written tool prepared for being implemented word by word. It is a process that is socially constructed by several actors, their negotiations and micro-activities. It also offers a new path towards opening the black-box (stated in Mintzberg et al., 1998) of strategy practicing.

S-As- A Social Practice: "Innovation" of The S-As-P Framework in Post-Mintzbergian Era

This part outlines the innovations that lie in premises of the S-As-P framework in a Post-Mintzbergian era. Just as management theories have evolved in an eclectic way since the classical perspective by building their arguments on what was missing to answer questions of their era, the S-As-P framework has also come up with new premises to solve and satisfy today's needs.

Old approaches and post-modern ones alike all reflect efforts to help managers manage better (Carter et al., 2008). In this spirit, the S-as-P approach seeks to improve strategic management practice (Johnson et al., 2007). For a long time, strategy research has been trapped by the modernist assumptions of its birthplace, in short, of the United States in the 1960s (Whittington, 2004). However the main challenge, posed in 1970s, was largely drawn from theoretical propositions unsuited to the understanding of the role of human action. The logic used by strategy completely isolated the individual from the so-called processes (Johnson et al., 2007).

According to Cartesian philosophy, mind is assumed to control matter. Adopting such orthodoxy, management is believed to seek to control the organization; the plan is believed to determine reality, or, strategy is believed to determine structure, form is believed to follow function. Thus this split between mind and body is reflected in the gap between strategy and operations. The main duties of management are analyzing, controlling, leading, thinking and planning; the other operational parts are inert and passive objects that have to be directed. Management as the 'head' creates visions, strategies and plans in order to dominate and lead the organization (the 'body'). Such a strategy grew into the gap between setting actual, clear goals in the face of possible, unpredictable futures; the gap between planning and specifically performing those plans; the gap between planned and instantaneous changes; the gap between means and ends; the gap between a head (management) and a body (organization) (Clegg et al., 2004). However, anticipating future developments in a world that is ever shifting, and the ignorance of the fundamental uncertainty characterizing every decision imply a gap between actual, clear goals and a possible, unpredictable future.

As soon as things become more complex, the formulated plans create a complexity with the problems of implementation thus the gap has enlarged between planning and performing (Clegg et al., 2004). Calculating and predicting futures instead of accepting an uncontrollable emerging future causes another gap between goals and unfolding but neglected opportunities. All of these could not be foreseen by sitting just in front of the computer, making analyses, presenting at the meetings and finally writing reports of all observations (Clegg et al., 2004). There is also a gap between seemingly stable ends and apparent rationality. Instead of being caught in these gaps, the notion of S-as-P is proposing an analytical cue for getting out of this dead-end (Clegg et al., 2004).

Another concern has arisen out of modernism with its enlightenment ideals. These ideals captured strategy within an epistemological straight jacket that valued scientific detachment over practical engagement, the general over the contextual, the quantitative over the qualitative. Today, though, post-modern skepticism has broken these epistemological constraints and modernism's monopoly is crumbling away (Clegg et al., 2004; Whittington, 2004). Thus, in the phase of post modernism the detached, quantitative generalizations of modernism are revealed as just one of the pathways forward for strategic management research. After modernism, there is no longer need to detach human beings through quantitative analysis of large and complex data sets; there is a much more intimate relationship with the subjects. As getting closer to practice, 'strategy 'is regarded as not only an attribute of firms but also an activity undertaken by people, so this implies an activity-based view of strategy (Johnson, Melin and Whittington, 2003; Whittington, 2004). In this context, Whittington argues that strategy is something people do, hence strategy can be seen as a social practice like any other practice with a wider constituency and wider repercussions than those of particular organizations (Carter et al, 2008; Whittington, 2004; Whittington et al., 2003).

Previously, the subject of strategy was dominated by a concern for strategy as what organizations have, wherein, people and what they do, and the effects of their interpersonal relations and political processes are missing. Moreover, strategy is defined as a concern for the competitive advantage and performance of the firm by simply applying economic theory to understanding strategic phenomena. Indeed, it was applying economic logic to choose strategies that generate superior economic performance (Barney, 2002; Johnson et al., 2007; Whittington, 2004). Accepting strategy as a social practice thus involves a refusal to privilege firm performance over that of either the field as a whole or its practitioners individually. From a managerial perspective, the concern shifts through to the actual activities of strategy's practitioners. Here, it is the performance of the strategists that matters, in the sense of how they perform their roles. In other words, applying the sociological sense to the strategy entails examining and assessing strategy not only from the top management perspective but also from the perspective of wider constituents such as the strategy consultants, gurus, leading academicians influencing the practice from outside of the organization (Whittington et al, 2003; Whittington, 2004). As referred by Toulmin (2001), scientists and practitioners can now be partners in putting 'Reason to work in the realm of Practice' (Toulmin, 2001 cited in Whittington, 2004). This is not a matter of simple post-modern rejection of the rational sciences; rather, it is about incorporating them within a broader enterprise of reasonable practice. So to say 'after modernism' is an altogether more inclusive and pragmatic formulation in which academic theory reconcile with managerial reality than its modern and post-modern rivals (Whittington, 2004). The management disciplines, in general, are losing their exclusive faith in modernist detachment and moving closer to the kind of engagement with practice that is characteristically 'after modern' (Whittington, 2004). In this era, the kinds of practical concerns that preoccupied the planning tradition are recovered and strategy research tends increasingly to look for the models beyond economics towards sociology. From the sociological viewpoint, strategy remains an activity that involves substantial resources and has significant consequences for society at large, however unintended (Jarzabkowski and Fenton, 2006). A coherent view of the firm and its activities as pluralism suggests has been mostly ignored. However, many practicing managers and academics ought to consider firms not only as coherent and focused strategic entities but also as pluralistic organizations with contradictory strategic foci (Jarzabkowski and Fenton, 2006).

TAKING STRATEGY SERIOUSLY: WHY DO WE NEED SUCH AN APPROACH?

For many years, strategic planning has been accepted as a rational approach with its diagnosing, forecasting, formulating and implementing motives, however it has also been criticized for not being able to reflect the uncertainty of strategy in practice. Thus, the gap between the theory of what people do and what people actually do has given rise to the 'practice' approach in the management literature (Carter et al., 2008; Jarzabkowski, 2002). The reasons for the emergence of such approaches are compelling.

From an economic perspective, markets are becoming more open, market entry is getting easier, resources are increasingly becoming tradable, information is more readily available, and labor is more mobile. Under these circumstances, sustainable advantage can be achieved through the interactive behaviors of people in organizations. The increasing pace of change in volatile markets has lead to a shift in strategy and decision making from being well-defined systems of episodic planning to a much more continuous process. Eisenhardt and Brown called this "patching", a process that is rooted in more everyday practices and involving more people throughout organizations (Eisenhardt and Brown 1998; Johnson et al., 2007). Since the landmark contributions by Michael Porter, strategy research has largely been based on the microeconomics tradition. As a consequence, research has both typically remained on the macro-level of firms and markets and reliant on the abstract categorization of activities and practices while reducing strategy to a few causally related variables in which there is little evidence of human action. In order to understand human agency in the construction and enactment of strategy, it is necessary to re-focus research on the actions and interactions of the strategy practitioner (Jarzabkwoski et al., 2007; Johnson et al., 2007). S-as-P may thus be seen as part of a broader concern to humanize management and organization research. This perspective places human interaction at the center, and with this configuration, it takes a different ontological position from mainstream strategy research (Pettigrew et al., 2002; Weick, 1979 cited in Jarzabkwoski et al., 2007; Johnson et al., 2007). In other words, from the mainstream point of view, human action and its contribution to strategizing has been explained from the macro-economic level. S-as-P differs from mainstream research by placing human action and interaction at the center. This view about the role of individuals with regard to strategy implies that individuals indeed play a key role in strategy development (Johnson et al., 2007).

To summarize, the practice-based approach investigates strategy formation through focusing on 'praxis, practitioners and practices' (Carter, Clegg and Kornberger, 2008). The following describes these terms along with the strategy text framework.

Praxis- Practices- Practitioner- Strategy Text Framework

Several important questions such as "What is strategy? Who is a strategist? What do strategists do? What does an analysis of strategists and their doings explain? How can existing organization and social theory inform an analysis of S-as-P?" have arisen in many conference tracks and workshops in the field to develop some cohesive frameworks (Jarzabkwoski et al., 2007). Therefore, S-as-P, is concerned with the study of strategy through the lenses of strategy praxis, practitioners, practices and the strategy text framework (Fenton and Langley, 2008; Jarzabkowski et al., 2007; Jarzabkowski and Whittington, 2008; Whittington, 2006). These terms and the strategy text framework are examined along with what they denote in the S-as-P approach.

Strategy: The Concept of 'Strategy' From S-as-P Perspective

Traditionally, strategy has been treated as a property of organizations. This view suggests that an organization has a strategy of some kind or other (Whittington et al., 2003; Whittington, 2006). However, the micro-strategizing view of strategy focuses on micro-activities that are often invisible to the traditional view of strategy but have significant consequences for the organization. This activity based view (Johnson et al., 2003) assumes that strategy is not something that an organization has but something its members/actors/people do (Whittington et al., 2003; Whittington, 2006). Mostly invisible to traditional strategy research, micro activities are believed to have significant consequences for organizations and those who work with them. For instance, as the economic environment becomes more competitive and dynamic, the advantage lies in human assets with their intellectual capital (Johnson et al., 2003; Johnson et al., 2007). Individual skills and capabilities lie not only in the periphery but also in the center thereby considering strategy-making (Johnson et al., 2003). For practice theory, people count because people 'make do' in everyday life, negotiating the constraints handed down to them through a constant stream of tricks, stratagems and maneuvers. Thus, actors become important because their practical skills make a difference (De Certeau, 1984 cited in Whittington, 2004; 2006). Also they may be creative agents offering novel and original solutions for daily practice, they may be artful interpreters of practices in different contexts, and not machines operated automatically (Jarzabkoswski, 2002; Jarzabkowski et al., 2007; Whittington, 2004; 2006). As a guiding mechanism, the discourse of strategy increasingly constitutes peoples' personal identities through their participation in strategic practices (Knights and Morgan, 1995).

The S-as-P approach views strategy as an activity enabling an improvement of something in which people personally, and society in general, have a great deal at stake (Carter et al., 2008; Fenton and Langley, 2008; Johnson et al., 2007). In this sense, an integrated understanding of strategy is regarded as both an intra-organizational and extra-organizational phenomenon that extends outside organizations with potential influence upon whole societies (Whittington, 2006). In the micro-phenomena, actors are believed to be not acting in isolation but drawing upon the regular, socially defined modes of acting/operating (customs, rules, tacit knowledge and explicit technologies) that arise from the plural social institutions to which they belong (Jarzabkowski, 2004; Jarzabkowski et al., 2007; Whittington, 2001). Thus strategy is conceptualized as a situated, socially accomplished activity, while strategizing comprises those actions, interactions and negotiations of multiple actors and the situated practices that they draw upon in accomplishing that activity (Jarzabkowski et al 2007). That's why the strategy field is not a passive domain, but a set of interdependent actors engaging with each other to pursue a range of objectives (Whittington et al., 2003).

Practice: The Concept of 'Practice' From the S-as-P Perspective

Carter and his colleagues explain the S-as-P approach from an epistemological point of view, in that practice implies being 'closer' to reality and delivering a 'more accurate' description of the real world (Carter, et al 2008). 'Practice' refers both to the situated doings of the individual human beings (micro) and to the different socially defined practices (macro) that the individuals are drawing upon in these doings (Jarzabkwoski et al 2007).

Practice is teleological, "an activity seeking a goal" whereas practices are the "ingrained habits or bits of tacit knowledge" which constitute the activity. Practice implies the actual activity, events, or work of strategy. In other words it refers the interactions and interpretations from which strategic activity emerges over time. Apart from practice, practices are those traditions, norms, rules, and routines through which the work of strategy is constructed. Practices could be seen as the infrastructure through which micro-strategy and strategizing occurs, but practice is the one generating an ongoing stream of strategic activity. 'The term "practice" implies repetitive performance in order to become practiced; that is, to attain repeated, habitual, or routinized accomplishments of particular actions' (Carter et al., 2008; Jarzabkowski, 2002; 2003; 2004). Further, practice is the application and interpretation of practices (Whittington, 2001).

However, there is no agreement on the definition of practice in the field. Practice has been argued to mean anything from routine, to event, from becoming, to structuration theory, from learning in macro-contexts, and thus, in the process, has become a concept that can explain almost everything (Carter et al., 2008). Notwithstanding this criticism on the wide ranging use of the term, Carter et al (2008) referred Veyne's view (1997), that practice 'is not some mysterious agency, some substratum of history, some hidden engine; it is what people do (the word says just what it means)'.

From various interpretations of practice, three quite common features emerge. Firstly it is a concern for people and their activities, rather than for organizations and their collective properties. Secondly, it is a concern with the skills and learning involved as people go about their activities. Thirdly it is an assertion of the fundamentally social nature of people's activity, skills and learning (Whittington, 2001). Strategy as a social practice explains how the practitioners of strategy really act and react, both through their social interactions such as information transmissions, resource exchanges, power relations with other actors and with recourse to the specific practices present within a context (Jarzabkowski, 2002; Kenis and Knoke, 2002 Whittington, 1996; Whittington et al., 2003).

All in all, Jarzabkowski and Whittington summarize strategy practices as the social, symbolic and material tools through which strategy work is done. These practices may include theoretically and practically-derived tools that have become part of the everyday lexicon and activity of strategy, such as Porter's five forces, decision modeling and budget systems, as well as material artifacts and technologies, such as PowerPoint, flipcharts and spreadsheets (Jarzabkowski and Whittington, 2008).

Two Key Practice Terms: Recursiveness and Adaptation

One of the enduring problems for theories of the firm is how a social system can be prone to both repetitive reconstitution of practice and also have the capacity for change (Jarzabkowski, 2003). Jarzabkowski referred Giddens to explain the routinized nature of practice by theories of social order, such as structuration in which the interaction between agent and structure is recursive. In this sense, structures are the collective systems within which human actors carry out their daily activities. Structures give direction for human action and are also created and re-created by actors who draw upon social structure in order to act. This reciprocity between agent (human) and structure enables the persistence of social order, and hence institutionalized practice.

However, institutional social structures with their tacit and experience based knowledge are incorporated in the daily practices that constitute action. The persistence of the structure provides actors "ontological security" (Jarzabkowski, 2002). At the same time, this stability is discussed to prevent the adaptive nature of practice and is also termed the problem of recursiveness. It means the socially accomplished reproduction of sequences of activity and action. The problem of recursiveness comes mainly from a paradox of stability and change. Firstly, there is a need for stable practices to secure the system, but also change and adaptation to new ones are required in dynamic environments full of volatile interactions, (Jarzabkowski, 2002). As social becoming theory suggest the interaction between agent and structure does not sustain sedimented behaviors; it is 'becoming', not became. There is an ongoing process of social becoming that is realized through a chain of social events, or practice. This view argues that organizations are involved in an ongoing, adaptive process of internal or within-firm social structure building, embedded within a wider context of external or environmental social structure building. In the process of becoming, existing frameworks take on new meanings that are highly contextual. However, firms need both recursive and adaptive practice to capitalize on routines of success as well as developing the capacity for reinvention (Jarzabkowski, 2002; 2004).

Apart from the mentioned social theories, there is also an activity theory in which practical activity is regarded as the appropriate place for analyzing interaction between actors and collective structures. As activity theory suggests in order to function as a system, different organizational constituents are required to interact with each other sufficiently to produce strategic action (Jarzabkowski, 2003). In activity theory, tools, language, social rules and the division of labor are considered mediating mechanisms that transform the relationships between individuals, communities and shared endeavor. Such factors are interwoven in a complex web of mutual interactions (Blackler, 1993). According to this view, practices enable constituents to interact with each other in shared practical activity which generates continuity. On the other hand, when this interaction and shared activity break down due to different interpretations, practices serve as mediators between competing views that affect changes in practice (Jarzabkowski, 2003). Mediating effects of such practices make it easier to solve such enduring problems of continuity and change for firms.

Praxis: The Concept of 'Praxis' From S-as-P Perspective

The Greek word 'praxis' refers to actual activity, what people do in practice. What the practitioners actually do is strategy praxis — all the various activities involved in the deliberate formulation and implementation of strategy. Thus, it refers to the work that comprises strategy (Jarzabkowski and Whittington 2008; Whittington, 2006). In this sense, strategy praxis is the intra-organizational work required for making strategy and getting it executed. This intra-organizational work can be seen as taking places in episodes or flow of activities such as board meetings, calculating, form-filling, management retreats, consulting interventions, team briefings, presentations, projects, and conversations that are situating the routines that make up organizational life (Jarzabkowski, Spee and Smets, 2013; Jarzabkowski and Whittington 2008; Westley 1990; Whittington, 2006). These social practices have the capacity either to stabilize existing strategic orientations or create variations that cumulatively generate change in strategic orientations (Jarzabkowski and Seidl, 2008). Thus, the domain of praxis is wide. It embraces the routine and the non- routine, the formal and the informal. Praxis refers to twofold activity both at the industry level with an exploitation focus and at the organizational periphery level with an exploration orientation of strategy activities (Regnér, 2003; Whittington, 2006).

Practitioner: The Concept of 'Practitioner' From S-as-P Perspective

Strategy has long been thought the core of the senior executive task, but there has been an academy-wide shift away from the pursuit of a natural science type of organizational theorizing towards a richer and more complex framework including rather than excluding people and their exclusive characteristics (Spender and Grant, 1996). From this perspective, strategy practitioners are now seen as strategy's prime movers, are those who do the work of making, shaping and executing strategies. These are not just the senior executives for whom strategy is the core of their work. These could be strategic planners, middle managers, outside strategy advisers such as strategy consultants, investment bankers, corporate lawyers and business school gurus (Whittington, 2006). Jarzabkowski refers to strategic practitioners as skilled actors who are engaged in knowing, some of it explicit, discursive or declarative, and some of it tacit, practical or procedural, but all of it occurring through the social medium of practice (Jarzabkowski, 2002; Whittington, 2003).

Practitioners use the past to conjecture the present and future and being spontaneously reflexive in expanding the repertoire in accordance with the outcomes attained. In order to understand skilled practice, there is a need to look not only at what strategy is but also at how strategy is done, thus revealing the skill by which practitioners make use of resources. Practice is assumed to be the art of combination (Jarzabkowski, 2002; Whittington, 2003). By making do and the artisan like inventiveness, actors produce their own intentful activities from the artifacts that structure everyday activity (Jarzabkowski, 2002).

This refers to bricolage, as an important skill that can occur during improvisation and it is defined as "making do with the materials at hand" (Moorman and Miner, 1998). Practitioners are crucial mediators between practices and praxis; any paralysis in this relation can profoundly fail the strategy. Practitioners also have the possibility of changing the ingredients of their praxis. By reflecting on their experience, practitioners are able to exploit existing practices, while at the same time, they are also able to taking advantage of new practices and combine them into the whole. Each element in this cobweb of relations has significant repercussions in itself (Whittington, 2006).

Strategy Text: The Concept of 'Strategy Text" From S-as-P Perspective

As in many disciplines, the strategy discipline has also its own language (lingua franca) and terminology (Clegg et al 2004). Common language using familiar terms makes the communication easier for strategists as both know what the other means. Barry and Elmes (1997) referred to strategy as a form of "fiction" which creates, a story about the future, that may or may not be realized (Fenton and Langley, 2011).

Accordingly, Fenton and Langley have added a further element to the praxis, practitioner and practice framework; the "strategy text". They argue that strategy texts often constitute an important element of strategy practice and mediate interactions among praxis, practices and practitioners. They assert that if strategy as practice focuses on what people do, an extended narrative perspective, with its focus on sense making explains how and why people do what they do in organizations (Fenton and Langley, 2008).

As mentioned above strategy praxis refers to what practitioners actually do in their particular everyday activities as they engage with strategy. According to this view, part of what they do involves telling stories, or mobilizing narrative in various forms. In other words, narrative can be a form of praxis implicated profoundly in the sense making currency of human relationships and sense giving about strategic direction (Boje, 1991; Fenton and Langley, 2008). However, in the literature, storytelling is considered a strategic tool or a formalized practice. A wide group of strategy practitioners are involved somehow in the process of defining and carrying out strategy within or outside of their organizations (Fenton and Langley, 2008; Whittington, 2006).

From micro-narratives about strategy and/or broader institutional discourses, legitimate practitioners of strategy could be easily understood (Fenton and Langley, 2008). Strategy praxis often generates written texts in the form of strategic plans that are the main documents of analyses. According to Fenton and Langley, these texts mediate the interaction between praxis, practices and practitioners. That's why the strategic plan is assumed to be a legitimate tool for understanding the raison d'etre of the organization and the clue for the future positioning of it. This infrastructure enables us to see strategy as practice as a multi-actor, multi-level process of actions and interactions between actors making sense of their role and the roles of others in relation to the carrying out of strategy (Fenton and Langley, 2008).

Elements of this framework may be summarized as follows. Practice implies the actual activity, events, or work of strategy, while practices are ways of doing things in an organization. Praxis is what people do in practice. Practitioners are strategy's prime movers, those who do the work of making, shaping and executing strategies. These skilled actors could be for example strategic planners, middle managers, outside strategy advisers like strategy consultants, investment bankers, corporate lawyers or business school gurus. Practitioners can change the ingredients of their praxis. Based on the elements of this framework, strategy is not something defined by the shape of written plans, it is actively created by set of interdependent actors. That's why, strategizing is comprised of actions, interactions and negotiations of multiple actors situated in practices. This approach brings a new perspective to the field where strategy is viewed not as a passive domain, but as a set of interdependent actors engaging with each other to pursue a range of objectives.

SOLUTIONS AND RECOMMENDATIONS

As Jelenc and Raguz (2016) argues that strategy has found its own way and divorced from strategic planning perspective since early 1990s and new perspectives has come to the front as practice, process and multilevel views for strategy. Even they called this era "neo-strategic management" in that many other disciplines have collaboration with strategic management. Among such disciplines, practice perspective and its main contribution to the understanding of strategy and management of it is the main focus of this part.

This perspective principally extends our understanding of the role of human beings in the formation and execution of strategy, especially argues strategy making as a socially constructed phenomenon. In parallel with Resource Based View, as change agents, individuals are considered critical micro assets under this approach, because they are hard to determine, impractical to trade and imitate, thus sustainable advantage could only exist in them (Sithole, 2011). Another important implication is that strategy is not only a core senior executive task as perceived before. Strategy is a phenomenon created as a result of many interactions, discussions and negotiations from all levels both inside and outside of the organization. Hence, today's managers are required to break hierarchy chains and more integrated into all levels. It is also hard to say that this integration is enough. They should also be more concerned with external players like professors from management schools, professionals from consultancy firms, nongovernmental organizations (NGOs), political actors etc.

In global economy, managers face serious problems of continuity and change. On the one side, there is a need to have institutionalized practices and frameworks for shaping individual and organizational behavior, but on the other side there is a need to change continuously in order to adapt emerging trends in the economy. This situation makes pure planning useless to satisfy new needs created from global dynamics. Under these circumstances, performance means more than economic one and evaluations should be made considering not only the organization but also different societal environments, different cultural contexts, different people both inside the organization and outside of it from diverse professions. This does not mean that planning loses its validity, however this approach discusses there is more to understand rather only detecting gaps occurred from what is projected and what has actually happened.

As getting closer to practice, beside detached, quantitative generalizations of modernism, this approach accepts there is a much more intimate relationship with subjects, so there is no longer detach human beings from researches conducted. In other words, it refers methodology concerning with the doing of strategy; who does it, what they do, how they do it, what they use and what implications this has for shaping strategy. From this mostly sociological perspective, strategy is defined as something linking the interior world of the organization to the exterior worlds of the environments in which it operates (Clegg, Carter, Kornberger, 2004). The developing field has taken the concern of "humanize management" seriously by bringing human actors to the center of the strategy (Jarzabkowski and Spee, 2009).

FUTURE RESEARCH DIRECTIONS

This study's ultimate aim is to offer new insights considering S-as-P. However, besides conceptual framework, case studies would be a good opportunity to understand how strategy is practiced in and outside the organization, which actors have part in shaping and executing strategy, what has happened in that process, how practices are socially constructed etc. Contextual influences would be another research avenue under this framework. Inclusion of researchers' point of view and accepting their important roles in conducting such researches will open new methodological orientations and philosophies that will contribute to the literature from several aspects. Furthermore, S-as-P is argued to extend the scope of the strategic management field beyond profit seeking organizations. This extension of application welcomes new participants that may be target of future studies. Of particular interest, may be how such new participants interact especially from a network perspective.

Future studies should consider the main paradox of continuity versus change and how organizations are trying to solve this dilemma. This is especially relevant as firms become more global in an operational sense, and must increasingly question how realistic it is to expect any continuity in practices. Even the necessity of continuity may be questionable under rapidly changing conditions. In the literature storytelling is now considered a strategic tool, even a formalized practice, thus strategy making texts are another interesting topic in the process of defining and carrying out strategy within or outside organizations (Fenton and Langley, 2008; Whittington, 2006).

CONCLUSION

This conceptual framework furnishes insights into the S-as-P approach. Increasingly, a key argument for management disciplines, including strategy, has been paying close attention to what people actually do (Whittington, 2006). As Mintzberg (1994, p. 114) stated "Strategy making is not an isolated process…it is a process interwoven with all that it takes to manage an organization". In keeping with this sentiment, the S-as-P framework in the Post-Mintzbergian era tries to improve strategic management practices by including the individual as an important actor in so-called processes (Johnson et al 2007).

S-as-P is essentially concerned with strategy as an activity in organizations and mainly considers strategy to be an interaction of people, rather than as the property of organizations (Johnson, et al 2007). A practice perspective on strategy principally considers how strategy "practitioners" (most often senior managers, board members and consultants but also others) draw on more or less institutionalized strategic "practices" (routines, tools or discourses at organizational and extra-organizational levels) in idiosyncratic and creative ways in their strategy "praxis" (specific activities such as meetings, retreats, conversations, talk, interactions, behaviors) to generate what is then conceived of as strategy (Chris et al., 2008; Fenton and Langley, 2008; Whittington, 2006). This approach provides new answers for some of the ongoing traditional questions of strategic management and organization theory.

One of the main outcomes of such a perspective is its capacity to change the approach of many researchers from testing theory at a distance towards a more participative understanding (Whittington, 2003). A practice perspective reveals a previously unnoticed reality that strategy is more than just the property of organizations. This is in sharp contrast to the mainstream strategic management view that tends to isolate the organization from people and serves to create a superficial entity above all the people both outside and inside the organization. (Whittington, 2006).

Individuals' everyday lived experiences including emotions, bodily actions and speech are reflected in the way they make sense of their world and interact with others, so S-as-P research inform us about these subtle processes of interaction and influence with its aim of humanizing management. The work, workers and tools of strategy are center stage in this stream and so become the focus for research on practice (Jarzabkowski and Whittington, 2008).

Traditional views on strategy and strategy making could cause paralysis in managerial processes. This approach provides new answers for some of the ongoing traditional questions of strategic management and organization theory. S-as-P studies have extended mainstream strategy research by bringing to light practices that have largely gone unnoticed in the past, and discovering in them effects that previously were not imagined (Vaara and Whittington, 2012). Although the definition and importance of strategy is very well known, how strategies are actually made is still unclear for scholars and practitioners. S-as-P aims to answer this question by examining the micro activities of strategists. The main concern for S-as-P is not strategy at the organizational level but rather the micro-practices of strategists and how they lead to the creation of organizational strategy. These strategists do not necessarily have to be at the top of their organizations. They can be present at all levels of the organization. Practitioners and managers can use S-as-P philosophy to better analyze the strategy making process within their organizations, recognize what they are actually doing in the name of strategy, who makes strategy and the reasons for doing it. This approach will enable practitioners to reflect on their strategy making process (Downs, 2014). Managers have to be aware of the contextual, behavioral and political processes in their organizations in order to understand the real nature of strategy making for their organizations. With this mindfulness and awareness, their strategy making processes and eventually performance can improve.

REFERENCES

Barry, D., & Elmes, M. (1997). Strategy retold Toward a narrative view of strategic discourse. *Academy of Management Review*, 22(2), 429–452.

Boje, D. M. (1991). The storytelling organization: A study of story performance in an Office-supply firm. *Admistrative Science Quarterly,* 106-126.

Carter, C., Clegg, S., & Kornberger, M. (2008). Critical strategy: Revising strategy as practice. *Strategic Organization*, 6(1), 83–99. doi:10.1177/1476127007087154

Chia, R., & MacKay, B. (2007). Post-processual challenges for the emerging strategy-as-practice perspective: Discovering strategy in the logic of practice. *Human Relations*, 60(1), 217–242. doi:10.1177/0018726707075291

Clegg, S., Carter, C., & Kornberger, M. (2004). Get up, I feel like being a strategy machine. *European Management Review*, 1(1), 21–28. doi:10.1057/palgrave.emr.1500011

Clegg, S. R., Carter, C., Kornberger, M., & Schweitzer, J. (2011). Strategy: Theory and Practice. *Sage (Atlanta, Ga.)*.

Down, J. (2014). *What is Strategy-As-Practice and why is it important?* Retrieved from http://drjason-downs.com/what-is-strategy-as-practice-and-why-is-it-important/

Eisenhardt, K. M., & Brown, S. L. (1998). Patching. Restitching business portfolios in dynamic markets. *Harvard Business Review*, *77*(3), 72–82. PMID:10387579

Fahey, L. (1981). On Strategic Management Decision Proces. *Strategic Management Journal*, *2*(1), 43–60. doi:10.1002/smj.4250020105

Fenton, C., & Langley, A. (2011). Strategy as practice and the narrative turn. *Organization Studies*, *32*(9), 1171–1196. doi:10.1177/0170840611410838

Furrer, O., Thomas, H., & Goussevskaia, A. (2008). The structure and evolution of the strategic management field: A content analysis of 26 years of strategic management research. *International Journal of Management Reviews*, *10*(1), 1–23. doi:10.1111/j.1468-2370.2007.00217.x

Hendry, J. (2000). Strategic decision making, discourse, and strategy as social practice. *Journal of Management Studies*, *37*(7), 955–977. doi:10.1111/1467-6486.00212

Jarzabkowski, P. (2003). Strategic practices: An activity theory perspective on continuity and change. *Journal of Management Studies*, *40*(1), 23–55. doi:10.1111/1467-6486.t01-1-00003

Jarzabkowski, P. (2004). Strategy as practice: Recursive, adaptive and practices-in-use. *Organization Studies*, *25*(4), 529–560. doi:10.1177/0170840604040675

Jarzabkowski, P., Balogun, J., & Seidl, D. (2007). Strategizing: The challenges of a practice perspective. *Human Relations*, *60*(1), 5–27. doi:10.1177/0018726707075703

Jarzabkowski, P., & Fenton, E. (2006). Strategizing and organizing in pluralistic contexts. *Long Range Planning*, *39*(6), 631–648. doi:10.1016/j.lrp.2006.11.002

Jarzabkowski, P., & Paul Spee, A. (2009). Strategy as practice: A review and future directions for the field. *International Journal of Management Reviews*, *11*(1), 69–95. doi:10.1111/j.1468-2370.2008.00250.x

Jarzabkowski, P., Paul Spee, A., & Smets, M. (2013). Material artifacts: Practices for doing strategy with 'stuff. *European Management Journal*, *31*(1), 41–54. doi:10.1016/j.emj.2012.09.001

Jarzabkowski, P., & Seidl, D. (2008). The role of meetings in the social practice of strategy. *Organization Studies*, *29*(11), 1391–1426. doi:10.1177/0170840608096388

Jarzabkowski, P., & Whittington, R. (2008). A strategy-as-practice approach to strategy research and education. *Journal of Management Inquiry*, *17*(4), 282–286. doi:10.1177/1056492608318150

Jarzabkowski, P., & Wilson, D. C. (2002). Top teams and strategy in a UK university. *Journal of Management Studies*, *39*(3), 355–387. doi:10.1111/1467-6486.00296

Jelenc, L., & Raguž, I. V. (2016). Past and Future: NeoStrategic Management. In I. V. Raguž, N. Podrug, & L. Jelenc (Eds.), *Neostrategic Management* (pp. 1–13). Springer International Publishing. doi:10.1007/978-3-319-18185-1_1

Johnson, G., Langley, A., Melin, L., & Whittington, R. (2007). *Strategy as Practice: Research Directions and Resources*. Cambridge, UK: Cambridge University Press. doi:10.1017/CBO9780511618925

Johnson, G., Melin, L., & Whittington, R. (2003). Guest editors" introduction: Micro strategy and strategizing: towards an activity-based view. *Journal of Management Studies*, *40*(1), 3–22. doi:10.1111/1467-6486.t01-2-00002

Kenis, P., & Knoke, D. (2002). How organizational field networks shape interorganizational tie-formation rates. *Academy of Management Review*, *27*(2), 275–293.

Knights, D., & Morgan, G. (1995). Strategy Under the Microscope: Strategic Management and It in Financial Services. *Journal of Management Studies*, *32*(2), 191–214. doi:10.1111/j.1467-6486.1995.tb00340.x

Lynch, R. (2009). Strategic Management (5th ed.). Pearson Education Limited.

Mintzberg, H., Ahlstrand, B., & Lampel, J. (1998). *Strategy Safari: A guided tour through the wilds of strategic management*. Free Press.

Mintzberg, H., & Waters, J. A. (1978). Patterns in strategy formation. *Management science, 24*(9), 934948. Mintzberg H & Waters J (1985). Of Strategies, Deliberate and Emergent. *Strategic Management Journal*, *6*(3), 257–272. doi:10.1002/smj.4250060306

Moorman, C., & Miner, A. S. (1998). Organizational improvisation and organizational memory. *Academy of Management Review*, *23*(4), 698–723.

Regner, P. (2003). Strategy creation in the periphery: Inductive versus deductive strategy making. *Journal of Management Studies*, *40*(1), 57–82. doi:10.1111/1467-6486.t01-1-00004

Shah, S. T. H., Jamil, R. A., Shah, T. A., & Kazmi, A. (2015). Critical Exploration of Prescriptive and Emergent approaches to Strategic management: A review paper. *International Journal of Information. Business and Management*, *7*(3), 91.

Sithole, K. (2011). *A Strategy-as-Practice perspective: A case study of a business unit within a multinational engineering organization* (Unpublished Doctoral Dissertation). Stellenbosch University.

Vaara, E., & Whittington, R. (2012). Strategy-as-practice: Taking social practices seriously. *The Academy of Management Annals*, *6*(1), 285–336. doi:10.1080/19416520.2012.672039

Varyani, M. E., & Khammar, M. (2010). *A Review of Strategy-as-Practice and the Role of Consultants and Middle Managers* (Unpublished Master's Thesis). Chalmers University of Technology, Göteborg, Sweden.

Westley, F. R. (1990). Middle managers and strategy: Micro-dynamics of inclusion. *Strategic Management Journal*, *11*(5), 337–351. doi:10.1002/smj.4250110502

Whittington, R. (1996). Strategy as Practice. *Long Range Planning*, *29*(5), 731–735. doi:10.1016/0024-6301(96)00068-4

Whittington, R. (2001). Learning to strategise: problems of practice. *SKOPE Research Paper*, 20.

Whittington, R. (2003). The work of strategizing and organizing: For a practice perspective. *Strategic Organization*, *1*(1), 119–127. doi:10.1177/1476127003001001221

Whittington, R. (2004). Strategy after Modernism: Recovering Practice. *European Management Review*, *1*(1), 62–68. doi:10.1057/palgrave.emr.1500006

Whittington, R. (2006a). Completing the practice turn in strategy research. *Organization Studies*, *27*(5), 613–634. doi:10.1177/0170840606064101

Whittington, R., Jarzabkowski, P., Mayer, M., Mounoud, E., Nahapiet, J., & Rouleau, L. (2003). Taking strategy seriously: Responsibility and reform for an important social practice. *Journal of Management Inquiry*, *12*(4), 396–409. doi:10.1177/1056492603258968

KEY TERMS AND DEFINITIONS

Activity Theory: a theory in that practical activity is regarded as the essential site for analyzing interaction between actors and collective structures. Suggests in order to function as a system, different organizational constituents are required to interact with each other sufficiently to produce strategic action.

Bricolage: making do with the materials at hand.

Recursiveness: the situated doings of the individual human beings (micro) and to the different socially defined practices (macro) that the individuals are drawing upon in these doings.

Strategy as Social Practice: view envisages strategy as something people do.

Strategy Practice(s): the situated doings of the individual human beings (micro) and to the different socially defined practices (macro) that the individuals are drawing upon in these doings.

Strategy Practitioner(s): intra-organizational work required for making strategy and getting it executed.

Strategy Praxis: actual activity, what people do in practice that is intra-organizational work required for making strategy and getting it executed.

Strategy Text(s): narrative perspective focusing on sense making and explaining how and why people do what they do in organizations.

Chapter 6
Efficacy of Organizational Learning and Social Capital in Online Communities of Practice:
Dualities and Intersections

Serkan Gürsoy
Beykoz University, Turkey

Murat Yücelen
Yeditepe University, Turkey

ABSTRACT

This chapter deals with the evolution of communities of practice by considering two key components which facilitate knowledge sharing: Organizational Learning and Social Capital. Dualities and intersections between the building blocks of these two components are investigated by discussing organizational learning in its explorative and exploitative forms, while considering social capital in its bridging and bonding forms. As a critical contemporary step of evolution, information and communication technologies are also elaborated in order to examine the impact of constant and instant tools on these facilitators of knowledge sharing. The study aims to derive proxies among these components of organizational learning and social capital in order to design an integrated framework that reflects the nature of online communities of practice.

INTRODUCTION

Be it individuals or communities, all entities that constitute the contemporary business environment are witnesses to the globalization of the world incessantly occurring everyday by means of new channels and forms of communication, and they have become an integral part of the digitalized world by handling the internet and other media conduits which eliminate the limitations of internal constraints posed by boundaries. In parallel with individuals who are able to act globally, communities also have the inherent ability to cross over boundaries. Communities are also able to comprise all related participants of the

DOI: 10.4018/978-1-5225-2673-5.ch006

global environment by establishing efficient channels and impelling them to be part of the evolution. As an example, Intel Corporation, while terminating its long lasting investment and R&D research collaboration in Cambridge, moved on to launch the Intel Labs Europe project which encompasses a multitude of partnerships dispersed among EU countries, with the main intent of fostering open innovation. The University of Cambridge, chair of Cambridge University's School of Technology, Ian White, declared (Sherriff, 2006) after severing the profound relationship that while the closure of the Cambridge research lab is unfortunate, their researchers will continue to work together, even though they are dispersed across the EU and beyond. In contemporary terms, these groups of geographically dispersed participants, in other words groups of individuals who share their experiences and expertise within the same or similar professional spheres, are called communities of practice (CoP). Literally, the first conceptualization of this term was introduced by a cultural anthropologist, Jean Lave and an educational theorist and computer scientist, Etienne Wenger in 1991. In their book, "Situated Learning: Legitimate Peripheral Participation (Learning in Doing: Social, Cognitive and Computational Perspectives)", the subject of community of practitioners receives much attention especially due to the evolving nature of learning, namely from apprenticeship to situated forms. Their assumption "that members of the community have different interests, make diverse contributions to activity and hold varied viewpoints" unseals new explorative opportunities not only for the concept of situated learning but also for CoP. Even only paraphrasing a small anecdote from the acknowledgements section of their book can be helpful here for highlighting the role of CoP in learning. In the acknowledgements part, they are grateful both to organizers and participants for the opportunity to discuss the idea. This discussion opportunity provides a collaborative basis not only for personal or professional development of the individual members, but also for further elaboration of the idea by sharing knowledge, expertise, experiences and best practices in a particular domain of common interests (Lave & Wenger, 1991). Presently, literature has increasingly engaged in expanding the implications of such opportunities (Wenger, McDermott, & Synder, 2002) by the inclusion of knowledge sharing activities held in online spaces. In other words, as a subject matter of the knowledge management field, CoP are one of the critical resources creation mechanisms of contemporary organizations, especially because they facilitate the establishment, management and access opportunities regarding unrestricted knowledge repositories.

For the organizations (reaping the benefits of CoP), the notion underlined here is the critical importance of the optimization of resources (or trade off) between exploring and exploiting efforts for not throwing up the sponge in a competitive environment. From the beginning of the industrial revolution to the days of information age, knowledge based competition has pushed business organizations to become co-located structures not only in cities but also in countries in order to fill their knowledge gaps while struggling to turn their accumulated knowledge into value. Even though knowledge considered as the most strategic resource generating competitive advantage (Grant, 1996) is not a new perception, rapid evolution in such critical aspects as the means of communication, the shared content, and the diversity in the sources of knowledge, render the issue to reconsideration. Focusing these aspects necessitates to deal with the changes in such fundamental conceptualizations about knowledge; e.g. sources of knowledge (where it appears) or forms of knowledge (how it appears). Not surprisingly, CoP is at the intersection (or it is a playground) of these conceptualizations due to a well-known fact: Development in an organization's knowledge base is highly correlated with the development of its intangible assets rather than physical ones. More succinctly, as an intangible asset, intellectual capital mostly based on human resource practices plays a key role as a source of knowledge. When the issue becomes about human resource practices which can be mostly conducted in informal ways, organizations need to find some ways to formalize the outputs. However, reluctant to compromise on informality, organizations are not ready enough to build and to manage CoP formally.

Even though CoP is an old concept[1], especially recent developments in information and communication technologies (ICT) (e.g., the introduction of Web 2.0[2]) provided them freedom from location based structures, as well as being instrumental in sobering up their organizations to overcome the managerial paradox of formalizing informality. Instead of a paradox, it can be better to term this process as "optimization." As a consequence of the structural specificities of these communities in which members mostly interact informally, managing or supervising them may destroy much of their natural advantages and spontaneous benefits. From some aspects, these phenomena may remind us of the "The Truman Show", a movie directed by Peter Weir in 1998, where the entire life of Truman Burbank takes place within an arcological (artificially created ecology) dome equipped with thousands of cameras that monitor his whole life. While in the movie, Truman is the only person not awakened about his life while being watched and serviced for audiences, in CoP, the heart of the matter is the need for all members to be watched. Thus, to preserve the natural atmosphere of the community, instead of cultivating and/or ruling them, managers may need to consider harvesting the benefits of the natural atmosphere that produces knowledge and practices formally or informally.

This chapter initially presents the progress of evolution (*Evolution of CoP*) of individuals' actions and CoP from location based to dispersed forms by considering knowledge sharing practices. In line with this evolution, enablers of change, in other words the expansion and changing nature (*Characteristics of CoP for Knowledge Sharing*) of CoP, are presented within the context of organizational learning (*Explorative and Exploitative Forms of Organizational Learning in CoP*) and social capital (*Bridging and Bonding Forms of Social Capital in CoP*) which is regarded as a critical catalyst for knowledge creation in communities. *The Role of ICT for CoP* is devoted to the role of ICT in between organizational learning and social capital by monitoring the effect of instant and constant tools separately. The use of CoP for knowledge sharing is herein considered as an indispensable environment for both organizational learning and social capital. Finally, in Section 5, the role of ICT as an enabler of change is discussed and presented with the aim of providing some strategic implications for organizations. An integrated framework of this study is presented in Figure 1 wherein the numbers correspond to the sections of this chapter.

Figure 1. Integrated framework of the concepts used in the study

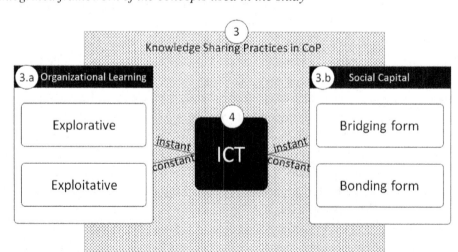

EVOLUTION OF COP

Even though the concept of CoP was introduced more than two decades ago by Lave & Wenger (1991), its history probably begins with cavemen meeting to discuss better ways/techniques for hunting or any other collective actions they perform. In early human history - let us say before the medieval ages - trading (Larson, 1979) was one of the main issues for which people met frequently to discuss about their shared interests or common issues. In Ancient Rome, the idea of *collegia opificum* (Walbank, Astin, Fredriksen, & Ogilvie, 1989), associations of interested players intending to access and control resources can be given as an example to early guild-like associations that were meeting to secure their future. As the first knowledge based structures, these groups - confraternities of textile workers, carpenters or incorporations of metalworkers - were the source of art, as well as being mysterious about their crafts. By serving some sort of social purpose (celebrating together, acting together) and business function (trading, training, exchanging) together, these groups were operated by members in line with such dramatic values embedded in their interactions. By acting together and helping each other, members could find various solutions for their common problems. They shared their experiences, insights, advices and aspirations to develop their techniques or to minimize their future risks. These early communities became platforms for collective learning, creating or designing, and sources of personal satisfaction by developing shared understanding and a sense of belonging to an interest group.

In the Middle Ages, guilds were serving similar values for artisans or merchants throughout Europe. Within the grant of an authority, they were getting together around a value for professional association, trade union, cartels and so forth. The profile of these practitioners was determined by such special classes as lawyers, architects, physicians and others who were the bodies of practical and theoretical knowledge in service of the elites (Larson, 1979). When the contrast between specialist elites and practitioners would become more visible, these classes had turned into institutionalized centers of learning as associations for students, teachers or guilds of learning. As a consequence of the functional process of resource accumulation, the value of these communities had reached an unprecedented scale because of the introduction of written documents which facilitated the spread of information by eliminating the mandate of face-to-face communication. In those days, public resources tended to be monopolized easily not only by monarchs, but also by a castle of scribes with unique powers vested in them. It is then easy to derive that all unique bodies of knowledge appearing in a class society could be monopolized by their creators and possessors. The value generated by those societies was exploited by small elites/guilds on whom specialists depended for their existence. Even though the fall of guilds can be addressed to the end of 15th century, they lost their influence in its entirety during the industrial revolution. Instead of moral attachments provided by symbols, myths or rituals in guilds, utilitarian attachment began to make people get together in modern organizations (Etzioni, 1961, cited in Kieser, 1989). Presumably, guilds reacted to economic crises by reinforcing their cartels (Kieser, 1989), while CoP expanded themselves to all classes and people. On the other hand, the transition of institutions from guilds to manufactories is also closely related with the evolution of the market for production factors, labor and capital.

In a nutshell, the institutional mechanisms of communities and labor markets coevolved. While division of labor had been implemented in the craft shops of monasteries in the early Middle Ages, together with the Renaissance, they evolved into special workplaces for urban dwellers. Sider (2005) claims that urban development –mostly presences with social unrest- was a large part of society during the Renaissance. Kieser (1989) noted that the transition of craft shops of monasteries to urban workhouses was triggered by the idea of engaging criminals and work dodgers with legally paid employment.

This transition provided an opportunity to bring production capacities under the control of especially merchants who constituted a larger portion of urban population. It also provided another opportunity for the community because new organizational forms emerged due to the failure of medieval economic thinking which acclaimed restrictive rules. The new era of economic thinking did not only legitimize profit making but also prepared an atmosphere for more relaxed, geographically extended, technically improved communities.

During the 18th century, improved communication and mobility together with rapid urbanization put an end to the isolation of the large numbers of provincial practitioners and shifted them up towards communities of professionals. When centered on shared practices, these communities which were built upon informal and personal bases could also be regarded as the "emergence of CoP". From the beginning of the industrial revolution, communities had started to develop their unique characteristics most importantly as the body of knowledge and practice within co-located boundaries of the office, city or country. Together with the rise of industrialization, locally organized practicing and learning has been gradually replaced by well-trained labor force practicing and learning in a strong societal environment. The larger CoP reformed themselves through the formation of apprentices. However, as a means of learning, apprenticeship began to lose its impact on learning in developing western economies and turned to a kind of guise for using cheap and unskilled labor. Even though situated learning (learning *in situ*) deals with the character of human understanding and highlights the importance of relationships between learning and the societal institutions, it was not enough to serve an acquisition of knowhow or abstract knowledge which are needed in an industrialized society and production processes. Lave & Wenger (1991) conceptualize situated learners as a certain kind of co-participants of work that are helpful for the acquisition of skills (but not abstract knowledge) by providing interactive and productive roles. This means that learners still need to possess the ability of transforming and reapplying knowledge. At this point, it is handy to recall Brown & Duguid's (1991) statements: There is an opposition perceived between working, learning and innovating. They underlined a gap between precepts and practice. While the precepts implies formal descriptions of work (procedures) and learning (subject matter), the practice implies actual practice (including abstract knowledge). Abstract knowledge makes actual practice meaningful not only because it increases productivity, but also in the sense of boosting creativity and innovation. In order to understand the value of "abstract knowledge", just remember Marx's statements on alienation of labor from work, process or from other labors. He contributes a famous description of this at the beginning of Capital (1965):

A spider conducts operations that resemble those of a weaver, and a bee puts to shame many an architect in the construction of her cells. But what distinguishes the worst architect from the best of bees is this, that the architect raises his structure in imagination before he erects it in reality.

He explains the situation of individuals. As social beings, they have to enter into relationships with each other regardless of their personal choices because of the necessity to work together to obtain what they need to live (Marx, 1844). Society does not consist of individuals, it is the sum of connections and relationships in which individuals find themselves (Marx, 1973). When society assigns a particular value to abstract knowledge in terms of the details of the practice which are nonessential, unimportant and detached from practice, this may distort intricacies of the practice and impedes individuals to enact and to be inspired. To overcome this deficiency, organizations are in search of effective ways of training, educating and supporting their members with proper techniques and technologies. However, practice is central to comprehend work related issues and needs to be well understood, engendered - through training - or enhanced - through innovation - (Brown & Duguid, 1991). For example, In Orr's (1996) study, "Talking about machines: An ethnography of a modern job", conducted on copy machine technicians, during meals, coffee breaks or while performing some other activities together, technicians' informal discussions took place in natural social interaction. The volume and nature of discussion supports knowledge transfers from more experienced technicians to the new ones.

The notion of "legitimate peripheral participation" (Lave & Wenger, 1991) shifts learning process from apprenticeship to collective and participatory learning. In order to overcome probable handicaps in apprenticeship (e.g., individual mentoring instead of group mentoring, excessive importance of pedagogy and teacher, stress of traditional way of doing versus necessity to innovate), legitimate peripheral participation offers some particular ways of learning by enabling learners engaged with others' practices and experts, and by distributing knowledge among co-participants. Succinctly, a community of practice reproduces itself through the reformation of apprenticeship and situated learning.

In parallel with these structural and cognitive changes in the communities, knowledge which is needed to survive in a competitive business environment has become an increasingly crucial asset since the beginning of the industrial revolution. Organizations have been facing the problem of managing and creating knowledge to become more flexible which is needed for responding effectively to changing business forms, from local to co-located. Instead of characterizing organizations as machines, the new metaphors tend to image organizations as organisms, brains, cultures, political systems and so forth (Morgan, 1977) because of the changes in information and energy patterns in the environment. When these patterns coupled with the developments in logistics and communication, sourcing of components and raw materials has been moved to low-cost areas around the world. Expectedly, this mobility is followed by transferring support services and other functional bodies of the company such as their call centers to cheap areas. Mirvis (1996) expresses the situation clearly: Since all life forms are subject to entropy, the problems of adaptation, conceptualized as the maintenance of equilibrium and "fit" of the organism with its environment, became a central concern to theorists. Sure, it was a central concern, not only for theorists, but also for managers in companies and organizations.

There had already been international trade activities since earlier times (e.g., East India Company in London to develop trade with the spice island in south-east Asia in 1599 or Dutch east India Company engaged in the same business as a rival). Their established practices on formal bases expanded by advancements in machinery and communication towards semi-formal bases due to their operations across the world, in various cultures and conditions. Behind the transition from local to dispersed business activities and from formal to semi-formal workforce structures, there can be found some dynamics such as globally dispersed customers and suppliers and the necessities to work in real time and on-demand. Factors forcing/motivating firms to operate internationally and/or globally are the subject of another discussion, however it is helpful to know the main axes in order to comprehend the dynamics of the transition of CoP towards dispersed forms. One of the conceptualizations was introduced by Yip, Loewe, & Yoshino (1988) as a model reflecting the factors that drive globalization in particular industries. According to this model, four axes catalyze internalization and globalization: Market factors, economic factors, environmental factors and competitive factors. These factors can be exemplified respectively as the global customers and distribution channels, sourcing efficiencies across the world and differences in country costs, falling transportation costs and improving communication, and finally, global moves of competitors and competitive interdependence among countries. In order to adapt to these new conditions, organizations are also renovated by specifying duties, dividing work and authority and exerting control overseas. In time, organizational roles are learned by members and role behavior becomes habituated (Mirvis, 1996). Lower costs, faster transactions and telecommunications, make inter-firm alliances and homogenization of work styles easier and smoother. This means that the global economy also refers to the integration of producers and customers within a network structure. Advances in technology can also be perceived as drivers of the new economy – knowledge economy - or global economy in the sense of changes in the traditional meaning of workforce. The workforce of the knowledge economy is characterized by groups of individuals interacting and mobilizing within communities. They are also engaging the problems of adaptation to rapid changes in the market. Within this environment, the capacity to innovate is the most important element in gaining and sustaining competitive advantage (Santos, Doz, & Williamson, 2004). Thus, the process of innovation not only depends on the capacity of organizations to use and to share knowledge (Kodama, 2005) but also requires better access to knowledge resources.

Upon this basis, organizations began to transform themselves towards becoming learning organizations. They also needed to transform the situation of learning and working, towards interrelated instead of separated activities. Thus, their members, as lifelong learners in a learning process, make the creation and use of knowledge meaningful and (Marsick & Watkins, 1999) facilitate knowledge sharing for performing their tasks better and more efficiently (Huysman & Wulf, 2006). Wenger (1998) discusses learning processes in three levels as for individuals, for communities and for organizations. While learning for individuals is an issue of engaging in and contributing to the practices of their community, it is an issue of refining practices and ensuring generations of members for the community. Beyond these perceptions, for organizations, learning is an issue of sustaining interconnected CoP. Thus, enabling an environment for the members to reap the benefits of networking can be one of the effective ways to facilitate learning for the organization. Generally, members tend to form networks of expertise naturally for their personal and professional learning, collaborating and for problem solving.

Briefly, it can be said that the industrial revolution has also reinforced a learning revolution, at least in Western economies since the beginning of internationalization. During the time of industry (industrial age), companies/organizations plodded away to control natural resources. In other words, these kinds of companies/organizations are known as resource-based organizations (Senge, 1993). It was the way, taken up seriously, to have bigger market share or to have bigger range of influence especially on resources. It is not difficult to say simply that the way is still valid but the perception of the resource is not. With the rise of the information age, organizations have begun to have and to use of knowledge effectively as if it is the most valuable resource. Practically, there can be found a tradeoff here in between tangible resources (e.g., physical capital) and intangible resources (e.g., knowledge capital). It is a substantial change if the knowledge era is compared with the industrial era, when tangible assets played a distinctive role. Presently, organizations still try hard to control knowledge resources; because of this they are now called as knowledge-based organizations.

Consequently, the expanding nature of trade and business operations, when coupled with industrial development followed by improvements in communication infrastructures, render these groups of individuals in CoP interconnected and priceless in todays' economy. The rising stress of competition and globalization makes these business operations knowledge-based and develops greater reliance especially on networking and practicing. As a research strand, CoP is kind of a meeting point for researchers working on organizational learning and social capital in the field of knowledge management.

CHARACTERISTICS OF COP FOR KNOWLEDGE SHARING

CoP has been utilized by organizations as a component of their purposes or strategies in which members come together formally or informally to discuss about recent concerns and/or to find solution to common problems. Their activities are mostly about learning, sharing knowledge and improving practices. Within a collaborative environment, learning takes place outside formal classroom environment. Even though CoP have various definitions, they all have common terms: collaborative environment, informal networks of professional practitioners, shared understanding, and specific knowledge domain. Onge & Wallace (2003) express their observations on CoP by a typology in three categories as; informal, supported, and structured. While informal CoP involve loosely organized members having common needs for improving their practices, in supported ones, members have more purposeful focus on developing new knowledge for their future practices. In structured CoP, members collaborate and learn within a purposefully generated content for contributing to an organization's development.

The fact lying behind all these attachments is shared identity (Wenger, 1998) which magnetizes members. This fact also causes a kind of duality for reaping the learning benefits: CoP can be a place where individuals learn from each other or CoP can be a place for collective improvement in the performance of collective practices. The notion of this duality makes sense when focused on organizations trying to find a balance between exploration and exploitation in organizational learning. As discussed in the previous section, the distinction between exploration and exploitation is fed by the distinction between abstract knowledge and actual practice. To overcome these dualities or constraints, organizational learning and social capital are two critical components of the knowledge management field. They help organizations not only to interact with their environment but also to preserve and develop its core competencies. However, both components have changing and dynamic natures since ICT becomes vital (not as an option) even in our personal daily lives. These dynamics force organizations to rethink their policies in order to sustain the functionality of these two key components.

To sum up, this section explores linkages between individual learning and organizational learning as a central issue for overcoming the duality of exploration and exploitation at individual, organizational and inter-organizational levels. The knowledge flow among these distinct levels (explorative way) ought to be turned into value (exploitative way) for sustaining competitive advantage. The first section deals with organizational learning while second section covers social capital within the frame of CoP.

Explorative and Exploitative Forms of Organizational Learning in CoP

Brown & Duguid (1991) base their research which is about the relationship between organizational learning and CoP on two central terms introduced by Bourdieu (1973): modus operandi (the productive activity of consciousness) and opus operatum (structured structure). Modus operandi can be simplified as the distinct or particular way of operation while modus operatum means an unvarying or habitual method of procedure (Allen, 1991). Bourdieu constructs his theory on an old issue involving objectivist and subjectivist debates. In 1845, with "The Theses on Feuerbach", Marx had criticized materialism (objectivism) which does not perceive human activity as practice, in a subjective way for the sensible world. On the contrary, idealism takes into account human activity in the sense of activity in an abstract way. Briefly, this critique is about habitus and the individual as human being: The habitus not only constrains practices, it is also a result of the creative relationships of human beings. Bourdieu (1977) explains habitus as invention or inventive dimension which depends on knowledgeable and creative actors. Thus, individuals are not the pure objects of the structures, they also have relative freedom to act (e.g., trial and error) for being creative and self-conscious. Within this context, Bourdieu perceives a practice as valuable when it is a praxis[3]. As it can be detected easily in between the lines of this explanation, the critical bottleneck lies here as to act freely or to act prescriptively. When organizational learning is remarked as the social process of cultivating practitioners from individuals engaged in knowledge sharing within a social context, the social construction of identity becomes critical.

Organizations are still in search for a balance between sharpening and blunting their individual members' distinctive abilities. Researchers Lave & Wenger, (1991) Brown & Duguid (1991) attempt to work on this matter by investigating organizational learning from a community perspective. Legitimate peripheral participation covers both individual and community learning by linking individual to community culture (Lave & Wenger, 1991). Further investigation by Brown & Duguid (1991) refers canonical and non-canonical practices. While the former implies an adherence to formal rules and procedures, the latter implies the informal routines that dominate day to day procedures. Brown & Duguid (1991) suggest that strict canonical focus inhibits problem solving capabilities of the organization. However, non-canonical focus as unstructured dialogue, particularly through storytelling, leads to innovation and problem solving. Similarly, Levitt, & March (1988) claim knowledge externalization process as the interpretation of events/practices. In other words, they propose a transition from tacit knowledge to explicit knowledge by highlighting three classical observations: Behavior in an organization is based on routines, organizational actions are history dependent and finally organizations are oriented to targets. Within the frame of these observations, they mention that organizations are seen as learning by encoding inferences from history into routines that guide behavior. Routines (forms, rules, procedures), independently from individuals, can be transmitted through socialization, education, training, imitation and so forth. They can also be recorded in a collective memory. However, the change in routines depends on interpretation of the history. Routines lead to favorable outcomes; but they are treated as fixed. A competency trap (Levitt & March, 1988) emerges here because routines may also lead to maladaptive specialization if newer ones are better than the older. Therefore, interpretations of experience need to be supervised by organizations for benefiting from individual learners. Organizations need to develop collective understanding to interpret history or experiences. They also need to focus on keeping these interpretations inside the collective or organizational memory. Levitt & March (1988) suggest to record all (rules, procedures, beliefs and cultures) in documents, accounts, files and rule books. The process of transforming experience into routines may have been a costly process almost three decades ago and it was sensitive to the cost of information technology. Even though today's technology provides giant advances when compared with the situation of those times, the amount of transfer cost still depends on the amount of tacit portion. The gap is still existent between individual learning and collective memory. Nonaka (1991) states this gap by setting a bridge between individual learning and organizational learning; the well-known knowledge conversion process from tacit to explicit. In the model (Nonaka, 1994), knowledge can be distributed with the help of information technologies once it goes through externalization processes. When information is interpreted by an individual, it turns into knowledge (Schoenhoff, 1993).

By considering knowledge as a dynamic human process of justifying personal belief toward the truth, Nonaka & Teece (2001) deal with two types of knowledge as explicit and tacit. They state that explicit knowledge can be expressed in formal and systematic language and shared in the forms of data, scientific formulas, specifications, manuals and such. On the other hand tacit knowledge emerges together with some cognitive barriers which makes the expression difficult (Hinds & Pfeffer, 2003). Because it is learned through experience and held at unconsciousness or semi-consciousness level (Polanyi, 1966 cited in Hinds & Pfeffer, 2003). Knowledge creation as the result of a complementary process of interactions between tacit form and explicit form transcends the boundary between individual and individual or between individual and community. This process can be observed in two directions from community to individual (macro level) or from individual to community (micro level). In order to comprehend the process of knowledge creation for the organization, one of the best choices is to focus on three elements introduced by Nonaka (1991) and constructed by Nonaka & Takeuchi (1995) and finally elaborated by Nonaka et al. (2001). These elements are known as the SECI process, *ba* and knowledge assets.

The SECI process involves four steps as socialization (tacit to tacit), externalization (tacit to explicit), combination (explicit to explicit) and internalization (explicit to tacit). These four steps of knowledge conversion helps an organization to create its own knowledge repository and to diffuse knowledge among its members. Briefly, it is a process that can be reiterated as the interpretation of an individual's mind by the organization to locate articulated knowledge and the interpretation of an organization's mind by an individual. With more emphatic words, it resembles the process of raining circle: Knowledge drops that are condensed from the individuals' lands vaporize towards the organizations' atmosphere and fall back again onto individuals' lands in drops.

The authors (Nonaka & Teece, 2001), describe socialization process as the conversion process of new tacit forms through shared experiences. They exemplify this process by mentioning traditional apprenticeship in which learners are guided and educated by experts (not by written documents). Moreover, socialization process refers to the process of interacting, spending time with other members, observing, imitating and practicing with others in a collective environment. CoP are particularly effective environments for running the socialization process thanks to experience-based characteristics. Saint-Onge & Wallace (2012) clearly spot CoP as a place where tacit knowledge will surface naturally and be shared with the people who really need to know it. As we touched upon previously, in the community of Xerox technicians as CoP, exchange of tacit knowledge took place within the context of storytelling. For organizations, storytelling not only helps to develop shared understanding but also to convert tacit form to explicit knowledge if and when the owner can codify what she knows.

The process of articulation of tacit knowledge, externalization, means translation of justified true beliefs to symbols, images, letters or written documents. Unavoidably, when tacit knowledge is externalized (is made explicit), a risk of losing some portions of it may emerge. However, for the rest of it, knowledge becomes available for articulation and can be shared by others even across the world's dispersed members. The success in externalization mostly depends on the sequential use of metaphors (Nonaka et al., 2001). All these solidifying efforts help tacit knowledge to permeate its cognitive barriers. This is also closely linked to Levitt and March's arguments about history dependent learning by interpreting previous experiences. This interpretation might be verbal, written or symbolized in such various ways: drawing, modelling or prototyping.

Combination process deals with knowledge transformation from an explicit form to another explicit form by converting, editing or processing it towards more systemic and complicated sets of new knowledge. It is a matter of synthesizing derived knowledge of an explicit form, from tacit forms with various sources, and making it ready to disseminate among the members of the organization. The use of database and IT networks help to facilitate this conversion by sorting, categorizing or linking acquired explicit knowledge with previous sources. This process also implies an integration (Yeh, Huang, & Yeh, 2011) or embodiment (Nonaka, 1991) of fragmented knowledge bodies into organizations' knowledge systems.

Finally, the last step of knowledge conversion, internalization is described as a process of embodying knowledge into tacit form. Because of the critical position of the role of the individual, it is closely related to learning by doing (Nonaka, 1994). When individuals combine or reconfigure explicit knowledge databases in action or practice, they link the circle by gaining their own new tacit knowledge. Internalization can also be perceived as an assimilation process of explicit knowledge by interpreting and then applying it in practice. Internalization also implies a process of recirculating organizations' set of combined knowledge repository by adding new insights.

The process of this conversion from one form to another - from tacit form to explicit and finally tacit again - helps organizations mostly to create new knowledge. On the other hand, each step may have some missing links: For instance; socialization process which needs to be supported by new knowledge keepers (e.g., individual having new/distinct stories) and the limits of conversion process from tacit to tacit is confronted with absorptive capacities of individuals. The risk of knowledge inertia may emerge unless the members meet other members from the outside of boundaries, and their absorptive capacity is supported by adequate amounts of explicit knowledge (observing, imitating, listening may not be enough to have abstract knowledge). As previously alluded to, externalization process of conversion may have been limited by the amount of symbols or methods used/known by people. Codification/solidification of tacit knowledge also has some risks concerning the translation which may be unintentionally far from the truth. We might learn just the documented history and old stories. However, this may probably not be the whole truth or all the history. They are merely a collection of someone's interpretations. One more example can be given about the combination process which needs to use an important dose of tacit knowledge (Adler, 1995). Not only the combination process, but all other processes of conversion need almost the same amount of tacit knowledge, as well. This approach makes SECI model seem as if it is blocked by some other knowledge type required for running knowledge conversion processes.

The other elements of the process between individual and organization is filled by *ba* and knowledge assets. Since knowledge has a context specific character which means, it may differ as to how, where or when it is used, and the character of participants have critical importance to trigger a knowledge creation process. According to Nonaka & Takeuchi (1995), *ba* refers to a shared context in which knowledge is shared, created and utilized. They also cite Suchman (1987) who proposes knowledge which cannot be understood without situated cognition and action.

Social, cultural and historical contexts are important for individuals (Vygotsky, 1986) because such contexts give the basis for one to interpret information to create meanings. As Friedrich Nietzsche argued, `there are no facts, only interpretations'. Ba is a place where information is interpreted to become knowledge (Nonaka et al, 2001).

Ba refers to a platform (physical or not) where interactions emerge between participants who are motivated around similar driving forces such as shared problems, shared practices, or shared benefits and so on. *Ba* is also a complicated and ever-changing platform without boundaries. However, the term of duality we used in previous sections, reappears here with respect to crucial importance of shared language, shared understanding and shared cognition for enabling *ba*. At the first glance, *ba* and CoP have similar meanings. However, Nonaka et al., (2001) state some differences between these two terms:

...community of practice is a place where the members learn knowledge that is embedded in the community, ba is a place where new knowledge is created. While learning occurs in any community of practice, ba needs energy to become an active ba where knowledge is created. The boundary of a community of

practice is firmly set by the task, culture and history of the community. Consistency and continuity are important for a community of practice, because it needs an identity.

As may be well remembered, the concept of "shared identity" was at the core of all these discussions. Because the boundary of *ba* is not constant, it is quickly and easily reformed by participants, it is not constrained by history or experiences, and shared identity does not exist in *ba*. It can be expressed that no shared identity means no limits caused by shared identity. Moreover, authors (Nonaka et al., 2001) underlined the level of change in CoP as mainly micro (change in individual composition – new participants are becoming full participants) while *ba* changes at both levels: micro and macro where the new members not only change the composition, but also change *ba* itself. They propose four types of interaction as (1) originating *ba*; face to face interaction between individuals, (2) dialoguing *ba*; a collective face to face interaction, (3) systemizing *ba*; collective virtual interaction and finally (4) exercising *ba*; face to face interaction between individuals. When these types of interactions overlap with the four steps of new knowledge creation (SECI), it makes sense. For instance, within the platform of originating *ba*, individuals can be socialized by sharing their experiences, stories, ideas or mental models. Then, in dialoguing *ba*, they can convert their shared contexts to models derived by common terms. This platform works for externalization and it makes face-to-face meetings necessary. Later, in systemizing *ba*, virtual interactions can be used for combining externalized knowledge with other various open sources. Virtually, on electronic networks, documentation and articulation have critical meaning here in the sense of not being limited by a boundary. Finally, in exercising *ba*; individuals have a chance to interpret articulated knowledge over the network by exercising on it in order to use it in action.

Consequently, the last element of the process is knowledge assets which means factors enabling "the knowledge creation process" to work properly. These are inputs, outputs and moderators (Nonaka et. al, 2001). The authors give trust as an example for enabling the process to function. As a last step of knowledge conversion process between individual and organization, they offer four types of knowledge which make organizations overcome the duality of learning or acting. These knowledge types are; experiential, conceptual, systemic and routine. While the first; experiential knowledge assets are composed of hands-on experiences among the individuals within the organization, the second; conceptual knowledge assets, are about the knowledge that can be articulated by symbols or images or written language. Systemic knowledge assets also refer to explicit knowledge formed in manuals, models, design, specifications and so forth. Finally, routine knowledge assets imply the knowledge routinized in actions or practices in the form of certain patterns or exercises used by organizational members.

Bridging and Bonding Forms of Social Capital in CoP

While the concept of social capital has been revisited by a multitude of researchers originating from various fields in the last century, it still does not have one single definition that embraces all facets of the intrinsic and applied implications that it encompasses (e.g., Hanifan, 1916; Jacobs 1965; Bourdieu, 1983; Coleman, 1988; Fountain, 1998; Nahapiet & Ghoshal, 1998; Woolcock, 1998; Putnam, 2000; Cohen & Prusak, 2001).

It has by now been widely articulated that social capital is a catalyst for developing knowledge capital between people by fostering the exchange of information and knowledge sharing. Nahapiet and Goshal (1998) presented social capital in three distinct dimensions: A series of connections between people (the structural dimension); trust and reciprocity (the relational dimension); and common context and understanding (the cognitive dimension). Similarly, two distinct categories of social capital have been pinpointed by Daniel, Schwier, & McCalla, (2003), namely a structural dimension referring "to the fundamentals of the network such as types of ties and connections and the social organization of the community", where the second dimension is the content dimension of social capital which "includes the types of norms, trust, shared understanding and those variables that hold people together."

As eloquently stated by Lesser & Prusak (2000), CoP play an indispensable role in managing and transferring knowledge. The authors attribute value to CoP because "they foster the development of social capital, which in turn is a necessary condition for knowledge creation, sharing and usage." In turn, Lesser & Storck's (2001) definition of a CoP in an organizational setting encompasses the structural and cognitive dimensions of social capital: "a group whose members regularly engage in sharing and learning, based on their common interests." The authors argue that while a lot of attention has been given to face-to-face interaction between people in analyzing social capital in CoP, there is no reason why distributed CoP whose participants utilize ICT tools should not be considered as part of the general definition of classical CoP. In fact their analysis of seven CoP reveals that the usage of ICT tools such as knowledge repositories, discussion databases and e-mail systems provided a boost to the structural dimension of social capital by giving community members the opportunity to "reveal" their expertise to others, and to obtain knowledge both internally and from external sources. This opportunity should remind us Wenger's words in his acknowledgement section expressing gratitude to all the participants for providing an opportunity. At this point, it is easier to understand why he thanks them and how this opportunity boosts knowledge sharing. Robert, Dennis & Ahuja (2008), propose that the structural dimension of social capital is particularly helpful when the face-to-face communication channel is not an option.

ICT usage also contributed to the relational dimension (obligations, norms, trust and identification) of social capital because community members could actively manage shared spaces, and begin evaluating and judging the trustworthiness and reciprocity of others based on members' contributions in the form of shared knowledge artifacts. In addition, Lesser & Storck (2001) observed taxonomies being developed in the knowledge repositories, by means of establishing common mechanisms for structuring and storing the collective memory of the community members. This observation can also be considered as positively influencing the cognitive dimension of social capital which is characterized by a shared context, meaning and understanding. Based on these propositions, it can be assumed that distributed or online CoP provide a suitable environment for developing social capital.

The working definition for social capital in virtual learning communities suggested by Daniel et al. (2003) supports this viewpoint by comprising all three proposed dimensions:

... common social resource that facilitates information exchange, knowledge sharing, and knowledge construction through continuous interaction, built on trust and maintained through shared understanding.

When analyzing how online CoP (oCoP) contribute to social capital development, another categorical approach proposed by Woolcock (1998) can also be helpful. Accordingly, social capital has three forms: bridging, bonding and linking. Putnam (2000) relates the first two of these to Granovetter's (1973) classification of weak ties and strong ties, respectively. Bridging social capital has an external connotation, in the sense that it suggests building weak ties with people who can be assumed to be different and who did not know each other before establishing a relationship. This results in information being transferred/shared by otherwise distinct external sources/communities, without having intimate relations. Bonding social capital, on the other hand, works inwards (has an internal orientation) based on strong ties established among people who know each other and focus on the same interests. Though the potential lack of diversity implies less new/different information being exchanged, bonding social capital also indicates "thick trust", solidarity, emotional support, and stronger interpersonal relationships/ connections (Kavanaugh, Reese, Carroll, & Rosson, 2005). It may be suggested that it is more common to see bonding social capital in highly cohesive communities where knowledge flows relatively more fluidly among members who trust each other.

There exist some researchers in the literature who investigated how the structural, cognitive and relational mechanisms trigger sustainable interactions in CoP. For instance, Inkpen & Tsang (2005) researched direct ties among individuals in order to realize the effect of interaction by focusing on relational and cognitive dimensions. According to the authors, these dimensions are mediators of knowledge exchange among members of a community. Therefore, it can be stated that weak ties provide a setting which allows more search for, and better access to, new information and resources (Granovetter, 1973). On the other hand, strong ties lead to more search for, and better access to, redundant or familiar information and resources (Hansen, 1999). This conceptualization leads us to set up a link between dimensions and forms of social capital, as well as organizational learning activities. In a nutshell, structural dimension can be perceived as an opportunity to develop relational and/or cognitive social capital if the participants continue to meet frequently. Thus, it can be derived that developing relational social capital provides grounds for nourishing bridging ties. These are highly eligible for explorative activities in organizational learning. On the other hand, cognitive social capital provides grounds for nourishing bonding ties. These ties are helpful to organizations for exploitative activities. Bonding and bridging ties can be effectively utilized by organizations to overcome the potential struggle posed by the duality between learning and acting or in other words, exploration and exploitation of knowledge. The distinction between exploration and exploitation can be clarified as the process of exploitation entails the deepening of a firm's core knowledge, while exploration implies a process broadening into non-core areas. Both for the exploration and exploitation process, networks and clusters offer opportunities and mechanisms by representing social capital (Burt, 2000).

While bonding social capital maintains the combination of trust and social cohesion in the community (Coleman, 1988) and enables members to receive social support from other members, it may limit the access to new connections overtime by making the members too dependent to the group (Woolcock & Narayan, 2001). On the other hand, bridging social capital provides access to new connections across the organizational boundaries. With the help of weak ties, bridging social capital provides trust and cohesion among members in different communities (Granovetter, 1973). Moreover, bonding social capital provides strong ties between members, facilitating forms of intergroup interaction and collective action, while bridging social capital provides ties between groups and other actors and organizations (Woolcock & Narayan, 2000). Briefly, bonding social capital refers to a trusting relationship between members in a single community (e.g., social capital in criminal gangs), bridging social capital refers a trusting network of relationships between members of different communities and between communities (e.g., social capital between sport clubs). At this point there is a need to revisit Granovetter (1973), who stresses that bonding and bridging social capital are correlated with strong and weak ties by maintaining existing relations (bonding) and extending networks or facilitating mobility (bridging). In this context it can be supposed that ICT may have a positive effect on the creation of bridging social capital while maintaining or reducing bonding social capital.

A countless amount of information is being produced by the minute in the virtual environment. The speed, volume and quality (trustworthiness) of the knowledge being shared are key especially in professional work related issues, specifically in planning and strategic decision making processes in organizations which may be fast or slow learners. Due to strong ties which imply intense emotional ties over a long period of time with high frequency contact and reciprocity (Wellman, 1982, cited in Kavanaugh et al., 2005), it can be suggested that bonding social capital embedded in oCoP will be a facilitator in the sharing of high quality and trustable knowledge among community members, although the content may lack diverse viewpoints. On the other hand, weak ties provide the opportunity to obtain new and diverse knowledge from external sources that may not be as trustworthy because of the short term nature of the relationship which by definition lacks emotional attachment and mutuality. Norris (2002) reports that the results a survey conducted among internet users, overall contact with different types of online groups like unions, community associations, and sports clubs, served both bridging and bonding functions, where the experience for reinforcing bonding was slightly higher overall. It is interesting to note that %50 percent of respondents had at one time or another used the internet to contact a trade or professional association – that can be considered in the realm of oCoP – and the same online group was reported by %24 of the respondents as the most frequently contacted among all other types of online groups investigated (Norris, 2002).

It can thus be proposed that oCoP provide a virtual environment which fosters the development of strong networking ties, consequently strengthening bonding social capital, and creating a learning environment where effective knowledge sharing and mutual learning can be nurtured among participants based on feelings of trust and reciprocity. It should still be recognized that trust will build over time and its strength will depend on the frequency and quality of the information being shared. Lesser & Storck's (2001) analyses suggest that distributed online communities are also instrumental in fostering bridging social capital, in the sense that they more often than not transpire organizational boundaries in the search for external knowledge by improving external linkages.

THE ROLE OF ICT FOR COP

Especially in the last two decades, the skills and capabilities of individuals have been increasingly noticed in terms of their ICT competencies. The ability to use ICT is no longer just important for practitioners in the ICT sector, but has become fundamental for everyday working practices. ICT have blended into the rhythms and routines of everyday working life. The skills needed here are not only technical, but more importantly, informational: skills that enable individuals to access, to process and to interpret information in useful ways. Within this frame, ICT can be considered as an important enabler in knowledge management (Davenport, 1997; Ruggles, 1998; O'Dell & Grayson, 1998). In other words, ICT facilitates knowledge transfer not only through the exchange of data but also the exchange of knowledge. Nonetheless, this requires a double transformation process from knowledge to information and then to data, and back from data to information, and finally, to knowledge. Bolisani & Scarso (1999) claim that the transfer of knowledge (especially in the tacit form) often requires proximity between the transmitter and the receiver. For example, videoconferencing and virtual chat rooms may aid the transfer of tacit knowledge by enabling virtual proximity between players, while the transfer of information (especially the codified form) can be distributed worldwide with the touch of a button.

The close relationship between knowledge sharing and social capital within the context of organizational learning directs a growing attention to the fundamental impacts of ICT on social capital (Blanchard & Horan, 2000; Wellman, 1997; Franzen, 2003; Uslaner, 2000; DiMaggio, Hargittai, Neuman, & Robinson, 2001; Hampton & Wellman, 2003; Quan-Haase & Wellman, 2004; Huysman & Wulf, 2006; Ellison, Steinfield, & Lampe, 2007). This attention to the impact of ICT on knowledge creation and skill diffusion makes clear that the ability to create, share and utilize knowledge is continuously upgraded by the advancement of ICT. While research communities are engaging in the clarification of blurred issues, fields of business have emerged to provide ICT services with a variety of solutions for organizational processes. ICT provides solutions for interaction, collaboration, learning and/or exploration as well as exploitation (Andersen 2004; Gilsing & Nooteboom, 2004; Nooteboom, 2004). In parallel with these advancements in organization, ICT introduces some other opportunities for organizations in the sense of possessing and managing their social assets (Millen & Patterson, 2003). Use of ICT in a virtual environment, including online communities, builds social norms and assets in geographically dispersed communities as well as location-based communities. With regard to CoP, online communities can be framed as a community which uses networked technology, especially the Internet, to establish collaboration across geographical barriers and time zones. An online community's main goal is to serve as a common ground for individuals who share the same interests as one another. Online communities exist according to the identification of an idea or task, rather than physical proximity. Members are organized around an activity, and they are formed when need arises (Squire & Johnson, 2000). Because the members cannot see each other, group norms are not dominant as much as in traditional communities, thus allowing for greater individual control. Therefore, researchers pointed out that online communities do not appear to be intimate social groups (Wellman, 1997; Cummings, Butler, & Kraut, 2002) and this causes a decrease in social capital (Putnam, 2000). On the other hand, analyses indicate that understanding an individual's full set of social behavior is crucial to examining her network relations, and building more effective software to support communication and social capital (Cummings et al., 2002; Preece, 2002). The value of the concept of social capital is to identify certain aspects of social structure by their function (Coleman 1988). Similarly, identifying certain functions of online social structure may be helpful to understanding the social phenomena.

Online communities can either be location-based, in which the electronic group is centered on the geographic locale, or dispersed, in which the electronic group is not (Blanchard & Horan, 2000). Location-based communities can also be defined as the individuals assembled around a central location who mostly communicate via intranet-based networks, while the members of a dispersed community mostly refer to a group of individuals from the outside of an organization, such as partners and third party players (Blanchard, 2004). Members of location-based communities mostly have a chance to meet face-to-face when they need to or in a regular fashion, and they mostly know each other directly or indirectly. Nonetheless, members of a dispersed community meet mostly online and they don't know each other in the real-world. Blanchard (2004) stresses that most members of location-based communities mostly indulge in both ways of interaction (face-to-face and online), and these communities are denser than dispersed communities. A higher level of social capital can be found in location-based communities when compared with dispersed ones, in terms of the easy flow of norms and trust in densely connected networks (Coleman, 1988). Similarly, Blanchard & Horan (2000) state that dispersed communities may decrease the social capital in location-based communities because they may decrease the density of the social networks of relationships in that community. With regard to the isolation effect of online communities on individuals (Putnam, 1995), members of dispersed communities may develop their own social capital in their online communities instead of developing it in their location-based communities if they sustain their online relationships within the existence of socio-emotional rewards (Blanchard, 2004). On the other hand, Wellman, Hasse, Witte, & Hampton (2001) found a positive correlation between the participation in online communities and the participation in traditional communities. According to the authors, participation in a dispersed community may not decrease some forms of social capital. In particular, increased Internet use is associated with an increase in civic group participation and it is significant because it may be a sign of increased activity in location-based networks of relationships. Although it has been argued that dispersed communities can decrease social capital and location based communities can increase it, this is not an accepted fact because of the fuzziness about the individuals who are developing a sense of community by interacting online (Blanchard, 2004).

With regard to the dimensional approaches to social capital, Pigg & Crank (2004) consider the functions of ICT supporting communication in various forms as well as information storage, retrieval, analysis and sharing. Each of these elements can be operationalized by means of software in a variety of forms with applications currently available in online communities. Considering ICT in two forms as information tools and communication tools may become necessary especially because of the fact that social capital is built upon "instrumental" and "expressive" information forms (Pigg & Crank, 2004). Beyond the information function, communication includes both cognitive and affective contents. Therefore, the written message itself is meaningless without considering both content and context (Raber & Budd, 2003). Along with these matters, ICT tools need to be formulated in line with their formats and content that communicate both the affective and cognitive elements (Pigg & Crank, 2004). Researchers attempted to classify ICT applications in line with the relationships facilitated among users (Pigg & Crank, 2004). They think it is the format of ICT that structures social ties between persons and connects them to activities. Altheide (1994) illustrates the relevance of organizational IT and formats for societal activities in which IT formats and an organizational context create an effective environment for problem solving which, in turn, creates a format and organizational solution appropriate to the societal context and activities of the entire process. According to the author, different formats, but the same information and communication technologies brought together allow "doing it" and "reporting it." On this basis, internet usage has created different formats for information technology that enables a flow of communication that isn't passive, but is a two-way transaction such as: e-mail, chatting and the use of social software. With regard to this classification DiMaggio et al. (2001) express that online communities interacting via the Internet have some differences when compared to earlier technologies. The internet offers different modes of communication (broadcasting, individual searching and group discussion) and different kinds of content (text, audio, visual images) in a single medium. Within this context, Quan-Haase & Wellman (2004) propose the use of social capital in two complementary meanings as social contact and civic engagement. They mention that social contact reflects interpersonal communication patterns, including visits, encounters, phone calls and social events, while civic engagement reflects the degree to which people become involved in their community, both actively and passively, including such political and organizational activities as political rallies or book and sports clubs. Pigg & Crank, (2004) differentiate between the information and communication functions. They propose that the communication function is multi-faceted and interactive, including text, audio and video, and it may as well be in real-time (as in VOIP) or asynchronous or archival/historical. According to them, the communication function refers to the acts of transmitting information of different types, e.g., ideas and feelings, from one person to another. The information function is complex because Internet-based information transfer can take place using a variety of features of the network (Pigg & Crank, 2004). The information transfer can be "active" in that people share information using various communication features of the Internet including e-mail and video conferencing, or it can be passive, based on one person's search for resources on the Internet and using, for example, its archiving or knowledge management capabilities. Based on these challenges for classifying ICT in sense of its format and the role in users' relations, Yuan, Zhao, Liao, & Chi (2013) consider the role of ICT tools for knowledge sharing. They gather ICT in three groups; communication tools, social media and long standing tools4 . While communication tools means functioning simply as a channel, social media tools generate knowledge sharing between users. Web 2.0 is one of the critical advancements for empowering ICT to generate two-way/interactive/mutual knowledge sharing within a community. Together with the introduction of this interactive environment, new possibilities such as distribution lists, photo directories, and advanced search engines, wikis, forums and more platforms can support online linkages with others to build new forms of social capital (Resnick, 2001). Kaplan & Haenlein (2010) define social media as "a group of Internet-based applications that build on the ideological and technological foundations of Web 2.0 and that allow the creation and exchange of user-generated content." Some of the important properties[5] of social media that make these platforms different than traditional media can be listed here as quality, space, frequency, accessibility, usability, immediacy and permanence. Beyond these properties, Vossen (2009) defines Web 2.0 in four dimensions. These are the social dimension, infrastructure dimension, functionality dimension and the data dimension. These dimensions technically are related with the Nonaka's (1994) process of knowledge sharing as socialization, externalization, combination and internalization.

With regard to Nonaka's (1994) statement about socialization – the process of creating tacit knowledge through shared experience - social dimension, is described as the software for sharing user-generated content or collaborative use of it (Vossen, 2009). This description of social media tools -Social Networking Sites (SNS) - refers to the applications for the interactions among users in which they create, share, and exchange information and ideas in online communities and networks. Another process of knowledge sharing is externalization -the conversion of tacit knowledge to explicit knowledge - (Nonaka, 1994), makes Wikis a conversational technology within the frame of meaningful dialogues (Andreano, 2008) externalizing practitioners experiences for submitting it to the Web 2.0 platforms (McAfee, 2006). According to Andreano (2008), wiki technology allows users to directly interact with the content they encounter. If a user using a best practices manual, for example, comes across a problematic or inaccurate piece of information, she can immediately edit the wiki to reflect her own recent experience. If another user finds something wrong with this edit, this other user can similarly change what appears on the wiki. The process of combination -the reconfiguration of existing information for having new knowledge by sorting, adding, re-categorizing, and re-contextualizing - (Nonaka, 1994), appears as forums in Web 2.0 technology (McAfee, 2006). Forums allow the users of the organization to arrange information and describe it in a way that makes sense to them and will aid them in their future discovery of relevant knowledge artifacts. It also serves better search functionality and the use of user-created tags (Andreano, 2008). The final process defined by Nonaka (1994) is internalization -conversion of explicit knowledge into tacit knowledge. For this process, Web 2.0 serves as blogs allowing users to express themselves through storytelling and narrative (Du & Wagner, 2006). The authors state that the process of expressing knowledge via blogs actually helps a content owner to construct knowledge because the conversation serves to refine and clarify knowledge of which the knower might have been unaware.

Consequently, the emergence of the Internet opens a new era of interaction by offering not only communication technologies but also new social aspects for daily life and business environment. Together with the various communication and social media tools, the Internet has extended the way of interaction among people to the era of interaction among users in such communities. With the rapid development in technologies and tools, it initially became a mediator of real world relations, but later it defined these relations with its own dynamics. Recent findings about the impact of ICT on social capital tend to support positive relationships between the constructs by underlining the sense of community in virtual spaces and enhancing its offline relations (Hampton & Wellman, 2003). Along with these findings, it can be derived that the impact of ICT on social capital depends on the type of technology selected by individuals and tools for interaction.

FUTURE RESEARCH DIRECTIONS

In order to reap the benefits of knowledge sharing in CoP more effectively, exploration and exploitation activities facilitated by organizations might be designed in accordance with the knowledge types created and articulated in the community. For example, experiential knowledge which derives from hands on experiences of an individual could be targeted by organizations as part of explorative activities, while conceptual, systemic and routinized knowledge created by individuals could be aligned with exploitative activities. The substance for future research in this field lies within the dynamics of knowledge conversion occurring in oCoP. Thus, other dualities embedded in these dynamics need to be visited.

Some unanswered questions:

- Which types of knowledge are served by bridging form of social capital in oCoP?
- Which types of knowledge are served by bonding form of social capital in oCoP?
- How do ICTs boost the cognitive dimension for facilitating bonding forms within the existing differences in identities between oCoP and CoP?

In the context of rapid and mostly unpredictable developments regarding CoP and ICT infrastructure, various dimensions branch out from the components of social capital, organizational learning and ICT. For instance, the form of social capital emerging in online communities needs to be reworked continuously by incorporating upcoming trends and technologies in ICT. As it has been presented in this study, oCoP may be emerge in both location based and dispersed forms. Regardless of the form of social capital, individuals interacting in the community mostly represent themselves as virtual identities. This means that there is no distinction on the basis of demographics, instead the diversity of the members may be reflected by their experiences and tenures. This example provides clues for future research directions, such as the undiscovered dualities in the identity representation of the members in oCoP. In addition, emerging types of knowledge need to be considered especially for oCoP. This new knowledge form is codified and be articulated as well as representing the cognitive characteristics of the creator. Finally, further dualities between knowledge types (*i.e.*, tacit knowledge in CoP versus synthetic knowledge in oCoP) need to be dwelled upon in the future.

CONCLUSION

CoP is a well-known concept for the knowledge management field. The popularity of the concept is mostly fed by the changing dynamics and composition of institutions and conditions. The evolution of CoP has been presented inappropriate detail to represent the changes in these dynamics. While CoP meant location based formations at the beginning, the concept turned into dispersed formations over time. This transition can be perceived as a breakthrough due to the changes of purposes, domains, identities and so forth. As time passes and different dynamics evolve, defining CoP is going to become more difficult. There is a need for reconceptualization of CoP in line with their changing nature. For example, availability of ICT not only for business operations but also our personal operations redefine our environment in terms of concept and context. At a micro level, most of us reserve much of our time for accessing knowledge what we need. At the macro level, organizations reserve a good portion of their resources for accessing our personal knowledge repositories. When organizational learning is perceived within the context of exploration and exploitation activities, organizational knowledge sharing dynamics necessitate such socio-organizational settings (i.e., social capital) as norms, culture, meanings, trust, common understandings and so forth. From this viewpoint, building and sharing social capital among CoP primarily help organizations to utilize internalized knowledge more effectively and productively together with the support of externalization efforts for diffusing, storing or sharing it. However, organizations are confronted with a duality of exploration and exploitation. In this study, the attempt to balance these two components of organizational learning was one of the central issues for elaborating the changing nature of CoP and social capital. In order to overcome the struggle between learning and acting, organizations follow particular models to harmonize explorative and exploitative activities in a contextual sphere to generate organizational learning. SECI, ba, and knowledge assets are some of the well-known models to convert individual knowledge into organizational knowledge and vice-versa. Moreover, in order to sustain competitive advantage, organizations use ba for setting effective networking especially in online spaces. As presented in this study, these two models, together with knowledge assets, make CoP and Social Capital highly important for the competitiveness of business firms.

Today's business models (e.g., geographically dispersed workplace formations) and advanced ICT infrastructures offer various opportunities for exploration and exploitation, as well as opportunities for internalization and externalization of knowledge. For instance, recent advancements in ICT engaged by oCOP provide some ways to reduce uncertainties and information asymmetries in transactions by handling and serving accessible data over networks. Sensors can collect and store various routines, procedures, acts, conversations and so on, thus serving users/organizations when needed. Online spaces make it possible to share these vital resources globally and make them available for the accession of every organizational member. However, the contrast between technological advancements and the organizational setting become clearer, especially because of the relatively slower responses of organizations to their rapidly changing environment. Besides the new opportunities of ICT supported cooperation for the generation of new knowledge and content sharing, organizations may need to realize and solidify some unresolved issues about organizational learning and their knowledge management processes. In order to make individuals knowledge (including tacit forms) in oCoP accessible for all the community or to codify transferred knowledge for reaping the benefits of its tacit aspects, organizations need to know how to set and serve social capital among all their agents.

REFERENCES

Adler, P. S., & Cole, R. E. (1995). Designed for learning: A tale of two auto plants. In I. McLoughlin, D. Preece, & P. Dawson (Eds.), *Technology, organizations and innovation: Critical perspectives in business and management* (pp. 1230–1245). London: Routledge.

Allen, R. E. (1991). *The concise Oxford dictionary of current English* (8th ed.). New York, NY: Oxford University Press.

Altheide, D. L. (1994). An ecology of communication: Toward a mapping of the effective environment. *The Sociological Quarterly, 35*(4), 665–683. doi:10.1111/j.1533-8525.1994.tb00422.x

Anderson, T. (2008). Teaching in an online learning context. In T. Anderson (Ed.), *Theory and practice of online learning* (2nd ed.; pp. 343–365). Edmonton, AB: AU Press.

Andreano, K. (2008). Knowledge Management 2.0? The Relationship between Web 2.0 Technologies and KM Theory. In *Knowledge about knowledge: Knowledge Management in Organizations* (pp. 15-22). Rutgers University. Retrieved May 6, 2016, from http://eclipse.rutgers.edu/wp-content/uploads/sites/30/2014/04/Knowledge.pdf#page=17

Blanchard, A. (2004). The effects of dispersed virtual communities on face-to-face social capital. In M. Huysman & V. Wulf (Eds.), *Social capital and information technology* (pp. 53–73). Cambridge, MA: MIT Press.

Blanchard, A., & Horan, T. (2000). Virtual communities and social capital. In E. L. Lesser (Ed.), *Knowledge and social capital: Foundations and applications* (pp. 159–178). Woburn, MA: Butterworth-Heinemann. doi:10.1016/B978-0-7506-7222-1.50010-6

Bolisani, E., & Scarso, E. (1999). Information technology management: A knowledge-based perspective. *Technovation, 19*(4), 209–217. doi:10.1016/S0166-4972(98)00109-6

Bourdieu, P. (1977). *Outline of a theory of practice* (Vol. 16). Cambridge University Press. doi:10.1017/CBO9780511812507

Bourdieu, P. (1983). Forms of social capital. In J. C. Richards (Ed.), *Handbook of theory and research for sociology of education* (pp. 241–258). New York, NY: Greenwood Press.

Brown, J. S., & Duguid, P. (1991). Organizational learning and communities-of-practice: Toward a unified view of working, learning, and innovation. *Organization Science, 2*(1), 40–57. doi:10.1287/orsc.2.1.40

Burt, R. S. (2000). The network structure of social capital. Re-print for a chapter. In B. M. Staw & R. I. Sutton (Eds.), *Research in Organizational Behavior* (Vol. 22). Greenwich, CT: JAI Press.

Cohen, D., & Prusak, L. (2001). *In good company: How social capital makes organizations work*. Boston, MA: Harvard Business School Press.

Coleman, J. S. (1988). Social capital in the creation of human capital. *American Journal of Sociology, 94*, 95–120. doi:10.1086/228943

Cummings, J. N., Butler, B., & Kraut, R. (2002). The quality of online social relationships. *Communications of the ACM, 45*(7), 103–108. doi:10.1145/514236.514242

Daniel, B., Schwier, R. A., & McCalla, G. (2003). Social capital in virtual learning communities and distributed communities of practice. *SANDBOX-Canadian Journal of Learning and Technology/La Revue Canadienne de l'apprentissage et de la Technologie, 29*(3).

Davenport, T. H. (1997). Ten principles of knowledge management and four case studies. *Knowledge and Process Management, 4*(3), 187–208. doi:10.1002/(SICI)1099-1441(199709)4:3<187::AID-KPM99>3.0.CO;2-A

DiMaggio, P., Hargittai, E., Neuman, W. R., & Robinson, J. P. (2001). Social implications of the Internet. *Annual Review of Sociology, 27*(1), 307–336. doi:10.1146/annurev.soc.27.1.307

Du, H. S., & Wagner, C. (2006). Weblog success: Exploring the role of technology. *International Journal of Human-Computer Studies, 64*(9), 789–798. doi:10.1016/j.ijhcs.2006.04.002

Ellison, N. B., Steinfield, C., & Lampe, C. (2007). The benefits of Facebook friends: Social capital and college students use of online social network sites. *Journal of Computer-Mediated Communication, 12*(4), 1143–1168. doi:10.1111/j.1083-6101.2007.00367.x

Etzioni, A. (1961). *A Comparative Analysis of Complex Organizations.* New York: Free Press.

Fountain, J. E. (1998). Social capital: Its relationship to innovation in science and technology. *Science & Public Policy, 25*(2), 103–107.

Franzen, A. (2003). Social capital and the new communication technologies. In J. E. Katz (Ed.), Machines that become us: The social context of personal communication technology (pp. 105-116). New Brunswick, NJ: Transaction Publishers.

Gilsing, B. N. V., & Nooteboom, B. (2004). Density and strength of ties in innovation networks: a competence and governance view. *CentER Discussion Paper, 2005*(40). Retrieved May 17, 2016, from https://pure.uvt.nl/ws/files/773647/40.pdf

Granovetter, M. (1973). The strength of weak ties. *American Journal of Sociology, 78*(6), 1360–1380. doi:10.1086/225469

Grant, R. M. (1996). Toward a knowledge-based theory of the firm. *Strategic Management Journal, 17*(S2), 109–122. doi:10.1002/smj.4250171110

Hampton, K., & Wellman, B. (2003). Neighboring in Netville: How the Internet supports community and social capital in a wired suburb. *City & Community, 2*(4), 277–311. doi:10.1046/j.1535-6841.2003.00057.x

Hanifan, L. J. (1916). The rural school community centre. *The Annals of the American Academy of Political and Social Science, 67*(1), 130–138. doi:10.1177/000271621606700118

Hinds, P. J., & Pfeffer, J. (2003). Why organizations don't "know what they know": Cognitive and motivational factors affecting the transfer of expertise. In M. S. Ackerman, V. Pipek, & V. Wulf (Eds.), *Sharing expertise: Beyond knowledge management* (pp. 3–26). Cambridge, MA: The MIT Press.

Huysman, M., & Wulf, V. (2006). IT to support knowledge sharing in communities: Towards a social capital analysis. *Journal of Information Technology, 21*(1), 40–51. doi:10.1057/palgrave.jit.2000053

Jacobs, J. (1965). *The death and life of great American cities*. Penguin Books.

Kaplan, A. M., & Haenlein, M. (2010). Users of the world, unite! The challenges and opportunities of Social Media. *Business Horizons, 53*(1), 59–68. doi:10.1016/j.bushor.2009.09.003

Kavanaugh, A. L., Reese, D. D., Carroll, J. M., & Rosson, M. B. (2005). Weak ties in networked communities. *The Information Society, 21*(2), 119–131. doi:10.1080/01972240590925320

Kieser, A. (1989). Organizational, institutional, and societal evolution: Medieval craft guilds and the genesis of formal organizations. *Administrative Science Quarterly, 34*(4), 540–564. doi:10.2307/2393566

Kodama, M. (2005). New knowledge creation through leadership-based strategic community – a case of new product development in IT and multimedia business fields. *Technovation, 25*(8), 895–908. doi:10.1016/j.technovation.2004.02.016

Larson, M. S. (1979). The rise of professionalism. *SA. Sociological Analysis, 233*. PMID:489184

Lave, J., & Wenger, E. (1991). *Situated learning: Legitimate peripheral participation*. Cambridge University Press. doi:10.1017/CBO9780511815355

Lesser, E., & Prusak, L. (2000). Communities of practice, social capital, and organizational knowledge. In J. A. Woods & J. Cortada (Eds.), *The knowledge management yearbook 2000-2001* (pp. 251–259). Amsterdam: Elsevier. doi:10.1016/B978-0-7506-7293-1.50011-1

Lesser, E. L., & Storck, J. (2001). Communities of practice and organizational performance. *IBM Systems Journal, 40*(4), 831–841. doi:10.1147/sj.404.0831

Levitt, B., & March, J. G. (1988). Organizational learning. *Annual Review of Sociology, 14*(1), 319–340. doi:10.1146/annurev.so.14.080188.001535

Marsick, V. J., & Watkins, K. E. (1999). *Facilitating learning organizations*. Gower.

Marx, K. (1965). *Capital: a critical analysis of capitalistic production* (Vol. 3). Progress Publishers.

Marx, K. (1973). *Grundrisse: Foundation of the critique of political economy* (M. Nicolaus, Trans.). Harmondsworth, UK: Penguin.

Marx, K. (2012). *Economic and philosophic manuscripts of 1844*. Courier Corporation.

McAfee, A. P. (2006). Enterprise 2.0: The dawn of emergent collaboration. *MIT Sloan Management Review, 47*(3), 21–28.

Millen, D. R., & Patterson, J. F. (2003). Identity disclosure and the creation of social capital. CHI'03 extended abstracts on Human factors in computing systems, 720-721. doi:10.1145/765891.765950

Mirvis, P. H. (1996). Historical foundations of organization learning. *Journal of Organizational Change Management, 9*(1), 13–31. doi:10.1108/09534819610107295

Morgan, G. (1997). *Images of organization*. London: Sage Publications.

Morgan, N., Jones, G., & Hodges, A. (2012). *Social media.* The Complete Guide to Social Media From The Social Media Guys.

Nahapiet, J., & Ghoshal, S. (1998). Social capital, intellectual capital, and the organizational advantage. *Academy of Management Review, 23*(2), 242–266.

Nonaka, I. (1991). The knowledge-creating company. *Harvard Business Review, 69*(6), 96–104.

Nonaka, I. (1994). A dynamic theory of organizational knowledge creation. *Organization Science, 5*(1), 14–37. doi:10.1287/orsc.5.1.14

Nonaka, I., & Teece, D. J. (Eds.). (2001). *Managing industrial knowledge: Creation, transfer and utilization.* Sage Publications.

Nooteboom, B. (2004). *Inter-firm collaboration, learning and networks: An integrated approach.* London: Routledge.

Norris, P. (2002). The bridging and bonding role of online communities. *The Harvard International Journal of Press/Politics, 7*(3), 3–13. doi:10.1177/1081180X0200700301

ODell, C., & Grayson, C. J. (1998). If only we knew what we know: Identification and transfer of internal best practice. *California Management Review, 40*(3), 154–174. doi:10.2307/41165948

Orr, J. E. (1996). *Talking about machines: An ethnography of a modern job.* Ithaca, NY: Cornell University Press.

Pigg, K. E., & Crank, L. D. (2004). Building community social capital: The potential and promise of information and communications technologies. *The Journal of Community Informatics, 1*(1), 58–73.

Preece, J. (2002). Supporting community and building social capital. *Communications of the ACM, 45*(4), 37–39. doi:10.1145/505248.505269

Putnam, R. (1995). Bowling alone: Americas declining social capital. *Journal of Democracy, 6*(1), 65–78. doi:10.1353/jod.1995.0002

Putnam, R. (2000). *Bowling alone: The collapse and revival of American community.* New York, NY: Simon Schuster. doi:10.1145/358916.361990

Quan-Haase, A., & Wellman, B. (2004). How does the Internet affect social capital. *Social Capital and Information Technology, 113,* 135–113.

Raber, D., & Budd, J. M. (2003). Information as sign: Semiotics and information science. *The Journal of Documentation, 59*(5), 507–522. doi:10.1108/00220410310499564

Resnick, P. (2001). Beyond bowling together: Sociotechnical capital. *HCI in the New Millennium, 77,* 247–272.

Ruggles, R. (1998). The state of the notion: Knowledge management in practice. *California Management Review, 40*(3), 80–89. doi:10.2307/41165944

Saint-Onge, H., & Wallace, D. (2012). *Leveraging communities of practice for strategic advantage.* Butterworth-Heinemann.

Santos, J., Doz, Y., & Williamson, P. (2004). Is your innovation process global? *Sloan Management Review, 45*(4), 31–37.

Schoenhoff, D. M. (1993). The barefoot expert. Westport, CT: Greenwood Press.

Senge, P. M. (1993). Transforming the practice of management. *Human Resource Development Quarterly, 4*(1), 5–32. doi:10.1002/hrdq.3920040103

Sherriff, L. (2006, October 26). *Intel to close Cambridge research centre.* Retrieved October 3, 2016, from http://www.theregister.co.uk/2006/10/26/intel_closing_cambridge/

Sider, S. (2007). *Handbook to life in Renaissance Europe.* New York, NY: Oxford University Press.

Squire, K., & Johnson, C. (2000). Supporting distributed communities of practice with interactive television. *Educational Technology Research and Development, 48*(1), 23–43. doi:10.1007/BF02313484

Suchman, L. (1987). *Plans and situated actions: The problem of human-machine communication.* New York, NY: Cambridge University Press.

Uslaner, E. M. (1998). Social capital, TV and the Mean World: Trust, optimism, and civic participation. *Political Psychology, 19*(3), 441–467. doi:10.1111/0162-895X.00113

Vossen, G. (2009). Web 2.0: A buzzword, a serious development, just fun, or what?. *SECRYPT,* 33-40.

Walbank, F. W., Astin, A. E., Fredriksen, M. W., & Ogilvie, R. M. (1989). *The Cambridge ancient history VII. 2: The rise of Rome to 220 BC.* Retrieved from http://www.jstor.org/stable/41655564

Wallace, D., & Saint-Onge, H. (2003, May). Leveraging communities of practice. *Intranets: Enterprise Strategies and Solutions,* 1-5.

Wellman, B. (1982). Studying personal communities. In P. Marsden & N. Lin (Eds.), *Social structure and network analysis.* Beverly Hills, CA: Sage Publications.

Wellman, B. (1997). An electronic group is virtually a social network. In S. Kiesler (Ed.), *Culture of the Internet* (pp. 179–205). Mahwah, NJ: Lawrence Erlbaum.

Wellman, B., Hasse, A., Witte, J., & Hampton, K. (2001). Does the Internet increase, decrease, or supplement social capital? Social networks, participation, and community commitment. *The American Behavioral Scientist, 45*(3), 436–459. doi:10.1177/00027640121957286

Wenger, E. (1998). *Communities of practice: Learning, meaning, and identity.* Cambridge University Press. doi:10.1017/CBO9780511803932

Wenger, E., McDermott, R. A., & Snyder, W. (2002). *Cultivating communities of practice: A guide to managing knowledge.* Harvard Business Press.

Woolcock, M. (1998). Social capital and economic development: Toward a theoretical synthesis and policy framework. *Theory and Society, 27*(2), 151–208. doi:10.1023/A:1006884930135

Woolcock, M., & Narayan, D. (2001). Social capital: Implications for development theory, research and policy. *The World Bank Research Observer, 15*(2), 225–249. doi:10.1093/wbro/15.2.225

Yeh, Y. C., Huang, L. Y., & Yeh, Y. L. (2011). Knowledge management in blended learning: Effects on professional development in creativity instruction. *Computers & Education, 56*(1), 146–156. doi:10.1016/j. compedu.2010.08.011

Yip, G. S., Loewe, P. M., & Yoshino, M. Y. (1988). How to take your company to the global market. *The Columbia Journal of World Business, 23*(4), 37–48.

Yuan, Y. C., Zhao, X., Liao, Q., & Chi, C. (2013). The use of different information and communication technologies to support knowledge sharing in organizations: From e-mail to micro-blogging. *Journal of the American Society for Information Science and Technology, 64*(8), 1659–1670. doi:10.1002/asi.22863

KEY TERMS AND DEFINITIONS

Bonding Social Capital: A form of social capital enabling its owners to utilize their existing resources by serving them a collaborative sphere (tight environment, synergy, trust, ability, opportunity, collaborative sphere, etc.).

Bridging Social Capital: A form of social capital enabling its owners to access new resources by serving them new ties mostly from outside (the boundaries).

Communities of Practice (CoP): Groups of individuals coming together and interacting around a common interest in order to improve their interrelated practices.

Constant ICT: information and communication technologies helping individuals to transfer their coded knowledge asynchronously.

Dispersed Communities of Practice: Groups of individuals who are geographically dispersed and interact online with relation to their shared interests in order to improve their interrelated practices.

Exploitative Form of Organizational Learning: Process of creating and utilizing new knowledge within the organization as a whole.

Explorative Form of Organizational Learning: Process of accessing new knowledge which exists in the environment.

ICT: Information and communication technologies helping individuals to transfer or store their coded knowledge.

Instant ICT: information and communication technologies helping individuals to transfer their coded knowledge synchronously.

Location-Based Communities of Practice: Groups of individuals who are geographically together using ICT to interact with relation to their shared interests in order to improve their relevant/interrelated practices.

Online Communities of Practice (oCoP): Groups of individuals using ICT to interact in relation to their shared interests in order to improve their relevant/interrelated practices.

Organizational Learning: Process of gathering and diffusing new knowledge within the organization as a whole.

Social Capital: A form of intangible capital emerging within a group of individuals interacting for their shared purposes.

ENDNOTES

[1] e.g., Academie Francaise (1635), Royal Society of London (1660), Academie des Sciences (1666) and Accademia dei Dissonanti di Modena (1683)

[2] The term Web 2.0 was coined in 1999 to describe web sites that use technology beyond the static pages of earlier web sites.

[3] The process by which a theory, lesson, or skill is enacted, embodied, or realized. "Praxis" may also refer to the act of engaging, applying, exercising, realizing, or practicing ideas.

[4] The authors also consider long-standing tools such as databases and digital archives that allow searching or communicating with document contributors; hence, their value for developing awareness of expertise distribution and social capital is limited. They report that more than half of their interviewees who use long-standing tools reported that their contributions to these databases were mandated by managers and hence may not contain as many details as when the contributions were more voluntary. According to authors, the lack of contextual information of knowledge stored in such databases calls for the integration of other ICT tools (Yuan et al., 2013).

[5] *Quality*: In industrial (traditional) publishing—mediated by a publisher—the typical range of quality is substantially narrower than in niche, unmediated markets. The main challenge posed by content in social media sites is the fact that the distribution of quality has high variance: from very high-quality items to low-quality, sometimes abusive content. *Space:* both industrial and social media technologies provide scale and are capable of reaching a global audience. Industrial media, however, typically use a centralized framework for organization, production, and dissemination, whereas social media are by their very nature more decentralized, less hierarchical, and distinguished by multiple points of production and utility. *Frequency*: the number of times an advertisement is displayed on social media platforms. *Accessibility*: the means of production for industrial media are typically government and/or corporate (privately owned); social media tools are generally available to the public at little or no cost. *Usability*: industrial media production typically requires specialized skills and training. Conversely, most social media production requires only modest reinterpretation of existing skills; in theory, anyone with access can operate the means of social media production. *Immediacy*: the time lag between communications produced by industrial media can be long (days, weeks, or even months) compared to social media (which can be capable of virtually instantaneous responses). *Permanence:* industrial media, once created, cannot be altered (once a magazine article is printed and distributed, changes cannot be made to that same article) whereas social media can be altered almost instantaneously by comments or editing (Morgan et al., 2012).

Chapter 7
Social Innovation in the For-Profit Organization:
The Case of Banca Prossima

Tindara Abbate
University of Messina, Italy

Angelo Presenza
University of Molise, Italy

Lorn Sheehan
Dalhousie University, Canada

ABSTRACT

Social entrepreneurship and social innovation are attracting increasing attention from policy makers, practitioners, as well as academics. They represent different ways of thinking and addressing social issues often overlooked by public/private organizations and also provide a viable means of responding to multiple social, economic and environmental crises. With this in mind, this chapter leads to a better understanding of social entrepreneurship and social innovation in the non-profit sector, using one specific case followed by a more generalized discussion. The case of "Banca Prossima" illustrates engagement in social problems and trying to find and apply new solutions that simultaneously meet a social need while also leading to new or improved capabilities and relationships and a better use of assets and resources.

INTRODUCTION

Social entrepreneurship has fast become a global phenomenon (Zietlow, 2002; Robinson et al., 2009), receiving increased attention from researchers (Doherty et al., 2014; Dees, 2012; Defourny and Nyssens, 2008; Haugh, 2007; Hockerts, 2006; Mair and Martí, 2006; Short et al., 2009), including identifying its relevant societal effects (Austin, 2006; Martin and Osberg, 2007) and moving towards the definition of innovative approaches and activities to solve certain social problems (Robinson et al., 2009).

DOI: 10.4018/978-1-5225-2673-5.ch007

Globalization of the social entrepreneurship phenomenon is strictly associated with the following key factors: wealth disparity at the global level; market, institutional and state failures; spread of the corporate social responsibility movement; technological developments and recognition of shared responsibilities (Zahra et al., 2008). Two additional reasons may further explain why social entrepreneurship has emerged so strongly in society. First, social entrepreneurship can help non-profit organizations define and work in innovative ways, improving efficiency in products/services and serving their communities better (Reis and Clohesy, 1999). Second, certain conditions are best served by alliances between corporate and non-profit organizations where cooperation can clearly produce a better quality of life (Jiao, 2011).

Intrinsically linked with social entrepreneurship is the concept of social innovation which refers to exploring and finding new products/services, new ways to meet social needs which are not satisfactorily met by the market or the public sector, or tackling societal challenges, empowering people and creating new social relationships and models of collaboration (European Union and The Young Foundation, 2010). These are contemplated as a major issue for the European Commission, and also considered an important opportunity to connect with citizens and to stimulate a better quality of life (Altuna et al., 2015). Consequently, the European Commission has committed to keep, define and develop the European Union social model (under a sustainable and inclusive growth agenda) to address major societal challenges through social innovation with the involvement and the collaboration of all social actors, including the public sector, large enterprises, small-medium enterprises, social economies, etc. (European Commission, 2010), utilizing the open innovation approach highlighted recently by Chesbrough (2003).

Beyond the role played by the European Union in social innovation and the emblematic cases of non-profit organizations and foundations created on an ad hoc basis, there is limited contribution from other actors, such as private sector firms. Additionally, in recent years the concept of social innovation is increasingly of interest to academics seeking to structure and to develop the field of social innovation in an appropriate way (i.e., Rüede and Lurtz, 2012; Howaldt and Schwarz, 2010; Zahra et al., 2009; Phills et al., 2008; Pol and Ville, 2009; Alvord, et al., 2004). But, the resultant empirical studies have mainly referred to cases dealing with not-for-profit organizations (Altuna et al., 2015). Relatively unexplored are other sectors and other actors involved in social innovation activities, which, better understood through empirical investigation, might lead to a better understanding of how they create, develop and launch social innovations.

To address this gap, the chapter presents and discusses a case study of Banca Prossima, a firm that is mainly involved in social innovation projects and initiatives. Banca Prossima is a for-profit independent bank within the Intesa Sanpaolo group which provides products and services to non-profit customer segments (such as social businesses, associations, foundations and religious organizations). The continuous commitment to, and focus on, social innovation activities makes this for-profit organization an ideal case for the exploratory purpose of this research. Additionally, this case represents an interesting example of a bank that has evolved its activities to ever more advanced financial services (Formisano et al., 2016), in response to the profound changes that have taken place in the last few years, such as globalization, technological innovation and increasingly demanding customers. In particular, banks are putting strategies in place to respond to increased competition and more sophisticated customer's needs (Formisano and Russo, 2011) and in doing so have begun to transition from a product orientation to a customer orientation, with the aim of better understanding and satisfying heterogeneous client needs.

In light of these trends, the chapter is structured into three sections. First, a brief review of the literature on social entrepreneurship and social innovation. Second, an analysis of the "Banca Prossima" case study, emphasizing the application of new solutions to social problems that simultaneously meet a social need while also leading to new or improved organizational capabilities and relationships and better use of assets and resources. Finally, conclusions with managerial implications and suggestions for future research.

BACKGROUND

The Concept of Social Entrepreneurship

Although social entrepreneurship appears an inevitable response to complex societal needs and problems, a decade ago Roberts and Woods (2005, p. 45) observed that social entrepreneurship was at an "exciting stage of infancy, short on theory and definition but high on motivation and passion. The challenge for academia is to turn an inherently practitioner-led pursuit into a more rigorous and objective discipline". In this regard, various definitions of social entrepreneurship have been developed (Christie and Honig, 2006; Nicholls, 2006; Certo and Miller, 2008; Thompson, 2008), with some focusing mainly on its mission (Dees, 2001), its multiple dimensions (Mort et al., 2003) and its processes or mechanisms (Chell, 2007; Robert and Woods, 2005). However, a number of "conflicting tensions" regarding the definitional boundaries still remain (see table 1), such as the content and the dimensions of social enterprises (Dacin et al., 2011; Santos, 2012; Zahra et al., 2009), which fuel a relevant debate involving both academics and policy makers (Leadbeater, 2007).

Accordingly to Zahra et al. (2009, p. 522), social entrepreneurship "encompasses the activities and processes undertaken to discover, define, and exploit opportunities in order to enhance social wealth by creating new ventures or managing existing organizations in an innovative manner". Another useful conceptualization is offered by Peredo and McLean (2006, p. 64) who, after an examination of social entrepreneurship in its common use, suggest the following comprehensive definition: social entrepreneurship is exercised where some person (or group) (1) aims at creating social value, either exclusively or at least in some prominent way; (2) shows a capacity to recognize and take advantage of opportunities

Table 1. The main tensions regarding the notion of Social Entrepreneurship

Is social entrepreneurship an individual or a collective phenomenon?	It appears that social entrepreneurship can be both an individual and a collective phenomenon.
Is social entrepreneurship shaped by social value rather than economic value?	The creation of social value is the essential feature of the initiatives, for the social entrepreneur's principal aim is to produce social change.
Is social entrepreneurship located only in the non-profit sector, or can it also be found in the for-profit and public sectors?	While many social entrepreneurship initiatives can be found in the non-profit sector, some social entrepreneurship "attitudes" also concern other sectors.
Does social entrepreneurship aim to achieve incremental social impacts, or is it meant to produce radical social transformations only?	It seems that if social entrepreneurship is a way to improve the quality of life of individuals and communities through social value creation and innovative paths, it is not essential to establish whether its impact has to be incremental or radical.
Is social entrepreneurship a local phenomenon or a global one?	While many initiatives happen at the local level, the impact and the repercussions that flow from that impact cannot be isolated, as there are ultimately global links.

Source: *(European Commission, 2010)*

to create that value ('envision'); (3) employs innovation, ranging from outright invention to adapting someone else's novelty, in creating and/or distributing social value; (4) is willing to accept an above-average degree of risk in creating and disseminating social value; and, (5) is unusually resourceful in being relatively undaunted by scarce assets in pursuing their social venture. From this perspective, social entrepreneurship seems to be one of the most deliberate, and potentially most effective, ways for social innovation to offer solutions to pressing social problems. This means that social enterprises seek to serve the community's interest (social, societal, and environmental objectives) rather than profit maximization.

This point is reinforced by Phills et al. (2008) who suggest that social entrepreneurs see new patterns and possibilities for innovation and are willing to bring these new ways of doing things to fruition even when established organizations are unwilling to try them. And enterprises are important because they deliver innovation. But ultimately, innovation is what creates social value. Innovation can emerge in places and from people outside of the scope of social entrepreneurship and social enterprise. In particular, large, established nonprofits, businesses, and even governments are producing social innovations.

As Phills et al. (2008) noted, the underlying objective of social entrepreneurs and social enterprises is mainly to create social value which entails the creation of benefits or reductions of costs for society – through efforts that address social needs and problems – in ways that go beyond the widely-held convictions of private gains and general benefits from market activity. In this respect, the European Commission perceives social enterprises as often having an innovative nature, through the goods or services they provide, and also through the operational or organizational methods they utilize, often employing society's most fragile (socially excluded) individuals (Pisano et al., 2015). In addition, Dees (2006) emphasizes that social entrepreneurs discover or create novel opportunities through processes of exploration, innovation, experimentation and resource mobilization, revealing an active, confused and highly decentralized learning process that is necessary if social innovations are to be practically discovered and implemented to solve social problems.

Social Innovation

The novelty of the concept and the heterogeneity of disciplines involved have led to the proliferation of various definitions of social innovation (Zapf, 1991; Alvord et al., 2004; Moulaert et al., 2005; Pol and Ville; 2009; Rüede and Lurtz, 2012), in an attempt to explain its different forms and practices (Howaldt and Schwarz, 2010). Phills et al. (2008) state that social innovation can be considered as follows: "a novel solution to a social problem that is more effective, efficient, sustainable or just than existing solutions, and for which the value created accrues primarily to society as a whole rather than private individuals. Alvord et al. (2004, p. 262) underline that social innovation can be defined as "innovative solutions to immediate social problems that mobilize ideas, capacities, resources, and social arrangements required for sustainable social transformations". Additionally, the Innovation Union Flagship describes social innovation as finding new ways of meeting social needs which are not adequately met by the market or the public sector or to tackle societal challenges, empowering people and creating new social relationships and models of collaboration (European Commission, 2010). Although, the project and initiatives of social innovation are generally encouraged by non-profit organizations and foundations, the European Commission (2012) states that social innovation can and must take place in all four sectors or as combination of them: (1) the non-profit sector; (2) the public sector (both in terms of policies and service models); (3) the private sector; and, (4) the informal sector.

As outlined by the European Commission, all actors and all regions should be involved in social innovation and there is actually an interesting sign that social innovations can increasingly be defined and developed by firms (European Commission, 2012, p. 29). In fact, the for-profit sector is increasingly showing concrete levels of social responsibility, a high level of social value creation and certain social entrepreneurship "attitudes" (OECD, 2010, p. 190) to develop and manage social innovation projects. Emblematic cases in this direction are the big companies like Apple, Siemens, Dell and others that may have created an environment of entrepreneurship or ancillary industries or processes to satisfy some social needs/problems of China (Salim Saji and Ellingstad, 2015).

Following a review of the literature, Caurlier-Grice et al. (2012) propose several common features and core elements of social innovation (see Figure 1). The core elements appear mainly necessary to define a social innovation, speaking to: novelty, where social innovation needs to be new in some way or applied in a new way; practical application, where social innovation has to address the practical application or implementation of a new idea financially sustainable in the medium- to long-term; meets a social need, explicitly considered as something that can cause serious harm or socially suffering when not met; effectiveness, implying that social innovation should be more effective by creating a measurable improvement in terms of outcomes from existing solutions; enhancement of society's capacity to act, determining new roles and relationships, developing assets and capabilities and/or better use of assets and resources. The main common features of social innovation are: cross-sectoral; grassroots and bottom-up; pro-sumption and co-production; mutualism; creation of new roles and relationships; better use of resources and assets; and development of assets and capabilities; and open and collaborative.

Regarding this last feature, it is interesting to note that social innovation seems to naturally reflect the open innovation principles (Chesbrough, 2003) because the development of successful social innovation projects/activities inevitably requires the involvement of different external actors, strongly committed to the social mission and social goals. In addition, social innovation activities need generally to create new social relationships or social collaborations (Murray et al., 2010). Similarly, open innovation is strongly focused on collaboration (Chesbrough et al., 2008), stressing opportunities to attract innovative ideas,

Figure 1. Common features and core elements of social innovation

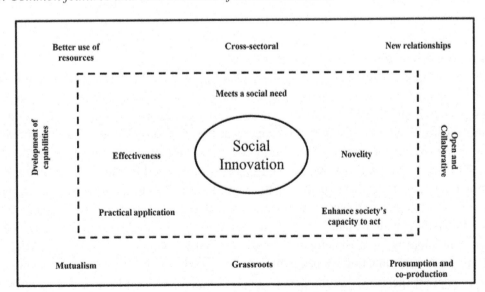

exchange knowledge among different actors, and work together through open and collaborative networks in order to develop products/services (Chesbrough, 2003) or to solve problems. In fact, according to the principles of open innovation, an organization does not innovate in isolation, but rather by engaging with different types of partners and acquiring ideas and resources from the external environment (Chesbrough, 2003).

With these definitional elements in mind, the chapter presents a case study that provides exploratory insights into the main characteristics and activities through which a for-profit organization can successfully define and develop social innovation involving particular segments of society (usually disadvantaged, marginalized or poor) and allowing all or part of the benefits derived by the innovation activity to accrue to that same segments of the society (Tan et al., 2005).

CASE STUDY

Banca Prossima: Overview

In 2007 Intesa SanPaolo emerged from the merger of Banca Intesa and Sanpaolo IMI. It has Italian leadership with context and a significant international presence focused on Central-Eastern European, Middle Eastern and North African Countries with approximately 1,200 branches and 8.1 million customers belonging to the Group's subsidiaries working in commercial banking in 12 countries (Intesa Sanpaolo, 2017). The bank is characterized by the Head Office Departments that consist of both the Corporate Social Responsibility (CSR) Department and the Bank and Society Laboratory (defined easily as "Laboratory"), which reflects the organizational structure oriented mainly to the definition and the development of social innovation projects and activities. Additionally, Banca dei Territori (the domestic commercial banking unit) is dedicated to retail customers, private customers and small-medium enterprises (SMEs). Within this division, there are different branches: Mediocredito (the bank oriented to SMEs activities), Banca Prossima (the independent bank dedicated completely to non-profit organizations) and other banks committed to specific client segments.

This chapter intends to focus on the case of Banca Prossima, which represents an emblematic experience of social entrepreneurship, operating in the not-for-profit sector, and of strong commitment and effort to generate new ideas and initiatives capable of transforming the economic, social and political context of marginalized groups and affect social change.

The mission of Banca Prossima is to meet and satisfy the needs and requirements of non-profit organizations (i.e., foundations, social businesses, associations and the religious world), by offering excellent products targeted to improving the quality of banking services and participating in the creation of social value. In this regard, it intends effectively "to support the best not-for-profit initiatives to spread culture diffusion and education, enjoyment and protection of the environment and art and to facilitate access to credit and to work" (Banca Prossima, 2017). In fact, as underlined by the CEO of Banca Prossima: "the decision to create a specialized bank to better serve the third sector is the result of the experience gained by the Laboratory in four years of collaboration with the non-profit. This is a project that affects the way we do business with a clientele usually neglected by banks, but that could soon take charge of many services no more supplied directly by the system of public welfare" (Altuna et al., 2015, p. 266).

Therefore, since its foundation, Banca Prossima has sought to ensure the highest level of service and ability to support the growth of the best initiatives, which are often limited and penalized by the conventional criteria of banking evaluation. To further this goal, it has revised the process of risk analysis by defining and adopting an innovative social enterprise rating model that integrates the traditional methods of banking with specific metrics to evaluate the sustainability of clients that present peculiarities different from those of "privates" or "companies". In fact, this new ad hoc rating is not in contrast with the bank's traditional analytical methods, but it also contemplates some qualitative elements, such as fund raising abilities, critical success factors related to projects funded by the Public Administration and Foundations, and the percentage of orders derived from individual benefactors. Specifically, this model enables Banca Prossima to take the peculiarities of the non-profit organizations into account when evaluating its clients on matters of debt sustainability and social projects. Additionally, Banca Prossima has developed a special risk fund (Fund for the Development of the Social Enterprise) from the company's profits. As specified in the statute, 50 per cent of these profits (100 per cent for the first ten years since its foundation in 2007) have to be devoted to this fund, which intends to intervene in particularly risky areas, considered highly relevant in terms of the social value generated. This fund is not considered as part of the bank equity and it would be given to charity in the event of dissolution of the company.

For these reasons, Banca Prossima has been placed among the organizations and institutions which primarily serve the specific needs of social enterprises and businesses with social and environmental objectives within "The Open Book of Social Innovation".

Banca Prossima: Initiatives and Projects

As noted above, Banca Prossima works partially on its own and partially in collaboration with Intesa Sanpaolo on numerous projects (Table 2), fostering socially innovative activities through the involvement and participation of external partners making innovative use of their capabilities and competences. It stimulates the creation of inter-organizational relationships and strategic alliances, explores new opportunities to better use existing resources (i.e., knowledge and capital), and also aims to improve or to solve social problems (i.e., health-related problems).

In fact, the definition and the development of these innovative initiatives demonstrate the profound belief and the relevant work of Banca Prossima in support of social projects that are pursued for their social impact, independent of the profits they can generate, and in support of disadvantaged social groups in terms of resolutions of their problems Such projects and the groups they serve are usually excluded from receiving credit. In contrast to commercial entrepreneurs, these groups have several difficulties in accessing or finding financial resources for innovation, as well as in attracting potential investors, such

Table 2. Examples of social innovation projects

A scheme for advancing payments from the Campania Region to a consortium of non-profits that won a regional auction for provision of healthcare services to old and disadvantaged people. This can be considered one of the first such schemes in the South of Italy.
A nursery centre project run jointly with a consortium of "social co-operatives" that would train the childcare workers, guaranteeing quality standards. Banca Prossima grants loans with no personal guarantee required. The resulting network is currently one of the country's largest, servicing over 8 000 3-year-olds and employing over 2000 women
A project for setting up residences to host mentally disabled people who have outlived their parents.
A project to finance volunteer organizations, whereby Banca Prossima provides loans guaranteed up to 20% by means of a fund set up by local centres servicing volunteer organizations in Lombardy and a Foundation.

Source: *(OECD, 2010)*

as venture capitalists, to support social innovation because they are legally restricted from distributing profits and, consequently, are unable to offer financial returns (Austin et al., 2006).

In this regard, a significant initiative developed by Banca Prossima is "Terzo Valore", a free web-based platform which provides new resources to the Third Sector and, at the same time, permits any private citizen to select and fund a non-profit project, amongst those pre-screened by Banca Prossima, either through specific donations or loans without intermediation. This crowdfunding initiative is particularly innovative in Italy because citizens' loans between peers (as is the case for non-profit institutions) were previously problematic to implement from a legal viewpoint. In fact, P2P platforms emerged, but most shut down, so "Terzo Valore" created a viable way to serve the market. The "Terzo Valore" loans are capital-guaranteed by Banca Prossima (this was not standard in previous cases) and Banca Prossima supplies at least a third, and up to 100%, of the financing. Through "Terzo Valore", 23 projects have been financed in education, religion, social welfare and cultural areas, for a total of 4.21 million euros, at an average interest rate of less than 3% (Banca Prossima, 2017).

Another important initiative of Banca Prossima is the "Foundation for Innovation in the Third Sector" (Fondazione Fits2014, 2017). It is proposed as "an enterprise venture established by Banca Prossima in 2011 with the aim of creating social value, starting with the voluntary sector and with our sights set on the entire community" (Fondazione Fits2014, 2017). This foundation does not intend to offer subsidies but exists to "monitor new social needs, develop flexible service models to meet rapidly evolving social demands, disseminate best practice across the region to generate efficiency and economies of scale, and attract interest from new social investors for public and private entities" (Fondazione Fits2014, 2017). This is because the social system intensely supports defining and developing different innovative models able to support the sustainability of organisations by improving efficiency and using diverse financial tools to facilitate and strengthen links with private, public and social enterprise supporters. Therefore, the roles of researching, monitoring and "its accompanying social planning, promotion and development of network systems among third-sector players, synergy with commercial entities and government agencies, and innovative welfare models are the modus operandi for FITS!" (Fondazione Fits2014, 2017). From this perspective, it is clear that the foundation assumes a critical role of an "aggregator" in terms of suitable experience and a "catalyst" for skills and competencies. The main achievements of the Foundation are principally developed around the following important areas: energy, Europe, social project financing, skills workshops and corporate social responsibility (see Table 3). These activities are the result of intense and qualified research that identifies social needs by digging into different information sources. This preliminary and relevant phase is followed by the so-called design activities (Altuna et al., 2015, p. 266), during which the intervention model is concretely defined because, once the main objective is defined, it is necessary to determine where and how to change and innovate the process of credit provision. Finally, the process concludes with the identification of the project partners that should be engaged. In effect, all the activities are developed in collaboration with on average two or three partners with specific competences important to the social project; with the majority (around 80 per cent of them) coming from the third sector.

Similar to these innovative social initiatives, it is useful to consider other two different areas of activities. Firstly, Banca Prossima has developed a stakeholder communication strategy for the Third Sector, identifying and defining appropriate mechanisms, such as collaboration with a national non-profit association named Vobis (Volunteer Bank for Social Initiatives), to put its expertise service through mentoring at the disposal of citizen and non-profit applicants. Secondly, within its organization Banca Prossima has introduced the so-called "Head of Relationship" program in recognition of managers who

Table 3. The principal activities of FITS!

Areas	Needs Analysis	Model of Intervention	Partners
Energy	Revising energy installations to reduce the waste associated with these activities and the cost savings; to support the development of renewable energy and to reduce the effects of pollution from fossil fuels. The need for access to qualified professionals to examine production systems and energy usage with low investment.	Analysis of energy efficiency needs for estates (i.e., offices, schools, sports facilities, etc.); Planning for installations required; Creation of Social Energy Service Companies; Use of financial mechanisms of the FITS! and Banca Prossima energy-efficiency programme.	FITS! Banca Prossima E.ON Connecting Energies (ECT)
Europe	There are 14.5 million people employed in the social economy in Europe (6.5% of the European Union population), but in relation to the major European economies, Italy has the highest number of employees as a percentage of the total economy (9.7%). The "Made in Italy" motto and the quality of life are rooted in the infrastructure of relationships and ties with the community. It is the share capital of the Italian territory that supplies production chains today, and without this it would be impossible to generate value. The presence and the widespread dissemination of non-profit organisations and social enterprises, even outside the national borders, therefore, becomes a major indicator of competition.	Participation in European tenders; Establishment of social enterprise networks, exploring market opportunities for social enterprises and/or members of these networks; Fostering synergies between companies and enterprises to generate economies of scale.	FITS! Banca Prossima
Social Project Financing	The current state of public finance in Italy, the demands from Europe and, in the case of municipalities, the obligations imposed by the Stability Pact, have induced legislators to introduce tools and mechanisms to engage private capital more effectively in the development of public works and public utilities.	Public-initiative financing and private-initiative financing. The public-initiative model of project financing requires a private institution (the promoter) to propose construction of a public utility work to the authorising government agency, where it is already included in its three-year schedule of work. Where it is not already included, but the authorising agency acknowledges the public utility of the scheme proposed by the private institution (the applicant), project financing is by private initiative.	FITS! provides access to its planning facilities and performs an advisory function. Banca Prossima: financial partner Companies and public institutions Private companies Joint stock companies with majority public holding Joint stock companies with majority private holding
Skills Workshop	Non-profit organisations have invested in training to strengthen the skills of their workforce and management. Priority training objectives: development of vocational skills for workers and managerial skills of corporate heads	Focus groups to identify training needs to inform training programmes that will be made available to organisations and institutions in the voluntary sector.	FITS! Intesa Sanpaolo Formazione
Corporate Social Responsibility	Company focus on corporate social responsibility has increased significantly in Italy. Social responsibility plays an important role in internal and external business communications and in positioning the company image, especially in the context of the territory and the sector in which it operates. The need arises to devise models of intervention that are oriented towards a new way of promoting company policies and increasing their social impact on the territory and on the community.	Implementation of initiatives in support of community welfare to selected corporate clients, to enhance their CSR policies.	FITS! Companies: Vodafone Foundation, Peppino Vismara Foundation, L'Oreal, E.ON Connecting Energies Srl Intesa SanPaolo Banca Prossima

Source: (Fondazione Fits2014, 2017).

distinguish themselves through their professional skills in managing relationships, not only with Third Sector clients but in their private life through their engagement in volunteer-related activities. These managers receive refresher courses and training to help them identify core decision making needed to understand both the process and areas of inter-organizational conflicts, and ultimately to pinpoint the most suitable solution for even the most complex problems.

SOLUTIONS AND RECOMMENDATIONS

As highlighted by the literature review and the case study 'Banca Prossima', the term "social entrepreneurship" is used to refer to the rapidly growing number of organizations that have created models for efficiently catering to basic human needs that existing markets and institutions have failed to satisfy. Social entrepreneurs solve several societal issues because they combine the resourcefulness of traditional entrepreneurship with a mission to change society. A few recommendations are key to support the growing number of social innovation initiatives across the globe. The most important concerns improving the capacity of social entrepreneurs to effectively apply open innovation principles (Chesbrough, 2003). Additionally, social innovation projects or activities inevitably require the involvement of different external actors, strongly committed to the social mission and social goals being pursued. This means that social entrepreneurs must be also comfortable and adept with concepts such as informal organization, trust, culture, social support, social exchange, social resources, embeddedness, relational contracts, social networks, and interfirm networks. All of these fall under the "umbrella concept" of social capital (Hirsch and Levin, 1999). This means that social entrepreneurs should take care to develop interpersonal trust and meet social expectations. The ultimate goal is to create value in their social innovation network by bonding similar people and bridging diverse perspectives.

FUTURE RESEARCH DIRECTIONS

Future research could include gathering additional empirical evidence, beyond this case study, on social innovation in for-profit organizations. Other sectors, beyond banking and financial services, with their own set of specific dynamics might also be investigated. It would be useful to understand the main motivations that stimulate these organizations to develop social innovation projects and the existence of any contextual factors that can affect the success of this kind of innovation.

CONCLUSION

This chapter contributes a focus on how for-profit organizations can develop, organize and deliver successful social innovation projects and initiatives. At the broadest level, it adds new insights to scholarly research focused on a relevant, although underdeveloped topic, namely the definition and implementation of social innovation in for-profit organizations. More specifically, the case study emphasizes that these organizations need to develop a set of resources and specific competencies to facilitate social innovation projects, such as the knowledge of societal needs of particular disadvantaged groups as well as the competences needed to define an appropriate model of intervention. For-profit organizations can help to solve social problems using their business competencies and resources, and through partnerships with government, create and maintain suitable relationships and collaborations with them in order to effectively solve community problems and social issues. Intrinsically linked with this, is the opportunity and necessity for these organizations to develop and implement an open business model (Chesbrough, 2003) that clearly fosters the involvement and participation of external stakeholders in their internal activities and processes.

The case study presented here provides some interesting suggestions to managers working in firms that are willing to develop products or services motivated by the goal of meeting a social need. They are shown to be able to solve social problems with innovative solutions that contribute to the creation of social value while also creating firm level profits. With the notion of a social mission, they have to select and adopt an appropriate approach to explore social value-opportunities and to administer their social innovation projects, in a way that overcomes organizational rigidities while acquiring the critical competencies for social innovation that for-profit organizations typically lack. These implications are highly relevant to achieving positive societal effects. Although social innovation is usually considered the principal domain of non-profit organizations, encouraging a superior engagement of for-profit organizations in this type of innovation activity represents a key opportunity for the generation of several benefits for society.

REFERENCES

Altuna, N., Contri, A. M., DellEra, C., Frattini, F., & Maccarrone, P. (2015). Managing social innovation in for-profit organizations: The case of Intesa Sanpaolo. *European Journal of Innovation Management, 18*(2), 258–280. doi:10.1108/EJIM-06-2014-0058

Alvord, S. H., Brown, D. L., & Letts, C. W. (2004). Social entrepreneurship and social transformation: An exploratory study. *The Journal of Applied Behavioral Science, 40*(3), 260–283. doi:10.1177/0021886304266847

Austin, J., Stevenson, H., & Wei-Skillern, J. (2006). Social and commercial entrepreneurship: Same, different, or both? *Entrepreneurship Theory and Practice, 30*(1), 1–22. doi:10.1111/j.1540-6520.2006.00107.x

Banca Prossima. (2017). *Information about Banca Prossima*. Retrieved January 13, 2017, from www.bancaprossima.it

Certo, S. T., & Miller, T. (2008). Social entrepreneurship: Key issues and concepts. *Business Horizons, 51*(4), 267–271. doi:10.1016/j.bushor.2008.02.009

Chesbrough, H. W. (2003). *Open Innovation: The New Imperative for Creating and Profiting from Technology*. Boston: Harvard Business School Press.

Christie, M. J., & Honig, B. (2006). Social entrepreneurship: New research findings. *Journal of World Business, 41*(1), 1–5. doi:10.1016/j.jwb.2005.10.003

Dacin, T. M., Dacin, P. A., & Tracey, P. (2011). Social entrepreneurship: A critique and future directions. *Organization Science, 22*(5), 1203–1213. doi:10.1287/orsc.1100.0620

Dees, G. J. (2001). *The meaning of social entrepreneurship*. Available at: www.caseatduke.org/ documents/dees_sedef.pdf

Dees, G. J. (2012). A tale two cultures: Charity, problem solving, and the future of social entrepreneurship. *Journal of Business Ethics, 111*(3), 321–334. doi:10.1007/s10551-012-1412-5

Defourny, J., & Nyssens, M. (2010). Conceptions of social enterprise and social entrepreneurship in Europe and the United States: Convergences and Divergences. *Journal of Social Entrepreneurship, 1*(1), 120–132. doi:10.1080/19420670903442053

Doherty, B., Haugh, H., & Lyon, F. (2014). Social Enterprises as Hybrid Organizations: A Review and Research Agenda. *International Journal of Management Reviews, 16*(4), 417–439. doi:10.1111/ijmr.12028

European Union and The Young Foundation. (2010). *Study of Social Innovation, A paper presented by the Social Innovation Exchange (SIX) and the Young Foundation for the Bureau of European Policy Advisors*. London: Young Foundation.

Fondazione Fits 2014. (2017). *Information about Fondazione Fits 2014*. Retrieved January 13, 2017, from Retrieved January 13, 2017, from www.fondazionefits2014.com

Formisano, V., Fedele, M., & Antonucci, E. (2016). Innovation in Financial Services: A Challenge for Start-Ups Growth. *International Journal of Business and Management, 11*(3), 149–162. doi:10.5539/ijbm.v11n3p149

Formisano, V., & Russo, G. (2011). Service Logic, Value Co-Creation And Networks in the Banking services. Giannini Editore.

Haugh, H. (2007). New Strategies for a Sustainable Society: The growing contribution of Social Entrepreneurship. *Business Ethics Quarterly, 17*(4), 743–749. doi:10.5840/beq20071747

Hirsch, P. M., & Levin, D. Z. (1999). Umbrella advocates versus validity police: A life-cycle model. *Organization Science, 10*(1), 199–212. doi:10.1287/orsc.10.2.199

Hockerts, K. (2006). Entrepreneurial opportunity in social purpose business ventures. In J. Mair, J. Robinson, & K. Hockerts (Eds.), *Social Entrepreneurship* (pp. 142–154). New York: Palgrave Macmillan. doi:10.1057/9780230625655_10

Howaldt, J., & Schwarz, M. (2010). *Social Innovation: Concepts, research fields and international trends*. Dortmund: Sozialforschungsstelle Dortmund.

Intesa Sanpaolo. (2017). *Information about Intesa Sanpaolo*. Retrieved January 13, 2017, from www.intesasanpaolo.it

Jiao, H. (2011). A conceptual model for social entrepreneurship directed toward social impact on society. *Social Enterprise Journal, 7*(2), 130–149. doi:10.1108/17508611111156600

Leadbeater, C. (2007). *Social enterprises and social innovation: strategies for the next ten years. A social enterprise think piece for the Office of the Third Sector*. Cabinet Office. Retrieved from http://www.sagepub.com/sites/default/files/upm-binaries/66035_Cnaan_Chapter_2.pdf

Martin, R. L., & Osberg, S. (2007). Social entrepreneurship: The case for definition. *Stanford Social Innovation Review, 5*(2), 29–39.

Mort, G. S., Weerawardena, J., & Carnegie, K. (2003). Social entrepreneurship: Towards conceptualization. *International Journal of Nonprofit and Voluntary Sector Marketing, 8*(1), 76–88. doi:10.1002/nvsm.202

Nicholls, A. (2006). Playing the field: A new approach to the meaning of social entrepreneurship. *Social Enterprise Journal, 2*(1), 1–5.

Phills, J., Deiglmeier, K., & Miller, D. (2008). Rediscovering Social Innovation. *Social Innovation Review, 6*(4), 1–11.

Pol, E., & Ville, S. (2009). Social innovation: Buzz word or enduring term? *Journal of Socio-Economics, 38*(6), 878–885. doi:10.1016/j.socec.2009.02.011

Reis, T., & Clohesy, S. (1999). *Unleashing New Resources and Entrepreneurship for the Common Good: A Scan, Synthesis and Scenario for Action.* Battle Creek, MI: WK Kellogg Foundation.

Roberts, D., & Woods, C. (2005). Changing the world on a shoestring: The concept of social entrepreneurship. *University of Auckland Business Review, 19*(1), 45–51.

Robinson, J. A., Mair, J., & Hockerts, K. (Eds.). (2009). *International Perspectives of Social Entrepreneurship.* London: Palgrave.

Rüede, D., & Lurtz, K. (2012). *Mapping the Various Meanings of Social Innovation: Towards a Differentiated Understanding of an Emerging Concept.* EBS University.

Santos, F. M. (2012). A Positive Theory of Social Entrepreneurship. *Journal of Business Ethics, 111*(3), 335–351. doi:10.1007/s10551-012-1413-4

Short, J. C., Moss, T. W., & Lumpkin, G. T. (2009). Research in social entrepreneurship: Past contributions and future opportunities. *Strategic Entrepreneurship Journal, 3*(2), 161–194. doi:10.1002/sej.69

Thompson, J. (2008). Social enterprise and social entrepreneurship: where have we reached?: a summary of issues and discussion points. *Social Enterprise Journal, 4*(2), 149–161. doi:10.1108/17508610810902039

Zahra, S. A., Gedajlovic, E., Neubaum, D. O., & Shulman, J. M. (2009). A typology of social entrepreneurs: Motives, search processes and ethical challenges. *Journal of Business Venturing, 24*(5), 519–532. doi:10.1016/j.jbusvent.2008.04.007

Zahra, S. A., Rawhouser, H. N., Bhawe, N., Neubaum, D. O., & Hayton, J. C. (2008). Globalization of social entrepreneurship opportunities. *Strategic Entrepreneurship Journal, 2*(2), 117–131. doi:10.1002/sej.43

Zietlow, J. T. (2002). Releasing a new wave of social entrepreneurship. *Nonprofit Management & Leadership, 13*(1), 85–90. doi:10.1002/nml.13107

KEY TERMS AND DEFINITIONS

Banca Prossima: It represents a relevant example of social entrepreneurship, whereby a for-profit organization (in this case a bank) also operates in the not-for-profit sector. It has a strong commitment to generating ideas and initiatives capable of improving the economic, social and political situation of marginalized groups and affect social change.

Open Innovation: Is a paradigm that assumes that firms can access and absorb external ideas as well as internal ideas, and internal and external paths to market, as they seek to advance their technology. More recently it has been described as distributed innovation process based on purposively managed knowledge flows across organizational boundaries.

Social Capital: Broadly refers to the resources accumulated through the relationships among people.

Social Entrepreneurship: Encompasses the activities and processes undertaken to discover, define, develop, and exploit opportunities in order to improve social wealth by creating new ventures or managing existing organizations in an innovative manner.

Social Innovation: New ways of meeting social needs which are not adequately met by the market or the public sector or to tackle societal challenges, empowering people and creating new social relationships and models of collaboration.

Chapter 8
Managing Business Ethics in a Global Environment:
The Impact of Cultural Diversities

Rossella Canestrino
Parthenope University of Naples, Italy

Pierpaolo Magliocca
University of Foggia, Italy

ABSTRACT

The aim of this chapter is to explore the how international players, acting at global level, may overcome a "moral gap" when it arises. In doing this, the linkage between culture and Business Ethics was examined in order to highlight the way values and believes differently affect a) the assumption about what is right or wrong, b) the individual/organizational moral reasoning, and c) the consistency between individual/ organizational behaviour and the moral standards that prevail in a given context. Relevant issues were investigated referring to all the levels – individual, corporate and systemic – within which a "moral gap" may arise. Accordingly, "Bridging" diversities was identified as a good solution to solve a "moral gap" at all the mentioned levels. Cross-cultural sensitivity and cross-cultural negotiation were finally claimed as necessary to look for a trade-off between universal norms and local particularism, as well as to finally identify new common standards respectful of the opposite positions.

INTRODUCTION

Both globalization and the growing of international competition have affected the complexity of academic inquiry about Business Ethic and firms' Social Responsibility. The interest of academics for the underlined subjects is, particularly, supported by the wide range of studies actually available about the topic.

In spite of this, further researches seem to be still necessary, mainly because of the complexity of the issues and the establishment of a wider global competitive environment.

The field of Business Ethic deals with questions about whether specific business practices are acceptable. It mainly relates to rules, standards, and moral principles regarding what is right or wrong in

DOI: 10.4018/978-1-5225-2673-5.ch008

specific situations (Ferrell and Fraedrich, 2015; De George, 1993). It also means that Business Ethics comprises the principles, values, and standards that guide both individual and organizational behavior in the world of business.

Many Scholars (Ferrell and Fraedrich, 2015; Alas et al., 2015; Donaldson and Dunfee, 1999, 1994; Robertson, 2002; De George, 1993) recognize the deep linkage between culture and the establishment of the mentioned (moral) standards, as well as between culture and individual/organizational ethical behavior (Vitell et al., 2013; Husted, 2000; Cohen et al., 1996; Wines and Napier, 1992).

Particularly, culture may influence Business Ethic, by

1. Shaping the assumption about what is right or wrong;
2. Influencing the individuals' moral reasoning (even within organizations) and, finally, by
3. Affecting the consistency between individual/organizational behavior and the moral standards that prevail in a given context.

Due to the globalization of markets and production processes, an increasing number of individual players and business organizations deals with ethical issues in cross-cultural settings.

Since countries differ in their cultures, socio-economic, political, and legal systems, as well as in their level of economic development, international players have to deal with ethical issues much more than before: they are exposed to different values and ethical norms, and are often criticized for their ethical misconduct (Armstrong et al., 1990).

When acting at global level, therefore, international players (be them individuals or organizations) keep in contact with different cultural contexts: from a cultural perspective, host contexts may be very different from the domestic ones. In such circumstances, moral standards may also differ, and a so-called "moral gap" may arise.

The above situations pose deep challenges for both individuals and organizations: every time a "moral gap" establishes, international players are claimed to manage it in order to avoid the negative consequences of national or international boycott initiatives and the failure of the whole business, at least. In order to prevent failures, organizations should identify the set of rules to respect in each situations, as well as what may be do or not in the undertaking business. In doing this, they need to get a deep knowledge of local culture, as well as of the way culture shapes the local "moral free space" (Donaldson and Dunfee, 1999).

According to the above considerations, the traditional approach to Business Ethic may be extended by the theoretical contributions coming out from Cross-Cultural Management studies, in order to widen the actual understanding about the way Business Ethic may be managed in a global environment.

Depending on the above consideration, the chapter aims to explain:

1. How cultural diversities may affect the establishment of moral standards, as well the hierarchy of values that prevail in given societies;
2. How international players (acting in a global environment) define the set of standards they choose to respect in each situation;
3. How international players may manage a moral gap when it arises.

The chapter is organized as follow: the next section proposes a literary review about the principles and the theories belonging to the field of *Business Ethics*, focusing on individual, organizational (Corporate Social Responsibility) and systemic level. A discussion about the linkage between culture and ethic is then developed, in order to explore the existing tie between cultural values, morality and firms' ethical behavior. In seeking to gain the chapter's goals, some advices about the way Hofstede' cultural dimensions may be used to understand cultural diversities, and to manage ethical conflicts, are also provided. Some suggestions to overcome the challenges arising by the international ethical conflicts are finally proposed.

LITERARY REVIEW: DEFINING BUSINESS ETHICS – FROM INDIVIDUAL'S MORAL CONDUCT TO CORPORATE SOCIAL RESPONSIBILITY

The study of ethic is an ancient tradition, rooted in religious, cultural, and philosophical beliefs (Canestrino, 2008, 2007). By the contrast, Business Ethics has attracted the attention of scholars only for more recent years. In the 1970s it began to develop as a field of study: at that time, both theologians and philosophers began to suggest that certain moral principles could be applied to business activities, laying the groundwork for the future development of the discipline. Time by time, they increased their involvement, building up the actual shape of the topic.

In general, Business Ethics concerns with what may be do or not in undertaking business (Ferrell and Fraedrich, 2015; Velasquez, 2012; De George, 1993), involving the rules that govern business activities and the values embedded in the business practice, as well. It deals with the basic philosophy and priorities of an organization in concrete terms (French, 1979) and contains the prohibitory actions at the workplace (Collier and Esteban, 2007).

From this perspective, Business Ethics equates with a kind of applied ethics (Broni, 2010) aiming at examining the ethical problems that arise in a business environment (Solomon, 1991) and that evaluates the moral principles to be applied in all the aspects of business conduct (Ferell and Fraedrich, 1997).

In accordance with the mentioned perspective Business Ethics does not only include the analysis of moral norms and moral standards, but it also try to apply the results of the mentioned analysis to the institutions, to the organizations and to all the business-oriented activities (Velasquez, 2012). In doing this, Business Ethics focus on three main issues – individual issues, corporate issues and systemic issues – in order to find the best solution for dealing with each of them. It means also that kinds of solutions that are appropriate for a given issue, may be not appropriate for another one (see table 1).

Particularly, Individual issues in business ethics mainly refer to the ethical dilemma[1] raised about individuals – as well as about their behaviors and decisions – acting in a company. Corporate issues refer to those ethical questions that arise and that need to be managed in a given organization, the last one considered as a whole. These may include the morality of corporate strategies, policies and practices. Finally, Systemic issues mainly refer to those ethical problems that may arise with reference to the economic, legal and institutional framework within which businesses act. The debate about the morality of capitalism or of the laws, of the worldwide distribution of wealth or of the industrial structure belong to this topic (Velasquez, 2012).

The distinction among Individual, Corporate and Systemic issues fits with the different (even overlapping) theoretical backgrounds within which ethical issues and the ethical dilemma are usually discussed. It's a matter of fact, that, at its first stage, Business Ethics always deals with individuals' morality, as well as with their perception of what is right or wrong, good and evil. At this level, people are claimed to solve ethical dilemmas through a reasoning process by which moral standards are applied to the situations and to the issues to face. Several decision making models have been developed using concepts, theories and evidences largely derived from social psychology, to picture the way people engage in moral behavior

Table 1. The issues of Business Ethics (our elaboration)

ISSUES	CORE TOPICS	RELATED THEORETHICAL FRAMEWORK
INDIVIDUAL	Individuals' moral reasoning and behavior	Cognitive Moral Development Theory (Kohlberg, 1976, 1969) Psychological Theory and Women's Development (Gilligan, 1982) Person-Situation Interactionist Model (Trevino, 1986) Issue-Contingent Model (Jones, 1991)
CORPORATE	Organization's social responsibility (strategies and policies)	Pyramid of CSR (Carroll, 1991)
SYSTEMIC	Morality of laws; distribution of wealth; political and institutional decisions	Theory of Moral Sentiment (Smith, 1759) Criticism to Capitalism (Marx, 1978) Institutional Framework for the Ethical Wealth of Nations (Jennings and Velasquez, 2015)

in their everyday life, as well as within business organizations (Jones, 1991; Dubinski and Loken, 1989; Trevino, 1986; Hunt and Vitell, 1986; Rest, 1986; Kohlberg, 1969).

At Corporate level, organizations have to face their own ethical dilemmas – that may be even very different from the individual ones – the last referring to the corporate's responsibility toward society.

At a wider level, Business Ethics finally deals with the morality of laws, norms, political and economic conditions that regulate firm's behavior within a given context.

Ethical dilemmas may particularly arise at each of the mentioned levels – individual, corporate and systemic – and need to be managed according to a reasoning process that always starts at individual level (in the writers view). Like a learning process, ethical decision making may be regarded as a moving up process through different levels - from the individual to the organization till communities and the larger networks. Since individuals are usually embedded in the organizational field, their moral reasoning is affected, not only by their own values and beliefs (that shape individual moral standards), but also by the other organizational players, as well as by the firm's own culture and policies. Moreover business organizations, in turn, are affected by the characteristics of the context within which they act, that means by the norms, rules and culture prevailing in the environment. In such circumstances, solving an ethical dilemma, applying moral concepts to organizations, became even more complex.

Not surprising, a strong struggles still remain in the field of Business Ethics among who – both scholars and practitioners – try to identify the drivers of ethical behavior and the way they may be managed in order to solve ethical problems at both corporate and systemic levels.

The Individual Level: The Ethical Decision Making Process Within the Organizations

As already noted, any ethical decision begins with the individual claimed at solving a given ethical dilemma. In general, people face ethical dilemmas every day, that is to say they apply their own moral standards to the situations and to the issues they ought to solve. In doing this, people usually refer to the values and beliefs they have learned, since they were children and that they have developed over the time, thanks to the experience.

Values and beliefs, as well as norms about the kinds of actions considered morally *right* or *wrong* belong to the set of moral standards or moral norms (Crane, 2000; Parker, 1998). The last ones distinguish from ethics by providing for the set rules according to which a given behavior is evaluated (as ethical or not) (Canestrino, 2008).

All individuals and communities have some kinds of moral standards, a basic sense of *right* or *wrong* in relation to particular activities. At first, they are typically absorbed within family, friends and societal influences like schools, church and associations. Later personal experience, learning and intellectual improvement allow individuals to evaluate and revise their own moral standards, as well as to develop new ones (Velasquez, 2012; Trevino and Nelson, 2011).

A lot of authors (Jones, 1991; Dubinski and Loken, 1989; Trevino, 1986; Hunt and Vitell, 1986; Rest, 1986; Kohlberg, 1976, 1969) examined the reasoning process by which individuals apply their own moral standards to the ethical dilemma they have to face, finally engaging in a given behavior. Among them, an important explanation comes from the moral reasoning research by Lawrence Kohlberg (1976), namely by his theory for Cognitive Moral Development[2].

Kohlberg's cognitive moral development model proposes that moral reasoning develops sequentially through three broad levels - Pre-conventional, Conventional and Post-conventional levels - each composed of two different stages (see table 2). By moving from the first level to the third one, individuals are aware of the reasons lying below their own, but they cannot comprehend reasoning more than one stage above their own.

At the pre-conventional level, individuals are very self-centered and view ethical rules as imposed from outside the self. Both the 1th and the 2nd stages seem to re-call the moral reasoning developed by children in their first age, when avoiding the punishment or gaining what they want (children's needs satisfaction) suggest for the right thing to do. In such circumstances, the individual is concerned with the concrete consequences of his actions, trying to avoid the penalties or to achieve personal interests. Concern for personal rewards and satisfaction become into particular consideration in the stage 2. As Trevino and Nelson (2011) note a small percentage of adults never advance beyond this stage.

At conventional level (including stage 3 and 4), the individual is still externally focused on others, but he is less self-centered than before. This is the case of the older children or younger adolescents living up by adhering to what is expected by their family, peer groups and society. Conformity to roles and the expectations of relevant others is significant in the stage 3, since peoples want firstly to be liked, though well of and approved by those close to them. The perspective broadens at stage 4 when right

Table 2. Kohlberg's Cognitive Moral Development

LEVELS	DRIVERS OF THE INDIVIDUAL'S MORAL DEVELOPMENT
LEVEL I - PRE-CONVENTIONAL	
Stage 1: Punishment and Obedience Orientation	Punishment Avoidance
Stage 2: Instrumental Purpose and Exchange	Getting Self-interest Rewards
LEVEL II – CONVENTIONAL	
Stage 3: Interpersonal Concordance Orientation	Getting Social Approval
Stage 4: Instrumental and Relative Orientation	Conforming to social order and authority (societal legitimization)
LEVEL III – POST-CONVENTIONAL	
Stage 5: Social Contract Orientation	Pursuing balance between societal good and individual rights
Stage 6: Universal Moral Principles Orientation	Following inner moral principle of right and justice

Our adaptation by Kohlberg (1969)

and wrong are based on loyalty to one's nation or society. At this stage persons recognize that rules and laws often exist for good reasons, and that following and respecting them is necessary for the wealth of the whole societal system.

At the post-conventional level (stage 5 and 6) people finally no longer accept values and norms of their group of reference in a simple way – be it family, peer group or society. They develop beyond the identification with others' expectations, rules, and laws to make decisions more autonomously. At stage 5 people become aware that all moral standards may be relative and are willing to question the law and to consider changing it for socially useful purposes. At stage 6 individuals, finally, look at the ethical principles of right and justice as criteria for evaluating the existing socially accepted norms and values.

The Cognitive Moral Development is useful to understand how individuals' moral capacity may develop, even in the field of business, that means even when ethical dilemmas concern business issues (Trevino, 1986). Kohlberg's theory of moral development has been extended by Trevino (1986) and by Jones (1991) to explain and predict the ethical decision making in organizations. Particularly, in her *Person-Situation Interactionist Model*, Trevino (1986) posits that the ethical decision making of the individuals within the organizations is explained by the interaction of individual variables (ego strength, field dependence and locus of control) and situational components (arising from the immediate job context and from the broaden organizational culture). More particularly, while individuals' decision, about what is right and what is wrong, depends on the stage of his own moral development (as it has been defined by Kohlberg), ethical behavior is affected by additional individual and situational moderators.

Following Trevino (1986), individuals' ethical decision making may be pictured as a multiple steps process aiming at solving a given ethical dilemma. In the first step (cognition), people advance a moral judgment according to their stage of moral development; after this they directly engage in a given behavior, that may be ethical or un-ethical (see figure 1).

Both individual and situational moderating factors, therefore, affect the consistency between the moral behavior and the moral judgment, that means between action and thought. At this step, moderators play a very important role causing un-ethical (or ethical) behavior, despite the previous moral evaluation[3].

Since moral actions always take place in a given social environment, they are the output, not only of the individuals' characteristics, but also of the interaction between individuals and environment (Higgins et al., 1984). According to the underlined point of views, Situational Moderating Factors – job context, organizational culture and characteristic of work – reasonably influence the individuals' ethical behavior, with the managers at Kohlberg's conventional level influenced to a greater extent (Trevino, 1986).

For the purpose of the writers, Organizational Culture[4] plays, among the others, a very important role.

Organizational Culture does not only moderate the cognition/behavior relationship (as it is showed in figure 1), but it also affects the cognitive moral development by providing for the collective norms about what is right or wrong. Even if Trevino (1986) has chatted the point somewhere in her paper, she never explicitly exploited the way organizational values and beliefs affect the individuals moral reasoning. At this step (according to the opinion of the writers), organizational culture moves individuals' orientation towards legitimization and approval by the other members belonging to the same organization: conforming to organizational goals and purposes may inspire, therefore, both the moral judgment and the undertaken actions.

Trevino's model was extended by Jones in 1991. The author particularly examined the impact that the characteristics of the ethical issue itself (labelled as moral intensity) have on the ethical decision making of the individuals within the organizations.

Figure 1. Interactionist model of ethical decision making in organizations (Trevino, 1986)

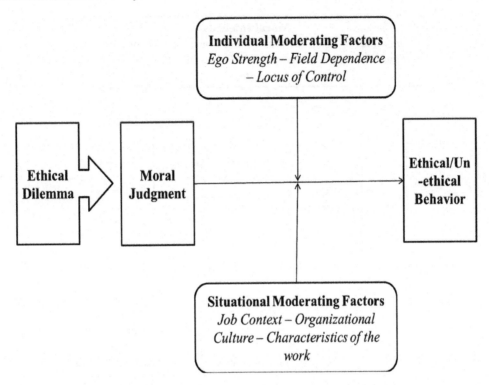

Figure 2 depicts Jones' model for ethical decision making. Individual Moderators and Situational Moderators (as they have been defined by Trevino) were added to the original model in order to get a wider understanding of the process.

Recognizing the moral issue is the starting point of the whole process. In order to identify it, individuals should, at first, recognize that they are moral agents and, secondly, that their actions affect the others. It doesn't mean, nevertheless, that people who fail in recognizing a moral issue do not make a decision, but that they do it by employing a different mental reasoning, like, for example, economic rationality. After having recognized the existence of a moral issue, people develop their own moral judgment. Jones explicitly incudes an additional step (between 2 and 4) whereby the decision maker establishes a moral intent before engaging in behavior. But central to the issue-contingent model is the notion of Moral Intensity, the last one never examined in the previous contributions about the topic.

Moral Intensity[5] is a construct able to capture the extent of issue-related moral imperative in a given situation. It is likely to vary substantially from issue to issue, with a few issues achieving high levels and many issues achieving low levels. Jones (1991) supports the idea that Moral Intensity positively relates to the moral decision making and behavior: the higher it is, the more sophisticated is the people's moral reasoning and the more frequent is their engagement in ethical behavior. The reason is quite simple: moral reasoning usually takes time and energy - to gather facts, to apply moral principles and to develop a moral judgment – thus moral agents economize their efforts and make use of external cues when perceiving a low stake for the issue they are dealing with (Taylor, 1975).

Depending on the above, Moral Intensity may be considered as a new moderating variable that adds to the Individual and Situational Moderating Factors introduced by Trevino (1986). Compared to these

Figure 2. The Issue- Contingent Model (our adaptation by Jones, 1991)

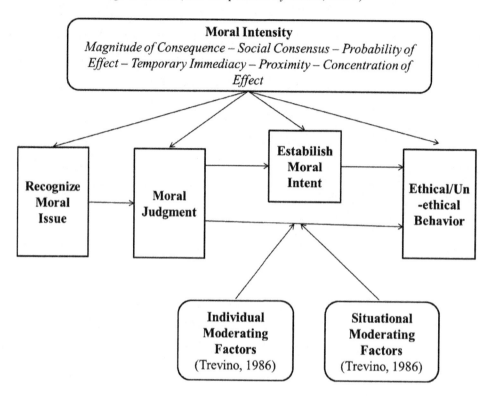

last ones, however, Moral Intensity is supposed to shape the recognition of the ethical issue, as well as the development of the moral judgment, thus suggesting for a revision of Kohlberg's theory. Even if discussing the effectiveness of the cognitive theory within the field of contingency model is not the aim of this paper, opportunities for future investigation may be underlined mainly referring to the development of a more comprehensive framework about the issue.

The Corporate Level: Understanding CSR

At corporate level Business Ethics deals with what a given organization may do or not, thus belonging to the field of the so-called Corporate Social Responsibility (CSR).

Carroll (1991) portrayed four components of CSR in his "Pyramid of CSR". The basic building block begins with firm's economic performance; then business is expected to respect the law, and after that, there is the business' responsibility to be ethical. At its most fundamental level, there is firm' obligation to do what is right, just, and fair, and to avoid or minimize harm to stakeholders (employees, consumers, the environment, and others). Finally, business is expected to be a good corporate citizen. This is captured in the philanthropic responsibility, according to which business is likely to support the social community and to improve the quality of life.

In summary, adopting a social responsible behavior means that firm should strive to make profits, obey the law, be ethical, and be a good corporate citizen. Similarly, according to the stakeholder perspective (Freeman and Evan, 1990; Freeman and Gilbert, 1988; Freeman 1984;), firms should go beyond profits' maximization and the shareholders' returns.

The proposed perspectives contrasted the classical economic argument - mainly sustained by Milton Friedman - that management has the only responsibility to maximize the profits of its owners or shareholders. Against the classical economic perspective, many scholars highlight the advantages of CSR. The adoption of CSR practices allows firms to achieve success by means of new products and technologies (Hedstrom et al., 1998); costs may be reduced and risks diminished (Hart and Milstein, 2003); firm's image improves with positive effects on firm's reputation and its market position (Jenkins, 2006). Within the same field of research, Lopez-Perez M.V. et al. (2009) identified the existence of a positive relationship between the adoption of social responsible practices and firms' R&D expenditures: the development of CSR practices may particularly affect investment decisions, and especially those related to R&D, lastly shaping firm' propensity to innovate.

Depending on the emerging changes, commitments to CSR has been soon interpreted as a global trend, as it is also supported by the growing number of international standards, such as ISO, GRI and the UN Global Compact, or, by the global span of company rating agencies such as the Dow Jones Sustainability Index.

Yet working against the trend toward global standardization is the fact that CSR depends on socio-political, national, cultural and other contextual factors (Halme, et al. 2009).

Matten and Moon (2004) were among the first scholars to theorize about the relationship between CSR and the wider national contexts. In their paper about "implicit" and "explicit" CSR, the authors conceptualize the differences between CSR in the United States and Europe, by referring to their institutional systems - that means to political, financial, educational and cultural systems (Matten and Moon, 2008)[6]. The context-dependency of CSR, therefore, is not surprising. It belongs to the wider discussion about the interplay between the contextual factors of a given environment and firms' ethical behavior.

In line with this perspective and following the leitmotiv of the proposed paper, the writers support the idea that, even at corporate level, both the notion of "good – or even bad – doing" and the propensity of firms to adhere to social responsible practices are culturally determined.

The Systematic Level: Utilitarianism vs. Deontology

At a wider level, Business Ethics deals with the morality of laws and norms, of economic and social systems, as well as of the governments' decisions and actions.

Business ethicists routinely deal with issues that have very broad economic and political significance, especially given the controversies that continue to rage over the appropriate role that the market should play in a democratic society, the power exercised by corporations within the public sphere, and the way that the vicissitudes of the labor market affects the life chances of individuals (Heath et al., 2010). Within this field, business ethicists are used to adopt tools and concepts developed within political philosophy in the attempt to answer to questions about the justifiability of the capitalist system or the national economic prosperity (Jennings and Velasquez, 2015; Donaldson, 2001): Locke's defense of private property as a natural right; Smith's *Theory of Moral Sentiments*[7]; Hume's and Mill's ideas about the morality of the developing free-enterprise economic system, but also Marx's[8] attack to the capitalism provide for the theoretical background of discussion.

In more recent years, Jennings and Velasquez (2015) examined how ethical values contribute to national economic prosperity, by widening the concept of "ethical wealth of nation" introduced by Donaldson in 2001. According to the authors, national economic performance increases every time political economy and institutions inspire to some ethical factors, namely fairer access to opportunities, better executed government, internalized aspirational morality and respect for civil society.

Even without neglecting the relevance of the mentioned contribution, the writers' opinion is that it lacks in providing any suggestions about the way institutions may act in an ethical manner at a more practical level.

What does happen, for example, when institutions or governments have to decide between conflicting moral standards? How do institutions or governments decide in such circumstance? Which kind of interests do prevail when individual or organizational interests contrast with economic or social ones?

When business ethics moves outside the individual or outside the organizational level, a lot of political actions find their own justification in the principle of economic survival, sounding morally repugnant for many. The reality is that there is no quick way to find solution to an ethical dilemma mainly when it involves the society to its larger extent. One example of the ethical dilemma that institutions had been - and are still - called to solve is provided by the experience of ILVA in Italy.

The ILVA case clearly reveals that the fair balance between the right to health and the protection of environment, on the one hand, and the right to work and production needs, on the other one, is very difficult to achieve (for a focus, see Table 3). From an ethical perspective, therefore, the Italian government's decision to allow ILVA to resume its steel production (Law Decree No. 207 of 3th December 2012) in spite of magistracy prohibition could be questioned about its inner "morality".

Table 3. ILVA's ethical dilemma

ILVA is the biggest steel production plant in Italy employing about 12,000 people and accounting for 75 per cent of the economic production in Taranto province.
Since 1997 the ILVA steel plant in Taranto was considered as "area at high risk of environmental crisis"; in the following years, the emergency situation in the territory of Taranto has become more and more evident, with serious consequences for health and environment. Surveys commissioned by the Court of Taranto, as well as studies carried out by public bodies and NGOs have shown heavy pollution of air, soil, surface and ground waters in the neighboring areas of the steel plant.
In June 2010, the Mayor of Taranto issued an ordinance stating that children should not play in Tamburu public gardens because of the presence of dioxin traces and other pollution particles. In 2012 the judicial authority ordered the closure of the plant's blast furnaces. But on the 3th of December 2012 the Italian Government issued the Law Decree No. 207 (the so called "Save ILVA Decree", then converted into Law No. 231), on "urgent measures to protect public health, the environment and employment levels in the event of a crisis in industrial establishments of strategic national interest", which allowed ILVA to continue the production activity and, at the same time, imposed to upgrade, within 36 months, the plant according to the requirements set out in the review of the Integrated Environmental Authorization (IEA).
The judge for preliminary investigations at the Court of Taranto and the Court of Taranto raised questions of constitutionality of Articles 1 and 3 of the "Save ILVA Decree"; however, the Constitutional Court ruled against both complaints.
ILVA employs thousands of people in Italy and the consequences of the potential closure or liquidation of steel plants would be dramatic. Moreover, the reduction of the steel production would also have significant effects on the whole Italian industry system. In this sense, State plays an essential role in order to guarantee national strategic capabilities and jobs, as well as the protection of fundamental rights enshrined in the Constitutions and in the Charter of Fundamental Rights of the European Union.
In spite of this, a critical issue belongs to the impact that ILVA's production for the environment and public health, as well as for agriculture and tourism.
ILVA is one of the European's biggest responsible in terms of greenhouse gas emissions. According to the Report of the European Agency for the Environment (2011), ILVA is the second most air polluting industrial facility in Italy. The presence of an un-healthy environment finds also support in the growing number of mortality rates and cancer diseases for both women and men. Agriculture was also affected in a negative way: emissions of dioxins (benzoapyrene and other cancer-causing chemicals) have poisoned fishing and farmland for miles around, with serious damages to export activities. As a consequence, the cultivation of mussels in the Mar Piccolo Bay of Taranto was banned in 2011 due to the pollution by dioxin. For the same reason, breeding and free pasture were prohibited in uncultivated areas within a radius of 20 kilometers from the industrial area. The impact on the tourism sector should also be taken into account. Taranto is a city with a great potential to attract tourists. However, the news in the international and national press on water pollution, soil contamination and air pollution caused by the ILVA's emissions have hampered, together with other reasons, the local tourism development.

Source: *Lucifora, A., Bianco, F. & Vagliasindi G.M. (2015)*. Environmental crime and corporate mis-compliance: A case study on the ILVA steel plant in Italy. Study in the framework of the EFFACE research project. Catania: University of Catania

ILVA case involves the relationship between judiciary, administrative and legislative powers, in order to establish the authority to be responsible in determining the balance between the protection of health and the environment on the one hand, and the public interest to the continuity of production and to employment on the other one. This balance is extremely difficult to achieve.

Within this field, philosophers have been wrestling with ethical dilemmas and moral decision making for centuries. As result, some important theories and principles have been identified to guide the individuals' choices, as well as organizations' and institutions' decisions. One set of theories were categorized as consequentialist and, among them, Utilitarianism (Bentham 1789; Mill, 1910) is probably the best-known theory. According to Utilitarianism actions and policies should be evaluated on the basis of the benefits and costs they produce for everyone in the society, that means that an ethical decision should maximize benefits to society and minimize harms.

In the empirical evidence of ILVA, the safeguard of the actual level of employment was evaluated as the best solution for everyone in the society (basing on the government's costs-benefits analysis). It is worth to mention that over the last twenty-five years, Italy already experienced the crisis of the large factory model and that the actual economic emergence (that has affected not only Italy, but all the Europe) requires for new actions, defensive of national competitiveness. By the contrast, environmental and health damages claim for a new way to evaluate both the costs and the benefits of alternative decisions, by taking into account, for the first time, the value of people's life and of their well-being.

Opposite to the Utilitarianism there is the Deontological Approach.

Rather than focusing on consequences, deontologists base their decisions on broad, abstract universal ethical principles or values such as honesty, fairness, loyalty, rights, justice, responsibility, compassion, and respect for human beings (Trevino and Nelson, 2011) According to some deontological approaches, certain moral principles are binding, regardless of the consequences: it means, therefore, that some actions would be considered wrong even if the consequences of the actions are good; by the contrast some actions would be considered right in spite of their negative consequences. It is like to say that certain rules or principles are morally right per se.

But how does a deontologist determine what rule, principle, or right to follow?

The most satisfactory foundation of moral rights is provided by Immanuel Kant (1785) in his *Groundwork of the Metaphysics of Morals*.

According to Kant good will is exercised by acting according to moral duty/law. The moral law consists of a set of moral maxims which are categorical in nature. A maxim is simply the reason that a people has to do something in a certain situation. This maxim becomes a universal law only if every person chooses to do the same thing, for the same reason, in the same situation.

Take the example of taking away the sand form the Pink Beach, in Italy. The Pink Beach is located in Budelli, a very small island of the La Maddalena Archipelago, in the northern of Sardina Region (Italy). Budelli has an area of just 1.6 km². Although its real name is "Cala di Roto", the popular name "spiaggia rosa" (Pink Beach) is given by the particular sand composition, thanks to a lot of skeletal remains of small, pink foraminifera, called Miniacina miniacea.

This sand is very pretty, so one immediately wants to take away a little bit of it to home, as a souvenir.

Using the formula of the universal law (categorical imperative), let's imagine the scenario if everyone were to adopt the maxim of taking away the pink sand from the beach, whenever he wishes. Do any irrationalities/contradictions arise from the adoption of such a maxim as universal law? Certainly, if everyone were to do this the beach would be damaged in a very short time, contrasting with the original reason for which you desire the sand (its beauty and uniqueness).

Unfortunately not all the people have equal moral rights or show as much respect for the protected interests of the others as they want others show for their own. In the example of the Pink Beach, Kant's categorical imperative failed in shaping individuals' behavior, so that in the 90s, thousand people came to this beach during summer, taking away the sand for souvenirs.

At a wider level, nevertheless, Kant's imperative seems to have well guided the institutions. These last ones decided to protect the beach from the theft of sand, by closing it to swimming and walking. The Pink Beach is nowadays the most protected zone and the flag of the National Park of La Maddalena: no one can reach anymore the beach due to the fact that the tourists were taking away the sands.

By this, the right of all human beings to enjoy a natural resource of unique beauty has been saved.

BUSINESS ETHICS AND CULTURE: UNDERSTANDING THE LINKAGE BETWEEN CULTURAL VALUES, MORALITY AND ETHICAL BEHAVIOUR

As already noted, many scholars recognize the deep linkage between culture and the establishment of the moral standards, as well as between culture and individual/organizational ethical behavior (Vitell et al., 2013; Husted, 2000; Cohen et al., 1996; Wines and Napier, 1992).

Culture may be considered as the set of driving-rules and core believes that develop in a society over time and that drive both individuals and firms' choices (Hofstede, 1980; Schein, 2004)[9].

As Resick et al. (2011) report, in business world when members of different cultures are faced with ethical dilemmas, individuals will frequently use their own cultural value systems to make ethical decisions. Moreover, cultural differences were found to impact individuals' ethical reasoning skills, with national culture recognized as having impact on various stages of the process (Rausch et al., 2014).

According to the above, culture may particularly influence *Business Ethics*, by

1. Shaping the assumption about what is right or wrong;
2. Influencing the individuals' moral reasoning (even within organizations) and, finally, by
3. Affecting the consistency between individual/organizational behavior and the moral standards that prevail in a given context.

Shaping the Assumption About What Is Right or Wrong

Right and wrong, just and unjust derive their meaning and true value from the attitudes of a given culture: some ethical standards are culture-embedded, and one should not be surprised to find that a given act, considered quite ethical in one culture, may be looked upon with disregard in another, nor that culture is also responsible for the hierarchy of values prevailing in each area (Canestrino et al., 2016; Canestrino, 2008).

Not surprising, some practices, like for example, software piracy, are differently perceived at global level, thus resulting in a different size from country to country.

It doesn't mean, however, that economic factors, like per capita income, unemployment's rate or the presence of foreign direct investments do not affect users' propensity for illegally copying and downloading software. As Marron and Steel (2000) pointed out, developed economies have more protection on intellectual property rights, with high-income countries showing lower piracy rates. Similarly, using cross-sectional dataset to investigate the relationship between income inequality and software piracy rates, Andres (2006) also found that efficiency of judicial system is a major factor when explaining the cross-national variations in software piracy rates. In 2007, Yang and Sonmenz found, not only that some culture variables, such as education expenditure, religions, and individualism could explain the most cross-national variations of software piracy rates, but also that a negative relationship between the gross national income (GNI) and software piracy rates exists.

Following researches' results a lot of drivers seem able to affect software piracy rates: nevertheless culture plays an important role in shaping the perception that users' have about of the *morality* of the mentioned practice, as it is showed in Table 4.

Influencing the Individuals' Moral Reasoning

After moral standards have established in a given context (be it a social or an organizational one), behaving ethically depends on the individuals' ability to recognize that ethical dilemma, or an ethical issue, exists.

Marta and Singhapakdi (2005) found systematic differences in the perception of ethic between groups of people from the U.S. and Thailand, since American managers were more likely to perceive unethical marketing behavior as a serious issue, than the Thai counterparts. From a cultural perspective, Thais are more collectivist than Americans and more accepting of enduring power differentials. This is the reason why "Thai managers do not perceive themselves as independent moral agents in work situations" (Jones, 1991, p. 390) and are less likely to discern the moral intensity in a given ethical scenario. This would, in turn, explain their lower perception of moral intensity.

The cultural dimension Masculinity vs Femininity also impact on the key issue of Business Ethics (Vitell et al., 2013). Societies that are characterized as masculine support individuals in getting success and ambitious goals, thus fostering the adoption of competitive behaviour. By the contrast, in feminine culture inter-personal relationship, quality of life and concern for the weak are evaluated to a great extent (Hofstede, 1991, 1980). The mentioned diversities significantly contribute to one's engagement in unethical behavior, simply because decision-makers coming from some cultures (as it is the case of masculine cultures) do not "perceive" certain ethical problems, that are not defined by their culture as involving ethics. As a consequence, businesspeople coming from countries characterised by a high masculinity score, like Austria or Italy, seem to be less influenced by ethical problems than businesspeople coming from feminine countries, like Netherlands and Sweden (Roxas and Stoneback, 2004; Robertson, 2002).

In field of CSR, Arslan (2001) sustained the existence of a strong relationship between the perception that individuals have of social responsibility and their Achievement Orientation[10]. The author compared the perception of social responsibility by English, Irish and Turkish managers, finding that a high level in the Achievement Orientation (that mainly characterizes Anglo-Saxon culture) encourages short terms and opportunistic behaviour, thus limiting the individuals' social responsibility concerns. Conversely, a low level of Power Orientation, that characterise, for example, some of Muslim Turkish culture, may lead to a greater sensitivity towards ethical achievements and CSR.

In more recent years, Rausch et al. (2014) investigated the relationship between cultural dimensions and the ethical decision making process in two groups of students form U.S. and German universities, by focusing on the perception that people have about moral intensity (as it has been defined by Jones in 1991) and its constituent parts. According to the research's results, the more individualistic nationals result in a superior ability to detect some components of moral intensity, namely probability of effect, temporary immediacy and concentration of effect. It means, therefore, that people from U.S. pay close attention to how many parts may be harmed, the probability of the damage and the amount of time until

Table 4. Software piracy around the world: A cultural perspective

Gophal and Sanders (2000) define software piracy as the mechanism by which individuals purchase a copy of the software at the market price and make copies in order to distribute them to the other group members.

Statistics on software piracy developed by the Business Software Alliance (BSA) provide international estimates on the size of the phenomenon. The BSA has been studying global trends in PC software piracy for more than ten years.

According to the collected information, reported into the ninth edition of the annual global piracy study, the global piracy rate for PC software hovered 42% in 2011. The commercial value of this shadow market of pirated software climbed from $58.8 billion in 2010 to $63.4 billion in 2011, a new record, propelled by PC shipments to emerging economies where piracy rates are highest.

The reason for the underlined growth lies into the expansion of PC market into higher piracy countries that has been faster than that into the lower piracy ones. The gap in spending on legal software in emerging and mature economies is stubbornly persistent. China, for example, spends less than a quarter of the amount that Russia, India, and Brazil spend on a per-PC basis, and just 7% of the total amount that the United States spends. The data below shows the software piracy rates recorded for the different geographical areas at worldwide level.

*Software Piracy Rate (*BSA Global Software Piracy Study 2011, Ninth Ed.*)*

	2011	2010
Asia Pacific	60%	60%
Central and Eastern Europe	62%	64%
Latin America	61%	64%
Middle East and Africa	58%	58%
North America	19%	21%
Western Europe	32%	33%
TOTAL WORLDWIDE	42%	42%
EUROPEAN UNION	33%	35%
BRIC countries*	70%	71%

*BRIC Countries are Brazil, Russia, India, and China

Within North America, the United States rate for software piracy is 19% of the total market, with Puerto Rico showing the highest level in the area (42%); it increases to 32% in Western Europe where the rate runs from the 20% of Luxembourg to the 61% of Greece; both Central and Eastern Europe and Latin America score surpasses 60% with the highest percentages reached by Georgia and Moldova (91% and 90% respectively) and by Venezuela (88%).

From a cultural perspective, many authors (Yoo et al., 2014; Swinyard et al., 2013; Shin et al., 2004; Moores, 2003; Lu, 2001) agree with the idea that software piracy is affected by cultural issues, since people coming from different countries consider copyright and the intellectual property in a very different way.

In the former Soviet Union, for example, Capitalism has substituted the State as the authority that tries to impose norms and regulations on intellectual property. Therefore the Soviets have developed a growing fear toward the control on the spread of knowledge, thus considering free transfer of ideas as an important value.

In Africa, where the society developed thanks to un-written culture for centuries and where artistic expression was mainly based on religion, copyright is considered a colonial concept, too abstract and contradictory. Any control over information is seen as an attempt by the richer areas to maintain the old colonial system.

In China and other Asian countries intellectual property is, finally, interwoven with the cultural make-up, which for two thousand years has considered imitation as the necessary basis for learning and transferring knowledge from generation to generation. In this context Confucianism inspires collective ideals in which individuals are asked to share their know-how (Canestrino, 2008).

In the attempt to understand the linkage between software piracy and cultural values prevailing in a given society, Yoo et al., (2014) explored the way differences on Hofstede's cultural indexes (Hofstede, 1980) can affect behaviors by comparing two countries – Vietnam and Korea – with similar level of COLL and masculinity but different levels of PD and UA. The importance of this study is in its revelation of these two factors as the most influential indexes in determining attitudes to piracy in the examined countries. Moores (2003) reported that more individualist and richer a society became, less software piracy rate develops; according to Donaldson (1996), Confucianism leads people to share their own knowledge with society, thus prompting some Chinese, or other Asian firms, to consider intellectual property as a symbol of Western countries technological monopoly; according to Shin et al. (2004) in collectivistic cultures software is naturally considered a resource to share with community in order to increase the overall group welfare. Not surprising, high-tech, high-collectivistic countries such as Indonesia (86% piracy rate), China (77%), and Thailand (72%) are extensively involved in piracy activities.

All the mentioned countries report for low level of IND, respectively 20 for both China and Thailand (lower than the Asian rank of 23) and 14 for Indonesia (lowest world score for IND). It means, therefore, that all the referred countries characterize for high levels of COLL.

COLL is often assimilated to utilitarianism, the last one strives for the greatest good to the greatest number of people, thus more utilitarian people are, more they are involved in software piracy (Gophal and Sanders, 1998).

a given impact is felt. Despite its limits, the mentioned work provides for a widening of the existing literature about the topic, suggesting a new explanation that takes into account, for the first time, the complex links between culture, moral intensity and individual's awareness about ethical dilemmas.

Affecting the Consistency Between Individual/Organizational Behavior and the Moral Standards That Prevail in a Given Context

After an ethical dilemma has been perceived, individuals usually develop their moral judgment (according to the moral reasoning process that has been previously described) in order to finally engage in an ethical behavior. At this step, Organizational Culture has been already considered an important moderating factor in Trevino's model (1986), even if the author never exploited the way culture affects peoples' final decision to act.

Particularly, the cultural dimension IND vs COLL seems to affect the individuals' ethical behavior to a great extent. As Husted (2000) noted, in individualistic cultures, like U.S., individuals see themselves as independent from the collective group within which they are embedded and are used to pursue their own interests. Moral standards develop in accordance with the prevailing values, reducing the gap between the personal interests (private self) and the collective ones (public self): autonomy and self-realization rise to moral principles, thus people are more likely to behave in accordance with judgments previously formulated. Following the above, a greater consistency between behavior and moral judgement exists in individualistic cultures rather than in collectivistic ones.

In exploring the importance of gender across cultures in ethical decision-making, Roxas and Stoneback (2004) highlighted that individuals - both men and women – embedded in masculine environments are more likely to break the rules. By the contrast feminine cultures inspire the respect of rules, thanks to peoples' tendency to emphasize the establishment of harmonious relationships and to do things well. Following the authors' considerations, therefore, it may be reasonably suggested that a greater consistency establishes between individuals' behavior and moral norms in feminine cultures than in masculine societies. The propensity of a given moral player to act consistently with previously defined standards has been also widely investigated at organizational level, in the field of CSR.

Researches in CSR have identified remarkable differences between the companies from different countries. In a comparative understanding of CSR, Matten and Moon (2008) pointed out that U.S. corporations usually made explicit their attachment to CSR, whereas European business responsibility tends to be more implicit. The mentioned differences are, even partially, due to the diversities between U.S. and European cultural systems, which generate different assumptions about society, business and government.

In U.S., CSR has been embedded in a system that leaves more incentives and opportunities for corporations to take comparatively explicit responsibility, than in the European one. As a consequence, U.S. firms usually adhere to voluntary corporate programs and strategies as a response to the stakeholders pressure; they often engage alliances with other corporations, with governmental and non-governmental organizations.

By the contrast, European firms do not explicit devote to CSR, mainly because of the embeddedness of the corporations role within the wider formal and informal institutions for society's interests and concerns. The cultural dimension IND also plays an important role in shaping explicit CSR. As the authors themselves noted, "Institutions encouraging individualism and providing discretion to private economic actors in liberal markets would be considered national systems in which one would expect to find strong elements of explicit CSR" (Matten and Moon, 2008, p. 410).

Referring to the linkage between Hofstede's cultural dimensions[11] and CSR, the researches' findings often contrast, mainly because of the differences in the adopted methodology, as well as in the sample (ex.: firms' characteristics, multinational dimension, etc.) used to develop the studies.

Peng et al. (2014), for example, suggest that all the four Hofstede's dimensions can predict firm's CSR engagement. Their particularly find that IND and UA positively relate with firm's CSR commitment, while PD and MAS negatively influence it.

UA particularly refers to the extent to which people feel threatened by uncertain or ambiguous situations (Hofstede, 1994). Strong uncertainty avoidance countries usually have more extensive written codes of conduct and laws that exactly stats what is allowed and what is not. For example, environmental legislation is much more extensive in countries high on this dimension (Katz, et al., 2001). In low uncertainty avoidance cultures, the ethical decision-making process and criteria are likely to be based on the interpretation of rules. As Peng et al. (2014) themselves noted:

In cultures stressing high uncertainty avoidance, people place great importance on keeping everything accountable or certain. As a business strategy that helps firms to develop long term sustainable relationship with its stakeholders, engaging CSR can be one of the effective ways to reduce the environmental uncertainties of the firms (p. 4).

BUSINESS ETHICS IN A GLOBAL ENVIRONMENT: WHEN DOES "MORAL GAP" ARISE?

All the referred literary contributions show the relevant influence that national culture has on the definition of moral standards, on the perception of business ethic issues, as well as on the consistency between moral judgment and ethical behavior, at both individual and organizational standpoint.

Since values and beliefs differ at worldwide level, new practical issues get up in response to both globalization and the growing international competition, thus affecting the complexity of academic inquiry about Business Ethics.

Ethical dilemmas may particularly arise every time firms must comply with multiple and sometimes conflicting moral standards, as in the case they internationalize countries with varying practices (Canestrino, 2008). In such circumstance, a so-called "moral gap" establishes, impelling the international players to choose which rules, "domestic" instead of "host", sometimes conflicting, they ought follow.

To illustrate, United States law forbids companies from paying bribes either domestically or overseas; however, in other parts of the world, bribery is a customary, accepted way of doing business (Jennings, 2000). Similar problems can occur with regard to child labor, employee safety, work hours, wages, discrimination, and environmental protection laws.

What does it happen, therefore, when international firms invest in those countries where moral standards significantly differ?

Figure 3 shows the two circumstances under which a "moral gap"[12] establishes: the larger the cultural distance among the partners is, the more evident is the "moral gap" when it occurs.

In general, a "moral gap" forms every time:

Figure 3. Moral gap in global environment (our elaboration)

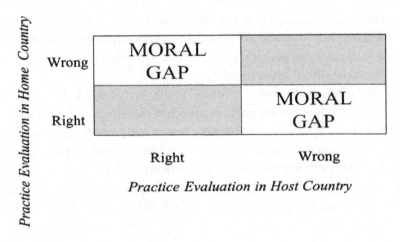

1. What is considered right into the firm's domestic country, is considered wrong into the host one; or
2. What is considered wrong into the firm's domestic country, is considered *right* into the host one (Canestrino, 2007),

    impelling international players to make a choice about the set of moral standards they will conform to.

    "Moral gap" may establish at individual, corporate, as well as at systemic level, every time domestic and host countries (of a given internationalization process) characterize for different and conflicting moral standards.

    At individual level, personal moral standards provide for the background upon which the individuals face an ethical dilemma, when it occurs, finally engaging in a given behavior.

    Imagine, for example, to be an American human resource management. You were chosen to manage a corporate division, located in a poor country where child labor is allowed, in order to execute the corporate firing program. Appalled to find that the subsidiary is using child labor in direct violation of the company's own ethical code, your American boss instructs you to replace the children with adults. By this the company would solve the "moral gap" emerging by the different evaluation of the practice in the home and in the host countries. But you also know that, far to be inspired by real moral principles, the corporate is trying to avoid the damages arising from international activists' protests organized against the company. You finds that a 12-yearold girl work in factory floor: she is an orphan, who is the only breadwinner for herself and her 6-year-old brother, and she would be unable to find another job. If you replace her, probably she should be forced to turns to prostitution (children prostitution – of both of males and females – is a dramatic social problem in the country where the company division locates). What do you decide to do? The moral standards prevailing in the country where you come from suggest you to replace the little girl, but in accordance to the your personal hierarchy of values you feel that refusing to fire the little girl is the only "right" thing to do. It could be damaging for you and your career advancements and the final decision is very difficult to be engaged anyway because of organizational pressures.

    Even at organizational level a "moral gap" may easily arise every time organizations move from national markets to foreign ones, as well as every time MNCs have to manage multicultural units.

What does it happen, for example, when an expatriate manager[13] is sent to a very different cultural context for an international assignment, replacing the local manager? How do employees perceive this change? Does the decision imply ethical concerns? For every expatriates, moving to a new country requires adjusting to local customs, languages and politics. But what happens when certain facets of a culture affect ones' moral or ethical assumptions?

Take as example the practice of "wasta". "Wasta" is the Arabic word used to define the clout, the connections, the influence, pull or favoritism. It is a practice morally accepted in many Middle Eastern countries where peoples with "wasta" acquire prestige, honor, and permits, get jobs, obtain favorable rulings from agencies, get government contracts and benefit from government rules that limit competition. Within the companies, family relationships and social networks can take priority in business decisions, including who gets hired or promoted. In other words, "wasta" is regarded as an intrinsic part of the culture and a way of conducting business across the Arab World (Hooker, 2008), but it is not the same in western countries. Here employers hire, promote and fire the workers on the bases of individual's skills, thus Westerners usually look at "wasta", at best, as favoritism, and at worse, as nepotism.

An American manager sent to a middle eastern division to manage human resources would face the moral gap arising by the contrast between his personal moral standards and the local ones. In such circumstance, in fact, "wasta" would evaluated as wrong by the expatriate even if it is an accepted practice (right) in the host country. In any case, "wasta" should be taken into consideration.

What about the American expatriate manager?

On one case, he could adapt to local "customs". Otherwise, the expatriate could decide to respect his own values by improving the management of employee performance, given that the tight-knit nature of many Middle Eastern business communities makes social or familial relationships very hard to avoid. In making such dramatic changes within a corporation, it is wise to use local trainers who understand the culture and can make the most effective case for the change. Employees may be reluctant to change if they view the effort as simply a way to 'comply' with the corporation's standards. Instead, they may be more receptive if they understand how the new practices are important to their careers and to the overall competitiveness or business mission of the company, without violating local customs or traditions.

At wider level, a "moral gap" may also deal with the morality of laws and norms, of economic and social systems, and with governments' decisions and actions (see ILVA case study).

Even at systematic level, different moral standards establish according to the prevailing values and beliefs, translating, not only into a different regulation of "questionable" practices, but also to a different evaluation (from a moral perspective) of the same. Take as example, the so-called Reproductive Tourism (RT) and its diffusion at European level.

RT is refers to a practice according to which people travel across national borders, in order to access to reproductive technologies and services, such as in vitro fertilization (IVF), gamete (sperm and egg) donation, sex selection, surrogacy, and embryonic diagnosis (Martin, 2009).

As Canestrino et al. (2016) reported the phenomenon is not restricted to U.S. or Australia, but it also occurs in Europe, where patients come from France, Germany or Italy travel to Belgium to gain treatments not available at home, like, for example, in vitro fertilization treatments (IVF) with oocyte or sperm donation or fertilization treatments for homosexuals, lesbians, or singles (not allowed in Italy, France and Germany).

Even if belonging to the same sovra-national context (namely EU), diversities in national and local standards allowed the flourish of - sometimes very different - national normative frameworks, fostering a huge debate about the morality of some practices like, for example: gamete donors, surrogacy and fertilization treatments for homosexuals. Within the mentioned debate, the emergence of a dual healthcare system (one for poor and one for rich) represents a key corner.

How do we evaluate the phenomenon and the lack of a uniform system of norms within UE? Is it right to impel people to look for a foreign country to receive medical treatments not allowed at home? What about the individuals who cannot go abroad for treatments, because of the high costs of travel and accommodation expenses? To what extent UE is responsible to grant the same healthcare rights to all European citizens? On the contrary, it would be right imposing to the single nations the adoption of uniform norms in contrast with the local accepted moral standards?

Obviously no "right formula" really exists. International players, be them individuals, organizations or institution, respond to "moral gap" in different ways, with different outcomes, and in doing this they may, alternatively, adopt an absolutist or a relativist approach.

Overcoming "Moral Gaps": The Relevance of Cross-Cultural Sensitivity and Cross-Cultural Negotiating Ability

Referring to the issue, an important premise needs to be pointed out (in the writers' opinion). Adopting an absolutist or e relativistic approach helps international players to make a decision about the rules to be applied every time that a "moral gap" establishes (home country or host country norms). It doesn't mean, therefore, that the "moral gap" reduces, since it mainly depends on the existing diversities among the prevailing values at global level.

Ethical absolutism, which has also been referred to as universalism, dictates that an omnipresent set of standards should be universally applied, being equally valid in all places and times (Qizilbash, 1997).

Ethical absolutism inspires to the deontology, directing that behavior should be evaluated by the same rules regardless of its consequences. Without neglecting the existence of multiple moral standards employed around the world, absolutists strongly believe that all moral principles and actions could be rooted in common universal norms, mainly based on the human beings' requirement of long-term survival (Harmon, 1984).

Cross-cultural ethical researches have provided some support for ethical absolutism. Comparisons about the ethical beliefs prevailing in American and Israeli business managers (Izraeli, 1988), Greek and American business students (Tsalikis and Nwachukwu, 1988), and South African and Australian managers (Abratt et al., 1992) all found that, despite differences in socio-cultural and political factors, ethical beliefs based on moral standards varied very little from culture to culture.

In spite of this, however, neglecting the relevance of cultural diversities may lead to negative consequences for business activities, mainly when international players try to apply norms that contrast with the embedded moral standards and local behavior (Canestrino, 2008). Referring to this issue, a useful example is provided by the "Italian Tax Mores" case study developed by Arthur Kelly in 1983 (See Table 5).

In spite of the reported case study, it has to be noted that adopting an absolutistic approach does not always imply negative consequences for firm. In some occasions, it is the right thing to do in the right moment for do it, as it is clearly showed by the experience of General Motors (GM), in South Africa (Table 6).

Table 5. The risks of Absolutism: Evidence from the Italian tax system

The Italian corporate tax system is very different from the American one, with only very few exceptions. Italian corporations are particular expected to underestimate their real income and profit to get tax facilities. This is the reason why Italian authorities are used to check for corporates' tax declaration and real income, about six months after the annual deadline, arranging a personal meeting with the corporate's representatives, in order to discuss about the discrepancies between the "expected" and "declared" profit.

It has to be noted that the tax amount established by the Italian Tax Department is several times higher than th amount resulted by the corporate's evaluation, since it bases on the assumption that firms always declare less profits than they have really gained. Moreover, the amount of tax paid by the corporate for a given year is supposed to be the starting point for future negotiations, that means the minimum level of taxes that the firm have to pay in the future.

Given the above background, consider the following example: A leading American bank opened a bank subsidiary in a major Italian city. At the end of the first-year activities, the bank was advised by its local lawyers and tax accountants, both from branches of U.S. companies, to fill in its tax declaration according to the "Italian-style" that means to underestimate its profits, before negotiation with local tax authorities.

Despite this, however, the American manager of the subsidiary (at first overseas assignment), refused to do it, mainly because the inconsistency between the Italian and the American practices (the last considered as the best one).

About six months after filling its "American-style" tax declaration, the bank received an "invitation to discuss" notice from the Italian Tax Department. About sixty days after, a tax assessment notice was sent to the bank, requesting a tax amount of approximately three times that shown on the bank's corporate tax declaration. After having refused to accept any kind of suggestion to manage the negotiation, the bank general manager was forced to pay the amount established by the original tax assessment and was soon recalled to the USA in order to be replaced.

Source: *Kelly A. (1983)*. "Case Study – Italian Tax mores". In: Donaldson and Werhane (Eds.), Ethical Issues in Business: A Philosophical Approach (2nd Ed.). Englewood Cliffs: Prentice Hall Inc.

Table 6. Adopting Absolutism against human rights violation

Between the late 1970s and 1980s GM developed significant activities in South Africa, where apartheid still existed, denying the basic political rights to the majority of the non-white population, in contrast with the most universally accepted human rights granted in developed nations (eg.: freedom of association, of speech, of assembly, etc.). At that time, GM adopted what has been called the Sullivan principles, named after Leon Sullivan, a black Baptist minister and a member of GM's board of directors. Sullivan argued that it was ethically justified for GM to operate in South Africa so long as two conditions were fulfilled: first, that the company should not obey the apartheid laws in its own South African operations (a form of passive resistance), and second, that the company should do everything within its power to actively promote the abolition of apartheid laws.

Sullivan's principles were widely adopted by U.S. firms operating in South Africa and their violation of the apartheid laws was ignored by South African government, which clearly did not want to antagonize important foreign investors.

Source: *Fisher, C.M., & Lovell, A. (2009)*. Business Ethics and values: Individual, corporate and international perspectives. Harlow: Pearson Education

Opposite to absolutism, ethical relativism emphasizes the idea that no principles are better than others, refusing the chance to define any universal norm (De George, 1993). Ethical relativists particularly claim that all values are relative to particular cultural contexts and that no ultimate universal ethical principles exist.

From a managerial perspective, therefore, international players, which inspire to relativism, are usually to adhere and to act in accordance with the host countries rules - almost like performing a "duty" (Beauchamp and Bowie, 2001) - agreeing with the guiding slogan of "When in Rome, do as the Romans do" (Larrison, 1998).

Like absolutism, ethical relativism is also subjected to criticism, to the extent to which it could lead to the acceptance of every practice, whatever a-moral it is: at its extreme, for example, ethical relativism could suggest that using slave labor, in a country, is right if slavery doesn't contrast with the local sense of justice.

Sometimes, far to be inspired by a moral reasoning model, multinationals seems to adhere to the host country moral standards more to get economic advantages, than to respect local culture.

In such circumstances, nevertheless, boycott activities may be arranged against organizations, with negative consequence at both local and global level: a lot of protests and boycott activities have been arranged, for example, against Coca Cola (see Table 7).

Taking into account the mentioned considerations, as well as the negative impacts that may come out by the adoption of both absolutist and relativist approaches for the business, an important premise to successfully act at global level is to not neglect the existence of multiple rules employed around the world, keeping always in mind, however, that these kinds of variables, culture-embedded, must be rooted in a common universal moral standard, the last one inspiring to the basic requirements of human being and of his environment's survival.

But how do international players overcome a "moral gap" when it arises?

Trevino and Nelson (2010) propose a sequence of eight steps to follow when solving an ethical dilemma (Gather the facts; define the ethical issue; identify the affected parties, that means identify the stakeholders; identify the consequences of the decision; identify the obligations; consider one's own character and integrity; think creatively about potential actions; check the gut)[14] that could be applied also to moral gaps resolution. In spite of its inner limits (the eight steps suggest a linear decision-making process, while the ethical decision making is often not linear), the sequence provides for useful suggestions helping to look for alternative solutions that "stay in the middle" between absolutistic and relativistic approaches.

Referring to the "moral gap" of the American manager sent to a subsidiary to replace children from the factories, for example, identify the consequences of the corporate decision could be useful to look for a solution that "save the corporate image" without compromising children rights, at the same time.

In the mentioned example, corporation could sign up an ethical code of conduct to regulate and limit child labor in societies where the lack of social safety net forces children to find a way to make a living to support themselves and/or their families. The code would stipulate that children should not be employed in physically taxing work - such as heavy lifting - should work fewer hours than adults, and receive pay commensurate with the work they are doing and not be seen as a cheap alternative to adult labor.

From a moral perspective, the proposed solution would mean "to bridge" between two contrasting moral standards ("respect individual freedom" in the developed American country vs "support the group

Table 7. Does Relativism pursue "Moral Values"? The boycott activities against Coca-Cola

Coca-Cola is charged to control water resources in a lot of under-developed countries, especially in India. New researches carried out in the Indian states of Rajasthan and Uttar Pradesh show that Coca-Cola's activities negatively impact water resource levels and environmental pollution. In the small and poor village of Kaladera in Rajasthan, water levels have seriously declined since Coca-Cola's arrival in 1999.

Other communities in India that live and work around Coca-Cola's bottling plants are experiencing severe water shortages as well as environmental damage.

Farmers are increasingly unable to irrigate their lands and sustain their crops, putting whole families at risk of losing their livelihoods, and Coca-Cola was unable to retrieve the negative consequences of its activities.

Several groups support Coca-Cola boycott, including the Service Employees International Union (SEIU), UNISON, the largest public service union in Great Britain, and Veterans for Peace. A lot of Universities in Europe and in the United States are now voting to ban Coca-Cola from operating on their campuses because of the company's abuses around the world. In December 2005 the University of Michigan stopped its contract with Coca-Cola because of Company's labor practices in Colombia and environmental impact in India. In the same month, a similar decision was taken by New York University, which accounts for more than 50,000 students. Student activists in the UK are also campaigning to ban Coca-Cola products sales in their campuses and student unions have already voted to end commercial relations at many universities in the U.K.

In Plachimada in the southern state of Kerala (India), Coca-Cola's plant was forced to close down in Mach 2004 after the village council refused to renew the company's license, because of the indiscriminate extraction, use, and contamination of the common groundwater.

Source: *Canestrino and Calvelli (2010)*

necessity" in many under-developed and collectivistic countries) by identifying a "new" common standard, respectful of the opposite positions. This new standard – labelled as "granting children survival" should be up-graded in the hierarchy of moral standards of both domestic and host countries, posing at a higher level.

"Bridging" diversities may be also a good solution (in the opinion of the writers) to solve "moral gap" at both organizational and systematic level.

With reference to the practice of "wasta" in Middle East countries, managers who want to introduce Western business models to the Middle East, cannot simply decree a "no nepotism" policy, in order to avoid the risk to be regarded as naïve or arrogant, and in either case, culturally insensitive. Even when an "alternative solution" to the available options cannot be found, it is important not to make implied value judgments about the practices of other cultures. In such situation could be useful, for example, to sponsor the making changes through a training program for employees that stresses job performance, while factoring in "wasta" or other local customs and practices. Meanwhile, Middle East employers could educate employees from different cultures on how their society values the importance of relationships, including trust and loyalty.

Similarly, at systematic level, managing moral gaps requires a global governance able to develop norms and rules respectful of all citizens' rights, even if the chance to find the right solution for all seems to be more a theoretical exercise than a really feasible option.

Taking into account the above discussion, therefore, cross-cultural sensitivity (Rodrigues, 1997; Schein, 1981) and cross-cultural negotiating abilities are, therefore, necessary to overcome the conflicts every time that values and believes collide and that different moral principles establish at worldwide level. Cross-cultural sensitivity particularly refers to ones' ability to decipher others' values (Rodrigues, 1997; Schein, 1981) and to understand a new environment using the situated and contextual knowledge (Shapiro, et al., 2008). The awareness of and knowledge about cultural differences also belong to the concept, as well as the ability to create trust and commitment among actors coming from in different cultural settings (Canestrino and Magliocca, 2016). Following Salacuse's studies about the ways that culture affects negotiating style (Salucuse, 1998), the cultural negotiating abilities may be reasonably defined as the international player's capacity to better understand and to interpret his counterpart behavior, finding the way to overcome cultural diversities.

Within the field of business ethics, cross-cultural sensitivity and cross-cultural negotiating abilities could support the international players to keenly understand the business environment in which they operate; to recognize cultural expectations and ethical dilemmas; to avoid conflict when possible; to balance the interests of various stakeholders in an ethical way; and to develop strategies for influencing partners.

FUTURE RESEARCH DIRECTIONS

Starting from the literary contributions about *Business Ethics*, on one hand and cultural studies, on the other hand, the chapter proposes a wide understanding of the way cultural dimensions may define different moral standards at worldwide level, affecting also individual, organizational and institutional propensity to adhere them. Despite this, It has been argued that the proposed suggestions do not provide for any simply solution to the ethical dilemmas that arise at global level. *Business Ethics* remains a very complex issue and this paper aims also to provide for a widen cultural-based picture of the phenomenon. Many questions are still un-answered, requiring for future investigations. Among them, it should not to be neglected the fact that even cross-cultural sensitivity and cross-cultural negotiation style themselves affected by culture (Canestrino and Magliocca, 2016; Salacuse, 1998). It means, therefore, that even individuals' ability to prevent and to manage moral gaps is itself cultural-embedded. Accordingly, new researches are necessary in this direction.

CONCLUSION

Both globalization and the growth of international competition have intensified the complexity of academic debate about the topic, mainly because the existing cultural diversities between and among countries. When acting in the global environment, therefore, international players keep in contact with different cultural contexts: every time it happens a "moral gap" may arises, the last one depending on the differences between the moral standards that prevail, respectively in the home and in the host countries. A "moral gap" may particularly arise every time cultural diversities shape the sense of morality of individuals, organizations and institutions as well, that means it may refers to all the three issues investigated within the field of business ethics, requiring for solution.

Managing a "moral gap" is not easy: in doing this, the international players, be them individuals, organizations or institutions - may adopt, alternatively an absolutist, or a relativist approach. According to the first one, they act in accordance with the rules and norms prevailing in their home country. By the contrast, the adoption of a relativistic approach lead the players to observe local rules, so the host countries' moral standards usually prevail in this situation.

As empirical evidences show, however, negative consequences for business may be determined by both absolutist and relativist approaches. Adopting an absolutist perspective usually imply a "cultural insensitiveness" usually followed by negative judgments of both rules and practices that prevail the host countries: home country norms are evaluated right and applied everywhere, regardless the diversities. In such circumstances, conflicts may easily arise mainly because of people reluctance to comply with "foreign" standards and negative consequences for business activities may be determined by the under-evaluation of the local traditions. By the contrast, the adoption of host countries norms, that characterizes the relativist approach, is usually perceived as a way for multinationals to get profits in many under-developing and rising economies, rather than the attempt to solve an emerging ethical dilemma. When it happens, boycott initiatives may be undertaken at global level, even mining the success of business activities.

Taking into account the negative consequences deriving from the adoption of both absolutist and relativist approaches, the chapter finally focus on the way international players may overcome the moral gaps that result from the individual, organizational and systematic level of business ethics.

It's a matter of fact that "moral gaps" cannot be reduced or avoided since, they are deeply rooted in a given culture. In spite of this, multiple actions may be undertaken to find novel and alternative solutions to the available options. These last ones act as "bridge" between contrasting moral norms by identifying "new" common standards, respectful of the opposite positions.

Looking for a trade-off between universal norms, and local particularisms, however, is not easy. In doing this, knowing culture and cultural diversities is a fundamental premise to prevent cultural conflicts (ex-ante), as well as to overcome them (ex post). Cross-cultural sensitivity is, therefore, necessary every time that values and believes collide and different moral principles establish at worldwide level. But being aware of diversities isn't the only premise to effectively manage a mora gap. Cross-cultural negotiating ability, belonging to the player's capacity to understand and to interpret his counterpart behavior is also fundamental for the development of a "new space" of cooperation within which common moral standards may be negotiated among the parties. When established, these standards up-grade in the hierarchy of moral standards that prevail in both domestic and host countries, posing at a higher level, as the output of a common share of ideas.

REFERENCES

Abratt, R., Nel, D., & Higgs, N. S. (1992). An examination of the ethical beliefs of managers using selected scenarios in a cross-cultural environment. *Journal of Business Ethics, 11*(1), 29–35. doi:10.1007/BF00871989

Alas, R., Gao, J., & Carneiro, J. (2015). Connections between ethics and cultural dimensions. *Engineering Economics, 21*(3).

Andrés, A. R. (2006). Software piracy and income inequality. *Applied Economics Letters, 13*(2), 101–105. doi:10.1080/13504850500390374

Armstrong, R. W., Stening, B. W., Ryans, J. K., Marks, L., & Mayo, M. (1990). International Marketing Ethics: Problems Encountered by Australian Firms. *Asia Pacific Journal of International Marketing, 2*(2), 6–15.

Arslan, M. (2001). The work ethic values of protestant British, Catholic Irish and Muslim Turkish managers. *Journal of Business Ethics, 31*(4), 321–339. doi:10.1023/A:1010787528465

Beauchamp, T. L., & Bowie, N. E. (2001). *Ethical Theory and Business*. Upper Saddle River, NJ: Prentice-Hall.

Bentham, J. (1789). *The principles of moral and legislation*. Cambridge, MA: Oxford University.

Broni, J. V. G. (2010). Ethical dimensions in the conduct of business: Business ethics, corporate social responsibility and the law. The" ethics in business" as a sense of business ethics. In *International Conference On Applied Economics–ICOAE* (p. 795).

Buono, A. F., Bowditsch, J. L., & Lewis, J. (1989). When cultures collide. The Anatomy of a Merger. *Human Relations, 38*(5), 477–500. doi:10.1177/001872678503800506

Canestrino, R. (2007, May). *Business Ethics and Firms' internationalization processes. The impact of culture on "moral gap"*. Paper presented at the IACCM Annual Conference "Cross-cultural Life of Social Values", Rotterdam, The Netherlands.

Canestrino, R. (2008). La dissonanza etica nei processi di internazionalizzazione delle imprese. In A. Calvelli (Ed.), *Cross Cultural Management* (pp. 167–240). Naples: Enzo Albano Editore.

Canestrino, R., & Calvelli, A. (2010, September). *Culture and Business Ethics: the impact on firms' management of value chain activities*. Paper presented at the EBEN annual conference, Which values for which organizations? Trento, Italy.

Canestrino, R., & Magliocca, P. (2016). Transferring Knowledge through Cross-border Communities of Practice. In *Organizational Knowledge Facilitation through Communities of Practice in Emerging Markets* (vol. 1, pp. 1-30). Academic Press. DOI: 10.4018/978-1-5225-0013-1.ch004

Canestrino, R., Magliocca, P., & Guarino, A. (2015). Environmental sustainability in the Italian organic wine industry: preliminary results. In Contemporary Trends and Perspectives in Wine and Agri-food Management. Academic Press.

Canestrino, R., Magliocca, P., & Nigro, C. (2015). Drivers and implications of medical tourism: a neo-institutional perspective. *Sinergie Italian Journal of Management*, 271-290.

Canestrino, R., Magliocca, P., & Nigro, C. (2016). Understanding medical tourism within the field of neo-institutionalism: An ethical insight. *International Journal of Environment and Health*, 8(1), 76-99. doi:10.1504/IJENVH.2016.077659

Carroll, A. B. (1991). The pyramid of corporate social responsibility: Toward the moral management of organizational stakeholders. *Business Horizons*, 34(4), 39–48. doi:10.1016/0007-6813(91)90005-G

Cohen, J. R., Pant, L. W., & Sharp, D. J. (1996). A methodological note on cross-cultural accounting ethics research. *The International Journal of Accounting*, 31(1), 55–66. doi:10.1016/S0020-7063(96)90013-8

Collier, J., & Esteban, R. (2007). Corporate social responsibility and employee commitment. *Business Ethics (Oxford, England)*, 16(1), 19–33. doi:10.1111/j.1467-8608.2006.00466.x

Crane, A. (2000). Corporate greening as amoralization. *Organization Studies*, 21(4), 673–696. doi:10.1177/0170840600214001

De George, R. T. (1993). *Competing with Integrity in International Business*. Oxford, UK: Oxford University Press.

Donaldson, L. (2001). The contingency theory of organizations. *Sage (Atlanta, Ga.)*.

Donaldson, T. (1996). Values in tension: Ethics away from home. *Harvard Business Review*, 74(5), 48.

Donaldson, T., & Dunfee, T. W. (1994). Toward a unified conception of business ethics: Integrative social contracts theory. *Academy of Management Review*, 19(2), 252–284.

Donaldson, T., & Dunfee, T. W. (1999). When ethics travel: The promise and peril of global business ethics. *California Management Review*, 41(4), 45–63. doi:10.2307/41166009

Dubinsky, A. J., & Loken, B. (1989). Analyzing ethical decision making in marketing. *Journal of Business Research*, 19(2), 83–107. doi:10.1016/0148-2963(89)90001-5

Ferrell, O. C., & Fraedrich, J. (1997). *Business Ethics* (3rd ed.). Boston: Houghton Mifflin Co.

Ferrell, O. C., & Fraedrich, J. (2015). *Business ethics: Ethical decision making & cases*. Nelson Education.

Ferrell, O. C., & Gresham, L. G. (1985). A contingency framework for understanding ethical decision making in marketing. *Journal of Marketing*, *49*(3), 87–96. doi:10.2307/1251618

Fisher, C. M., & Lovell, A. (2009). *Business Ethics and values: Individual, corporate and international perspectives*. Pearson Education.

Frederick, W. C., Davis, K., & Post, J. E. (1988). *Business and society: Corporate strategy, public policy, ethics* (6th ed.). New York: McGraw-Hill.

Freeman, R. E. (1984). The politics of stakeholder theory. *Business Ethics Quarterly*, *4*(4), 409–421. doi:10.2307/3857340

Freeman, R. E., & Evan, W. M. (1990). Corporate Governance: A Stakeholder Interpretation. *The Journal of Behavioral Economics*, *19*(4), 337–359. doi:10.1016/0090-5720(90)90022-Y

Freeman, R. E., & Gilbert, D. R. (1988). *Corporate strategy and the search for ethics (No. 1)*. Englewood Cliffs, NJ: Prentice Hall.

French, P. A. (1979). The corporation as a moral person. *American Philosophical Quarterly*, *16*(3), 207–215.

Gjølberg, M. (2009). Measuring the immeasurable?: Constructing an index of CSR practices and CSR performance in 20 countries. *Scandinavian Journal of Management*, *25*(1), 10–22. doi:10.1016/j.scaman.2008.10.003

Gjølberg, M. (2011). Explaining regulatory preferences: CSR, soft law, or hard law? Insights from a survey of Nordic pioneers in CSR. *Business and Politics*, *13*(2), 1–31. doi:10.2202/1469-3569.1351

Gopal, R. D., & Sanders, G. L. (2000). Global software piracy: You cant get blood out of a turnip. *Communications of the ACM*, *43*(9), 82–89. doi:10.1145/348941.349002

Halme, M., Roome, N., & Dobers, P. (2009). Corporate responsibility: Reflections on context and consequences. *Scandinavian Journal of Management*, *25*(1), 1–9. doi:10.1016/j.scaman.2008.12.001

Harmon, G. (1984). Is there a single true morality? In *Krausz, M. (1989), Relativism: Interpretation and Confrontation*. Notre Dame, IN: University of Notre Dame Press.

Hart, S. L., & Milstein, M. B. (2003). Creating sustainable value. *The Academy of Management Executive*, *17*(2), 56–67. doi:10.5465/AME.2003.10025194

Heath, J., Moriarty, J., & Norman, W. (2010). Business ethics and (or as) political philosophy. *Business Ethics Quarterly*, *20*(03), 427–452. doi:10.5840/beq201020329

Hedstrom, G., Poltorzycki, S., & Strob, P. (1998). *Sustainable develop- ment: the next generation of business opportunity*. Available at: http://www.resourcesaver.com/file/toolmanager/O16F4954.pdf

Higgins, A., Power, C., & Kohlberg, L. (1984). The relationship of moral atmosphere to judgments of responsibility. *Morality, moral behavior, and moral development*, 74-106.

Hofstede, G. (1984). *Culture's consequences: International differences in work-related values* (Vol. 5). Los Angeles, CA: Sage Publication.

Hofstede, G. (1994). The business of international business is culture. *International Business Review*, *3*(1), 1–14. doi:10.1016/0969-5931(94)90011-6

Hofstede, G., Hofstede, G. J., & Minkov, M. (1991). *Cultures and organizations: Software of the mind* (Vol. 2). London: McGraw-Hill.

Hooker, J. N. (2008). *Corruption from a Cross-Cultural Perspective*. Retrieved from http://ethisphere.com/a-cross-cultural-view-of-corruption

Hunt, S. D., & Vitell, S. (1986). A general theory of marketing ethics. *Journal of Macromarketing*, *6*(1), 5–16. doi:10.1177/027614678600600103

Husted, B. W. (2000). *Toward a model of cross-cultural business ethics: The impact of individualism and collectivism on the ethical decision-making process*. Academy of Management Proceedings.

Izraeli, D. (1988). Ethical beliefs and behavior among managers: A cross-cultural perspective. *Journal of Business Ethics*, *7*(4), 263–271. doi:10.1007/BF00381831

Jenkins, H. (2006). Small business champions for corporate social responsibility. *Journal of Business Ethics*, *67*(3), 241–256. doi:10.1007/s10551-006-9182-6

Jennings, P. L., & Velasquez, M. (2015). Towards an Ethical Wealth of Nations: An Institutional Perspective on the Relation between Ethical Values and National Economic Prosperity. *Business Ethics Quarterly*, *25*(04), 461–488. doi:10.1017/beq.2015.42

Jones, T. M. (1991). Ethical decision making by individuals in organizations: An issue-contingent model. *Academy of Management Review*, *16*(2), 366–395.

Kant, I. (1785). Groundwork for the Metaphysics of Morals. Academic Press.

Katz, J. P., Swanson, D. L., & Nelson, L. K. (2001). Culture-based expectations of corporate citizenship: A propositional framework and comparison of four cultures. *The International Journal of Organizational Analysis*, *9*(2), 149–171. doi:10.1108/eb028931

Kelly, A. (1983). Case Study -- Italian Tax Mores. In *Ethical Issues in Business: A Philosophical Approach* (2nd ed.). Englewood Cliffs, NJ: Prentice Hall Inc.

Kohlberg, L. (1969). Stage and sequence: the cognitive-developmental approach to socializa- tion. In D. A. Goslin (Ed.), *Handbook of socialisation theory and research* (pp. 347–480). Chicago: Rand McNally.

Kohlberg, L. (1976). Moral stages and moralization: The cognitive-developmental approach. *Moral development and behavior: Theory, research, and social issues*, 31-53.

Larrison, T. (1998). Ethics and international development. *Business Ethics (Oxford, England)*, *7*(1), 63–67. doi:10.1111/1467-8608.00089

Locke, J. (1924). *An essay concerning human understanding*. Academic Press.

Lopez-Perez, M. V., Perez-Lopez, M. C., & Rodriguez-Ariza, L. (2009). Corporate Social Responsibility and Innovation in European Companies. An empirical research. *Corporate Ownership & Control*, *7*(1), 274–285. doi:10.22495/cocv7i1c2p3

Lu, X. (2001). Ethical issues in the globalization of the knowledge economy. *Business Ethics (Oxford, England), 10*(2), 113–119. doi:10.1111/1467-8608.00221

Lucifora, A., Bianco, F., & Vagliasindi, G. M. (2015). *Environmental crime and corporate and corporate mis-compliance: A case study on the ILVA steel plant in Italy. In Study in the framework of the EFFACE research project.* Catania: University of Catania.

Marron, D. B., & Steel, D. G. (2000). Which countries protect intellectual property? The case of software piracy. *Economic Inquiry, 38*(2), 159–174. doi:10.1111/j.1465-7295.2000.tb00011.x

Martin, L. (2009). Reproductive tourism in the age of globalization. *Globalizations, 6*(2), 249–263. doi:10.1080/14747730802500398

Marx, K. (1978). *Wage Labour and Capital.* Peking: Foreign Language Press.

Matten, D., & Moon, J. (2004). Corporate social responsibility education in Europe. *Journal of Business Ethics, 54*(4), 323–337. doi:10.1007/s10551-004-1822-0

Matten, D., & Moon, J. (2008). Implicit and explicit CSR: A conceptual framework for a comparative understanding of corporate social responsibility. *Academy of Management Review, 33*(2), 404–424. doi:10.5465/AMR.2008.31193458

Mill, J. S. (1910). *Utilitarianism, Liberty, Representative Government.* London: Dent.

Moon, J., Crane, A., & Matten, D. (2005). Can corporations be citizens? Corporate citizenship as a metaphor for business participation in society. *Business Ethics Quarterly, 15*(03), 429–453. doi:10.5840/beq200515329

Moores, T. T. (2003). The effect of national culture and economic wealth on global software piracy rates. *Communications of the ACM, 46*(9), 207–215. doi:10.1145/903893.903939

Parker, D. B. (1998). *Fighting Computer Crime–A New Framework for Protecting Information.* Wiley Computer Publishing.

Peng, Y., Dashdeleg, A., & Chih, H. L. (2014). National Culture and Firm's CSR Engagement: A Cross-Nation Study. *Journal of Marketing and Management, 5*(1), 38–49.

Qizilbash, M. (1997). Needs, incommensurability and well-being. *Review of Political Economy, 9*(3), 261–276. doi:10.1080/751245295

Rausch, A., Lindquist, T., & Steckel, M. (2014). A Test of US versus Germanic European Ethical Decision-Making and Perceptions of Moral Intensity: Could Ethics Differ within Western Culture? *Journal of Managerial Issues, 26*(3), 259.

Resick, C. J., Martin, G. S., Keating, M. A., Dickson, M. W., Kwan, H. K., & Peng, C. (2011). What ethical leadership means to me: Asian, American, and European perspectives. *Journal of Business Ethics, 101*(3), 435–457. doi:10.1007/s10551-010-0730-8

Rest, J. R. (1986). *Moral development: Advances in research and theory.* New York: Praeger publishers.

Robertson, D. C. (2002). Business ethics across cultures. In The Blackwell handbook of cross-cultural management, (pp. 361-392). Blackwell Business.

Rodrigues, C. A. (1997). Developing expatriates cross-cultural sensitivity: Cultures where your cultures OK is really not OK. *Journal of Management Development, 16*(9), 690–702. doi:10.1108/02621719710190211

Roxas, M. L., & Stoneback, J. Y. (2004). The importance of gender across cultures in ethical decision-making. *Journal of Business Ethics, 50*(2), 149–165. doi:10.1023/B:BUSI.0000022127.51047.ef

Salacuse, J. W. (1998). Ten ways that culture affects negotiating style: Some survey results. *Negotiation Journal, 14*(3), 221–240. doi:10.1111/j.1571-9979.1998.tb00162.x

Schein, E. H. (1981). Improving face-to-face relationships. *Sloan Management Review, 22*(2), 43–52. PMID:10250386

Schein, E. H. (2004). *Organizational culture and leadership* (3rd ed.). San Francisco: Jossey-Bass.

Shapiro, J. M., Ozanne, J. L., & Saatcioglu, B. (2008). An interpretive examination of the development of cultural sensitivity in international business. *Journal of International Business Studies, 39*(1), 71–87. doi:10.1057/palgrave.jibs.8400327

Shenkar, O., & Zeira, Y. (1992). Role Conflict and Role Ambiguity of Chief Executive Officers in International Joint Ventures. *Journal of International Business Studies, 23*(1), 55–75. doi:10.1057/palgrave.jibs.8490259

Shin, S. K., Gopal, R. D., Sanders, G. L., & Whinston, A. B. (2004). Global software piracy revisited. *Communications of the ACM, 47*(1), 103–107. doi:10.1145/962081.962088

Singhapakdi, A., & Marta, J. K. (2005). Comparing marketing students with practitioners on some key variables of ethical decisions. *Marketing Education Review, 15*(3), 13–25. doi:10.1080/10528008.2005.11488918

Smith, A. (1759). The Theory of Moral Sentiments. Cambridge, UK: Cambridge University Press.

Solomon, R. C. (1991). Business ethics, literacy, and the education of the emotions. *The Ruffin Series in Business Ethics*, 188-211.

Swinyard, W. R., Rinne, H., & Kau, A. K. (2013). The Morality of Software Piracy: A Cross-Cultural Analysis. In *Citation Classics from the Journal of Business Ethics* (pp. 565–578). Springer Netherlands. doi:10.1007/978-94-007-4126-3_29

Taylor, S. E. (1975). On inferring ones attitudes from ones behavior: Some delimiting conditions. *Journal of Personality and Social Psychology, 31*(1), 126–131. doi:10.1037/h0076246

Trevino, L. K. (1986). Ethical decision making in organizations: A person-situation interactionist model. *Academy of Management Review, 11*(3), 601–617.

Trevino, L. K., & Nelson, A. K. (2011). *Managing business ethics: Straight talk about how to do it right.* Hoboken, NJ: Wiley.

Tsalikis, J., & Nwachukwu, O. (1988). Cross-cultural business ethics: Ethical beliefs difference between blacks and whites. *Journal of Business Ethics*, 7(10), 745–754. doi:10.1007/BF00411021

Velásquez, T. A. (2012). The science of corporate social responsibility (CSR): Contamination and conflict in a mining project in the southern Ecuadorian Andes. *Resources Policy*, 37(2), 233–240. doi:10.1016/j.resourpol.2011.10.002

Vitell, S. J., Nwachukwu, S. L., & Barnes, J. H. (2013). The effects of culture on ethical decision-making: an application of Hofstede's typology. In *Citation Classics from the Journal of Business Ethics* (pp. 119–129). Springer Netherlands. doi:10.1007/978-94-007-4126-3_6

Wines, W. A., & Napier, N. K. (1992). Toward an understanding of cross-cultural ethics: A tentative model. *Journal of Business Ethics*, 11(11), 831–841. doi:10.1007/BF00872361

Yang, D. L., & Sonmez, M. (2007). Economic and Cultural Impact on Intellectual Property Violations: A Study of Software Piracy. *Journal of World Trade*, 41, 731–750.

Yoo, C. W., Sanders, G. L., Rhee, C., & Choe, Y. C. (2014). The effect of deterrence policy in software piracy cross-cultural analysis between Korea and Vietnam. *Information Development*, 30(4), 342–357. doi:10.1177/0266666912465974

Zahra, S. A. (1989). Executive values and the ethics of company politics: Some preliminary findings. *Journal of Business Ethics*, 8(1), 15–29. doi:10.1007/BF00382013

KEY TERMS AND DEFINITIONS

Business Ethics: A specialized study of moral right and wrong that concentrates on moral standards as they apply to business institutions, organizations, and behavior.

Cognitive Moral Development: Theory of moral reasoning proposed by Kholberg in 1976 to explain the way people think and decide to act about what they perceive ethically right.

Corporate Social Responsibility: Business practices aiming, not only, to get profits, but also to obey the law, to be ethical, and to be a good corporate citizen.

Cross-Cultural Sensitivity: One's ability to decipher others' values.

Cultural Negotiating Ability: One's capacity to better understand and to interpret his counterpart behavior, finding the way to overcome cultural diversities.

Culture: Programming of the mind that distinguishes the members of one group or category of people from others.

Ethical Dilemma: Condition that involves a conflict between moral imperatives, in which to obey one means to break another. In an ethical dilemma two or more ''right'' values are in conflict.

Moral Gap: Condition according to which what is considered right in one context, is considered wrong in another context.

Moral Standards: Set of principles according to which actions (ethic or un-ethic) are evaluated; they arise from local traditions and are deeply rooted in a context.

Organizational Culture: Common set of assumptions, values and beliefs shared by organizational members and manifests itself in norms, rituals, legends and organization's choice for heroes and heroines.

ENDNOTES

[1] An ethical dilemma arises every time a decision (to solve a given problem) involves a conflict between moral imperatives, in which to obey one means to break another. In an ethical dilemma two or more "right" values are in conflict (Trevino and Nelson, 2011).

[2] Kohlberg (1976) focused on the way people think and decide to act about what they perceive as ethically right. He interviewed 58 American boys – all aged between 10 and 16. Responses were analyzed and resulted in new understanding of how moral reasoning in human beings, gradually develops over time through brain development and life experience.

[3] Within the Individual Moderating Factors, individuals high on Ego Strength are expected to respect their own moral conventions more than individuals with low ego strength, thus resulting in high consistency between action and thought in the organizational field. Field Dependence depicts the individual tendency to make use of external referents to reduce the ambiguity of a given ethical dilemma. In accordance, as Trevino noted, people (and managers) high on Field Dependence show a less consistency between moral action and moral judgment, mainly because they lack for autonomy and are easily to look for external source of information. Locus of Control finally describes to what extent people perceive themselves able to control external events. People with "internal" Locus of Control believes that outcomes depend on their own efforts, otherwise they are beyond control and depend on the fate, luck and destiny. As consequence, people whose Locus of Control is internal are more likely to act in coherence with their moral judgment than people characterized by "external" Locus of Control.

[4] Organizational Culture may be defined as "a pattern of shared basic assumptions that a group has learned as it solved its problems of external adaptation and internal integration, that has worked well enough to be considered valid and therefore, to be taught to new members as the correct way to perceive, think, and feel in relation to those problems" (Schein, 2004, p. 17). It mainly refers to the common set of assumptions, values and beliefs shared by organizational members and manifests itself in norms, rituals, legends and organization's choice for heroes and heroines.

[5] The construct of Moral Intensity includes six components: Magnitude of consequences, social consensus, probability of effects, temporal immediacy, proximity, and concentration of effects. The magnitude of consequences of the moral issue is defined as the sum of the harms, or benefits, done to victims, or beneficiaries, of the moral act in question; the social consensus refers to the evaluation of a moral action (right or wrong) by the social group within which people are embedded; the probability of effects is a joint function of the probability that a give action will cause the predicted harms; temporal immediacy is the length of time between the present and the onset of consequences of the moral act (shorter length of time implies greater immediacy); the proximity is the feeling of nearness (social, cultural, psychological, or physical) that the moral agent has for victims or for the beneficiaries of the evil act in question; the concentration of effects finally is an inverse function of the number of people affected by an act of given magnitude.

[6] Similarly, Gjølberg (2009) developed two indexes: one measuring CSR practices and one measuring CSR performance in 20 different OECD nations. The indexes reveal striking differences among 20 nations, suggesting for a better investigation of CSR at national level.

[7] Smith (1759) wrote is "Theory of Moral Sentiment" before the "Wealth of the Nation". The work is an essay towards an analysis of the principles by which men naturally judge concerning the conduct and character, first of their neighbors, and afterwards of themselves.

8   For Marx (1978) the problem with capitalism was that most of the benefits were reaped by the few, when there was enough to better the lot of all. His critique has still followers today.

9   Hofstede et al. (1990) highlights that there is a significant difference between national and organizational culture. But organizations are embedded into societies, which can be defined by certain national values; moreover they consist of individuals who introduce their own beliefs (arising at societal level) into the organization. In view of the above, national culture may reasonably provide for indications about both organizational and individual culture.

10   Trompenaars (1996) defines the Achieved/Ascribed Orientation by identifying the way by which people reach power positions; by obtaining "a result" or by recognition for something with success being naturally attributed.

11   Hofstede (1980) clustered more than 70 countries, by analyzing IBM respondents between 1967 and 1973. Since 2001, scores have been listed for 74 countries and regions, partly based on replications and extensions of the original IBM. Hofstede clustered the different countries according to some cultural dimensions, namely, Power Distance; Individualism vs collectivism, Masculinity vs Femininity and Uncertainty Avoidance. A fifth dimension, Long-term Orientation, was added to the original model, after conducting an additional international study with a survey instrument developed with Chinese employees and managers. Hofstede's Power Distance (PD) index measures the extent to which the less powerful members of organizations and institutions (like the family) accept and expect that power is distributed unequally. Individualism vs Collectivism (IND vs COLL) refers to the degree to which individuals are embedded into their own social group. While individualistic people are self-oriented and take primarily care of themselves, collectivistic people are deeply embedded into their social group. Collective interests prevail over the individual ones; extended families (with uncles, aunts and grandparents) protect them in exchange for unquestioning loyalty. The Masculinity (MAS) vs Femininity dimension describes how cultures differentiate on not between gender roles. Masculine cultures tend to be ambitious and need to excel. In workplaces employees emphasize their work to a great extent (live in order to work) and they admire achievers who accomplished their tasks. Feminine cultures consider quality of life and helping others to be very important. Working is basically to earn money which is necessary for living. In business as well as in private life they strive for consensus and develop sympathy for people who are in trouble. Uncertainty Avoidance (UA) deals with a society's tolerance for uncertainty and ambiguity. If Uncertainty Avoidance is strong, changes are felt as dangerous, and "what is already known" is preferred to changes: both individuals and organizations adopt procedures for predicting and reducing the uncertainty of future events. Long-term Orientation (LTO) exists when individuals focus more on the future, than on the present. Long term oriented people delay short-term material or social success or even shot-term emotional gratification in order to prepare for the future. They value persistence, perseverance, saving and being able to adapt. The scale for each dimension runs from 0 - 100 with 50 as a midlevel. The rule of thumb is that if a score is under 50 the culture scores relatively low on that scale and if any score is over 50 the culture scores high on that scale (Hofstede, 1980).

12   It has to be noted that even if "moral gap" depends on cultural diversities, it does not overlap with the so-called "intercultural gap". The "moral gap" always refers to the ethical evaluation of the actions that international players put, or are willing to put, into practice, in accordance to the set of moral standards prevailing in a given context (home vs host country). By the opposite the "intercultural gap" may establish every time values and beliefs significantly differ, even without referring to any

moral standard. When partners come from different countries differences in language, communication style (both verbal and non-verbal), organizational routines and propensity to cooperate increase the risk of a cultural collision: in such circumstances, international players may feel frustrated, shaping the conditions for a cultural shock (Buono et al., 1989), conflicts misunderstandings and low performances, as well (Shenkar and Zeira, 1992). In spite of no moral judgment is developed under the mentioned circumstances. No one could evaluate, for example, as wrong using the red color, instead of white, for weddings, neither the Japanese physical exercises before working: these are cultural embedded-practices, even if they cannot be connected to any moral standard.

[13] Expatriation is the process by which an employee is sent abroad for an international assignment and it a quite common practice employed in the MNCs to transfer useful knowledge to the geographically dispersed units (Canestrino and Magliocca, 2010).

[14] For a full examination of the eight-step process, see Trevino, L. K., & Nelson, K. A. (2010). Managing business ethics. John Wiley & Sons.

Chapter 9
Project and Risk Management in a Global Context:
The Importance of Cultural Risk

Mirko Perano
Reald University of Vlore (ASAR), Albania

Bice Della Piana
University of Salerno, Italy

Gian Luca Casali
Queensland University of Technology, Australia

ABSTRACT

Project management is one of the possible ways to improve the organizational reputation and create value. The control achievable on each project' constrains (time, cost and quality) and the actions consequent by assessment process can represent in theory a guarantee for the success of a project. In practical, there are many risks capable of upsetting the project dynamics leading to failures. Risk management, or the specific area of knowledge of Project Risk Management, are useful to prevent this possible occurrence. The global dimension of organizations' networks that use PM, moves this quality to the project that this organizations do. A definition of global project is provided as well as also the consequent considerations about the cross-cultural aspect within the peoples involved in this type of project. It is framed and proposed a new category of risk related to management of global project: cultural risk analysis.

INTRODUCTION

Project management is a useful discipline that among other things can reduce the project complexity and, maximize the knowledge and control on each activities. What makes the process complex is the fact that each activity is under the constraints of three important variables: costs, time and quality. Through the evolution of project management (PM), knowledge and models have moved continuously between conceptual and empirical research. Under the social point of view, "projects are complex social settings

DOI: 10.4018/978-1-5225-2673-5.ch009

characterized by tensions between unpredictability, control and collaborative interaction among diverse participants on any projects" (Cicmil et al. 2006, p. 676). From other hand, one of the substantial characteristic of project is the innovation considering that the life cycle of general innovation outcomes is increasingly shorter.

The organizations operating in global context are seeking to fight the high level of complexity in managing projects. Although a lot of researcher (as in e.g. Pinto, Slevin, 1988; Baccarini, 1996; Vidal, Marle, 2008 and others) have made effort to investigate on complexity projects factors, but the identification of a solution for a problem in continuously moving is an hard goal to achieve.

Assuming that the society is complex, that the environment is complex, the competition is complex and the projects are complex, is it possible to argue that with this high general level of complexity and with this global "complexition" (competition and high level of complexity), the modern project management is really adequate to manage all the activities?

The management of cultural diversity is a hard topic starting from the globalization' phenomena. This is not only the case of international management, or the case of negotiation between two or more parts from different part of the world and different culture. With facilitation of transit of people and things the global collaboration on big (o mega) project has been facilitated. The management of this big project has increasingly involved international stakeholders and project team (PT) members involved from different part of the world. This is, also, the case of the cross cultural aspect in project management operating in global context.

The aim of this work is to provide a different perspective to understand the complexity projects. Starting from the definition of project before provided (Cicmil et al. 2006) and acknowledging that project can be defined as "global" (Binder, 2016), the authors argue that is possible to read the project complexity also under the lens of cultural aspect in order to reduce it in reducing the cultural risk in managing projects. Cultural aspect is linked to contextuality and this relation influences the project complexity (Koivu et al, 2004).

The work is structured as follow: the first part describe the modern PM; the second describe the Project Risk Management (PRM); the third discusses the cultural aspect and the related cultural risk. The work end with indication of future research and with conclusions.

PROJECT MANAGEMENT IN GLOBAL CONTEXT

The Project Management (PM) is defined as "systemic management of a complex, unique and a fixed time lasting enterprise, aiming at reaching a clear and pre-set goal, by a continuous process of planning and control of different resources having interdependent constraints of costs-time-quality" (Archibald, 2004, page 29). In more details, quality, time, costs and resources are the management variables (or constrains) around which the methodology of the PM operates. In addition, it is possible to identify elements: structural such as project, programs, processes, tasks, and main actors (or project stakeholders) such as Project Manager (PMr), Sponsor and Project Team (PT).

The terms program/project/process/performance (task) are often used as synonyms, even if they have a different semantic meaning.

In this sense, we assume that program is a long-term action, normally involving more than one project.

The process, instead, is a whole of activities carried out with continuity or made by a sequence of known operations, which are repeated whenever circumstances require it.

The performance or task is a short-term effort (ranging between a week and some months) made by an organization, which together with other tasks, can be a process or even a project.

The project refers to a whole of correlated activities aiming at reaching a unique goal, by the use of human, financial, material and technological resources and inconformity of pre-set constraints of time, costs and quality. The projects can have some common characteristics:

- Clear and definite goals;
- Uniqueness: innovative;
- Provisional character: market windows, that is a date of starting and ending, being both scanned by the project life cycle;
- Progressive processing intended as development obtained along successive and incremental stages;
- Multidisciplinary approach;
- Limited resources.

Scope/Quality, Costs/Resources and Schedule/Time are the constraints of a project and in order to realize a successful project, a PMr must consider and search an harmony between these three often-competing goals (Schwalbe, 2007, p.8), even with the positive evaluation of quality output by customer (Kerzner, 2009, p.3). The life of a generic project starts with the identification of one or more (totally or partially) unsatisfied or latent needs and develops through different stages concerning the identification of opportunities, feasibility evaluations, planning, construction and tests, exercise and preservation.

Therefore, it is commonly referred to as the "Project Life Cycle" a series of three stages (initial stage, intermediate stage, and final stage) that connects the beginning and the end of the project with each other. Each stage of the project has its own characteristics aiming at producing specific intermediate outputs representing input being fundamental for the prosecution and completion of the activities of the following stages.

The project stakeholders are people or firms that can either being actively involved in the project, being influenced by the project's outcomes or they can also influence the goals and results of the project. The main stakeholders of a project include:

- **Project Manager:** The person responsible for the management of the project.
- **Client/User:** Person or organizational structure that will use the product of the project. Two different levels of clients can exist.
- **Performing Organization:** Business having employees who are more directly involved into the carrying out of works.
- **Members of the Project Group:** Group being in charge of the carrying out of the work provided by the project.
- **Project Management Group:** Members of the project group who are directly involved in PM activities
- **Sponsor:** Person or group providing cash or in kind financial resources, being necessary for the project.
- **Influential Entities:** People or groups who are not directly linked to the purchase or use of the product of the project but who, because of the role played in the organizational structure of the

client or in the Performing Organization, can positively or negatively influence the project carrying out procedure.

Besides these main stakeholders there are a variety of project both internal and external stakeholder categories, such as owners and investors, suppliers and contractors, members of the working group and their "families", government agencies and representatives of the media, individual citizens, provisional or permanent lobbies, organizational structures and companies in their whole. In the case of global projects, the correct identification of all stakeholders in the planning stage is very important. Realizing that one stakeholder was not included, require adding this last and all the project requisites required in the course of work, it could seriously affect the success of the project (Bassi, 2007, page 207) in terms of impact on triple constraints.

Managing project in the global context, all of these stakeholders can work at very high distances. This is not only a problem of project organization that can be easily fixed with technology (where it is possible), or a problem of time zone for the organization of team work, but the main problem is the cross cultural differences/diversity between all this part involved. This aspect represent a real dimension of the project, a variable that should be measurable in order to have greater control of risks and ensure a better project management.

The main figure in the development of a project is the PMr an entity being entrusted by the organization, of reaching the goals through a project structure. The PMr plays the double role of sole Manager of the success of the project and of point of reference for the Buyer, the Business Management and the whole PT. His tasks are:

- To plan the project in terms of times and costs, ensuring the technical consistency between the different components of the project;
- To ask the business Organizational Units for the resources necessary for the project, negotiating, agreeing and formalizing the assignment of the budgeted resources, time, costs and characteristics of the goods to be produced;
- To check the carrying out of the working stages and of the activities being necessary for the delivery of the well working product (testing, training of users, preparation of the technical and operational documents supporting the management, use and maintenance, etc, of the product), performing the most suitable actions in order to reach the goals.

The first goal of the PMr is that of getting a project be carried out according to the commitment expectations, succeeding in completely satisfying his needs, also using an approach that could first provide support to the commitment himself, as regards the clarification and definition in a precise and organic way, of the requirements needed. The PMr shall also have special technical, management, relational and personal characteristics (with reference to the sector typical of the project), (human management) and special professional competences about the management of the personnel, the programming systems and the control of activities and the use of information systems (Perano, 2012, p. 333). While the PMr is responsible towards the company for the carrying out of a project, the Project Sponsor has the business responsibility of the project.

The Sponsor is in the middle of a system of relations putting in contact different and various organizations (the client organization, or however the organization being the receiver of the deliverable products of the project, the permanent organization belonging to the PT, the PT itself as provisional enclave of an "adhocratic" kind, meant for carrying out the project).

The Sponsor shall:

- Provide a point of reference and guide both towards the PMr and the PT;
- Guarantee that all the involved parties (stakeholders) participate into the project and are suitably represented in the project organizational structure;
- Ensure that all the business managers of the involved resources and budgets devoted to the project, are suitably involved;
- Ensure that all the business policies provided for the governance are carried out;
- Inform the management about the state of the project in course, about the estimated completion time and the consequent decisions, according to the systematic information produced by the PMr (state of work progress);
- Guarantee that the PMr plays a suitable role and has enough power to autonomously manage the project, exceptions to be evaluated, from time to time, with the Coordination Committee;
- Ensure that the PMr understands its role and tasks and avails itself of escalation procedures in all those cases in which he has not got enough power to intervene;
- Negotiate with the main stakeholders the questions not falling within the authority of the PMr;
- Decide the actions of quality assurance aiming at ensuring that the project is conforming with all the provided standards, particularly how and by whom they will be carried out;

Project team (PT) is usually seen as a combined effort to reach the goals provided by the project-through the coordination of the PMr. The PT, substantially unites people coming from inside the organization or from its external suppliers, who help the success of the project, according to the experience, the technical skill and personal commitment, it is also responsible for the activities of the PM such as the planning, control and ending of the project. The team works when goals and methods are clear and shared and when the whole group is able to manage time, fix and respect roles, procedures and rules.

To create a united team is one of the fundamental rules to manage a project with success. No working methodology can guarantee the success of a project without the presence of a motivated and well matched team. Before really starting the carrying out of the project is then necessary to meet each other, to fix the team goals, to fix tasks and responsibilities for each entity, to define the working standards, to plan the communication flows, to make sure that everyone well knows the contents of the project plan, to obtain the commitment of everyone.

The PM is implemented by the application and integration of the PM processes for the start up, planning, carrying out, monitoring, control and ending activities.

The startup starts a project or a stage of the project and the output defines its purpose, it sets the goals and authorizes the PMr to start the project itself. The purpose of this stage is determining the link between the motivations and the benefits expected from the project and the essential elements qualifying the solution, that is the fundamental characteristics of the output and the project. During the start up stage the following is also specified: the initial description of the field, the deliverables, the project duration, the resources that the organizational structure is ready to invest, the PMr is chosen among the possible candidates, the initial assumptions and constraints are documented. All these information are concentrated into the Project Charter and, once it has been approved, the project receives the official validation.

The activity of planning (see Table 1) is an estimate and evaluation operation of the project activities (duration, interconnections, resources and means being available for the carrying out).

This hierarchic desegregation results to be useful, since it allows to have a complete, and at the same time detailed picture of the project, thus minimizing possible mistakes or omissions in the assignment of responsibilities (mitigation of the risk project degree), and making the control activity simpler and more accurate during the carrying out of the project. The following step is the identification of the resources devoted to the project – people, equipment, spaces or structures – as well as their allocation to different activities. At this point it is possible to draw up a project budget by considering all the costs being directly referable to the project activities. Once the activities, the people, the roles and costs have been identified, it is possible to create an outline plan, prepared by the project leader.

The project plan is an official document in which project goals are described together with the elements being necessary to reach them, and it is updated as the progress of the project goes on in its activities and stages. It is then a reference plan with which to check, during the carrying out process, the discrepancies with the partial results, in comparison with the provided purposes. During the project planning, all the necessary stakeholders are involved, since they are the repositories of skills and knowledge useful for the development of the PM plan and according to their influence on the project and its results.

During the carrying out stage all the resources are planned, the human and material ones, they are implemented to reach the goals described in the project plan, carrying out, if necessary, all the necessary revisions following a suitable checking activity. The latter consists of sub-stages, such as the work coordination and management, the management of quality, the management of the PT and of human resources, the project communication and documentation, the selection and management of suppliers.

Monitoring and control coexist for the observation of the project carrying out, in order to timely identify the possible problems and adopt the right correction measures. Continuous monitoring provides the PT with the information concerning the project conditions and shows the possible areas requiring special care. In this stage changes are globally controlled; the context is checked and verified; scheduling, costs and quality are checked; a reporting of performances is carried out, as well as the management of stakeholders and the team.

The ending is when the project is completed. A project is considered to be ended when the project goals have been reached, both if the ending has been made for difficulties found (reduction of the budget, budget overshooting or breach of constraints). The ending stage is that when the output and the budgeted

Table 1. Planning Activities

Formalization of goals;	Determination of the resources (people and materials) and in which amount they shall be used	Planning of the intra and extra team project
Division of the main project into components being more detailed, smaller and better manageable;	Identification and attribution of roles, responsibilities and of the mutual project relationships	Determination and assessment of risks/critical points of the project and preparation of prevention actions
Creation of a risk plan;	Cost estimate and expense calendar	Identification of the quality standards being relevant for the project
Scheduling of the activities and definition of the precedence relationships between the activities themselves, the estimate of their duration and the fixing of the starting and ending dates;	Definition of the PT with the appointment of a manager	Creation of a document that guides both the carrying out and the control of the project

resources are to be released, while evaluating the degree of success in reaching the pre-set goals and capitalizing the acquired experience. The ending process is officialized by the formal acceptation of the project by the client (purchaser/user). The ending of a project is then the natural completion of a set of processes that are started since the beginning of the project itself and aiming at allowing, within the scheduled times, to enjoy what has been carried out.

The management of projects requires an interfunctional structure based on the sharing of the project goals and on the motivation of the team to reach the efficiency, a structure in which responsibility is shared at different levels by the PMr with the whole team.

Such a structure provides two kinds of managers, the "function" manager and the provisional "project" manager: the function manager has the task to censure specialization and the competences of the typical resource of the function; it is a task of the PMr, instead, to take advantage at best, of the competences of the resource within the project.

The structures providing two kinds of managers are also called matrix organizational structures where the dependence on the PMr allows them to use and fully exert its power, regardless of the structures to which the resources coordinated by them, belong.

In this kind of structure there is no one who finally decides (then the possible conflict between managers is institutionalized) and the people belonging to a function can participate into more groups at the same time, following one or more projects. One of the advantages of a matrix structure is that more balanced and competitive choices can be made, because they are the product of the contribution of more different points of view.

According to the "weight" of the PMr compared with the function manager four kinds of structure exist, each of them drastically influences the PM:

- Weak, in which the power and the roles of the permanent structure are not changed and the PMr is only a coordinator of the resources involved into the project;
- Balanced, in which the function manager allocates resources to the project, defines the interfaces, manages the resources and checks the budgets of the plan;
- String, in which the PMr has got the control over the resources in comparison with the function manager, who allocates them to the project and takes charge of them at the end of the project;
- Pure, which deeply changes the structure, roles and powers of the permanent functions. It is characterized by the strong interaction between the members of the PT who are physically in the same office and by their ability to face the critical points of the project thanks to the formal authority and autonomy of the PMr.

The maturity model of PM has produced a variety of tools and techniques, widely used and implemented according to the experience and the social and organizational changes of our society. A lot of this tools and techniques can be used to manage the complexity of the project. This complexity depend by multiple factors: firstly the "public project are often more complex than those in the private sector" (Kerzner, 2013) although the "private sector project managers like to assume that their work is more demanding than project in the public sector" (Wirick, 2009, pp 8-19); secondly the complexity factors can depend directly by people involved in the management of project. This may concern all figures involved in all project levels included the stakeholders. In the big project peoples interact and exchange data and information with a number of exchange that require technical knowledge (not only about PM) and mind projected in one direction shown by PMr. It is important that in doing PM, peoples rowing in the same direction, implying that this peoples have the same understand about the direction dictated by PMr. It is right in this circumstance that the difference/diversity of cultural aspect (cross cultural) can have influence in determining the project success or less, or failure.

PROJECTS IN A GLOBAL CONTEXT

Organizations that adopt the PM as a culture for create value through project, generally have similar characteristics: internal formal procedures shared between all divisions or departments, common knowledge about PM and clear idea of potential but also about the risks, the organizational structure adapted to PM needs (i.e. PM office, etc...), and others.

Not always, however, this knowledge can contrast the effects of some problem arising from particular characteristics, as i.e. the global reach of the project. Starting from literature and from the body of knowledge of PM and according to Binder (2016), we can define five types of project/program in terms of project reach:

From Table 2 project and program classification according to the reach, it is possible to catch real elements that can enrich the body of knowledge of PM, allow a better comprehension of project and program, contribute to facilitate the understanding the complexity of the projects with the advantage to better mitigate the risks. The interesting aspect (at the moment not more investigate in PM), is that emerge from point 4 of Table 2, or cross cultural risk in project management related to the project in global context. Following, from literature, the factors that characterize the complexity of the projects.

Between standard project and global project there are a lot of differences.

PROJECT COMPLEXITY FACTORS

In order to understand the key factors of project complexity, a literature review has been realized. "Complex" is a composite Latin term "Com: together" and "plex: woven". Complexity describes the behavior of a system or model whose components interact in multiple ways and follow local rules, meaning there is no reasonable higher instruction to define the various possible interactions (Steven, 2001, p. 19 from wikipedia.org). "Project are becoming complex, traditional project management methods are providing

Table 2. Definitions of project/program in global context

	TERMS	DEFINITION
1	*Distributed project*	Most of team members working in the same organization and in different locations
2	*International project*	Team members working in the same organization and in different countries;
3	*Virtual project*	Most of team members working in different organizations and in different locations
4	*Global project*	"Project managed across borders, with team members from different cultures and languages, working in different nations around the globe"
5	*Global program*	"A group of related projects with aligned strategic benefits normally associated with tactical organization change, whose stakeholders are located in different countries"

Source: *(Binder, 2016)*

inadequate, and new methods of analysis and management are needed" (Williams, 1999 from Levin & Ward, 2011, p. 6). From literature emerge that one of the category factors that influence the complexity of project is the dimension (Christoph, Konrad, 2014, p. 169). Other factor emerged from literature is the contextuality of project. Chun at al. (2003) highlight that contextuality is a relevant characteristic of complexity; the authors consider the contextuality as a common denominator of complex systems. Koivu et al. (2004) proposed the concept of project complexity context-dependence, and the idea that "the context and practices that apply to one project are not directly transferable to other projects with different institutional and cultural configurations, which have to be taken into account in the processes of project management and leadership". From other studies emerge that cultural complexity was combined with the organizational complexity (number of organizational structure hierarchies; number of organizational units and departments) (Lan, et. Al., 2015, p. 1701). From literature review emerged that project dimension, contextuality and cultural aspect have an impact on project complexity.

Assuming that global project/program (as defined in point 4 of Table 2) involve a lot of people (PT members, stakeholders) with different cultures and languages working in different nations, it is logical to imagine that the cross cultural aspect can concretely be not merely a factor of project complexity, but also a real element of risk. This leads to imagine the area of risk of PM and open to "cross cultural risk" as a new specific risk topic of PM.

PROJECT AND RISK MANAGEMENT

The subject of risk has been for a long time debated in the economic-business literature mostly due to the lack of a general view, but each event can be assessed differently (risky or less) based on the type of aspects that have been measured and the specific point of view with which the event was observed. As regards the meaning of the term risk too, even if it can be guessed, today it is still difficult to identify in the literature a univocal and generally shared definition of it by the scientific community. According to some scholars, the risk is naturally involved in an enterprise activity, it is an element that is transferred to projects where the enterprise adopts a project oriented policy for the creation of value and its maintenance, for survival. Others, according to a business point of view, interpret it as a "factor of business production" (Ferrer, Paccess, 1974, page 119 and the following). Others deal with the subject of risk and uncertainty, like Knight (1921), providing hints on the relationships existing between them. The activities of identification, evaluation and definition of risk priorities, belonging to a process based on a risk oriented culture, are today explained in the more famous study field of the Risk Management which, born around the '50s, has had its evolution characterized by the birth of two thought trends: the Financial Risk Management and the Business Risk Management (Gaudenzi, 2006, page 224). It was then analyzed from a global point of view, by distinguishing the pure risks (events causing losses) from the entrepreneurial ones (events causing losses or gains). Connected with the approach of the Financial Risk Management the more recent idea of Enterprise Risk Management (ERM) (CoSo, 2004) emerges, which emphasizes the holistic value of the risk management process, thanks to the use of the adjective "enterprise", and of giving more emphasis to the integration of the process in all the business activities" (Gaudenzi, 2006, page 227) besides transversally involving, within the process of risk management, different actors such as the top management, the middle management and other key entities. An interesting interpretation of the risk from a supply chain point of view, is also offered by what is today called the supply chain risk management (SCRM) (Rowat C., 2003, page 68-69) of the organization.

First standardization hypotheses of processes of risk management have been formulated, which can be adopted by organizations working in different sectors. In 2009 the ISO (International Standard Organization) has defined a standard for the Risk Management which consists of a whole of general principles and guidelines, for the identification, evaluation and definition of risk priorities and their management, which can be adopted by any public, private, social organization, association, groups or individuals: the ISO 31000:2009. The rule – structured in 4 big sections (the vocabulary used, the principles established within the rule; the organizational framework; the process of risk management) – defines the risk as the effect of the uncertainty of goals (Motet, 2009, page 3) that an organizations has set to reach. This shared interpretation of the idea of risk, focuses the attention on a possible relationship between the goals that an organization aims at reaching and the risks deriving from a determinable (or sometimes) not determinable distribution of probabilities, which can be referred to events being not certainly due to occur.

The Project Risk Management (PRM) can be defined as "the systematic process of identification, analysis and response to project risks" (Tonchia, 2007, page 193). The specific goals of the PRM "are that of increasing the probability of positive events and de-creasing the probability and impact of events adverse to the project goals" (PMBOK Guide 4th ed., page 340). The risk nature of the project is justified by three fundamental reasons which are to be well understood for a correct project management:

1. Common characteristics (uniqueness, complexity, hypothesis and constraints, people, stakeholders, change), which represent risks to be eliminated by evaluations and the following actions;
2. Deliberated design, the carrying out of a project output cannot avoid to undergo a (mainly) controlled risk management;
3. External environment, projects live within a general environment and within a specific context, full of elements and factors with which the project itself can come in contact, in case of conflict with the purpose or the specific project goals, risks are born, which are to be considered in its management.

The PRM process has to identify individual risk events within the project, in order to allow its right management, as well as the "project risk" which is used to describe the joint effect of risky events and other sources of uncertainty. The risks of a project can be internal or external.

The main component of a risk referred to a certain event, are the probability of occurrence of such event and its impact, that is the consequences caused by the event, in the case the latter should really occur.

The PRM is structured in stages, each of them has to produce an output, and it provides the intervention of different entities, each one with its own responsibilities and the use of specific techniques (PMI, 2009, p. 19). The stages of the PRM, from literature (included PM Book) on PM topic, are the following:

- **The Planning of Risks:** It fixes the procedure according to which it is possible to identify (as regards their nature and quantity), monitor and control risks. Such process is normally managed by the PMr (Project Manager) who guides its dynamic development in relation to its cultural approach and to the context. In this activity is important involve the commitment because the its priority and thinks can influence the methodology used to address the risks (Nokes, Kelli, 2008, p. 295);
- **The Identification of Risks:** It is a repetitive process managed by PMr, by the stakeholders, by the sponsor (if existing), and by the PT who work at identifying as many risks as possible. During this stage the revision of the project documents is carried out together with the collection of infor-

mation by suitable techniques (questionnaires, focus-groups, Delphi technique, SWOT analysis, etc.) and, by special analyses, (Analysis of the check-list, Analysis of assumptions). "Risk identification is a fundamental part of defining and analyzing scope, schedule, costs and other project plans" (Kendrick, 2015, p. 35);

- **The Qualitative Analysis:** It is a process by which the PMr provides for assigning a weight, a degree of dangerousness to the category and the single risk concerning the project, together with the probability of impact (minimum, medium, high);
- **The Quantitative Analysis:** This stage provides the attribution of a numeric assessment on the probability and impact of the most important risks (Nokes, Kelly, 2008, pp. 306-307).
- **The Plan of Response to Risks:** This stage is aimed at identifying the best response to each main risk falling within the risk management as a component, and at deter-mining the actions allowing to improve the opportunities and reduce the threats to the project goals;
- **Risk Monitoring and Control:** It represents the final stage of the PRM characterized by the whole of the activities aiming at identifying the first effects produced by the occurrence of an expected event (risk) and at implementing the right countermeasures.

The analysis and management of the risks process consists in using methods, techniques and instruments being different for the different stages characterizing the PRM.

As a basic principle, the techniques of the PRM can be distinguished in two categories:

- Statistical techniques, which analyze the historical series of data concerning the past occurrences of risks, in order to deduce the frequency and the seriousness with which each risky event could occur in the future.
- Discretional techniques, used in the cases in which the historical series of data are inadequate and avail themselves of evaluation criteria strongly based on the human factor, that is on intuition, the personal ability and the experience of whom manages the risk analysis.

Among the discretional techniques there are both quantitative techniques, their purpose is that of estimating the distribution of the chance variables of business risks, being the subject of investigation by statistical analyses carried out by highly complex mathematic and probabilistic models, and qualitative techniques measuring the low difficulty risks, which do not result to be immediately and easily quantifiable, by the help of descriptive scales for the representation of the occurrence probability related to them. A detailed review of the instruments, techniques and methods used in the management of risk and distinguished for each stage, is shown below (Table 3). Planning, identification, qualitative and quantitative analyses, planning of responses, monitoring and control of which the PRM consists, as the following table shows. Methods, techniques and instruments have been selected according to the directions of the PMBOK®, the PMI, the ISO 31000:2009 and with reference to a survey whose addressees have been Project Managers (questionnaire sent to 995 managers working in different organizations) (White, Fortune, 2002).

From Table 3, following the description of the most relevant tools, methods and techniques used in PRM.

The analysis of methodologies, both the ETA – *Event Tree Analysis* – and the FTA – *Fault Tree Analysis* – and the DTA – *Decision Tree Analysis* – they are used in the probabilistic evacuation of risk, and in particular, in the identification of the system interrelations due to shared events.

Table 3. Tools supplied to the PRM

Tools & Techniques	RISK MANAGEMENT STAGES				
	Planning	Identification	Qualitative and Quantitative Analyses	Response Planning	Monitoring and Control
Event Tree (Event Tree Analysis)		X	X		
Fault Tree (Fault Tree Analysis)		X	X		
Decision Tree (Decision Tree Analysis)	X		X	X	
Analysis of cause at their roots	X	X		X	
Analysis of the technical performance					X
Analysis of reserves					
Brainstorming	X	X		X	
Checklist	X	X		X	
CCPM (Critical Chain Project Management)	X			X	
CPM (Critical Path Method)		X	X		
Delphi	X	X		X	
Cause-effect diagram (Ishikawa or fishbone diagram)		X			
EMV (Expected Monetary Value)	X		X	X	
EVM (Earned Value Management)			X	X	X
Expert Judgement		X	X		
GERT			X		
The Interviews	X	X		X	
Probability and Impact Matrix (P-I Matrix)			X		
PDM (Precedence Diagramming Method)			X		
PERT (Program Evaluation and Review Technique)		X	X		
Project Risk Management Plan	X			X	
RBM (Risk Break-down Matrix)		X	X		
RBS (Risk Breakdown Structure)	X	X		X	
Risk Register			X	X	X
State of the project meetings					X
Monte Carlo simulation			X		
SWOT Analysis		X			
Risk assessment and revision					X
What-if Analysis		X			

Source: *(White, Fortune, 2002)*

The technique of the *Event Tree* is used in order to identify the consequences that can come out from the occurrence of an event being potentially dangerous. The Fault Tree Analysis is to be included among the analysis methods of a deductive kind, since, starting from a "general" and whole analysis of the kind of fault (or undesired event occurred on the system), results into the identification of faults on its components.

The *Root Cause Analysis* (RCA) is a structured investigation, which has the aim of identifying the real cause of a problem and the actions being necessary to eliminate it (Anderson, Fagerhaug, 2000). The *analysis of performances* aims at ensuring the comparison between the estimated technical performances and the real ones, in order to carry out the necessary adjustments (Russel D. Archibald, 2004, page393). The shifts occurred in the technical performances can show a new risk, which must be, then, investigated and analyzed, in order to find the necessary answers (Loosemore M., et al. 2006).

The *analysis of reserves*, allows to monitor the state of erosion of the financial reserves granted to the different activities carried out along the whole time range provided for each activity. The *brainstorming* is a decision making procedure created by Osborn in 1967 and its purpose if that of encouraging as many ideas as possible to emerge within the group meetings, in a free and spontaneous way, in order to find the solution of a problem and to identify an optimal strategy. It allows collecting data and information for the identification of risks, the definition of solutions or the collection of ideas by asking for the advice of experts in the field.

Checklist are lists where what to check undergoes special check questions, they are ordered according to the project typology, they are based on the risk factors of the project and on the previous business experiences allowing to list all the situations or aspects which could imply possible risks. The *Critical Chain Project Management* (CCPM) is a method for the planning, carrying out and management of projects in single and multi-project environments, which is born from the need of remedying a number of negative factors, which are often the cause of the failure of projects.

The *Critical Path Method* (CPM) in the area of risk helps to guarantee an efficient management of project costs, underlining the problem areas. The method of critical path, based on a network technique implementing an algorithm of deterministic calculation, allows the planning the times of the project activities and their costs and resources. With reference to risk management, such instrument, consisting of the project scheduling, allows the PT, to anticipate and mitigate the impact of risky events, therefore it results to be a key element for risk assessment (Hulett, 1995, pp. 21-31). Its use allows identifying the interdependence between the project activities considering, for each of them, an acceptable estimated delay level (float), and provides a scheduling of the activities, defining a relationship of end/start between them.

Delphi method is a repetitive investigation method having the purpose of obtaining information, opinions and answers by a group of independent and autonomous experts (panel), in order to reach a general agreement about the identification and planning of the project risks (Tonchia, Nonino, 2007, page 197).

K. Ishikawa has developed the *cause-effect diagram*, also called fishbone, in Japan in 1943, and it is a managerial technique, which allows analyzing and assessing the most probable casual chain of the problems arising during the carrying out of the project. The *Expected Monetary Value* (EMV) refers to a specific analytical technique in which a calculation, in order to determine the average of all possible results is carried out when the future is expected as a variety of uncertain events which may or not occur. It is a technique of risk management, which can help with the quantification, and comparison of risks in many aspects of the project. By using the EMV, it is possible to quantify each risk, in order to decide if numbers supports the qualitative analysis.

The *Earned Value Management* (EVM) is a cost control methodology, being commonly accepted to objectively communicate the progress of a project. It allows carrying out a financial analysis to assess and measure the performances along the stages of the project life cycle. The technique based on the "judgement expressed by experts", *Expert Judgments*, is useful above all for quantifying the failure (or success) risk of the project, intended as a whole. The expert judgement is usually the crucial point in the estimate of costs and times of a project, while it becomes a weak point in the quantification concerning the management of a process.

The *Graphical Evaluation and Review Technique* (GERT) allows the non-determinability of paths explicit, with the consequent possibility of representing more conclusions. Therefore, it is a suitable technique to analyze the "uncertainty" factor, focusing the attention on project risks, and provides, consequently, a probabilistic estimate of the general size of the risk connected with the interrelations and paths of the single activities. This technique is useful as an approach for measure the project complexity.

The *interviews*, carried out by meetings with entities having got important information, which can offer a precious contribution to come to know events and judgements, also allow to know conditions and opinions being necessary for the identification of the project risks.

The most widespread technique for the analysis of risks as occurrence probability and seriousness of consequences which can derive from it, is the *Impact-probability Matrix*, by which it is possible to identify priority risks by the assignment of the character of priority, according to their potential implications to reach the goals. It represents the final stage of the risk qualitative analysis of a project.

The *Precedence Diagramming Method* (PDM) is a technique of network analysis that is very useful above all in the analysis stage of a project, since it helps to define the critical path and the amount of time being necessary to carry out pre-fixed activities, defining among them, the dependence/priority constraints and identifying possible delays.

The *Program Evaluation and Review Technique* (PERT) is a planning technique used in the PM, which can be also adopted in the management of project risks. PERT technique, associated with the risk management, will allow focusing the attention on the analysis and monitoring of sequence constraints, times and resources. The use of PERT allows the identification of the most delicate and critical activities, which could cause risks.

The *Project Risk Management Plan* is used by the PRMr and/or by the PT, in order to identify, classify and assign priorities, plan and monitor the risk in a project for the life cycle of the same. It provides a complete model specifying the method, the elements and resources- conforming both with the risk level and the project complexity to be applied to risk management.

The combined use of RBS and WBS can be used to give place to a matrix structure, allowing managing risk at a level of specific detail. To produce such combined matrix, risk analysis is carried out before identifying and classifying risks by the use of RBS, directly or by the use of other identification methods, as brainstorming or the interviews. The lowest levels of the RBS are then connected to the work packages (WP) in the WBS, producing a bi-dimensional matrix (Hillson D., 2003, page111) called "*Risk Breakdown Matrix*" (RBM). This matrix allows to classify risks ac-cording to numeric values, therefore it allows to identify the activities having more risks connected to it, to identify the most important risk, that is the one having a higher numeric value.

The *Risk Breakdown Structure* (RBS) provides a hierarchical representation of the project risks, structured by categories, emphasizing those being the most critical ones. Once the risks, which can have a negative impact on the project, have been identified, it is necessary to compare them with each other, to eliminate the overwhelming ones, to add the forgotten ones, to break down those, which are mere effects of primary causes, to gather together those being similar to each other, which have been uselessly separately detailed. The final step of the drawing up of the RBS is the collection of risks in two homogeneous categories according to their typology. The Risk Register includes a list of all the risks identified for a project. It includes the identification of risks with the probability assigned to them, and their related responses/actions, therefore it is a fundamental instrument for the project managers.

Monte Carlo simulation aims at reducing the uncertainty level, by a repeated number of simulations. It is an analysis using the network diagram and the estimates to carry out a number of simulations on the costs and planning of the project. It can assess the general project risk and supplies a finished percentage value within a certain date or for a specific cost.

What results from such activity is not a single estimate, but a big number of estimates, each of them is associated with a level of probability according to which it may occur as accurate, thus defining what is statistically called "level of confidence".

The *SWOT Analysis* is an tool supporting the decision making process during strategic planning, which used in order to determine the strong points, weak points, opportunities and threats of a project or an enterprise. The assessment and revision of risks allows to confirm and apply risk response actions, being initially implemented or to change them in case changes have occurred, such as the actions being initially planned that have lost their validity.

The *What-If Analysis* is a technique allowing identifying all the potential risk situations and the consequences of such risks, with the later configuration of possible situations and correction solutions, countermeasures or the necessary changes to the project. The added value to this methodology is that of reducing the response time in case a situation foreseen by the analysis occurs with the consequent reduction of costs and potential problems.

The field of risk modelling has rapidly developed over the last years up to become a key factor in the systems of risk management by many above all financial organizations (Branger, Schlag, 2004, page 1).

The risk model generally stands for the potential mistake made on facing a certain phenomenon by some "cognitive instrument" (which is the model) because of limits in the modelling and/or not precise assumptions, which are dated or simply not valid in "extreme" real conditions. The risk model is meant for intervening in the solution of certain mistakes and not precise results, which may characterize a project.

Risk modelling is normally a methodological choice, following a foregoing one made by the organization, in order to analyze in depth, make the business culture homogeneous about the subject, and adopt internal formalized procedures. The organizations which do not adopt a project oriented logic normally adopt standards for risk management among which there is the ISO 31000:2009. In the organizations working by projects/programs using the study field of the PMr, as regards risk modelling refer to the area of risk management included again in the PMBOK® (or in other standards), even if not seldom on the construction of a risk model, both standards (ISO 31000:2009 and PM standard) are referred to.

Risk modelling can be an important instrument to support the management of a variety of strategic, operational, economic-financial decision, but it is often not properly used and not well understood by managers. To promote and include the risk model in the risk management process, can allow a better development of emergency plans allowing a rapid response to crises and potentially offer the opportunity of transforming negative risks into leading factors for future growth.

All this tools, methods and techniques, from literature and PMBOK©, are the most used in the project risk management and in the risk management area. However, managing project in a global context presents more complexity emerging by multiple factors, included the cultural aspect derived from project dimension of project. Despite in the last version of PMBOK© (fifth ed.) the cultural aspect was been addressed but still undervalued. The cultural aspect in PM can lead to risks depending on the level where the event will occur (between PM and Team leader; PM and team members; Team leader and Team leaders; team members and team members). The implications flowing from cultural factor can weigh heavily on the project/program success. As it is possible to imagine, the PMr have final responsibility about this type of risk; but until now, there is not tool, technique or instrument that can help to mitigate the cultural risk in managing project. The relevance of cross cultural management and related risks needs more attention in PM in order to precede risky events also with the support of specific cross cultural tools able to help for an appropriate cultural risk analysis.

CROSS CULTURAL RISK IN MANAGING GLOBAL PROJECT

Cross Cultural Management

Over the last decades, growing internationalization of the economy and related globalization of competition and business strategies have generated increasing interest in international management research, and in particular in comparing management practices across different cultures and nations (Werner, 2002; Tsui et al., 2007). A corollary to this development is the ever increasing of publications that deal with a wide range of issues concerning cross-cultural management (Schollhammer, 1973).

The more comprehensive definition of Cross Cultural Management is the following:

Cross-cultural management explains the behavior of people in organizations and shows people how to work in organizations with employee and client populations from many different cultures. Cross cultural management describes organizational behavior within countries and cultures; compares organizational behavior across countries and cultures; and, most important, seeks to understand and improve the interaction of co-workers, managers, executives, clients, suppliers, and alliance partners from different countries and cultures around the world (Adler, Gundersen, 2008: 13).

A recent systematic literature review (Capaldo et al., 2012) of 317 articles published on 40 top leading management journals highlights that the themes that incorporate the "tradition" of cross-cultural management studies are "interaction, collaboration & negotiation" and "cross-cultural training & international assignments". The authors labeled these themes as cross cultural management research's core themes. As is evident, the main issues arising from the selected core themes are the following:

- Cross-cultural training;
- International assignments;
- Interaction;
- Collaboration;
- Negotiation.

The authors also proposed a relationship between them as it follow.

The "international assignment" refers to the specific tasks of expatriates. The term expatriate refers to an employee who is on a long-term assignment outside his/her home country (Mayerhofer et al., 2004). Therefore, the expatriate interacts with other people from different cultures (Harris & Moran,

1999; Mendenhall & Stahl, 2000). Consequently, the relevance of the theme "international assignment" in cross cultural management studies derives from the need to adjust to a different climate, a new culture, and a variety of language barriers (Hechanova et al., 2002), The "Interaction" is aimed at the joint implementation of activities. Therefore, it requires some amount of collaboration. The "Collaboration", in turn, is based on some kind of agreement among the collaborating parties. Achieving an agreement requires a process of "negotiation". Thus, the agreement represents the concluding phase of the negotiation process (Graham et al. 1994;). Previous studies have shown that negotiations conducted by expatriate belonging to different cultures often fail due to problems related to cross-cultural differences (Black, 1987; Tung, 1984). These differences may create distortions in the early stages of the cross-cultural negotiation process, thus affecting the achievement of the agreement and, therefore, the various opportunities arising from collaboration (Metcalf et al. 2006; Gatti et. al. 2008; Della Piana & Testa, 2009). In order to support effective interaction between people of different cultures, the effectiveness of the negotiation process and, more generally, the success of international assignments, some activity of "cross-cultural training" is needed. The aim of this activities is to facilitate effective cross-cultural interactions (Mendenhall and Oddu, 1986). Supported by the systematic literature review, Capaldo et al. (2012) believe that cultural differences create many difficulties in the negotiation process and that this implies the need for specific training programs in order to increase for the expatriates their cultural background on the target culture, thus minimizing the risk of their ineffective conduct. This consideration seems even more relevant when considering that in global projects there many stakeholders, so the risks of not understanding or misjudgment of others' behavior due to cultural differences can exponentially increase. This is what it is possible to call "cultural risk" in Project Management. According to the risk perception process (Douglas and Wildavsky 1982; Rayner 1990; Schwarz and Thompson 1990), cultural beliefs and world-views determine also how people experience and interpret risks but this aim is out of the purpose of this work (Renn and Rohrmann, 2000).

Cross Cultural Training for the Effectiveness of a Cross Cultural Negotiation in Managing Global Projects

When the project spread its influence into foreign countries and the related activities take on increasingly complexity, the need for a deeper understanding as to how cultural factors influence the global team functions becomes relevant. Cultural factor is an element of context related to both dimension of project complexity (organizational and technological). This factor can have a significant impact also on decision assumed in the project. The information (about a decision) can be altered by "cultural variety, staff diversity and staff interdependences. As a consequence, when turning this decision into an action (at the end of the information transmission process), the real action can be different from the action the project manager wanted" (Vidal, Marle, 2008).

Cross Cultural Training and Cross Cultural Negotiation can be considered as relevant issues to take into account in managing global projects and, overall, their related risks.

Cross Cultural Negotiation in a global project means actively working towards the purpose of the project that satisfies all parties that start from culturally different positions. This requires that the PMr must be able to uncover latent differences and dealing with them openly, while also capitalizing on common ground and building the relationship upon it. Therefore, PMr needs to find a balance between the unconditional acceptance of another person's culture (cultural hypocrisy) and the tendency towards imposing on the other party, even though unwittingly, one's own culture (cultural imperialism).

"Cross-cultural training enables the individual to learn both content and skills that will facilitate effective cross-cultural interaction by reducing misunderstandings and inappropriate behaviors" (Black and Mendenhall, 1990: 120). Cross-cultural training tend to increase the capability to improve cross-cultural interactions. More specifically, it is assumed to have a positive impact on the individual's development of cross-cultural skills, on the team members adjustment to cross-cultural situations.

Implementing a cross-cultural training program before starting the core PM activities can be seen as an integral part of the process. Thus, cross-cultural training enhances the capabilities of PM Group on international business assignments. Drawing on the four areas of expatriate training identified by Weaver (1998), it is possible to contextualize these areas to the global project and consider that cross cultural training should assist PM group in:

- Anticipating the stress of cross-cultural adjustment;
- Facilitating the development of coping strategies;
- Helping the team members feel confident that they will be able to adjust successfully to the new culture;
- Assisting them in understanding the process of cross-cultural adaptation.

Cultural Risk Analysis

Performance and success in a global project characterized from unfamiliar cultures requires adaptation in the way to do business. When project managers select team members, assign roles and responsibilities and overall evaluate the risks of a project in a global context have to take into account different cultural values and behaviors.

It is important that PMr prepares its team members for integration into their new team. He must help them to adapt, communicate and interrelate at the highest level with team members from different cultures. By this way, they should perceive the reduction of the psychological effects brought on by disorienting situations; at the same time, they should realize that it is possible to lead to an increase in performance and success.

Just to give some examples of how different cultural values may affect human interactions in a global project, Binder (2016: 24) highlights the following questions:

- Is it acceptable to book a meeting during the lunch hour or to organize it starting at 6pm on a summer Friday afternoon?
- Are project managers more effective when they use their hierarchical position or their competencies?
- How important is the performance orientation instead of the humane orientation in a global teamwork?
- What is the preferred leadership style for project managers when they interact with people from different cultures in the same project?

Sometimes specific cultural tools that help make better decisions are needed. To this end, customized processes using both rigorous research and real-world experience may support the team leader to rich a formula for achieving the highest level of performance, ultimately reducing operation time and cost.

More precisely, if the team members understand the role culture exerts on building successful global business relationships, the global project's effectiveness with global customers, suppliers, and partner increases because reduce risk in international business encounters gaining cultural self-awareness and recognizing potential cultural challenge.

The increase of cross cultural competence of the project group members who are directly involved in PM activities (Project Management Group) is just the first essential step to achieve the goals of project with an international scope and scale. The second essential step is to understand, adapt and integrate the cultural values of the whole Project Team (PT) that substantially unites people coming from inside the organization and/or from its external suppliers. The third essential step regards this kind of alignment considering other relevant project stakeholders, the Influential Entities. Even if these people or groups are not directly linked to the project they can positively or negatively influence the project carrying out due to their role in the Client or in the Performing Organization. Not least is the opinion of the working group's families, government agencies, the media and the lobbies.

Considering a global context, the PMr shall have special technical, management, relational and personal characteristics (with reference to the sector typical of the project), special professional competences about the human resource management, the programming systems, the use of information systems and overall an high level of cross cultural competence.

In order to enhance his/her global mindset, it is expected that the PMr improve the following skills:

- Gain self-awareness of the global leadership competencies.
- Understand cultural expectations, develop alternative views of leadership from around the globe and adapt the leadership style.
- Understand how to effectively build trust in international teams.
- Effectively lead the international team and build intercultural business relationships.

Overall the PMr need to create a "cultural comfort zone" until the project ends. A situation where the project stakeholders feel safe. Specifically, a behavioral state within which the team members operate in an anxiety-neutral condition usually without a sense of risk (White, 2009). A comfort zone is a type of mental conditioning that causes a person to create and operate mental boundaries. Such boundaries create an unfounded sense of security. Like inertia, a team member who has established a comfort zone in a particular axis of the project, will tend to stay within that zone without stepping outside of it.

By this way, the PMr may reduce costs, time, and risk in international business encounters.

FUTURE RESEARCH

The main aim of this exploratory study was to provide initial elements to support the need for further research on this topic. From the literature review a large number of factors have been highlighted and identified as possible reason behind the high level of complexity in the current status of project management discourse. Another important highlight of this study has been the discussion about the pivotal role of cross cultural aspect between the project dimension and the context factors. The cross cultural factors in managing global project can constitute the start point for a future research in better understanding "how cross cultural risk can impact on project complexity and how it is possible to manage and mitigate that risk".

CONCLUSION

The management of global project require particular attention in order to control the complexity deriving from the global reach of the project. According to Laszlo (1994), Thomas (2000), Hodgson, Cicmil (2000), the model of PM is not quite adequate to manage, with tools and actual techniques, the actual project complexity. Many complicated projects are managed with inadequate tools, methods and techniques (in terms of scale, heterogeneity, etc…) or only have ambiguous goals. It is simple to think that this projects shortly will become complex. Around the topic of project complexity scholars put attention in order to catch (often with a quantitative analysis) the project complexity factors. A lot of this research constitute the base of knowledge of this work.

The definition of global project/program, characterized by team members from different cultures and languages that working in different nations around the globe, raises a need to have a comprehension of a new aspect that can help to better investigate the project complexity. Starting from this definition of global project and also consider the project dimension and cross cultural as project complexity factors bring to a conclusion that cross cultural project can be consider as a project complexity factor and can constitute a single risk that should be considered in the area of PRM. The cross cultural project risk analysis can support to manage project in global context, or manage global project with a different level of complexity or risk and it can help to achieve better the primary project objective in terms of costs, time and quality.

REFERENCES

Adler, N. J., & Gundersen, A. (2008). *International dimensions of organizational behavior* (5th ed.). Mason, OH: Thomson Higher Education.

Anderson, B., & Fagenhaug, T. (2000). *RCA: Simplified tool and techniques*. Milwaukee, WI: ASQ Quality Press.

Archibald, R. D. (2004). *Project Management: la gestione di progetti e programmi complessi*. Milano, Italy: Franco Angeli.

Baccarini, D. (1996). The concept of project complexity – a review. *International Journal of Project Management, 14*(4), 201–204. doi:10.1016/0263-7863(95)00093-3

Bassi, A. (Ed.). (2007). *Gestire l'innovazione nelle PMI. Il project management come competenza manageriale*. Milano, Italy: Franco Angeli.

Binder, J. (2016). *Global Project Management. Communication, Collaboration and Management Across Boarders*. New York: Routledge.

Black, J. S. (1987). Japanese/American negotiations: The Japanese perspective. *Business and Economic Review, 6*(1), 27–30.

Black, J. S., & Mendenhall, M. (1990). Cross-Cultural Training Effectiveness: A Review and a Theoretical Framework for Future. *Academy of Management Review, 15*(1), 113–136.

Branger, N., & Schlag, C. (2004). *Model Risk: A Conceptual Framework for Risk Measurement and Hedging.* Retrieved October, 15, 2016, from https://www.wiwi.uni-muenster.de/fcm/downloads / forschen/2004_Model_Risk.pdf

Capaldo, A., Della Piana, B., Monteleone, M., & Sergi, B. (2012). *Cross-Cultural Management: A Mosaic of Words and Concepts.* Milano, Italy: McGrawHill.

Capaldo, A., Della Piana, B., & Vecchi, A. (2012). Managing across cultures in a globalized world. Findings from a systematic literature review. In *The Global Community* (Vol. 1, pp. 7–40). New York: Oxford University Press.

Chu, D., Strand, R., & Fjelland, R. (2003). Theories of complexity – Common denominators of complex systems. *Essays & Commentaries. Complexity, 8*(3), 19–30. doi:10.1002/cplx.10059

Cicmil, S., Williams, T., Thomas, J., & Hodgson, D. (2006). Rethinking Project Management: Researching the actuality of projects. *International Journal of Project Management, 24*(8), 675–686. doi:10.1016/j. ijproman.2006.08.006

Committee of Sponsoring Organization (CoSo). (2004). *Enterprise Risk Management – Integrated Framework.* New York: COSO.

Crtistoph, A. J., & Konrad, S. (2014). Project Complexity as an Influence Factor on the Balance of Costs and Benefits in Project Management Maturity Modeling. *Procedia: Social and Behavioral Sciences, 119*(March), 162–171. doi:10.1016/j.sbspro.2014.03.020

Della Piana, B., & Testa, M. (2009). L'efficacia dei processi di negoziazione crosscultural nei business internazionali. *Sviluppo & Organizzazione, 235*(1), 2–21.

Douglas, M., & Wildavsky, A. (1982). *Risk and culture.* Berkeley, CA: University of California Press.

Ferrer Paccess, F. M. (1974). *I sistemi d'impresa.* Bologna, Italy: Il Mulino.

Gatti, M., Della Piana, B., & Testa, M. (2008). Cross-cultural practices in international negotiation process. The Alenia Aeronautica case. *EIASM Proceedings on 5th Workshop on International strategy and cross-cultural management.* Instanbul, Turkey: KOC University.

Gaudenzi, B. (2006). Nuovi approcci di gestione dei rischi d'impresa: Verso l'integrazione tra imprenditore e management. *Sinergie: Italian Journal of Management, 71*(Sep), 221–243.

Graham, J. (1985). The influence of culture on the process of business negotiations, an exploratory study. *Journal of International Business Studies, 16*(1), 81–96. doi:10.1057/palgrave.jibs.8490443

Graham, J. L., Mintu, A. T., & Rodgers, W. (1994). Explorations of Negotiation Behaviors in Ten Foreign Cultures Using a Model Developed in the United States. *Management Science, 40*(1), 72–95. doi:10.1287/mnsc.40.1.72

Harris, P. R., & Moran, R. T. (1999). *Managing Cultural Differences: Leadership Strategies for a New World of Business* (5th ed.). Burlington, MA: Gulf Professional Publishing.

Hechanova-Alampay, R., Beehr, T. A., Christiansen, N. D., & Van Horn, R. K. (2002). Adjustment and Strain among Domestic and International Student Sojourners. A Longitudinal Study. *School Psychology International, 23*(4), 458–474. doi:10.1177/0143034302234007

Hillson, D. (2003). *Effective Opportunity Management for Projects Exploiting Positive Risk.* New York: Marcel Dekker Inc. doi:10.1201/9780203913246

Hodgson, D., & Cicmil, S. (Eds.). (2006). *Making projects critical.* New York: Palgrave McMillan Publishing. doi:10.1007/978-0-230-20929-9

Hulett, D. T. (1995). Project Schedule Risk Assessment. *Journal of Project Management, 26*(1), 21–31.

Kendrick, T. (2015). *Identifying and Managing Project Risks: essential tools for failure-proofing your project* (3rd ed.). Amacon.

Kerzner, H. (2009). *Project Management* (10th ed.). Hoboken, NJ: John Wiley & Sons, Inc.

Kerzner, H. (2013). *Project Management* (11th ed.). Hoboken, NJ: John Wiley & Sons, Inc.

Knight, F. (1921). *Risk, Uncertainty, and Profit.* Boston, MA: Hart, Schaffner and Marx, Houghton Mifflin.

Koivu, T., Nummelin, J., Tukiainen, S., Tainio, R., & Atkin, B. (2004). *Institutional complexity affecting the outcomes of global projects.* Working Papers 14. VTT.

Lan, L., Qing-hua, H., & Long-long, S. (2015). Identifying the Project Complexity Factors of Complex Construction Projects. *Proceedings of International Conference on Management Science & Engineering (22th)* (pp. 1697-1702). Retrieved October 07, 2016 from http://icmse.hit.edu.cn/icmsecn /ch/reader/ create_pdf.aspx?file_no=L2015090226&flag=2

Laszlo, E. (1994). The evolutionary project manager. In D. I. Cleland & R. Gareis (Eds.), *Global project management handbook* (International Editions). New York: McGraw-Hill.

Levin, G., & Ward, J. L. (2011). *Project Management Complexity. A Competency Model.* Taylor & Francis Group.

Loosemore, M., Raftery, J., Reilly, C., & Higgon, D. (2006). *Risk Management in Projects.* New York: Taylor & Francis.

Mayerhofer, H., Hartmann, L. S., Michelitsch-Riedl, G., & Kollinger, I. (2004). Expatriate Assignments: A Neglected Issue in Global Staffing. *International Journal of Human Resource Management, 15*(8), 1371–1389. doi:10.1080/0958519042000257986

Mendenhall, M., & Oddou, G. (1986). Acculturation profiles of expatriate managers: Implications for cross-cultural training programs. *The Columbia Journal of World Business, 21*(4), 73–79.

Mendenhall, M. E., & Stahl, G. K. (2000). Expatriate training and development: Where do we go from here? *Human Resource Management, 39*(2), 251–265. doi:10.1002/1099-050X(200022/23)39:2/3<251::AID-HRM13>3.0.CO;2-I

Metcalf, L. E., Bird, A., Shankarmahesh, M., Aycan, Z., Larimo, J., & Valdelamar, D. D. (2006). Cultural tendencies in negotiation: A comparison of Finland, India, Mexico, Turkey, and the United States. *Journal of World Business*, *41*(4), 382–294. doi:10.1016/j.jwb.2006.08.004

Motet, G. (2009). Les cahiers de la sécurité industrielle. *La Norme ISO*, *31000*, 10.

Nokes, S., & Kelly, S. (2008). *Il project management. Tecniche e processi*. Milano, Italy: FT Prentice Hall.

Perano, M. (2010). Il Project Management. In M. Pellicano & M. V. Ciasullo (Eds.), *La visione strategica dell'impresa* (pp. 321–355). Torino, Italy: Giappichelli Editore.

Pinto, J. K., & Slevin, D. P. (1988). Critical success factors across the project life cycle. *Project Management Journal*, *19*(3), 67–75.

PMI (Project Management Institute). (2009). *Practice Standard for Project Risk Management*. Philadelphia: PMI.

Rayner, S. (1990). *Risk in cultural perspective: Acting under uncertainty*. Norwell, MA: Klewer. doi:10.1007/978-94-015-7873-8_7

Renn, O., & Rohrmann, B. (2000). Cross-cultural risk perception: State and challenges. In O. Renn et al. (Eds.), *Cross-Cultural Risk Perception. A survey on empirical studies*. Dordrecht, The Netherlands: Kluwer. doi:10.1007/978-1-4757-4891-8_6

Rowat, C. (2003). LRN supply-chain risk and vulnerability workshop. *Logistics & Transports Focus*, *5*(2), 68–69.

Schollhammer, H. (1973). Strategies and Methodologies in International Business and Comparative Management Research. *Management International Review*, *13*(6), 17–31.

Schwalbe, K. (2007). *Information Technology Project Management* (5th ed.). Boston, MA: Thomson Course Technology.

Schwarz, M., & Thompson, M. (1990). *Divided we stand: Redefining politics, technology, and social choice*. Philadelphia: University of Pennsylvania Press.

Shepard, M. (2012). *Il nuovo standard internazionale di project management: ISO 21500. Il Project Manager, 11*.

Steven, J. (2001). *Emergence: The Connected Lives of Ants, Brains, Cities and software*. New York: Scribner.

Thomas, J. (2000). Making sense of project management. In R. Lundin, F. Hartman, & C. Navarre (Eds.), *Projects as business constitutents and guiding motives*. London, UK: Elsevier Academic. doi:10.1007/978-1-4615-4505-7_3

Tonchia, S. (2007). *Il Project Management*. Milano, Italy: Il Sole24Ore.

Tonchia, S., & Nonino, F. (2007). *Il Project Management*. Milano, Italy: Il Sole24Ore

Tsui, A. S., Nifadkar, S. S., & Ou, A. Y.Amy Yi Ou. (2007). Cros-snational, cross-cultural organizational behavior research: Advances, gaps, and recommendations. *Journal of Management, 33*(3), 426–478. doi:10.1177/0149206307300818

Tung, R. L. (1984). *Business negotiations with the Japanese.* Lexington, MA: Lexington Books.

Vidal, L.-A., & Marle, F. (2008). Understanding project complexity: Implications on project management. *Kybernetes, 37*(8), 1094–1110. doi:10.1108/03684920810884928

Weaver, G. R. (1998). The Process of Reentry. In G. R. Weaver (Ed.), *Culture, Communication, and Conflict: Readings in Intercultural Relations* (2nd ed.; pp. 230–238). Simon & Schuster Publishing.

Werner, S. (2002). Recent developments in international management research: A review of 20 top management journals. *Journal of Management, 28*(3), 277–305. doi:10.1177/014920630202800303

White, A. (2009). *From comfort zone to performance management.* White & MacLean Publishing.

White, D., & Fortune, J. (2002). Current practice in project management – an empirical study. *International Journal of Project Management, 20*(1), 1–11. doi:10.1016/S0263-7863(00)00029-6

Williams, T. M. (1999). The need for new paradigms for complex projects. *International Journal of Project Management, 17*(5), 269–273. doi:10.1016/S0263-7863(98)00047-7

Wirick, D. W. (2009). *Public-Sector Project Management.* Hoboken, NJ: Wiley. doi:10.1002/9780470549131

Chapter 10
Water–Related Price Risks:
Implications for Company Competitiveness

Ninel Ivanova Nesheva-Kiosseva
New Bulgarian University, Bulgaria

ABSTRACT

This chapter presents the issue of the risks associated with the increase of the price (tariffs) of water, which are, and promise to be, a growing challenge for the sustainable management of the companies. At the beginning of the chapter the term risk is operationalized and water-related risks are classified. The reasons and their specific characteristics for the raising of water prices and the objective risks they create for the companies have been identified in the main part of the chapter. This part informs the company management about the possible causes of unjustified increase in the price of the water used in their activities. Several informational and analytical solutions and guidelines for the management have been marked in the end. These can prove useful in preventing and reducing the abovementioned risks and in aiding the sustainable management of the companies.

INTRODUCTION

This chapter examines the causes and sources of the increase in water prices and the risk they pose to competitiveness. There is no company that does not use water in its production and sanitary needs for economic and household purposes. The constant increase of the price of the water used as a resource in production, the complex methodology of water price formation represents a challenge to the sustainable management of companies, as is included in the cost of production. The purpose of the text is to aid management in making informed decisions to optimize water use for sustainable management and the successful performance of companies in financial and social terms.

DOI: 10.4018/978-1-5225-2673-5.ch010

BACKGROUND

Practical problems of water management date back to ancient times with the creation of the first irrigation and urban water systems in Mesopotamia, China, Ancient Egypt, the Roman Empire. With industrialization, the growth of world population and the development of the processes of globalization, which move huge masses of people and industries to urban and industrial areas, combined with the needs of agricultural production, the issues of water management have acquired new aspects and have become more acute. In fact, research on "water issues" have never ceased and have been made from different angles - engineering, chemical, environmental, managerial and economic, social, environmental. The main question is "Is water a commodity, an economic good (and how do we define an "economic good"), a gift of nature that cannot be priced and a human right?" Ecologists, social scientists, and economists are divided on the answer to this question. Each has argued their case with the tools of their trade and within their science. In fact, water is all that and much more, it is the very existence of life in all its manifestations. Water is life itself.

This unique nature of water and the pressure of the challenges of the industrialized and globalized world, put the different scientific areas and socio-political system in the position to find a complex balance between the various uses, the limited quantities, qualities, water needs, combined with existing incomes. This, indeed, is an impossible task, but the lack of a new Newton to come forth with the universal law of the socio-ecological-economic universe of water is evident. In an attempt to solve the water issue the oldest common system of its management is being used, that of centralized regulation. But the scarcity of water, the investments that the utility companies providing water supply (WSO) have made in extracting, purifying, treating and delivering it to the consumers requires the use of new methods in the balance formation, the methods of regulatory pricing coupled with the requirement that water be seen as a human right - the right of life.

The apparent lack of the new Newton has led to the laboratory creation of multiple methods for water pricing that combine market components, recover the costs of water companies, and provide the vital minimum of water supply to the poor, as well as to meet environmental requirements. The application of these methods in practice, however, leads to the result of constantly raising water prices and coercive measures for the reduction of its consumption not only for agricultural and industrial needs but also for household needs.

On the demand side are the businesses and households that can neither live nor exist without water. All this is a challenge to the management of companies placed in an environment of intense and growing competition in terms of globalization and requires taking unconventional decisions. But in order to make the right decision, you need true and accurate data on reflecting the entire complexity of the problems.

In response to this challenge, this chapter presents in an accessible way the main sources of the increase of the price of water. The goal is the text to serves as a basis for successfully management the water issues from the companies.

MAIN FOCUS OF THE CHAPTER

It is impossible to review the entire literature on "water issues". However, if there should be a review of the literature it should start from around 53 000 BC. Since water price risk for companies is not among the issues on which to focus research there is practically no systematic scientific literature on the risks for companies coming from the price of water. In practice these price risks are outsourced by businesses and their management, and is dealt with by consulting firms as part of their research and development rather than treated as company research projects.

Risk of Increasing of the Price of Water for Businesses

Risk is a possible deviation from expectations. It can be both positive and negative. When the result of the risk is negative, the business is likely to lose.

Frank Knight defines risk as "uncertainty":

The word "uncertainty "seemed best for distinguishing the defects of managerial knowledge from the ordinary" risks "of business activity, which can feasibly be reduced if not eliminated by applying the insurance principle through some organization for grouping cases (Knignt, 1964, p. 1ix).

Water risks in the economy can be viewed from three sides.

- On the demand side: from the perspective of water consumers and water services;
- On the supply side: the side of the suppliers of water (WSO)
- On the side of the regulatory authorities, who must balance the needs of consumers and suppliers -WSO.

The author addresses the issue of rising water prices from the perspective of the managers of the companies-consumers of water services.

Managing the demand for water for industrial and agricultural needs is a strategic management activity that aims to achieve efficient and sustainable water use and with it financial stability for the companies using water supplies for their activities.

The cost of water used in production is part of the companies' economic risk, the trend being the increase of its delivery price. The critical study, the defining of this risk by the companies is in favor of creating informed strategic management decisions in the era of the Second Globalization.

Classification of Water Risks for Companies

The risks associated with water for the companies have different and various classifications.

In Water: The New Business Risk (China Water Risk, 2010) the following risks are differentiated:

1. Physical/Operational risk.
2. Regulatory risk.
3. Economic risk.
4. Reputational risk.
5. Social risk.
6. Supply chain risk.
7. Investment risk.
8. Risks in combination.

The Swedish organization for water analysis - Swedish Water House (SIWI), part of the Stockholm International Water Institute, recognizes the following related to water risks for businesses:

1. **Operational Risks:** These are risks that lead to an increase in the companies' production prices.
2. **Market Risks:** Risks associated with loss of market share; they are mainly due to loss of competition with companies, which reduce their water footprint.
3. Reputational risks.
4. Regulatory risks.
5. Financial risks.

Financial risks reduce revenue, access to capital, leading to higher interest rates and insurance premiums for companies ("Water as a financial risk", n.d.).

In addition to this SIWI establishes the group "Corruption Risks in Water Licensing" (Water: The New Business Risk, Part II, 2010).

Risks in this group are reduced to the following: license application process; the content of the license; bidding and trading procedures; enforcement of license (Warner et al., 2009).

There is potential for corruption, creating risk in these circumstances, is due to monopoly and the state regulation of WSO.

Therefore, the corruption risk is also a regulatory risk as it derives from the decisions of regulatory authorities - national regulatory commissions – The Commissions for energy and water regulation or the ministries, responsible for the regulation of the water sector. Worldwide, the corruption factor in the field of water supply is indeed immense.

The Water Integrity Network estimated in its report "Water Integrity Global Outlook 2016" (Das, Fernandez, Van der Gaag, McIntyre & Rychlewski, 2016) that $75 billion dollars of water investments are lost to corruption annually at various levels - corporate, political, municipal, etc. (assuming corruption is only 10% of all investments).

The SASB Climate Risk Framework includes risks associated with water to Climate Risk Categories, which have a corresponding financial impact on businesses. The risk factors for water are: physical effects, transition to a low-carbon resilient economy and climate regulation, which create an impact on companies in cash flow, asset value impacts and financing impact. (Sustainability Accounting Standards Board, 2016).

When it comes to increasing the price of "a resource, a good and a human right", such as water is, in terms of classification of financial risks, it is usually called "commodity price risk".

Water-Related Price Risk for Companies: Causes and Identification

The price risk is inherently an economic risk. Here the author uses the term "price" because in an economy based on market principles, the price is "a magic crystal, which reflects all economic activity." The term "price risk" concentrates in itself the diversity of types and classifications of risk. Ultimately, rising water prices and the variety of water regimes, different in almost every town and village, are reflected in the price of the products and services manufactured and sold by the company.

The global trend in the price of water is towards a constant increase. The calculation of the rising water prices in the cost of goods causes for the companies a price risk related to water.

GWI estimates that global water rates have increased with an average of 6.8 percent in just one year (between July 2010 and 2011) at a constant exchange rate (Global Water Tariffs Continue Upward Trend, 2011).

The author considers the term "price risk" more convenient to use and analyze micro and small enterprises that neither have centers for R & D, nor financial resources for technological and scientific optimization of water use, compared with large corporations.

The price risk associated with water:

- Is a systematic and continuous risk.
- Is a risk posed by the cost of water at the entrance: it occurs in adverse movements in the price of resources (water) needed to produce goods and services, resulting in increased costs to businesses.
- Creates business "revenue at risk" (RAR) (Thayer, Bruno & Remorenko, 2013; Hardcastle, 2015).
- Creates negative cash flow impact for businesses.

Therefore, the price risk of increasing the price of water leads to a risk for the creation of a competitive price of the goods and services that the company produces.

The price risk in the enterprise is practically connected with the:

- Pricing of resources, including water.
- Pricing of goods and/or services to be sold.

A study by Price Waterhouse Coopers, shows that 86 percent of a company's senior management believes that the "commodity price risk" (which includes price risk and water), is very important for the profits of enterprises. (PricewaterhouseCoopers, 2009).

The same study indicates that to manage price changes, 81 percent expect to reduce the total cost, 79 percent rely on a guide to purchases, 49 percent of the production changes, 35 percent hedging and 33 percent of hedging and portfolio optimization (Warford, 1997).

In the mid 70's the price of industrial water in Japan is estimated to have grown drastically. This forces Japanese companies to undertake an investment program for the processing of water by creating their own corporate system for this purpose, and usually reducing its consumption.

There are already a number of examples of enterprises in industry that have benefitted greatly from the rational use of water, such as Coca Cola, the Campbell Soup Company etc. Agricultural business can generate even more profit from the sustainable use of water (Burritt & Christ, 2014).

Water: Both a Local and Global Problem

The nature of water as a vital resource and good, necessary for every vital function and activity, the fact that it is both global and local, renewable and non-renewable, creates an uncertainty in its management, and hence, uncertainty in its users.

Water is essential for human existence as well as for economic activity a "finite and vulnerable resource, essential to sustain life, development and the environment", (The Dublin Statement on Water and Sustainable Development (DSWSD], Principle No. 4, 1992), which is the basis of life and any business on Earth.

In business analysis and scientific literature more importance is attached to the risks associated with stock market fluctuations, monetary policy, interest rates, the prices of energy for the companies than with the risks generated by water management issues.

Financial instruments, money and energy are felt as a global problem to a greater extent than water because they are traded on world markets, which have their price-makers and coordinate worldwide prices. The situation with water is different. There are no global markets of industrial water. Every living being needs water here and now, in a specific place, in this specific limited time and its availability for the people and businesses depends on local factors. Access to water and the provision of the necessary amounts of water are different in different locations. They are not fixed, nor can they always be managed flexibly, such as the amount of money today. Water is a global and local issue at one and the same time where the ability to coordinate a time and place between the global and the local in addressing water issues is absent. And this makes it a specific, a special resource, from which arise specific and particular risks for the companies.

But local water problems, which are the key to life and business are global problems, they are also long-term problems. This is to say that from a management point of view they are strategic management problems. That is why governmental authorities and businesses alike should come up with strategic solutions for water management.

Water as an Economic Resource and a Human Right: The Concept of Affordability -Theoretical and Practical Problems

Water is determined as a fundamental, inalienable human right and along with this as the "economic asset of economic value." The fourth principle, proclaimed by the Conference on Water in Dublin in 1992, which is fundamental in its treatment and management reads "Water has an economic value in all its competing uses and should be recognized as an economic good". (DSWSD, Principle No. 4, 1992)

Consideration of water as a fundamental human right, proclaimed at the highest international level has led to the fact that two conditions have been taken into account in the regulatory pricing of water - the price of drinking water to be accessible (affordable) as this principle does not apply to industrial water and water for irrigation. Even if in a number of countries the latter is not subjected to stringent treatment as drinking water, industrial and water used for irrigation purposes is more expensive than drinking (tap) water. Once after the demands for drinking water have been satisfied as basic needs, water should be used on a competitive basis as a productive and limited resource; its allocation should be based on the highest value (utility) that it could create.

These principles have been applied in practice to show that water supply for economic use may be stopped in the event of a grave water crisis. Such a crisis occurred in Venezuela in 2016 and companies using larger amounts of water in their production were stopped by virtue of a government decision. (Follett, 2016). But this has not resolved the problems. There are different theoretical views on the economic role of the price of water and various practical techniques for its pricing.

Under normal conditions, when no acute water crisis exists, the regulators determining the price of water are of a different opinion. The price of water supply, unlike the prices of other goods and services does not perform the function for optimizing the allocation of resources (in this case water) with a view to more effective use. The price of water is to a larger extent a tool in achieving the stability of the suppliers (WSO), which are able to continue deliveries and have funds for repairs and maintenance as well as an ability to invest. The viewpoint of the regulators is that they have been called upon to correct market prices and to bring effectiveness in water consumption. When the price does not fulfill such a function, it does not give the usual information to consumers and producers. In this way, a high risk for both producers and consumers arises.

Strengthened Individual and Intersectoral Competition Among Water Users: A Steady Increase in Demand for Water for Industrial Purposes.

Companies in the fields of agriculture, energy, transport, industry, the businesses of "free time" (leisure), and of course - households that take precedence in determining the regulatory cost and access to water compete for water resources. The largest industrial users of water are the sectors of energy and industry.

The priorities of the government's economic policy, the traditions in the economic system, various public organizations with influence, political and business lobbies that are able to provide greater access at a better price to a single sector and in detriment to another influence the competition for water. Actual water consumption on the planet has been estimated at 9 000 cubic km. per year. Water is the most widely used resources, its consumption exceeds 30 times the industrial consumption of all other resources and this tendency keeps growing at a rapid pace (Helmer, 1997).

As a volume, the larger bulk of the water is used for industrial needs. This amounts to about 65 percent of the water consumed by mankind and the remaining 35 percent are used for the needs of agriculture and households.

In recent years, there has been a rapid increase in the volume of water consumed for drinking, while the rate of water consumption for agricultural and industrial use has decreased.

According to the European statistical office Eurostat, the EU industry uses about 40 percent of the raw water that comes mainly from public (WSO) suppliers. In addition, the industrial sector is the main pollutant of water responsible for about 60 percent of the pollution, according to incomplete data (Förster, 2014).

Also, according to Eurostat, the four largest industrial sectors in the EU are supplied for their production from 2 percent to 50 percent by public water suppliers and from own water sources, according to data for 2011 (Förster, 2014). (In addition, these facts show the great role of the state regulatory authorities in defining the price of water as recourse for industry.)

In the member states of the EU there is a constant trend towards water price increase in the medium-term future. In England and Wales, the average prices for water services have increased by 35 percent in the period 1989 - 2006; in 2009 in Spain the price of drinking water increased by 100 percent compared to 2000 (European Environment Agency, 2013).

The price of the water extracted for the industry has large variations in terms of who delivers it. According to forecasts of "Veolia"- the giant in the water business, the global GPD will increase with 70 percent in 2050 compared to 2010, which will be produced in water scarce regions (Veolia Water, 2014a).

According to the study of Environmental Outlook Baseline (OECD, 2012) the demand for the so-called "blue water" – the use of water from different sources such as rivers, lakes and groundwater will grow by 55 percent from 2000 to 2050. (Note: "Blue water" is the freshwater from lakes, rivers and groundwater; "green water" – water from rainfall; "gray water" (sullage) - wastewater.)

The industry will have the largest share in this growth with an increase of 400 percent or 1,000 cubic km. The largest industrial users of water are energy and manufacturing). The energy industry will further increase its consumption of water with 140 percent or 300 cubic Km. Due to the growth of the world's population (about 40 percent in 2050, or approximately 80 million/per year) household use of water will increase seriously with a demand of 130 percent, also about the same as the electricity sector (OECD, 2012).

The use of water for agricultural production and livestock production accounts for about 70 percent of the use of fresh water on the planet. Its relative share has large variations in high- and low-development economies. In some of the low-developed economies this use comes up to 90 percent of the usage of blue water, while in the developed industrialized countries the situation is vice versa. For example, according to Eurostat, in Belgium water for agricultural needs is around 9 percent of the amount of water for industry, and in the Netherlands this is only 3 percent.

The water used for agricultural purposes in the world derives (world average) from 80 percent rainfall (the so-called "green water") and only 20 percent of "blue water" (Molden, 2007).

Increasing demand for water as a result of increased competition for water, poses a serious price risk, that of increasing the price of water for agricultural, industrial and domestic consumers. This increased demand will put pressure on the water infrastructure and its prices as well as on the components of its service.

Price Sensitivity of the Users to Water Prices: Price Elasticity of Water Demand

The price of water is not elasticity of demand. In itself, the rigidity of water demand is a risk that firms must bear in mind in the present, in their future plans and at any one time.

There is no firm that does not use water to a greater or to a lesser extent. There is no substitute for water and water is beyond any comparison. Therefore, the industrial and agricultural users of water are extremely sensitive in this respect.

Users of water in agriculture and industry depending on the region where they operate may be more sensitive to the price of water if in their region there are no possibilities for the creation of reserves of water in reservoirs or dams. They are also at risk of reduced water reserves due to climate reasons.

Water, however, has a small share in the total costs incurred by companies for resources and constitutes a fraction of the price of the final goods produced.

There are companies that have lowered to zero the risk of price fluctuations of the water, have established their own systems for a complete water cycle, including purifying their own water sources.

Therefore, the risks for the different regions and companies are different. For these reasons, the choice of pricing and pricing methods concerning water price risks are different for the different companies.

Consumer sensitivity to the price of the water supplied therefore varies to a large degree, and varies between individual users depending on their income and technological optimization in the use of water, and also varies seasonally, especially for agricultural purposes. Consumer sensitivity to water is captured by the measure "price elasticity of demand". This indicator gives us an idea of how much the demand will change as a percentage at a given percentage change in price. It is calculated using the following known formula as part of the percentage change in the amount of demand and the percentage change in the price of supply.

$$E^P_D = (Q_1 - Q_0)/(Q_1 + Q_0) /(P_1 - P_0)/(P_1 + P_0)$$

This elasticity, i.e., the change of the amount of water that the consumer can afford in case (increase in our case) the price of water depends on whether the product or service has a substitute. With water this is the worst possible scenario since it has no substitute and is usually supplied by the firms - regional monopolies.

The elasticity of demand for water is estimated theoretically between 0 and -1 i.e. water demand is inelastic or relatively inelastic. The baseline scenario for the elasticity of demand to price is that even large changes in the offer price of water will not cause a drastic change in its demand because it is a vital resource. This is good for companies supplying water services but not good for consumers, especially in terms of supplier-monopoly de jure. This elasticity shows that if the price of water increases by 200 percent, then to maintain the same final price of the goods produced with it, manufacturers must reduce their use of water for the production by 100 percent. This is impossible unless in full recycling.

The model of water pricing is also influenced by the elasticity of water demand. If "block tariffs (rates)" are used (these will be mentioned later) elasticity has certain variations, if other methods are used the variations are different. Along with this, even block tariffs produce different variations of elasticity due to different "volumetric steps" which are taken in different countries. But what price does the block include - just payment for clean water separately or price of clean water together with price for its purification and wastewater? Climate conditions also influence elasticity and rainy or dry years and months, which has been well proven in the calculations of Klaiberet et al. (2010).

Other studies have shown that the demand for water for irrigation becomes inelastic below a certain threshold and elastic above another price threshold. (Varela-Ortega, Sumpi, Garrido, Blanco & Iglesias, 1998). This is quite logical. A study conducted on the basis of three river basins in Spain and using mathematical modeling, shows that in one region (Andalusia) water demand becomes elastic at prices ranging between 4 to 30 peseta/m³ (about 8 US cents/m³ - 1998). For the second region (Castilla) demand is inelastic at low cost and it becomes elastic at a price over 17 peseta/m³. In the region of Valencia, demand is completely inelastic even when there is a great price increase to a level of 35 peseta/m³. (Varela-Ortega at al., 1998). These dramatic regional differences are described by other authors and confirm the strictly regional elasticity of the price of water.

The reasons for these differences can be explained by the effectiveness of the technology of irrigation and the farmers' income. The better the performance of new water supply facilities, the smaller elasticity is, due to the greater efficiency of its irrigation systems that have less water loss, and vice versa. (Varela-Ortega at al., 1998).

Other authors have estimated elasticity of water at -0.2 in countries in transition in EU (Fankhauser & Tepic, 2007). This means that every increase of 1 percent in the cost of water will result in a 2 percent reduction in water consumption. This conclusion is unlikely under normal conditions, since according to it, water demand is elastic and the demand changes more than the amended price. Goods with such elasticity are of no importance to the user, which is not the case when speaking of water. Explanation of this ratio may be searched during chaos in the countries in transition in Eastern Europe, including in the regulation and accountability of water during the survey period, as well as the deep drop in income, which has been observed in transitive economies.

The assumption that under normal conditions water demand is inelastic and is closer to 0 for the various water needs - between 0 and -1, as is characteristic of commodity nutrient and there is no substitute, which is typical of water.

$$-1 < E^P_D < 0$$

As a formal summary of water demand, we can deduce the following formula: Water demand is a function of the price P, consumer income I, expectations W (for business users), the amount of users N (reductions or increases), and other non-price factors T, in this case the technological capabilities that increase efficiency in water use. The non-price factors move the demand curve to the right or to the left, i.e. they increase or reduce it.

$$Q_D = f (P, I, W, N, T)$$

Price Risk Associated with Regulatory Methods of Water Pricing

The methods of pricing and the quality of the regulation of water pricing are key issues in creating price risks for companies. In different countries, there are "weak" and "strong" regulators who are independent by law, but some of them are subjected to different influences by external factors. Non-economic factors such as corruption and lobbyism are intertwined in regulatory pricing as well as accessibility to the available quantities of water for the population with low and non-rising incomes. Water pricing and methods of formation of tariffs are important tools in the management of water consumption (water demand) on a regional and macro level. As a whole the companies work in great uncertainty concerning the actions of regulatory authorities.

It is difficult to determine the quantitative effect of the regulatory methods of pricing on producer prices, including the price of water in the cost of their goods. The reason for this is the lack of complete and comparable statistics and the many variations of pricing, applied in different countries. In EU, water prices vary over a large range with amplitudes of about 75 percent. The cheapest water is in Milan and the most expensive is in Zurich and Geneva (Lallana, 2003, p. 4, p. 7).

The prices of industrial water, the water for household and agricultural needs also varies. The differences vary from country to country to a large extent. For example, in the Netherlands the price of drinking water is around 3.25 Euro higher than that of the price of water for industrial needs and about 2 Euro higher than that for agricultural purposes, per cubic meter. The difference is even greater in France. While in Turkey, Portugal and Hungary the price of industrial water considerably exceeds the price of water for household and agricultural needs (Lallana, 2003, p. 5).

We believe these enormous differences everywhere are mostly due to the methods used for pricing applied by the regulators, the regulators' assessment of the actual costs of the suppliers (WSO) and the existence of cartels. When the conditions of the water resources are normal, the price of water should be formed by the extraction cost, costs for its purification and other treatments, its transportation and delivery costs to the consumer.

Water tariffs must simultaneously be economically and socially founded and meet the criteria for quality of life and cost of this quality. The profits of the water providers (WSO) should cover the needs for investment rather than current spending needs.

In various countries, various methods are used in the pricing of electricity and heating and the pricing of water.

Methods of regulatory pricing, most commonly used are:

- Rate of return regulation/Cost plus
- Price cap/Revenue cap regulation
- Yardstick

In addition, in different countries various solutions are applied, for example:

- Water Markets - or water cap-and-trade scheme regulation
- Marginal opportunity cost pricing

In Rate of return, prices and profit based on cost plus return on assets. The ratio of Stock price/ Revenues based on cost-plus return on assets. The determination of tariffs has 3 phases - determining the amount of operating costs, determining the amount of investment and determining the rate of profit.

This method ignores competition. This is a non-competitive method that can bring about a steady increase in the price of water if applied in a "natural monopoly". This method creates substantial risk for corruption. It does not create conditions for increasing efficiencies for the water supplier, resulting in equal conditions to reduce the price of water by reducing losses in the system of delivery, since the company supplying water does not increase its efficiency.

Another downside of the application of this method of water pricing is the possibility of overcapitalization and the emergence of the so-called "Averch-Johnson Effect" or "AJ- Effect") (Averch & Johnson, 1962) named after the two economists who developed an abstract model of a company located in regulation and using the "Rate of return". (The model Averch-Johnson shows that when companies are subject to regulation by the method of Rate of Return, if permitted their return is greater than the required return on capital, and firms will tend to overinvest in their capacity).

Symbolic method Rate of return (Operating costs plus) can be recorded as follows:

$$P \text{ (delivery)} = AIR / (AQW - MATLW)$$

- **AIR:** Annual income needed for the particular water operator (WSO). Annual revenues approved the company's costs (related activities) that it may recover through the sale of its service. Allowable costs include the operating and maintenance costs (OPEX or O & M) plus capital expenditures CAPEX (depreciation and return).
- **AQW:** Quantity of water (annual amount) at the entrance of the water system for the previous year.
- **MATLW:** The maximum allowable total loss of water, according to the annual target level for the water system.

Since this method does not involve the consideration of any market conditions by the operators, it leads to the creation of an overvalued service. In this method, there is a plurality of possible abuses in the measurement of the incoming water, and in consideration of the water losses in the system.

If there were an honorable contract, bilaterally acceptable for both parties, between the provider of water and the clients, and if compliance were assured, this risk would not exist. In this respect, the new IFRS 15, which is coordinated with US GAAP, set to begin in 2018 moves us in the right direction.

In order to determine the return on investment, this regulatory method uses the RAB method (based on adjusted return on invested capital) (ERRA, 2009).

This is a method of forming tariffs aimed at attracting investments so as to improve and expand the system. The RAB suppliers of water (WSO) receive a guaranteed return on investment, which would be sufficient to service their loans and to obtain profit. The savings remain available to the company.

RAB has a number of disadvantages. It is a complex process that requires the development and coordination of a long-term investment program. There is also the problem with the objectivity and independence of the evaluation of the assets. It is necessary to introduce the statement of investment policy. The regulators also have to establish the fulfillment of the long-term investment parameters. The danger of presenting operating costs as investment costs exist, as practice shows. Altogether, RAB shows a tendency towards a continuous increase of the price of water.

$$RAB = A\text{-}F\text{-}D + NWC$$

- **RAB:** Regulatory asset base
- **A:** Value of assets used and useful lives
- **F:** Value of assets acquired gratuitously funded by the state or municipality
- **D:** Accumulated depreciation over the previous period of used assets
- **NWC:** Needed working capital.

The RAB (opening value) is taken as a basis for the new regulatory period from the previous one. In such a way, the RAB for the new regulatory period is:

$$RAB \text{ (new)} = RAB \text{ (opening)} + RAB \text{ (additions)} - RAB \text{ (depreciation)} + Disposals$$

(Determination of RAB after asset revaluation, 2009)

The methodology of pricing with RAB practically admits inaccuracies, especially with weak regulators and corruption among the control and regulatory authorities as they may recognize O & M costs for investment costs. There is an abundance of such cases. The performance of the operator in an environmental aspect does not improve, because investments have not been made, and the price of water keeps growing steadily and is unjustified.

The other pricing method is "Yardstick regulation".

The Yardstick regulation is a regulatory method putting the companies in comparative competition on certain indicators. This type of regulation requires the revenue of the water provider to be indexed with the index of average productivity of companies in the industry. This regulation is less common for countries such as Chile, Colombia, Australia, England and Wales, Portugal. There are different options according to which this method can be applied. Close to it are the "cost-proxy models". They include pricing and overall long-term additional costs for the supply of water.

Yardstick regulation is recommended as a way to weaken the regional monopolies in the supply of water, as the regulator should have access to the complete information and can compare their performance. The controller can compare specific expenses of companies with average-sectorial, and require them to achieve certain levels of performance.

$$AC_i = Sum \ (AC_j)/(n\text{-}1), \ j \neq i$$

In some cases, this method of adjusting results by reducing the price of water achieves higher cost efficiency.

However, the positive results can be achieved only on condition that the regulator is strong and independent, not susceptible to corruption and there is no existing cartel agreement between the companies monopolists. In other words, the Yardstick regulation is likely to lead to a positive result if the regulators of public services and the regulatory authorities in the competition are strong, independent and uncorrupted.

It is estimated that the Yardstick regulation will eliminate the inefficient companies, due to the fact that it is based on an analysis of the performance of the companies.

Cap price regulation or CPI-X regulation. (Adjustment through price limits) is the other pricing method.

In theory, this method of regulation establishes a ceiling on the price or profit of the suppliers (WSO). It simulates the market situation as the yardstick does but by using other improved technology.

The method aims to force companies supplying water (WSO) to reduce their dependents, from where the cost of water supply can be reduced. Companies have to reduce their costs by increasing their efficiency to meet the requirements of the regulator for a certain level of water price, which they should not exceed. The company has the incentive to assign to itself all profits received. Therefore, it seeks to increase its efficiency. That is the way things stand in theory.

The coefficient of efficiency *X* plays a major role in this method of pricing.

There are different variants of the method. One of the most common is limiting the rise in water prices through the growth of the consumer price index and reduction of the cost by deducing the factor of performance *X*.

In general, the formula is as follows:

$$P_t = CPIX + K + Q$$

- **CPI:** Consumer Price Index
- **X:** Required efficiency
- **Q:** Standards of quality
- **K:** Network expansion – i.e. investment in Fixed Assets.

Or:

$$P_t = P_{t-1}*(1 + I - X)_t$$

- **P:** prices offered by the water and sewerage operator;
- **I:** Inflation for the previous period, which affects the cost of water and sewerage operator
- **T:** Time index;
- **X:** Factor for improving efficiency.

Price period is for 1 year or more.

This model is a variant of the price cap regulation main formula, as it looks like a simple formula CPI-X+ K+Q, where the terms reflect adjustments for price inflation, productivity, network expansion, and improved quality of service. In practice, with baskets other features, the formal representation of the formula can be quite complicated.

There are a number of hazards in the application of the method, however:

If the company - monopoly does not account for increased efficiency, the *X* factor would be equal to 0 and then prices will not fall, but will grow continually. There are a number of such cases in which the index *X* is not considered and this enables companies to increase prices and assign the entire profits to themselves along with this.

More and more European countries use variants of Cap price in different varieties; the main being Individual price cap, Revenue cap (Fixed revenue cap, Average revenue cap, Hybrid revenue cap) and Tariff basket.

Block tariffs are the other pricing method. There are increasing and decreasing block tariffs (rates).

This method follows growing - reducing steps of fixed volumes of water consumption or pollution, according to which increases-decreases the price of water.

Water markets or Water cap-and-trade scheme regulation is the newest tool in this field. Trade with water rights has already been introduced in several countries. A limited number of countries, in combination with regulated pricing introduced trading with water rights, which is the sale of a right of access to water. Such trade has been conducted in Australia, USA, Canada, Chile, Armenia, and Iceland. These programs are local and have the ambition to expand their number to about 20 ("Cap and Trade", 2017). Australia has developed accounting standards for the preparation and publication of water accounting reports for entities including regulation and accountability in the marketing of water rights in AWAS1 and AWAS2.

Chapter "Water rights, water allocations and water restrictions", Art. 163, Chapter 164 and "Water market activity", Art. 165-167. 1 of AWAS accurately regulates reporting trade with water rights and claims to water in the water accounts of companies (Water Accounting Standards Board, 2010).

The trade in water rights is a transfer of water licenses for a given period. Usually the period is one fiscal year. (O'Brien, 2010). These market-based instruments regulating the price of water include components of its quality and quantity, taking into account the extent of pollution and contaminants that users of water resources cause. It is believed that these instruments contribute to the proper allocation of water resources and control water pollution. Trade in water rights allows companies that have a surplus of water to sell it to the needy and thus profit (Burritt & Christ, 2014a).

Price Risks Related to Reforms in the Water Sector

A great uncertainty and the associated with it risk for companies are the reforms in the water sector carried out and planned to be carried out in the future. In many industrialized countries, the system of water pricing and the institutional status of the water regulatory authorities has changed.

Australia envisages the expansion of trade with "water rights", relying to add a greater market element in the pricing of water.

Russia changed its Water code in 2006 and amended it more than dozen times till 2016. (Vodniy Codex Rossiiskoy Federaciy).

Article 20 of the Code says that water use shall be subject to payment and is based on a contract, irrespective of the fact whether a body or parts of it are concerned and prohibits monopolization in the water sector. During the latest reform of the water regulation in the Russian Federation the Commission for Energy and Water was transformed into a Department of the State Competition Commission and its functions were linked to the problems of competition.

In the EU countries, these commissions are separate from the Competition Commission. This diversity and variety in the philosophy and technology of water pricing can create risks for profit enterprise groups operating transnationally.

As a whole, the pricing of water on the principle of "user pays", "polluter pays" and the use of "full-cost pricing" (Christian-Smith, Gleick & Cooley, 2011, p. 144) is undergoing reforms in the highly-industrialized countries apart from China and Russia. These reforms are combined with the necessary requirements for these pricing systems - detailed water accounting and reporting, and "full-cost recovery" of the costs of water infrastructure and service delivery and treatment of water, increasing the efficiency of irrigation of agricultural areas through new methods of drip irrigation, etc. (Christian-Smith, et al, 2011, p. 146).

What are some of the dangers that these reforms pose?

Using the "Full Cost Pricing Method": full cost pricing (or fully distributed cost pricing) includes the distribution share of the overall business costs in the final price of goods and services.

According to the European Environment Agency (EEA):

The full cost comprises three elements as also set out in the WFD [Water Framework Directives, EC, 2000]:

1. **Environmental Costs:** The costs of damage that water uses impose on the environment and eco-systems and those who use the environment, e.g. a reduction in the ecological quality of aquatic ecosystems or the salinization and degradation of productive soils.
2. **Resource Costs (Opportunity Costs):** The costs of foregone opportunities which other uses suffer due to the depletion of the resource beyond its natural rate of recharge or recovery, e.g. linked to the over abstraction of groundwater.
3. **Financial Costs:** The costs of providing and administering these services. They include all operation and maintenance costs, and capital costs (principal and interest payment), and return on equity where appropriate.) (EEA Report No. 1, 2012, pp. 31-32).

It is important to note that the Resource Costs (opportunity costs) increase while reducing the resource, which is a prerequisite for raising the price of water supply. The EU envisages a pricing tool called "true cost" based on its water directive (Werner & Collins, 2012, p. 8). For the time being it is not entirely clear what "true cost" is. There are various metrics and views with this water pricing.

"Veolia" has offered the water-pricing instrument called "True Cost".

Apart from the standard costs - Direct Costs in which it has included "price of water", Operational Costs (OPEX) and Investments (CAPEX), Indirect Costs which include the cost for CSR of the Company.

In the forming of the final price "Veolia" has included the use of this tool, as well as "Costs related to risks":

- Operational risks: e.g. water shortages, flooding;
- Financial and regulatory risks;
- Costs related to reputational risks: e.g. temporary loss of license to operate, boycotts;
- Penalties due to water pollution enhance regulation. (Veolia Water, 2014b)

The water pricing in China is based on "Marginal opportunity cost pricing".

In 2006 together with the World Bank, the National Development and Reform Commission of the People's Republic of China, China introduced the scheme of pricing of water based on the principle of China Water Risk (2010). A feature of this pricing is that the full costs are not paid by the user of water services and water sources, but are shared between the state budget and the consumers. The users pay only the operational, maintenance and disposal costs, and the state budget pays the portion that covers the capital, investment and infrastructure costs for water supply. The pricing system uses "marginal opportunity cost", the price does not include fixed costs that are not specific to this product. This cost sharing is based on experience in water pricing, which shows that prices equal to marginal costs lead to losses for the companies supplying water (WSO).

MOC = MPC + MUC + MEC

- **MPC:** Marginal private cost,
- **MUC:** The marginal user (or depletion) cost, and
- **MEC:** The marginal externalities (social, environmental) costs. (Warford, 1997).

The price of water is largely dependent on the water stocks of the region.

Countries in Africa and some Latin American countries have insufficient water resources. The application of the methods of full costing and full cost recovery is not possible because they can cause a humanitarian catastrophe for the poor.

The distribution of water across the globe is uneven. In Europe and Asia, where 70 percent of the world's population lives are 39 percent of the water supplies. (Wurbs, 2005; Wang, Fang & Hipel, 2008; Kumar, 2008). Water losses increase due both to accidents, the poor state of the water network but also to a large extent these are due to climate changes. The risk that climate poses is a major long-term one for users of water for household and industrial purposes.

There are risks associated with a lack of common standards for the accounting of costs in environmental accounting systems, both for WSO and for consumer companies. There is no uniform standard for environmental reporting for the countries using MSFA.

In Russia, environmental bills are common with financial counts in a financial state regulated single accounting chart. China uses a Chinese standard, in Japan - Japanese rules apply. In some countries, even in the EU (e.g. Bulgaria, Romania, Greece) there are no national standards for environmental accounting.

In general not only lack of opportunity for the compatibility of accounting data is observed, but there are many methodological and terminological differences in the conventional accountancy systems of states and noticeable differences in this respect between developed and developing countries. This creates additional difficulties for the companies based in different countries, when alignment and compatibility of data is sought.

This section deals with the differences existing between IFAS and GAAP, as well as between them and other accounting standards on accounting in recognition of revenue in terms of the use of certain accounting methods.

There is a difference between "Cost recovery principle of water pricing" and "Cost-recovery accounting method for recognition of revenue".

"Cost recovery principle of water pricing" is the principle that through water rates defined by regulation, provides financial reimbursement for the firms WSO for extraction, treatment and discharge of water to consumers. Reimbursement is defined as the ratio between revenue from water supply and sewerage services and the costs for these by the WSO (Van den Berg, 2015). Cost Recovery Principle means in fact full cost recovery. "Cost recovery for water services might read: to recover all of the costs associated with a water system, programme or service to ensure long-term sustainability". (Cardone & Fonseca, 2003).

The accounting method Cost Recovery is used for the suppliers of water. This method is used in cases when there is a high probability of default of the delivered products. According to the method quoted, first payments received from customers are used to cover the cost of production and only after full cost recovery, the remaining payments are recognized as gross profit.

In the utilities of water supply there is a really high probability of default. It arises from the fact that water is an inalienable human right and there are price caps called affordability for the price of water for households.

The EU Water Directives have announced the "Cost recovery principal" which is based on the fact that the water services rendered must be paid (EU Water Framework Directive, 2000, p. 29).

The costs are covered by the tariffs in the water bills of consumers. If the cost of water supply and the invoices are higher than the thresholds of affordability of the consumers and the consumers are unable (or unwilling) to pay, the companies supplying the utility service actually do two things – transfer the unpaid water bills of the households that cannot afford to pay to the accounts of the consumers that can pay; or they transfer the unpaid costs of supply to the households in the water prices (bills) for business, so that the water for industry is more expensive than household water, as it is in many countries. Besides this the water providers continue to want and receive an increase in the price of water from regulators. The "reasons" are always needs of new investment; covering debts to creditors etc. Water suppliers have agreed upon a certain percentage of profits with the regulator. For example, the fixed percentage of profit that is agreed between the regulator and "Sofia Water" ("Veolia") in Bulgaria is 17 percent of the annual net profit.

A research on the effectiveness of the application of Cost recovery shows that in agriculture the costs are between 20 percent and 80 percent worldwide, and about 50 percent on average in the Mediterranean EU countries. (Assessment of cost recovery through water pricing, 2013). Thus, if subsidies are not applied, the suppliers must inflate the bills of their regular household and industrial customers.

Another problem is the possibility of use of various methods for evaluation of the value. Accounting standards allow the use of "historical cost" (book value) and "fair price". Historical cost is the cost of acquisition, the "fair value" is the result of assessment, subject to objective and subjective criteria, not a single concept, and there are numerous "fair prices". "Fair is the price that would be received to sell an asset or would be obtained upon delivery of the obligation in terms of the usual operations between market participants at the measurement date." (*IFRS No* 13 Fair Value Measurement, 2011).

The fair value is the "input price", while the historical cost (book value) is priced as "output price". Both approaches used simultaneously in different countries, bring about differences in the value of equity investments and assets. This in turn affects negatively the application of regulatory methods such as RAB, assessing the value of investments of the companies-suppliers of water and the value of their capital. Usually (except in a profound crisis), the fair value is higher than the historical price. In practice the use of the fair price method only leads to an overinvestment of the companies-water suppliers, proven in the mathematical model Averch - Johnson at Rate of return. And the investments of these companies are paid for by the bills of the users.

The design of water tariffs is even more diverse. Companies operating in different cities located even in the same country can hardly navigate through the differences in the formation of tariffs. Even if the method of pricing given by the regulator is unified, even if the principle of formation of tariffs for a country is based on a general principle, different cities have different and varying tariffs - formation of final price of water supply.

Projects IBNet Tariffs DB (joint product of Global Water Intelligence (GWI) and International Benchmarking Network of the World Bank (IBNet) collect and display information about tariffs in different regions, countries and cities- 2994 numbers of tariffs. 2817 of them are volumetric, 96 Flat rate, Jump tariff - 11 and others -70. (IBNet Tariffs DB, n.d.)

Most countries use tariffs with fixed or a volume component and a variety of block tariffs, but pricing structures vary greatly. In the designs of the tariffs there are differences in terms of whether the cost of treatment is separate from the price for the supply of water. The types of rates used in the world can be described generally so (Table 1).

Risk of Cartel Prices

Due to the regional nature of water, in the majority of cases the supply of water is carried out by companies that are "Monopoly De Jure" in the region (city, region, parts of the country).

The private companies for water supply can be segmented into 6 groups in Europe:

1. The French water giant "Veolia", "Suez", "Lyonnaise des eaux" and "SAUR";
2. The large Spanish multinational construction companies which build water infrastructure and deal with water management ("Fomento de Construcciones y Contratas S.A." (FCC), "Sacyr Vallehermoso", "Acciona S.A.", "Ferrovial");
3. The German and Austrian companies like "Gelsenwasser AG" and "Energie AG";
4. The private equity companies in the UK and EECA operating on a national level;
5. The domestic companies operating only in their home country;
6. Asian multinationals operating in the UK, and owning large British companies, suppliers of water – "Wessex Water" (Malaysian), "Bournemouth and West Hampshire Water" (a Singapore based company). (Urban Water Consortium, 2014).

Table 1. Summary of the models used in water tariffs

	General Type	Without metering	With metering (volumetric)	Not fixed charge	+ Minimum charge	+ Fixed charge	Blocks
1	Flat fee (flat rate)	X					
2	Constant volumetric		X	X			
3	Constant volumetric rate		X			X	
4	Constant volumetric rate		X		X		
5	Increasing blocks		X	X			X
6	Increasing blocks					X	X
7	Increasing blocks				X	X	X
8	Decreasing blocks			X			X
9	Decreasing blocks					X	X
10	Decreasing blocks				X	X	X

Source: (OECD, 2010)

In fact, these giants have strongly intertwined their activities. For example, "Veolia" owns "Folkestone and Dover", "Three Valleys", "Tendring Hundred" in the UK (Hall & Lobina, 2012a, p. 7).

Everywhere the prices that these companies are levying are constantly increasing.

For example, in Paris, the price of water has doubled for the last 25 years (Hall & Lobina, 2012b, p. 30) for water supplies from "Suez" and "Veolia".

In Berlin, water prices have almost tripled for the delivery of water to the city by a consortium of "Veolia" and the German multinational (RWE). The Commission for Competition in Germany has found out that the real price is 19 percent lower. (Hall & Lobina, 2012b, p. 32).

In 2011, the CEC imposed on Suez Environment and its subsidiary Lyonnaise des Eau a fine of € 8,000,000. Suez was fined € 8 million for breaking a seal during an inspection in 2011.

In 2012, the European Commission initiated a procedure for price-fixing against Saur, Suez and "Veolia". The press release reads as follows:

The European Commission has opened formal antitrust proceedings to investigate whether the French companies SAUR, Suez Environnement/Lyonnaise des Eaux and Veolia, together with their trade association Fédération Professionnelle des Entreprises de l'Eau ("FP2E"), have coordinated their behaviour on French water and waste water markets, in breach of EU antitrust rules. (European Commission, Press release, 2012).

Along with this the water supply giant Veolia constantly maintains a high level of debt due to which it will have to change its pricing policy in the near future (along with restructuring and sale of its assets, now being carried out). Due to the pressure imposed by consumers, the global trend in ownership of water providers is already in the process of remunicipalization. (Hall & Lobina, 2012a, p. 5).

In this way, there is a general trend of uncertainty in pricing and the price of water is being formed due to the uncertainty about the future of ownership of the supplier companies and their indebtedness. While public administrations have altruistic goals, the private companies' goals are to maximize profit.

The continuing process of privatization of the water utilities would go on with the increase of prices, especially if they were able to log in to cartel unions. If the trend on remunicipalization prevails, the altruistic public purposes of the administration would prevail and public companies would be guided, first and foremost, by the principle of affordability for home users. But municipal budgets are limited, and strict adherence to the principle of affordability would lead to increased water prices for household users, if new sources of financing municipal expenditures are not found, which, as a rule, occurs through tax increases and is an unpopular measure.

FUTURE RESEARCH DIRECTIONS

With water prices there is great uncertainty and invariability causing price risk for the companies. The main source of information for management decisions related to water price risk is to create a competitive price for the companies in the field of environmental accounting and even creating, as Australia has done, Water Accounting and Reporting. This can give a reliable base for management decisions to reduce price risk associated with rising water prices for the companies. Public water reporting presentation has reduced the options for a "reputational risk" that adversely affects the company's sales. Roger Burritt writes:

The future will see accountants called upon to provide clients with analysis regarding the economic costs associated with water-related decisions. This suggests there is an opportunity for accountants and accounting firms to position themselves as global experts in the area of corporate water risk and water trading opportunities. (Burritt & Christ, 2014b).

Special attention should be given to the theory of costs, the practice of their reporting and the development of the tool full costing, the Cost Recovery method and the Cost Recovery Principal.

The use of various risk management techniques, developed in compliance with the specific case is also necessary. Here is a large assortment of tools, depending on the specific case.

- Measure Revenue at Risk (RAR);
- Measurement of market risk;
- Dynamics of the share market.

For managerial decision-making in water-related price risks, the management may solve 2 types of tasks in connection with the specific character of water-related risks as mentioned above:

1. Tasks in which quantitative relations are almost completely unknown (unstructured or qualitatively expressed objectives);
2. Tasks, which contain both quantitative and qualitative elements (poorly structured or mixed problems) (Popchev, 2016).

We should resort to Task 2 in cases where the price of water is growing largely due to the inclusion in it, besides quantitative, qualitative elements such as the quality of the water, its degree of contamination after production when the water is sent to the purifying system.

Possible solution option: When environmental factors are characterized by uncertainty, due to the lack of sufficiently reliable methods or means for measurement and the presence of disturbing factors with unstable statistical characteristics, etc., the choice is in conditions of uncertainty.

Selecting decisions under risk a majority of optimal criteria is formed and are functions of different variables (arguments). A numeric value of this criterion is mainly based on two groups of factors.

The first group of factors depends on the individual decision maker and is called "elements of the decision". The elements of the decision are the management's quality and preparation, its understanding of the importance of water-related price risks.

The second group of factors characterizes the conditions in which the company operates. These are the regulatory, accounting, local characteristics of the area where the entity operates. With regard to this group, there are different strategies (Popchev, 2016).

Factor 1 cannot affect factor 2.

There are different criteria for choosing a solution:

1. Characterizing profit in the adopted solution: the greater the value of the criterion, the better the solution (maximization of criterion);
2. Characterizing expenses (losses) in the adopted solution, with an obvious necessity to achieve the lowest possible cost-losses (minimization of criterion)

When it comes to ranking projects in terms of risk and uncertainty, the construction and use of models, algorithms and software tools for the achievement of a Multi-criteria decision is recommended.

When assessing projects to reduce water use such as the recycling systems using their own water, etc., methods for risk assessment of investments in real assets can be used, dynamic methods such as the method factor "income/expenses", static methods such as method of minimum cost, etc.

The models for risk management should be selected in view of the specifics. For example, in Bulgaria V. Kasurova summarizes significant experience in implementing various models for risk management. The study indicates that the application of different models for assessing the risk of bankruptcy for one and the same Bulgarian company gives different, sometimes even contradictory results (Kasurova, 2010).

CONCLUSION

The associated water price risk for companies is reflected in the increase in water prices, which are determined and governed locally by different methods and techniques. Raising water prices constantly increases the costs of the companies and represents a problem for sustainable management. Water prices should be the focus of managerial effort to win a competitive position on the globalizing markets. A major problem facing management is conforming the management of local water prices with global markets.

The companies' management needs to better understand the methods and tools of water pricing. This is necessary for it to be able to identify the "centers of responsibility" of their growth. Many of these factors for the increase in water prices are objective and cannot be influenced by management, but others can be adjusted. So the task before management is to find a means of controls both for the external environment and also for the optimization of the internal environment. This is a new strategic task, representing a serious challenge. It cannot be decided without the joint efforts of all water users, which should combine their efforts for the sake of transparency and correctness of water pricing. Their efforts for better water risk management must combine "the local and the global – the environmental and the economic." The risk for every business is strictly local and specific, and it requires very specific solutions, consistent with strategic global environmental requirements.

REFERENCES

Averch, H., & Johnson, L. (1962). Behavior of the Firm Under Regulatory Constraint. *The American Economic Review*, 52(5), 1052–1069.

Burritt, R., & Christ, K. (2014). *Taking Water Into Account*. Retrieved January 15, 2017, from: http://www.accaglobal.com/vn/en/technical-activities/technical-resources-search/2014/september/taking-water-into-account.html

Burritt, R., & Christ, K. (2014). *Water Accounting: A Short-Term Drought?* Retrieved January 15, 2017, from: https://www.charteredaccountantsanz.com/en/Site-Content/Business-Trends-Insights/Acuity/December-2014/Water-accounting-a-short-term-drought.aspx#.Vs9c2vl97IU

Cap and Trade. (n.d.). Retrieved January 26, 2017, from: http://12.000.scripts.mit.edu/mission2017/solutions/economic-solutions/cap-and-trade-2/

Cardone, R., & Fonseca, C. (2003). *Financing and Cost Recovery. Thematic Overview Paper*. Retrieved January 15, 2017, from: http://www.unep.or.jp/ietc/kms/data/1972.pdf

China Water Risk. (2010). *Water: The New Business Risk Part II*, 1-13. Retrieved from: http://chinawaterrisk.org/wp-content/uploads/2011/06/Water-The-New-Business-Risk-Part-2.pdf

Christian-Smith, J., Gleick, P. H., & Cooley, H. (2011). *US Water Policy Reform, Pacific Institute, World's Water series along with select content from the newest release*. Retrieved January 15, 2017, from: http://ceowatermandate.org/accounting/about/preface/

Das, B., Fernandez, C. F., Van der Gaag, N., McIntyre, P., & Rychlewski, M. (2016). *Water Integrity Global Outlook*. Retrieved January 15, 2017, from: http://www.womenforwater.org/uploads/7/7/5/1/77516286/water_integrity_global_outlook__book_2016_full__1_.pdf

Energy Regulators Regional Association (ERRA). (2009). *Determination of RAB after Asset Revaluation. (ERRA)*. Retrieved January 15, 2017, from: http://www.erranet.org/wp-content/uploads/2016/03/ERRA_Regulatory_Asset_Base_final_report_STC.pdf

EU Water Framework Directive WFD. (2000). Official Journal of EU, L 327, 22 December. *Article, 9*, 29.

European Commission. (2012). *Antitrust: Commission opens proceedings against companies in French water sector*. Retrieved January 15, 2017, from: http://europa.eu/rapid/press-release_IP-12-26_en.htm

European Environment Agency. (2013). *Assessment of Cost Recovery Through Water Pricing* (Technical Report No 16). Retrieved from: www.eea.europa.eu/publications/assessment-of-full-cost-recovery/download

Fankhauser, S., & Tepic, S. (2007). Can Poor Consumers Pay For Energy And Water? An Affordability Analysis for Transition Countries. *Energy Policy, 35*(2), 1038–1049. doi:10.1016/j.enpol.2006.02.003

Follett, A. (2016, March 17). Venezuela Shuts Down for a Week due to Water, Power Crisis. *The Daily Caller*. Retrieved from: http://dailycaller.com

Förster, J. (2014). Water use in industry. *Statistics in Focus, 14*. Retrieved from: http://ec.europa.eu/eurostat/statistics-explained/index.php/Water_use_in_industry

Hall, D., & Lobina, E. (2012a). *The Birth, Growth and Decline of Multinational Water*. University of Greenwich. Retrieved from: http://www.right2water.eu/sites/water/files/the%20birth,%20growth%20and%20decline%20of%20water%20MNCs%20-D.%20Hall%20May%202012.pdf

Hall, D., & Lobina, E. (2012b). *Water Companies and Trends in Europe*. University of Greenwich. Retrieved from: http://www.epsu.org/sites/default/files/article/files/2012_Water_companies-EWCS.pdf

Hardcastle, J. (2015, August 26). Water Scarcity Puts Revenue At Risk. *Environmental Leader*. Retrieved from http://www.environmentalleader.com

Helmer, R. (1997). Water Demand and Supply. In *Proceeding of the IAEA, Symposium, Tajeon, Republic of Korea* (pp. 15–24). Vienna, Austria: IAEA

IBNet Tariff Database. (n.d.). *Tariff list*. Retrieved from https://tariffs.ib-net.org/TariffTable?countryId=0

International Accounting Standard Board. (2011). *IFRS No 13 Fair Value Measurement*. Author.

Kasurova, V. (2010). *Modeli i Pokazateli za Analiz na Finansovata Ustoiychivost na Kompaniyata* [Models and Indicators for Analysis of Financial Stability of the Company]. Unpublished manuscript, New Bulgarian University, Sofia, Bulgaria. Retrieved from: http://eprints.nbu.bg/637/1/FU_1_FINAL.pdf

Klaiber, H., Smith, V., Kaminsky, M., & Strong, A. (2010). *Estimating the Price Elasticity of Demand for Water with Quasi Experimental Methods*. Paper presented at 2010 Annual Meeting of Agricultural and Applied Economics Association, Denver, CO. Retrieved from: http://ageconsearch.umn.edu/bitstream/61039/2/010260.pdf

Knight, F. (1964). *Risk, Uncertainly and Profit*. Retrieved from: https://mises.org/sites/default/files/Risk,%20Uncertainty,%20and%20Profit_4.pdf

Kumar, L. V. (2008). Urban infrastructure and water resources. *Water and Energy International*, 65(3), 77–80.

Lallana, C. (2003). *Water Prices* [Fact Sheet]. Retrieved from: http://www.eea.europa.eu/data-and-maps/indicators/water-prices/water-prices

Molden, D. (Ed.). (2007). *Water for Food, Water for Life: A Comprehensive Assessment of Water*. Routledge.

O'Brien, B. (2010). *Water licenses valued at A$2.8 billion traded in Australia's emerging water markets*. Retrieved January 26, 2017, from: http://voxeu.org/article/price-precious-commodity-water-trading-australia

OECD. (2010). *Pricing Water Resources and Water and Sanitation Services*. OECD. doi:10.1787/9789264083608-en

OECD. (2012). *OECD Environmental Outlook to 2050: The Consequences of Inaction*. Retrieved from: https://www.oecd.org/env/indicators-modelling-outlooks/49846090. pdf

Popchev, I. (2016). *Shest Temi po Upravlenie na Riska* [Six Themes on Risk Management]. Bulgarian Academy of Science. Retrieved from: http://is.iinf.bas.bg/I_Popchev/6_themes_on_Risk_Management.pdf

PricewaterhouseCoopers. (2009). *Navigation: Managing commodity risk through market uncertainty* (in-depth discussion). Retrieved from: https://www.pwc.com/gx/en/metals/pdf/managing-commodity-risk.pdf

Sustainability Accounting Standards Board. (2016). *Climate Risk* (Technical Bulletin TB001-10182016). Retrieved from: http://using.sasb.org/wp-content/uploads/2016/10/Climate-Risk-Technical-Bulletin-101816.pdf

Thayer, C., Bruno, J., & Remorenko, M. (2013). Using data analytics to identify revenue at risk. *Healthcare Financial Management Magazine*, 67(9), 72-80. Retrieved from: https://www2.deloitte.com/content/dam/Deloitte/us/Documents/life-sciences-health-care/us-lshc-hfm.pdf

The Dublin Statement on Water and Sustainable Development. (1992). *Principle No.1*. Retrieved from: http://www.un-documents.net/h2o-dub.htm

UrbanWater Consortium. (2014). *The European Water Market Analysis* (Deliverable 1.1). Retrieved from http://urbanwater-ict.eu/wp-content/uploads/2014/08/URBANWATER-D1.1-The-European-Water-Market-Analysis.pdf

Van den Berg, C. (2015). Pricing Municipal Water and Wastewater Services in Developing Countries: Are Utilities Making Progress Toward Sustainability? In A. Dinar, V. Pochat, & J. Albiac-Murillo (Eds.), *Pricing Experiences and Innovations* (pp. 443–462). doi:10.1007/978-3-319-16465-6_23

Varela-Ortega, C., Sumpi, J. M., Garrido, A., Blanco, M., & Iglesias, E. (1998). Water pricing policies, public decision making and farmers response: Implication for water policy. *Agricultural Economics, 19*(1-2), 193–202. doi:10.1016/S0169-5150(98)00048-6

Veolia Water. (2014a). *Finding the Blue Path for a Sustainable Economy* (White Paper). Retrieved from: http://www.veolianorthamerica.com/sites/g/files/dvc596/f/assets/documents/2014/10/19979IFPRI-White-Paper.pdf

Veolia Water. (2014b). *The True Cost of Water. An Economic Evaluation of Risks and Benefits Related to Water Use* [Brochure]. Retrieved from: http://www.veoliawatertechnologies.com/sites/g/files/dvc471/f/assets/documents/2014/10/32794True-Cost-of-Water-2014-LR_0.pdf

Vodniy Codex Rossiiskoy Federaciy (Water Code of the Russian Federation). (2006). Retrieved on January 27, 2017, from: http://pravo.gov.ru/proxy/ips/?docbody=&nd=102107048

Wang, L., Fang, L., & Hipel, K. (2008). Basin-wide cooperative water resources allocation. *European Journal for Operational Researches, 190*(3), 798–817. doi:10.1016/j.ejor.2007.06.045

Warford, J. (1997). Marginal Opportunity Cost Pricing for Municipal Water Supply (Special Paper). Ottawa, Canada: International Development Research Centre. Retrieved from https://idl-bnc.idrc.ca/dspace/bitstream/10625/32032/7/118129.pdf

Warner, J., Butterworth, J., Wegerich, K., Mora Vallejo, A., Martinez, G., Gouet, C., & Visscher, J. T. (2009). *Corruption Risks in Water Licensing with Case Studies from Chile and Kazakhstan* (SWH Report No. 27). Retrieved from: http://www.swedishwaterhouse.se/wp-content/uploads/1259084220867Corruption-Risks-in-Water-Licensing.pdf

Water Accounting Standards Board. (2012). *Preparation and Presentation of General Purpose Water Accounting Reports* (Australian Water Accounting Standard 1). Retrieved from: http://www.bom.gov.au/water/standards/documents/awas1_v1.0.pdf

Water as a Financial Risk. (n.d.). Retrieved January 27, 2017, from: http://www.swedishwaterhouse.se/en/cluster-groups/water-financial-risk/

Werner, B., & Collins, R. (2012). *Towards efficient use of water resources in Europe*. Retrieved January 15, 2017, from: http://www.enorasis.eu/uploads/files/Water%20Governance/2.EEAreport.pdf

Wurbs, R. A. (2005). Modeling river/reservoir system management, water allocation, and supply reliability. *Journal of Hydrology (Amsterdam), 300*(1-4), 100–113. doi:10.1016/j.jhydrol.2004.06.003

Zetland, D. (2011). Global Water Tariffs Continue Upward Trend. *Global Water Intelligence, 12*(9), 35-40. Retrieved from: https://www.globalwaterintel.com/global-water-intelligence-magazine/12/9/market-profile/global-water-tariffs-continue-upward-trend

KEY TERMS AND DEFINITIONS

Environmental Accounting: A new stage in the development of accounting and reporting, based on the principle of traditional accounting and reporting, but recording, analyzing and reporting environmental costs and benefits for companies.

Regulator (Water Regulator): Generally, independent of the government administrative body which performs the tasks of water pricing. Regulators are often a common authority for the pricing of water, energy and heating. They are empowered to control the quality of the water (energy and thermal) services of the suppliers (WSO).

Regulatory Pricing of Water: Different methods of formation of the price of water by the regulators, including pricing models, principles, laws and rules for their application.

Water and Sewage Operator (WSO) or Water Utilities Companies: companies engaged in the production, treatment, safety, and delivery to users of water for household and economic needs.

Water-Related Price Risk: A concept, concentrating in itself the names of risks facing companies (such as regulatory, operational, reputational, market and corruption risks, plus part of the definition of financial risk). Concentrates in itself in bulk all the above risks in a risk of forming an uncompetitive price of goods and services due to increasing water prices and lack of optimization of water resources by the management of businesses. By nature, an economic risk.

Chapter 11
National Income Inequality, Society, and Multinational Enterprises

Nathaniel C. Lupton
University of Lethbridge, Canada

Guoliang Frank Jiang
Carleton University, Canada

Luis F. Escobar
University of Lethbridge, Canada

ABSTRACT

This chapter calls for understanding the perspective of multinational enterprises (MNEs) on international differences in income inequality. The authors set a research agenda on how national differences in income inequality influence MNE expansion strategies. Applying a transaction cost framework, both negative and positive economic outcomes of income inequality, from the MNE's perspective, are identified. Low levels of income inequality may deter foreign investment, as MNEs prefer countries where they incur lower levels of transaction costs arising from interactions with various market and non-market actors. However, the positive effect of income inequality on location attractiveness will likely diminish at higher levels of inequality when benefits are increasingly offset by additional monitoring, bargaining and security costs owing to instability and conflict. The chapter further explores the implications for level of MNE equity applied in the choice of entry mode under different levels of income inequality.

INTRODUCTION

In this chapter, we begin a discussion, and call for novel research, on how multinational enterprises (MNEs) respond to national income inequality worldwide. Prior research on MNE strategy has detailed how location characteristics, comprised of land, labor, infrastructure and capital endowment, along with institutional quality, impact the 'where' and 'how' of international expansion (Nielsen, Asmus-

DOI: 10.4018/978-1-5225-2673-5.ch011

sen & Weatherall, 2017). The role of societal characteristics, however, receives much less attention. One societal characteristics that has received much attention lately is income inequality. Recent studies provide evidence that long-term rise of income inequality leads to slower economic growth (OECD, 2015), implying that there is a more direct relationship between economic investments and inequality. Our goal, therefore, is to motivate a research agenda aimed at understanding the MNEs' preferences for varying levels of income inequality (i.e. location attractiveness), and how it impacts the MNEs' expansion strategies (i.e. cost and benefits of inequality).

Figure 1 depicts a simplified overview of what is known about the interrelations between income inequality, society and the firm. Income inequality impacts social conditions including crime, quality of life, and unrest, and also impacts economic growth and political stability (Neckerman & Torche, 2007). The firm affects inequality as it is the primary mechanism through which incomes are provided (Cobb, 2016). What is so far missing from current research is the effect that the societal impacts of income inequality have on the functioning of business operations. Our chapter thus aims to flesh out this relationship by applying a transaction cost lens to predict how the social outcomes of different degrees of income inequality impact the economic interests of the MNE. By better understanding this relationship, we will be able to predict how income inequality impacts MNE decisions on international expansion, such as location choice and entry mode.

Following this introduction, we briefly define income inequality, its measurement, and its known outcomes. Next, we review literature on MNE expansion strategies to deduce how the social consequences of both low and high income inequality will impact them. In this section, we apply a transaction cost lens (Williamson, 1985) to relate the social and economic consequences of income inequality to economic costs and potential benefits for firms. We follow this with a section outlining our tentative predictions on the extent to which the MNE will exhibit a preference for income inequality, depending on its economic motives for expansion. This section also directs future research on how the MNE may use organizational structure, namely entry modes such as wholly-owned subsidiaries, joint ventures, etc., to buffer the firm from the negative consequences of social conditions induced by income inequality. Finally, we call for research on how MNE experience, including the nature of its home country income inequality and international experience will also shape the MNE's general preferences towards income inequality.

Figure 1. The position of the multinational enterprise between inequality and society

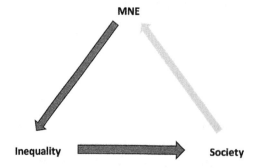

BACKGROUND

National Income Inequality Defined and Measured

National income inequality refers to the distribution of total wage earnings amongst a country's workers, including wages from employment, business income and earnings from investment. The extant inequality research has mainly focused on its negative impacts on individual wellbeing and societal functioning (Neckerman & Torche, 2007; Pickett & Wilkinson, 2015). While the factors that contribute to income inequality are multifaceted, income inequality is an inevitable outcome of wage differentiation based on profession, qualifications and/or productivity levels (Jacoby, 2005). Such differences are to be expected, as wage setting is a key mechanism for increasing employee motivation and skills upgrading (Simpson, 2009).

Measurement of income inequality can be approached in different ways, although most techniques involve use of either point estimates or coefficient of variation (Cobb, 2016). Point estimates compare the proportion of cumulative wealth above and below specific thresholds, for example, the share of cumulative earnings of the top 1% of wage earners compared to the other 99%, or the number individuals whose combined wealth equals that of the bottom half of earners worldwide (Atkinson, 1975). At the time of this writing, the eight wealthiest persons of the world had a combined wealth equal to that of the bottom half of the world's population (Mullany, 2017). Point estimates typically tend to depict inequality in sharp relief while ignoring the characteristics of the middle of the distribution. As such, these estimates tend to depict conditions which do not entirely reflect the experience of the middle class. The OECD (Lopez Gonzalez, Kowalski & Achard, 2015), for example, points out that while globally the gap between middle and bottom earners is widening, the gap between middle and high earners is shrinking.

Coefficients of variation, such as the Gini coefficient, are less sensitive to the extreme points in the distribution and thus better capture the shape of a distribution throughout all ranges. Recent work by Solt (2009) provides the most comprehensive and comparable data on worldwide national income inequality. Nonetheless, all measures of inequality are currently limited in that it is impossible to divide the proportion of income derived from non-labor earnings from labor earnings due to national differences in tax reporting of investment income. Likewise, most income inequality data are currently aggregated to the national level, and therefore do not allow examination of sub-national variation, such as the sharp contrast between rural and urban populations in India, or the population whose economic activity is primarily informal, and hence not observable.

Figures 2 and 3 depict trends in inequality in a sample of emerging (i.e. BRIC) and developed (i.e. G7) countries, respectively. The most noticeable difference between the two graphs is average level of inequality. While G7 countries tend to be more vocal about rising inequality, BRIC economies are overall much higher on this dimension. Furthermore, while some G7 countries have experienced increases in inequality (i.e. Canada, the U.S., and Germany), these changes are quite gradual compared to the more volatile shifts in BRIC countries. China, for example, saw a large spike in inequality around 2000, which coincided with its ongoing economic liberalization, perhaps indicating the rise of capitalism. India, also

Figure 2. Income inequality trends in BRIC countries

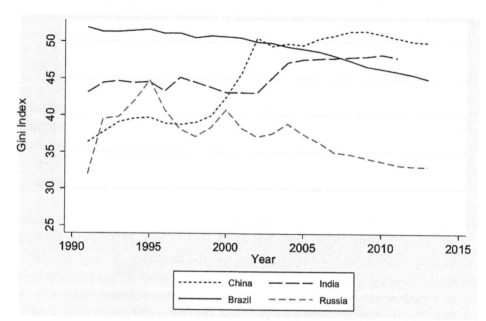

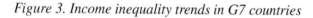

Figure 3. Income inequality trends in G7 countries

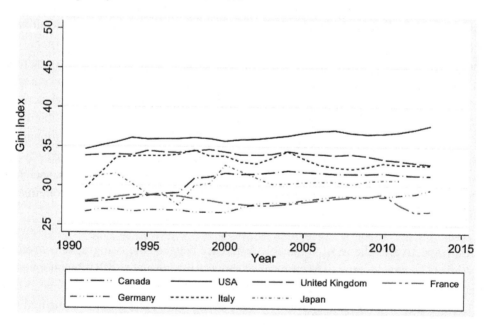

possessing high economic growth rates, has similarly experienced an income inequality spike, albeit less pronounced than in China. Although economic growth in Brazil has not met the more optimistic of predictions, its income inequality has declined since late 1990s. This cursory analysis cannot begin to explain national income inequality differences and trends, and indeed a substantial body of literature we review later suggests the causes are complex and highly interrelated. For the purposes of this chapter, it is important to note that differences in levels and trends in income inequality between countries vary widely, and that economic globalization, comprised of substantial foreign direct investment and liberal economic policies, appears to play a role. We next examine what is known about the outcomes of income inequality for society. The specific role of the MNE is examined later.

Income Inequality and Society

Growing income inequality in societies around the world, and its relationship with social ills such as damaged trust, lack of social mobility, negative health consequences, high crime rate and stagnating wages, is garnering substantial attention in mainstream (e.g. Irwin, 2014; Piketty, 2014) and academic discourse alike (e.g. Alvaredo et al, 2013). Even long-time stalwarts of competitive business strategy have raised alarm over the potential for a downward economic spiral with business at the helm (e.g. Porter & Kramer, 2011). The causes of income inequality are many, and these vary by country, and between countries, as discussed earlier. Some of the more widely cited influences on increasing income inequality are the increasing reliance on mechanization and automation, the decline of unionization and collective bargaining, and globalization (Van Reenen, 2011; Wolff, 2015).

Technological change influences wage distribution through increasing the marginal productivity of skilled workers, who are paid more, while the wages of less-skilled labor remain stagnant. The often-cited Kuznets curve (Kuznets, 1955) assumes that demand for skilled workers exceeds supply and thus, in the short term, technological change widens the earnings gap. Inequality is then the unintended consequence of technological developments.

While technological progress can increase inequality by displacing less-skilled workers from higher paying jobs, unions are largely credited with raising the wages of lower income earners at a faster rate than upper wage earners, thereby narrowing income gaps in the middle of the wage spectrum (Alderson & Nielsen, 2002). Countries like Spain, Ireland, Mexico and Chile have experienced an increase in union memberships. Chile, for example, has doubled the number of workers unionized since 1981 (Economist, 2015). The traditional economic view suggests that an increase in union membership would lead to higher bargaining power of the members, which in return allows them to secure higher wages (Lommerud, Meland & Sorgard, 2003). For rich countries, however, labor union memberships are at historic lows. In the United States for example, membership dropped by almost 30% from 1979 to 2013 (Economist, 2015). Declining unionization is largely cited as a source of widening income gaps in the United States over the latter half of the twentieth century.

Finally, globalization is often targeted as the primary driver of wage stagnation, as manufacturing jobs are transferred overseas to lower wage countries, thereby placing downward pressure on the lower end of the wage spectrum while the upper end continues to rise (Hellier & Chusseau, 2010; Smeeding, 2005). However, while jobs have been displaced in developed economies, these losses have been found to pale in comparison to those caused by mechanization and automation of production (Lehmacher, 2016). As MNEs move parts of their operations around the globe in order to obtain greater efficiency, higher productivity, higher revenues and tax advantages, they impact income inequality not only at home, but also between and within countries abroad. In the next section, we summarize the findings on research that examines the link between the MNE's investment activity and its impact on national income inequality.

Income Inequality and the MNE

Business is one of the primary mechanisms affecting social inequality given its proximal relationship with value creation (Davis & Cobb, 2010). Most research has focused on the impact of foreign direct investment (FDI) on national income inequality. In addition, prior studies on the relationship between income inequality and FDI typically rely on aggregate investment data (Basu & Guariglia, 2007; Deng & Lin, 2013; Jensen & Rosas, 2007; Lin, Kim & Wu, 2013; Wu & Hsu, 2012) and thus do not provide direct answers to the question of how an individual firm's expansion strategy may either benefit from or be constrained by income inequality.

Research on the impact of FDI on income inequality has produced mixed and sometimes contradictory results (Jensen & Rosas, 2007; Mah, 2012; Mahler, Jesuit & Roscoe, 1999; Peluffo, 2015; Tomohara & Yokota, 2011). These inconsistencies have been attributed to national differences in human capital endowment, the technological capability of local industries, and a variety of other institutional and economic conditions in the host country (Lin et al., 2013; Tsai, 1995; Wu & Hsu, 2012). The lack of consensus within this literature implies that both the portion of economic gains from FDI captured by the MNE and the portion distributed to different income segments and stakeholders varies between countries (Tsai, 1995). This means that as an MNE considers a foreign investment the attractiveness of a target location depends on how much of the economic gains the MNE expects to capture. This MNE perspective on the societal conditions produced by income inequality is necessary to better understand the role of the MNE in shaping national and cross-national income inequality. We next introduce transaction cost economics (TCE) to better understand location attractiveness; and then use this framework to understand the implications of income inequality on the MNE's expansion strategy.

CLOSING THE LOOP: SOCIETAL QUALITY AND BUSINESS FUNCTIONING

Transaction Cost Economics (TCE) and International Expansion

Transaction cost theory is useful for understanding business decisions in general, and the impact of inequality on the MNE as it internationalizes, in particular. TCE has long played a crucial role in the research on strategic management and international business (Coase, 1937; Macher & Richman, 2008; Williamson, 1979; Williamson, 1985). TCE holds that markets, firms, and intermediate organizational forms (e.g. strategic alliance) are discrete, efficient governance structures that match different types of economic transactions. Based on the two key assumptions of bounded rationality and opportunism, the theory focuses on three transaction attributes, namely asset specificity, uncertainty, and frequency. TCE predicts that various governance forms have different impacts on minimizing the costs associated with bargaining, governing and monitoring transactions (Williamson, 1985). The theory is at the core of several lines of research on strategic management in the global economy.

The theory of the MNE, especially the internalization framework, draws directly on transaction cost theory (Buckley & Casson, 1976; Hennart, 1982; Rugman, 1981). According to TCE, the MNE and the market are alternative governance structures for organizing interdependent economic activities across countries. The internalization framework argues that, due to market imperfections (especially for intermediate products), the firm is inclined to undertake economic activities internally (e.g. the transfer of proprietary technology) than through markets, as the latter is subject to higher transaction cost.

Internalization allows the MNE to retain competitive advantage derived from its tangible and intangible capabilities that cannot be readily transferred internationally using market mechanisms such as in the cases of exporting and licensing (Rugman & Verbeke, 1992). Thus, MNEs exist mainly as a governance solution to exploit opportunities arising from the integration of ownership advantages (e.g. proprietary technology) and location advantages (e.g. resource endowments and favorable state regulations) (Dunning, 1988; Hennart, 1982).

While host countries may offer economic advantages, such as access to low-cost natural resources or subsidy to set up operations, the countries' socio-political and institutional environment can potentially increase the cost of doing business. Political hazards such as seizure of assets and adverse changes in taxes and regulations can diminish the economic gains captured by the MNE. From a TCE's point of view, the socio-political environment of a country market determines how costly it is for MNEs to engage in economic investment and political activities (Henisz & Zelner, 2004; North, 1990). Uncertain environment implies higher transaction costs because frequent shifts in government policies or in agreements with other stakeholders such as organized labor mean frequent re-negotiation of new arrangements (Anderson & Gatignon, 1986) and this will present the social and political actors with many occasions to behave opportunistically to shift rents from the foreign investor to local stakeholders (Henisz & Williamson, 1999).

Transaction costs, comprised of contract negotiation, monitoring and enforcement costs, are incurred to mitigate ex-post opportunistic behaviors by transacting parties (Hennart, 1991). MNEs are particularly subject to hold-up by external actors such as the state (e.g. changing royalty regime for a refinery) due to the lengthy investment horizon and the fact that the assets invested are not easily redeployed (Henisz, 2000; Hennart, 1982; Jensen, 2006; Rugman & Verbeke, 2005; Williamson, 1981). MNEs thus incur substantial transaction costs to mitigate threats, and sometimes forgo investing in a potential host country in favor of locations that offer lower transaction costs. The extent to which the MNE leverages ownership and location advantages through internalization thus depends on the economic and institutional conditions of the host country, which directly influence transaction costs. For instance, more stable institutional environments characterized by firm rule of law, reliable property rights protection and political stability tend to reduce these transaction costs (Henisz, 2000). All else being equal, locations in which MNEs incur lower transaction costs are more attractive. We next examine how societal outcomes of income inequality can impact these costs, and therefore contribute to the investment attractiveness of a country.

The Costs and Benefits of Income Inequality From the MNE Perspective

Drawing upon income inequality research in the fields of labor economics, sociology and organization theory, we highlight the costs of both high and low inequality, which may detract indirectly from the MNEs overall cost efficiency. These costs, amongst others, impact the extent to which the expected gains from international expansion are realized. Employees are a primary group of stakeholders impacting the MNEs' decisions, but given the impact of income inequality on social functioning, the role of secondary stakeholders including government, civil society organizations (CSO) and local citizenry in general are also considered. We therefore examine the impact of income inequality on location attractiveness by exploring the transaction cost implications of labor market rigidity, political engagement of market and non-market actors, and labor supply characteristics in host countries. We later argue that the costs and benefits of inequality and their effect on transaction costs impact the MNE's expansion decisions regarding where to invest (i.e. location choice) and how to invest (i.e. through direct investment or non-equity alliances). To these discussions we further add the contingent effects of MNE investment motives, and the roles of international and home country experience, which may alter the MNE's responses to income inequality.

Direct and Indirect Labor Costs

The cost of labor comprises a substantial portion of the MNE's overall operating costs. While reducing labor cost is not the only motive for international expansion and offshoring, it is a key MNE consideration in moving production operations to a new country. Indeed, moving jobs offshore is highly objected to by those holding an anti-globalization perspective. All else equal, income inequality indicates a wide distribution of wages levels, i.e. fat tails (Spilimbergo, Londono & Szekely, 1999). Here, income inequality is often a direct manifestation of a large and underemployed workforce. The rapid economic expansion in China, for example, was fueled both by an increased focus on industrialization and enticing the vast potential workforce from rural areas into the manufacturing sector. Due to persistent downward pressure on wages at the lower end of the earnings spectrum, income inequality tends to remain persistent (Hellier & Chusseau, 2010). In a less abundant labor market, conversely, the lower wages would rise more rapidly as local firms and MNEs competed for labor resources. High rates of unemployment thus work in conjunction with already low wages to further stifle wage growth, especially in the absence of more stringent labor regulations. This presence of abundant low-cost labor creates an attractive condition for MNEs seeking to maintain bargaining power over labor, which not only reduces wages but also the costs involved in locating and retaining a more cooperative workforce.

While it is generally assumed that the MNE seeks to lower labor costs simply by moving to lower-wage countries, that perspective overlooks the fact that these costs also depend on the efficiency of bargaining, monitoring and enforcing employment contracts. In addition to lower wages, the MNE can increase the efficiency of its operations by capitalizing on a more flexible labor market (i.e. less rigid markets). The term labor market *rigidity* refers to the extent that constraints imposed by labor institutions on the firm's ability to alter wages and staffing levels in response to changing business conditions, such as fluctuations in global demand (Cuñat & Melitz, 2012). Stringent policies at the national level regarding job protection and the use of collective bargaining, are the main factor leading to increased labor market rigidity, and consequently lower income inequality (Siebert, 1997). Research has also shown that rigid labor markets formed through high levels of unionization, centralized collective bargaining, government regulations restricting layoffs and contract extension policies create higher direct and indirect costs for firms (Belderbos & Zou, 2009; Gross & Ryan, 2008; Lafontaine & Sivadasan, 2009). In the case of collective bargaining, for example, firms must invest time and resources into negotiations with labor organizations. In 2016, for example, workers at the former appliance division of General Electric rejected a new contract, spurning an attempt by the new owner, China's Haier Group, to cut labor costs at a factory in Kentucky (Mann, 2016). Need for approval from these organizations before making staffing changes that impact either staffing levels, wages or both limits the firm's responsiveness to market conditions. Government policies on layoffs also create compliance costs, and limit the firms' flexibility in staffing decisions. Higher inequality arising from less rigid labor markets should thus be more attractive to MNEs because they create more conducive environments for labor cost economizing.

Political Engagement of CSOs

Other stakeholders, such as consumer and environmental advocacy groups, also exert demands to which the MNE may ultimately need to respond. When the MNE seeks to expand its operations abroad, there are costs and benefits which are unevenly distributed amongst various stakeholders (Jensen, 2006). For instance, foreign acquisition brings with it the possibility of job losses, which have both direct and indirect effects on the local economy, including lower wages and downward pressure on overall wage levels (Mann, 2016). Firms must also meet local product quality and labelling requirements, environmental performance standards, expectations to invest in the local community, and other issues that add to the cost of investment. Hence, MNEs consider regulations imposed by the state, such as local content requirements, quality and quantity of employment and overall economic development as detracting from overall firm profitability (Saka-Helmhout, Deeg & Greenwood, 2016).

Similarly, local governments are faced with conflicting demands from different segments of society. For example, investment by foreign firms can bring new jobs, injects capital, and hopefully stimulates the overall economy, yet their constituents may raise numerous concerns which cannot be ignored such as adverse effects of production on the natural environment. Policymakers are thus pressured by various groups to mitigate potential job losses, protect domestic industry, reduce resource exploitation, and limit profit repatriation, while encouraging investment in local communities. The more politically engaged these interest groups are, the more constraints the MNE will face in pursuing its economic goals (Jensen, 2006; Solt, 2008).

While it is apparent that these policy requirements will produce friction in firms' abilities to achieve economic objectives, income inequality is also likely to have an effect on the vigilance of CSOs. Relative bargaining power theory demonstrates that both individual and organizational constituents of a society are less likely to voice their concerns, seek concessions and so forth when they are simply not accustomed to having their demands met (Goodin & Dryzek, 1980; Solt, 2008). High levels of income inequality are likely to lead to a reduction in these sort of societal pressures, as large numbers of individuals increasingly interpret the social system as being 'rigged' against them, thereby inducing them to disengage, politically (Uslaner & Brown, 2005).

As income inequality increases, engagement with the political process for many stakeholders declines, due to the positive connection between wealth and political power (Solt, 2008). Simply put, the higher the income inequality of a country, the lower the level of interest amongst the non-elite to improve their standing through political processes. As a result, the political process becomes less competitive and the relative political bargaining power of the MNE consequently increases. Hence, it will be easier for the firm to create alignment between its interests and those of local policymakers (Bonardi, Holburn & Bergh, 2006). The MNE can focus on a smaller subset of requirements such as job creation and technology provision, and sometimes political contributions (Boddewyn, 1994). A lower level of political engagement amongst CSOs thus allows the firm to reap greater benefits from its economic activities, as it faces a more muted policy response for environmental protection, setting labor standards, increasing domestic content, supporting local industry and so forth. Conversely, under conditions of low income inequality, the firm faces arduous negotiations and lengthy bargaining sessions with the state and CSOs, thus incurring higher transaction costs. As the MNE seeks to expand, it will thus likely seek out locations with less politically engaged constituents, which ultimately means that countries exhibiting higher income inequality will appear more attractive.

The Costs of Social Unrest

To this point, we have argued that income inequality, as socially unpopular as it may be, may be perceived favorably by foreign investors. However, the positive effects we have argued for are likely characteristic of more economically developed countries, where income inequality is low to moderate. The negative societal conditions noted by sociologists, including increased crime, negative health outcomes, lack of trust, and general social unrest, are more likely to manifest as income inequality increases. As general society becomes less cooperative, more suspicious of business interests, and generally more violent, there are real costs borne by firms. In this section, we therefore argue that although higher inequality countries may be more attractive for conducting business, the benefits associated with income inequality diminishes as increasing inequality can become a socially intolerable and economically unattractive location attribute.

There is a growing sentiment that rising inequality is a form of economic injustice brought about by global capitalism, and MNEs are often seen as central actors in fostering this process (Alvaredo, Atkinson, Piketty & Saez, 2013). Higher levels of inequality are often considered the cause of social unrest, (Alesina, 1996; Uslaner, 2008) resulting in increased societal conflict and political dysfunction (Alesina & Rodrik, 1994; Uslaner, 2008). This socio-political unrest tends to stifle economic growth (Alesina & Perotti, 1996), produce a less healthy population (Kawachi, Kennedy & Wilkinson, 1999; Pickett & Wilkinson, 2015), and entrenches income inequality across generations by restricting economic mobility (Pickett & Wilkinson, 2007). These poor-functioning societies, brought about by rising income inequality, are characterized by constituents exhibiting mistrust of authority figures such as, police and government, and diminished inclination towards cooperation. Aside from making life less pleasant for their members of these societies, this dysfunction is likely to make conducting business transactions more arduous. The efficiency of collecting payments, negotiating and reinforcing contracts, monitoring employees and business partners, will all be reduced, leading to higher transaction costs for firms (Flores & Aguilera, 2007; Knack & Keefer, 1997). As well, there is likely to be an increased need to protect against crime, thus increasing security costs incurred in guarding the firm's assets (Kawachi et al., 1999).

Increasing Risk of Political Violence

Political risks involve the degree of instability of policies concerning taxation and expropriation, but also the risk that a government may lose power through the use of force. The political tension fuelled by higher income inequality produces greater uncertainty for business investors regarding future costs (Alesina & Perotti, 1996; Alesina & Rodrik, 1994). For example, taxation may increase in high income inequality countries as those controlling the state seek to increase their benefits at the expense of the general public, or in more extreme cases, by seizing the assets of the firm (Habib & Zurawicki, 2002). This increases the uncertainty faced by firms, increasing the costs they incur in monitoring their local environment, in particular the emerging desires of the state. While aligning with the states' interests is often beneficial for foreign firms, it can become a liability as governments become less stable. Since the policy decisions of a destabilizing government tend to become more erratic, alignment with the state threatens the firm's assets and even survival when the government changes hands (Siegel, 2007).

The instability of high income inequality societies may further manifest itself in overt political activity including, in the extreme, political violence (Fowles & Merva, 1996; Keefer & Knack, 2002). In essence, while increasing inequality tends to reduce political engagement, further increasing inequality may result in *actively* disengaged constituents, more prone to political upheaval. As these threats increase to the point of manifestation, the functioning of the state is greatly impeded and may ultimately fail. Without the ability to use its authority, the state is less able to enforce laws, thus leading to increased crime, violence and corruption. These fractious societies experience a higher frequency and severity of vandalism and violent crimes (Kawachi et al., 1999). MNE employees and other assets may be specifically targeted because they are increasingly viewed as perpetrators of inequality through their use of offshoring and their political alignment with the state. The firm thus finds its indirect costs of production on the rise, as expenditures are increasingly needed on safeguards and security such as police protection (Hakkala, Norback & Svaleryd, 2008). These violent conditions need not be manifest for the MNE to be induced to make additional security investments. Even in countries where conflict is actively suppressed by the state or military, the increasing threat of violence is likely to induce the firm into making larger investments to secure its assets.

FUTURE RESEARCH DIRECTIONS

Investment Location Attractiveness

We have argued that income inequality would be generally viewed as positive, given that firms enjoy the benefits of more flexible labor markets and operate more efficiently in environments that do not place too many additional, sometimes conflicting demands on their resources. However, reduced levels of trust, declining cooperation, socio-political instability, and the dysfunctional nature of high inequality societies are unattractive from both a social and business perspective.

Of course, the more serious breakdown of society resulting from these effects is, in recent times, more of an exception than the norm. We thus believe that, given current cross-country differences in levels of income inequality, MNEs would generally maintain an overall positive perspective on income inequality, all else equal. This perspective would manifest itself in, for example, choosing locations with higher income inequality in which to establish more efficient operations. The more unfortunate effects of income inequality on society are likely to manifest only in countries with the highest levels of income inequality. In these countries, the increasing costs incurred to mitigate against crime, violence and general lack of cooperation will begin to outweigh the benefits, directly reducing the MNE's ability to capitalize on efficiency gains. Thus, while income inequality will be viewed as generally positive by firms, we expect that this effect will diminish at higher levels. The following are initial predictions on how inequality impacts MNE expansion strategy based on available evidence to date. Future research needs to test these empirically, and provide a more nuanced understanding of how income inequality impacts the location decisions of MNEs. Such research will help not only MNE investors, but also policymakers interested in reducing inequality while encouraging foreign direct investment.

While we think that MNEs in general will favor higher inequality countries (i.e. the benefits of inequality outweigh its cost), we believe the impact of inequality on location attractiveness will depend on its economic motives. Dunning (2000) classifies motives for investment into resource-, efficiency-, market- and strategic asset-seeking. Each of these motives may alter the relationship between income inequality and location attractiveness, thus contributing to cross-country imbalances in the types of foreign investment. The reasons for these expected differences lie in the fact that different motives create economic value through different mechanisms. For example, efficiency-seeking investments are focused on achieving cost reductions, often through accessing lower cost labor, while market-seeking investments seek to expand revenues and achieve market penetration in the local market.

Efficiency-seeking investment can achieve cost reductions through enhanced access to larger labor pools and/or increased labor productivity. MNEs seeking to improve their efficiency through international investment will experience the most friction from low inequality countries, due to increased labor rigidity and the increased bargaining power of lobbyists and CSOs. This is because labor market rigidity limits the MNE's ability to adjust employment levels and conditions in response to fluctuating demand levels, and changing global market conditions. In general, MNEs seeking to create new value through increased cost efficiency will benefit the most from cost advantages realized through investing in higher income inequality locations. Nonetheless, relative efficiency is an important consideration for nearly any type of investment, and so we do not expect that different motives will change the MNE's overall preference for higher inequality, at least within the current context of liberal market capitalism.

MNEs can also improve their performance by more fully leveraging the MNE's tangible and intangible assets to achieve economies of scale, which in turn enhances its market power (Dunning, 1993). Research establishes that market-seeking investments are most attracted not only to the availability of sufficiently large and affluent market segments, but also levels of economic growth, which in turn signal increasing consumer demand (Lei & Chen, 2011). Higher inequality countries often experience more stagnant growth. This is because socio-political conflict, pressures for redistribution through taxation, tend to lead governments to favor policies that do not encourage economic growth but redistribution of wealth (Alesina & Perotti, 1996; Rodrik, 1999). Thus, when MNEs consider the growth potential of a market, gains from the reduced labor market rigidity are at least partially offset by the reduced market potential.

The benefits of higher inequality for market seeking investments are further eroded through adverse reputational effects. These investments typically require the firm to work more closely with market and non-market actors in the host country such as consumers, wholesalers, retailers, advocacy groups, and non-governmental organizations. This increases the number of situations in which bargaining situations arise (Hakkala et al., 2008), thus exposing the MNE to more threats of opportunism and consequently higher operating cost. In essence, the MNE becomes more exposed, on more fronts, to the negative aspects of high inequality countries, in which mistrust and political instability more readily prevail (Adger, 2000; Dai, Eden & Beamish, 2013). The MNE in turn is compelled to invest more resources in building political coalitions and securing property and persons (Boddewyn, 1994). At the extreme, MNEs may choose to avoid the market altogether, in favor of a commercially less promising but safer locale for market expansion.

Another motive for investment is to develop the strategic, intangible assets of the firm, most notably through hiring skilled workers and conducting R&D. This type of investment is focused on enhancing the MNE's competencies, rather than exploiting them (Cantwell & Mudambi, 2005). Through these investments, the MNE seeks to augment its capabilities by tapping into geographically dispersed sources of strategically valuable knowledge and knowledge workers (Le Bas & Sierra, 2002; Tallman & Chacar, 2011).

In order to gain a strategic advantage in more knowledge-intensive functions, the MNE needs to access skilled workers and keep them motivated to share their knowledge and collaborate. These two objectives are difficult to achieve in higher inequality countries. First, these countries are more often characterized by reduced access to education, making them less attractive to firms seeking knowledge workers. In addition, higher inequality can lead to fewer incentives for knowledge sharing amongst individuals because they tend to closely guard any source of advantage they possess (Dyer & Nobeoka, 2000). Therefore, the reduced trust and the lack of norms for collaboration limit employees' ability and motivation to integrate knowledge (Minbaeva et al., 2003). Moreover, MNEs will find it difficult to become more socially embedded in these fractious socio-political environments, which in turn complicates knowledge absorption and assimilation (Heidenreich, 2012). Hence, the competence-enhancing potential for learning and capability development is limited, ultimately reducing opportunities for innovation (Dodgson, 1993).

In addition to building new capabilities, MNEs are also more cautious about sharing their existing proprietary knowledge through subsidiaries, as this tends to increase contract monitoring and enforcement costs (Oxley, 1999). Faced with greater risk of political unrest, policy uncertainty, and most pertinently, concerns about property rights protection (Easterly, Ritze & Woolcock, 2006), MNEs seeking to enhance their competencies may be less inclined to invest in higher income inequality countries.

In summary, the costs and benefits of income inequality are borne unequally by MNEs motivated by different investment objectives. Cost reduction is most significant to efficiency-seeking investments, and thus the positive relationship between income inequality and location attractiveness is likely to be more pronounced. In the case of market-seeking and more so in competency-enhancing mandates, the costs of inequality begin to weigh heavily on the benefits, thus eroding the attractiveness of higher inequality locations for these purposes.

Entry Mode Choice

Firms may use strategies and organizational structure to buffer the costs of income inequality, for example by choosing to enter via equity joint venture or alliance rather than wholly owned subsidiary. MNEs face an array of entry modes including wholly-owned subsidiary, joint venture, or non-equity investments such as licensing. As a general rule, an entry mode is preferable when it offers long-term efficiency in managing and controlling economic activities overseas. A large body of research investigating the choice of entry mode into a foreign market from a transaction cost perspective generally agrees that different modes of entry entail different levels of control (Brouthers, 2002; Brouthers & Brouthers, 2001; Madhok, 1997). For instance, Anderson and Gatignon's (1986) seminal paper proposed that firms possessing highly specific assets and stronger brand names will be better served by choosing entry modes offering higher degrees of control, such as wholly-owned subsidiary, and that the benefits will be greater when external environment is uncertain. Recent meta-analysis has largely confirmed this predictive strength of TCE in explaining entry mode choices (Zhao, Luo & Suh, 2004).

A related body of research extends the transaction cost framework to examine inter-firm relationship and governance arrangements, especially within a strategic alliance or a joint venture (Pisano, 1989; Sampson, 2004). These studies show that the importance of protecting transaction-specific assets such as intellectual property determines the structure of alliance relationship and that misaligned governance choices such as excessive bureaucracy can lead to higher transaction costs between alliance partners and inferior economic performance. However, research that draws on relational exchange theory and institutional theory, has shown that trust between transacting parties can lower transaction costs, facilitate investment in transaction-specific assets, increase the use of joint action agreements, and hence improve firms' economic performance (Dyer, 1996a, 1996b; Gulati, 1998; Zaheer, McEvily & Perrone, 1998). Therefore, the interplay of transaction attributes and social and environment conditions is important to the understanding of firms' strategies and performance.

According to relational exchange and institutional theories, it appears likely that in low income inequality countries, where firms face more arduous relationships with labor organizations and more politically active CSOs, a higher equity stake would be preferable. Wholly-owned subsidiaries offer the highest degree of control and hence lowest transaction costs, but cooperating with a local partner also has benefits. Working with local partner can be beneficial for building trust and legitimacy, and learning how to successfully manage external stakeholders. Hence, MNEs seeking to work with a more locally experienced partner may choose majority-owned joint ventures. At the opposite end of the inequality spectrum, since MNEs face heightened uncertainty surrounding political risk and socio-political unrest in the highest income inequality countries, it would appear that these environments too would predict use of higher equity stakes. Since wholly-owned subsidiaries offer the most control, this may be the preferred method for entry, although such an approach also creates the greatest risk in terms of loss of investments, or expropriation.

Finally, it would seem that equity entries would be most efficient in a moderate inequality location, where labor markets are more flexible, other stakeholders are less politically engaged, and society is generally more trusting. That said, there are numerous other considerations, especially the MNEs preferences towards certain modes and its economic reasons for international expansion that will bear upon the entry mode decision. Hence, we would predict that in moderate income inequality countries, the probability of choosing a particular entry mode is less affected by differences in inequality. Indeed as we argued previously, these are likely the most desirable FDI locations, all else equal, from a strategic perspective.

MNE Experience, Home and Abroad

Learning from experience changes a firm's strategic behavior (Nelson & Winter, 1982). As a firm repeatedly engages in an activity, its ability to efficiently manage the activity improves because the firm can infer from previous outcomes and adjust its actions accordingly (Cyert & March, 1963). MNE experience alters its perception of location attractiveness and consequently affects its foreign investment strategy (Delios & Henisz, 2003; Jiang, Holburn & Beamish, 2014). Learning based on direct experience has been found to be an important source of competitive advantage and superior performance for MNEs (Barkema, Bell & Pennings, 1996; Vermeulen & Barkema, 2001). We highlight two types of firm experience, namely international experience and home country experience, which may both influence MNEs' strategic responses to national income inequality.

The prevalent Uppsala internationalization process model suggests that MNEs gradually increase their commitment to foreign markets as their experience of international operation accumulates (Johanson & Vahlne, 1977). International experience helps resolve uncertainties about stakeholders, institutions, and market conditions in unfamiliar countries, which reduces perceived risks and associated operating cost in prospective projects, thereby increasing the probability of subsequent investment overseas (Eriksson, Johanson, Majkgard & Sharma, 1997). MNEs acquire and refine their competencies for operating overseas with every new foreign investment. As these competencies are redeploy in new locations the MNE incur lower transaction cost because they become more knowledgeable in engaging with various local stakeholders. A stylized finding from the internationalization process literature is that experience gained through prior foreign investments positively influences the MNE's propensity and pace of subsequent investment (Barkema & Drogendijk, 2007; Chang, 1995; Davidson, 1980). In general, MNEs more globally diffused and with more years of international operation, are typically more experienced with the challenges of operating in more hostile environments (Barkema et al., 1996; Nielsen et al., 2017).

However, prior studies have paid limited attention to the firm's home country experience. Yet, the firm's structure and strategy are history dependent (Nelson & Winter, 1982; Stinchcombe, 1965). The firm evolve to function effectively in its home country's market and institutional environments. Therefore, social, technical, and economic conditions of the home country to a large degree determine the MNE's competencies and its preferences for location attributes of foreign countries. For instance, Cuervo-Cazurra (2006) finds that foreign investors that have been exposed to bribery at home may not be deterred by corruption in potential host countries, but instead seek countries where corruption is prevalent. Similarly, Holburn and Zelner (2010) find that MNEs from home countries with higher policy certainties, or more intense policy competition among interest socio-economic and ethnic groups are less sensitive to host-country policy risk.

In the case of income inequality, we expect that both international experience and home country experience will influence how MNEs respond to and cope with income inequality in foreign countries. We expect that international experience will overall lower transaction costs associated with income equality, especially in host countries with higher level of socio-political instability attributed to income inequality. Yet, the extent of this impact will likely depend on the level of inequality in the MNE's home country. Since countries at both ends of the inequality spectrum presents higher level of transaction costs to MNEs, we expect that firms from home countries with moderate level of income inequality will particularly benefit from international experience because they likely lack sufficient home country experience in dealing with transaction costs arising from inequality.

CONCLUSION

In this chapter, we have proposed that national income inequality influences MNEs' foreign expansion strategies, due to the various economic and social consequences of inequality which can be translated to transaction costs for the firm. In doing so, we address calls to embed studies of inequality in the context of institutions and organizations (Morris & Western, 1999; Neckerman & Torche, 2007).

If our predictions are at least partially correct, then the costs and benefits of income inequality for MNEs will have consequences on overall firm profitability. By the same token, the preferences of the MNE will be at least partially manifested in their choice of locations for expansion. Future empirical research therefore needs to establish the existence of a link between income inequality and location attractiveness. Research on the contingent role of investment motives will also help to demonstrate how transaction cost considerations come to bear on these issues. A closer examination of investment motives will directly respond to recent calls for in-depth analysis of the role of managerial intentionality in the internationalization process (Buckley, Devinney & Louviere, 2007; Hutzschenreuter, Pedersen & Volberda, 2007)

That said, transaction costs arising from income inequality are only one of many considerations for the MNE. Thus, to the extent to which firms can use organizational structure as a buffer against transaction costs, income inequality may be a partial influence on entry mode considerations. In some cases, the control afforded by higher equity stakes may be the key to achieving these buffers, in others it may be the experience and relational capital of a local partner. Finally, more internationally experienced firms may shun locations with exceptionally low or high income inequality because they appreciate the economic costs of these locations, while less experienced firms may not be able to assess or cope with the risks, thus also choosing to shun these locations. However, more internationally experienced firms may already have developed stronger political and relational capabilities in foreign markets that would help them counter the costs of income inequality. Likewise, experience dealing with income inequality in the home country should help in similar fashion.

By shining a spotlight on the MNE's potentially differential preferences towards income inequality, we hope this chapter begins a discussion which has the potential to help researchers better understand how firms impact national income inequality. Prior research has helped us to better understand how location characteristics, typically cast as macroeconomic factors such as level of economic development, technological sophistication, etc., moderate the effect which aggregate FDI has on income inequality. This chapter brings MNE investors' economic motivations into the discussion. By better understanding how these motivations impact investment decisions, investment policy makers are better equipped to prioritize amongst investment types, and set objectives for attracting them.

REFERENCES

Adger, W. N. (2000). Social and ecological resilience: Are they related? *Progress in Human Geography*, *24*(3), 347–364. doi:10.1191/030913200701540465

Alderson, A., & Nielsen, F. (2002). Globalization and the great u-turn: Income inequality trends in 16 oecd countries. *American Journal of Sociology*, *107*(5), 1244–1299. doi:10.1086/341329

Alesina, A., & Perotti, R. (1996). Income distribution, political instability, and investment. *European Economic Review*, *40*(6), 1203–1228. doi:10.1016/0014-2921(95)00030-5

Alesina, A., & Rodrik, D. (1994). Distributive politics and economic-growth. *The Quarterly Journal of Economics*, *109*(2), 465–490. doi:10.2307/2118470

Alvaredo, F., Atkinson, A. B., Piketty, T., & Saez, E. (2013). The top 1 percent in international and historical perspective. *The Journal of Economic Perspectives*, *27*(3), 3–20. doi:10.1257/jep.27.3.3

Anderson, E., & Gatignon, H. (1986). Modes of foreign entry: A transaction cost analysis and propositions. *Journal of International Business Studies*, *17*(3), 1–26. doi:10.1057/palgrave.jibs.8490432

Atkinson, A. B. (1975). *The Economics of Inequality*. Oxford, UK: Clarendon Press.

Barkema, H., Bell, J. H. J., & Pennings, J. M. (1996). Foreign entry, cultural barriers, and learning. *Strategic Management Journal*, *17*(2), 151–166. doi:10.1002/(SICI)1097-0266(199602)17:2<151::AID-SMJ799>3.0.CO;2-Z

Barkema, H., & Drogendijk, R. (2007). Internationalising in small, incremental or larger steps? *Journal of International Business Studies*, *38*(7), 1132–1148. doi:10.1057/palgrave.jibs.8400315

Basu, P., & Guariglia, A. (2007). Foreign direct investment, inequality, and growth. *Journal of Macroeconomics*, *29*(4), 824–839. doi:10.1016/j.jmacro.2006.02.004

Belderbos, R., & Zou, J. L. (2009). Real options and foreign affiliate divestments: A portfolio perspective. *Journal of International Business Studies*, *40*(4), 600–620. doi:10.1057/jibs.2008.108

Boddewyn, J. J. (1994). International-business political-behavior: New theoretical directions. *Academy of Management Review*, *19*(1), 119–143.

Bonardi, J. P., Holburn, G. L. F., & Bergh, R. G. V. (2006). Nonmarket strategy performance: Evidence from US electric utilities. *Academy of Management Journal*, *49*(6), 1209–1228. doi:10.5465/AMJ.2006.23478676

Brouthers, K. D. (2002). Institutional, cultural and transaction cost influences on entry mode choice and performance. *Journal of International Business Studies*, *33*(2), 203–221. doi:10.1057/palgrave.jibs.8491013

Brouthers, K. D., & Brouthers, L. E. (2001). Explaining the national cultural distance paradox. *Journal of International Business Studies*, *32*(1), 177–189. doi:10.1057/palgrave.jibs.8490944

Buckley, P., & Casson, M. (1976). *The Future of Multinational Enterprise*. London: Macmillan. doi:10.1007/978-1-349-02899-3

Buckley, P. J., Devinney, T. M., & Louviere, J. J. (2007). Do managers behave the way theory suggests? A choice-theoretic examination of foreign direct investment location decision-making. *Journal of International Business Studies*, *38*(7), 1069–1094. doi:10.1057/palgrave.jibs.8400311

Cantwell, J., & Mudambi, R. (2005). Mne competence-creating subsidiary mandates. *Strategic Management Journal*, *26*(12), 1109–1128. doi:10.1002/smj.497

Chang, S. J. (1995). International expansion strategy of Japanese firms - capability building through sequential entry. *Academy of Management Journal*, *38*(2), 383–407. doi:10.2307/256685

Coase, R. H. (1937). The nature of the firm. *Economica-New Series*, *4*(16), 386–405. doi:10.1111/j.1468-0335.1937.tb00002.x

Cobb, J. A. (2016). How firms shape income inequality: Stakeholder power, executive decision making, and the structuring of employment relationships. *Academy of Management Review*, *41*(2), 324–348. doi:10.5465/amr.2013.0451

Cuervo-Cazurra, A. (2006). Who cares about corruption? *Journal of International Business Studies*, *37*(6), 807–822. doi:10.1057/palgrave.jibs.8400223

Cuñat, A., & Melitz, M. J. (2012). Volatility, labor market flexibility, and the pattern of comparative advantage. *Journal of the European Economic Association*, *10*(2), 225–254. doi:10.1111/j.1542-4774.2011.01038.x

Cyert, R. M., & March, J. G. (1963). *A Behavioral Theory of the Firm*. Malden, MA: Blackwell.

Dai, L., Eden, L., & Beamish, P. W. (2013). Place, space, and geographical exposure: Foreign subsidiary survival in conflict zones. *Journal of International Business Studies*, *44*(6), 554–578. doi:10.1057/jibs.2013.12

Davidson, W. H. (1980). The location of foreign direct investment activity: Country characteristics and experience effects. *Journal of International Business Studies*, *11*(2), 9–22. doi:10.1057/palgrave.jibs.8490602

Delios, A., & Henisz, W. J. (2003). Political hazards, experience, and sequential entry strategies: The international expansion of Japanese firms, 19801998. *Strategic Management Journal, 24*(11), 1153–1164. doi:10.1002/smj.355

Deng, W. S., & Lin, Y. C. (2013). Parameter heterogeneity in the foreign direct investment-income inequality relationship: A semiparametric regression analysis. *Empirical Economics, 45*(2), 845–872.

Dodgson, M. (1993). Learning, trust, and technological collaboration. *Human Relations, 46*(1), 77–94. doi:10.1177/001872679304600106

Dunning, J. H. (1988). The eclectic paradigm of international production: A restatement and some possible extensions. *Journal of International Business Studies, 19*(1), 1–31. doi:10.1057/palgrave.jibs.8490372

Dunning, J. H. (1993). *Multinational Enterprises and the Global Economy*. Workingham, UK: Addison Wesley.

Dunning, J. H. (2000). The eclectic paradigm as an envelope for economic and business theories of mne activity. *International Business Review, 9*(2), 163–190. doi:10.1016/S0969-5931(99)00035-9

Dyer, J. H. (1996a). Does governance matter? Keiretsu alliances and asset specificity as sources of Japanese competitive advantage. *Organization Science, 7*(6), 649–666. doi:10.1287/orsc.7.6.649

Dyer, J. H. (1996b). Specialized supplier networks as a source of competitive advantage: Evidence from the auto industry. *Strategic Management Journal, 17*(4), 271–292. doi:10.1002/(SICI)1097-0266(199604)17:4<271::AID-SMJ807>3.0.CO;2-Y

Dyer, J. H., & Nobeoka, K. (2000). Creating and managing a high-performance knowledge-sharing network: The Toyota case. *Strategic Management Journal, 21*(3), 345–367. doi:10.1002/(SICI)1097-0266(200003)21:3<345::AID-SMJ96>3.0.CO;2-N

Easterly, W., Ritze, J., & Woolcock, M. (2006). Social cohesion, institutions and growth. *Economics and Politics, 18*(2), 103–120. doi:10.1111/j.1468-0343.2006.00165.x

Economist. (2015). Why trade unions are declining. *The Economist.*

Eriksson, K., Johanson, J., Majkgard, A., & Sharma, D. D. (1997). Experiential knowledge and cost in the internationalization process. *Journal of International Business Studies, 28*(2), 337–360. doi:10.1057/palgrave.jibs.8490104

Flores, R. G., & Aguilera, R. V. (2007). Globalization and location choice: An analysis of US multinational firms in 1980 and 2000. *Journal of International Business Studies, 38*(7), 1187–1210. doi:10.1057/palgrave.jibs.8400307

Fowles, R., & Merva, M. (1996). Wage inequality and criminal activity: An extreme bounds analysis for the United States, 19751990. *Criminology, 34*(2), 163–182. doi:10.1111/j.1745-9125.1996.tb01201.x

Goodin, R., & Dryzek, J. (1980). Rational participation: The politics of relative power. *British Journal of Political Science, 10*(Jul), 273–292. doi:10.1017/S0007123400002209

Gross, D. M., & Ryan, M. (2008). FDI location and size: Does employment protection legislation matter? *Regional Science and Urban Economics, 38*(6), 590–605. doi:10.1016/j.regsciurbeco.2008.05.012

Gulati, R. (1998). Alliances and networks. *Strategic Management Journal, 19*(4), 293–317. doi:10.1002/(SICI)1097-0266(199804)19:4<293::AID-SMJ982>3.0.CO;2-M

Habib, M., & Zurawicki, L. (2002). Corruption and foreign direct investment. *Journal of International Business Studies, 33*(2), 291–307. doi:10.1057/palgrave.jibs.8491017

Hakkala, K. N., Norback, P. J., & Svaleryd, H. (2008). Asymmetric effects of corruption on FDI: Evidence from Swedish multinational firms. *The Review of Economics and Statistics, 90*(4), 627–642. doi:10.1162/rest.90.4.627

Heidenreich, M. (2012). The social embeddedness of multinational companies: A literature review. *Socio-economic Review, 10*(3), 549–579. doi:10.1093/ser/mws010

Hellier, J., & Chusseau, N. (2010). Globalization and the inequality-unemployment tradeoff. *Review of International Economics, 18*(5), 1028–1043. doi:10.1111/j.1467-9396.2010.00924.x

Henisz, W. J. (2000). The institutional environment for multinational investment. *Journal of Law Economics and Organization, 16*(2), 334–364. doi:10.1093/jleo/16.2.334

Henisz, W. J., & Williamson, O. E. (1999). Comparative economic organization: Within and between countries. *Business and Politics, 1*(3), 261–277. doi:10.1515/bap.1999.1.3.261

Henisz, W. J., & Zelner, B. (2004). Explicating political hazards and safeguards: A transaction cost politics approach. *Industrial and Corporate Change, 13*(6), 901–915. doi:10.1093/icc/dth036

Hennart, J. F. (1982). *A Theory of Multinational Enterprise*. Ann Arbor, MI: University of Michigan Press.

Hennart, J. F. (1991). The transaction costs theory of joint ventures: An empirical study of Japanese subsidiaries in the United States. *Management Science, 37*(4), 483–497. doi:10.1287/mnsc.37.4.483

Holburn, G. L. F., & Zelner, B. A. (2010). Political capabilities, policy risk, and international investment strategy: Evidence from the global electric power generation industry. *Strategic Management Journal, 31*(12), 1290–1315. doi:10.1002/smj.860

Hutzschenreuter, T., Pedersen, T., & Volberda, H. W. (2007). The role of path dependency and managerial intentionality: A perspective on international business research. *Journal of International Business Studies, 38*(7), 1055–1068. doi:10.1057/palgrave.jibs.8400326

Jensen, N. M. (2006). *Nation-states and the Multinational Corporation: A Political Economy of Foreign Direct Investment*. Princeton, NJ: Princeton University Press.

Jensen, N. M., & Rosas, G. (2007). Foreign direct investment and income inequality in Mexico, 19902000. *International Organization, 61*(3), 467–487. doi:10.1017/S0020818307070178

Jiang, G. L. F., Holburn, G. L. F., & Beamish, P. W. (2014). The impact of vicarious experience on foreign location strategy. *Journal of International Management, 20*(3), 345–358. doi:10.1016/j.intman.2013.10.005

Johanson, J., & Vahlne, J. (1977). The internationalization process of the firm: A model of knowledge development and increasing foreign market commitments. *Journal of International Business Studies, 8*(1), 23–32. doi:10.1057/palgrave.jibs.8490676

Kawachi, I., Kennedy, B. P., & Wilkinson, R. G. (1999). Crime: Social disorganization and relative deprivation. *Social Science & Medicine, 48*(6), 719–731. doi:10.1016/S0277-9536(98)00400-6 PMID:10190635

Keefer, P., & Knack, S. (2002). Polarization, politics and property rights: Links between inequality and growth. *Public Choice, 111*(1-2), 127–154. doi:10.1023/A:1015168000336

Knack, S., & Keefer, P. (1997). Does inequality harm growth only in democracies? A replication and extension. *American Journal of Political Science, 41*(1), 323–332. doi:10.2307/2111719

Kuznets, S. (1955). Economic growth and income inequality. *The American Economic Review, 45*(1), 1–28.

Lafontaine, F., & Sivadasan, J. (2009). Do labor market rigidities have microeconomic effects? Evidence from within the firm. *American Economic Journal. Applied Economics, 1*(2), 88–127. doi:10.1257/app.1.2.88

Le Bas, C., & Sierra, C. (2002). Location versus home country advantages in R&D activities: Some further results on multinationals locational strategies. *Research Policy, 31*(4), 589–609. doi:10.1016/S0048-7333(01)00128-7

Lehmacher, W. (2016). *Don't blame china for taking u.S. Jobs*. Fortune.

Lei, H. S., & Chen, Y. S. (2011). The right tree for the right bird: Location choice decision of Taiwanese firms FDI in China and Vietnam. *International Business Review, 20*(3), 338–352. doi:10.1016/j.ibusrev.2010.10.002

Lin, S. C., Kim, D. H., & Wu, Y. C. (2013). Foreign direct investment and income inequality: Human capital matters. *Journal of Regional Science, 53*(5), 874–896. doi:10.1111/jors.12077

Lommerud, K. E., Meland, F., & Sorgard, L. (2003). Unionised oligopoly, trade liberalisation and location choice. *The Economic Journal, 113*(490), 782–800. doi:10.1111/1468-0297.t01-1-00154

Lopez Gonzalez, J., Kowalski, P., & Achard, P. (2015). Trade, global value chains and wage-income inequality. *OECD Trade Policy Papers*, (182).

Macher, J. T., & Richman, B. (2008). Transaction cost economics: An assessment of empirical research in the social sciences. *Business and Politics, 10*(1), 1–63. doi:10.2202/1469-3569.1210

Madhok, A. (1997). Cost, value and foreign market entry mode: The transaction and the firm. *Strategic Management Journal, 18*(1), 39–61. doi:10.1002/(SICI)1097-0266(199701)18:1<39::AID-SMJ841>3.0.CO;2-J

Mah, J. S. (2012). Foreign direct investment, labour unionization and income inequality of Korea. *Applied Economics Letters, 19*(15), 1521–1524. doi:10.1080/13504851.2011.637888

Mahler, V. A., Jesuit, D. K., & Roscoe, D. D. (1999). Exploring the impact of trade and investment on income inequality: A cross-national sectoral analysis of the developed countries. *Comparative Political Studies, 32*(3), 363–395. doi:10.1177/0010414099032003004

Mann, T. (2016, Nov. 14). GA appliance workers reject contract offer from Chinese owner. *Wall Street Journal*.

Morris, M., & Western, B. (1999). Inequality in earnings at the close of the twentieth century. *Annual Review of Sociology, 25*(1), 623–657. doi:10.1146/annurev.soc.25.1.623

Mullany, G. (2017, January 16). World's 8 richest have as much a wealth as bottom half, Oxfam says. *New York Times.*

Neckerman, K. M., & Torche, F. (2007). Inequality: Causes and consequences. *Annual Review of Sociology, 33*(1), 335–357. doi:10.1146/annurev.soc.33.040406.131755

Nelson, R. R., & Winter, S. G. (1982). *An Evolutionary Theory of Economic Change.* Cambridge, MA: Belknap Press.

Nielsen, B., Asmussen, C., & Weatherall, C. (2017). The location choice of foreign direct investments: Empirical evidence and methodological challenges. *Journal of World Business, 52*(1), 62–82. doi:10.1016/j.jwb.2016.10.006

North, D. C. (1990). *Institutions, Institutional Change and Economic Performance.* Cambridge, UK: Cambridge University Press. doi:10.1017/CBO9780511808678

OECD. (2015). *In it together: Why Less Inequality Benefits All.* doi:10.1787/9789264235120-en

Oxley, J. E. (1999). Institutional environment and the mechanisms of governance: The impact of intellectual property protection on the structure of inter-firm alliances. *Journal of Economic Behavior & Organization, 38*(3), 283–309. doi:10.1016/S0167-2681(99)00011-6

Peluffo, A. (2015). Foreign direct investment, productivity, demand for skilled labour and wage inequality: An analysis of Uruguay. *World Economy, 38*(6), 962–983. doi:10.1111/twec.12180

Pickett, K. E., & Wilkinson, R. G. (2007). Child wellbeing and income inequality in rich societies: Ecological cross sectional study. *British Medical Journal, 335*(7629), 1080–1085. doi:10.1136/bmj.39377.580162.55 PMID:18024483

Pickett, K. E., & Wilkinson, R. G. (2015). Income inequality and health: A causal review. *Social Science & Medicine, 128,* 316–326. doi:10.1016/j.socscimed.2014.12.031 PMID:25577953

Pisano, G. (1989). Using equity participation to support exchange: Evidence from the biotechnology industry. *Journal of Law Economics and Organization, 6*(1), 109–126.

Rodrik, D. (1999). Where did all the growth go? External shocks, social conflict, and growth collapses. *Journal of Economic Growth, 4*(4), 385–412. doi:10.1023/A:1009863208706

Rugman, A. M. (1981). *Inside the Multinationals: The Economics of Internal Markets.* New York: Columbia University Press.

Rugman, A. M., & Verbeke, A. (1992). A note on the transnational solution and the transaction cost theory of multinational strategic management. *Journal of International Business Studies, 23*(4), 761–771. doi:10.1057/palgrave.jibs.8490287

Rugman, A. M., & Verbeke, A. (2005). Towards a theory of regional multinationals: A transaction cost approach. *Management International Review, 45*(S1), 5–17.

Saka-Helmhout, A., Deeg, R., & Greenwood, R. (2016). The MNE as a challenge to institutional theory: Key concepts, recent developments and empirical evidence. *Journal of Management Studies, 53*(1), 1–11. doi:10.1111/joms.12172

Sampson, R. C. (2004). The cost of misaligned governance in R&D alliances. *Journal of Law Economics and Organization, 20*(2), 484–526. doi:10.1093/jleo/ewh043

Siegel, J. (2007). Contingent political capital and international alliances: Evidence from South Korea. *Administrative Science Quarterly, 52*(4), 621–666. doi:10.2189/asqu.52.4.621

Smeeding, T. M. (2005). Public policy, economic inequality, and poverty: The United States in comparative perspective. *Social Science Quarterly, 86*(5), 955–983. doi:10.1111/j.0038-4941.2005.00331.x

Solt, F. (2008). Economic inequality and democratic political engagement. *American Journal of Political Science, 52*(1), 48–60. doi:10.1111/j.1540-5907.2007.00298.x

Solt, F. (2009). Standardizing the world income inequality database. *Social Science Quarterly, 90*(2), 231–242. doi:10.1111/j.1540-6237.2009.00614.x

Spilimbergo, A., Londono, J. L., & Szekely, M. (1999). Income distribution, factor endowments, and trade openness. *Journal of Development Economics, 59*(1), 77–101. doi:10.1016/S0304-3878(99)00006-1

Stinchcombe, A. L. (1965). Organizations and social structure. In J. G. March (Ed.), *Handbook of Organizations*. Chicago: Rand-McNally.

Tallman, S., & Chacar, A. S. (2011). Knowledge accumulation and dissemination in MNEs: A practice-based framework. *Journal of Management Studies, 48*(2), 278–304.

Tomohara, A., & Yokota, K. (2011). Foreign direct investment and wage inequality: Is skill upgrading the culprit? *Applied Economics Letters, 18*(8), 773–781. doi:10.1080/13504851.2010.491448

Tsai, P. L. (1995). Foreign direct-investment and income inequality: Further evidence. *World Development, 23*(3), 469–483. doi:10.1016/0305-750X(95)00136-Z

Uslaner, E. M. (2008). *Corruption, Inequality, and the Rule of Law: The Bulging Pocket Makes the Easy Life*. New York, NY: Cambridge University Press. doi:10.1017/CBO9780511510410

Uslaner, E. M., & Brown, M. (2005). Inequality, trust, and civic engagement. *American Politics Research, 33*(6), 868–894. doi:10.1177/1532673X04271903

Van Reenen, J. (2011). Wage inequality, technology and trade: 21st century evidence. *Labour Economics, 18*(6), 730–741. doi:10.1016/j.labeco.2011.05.006

Vermeulen, F., & Barkema, H. (2001). Learning through acquisitions. *Academy of Management Journal, 44*(3), 457–476. doi:10.2307/3069364

Williamson, O. E. (1979). Transaction-cost economics: The governance of contractual relations. *The Journal of Law & Economics, 22*(2), 233–261. doi:10.1086/466942

Williamson, O. E. (1981). The economics of organization the transaction cost approach. *American Journal of Sociology, 87*(3), 548–577. doi:10.1086/227496

Williamson, O. E. (1985). *The Economic Institutions of Capitalism: Firms, Markets, Relational Contracting*. New York, NY: Free Press.

Wolff, E. N. (2015). Inequality and rising profitability in the United States, 19472012. *International Review of Applied Economics, 29*(6), 741–769. doi:10.1080/02692171.2014.956704

Wu, J. Y., & Hsu, C. C. (2012). Foreign direct investment and income inequality: Does the relationship vary with absorptive capacity? *Economic Modelling, 29*(6), 2183–2189. doi:10.1016/j.econmod.2012.06.013

Zaheer, A., McEvily, B., & Perrone, V. (1998). Does trust matter? Exploring the effects of interorganizational and interpersonal trust on performance. *Organization Science, 9*(2), 141–159. doi:10.1287/orsc.9.2.141

Zhao, H. X., Luo, Y. D., & Suh, T. (2004). Transaction cost determinants and ownership-based entry mode choice: A meta-analytical review. *Journal of International Business Studies, 35*(6), 524–544. doi:10.1057/palgrave.jibs.8400106

KEY TERMS AND DEFINITIONS

Entry Modes: Mechanism through which firms internationalize. They can be classified as non-equity (e.g. direct export, licensing, franchising, strategic alliance) and equity modes of entry (e.g. joint ventures and wholly-owned subsidiaries). Non-equity entry modes entail less commitment and control from the parent company than equity modes.

Foreign Direct Investment (FDI): The investment of financial capital, made by a firm, into business operations or assets located in another country.

Income Inequality: The extent to which the distribution of total income amongst a country's employees deviates from perfect equality.

Location Attractiveness: Extent to which a location attracts foreign direct investment due to its endowment of natural resources, skilled or unskilled labor, and/or sizeable markets.

Location Choice: It refers to the decision that MNE managers face when deciding which location is best for a foreign investment. One of the most used theoretical frameworks, to evaluate different locations, among international business scholars is transaction costs economics.

Multinational Enterprise (MNE): A business organization which owns or controls assets in more than one country.

Transaction Costs: Costs incurred by a firm for engaging in an economic transaction. These typically include, identifying potential suppliers, bargaining for price, negotiating contracts, monitoring the quality of the service or product provided by the supplier, and enforcing contracts.

Chapter 12

Low vs. High Income Entrepreneurial Households:
Heterogeneous Response to Common Institution Environment in Developing Countries

Stelvia Matos
University of Nottingham, UK

Vernon Bachor
Winona State University, USA

Jeremy Hall
University of Nottingham, UK

Bruno S. Silvestre
University of Manitoba, Canada

ABSTRACT

We explore how income differences influence heterogeneous entrepreneurial responses to the institutional environment in Brazil shapes low-income entrepreneurs' propensity to exploit the informal rather than the formal economy. Drawing on the Brazilian Global Entrepreneurship Monitor (GEM) data, entrepreneurship discourse and institutional theory, we discuss the influence of inadequate preparedness and barriers to institutional support influencing entrepreneurs' abilities to engage in productive economic activities. We contribute to the entrepreneurship discourse by suggesting that concepts developed within the context of relatively prosperous settings do not adequately reflect how low-income entrepreneurs respond to institutional settings.

INTRODUCTION

In this chapter, we compare relatively low versus high-income entrepreneurs. Although they all share a common institutional environment, differences between these segments play a role in how entrepreneurs respond to, and operate under, institutional structures. We build on Baumol's (1990) and North's (1990) arguments that institutional incentives and structures play a key role in fostering entrepreneurial development. Lawrence et al. (2002: 282) define institutions as "relatively widely diffused practices, technologies, or rules that have become entrenched in the sense that it is costly to choose other practices,

DOI: 10.4018/978-1-5225-2673-5.ch012

technologies, or rules". We postulate that, while the institutional environment may be relatively homogenous within a given country, the degree of poverty (as measured by self-reported household income level) shapes how entrepreneurs engage in business activities, which in turn affect how they respond to, and are supported by, the institutional setting. Our objective is thus to describe how entrepreneurial behavior differs between low-income and high-income entrepreneurs, and how the institutional setting may influence such behavior. We contribute to the entrepreneurship discourse by suggesting that the concepts and theories developed within the context of relatively prosperous settings do not adequately reflect how low-income entrepreneurs will respond to institutional settings, and provide insights on why lower income entrepreneurs often prefer to exploit opportunities within the informal economy.

This chapter supplements the empirical literature on entrepreneurship in weak institutional environments (Aidis et al., 2008; Johnson et al., 1999, 2000; McMillan and Woodruff, 1999, 2002; Djankov et al., 2005, 2006; Webb et al., 2009), but differs by emphasizing that there are heterogeneous responses to the institutional environment by entrepreneurs, depending on their level of income. It is also a partial response to Bruton et al.'s (2012) call for the "need for an indigenous examination of the firms and managers in institutional settings where informal firms dominate."

The role of institutions in fostering entrepreneurial development has been widely recognized (Aldrich and Fiol, 1994; Sine et al., 2005). For example, North (1990) argues that economic growth is driven by the incentive structures that encourage individual effort and investment, which in turn is determined by institutions, i.e. society's 'rules of the game', the establishment of which shapes future productive structures (Bygrave and Minniti, 2000). Baumol (1990) argues that, while the supply of entrepreneurial talent is roughly constant, institutions mostly determine entrepreneurial growth that can either encourage productive, unproductive or destructive outcomes. He suggests that productive entrepreneurship will be hindered if the institutional incentives supporting more productive outcomes are weak.

This study considers entrepreneurs in Brazil, a major 'BRIC' (Brazil, India, Russia and China) emerging economy (Wilson and Purushothaman, 2003), yet one dealing with social inequality (Griesse, 2006; Hall et al., 2008; 2011). We utilize data collected through the Global Entrepreneurship Monitor (GEM) database to explore the differences between the country's highest income and lowest income entrepreneurial households. Our objectives are threefold. First, we provide a description of the differences between low and high-income entrepreneurs in Brazil in terms of their socio-demographic and perceptual factors such as entrepreneurial skills and experience, fear of failure, perception of opportunities and social capital. Second, we describe how these factors influence (i.e., magnitude and direction of affect) an individual's decision to get involved in a startup business, when analyzing low high-income groups separately. Finally, we explore how these differences lead to heterogeneous responses to common institutional settings.

The remainder of this chapter is structured as follows. In the next section, we provide an overview of the entrepreneurship literature and institutional theory as a theoretical foundation for our empirical analysis. Then we use the entrepreneurship literature to explore the importance of entrepreneurship in developing countries and factors that influence entrepreneurial behavior. We describe our data and method, which is then followed by our comparative analysis of low versus high-income groups and their entrepreneurial behavior. We conclude with discussions on the implications of our work for research and entrepreneurship policy.

BACKGROUND

Entrepreneurship and Institutions in Economic Development

According to Levie and Autio (2008), the role of the entrepreneur in economic development has been recognized since at least Schumpeter (1934), who regarded entrepreneurs as agents of transformation. He suggested that, through innovation, entrepreneurs create profit-making opportunities by establishing temporary monopolies through organizational and technological innovation, which in turn are eroded by new innovations. Schumpeter (1942) referred to this process as "creative destruction", which improves productivity and thus greater economic growth. More recently the 'Schumpeterian entrepreneur' has been recognized (e.g., Acs et al. 2004; Audretsch et al. 2006) as an agent able to convert knowledge into economic value, and thus a significant contributor to economic growth.

Kirzner (1997) provides another perspective on entrepreneurship and economic growth by suggesting that 'alert entrepreneurs' discover arbitrage opportunities in the market. According to Shane et al. (2003), Kirznerian entrepreneurs differ from Schumpeterian entrepreneurs by being less dependent on knowledge creation but rather the exploitation of existing information, and thus are a much more common form of entrepreneurship. Sautet (2013) in the context of developing countries notes the opportunity of entrepreneurs to grow beyond the local context is often constrained, particularly those from within impoverished communities. Thus, the context within which an entrepreneur operates plays an important role.

Institutional theory has proven to be a useful theoretical foundation for exploring the context under which entrepreneurs operate (Bruton et al., 2010). Leibenstein (1968: 78) suggests that "socio-cultural and political constraints" shape entrepreneurship within a given country. Such constraints include national cultural or universal values (Smith et al., 2002), relative wealth, type of government (e.g., centralized planning versus open economy), population growth (Hunt and Levie, 2004; Levie and Hunt, 2005), the economy's growth rate (Acs and Amoro, 2008) among others. DiMaggio and Powell (1983) see institutions as critical in reducing the uncertainty in a society as the institutions encompass the structures that provide the incentives for different types of economic activity (Aldrich and Fiol, 1994; North, 1990). Casero et al. (2013) using multiple countries of GEM data for 2006 and 2007 found that institutional quality influences total entrepreneurial activity and this activity contributes to economic development.

Scott (1995) introduced three institutional pillars (regulative, cognitive, and normative) that provide the stability and incentives that promote or inhibit social behavior in an economy. Each of these institutional pillars impacts firm legitimacy, "a generalized perception or assumption that the actions of an entity are desirable, proper, or appropriate within some socially constructed system of norms, values, beliefs, and definitions" (Suchman, 1995: 574), and these institutional pillars are considered critical for understanding entrepreneurship development in emerging economies (Peng and Zhou, 2005). Etzioni (1987) found that legitimacy increases the availability of resources that support new firm formation and growth, thus increasing the demand and supply of entrepreneurial activity. The formal and informal institutions establish legitimacy through the incentives and restrictions that encompass business rent-seeking activity (North, 1990). Webb et al. (2009) distinguish between entrepreneurs that engage in the formal economy (legal and legitimate means that produce legal and legitimate ends), informal economy (legitimate ends but illegal means) and the renegade economy (illegal and illegitimate means and ends). North (1990) suggests that entrepreneurs weigh the incentives and restrictions in the environment as represented by regulations (i.e., formal rules) as well as in terms of the prevailing cultural values and norms (i.e., informal rules).

Baumol (1990) argues that in an environment where the benefits and rewards for rent-seeking activities outweigh their costs, unproductive entrepreneurship (i.e., entrepreneurship that benefits the entrepreneur but not the economy) will flourish. Acs and Szerb (2007) discuss the aspects of societal wide institutions implemented through public policy and regulation that are intended to be available to all equally, but in practice access to the resources made available by such policy and regulation are limited for the poor and, more importantly, frequently these same institutional factors erect barriers to the poor. Two important specific examples of policy and regulations are property rights and protection and access to the legal systems that ultimately facilitate access to legitimate financial market (Aidis, 2005; Sautet, 2013; Webb et al., 2009).

Institutional Effects on Entrepreneurial Behaviour in Low Income Group

Studies on entrepreneurship have emphasized that demographic and economic factors such as education, age, wealth, and employment status are important drivers of entrepreneurial behavior (Blanchflower, 2004; Brush, 1992; Reynolds et al., 2003). More recently, Arenius and Manniti (2005) propose the incorporation of a set of variables describing the entrepreneur's subjective perceptions such as presence of role models or whether they know other entrepreneurs (e.g., Begley and Boyd, 1987), confidence in one's skills and abilities (Baron, 2000), risk propensity (e.g., Kihlstrom and Laffont, 1979), and alertness (Kirzner, 1973, 1979). Arenius and Manniti (2005) call these perceptual variables and argue that, although often biased, these variables are correlated with an entrepreneur's decision to start a business.

However, another stream of the entrepreneurship literature argues that perceptual variables are significantly influenced in emerging economies by the institutional environment (Ahlstrom and Bruton, 2002; Peng and Heath, 1996; Smallbone and Welter, 2001, 2006). According to Molonova et al. (2008), institutions provide sets of norms and expected behaviors that are reinforced by a system of rewards and sanctions to ensure compliance and influence social interactions in a given community. We classify institutions into three different categories (DiMaggio and Powell 1983; North 1990): Regulatory institutions refer to the formally codified, enacted, and enforced structure of laws in an environment; Normative institutions are less formal and usually manifest in commercial conventions and business practices; and Cognitive institutions are the beliefs about the expected standards of behavior specific to a culture and are typically learned through social interactions by living or growing up in a community.

We argue that within the same country with common regulatory institutions, heterogeneity can be observed in terms of normative and cognitive institutions. In countries like Brazil, with a long historical legacy of inequality (Griesse, 2006), this heterogeneity can be significantly accentuated. Although regulatory institutions are the same throughout the country, an impoverished entrepreneur living under circumstances where the rule of the game is to survive and informality is the norm, will likely behave very differently from entrepreneurs from wealthier communities that have access to formal education, financial services, etc. Consequently, in countries such as Brazil, with high levels of social and wealth disparity, the income level and social class from which the entrepreneur comes from are important. More specifically, we argue that entrepreneurs from extreme income distributions (upper and lower) have different behavior because they are exposed to different normative and cognitive institutions as they are immersed in different social contexts, thus institutions will affect their business performance in very diverse ways and this heterogeneity becomes clear on at least four dimensions.

First, the level of education vary considerably between those from impoverished communities and those that are not. Those from impoverished communities are often forced to start working earlier in life (e.g., sometimes before 12 years of age) at the expense of their formal education (Barros et al., 1994). Moreover, the schools located in impoverished communities tend to be of an inferior quality in comparison to the schools of those within wealthier communities (Schwartzman, 2005).

Second, law enforcement and property rights tend to be problematic as lower income entrepreneurs often participate in the informal (Webb et al., 2009) or "unofficial economy" (Johnson et al., 1997). This is particularly relevant in developing countries where black and gray markets (i.e., illegitimate) are established (Aidis and van Praag, 2007). In developing countries, like Brazil, lower income entrepreneurs usually become street vendors, selling commodity merchandise or food at a low price, and they usually do not have adequate money or knowledge to create a formal business following legitimate channels (IBGE, 2007). In the informal markets, low-income entrepreneurs often sell counterfeit merchandise (e.g., knock-off glasses, CDs and DVDs) without considering that such an activity is illegal (Andrade, 2004; Stephen et al., 2011). The formal structure (regulatory institutions) cannot identify these entrepreneurs properly as they are not registered as a business and do not pay taxes, and as a result they do not have access to labor rights such as paid vacations, parental leave, or retirement plans (Dasgupta, 2003).

Third, these entrepreneurs pursue business opportunities through the informal market, thus the financial system does not recognize them as legitimate entrepreneurs (de Soto, 2000), and since they do not appear in the official statistics, have bank accounts or a lending history, it makes it difficult for them to access the needed capital to legalize or expand their business (Reficco and Marquez, 2009). According to Parente (2003), low-income populations in Brazil have historically not had access to credit, either as consumers or entrepreneurs, while upper income entrepreneurs traditionally have access to a sophisticated financial system.

Fourth, low-income entrepreneurs often live in improvised areas consisting of squatter communities or shantytowns that lack property rights, have businesses that mostly operate informally, and are known for extreme poverty and crime, for example the infamous "favelas" in Brazil (Hall et al., 2008). These communities are often led by criminals, such as drug dealers, who control illegal activities and act as the established power by solving problems for that community (Morais, 2006). Thus, the behavioural norms under which these entrepreneurs learn through social interactions are usually unaccepted by regulatory institutions and are often considered to be illegitimate. The media creates illusory stereotypes of criminal offenders (Zafaroni, 2003 and Morais, 2006), especially drug dealers, which impressionable youth living in poor communities identify as role models because criminals are constantly on the news. Consequently, the effect of normative and cognitive institutions under which low-income entrepreneurs operate will differ from high-income entrepreneurs, and will likely create barriers for low-income entrepreneurs to create and maintain a viable business.

Social resources theory (Lin, 1982) sheds light on resources embedded within social networks by examining what these resources are, how these resources can be accessed, how these resources can be mobilized and thus can potentially help individuals to enhance their social status (Lin, 1999). Social capital theory (Bourdieu, 1985; Coleman, 1988; Portes, 1998) regards social networks as capital in an economic sense (i.e., as a resource that can contribute to better economic outcomes) and the information and obligations generated as a result of sustained interactions between network members raises reciprocity (Herreros, 2004). Hills et al. (1997) found networks to be important for access to resources (e.g., information, finance and labor) thus enhancing the opportunity recognition capabilities of the entrepreneur. A reliance on a small number of information sources may economize on information processing but can potentially introduce serious biases in the information received (Kahneman and Lovallo, 1993; Payne et al., 1992; Tversky and Kahneman, 1974). Thus, individuals in a low-income context tend to have less opportunity to establish and maintain close ties with a broad network of others as a result of poverty and low literacy constraints.

The concept of self-confidence (i.e., self-efficacy – an individual's self-assessment of their ability to succeed in specific situations) is mostly influenced by an individual's beliefs about their previous performance on similar or related tasks (Bandura, 1997; Compeau and Higgins, 1995). Individuals when reporting high self-confidence towards a particular task were found to invest greater effort in pursuing goals, in effective problem solving, in continued task interest, in persistence when faced with setbacks, and in a task orientation approach rather than avoidance. Low levels of literacy, typical of individuals living in low-income settings, would be expected to result in lower levels of self-confidence in entrepreneurial decision-making then those individuals with higher income.

Some entrepreneurs deliberately limit their business growth as they may expect some negative consequences from growth that potentially are in conflict with their goals (Kolvereid, 1992; Storey, 1994). Shane et al. (2003) suggest that an entrepreneur's aspirations of growth is the result of environmental conditions and entrepreneurial opportunities, and the motivations and ability of particular people might lead to different types of entrepreneurial actions under the same environmental conditions. Given the majority of informal businesses are run by or contemplated by low-income entrepreneurs, they may want to minimize exposure beyond their established market domain to avoid attracting the attention of regulatory institutions (Sautet, 2013). Thus, low-income entrepreneurs may choose to limit growth to avoid the costs of becoming formal.

Alertness is also crucial to understanding entrepreneurial behaviour (Kirzner, 1973, 1979). Alert entrepreneurs are those that are explorative, take broad intuitive perspectives that incorporate multiple inputs and tend to be more effective in recognizing and acting on business opportunities (Ardichvili et al., 2003; Bygrave et al., 1997; Kaish and Gilad, 1991); conversely those that fail in recognizing entrepreneurial opportunities often misjudge the context and the type of behavior required in a given situation (Gaglio and Katz, 2001). According to Gaglio and Katz (2001), the theory of alertness suggests that entrepreneurs, given the context in which they are immersed, make their decisions based on their ability to see opportunities. Therefore, we suggest that while entrepreneurs differ because the environment equips them with different information, their level of alertness to opportunity may be the same.

DATA AND EMPIRICAL METHOD

Much of the issues identified in the previous section have been explored using the GEM dataset, an ongoing multinational project created to investigate the incidence and causes of entrepreneurship within and between countries (Reynolds et al., 2005). The GEM surveys rely on stratified samples of at least 2000 individuals per country drawn from the entire working age population of 59 countries, capturing both entrepreneurs and non-entrepreneurs, and collect data on a number of individual social and economic characteristics and perceptions. Acs and Szerb (2007: 119) observe that for developed economies, reducing entry regulations, in most cases, will not result in more high-potential startups, but instead labor market reform and deregulation of financial markets is required to support growth of high-performance ventures. In this study, we use individual-level survey data collected between 2005 and 2009 in Brazil for the GEM Project. This period was selected because data by different levels of income is not available for previous years. The GEM model suggests the relationship between new business activity and the institutional environment is mediated by opportunity perception and the individual's perception of start-up skills (Levie and Autio, 2008).

The GEM survey identifies individuals' entrepreneurial activities as the outcome of a series of factors that influence their decisions including socio-demographic and perceptual factors. Socio-demographic variables include gender, age, income, work status, educational attainment and social network. The latter was measured by asking if the individual knows other entrepreneurs. Perceptual variables include subjective evaluations of the respondent about themselves and their entrepreneurial environment. These include them assessing their own skills, knowledge and ability regarding to start a business, their assessment of the existence of a business opportunity and the extent to which fear of failing affect their decision to start a business. The survey also collects data on the motivation to be engaged in an entrepreneurial activity as whether the individual is taking advantage of an opportunity or has no better employment choices (i.e., out of necessity).

Although the GEM dataset splits income distribution data into the lowest, medium and highest 33%, we decided to exclude the medium range to avoid blurring of marginal differences between the middle 33% with those at the upper and lower levels. Table 1 provides information on the general characteristics of the two selected groups.

Brazil is a useful country to study the difference in entrepreneurial behavior across income groups for the following reasons. First, the country is a major emerging economy (Wilson and Purushothaman, 2003), yet one dealing with social inequality (Griesse, 2008; Hall et al., 2011; Neri, 2009). Brazil's income distribution is heavily skewed towards the wealthy, where the top 10% of the population control 44% of the national income, whereas the bottom 40% of the population control only 10% of the national income (IBGE, 2010). In addition, many Brazilian policy makers now recognize entrepreneurship as a potential solution to social improvement (Hall et al., 2011). To determine whether there are differences between the upper and lower income groups, we apply the Chi-square ($\chi2$)-test, with statistical signification at the 5 percent level ($p < 0.05$; two-tailed).

Table 1. General characteristics of the cross-income sample

	Lowest 33%		Upper 33%	
	Mean*	**SD**	**Mean***	**SD**
Gender	.46	.489	.53	.50
Age	36.98	13.42	36.49	12.55
Educational attainment	.72	.448	.27	.468
Work status	.50	.500	.68	.468
Involved in start-up	.03	.164	.05	.215
Manages/owns business (up to 42 months old)	.08	.267	.11	.312
Manages/owns business (older than 42 months)	.09	.292	.16	.386
Reason - start up (opportunity)	.50	.50	.64	.481
Reason - business (opportunity)	.30	.46	.63	.482
Number of observations	6216		2435	

  * Mean values reflect the proportions of the referred discrete variable: (gender: 1 male, 0 female); (work status: 1 full/part time, 0 not working, retired or student); (start-up and manages/owns business: 1 yes, 0 no); (Reason: 1 opportunity, 0 necessity).

We divided our analysis into two parts. First we investigated the descriptive characteristics of each income group, regarding socio-demographic and perceptual variables and entrepreneurial decisions, to identify what variables are statistically significantly different using cross-tabulation analysis. Second, we investigated the influence of socio-demographic and perception variables in the entrepreneurial decisions of the two groups. For example, we aimed to identify which variables influence the decision of a low-income individual to become involved (or not) in a start-up, and if this influence differs between the lower and upper income groups. We use a Probit model to estimate the probability that individuals from low and high-income levels will get involved in a start-up against individual variables.

Brazilian Gem Data Analysis

Table 2 shows that for those involved in start-ups, 5 of the 10 variables are significantly different for socio-demographic and perceptual variables of low and high-income. Low-income start-up entrepreneurs are mostly female, older, less educated, have less confidence in their skills and know fewer entrepreneurs than the high-income group. Table 3 shows that fewer low-income entrepreneurs are involved in established business when compared to high-income entrepreneurs. We suggest these results could be due to heterogeneous responses to normative and cognitive institutions between the low and high-income groups, which may in turn negatively impact the low-income entrepreneur's capabilities and motivations to create and sustain a business.

Table 2 also shows the motivation for starting a business for the low-income groups is equal for either out of necessity or opportunity exploitation. However, when the motivation is analyzed for established businesses, the data in Table 3 shows the majority of low-income entrepreneurs are involved in business by necessity rather than opportunity recognition. In contrast, the majority of high-income individuals are involved in both start-up and established businesses for opportunity exploitation rather than out of necessity. This finding also alludes to differences in success between the two income groups, where low-income entrepreneurs may be forced to continue a mediocre business due to a lack of other options. The corresponding $\chi 2$ for the motivation to be involved in established business equals 163.94, while for a start-up business is 3.44, suggesting the difference in motivation between the two groups increases as the expectations of success decreases with business experience for the low-income individuals. Indeed, within the low-income group, fewer entrepreneurs have successfully created businesses, where only 9.4% are running established businesses versus 16.2% of the corresponding high-income entrepreneurs.

Table 2 also allows us to identify the differences in how the two groups of income perceive themselves and their environment. Consistent with the literature, the results show that fewer respondents of the low-income group seem to know other entrepreneurs when compared to the high-income group. Although this finding provides limited information about the social capital of low-income population in our sample, it does suggest they may have fewer opportunities to establish ties with other entrepreneurs. The results also show the low-income group scores low in subjective perception self-efficacy to start a business as well as in expectations to grow.

The results about the perception of future opportunities shown in Table 4 the majority of those involved in start-ups have positive expectations and were not significantly different between low and high-income entrepreneurs and the analysis indicates the perception of future opportunities is the most important covariate for the low-income group with a coefficient of 29.25. Although this result is by no means a comprehensive measure of alertness, it does suggest that opportunity perceptions may not dependent on educational level. This contrasts with some of the literature, for example Levie and Autio

Table 2. Chi-square tests of differences in proportions of those involved in start-ups

	Lowest 33%	Upper 33%	Chi-square
Gender	44.4	70.3	18.92***
Age	76.0	83.9	2.632
Work status	72.6	81.7	2.72
Low education attainment	58.3	18.6	44.83***
Knows entrepreneurs	58.8	75.0	7.97***
Sees good opportunities	70.1	63.8	1.24
Knowledge/skills	87.3	94.7	4.30**
Fear of failure	20.0	21.4	0.08
Reason – start-up (opportunity)	50.0	62.5	3.44**
Expects to grow	72.5	86.5	2.86
Actively involved in start-up	2.8	4.8	23.78***
Number of observations	171	118	

Gender: 1 male; Work status:; 1 = working full or part time, 0 = not working; Age up to 54yrs; Reason: 1 = opportunity, 0 = necessity; Expects to grow: 1 = yes, 0 = No

Table 3. Chi-square tests of differences in proportions of those involved in established business (older than to 42 months)

	Lowest 33%	Upper 33%	Chi-square
Gender	45.2	55.5	7.18***
Age	68.3	69.9	0.52
Work status	94.6	94.1	0.139
Low education attainment	74.2	34.6	261.36***
Reason (opportunity)	31.4	63.2	163.94***
Expects to grow	53.4	75.0	14.82***
Manages and owns an established business	9.4	16.2	79.44***
Number of observations	586	394	

(2008), by showing that educational level does not always positively relate to alertness. However, this finding is consistent with Webb et al.'s (2009) argument that the informal economy provides ample opportunities for alert entrepreneurs.

Finally, Table 4 shows the differences between income groups in how the variables influence the decision of individuals to start a business. Gender seems to influence both groups, although women are more likely to get involved in a start-up in the low-income group than men. Age seems to matter for the high-income group, especially in the 35 to 45 years old range, while age does not have a significant affect in the entrepreneurial decision of the low-income group. The likelihood of getting involved in a start up is positively related to being full or part time employed for the low-income group but does not seem to affect the high-income group. There were also differences in influence amongst the perceptual variables. Table 4 shows that for the low-income group, the coefficients of the perceptual variables

Table 4. Probability of an individual to get involved in a start up (no)

	Lower 33%			Upper 33%		
	Estimate	ChiSq	Prob>ChiSq	Estimate	ChiSq	Prob>ChiSq
Gender (male)	.199	4.81	.0284*	-.390	8.07	.0045*
Age [18-24]	-.064	.13	.7159	-.419	2.57	.1087
Age [25-34]	-.013	.77	.3805	-.231	.97	.3239
Age [35-44]	.030	2.61	.1061	-.706	9.34	.0022*
Age [45-54]	-.152	.65	.4217	.425	1.69	.1942
Work status (Full or part time)	-.166	.89	.3467	.073	.08	.7721
Work status (Part time only)	-.729	8.72	.0031*	.186	.20	.6530
Work status (Retired; disabled)	.760	2.15	.1426	-.128	.07	.7968
Work status (Homemaker)	0.5911	4.09	.0432*	.228	.12	.7246
Work status (Student)	-.664	2.71	.0997	.157	.08	.7748
Education attainment (none)	.888	3.02	.0823	.397	.64	.4221
Education attainment (some secondary)	.342	3.14	.0762	.226	.54	.4610
Education attainment (secondary)	.092	.02	.6586	-.360	3.00	.0834
Education attainment (post-secondary)	-.608	3.30	.0691	-.043	.02	.8837
Knows entrepreneurs (no)	.174	3.88	.0488*	.188	1.92	.1659
Sees good opportunities (no)	.509	29.25	<.0001*	.178	2.19	.1385
Knowledge/skills (no)	.678	28.65	<.0001*	1.16	19.36	<.0001*
Fear of failure (no)	-.480	19.16	<.0001*	-.353	5.51	.0189*
Model diagnostics						
RSquare	.1461			.1489		
Log-Likelihood (difference)	-95.714			19.334		

* Significant values at the 95% confidence or above

'perception of future opportunities', 'ability to start a business', and 'fear of failing' were all significant with the latter being negative, as expected. Thus, with the exception of 'knowing other entrepreneurs', perceptual variables significantly influence entrepreneurial decisions of the low-income group. For the high-income group, only the variables 'ability to start a business' and 'fear of failing' were significant. In particular, the difference in magnitude of the coefficient of 'fear of failing' of the two groups suggest that high-income entrepreneurs tend to be less risk adverse than their low-income counterparts.

SOLUTIONS AND RECOMMENDATIONS

Our study indicates that low-income entrepreneurs with low levels of education can be as alert as high-income ones, thus there is entrepreneurial potential throughout the system. However, in response to institutional disadvantages, these low-income entrepreneurs may be drawn towards the informal economy. We suggest that policymakers need to recognize that entrepreneurial behavior differs depending on income levels, and specifically that responses to institutions will vary. They thus need to develop mechanisms that encourage formal and productive entrepreneurship that reflects the heterogeneity of such impacts. More specifically, we suggest that policies that assume that all strata of society will respond equally to the institutional environment – a 'one size fits all' approach – will result in at best a continued legitimization of informal activities, or at worse encourage destructive entrepreneurship. Finally, policymakers need to understand that cognitive (i.e., cultural) influences have the largest impact on opportunity-based entrepreneurial activity.

FUTURE RESEARCH DIRECTIONS

Our study is limited due to the use of one data source. Although the GEM program is one of the most comprehensive series of studies on entrepreneurship, there is a potential sample bias. For example, informal entrepreneurs may be hesitant to participate in such studies because they would prefer to maintain a low profile. Indeed, this may be one of the most difficult challenges of studying low-income entrepreneurship, where the boundaries of informal, illegitimate, illegal, and even criminal activities may be open to interpretation.

Further research could explore how skills to support productive entrepreneurship can be incorporated into educational systems and programs designed to promote entrepreneurship within poor communities. Further research also needs to explore how entrepreneurial alertness is related to productive outcomes, and how institutions can be aligned to veer poor entrepreneurs away from the informal economy. For example, our study alluded to how alert entrepreneurs within impoverished communities may be influenced by negative references, leading to destructive outcomes. A formal test between such negative references and destructive outcomes would thus provide valuable insights in how activities within the informal economy can be avoided.

CONCLUSION

Our motivation for this research is based on the argument that entrepreneurial outlook and behavior differs considerably between low and high-income entrepreneurs in emerging economies. We postulate that while institutions are important to entrepreneurial behavior, such differences will result in different responds by, and support for, entrepreneurs. We draw on entrepreneurship and institutional theories and the GEM survey conducted in Brazil to examine how and why different income segments of the population differ in terms of entrepreneurial behavior.

Consistent with the literature, we found that, within upper income levels, men dominate most entrepreneurial activity. However, counter to the literature, we found that women are more dominant in lower income levels. Although further research is needed to understand why, we speculate that one reason could be due to men being more likely to be engaged in criminal activities, and thus unlikely to participate in the surveys in an attempt to maintain a low profile (see research limitations above). Another reason may be due to the influence of conditional cash transfer programs such as *Bolas Familia* where the recipients of the funds are exclusively mothers providing them with a small revenue stream that can be used as start-up money for a new venture.

As expected, our results show that low and high-household income entrepreneurs are significantly different in terms of socio-demographic characteristics, self-perceptions regarding their entrepreneurial skills, the social network and entrepreneurial environments in which they operate, and their motivations to get involved in business. These differences in turn are likely to reflect differences in how entrepreneurs are able to exploit cognitive and normative institutions. As a result, low-household income entrepreneurs may be at a disadvantage within the formal economy, as shown by our findings that fewer low-income entrepreneurs are able to maintain a business than those with higher incomes. Furthermore, in contrast to high-income entrepreneurs, as time progresses low-income individuals maintain their business increasingly out of necessity rather than perceived opportunity. However, in spite of these disadvantages, we also found that low-income entrepreneurs are starting businesses at the same rate as those with higher income levels, but are unlikely to succeed due to their lack of preparedness. Finally, we suggest that, in response to these institutional disadvantages, low-income entrepreneurs are drawn towards the informal economy, a problem that policymakers may be able to address by developing mechanisms that take in consideration heterogeneous responses to common institution environments.

REFERENCES

Acs, Z., & Szerb, L. (2007). Entrepreneurship, economic growth and public policy. *Small Business Economics, 28*(2/3), 109–122. doi:10.1007/s11187-006-9012-3

Acs, Z. J., & Amoros, J. E. (2008). Entrepreneurship and competitiveness dynamics in Latin America. *Small Business Economics, 31*(3), 305–322. doi:10.1007/s11187-008-9133-y

Acs, Z. J., Audretsch, D. B., Braunerhjelm, P., & Carlsson, B. (2004). *The missing link: The knowledge filter, entrepreneurship and endogenous growth.* Discussion Paper, No. 4783, December. London, UK: Center for Economic Policy Research.

Ahlstrom, D., & Bruton, G. (2002). An institutional perspective on the role of culture in shaping strategic actions by technology-focused entrepreneurial firms in China. *Entrepreneurship Theory and Practice, 26*(4), 53–70.

Aidis, R. (2005). Institutional Barriers to Small- and Medium-Sized Enterprise Operations in Transition Countries. *Small Business Economics, 25*(4), 305–318. doi:10.1007/s11187-003-6463-7

Aidis, R., Estrin, S., & Mickiewicz, T. (2008). Institutions and entrepreneurship development in Russia: A comparative perspective. *Journal of Business Venturing, 23*(6), 656–672. doi:10.1016/j.jbusvent.2008.01.005

Aidis, R., & van Praag, M. (2007). Illegal entrepreneurship experience: Does it make a difference for business performance and motivation? *Journal of Business Venturing, 22*(2), 283–310. doi:10.1016/j.jbusvent.2006.02.002

Aldrich, H. E., & Fiol, C. M. (1994). Fools rush in? The institutional context of new industry creation. *Academy of Management Review, 19*, 645–670.

Alwitt, L. F. (1995). Marketing and the poor. *The American Behavioral Scientist, 38*(4), 564–577. doi:10.1177/0002764295038004007

Andrade, J. (2004). Brazil's Piracy, a Cultural Challenge. *Brazzil*. Retrieved from http://www.brazzil.com/2004/html/articles/aug04/p141aug04.htm

Ardichvili, A., Cardozo, R., & Ray, S. (2003). A theory of entrepreneurial opportunity identification and development. *Journal of Business Venturing, 18*(1), 105–123. doi:10.1016/S0883-9026(01)00068-4

Arenius, P., & Minniti, M. (2005). Perceptual Variables and Nascent Entrepreneurship. *Small Business Economics, 24*(3), 233–247. doi:10.1007/s11187-005-1984-x

Audretsch, D., Keilbach, M., & Lehman, E. (2006). *Entrepreneurship and economic growth*. Oxford, UK: Oxford University Press. doi:10.1093/acprof:oso/9780195183511.001.0001

Bandura, A. (1997). *Self-efficacy: The Exercise of Control*. New York: WH Freeman.

Baron, R. (2000). Psychological Perspectives on Entrepreneurship: Cognitive and Social Factors in Entrepreneurs Success. *Current Directions in Psychological Science, 9*(1), 15–19. doi:10.1111/1467-8721.00050

Barros, R., Mendonca, R., & Velazco, T. (1994). Is poverty the main cause for child work in Brazil? Rio de Janeiro: Ipea.

Baumol, W. J. (1990). Entrepreneurship: Productive, unproductive, and destructive. *Journal of Political Economy, 98*(5), 893–921. doi:10.1086/261712

Begley, T., & Boyd, D. (1987). Psychological Characteristics Associated with Performance in Entrepreneurial Firms and Small Businesses. *Journal of Business Venturing, 2*(1), 79–93. doi:10.1016/0883-9026(87)90020-6

Blanchflower, D. G. (2004). *Self-Employment: More May Not Be Better*. NBER Working Paper No. 10286.

Bourdieu, P. (1985). The forms of capital. In J.G. Richardson (Ed.), Handbook for Theory and Research for the Sociology of Education (pp. 241–258). Academic Press.

Brush, C. G. (1992). Research on Women Business Owners: Past Trends, a New Perspective and Future Directions. *Entrepreneurship Theory and Practice, 16*, 5–30.

Bruton, G., Ahlstrom, D., & Li, H. (2010). Institutional Theory and Entrepreneurship: Where Are We Now and Where Do We Need to Move in the Future? *Entrepreneurship Theory and Practice, 34*(3), 421–440. doi:10.1111/j.1540-6520.2010.00390.x

Bruton, G. D., Ireland, R. D., & Ketchen, D. J. Jr. (2012). Toward a Research Agenda on the Informal Economy. *The Academy of Management Perspectives, 26*(3), 1–11. doi:10.5465/amp.2012.0079

Busenitz, L. W. (1996). Research on entrepreneurial alertness. *Journal of Small Business Management, 34*(4), 35–44.

Bygrave, W., Brush, C., Davidsson, P., Fiet, F., Greene, P., Harrison, R., & Zacharackis, A. et al. (1997). *Frontiers of Entrepreneurship Research*. Wellesley, MA: Babson College Press.

Bygrave, W., & Minniti, M. (2000). The social dynamics of entrepreneurship. *Entrepreneurship Theory & Practice, 24*, 25–36.

Casero, J. C. D., González, M. A., Escobedo, M. C. S., Martínez, A. C., & Mogollón, R. H. (2013). Institutional variables, entrepreneurial activity and economic development. *Management Decision, 51*(2), 281–305. doi:10.1108/00251741311301821

Coleman, J. S. (1988). Social capital in the creation of human capital. *American Journal of Sociology, 94*, S95–S120. doi:10.1086/228943

Compeau, D. R., & Higgins, C. A. (1995). Computer self-efficacy: Development of a measure and initial test. *Management Information Systems Quarterly, 19*(2), 189–211. doi:10.2307/249688

Dasgupta, S. (2003). Structural and behavioural characteristics of informal service employment: Evidence from a survey in New Delhi. *The Journal of Development Studies, 39*(3), 51–80. doi:10.1080/0 0220380412331322821

de Soto, H. (2000). *The Mystery of Capital: Why Capitalism Triumphs in the West and Fails Everywhere Else*. New York: Basic Books.

De Vita, L., Mari, M., & Poggesi, S. (2014). Women entrepreneurs in and from developing countries: Evidences from the literature. *European Management Journal, 32*(3), 451–460. doi:10.1016/j.emj.2013.07.009

DiMaggio, P. J., & Powell, W. W. (1983). The iron cage revisited: Institutional isomorphism and collective rationality in organizational fields. *American Sociological Review, 48*(2), 147–160. doi:10.2307/2095101

Djankov, S., Miguel, E., Qian, Y., Roland, G., & Zhuravskaya, E. (2005). Who are Russias Entrepreneurs? *Journal of the European Economic Association, 3*(2/3), 587–597. doi:10.1162/jeea.2005.3.2-3.587

Djankov, S., Qian, Y., Roland, G., & Zhuravskaya, E. (2006). Who Are Chinas Entrepreneurs? *The American Economic Review, 96*(2), 348–352. doi:10.1257/000282806777212387

Etzioni, A. (1987). Entrepreneurship, adaptation and legitimation. *Journal of Economic Behavior, 8*(2), 175–189. doi:10.1016/0167-2681(87)90002-3

Gaglio, C. M., & Katz, J. A. (2001). The psychological basis of opportunity identification: Entrepreneurial alertness. *Small Business Economics, 16*(2), 95–111. doi:10.1023/A:1011132102464

Griesse, M. (2006). The geographic, political, and economic context for corporate social responsibility in Brazil. *Journal of Business Ethics, 73*(1), 21–37. doi:10.1007/s10551-006-9194-2

Hall, J., Matos, S., & Langford, C. (2008). Social exclusion and transgenic technology: The case of Brazilian agriculture. *Journal of Business Ethics, 77*(1), 45–63. doi:10.1007/s10551-006-9293-0

Hall, J., Matos, S., Silvestre, B., & Martin, M. (2011). Managing the Technological, Commercial, Organizational and Social Uncertainties of Industrial Evolution: The Case of Brazilian Energy and Agriculture. *Technological Forecasting and Social Change, 78*, 1147–1157. doi:10.1016/j.techfore.2011.02.005

Hawley, A. (1968). Human Ecology. In D. L. Sills (Ed.), *International Encyclopedia of the Social Sciences*. New York, NY: Macmillan.

Haynie, M. J., Shepherd, D., Mosakowski, E., & Earley, C. (2008). A situated metacognitive model of the entrepreneurial mindset. *Journal of Business Venturing, 25*(2), 217–229. doi:10.1016/j.jbusvent.2008.10.001

Herreros, F. (2004). *The Problem of Forming Social Capital: Why Trust?* New York: Palgrave/Macmillan. doi:10.1057/9781403978806

Hills, G. E., Lumpkin, G. T., & Singh, R. P. (1997). *Opportunity recognition: perceptions and behaviors of entrepreneurs. In Frontiers of Entrepreneurship Research*. Wellesley, MA: Babson College Press.

IBGE. (2010). Instituto Brasileiro de Geografia e Estatística. Sintese de Indicadores Sociais. *Uma analise das condicoes de vida da populacao Brasileira*. Governo do Brasil. Rio de Janeiro. Retrieved from http://www.ibge.gov.br/home/estatistica/populacao/condicaodevida/indicadoresminimos/sinteseindicsociais2010/SIS_2010.pdf

Johnson, S., Kaufmann, D., Shleifer, A., Goldman, M. I., & Weitzman, M. L. (1997). The unofficial economy in transition. *Brookings Papers on Economic Activity*, 2(2), 159–240. doi:10.2307/2534688

Johnson, S., Kaufmann, D., & Zoido, P. (1999). *Corruption, Public Finance, and the Unofficial Economy.* World Bank Policy Research Working Paper No. 2169. Available at SSRN: http://ssrn.com/abstract=192569

Johnson, S., McMillan, J., & Woodruff, C. (2000). Entrepreneurs and the Ordering of Institutional Reform: Poland, Slovakia, Romania, Russia and Ukraine Compared. *Economics of Transition*, 8(1), 1–36. doi:10.1111/1468-0351.00034

Kahneman, D., & Lovallo, D. (1993). Timid choices and bold forecasts: A cognitive perspective on risk-taking. *Management Science*, 39(1), 17–31. doi:10.1287/mnsc.39.1.17

Kaish, S., & Gilad, B. (1991). Characteristics of Opportunities Search of Entrepreneurs vs Executives: Sources, interests, and general alertness. *Journal of Business Venturing*, 6(1), 45–61. doi:10.1016/0883-9026(91)90005-X

Kihlstrom, R., & Laffont, J. (1979). A General Equilibrium Entrepreneurial Theory of Firm Formation Based on Risk Aversion. *Journal of Political Economy*, 87(4), 719–740. doi:10.1086/260790

Kirzner, I. M. (1973). *Competition and Entrepreneurship*. Chicago, IL: University of Chicago Press.

Kirzner, I. M. (1979). *Perception, Opportunity, and Profit*. Chicago, IL: University of Chicago Press.

Kolvereid, L. (1992). Growth aspirations among Norwegian entrepreneurs. *Journal of Business Venturing*, 5(3), 209–222. doi:10.1016/0883-9026(92)90027-O

Langowitz, N., & Minniti, M. (2007). The entrepreneurial propensity of women. *Entrepreneurship Theory and Practice*, 31(3), 341–364. doi:10.1111/j.1540-6520.2007.00177.x

Lawrence, T. B., Hardy, C., & Phillips, N. (2002). Institutional effects of interorganizational collaboration: The emergence of proto-institutions. *Academy of Management Journal*, 45(1), 281–290. doi:10.2307/3069297

Leibenstein, H. (1968). Entrepreneurship and development. *The American Economic Review*, 58(2), 72–83.

Levie, J., & Autio, E. (2008). A theoretical grounding and test of the GEM model. *Small Business Economics*, 31(3), 235–263. doi:10.1007/s11187-008-9136-8

Levie, J., & Hunt, S. (2005). *Culture, Institutions and New Business Activity: Evidence from Global Entrepreneurship Monitor*. Babson College. Retrieved from http://fusionmx.babson.edu/entrep/fer/fer_2004/web-content/Section%20XIX/P2/XIX-P2_Text.html

Liao, J., & Welsch, H. (2003). Social capital and entrepreneurial growth aspiration: A comparison of technology- and non-technology-based nascent entrepreneurs. *The Journal of High Technology Management Research, 14*(1), 149–170. doi:10.1016/S1047-8310(03)00009-9

Lin, N. (1982). Social resources and instrumental action. In M. Peter & N. Lin (Eds.), *Social Structure and Network Analysis* (pp. 131–145). Beverly Hills, CA: Sage.

Lin, N. (1999). Social networks and status attainment. *Annual Review of Sociology, 25*(1), 467–488. doi:10.1146/annurev.soc.25.1.467

Manolova, T. S., Eunni, R. V., & Gyoshev, B. S. (2008). Institutional Environments for Entrepreneurship: Evidence from Emerging Economies in Eastern Europe. *Entrepreneurship Theory & Practice, 32*(1), 203–218. doi:10.1111/j.1540-6520.2007.00222.x

McMillan, J., & Woodruff, C. (1999). Interfirm Relationships and Informal Credit in Vietnam. *The Quarterly Journal of Economics, 114*(4), 1285–1320. doi:10.1162/003355399556278

McMillan, J., & Woodruff, C. (2002). The Central Role of Entrepreneurs in Transition Economies. *The Journal of Economic Perspectives, 16*(3), 153–170. doi:10.1257/089533002760278767

Minniti, M. (2004). Entrepreneurial alertness and asymmetric information in a spin-glass model. *Journal of Business Venturing, 19*(5), 637–658. doi:10.1016/j.jbusvent.2003.09.003

Morais, M.N. (2006). Uma análise da relação entre o Estado e o tráfico de drogas: O mito do Poder Paralelo. *Revista Ciências Sociais em Perspectiva*, 117-136.

Naffziger, D., Hornsby, J. S., & Kuratko, D. F. (1994). A proposed research model of entrepreneurial motivation. *Entrepreneurship Theory and Practice, 18*(3), 29–39.

Neri, M. (2009). Income Policies, Income Distribution, and the Distribution of Opportunities in Brazil. In L. Brainard & L. Martinez-Diaz (Eds.), *Brazil as an Economic Superpower?: Understanding Brazil's Changing Role in the Global Economy*. Washington, DC: Brookings Institution Press.

North, D. C. (1990). *Institutions, institutional change and economic performance*. New York: Cambridge University Press. doi:10.1017/CBO9780511808678

Parente, S. (2003). O mercado financeiro e a população de baixa renda. *Comissão Econômica para América Latina e o Caribe – CEPAL*.

Payne, J. W., Bettman, J. R., & Johnson, E. J. (1992). Behavioral decision research: A constructive processing perspective. *Annual Review of Psychology, 43*(1), 87–131. doi:10.1146/annurev.ps.43.020192.000511

Peng, M., & Zhou, J. (2005). How network strategies and institutional transitions evolve in Asia. *Asia Pacific Journal of Management, 22*(4), 321–336. doi:10.1007/s10490-005-4113-0

Peng, M. W., & Heath, P. S. (1996). The growth of the firm in planned economies in transformation: Institutions, organizations and strategic choice. *Academy of Management Review*, *21*, 492–528.

Portes, A. (1998). Social capital: Its origins and applications in modern sociology. *Annual Review of Sociology*, *24*(1), 1–24. doi:10.1146/annurev.soc.24.1.1

Prahalad, C. K. (2005). *The Fortune at the Bottom of the Pyramid*. Upper Saddle River, NJ: Wharton School Pub.

Reficco, E., & Marquez, P. (2009). Inclusive networks for building BOP markets. *Business & Society*, *48*, 140–172.

Reynolds, P., Bosma, N., Autio, E., Hunt, S., De Bono, N., Servais, I., & Chin, N. et al. (2005). Global Entrepreneurship Monitor: Data collection design and implementation 1998–2003. *Small Business Economics*, *24*(3), 205–231. doi:10.1007/s11187-005-1980-1

Sambharya, R., & Musteen, M. (2014). Institutional environment and entrepreneurship: An empirical study across countries. *Journal of International Entrepreneurship*, *12*(4), 314–330. doi:10.1007/s10843-014-0137-1

Sautet, F. (2013). Local and Systemic Entrepreneurship: Solving the Puzzle of Entrepreneurship an Economic Development. *Entrepreneurship Theory and Practice*, *37*(2), 387–402. doi:10.1111/j.1540-6520.2011.00469.x

Schumpeter, J. (1934). *The Theory of Economic Development*. Harvard University Press.

Schumpeter, J. (1942). *Capitalism, Socialism and Democracy*. New York: Harper and Row.

Schwartzman, S., & Brock, C. (Eds.). (2005). *Os desafios da educação no Brasil*. Rio de Janeiro: Nova Fronteira.

Scott, W. R. (1995). *Institutions and organizations*. Newbury Park, CA: Sage.

Shane, S., Locke, E., & Collins, C. J. (2003). Entrepreneurial motivation. *Human Resource Management Review*, *13*(2), 257–279. doi:10.1016/S1053-4822(03)00017-2

Sine, W. D., Haveman, H. A., & Tolbert, P. S. (2005). Risky Business? Entrepreneurship in the New Independent-Power Sector. *Administrative Science Quarterly*, *50*(2), 200–232. doi:10.2189/asqu.2005.50.2.200

Smallbone, D., & Welter, D. (2001). The distinctiveness of entrepreneurship in transition economies. *Small Business Economics*, *16*(4), 249–263. doi:10.1023/A:1011159216578

Stephen, A., Stumpf, P. E., & Chaudhry, L. P. (2011). Fake: Can business stanch the flow of counterfeit products? *The Journal of Business Strategy*, *32*(2), 4–12. doi:10.1108/02756661111109725

Storey, D. (1994). *Understanding the Small Business Sector*. London: Routledge.

Suchman, M. C. (1995). Managing legitimacy: Strategic and institutional approaches. *Academy of Management Review*, *20*, 571–610.

Tang, J., Kacmar, K. M., & Busenitz, L. (2012). Entrepreneurial alertness in the pursuit of new opportunities. *Journal of Business Venturing, 27*(1), 77–94. doi:10.1016/j.jbusvent.2010.07.001

Tominc, P., & Rebernik, M. (2007). Growth aspirations and cultural support for entrepreneurship: A comparison of post-socialist countries. *Small Business Economics, 28*(2-3), 239–255. doi:10.1007/s11187-006-9018-x

Tversky, A., & Kahneman, D. (1974). Judgment under uncertainty: Heuristics and biases. *Science, 185*(4157), 1124–1131. doi:10.1126/science.185.4157.1124 PMID:17835457

Valliere, D. (2013). Towards a schematic theory of entrepreneurial alertness. *Journal of Business Venturing, 28*(3), 430–442. doi:10.1016/j.jbusvent.2011.08.004

Viswanathan, M. (2007). Understanding Product and Market Interactions in Subsistence marketplaces: A study in Southern India. *Advances in International Management, 20*, 21–57. doi:10.1016/S1571-5027(07)20002-6

Viswanathan, M., Sridharan, S., & Ritchie, R. (2010). Understanding consumption and entrepreneurship in subsistence marketplaces. *Journal of Business Research, 63*(6), 570–581. doi:10.1016/j.jbusres.2009.02.023

Webb, J., Tihanyi, L., Ireland, D., & Sirmon, D. (2009). You say illegal, I say legitimate: Entrepreneurship in the informal economy. *Academy of Management Review, 34*(3), 492–510. doi:10.5465/AMR.2009.40632826

Williams, C. C., & Youssef, Y. (2013). Evaluating the Gender Variations in Informal Sector Entrepreneurship: Some Lessons From Brazil. *Journal of Developmental Entrepreneurship, 18*(1), 16p. doi:10.1142/S1084946713500040

Wilson, D., & Purushothaman, R. (2003). *Dreaming with BRICs: the path to 2050. Global Economics Paper 99*. Goldman Sachs.

Woolcock, M. (2001). Microenterprise and social capital: A framework for theory, research, and policy. *Journal of Socio-Economics, 30*(2), 193–198. doi:10.1016/S1053-5357(00)00106-2

Zafaroni, E.R. (1997). *Manual de Direito Penal Brasileiro: Parte Geral*. São Paulo: RT.

KEY TERMS AND DEFINITIONS

Destructive Entrepreneurship: Entrepreneurial activities that lead to societal detriment (e.g. criminal activities).

High-Income Entrepreneur: A Global Entrepreneurship Monitor (GEM) categorical variable that classifies individuals in three income thirds (low, medium and high), with high being an entrepreneur within the higher 33tile.

Innovation: The commercialization of invention that provides net societal benefits.

Institutional Environment: Rules and requirements to which entrepreneurs must conform in order to receive legitimacy and support.

Low-Income Entrepreneur: A Global Entrepreneurship Monitor (GEM) categorical variable that classifies individuals in three income thirds (low, medium and high), with low being an entrepreneur within the lower 33tile.

Productive Entrepreneurship: Entrepreneurial activities that lead to net societal gain (e.g. innovation).

Unproductive Entrepreneurship: Activities that do not create socially beneficial improvement, but instead seek rents through for example the exploitation of legal loopholes.

Chapter 13
Determining Influencing Factors of Currency Exchange Rate for Decision Making in Global Economy Using MARS Method

Hasan Dinçer
Istanbul Medipol University, Turkey

Ümit Hacıoğlu
Istanbul Medipol University, Turkey

Serhat Yüksel
Istanbul Medipol University, Turkey

ABSTRACT

The aim of this study is to identify the determinants of US Dollar/Turkish Lira currency exchange rate for strategic decision making in the global economy. Within this scope, quarterly data for the period between 1988:1 and 2016:2 was used in this study. In addition to this aspect, 10 explanatory variables were considered in order to determine the leading indicators of US Dollar/Turkish Lira currency exchange rate. Moreover, Multivariate Adaptive Regression Splines (MARS) method was used so as to achieve this objective. According to the results of this analysis, it was defined that two different variables affect this exchange rate in Turkey. First of all, it was identified that there is a negative relationship between current account balance and the value of US Dollar/Turkish Lira currency exchange rate. This result shows that in case of current account deficit problem, Turkish Lira experiences depreciation. Furthermore, it was also concluded that when there is an economic growth in Turkey, Turkish Lira increases in comparison with US Dollar. While taking into the consideration of these results, it could be generalized that emerging economies such as Turkey have to decrease current account deficit and investors should focus on higher economic growth in order to prevent the depreciation of the money in the strategic investment decision.

DOI: 10.4018/978-1-5225-2673-5.ch013

INTRODUCTION

Globalization means that eliminating economic barriers between countries (Dunning, 2002). It was effective almost all over the world especially after 1970. As a result of this aspect, economies of different countries became interconnected. This situation brought many advantages to the countries with respect to the economic growth. On the other hand, globalization also led to many risks for these countries, such as volatility in the market. In other words, economies of the countries became more fragile to the extraordinary changes in other countries owing to the globalization. In addition to the negative effects for the economic stability of the country, these kinds of problems also affect the decisions of the investors negatively (Yüksel et. al., 2015).

Within this context, the stability of the currency exchange rate is very significant for the economies of the countries. The main reason behind this situation is that the exchange rate affects many important factors in the economy such as export, economic growth, and foreign direct investments (Bacchetta and Van Wincoop, 2000). Therefore, countries always prefer a stable exchange rate in order to prevent volatility in the market. Otherwise, countries may experience important losses due to high amount of increase or decrease in the value of exchange rate. In the past, there were many economic crises which were occurred because of this problem. For example, Southeast Asian countries had important losses in 1998 due to the high amount of changes in currency exchange rate (Corsetti et. al., 1999).

Turkey is also a country which experienced two different economic crises in 1994 and 2000. During this period, Turkey had significant amount of losses due to high amount of increase in US Dollar/Turkish Lira currency exchange rate. Many companies went bankruptcy owing to the fact that they cannot manage this increase. As a result of this situation, a lot of people lost their jobs. The effect of this crisis was so severe that lots of banks were taken over by the Savings Deposit Insurance Fund (SDIF) in this period (Yüksel, 2016b).

Because of this situation, it can be said that the studies aimed to identify the determinants of the exchange rate is essential. Parallel to this aspect, the purpose of this study is to define the influencing factors of US Dollar/Turkish Lira currency exchange rate. In order to achieve this objective, Multivariate Adaptive Regression Splines (MARS) method was used in this study. With respect to the originality concept, the most important property of this analysis is that MARS method was used for this subject firstly in this study. As a result of this analysis, it will be possible to make recommendation so as to have more stable US Dollar/Turkish Lira currency exchange rate.

The paper is organized as follows. After introduction part, information about the similar studies in the literature was given. Additionally, the third part gives information about Multivariate Adaptive Regression Splines (MARS) method. In this part, firstly general information and model creation process will be explained. After that, studies in which this method was used will be explained. Moreover, fourth part includes research and application to understand the determinants of US Dollar/Turkish Lira currency exchange rate. Finally, the results of the analysis were given at conclusion.

BACKGROUND

Because the subject of determining the value of the exchange rate is very important, there were many studies in the literature which focused on this subject. Some of these studies were explained on Table 1.

Table 1. Similar studies in the literature

Author	Scope	Method	Result
Edwards (1988)	12 developing countries	Regression	It was concluded that macroeconomic factors influence real exchange rate.
Gagnon (1993)	USA	Descriptive Statistics	Exchange rate variability has a negative effect on the level of trade.
Campa (1993)	USA	Tobit	It was identified that there is negative correlation between exchange rate volatility and with the number of foreign investors.
Devereux (1997)	Canada	Regression	Macroeconomic factors such as GDP growth and inflation rate affect real exchange rate.
MacDonald (1998)	G7 countries	VAR	Foreign trade and real interest rate are the significant determinants of real exchange rate.
Darby et. al. (1999)	France, Germany, Italy, UK and USA	Regression	They analyzed the situations in which exchange rate uncertainty affect the level of investment or not for different countries.
Berument (2002)	Turkey	VAR	There is a direct relationship between inflation rate and foreign exchange rates.
Juhn and Mauro (2002)	IMF member countries	Probit	The size of the economy has a significant effect on exchange rate.
Bilgin (2004)	Turkey	Regression	It was defined that there is a strong relationship between foreign exchange rate and unemployment.
Şimşek (2004)	Turkey	ARDL Test	It was concluded that net foreign assets, M2 money supply[1*] and trade balance influence the real exchange rate in Turkey.
Morales-Zumaquero (2006)	Canada, Japan, USA	SVAR	Fluctuations in real exchange rate are explained by inflation rate.
Gül and Ekinci (2006)	Turkey	Granger Causality Test	It was determined that there is a relationship between exchange rate and inflation.
Candelon et. al. (2007)	8 EU member countries	Regression	It was analyzed that higher inflation affects exchange rate.
Mark (2009)	USA	Regression	Output gaps and expected inflation are the main determinants of exchange rate.
Cayen et. al. (2010)	Australia, Canada, New Zealand	Regression	Commodity price levels are very significant so as to determine real exchange rate.
Savaş and Can (2011)	Turkey	Granger Causality Test	Changes in BIST 100 Index affect foreign exchange rate.
Hamori and Hamori (2011)	Japan	SVAR	Real shocks play a dominant role in explaining the real exchange rate fluctuations.
Dilbaz Alacahan (2011)	Turkey	Descriptive Statistics	High interest rate causes a decrease in foreign exchange rates.
Acar Balaylar (2011)	Turkey	Descriptive Statistics	It was identified that foreign currency rate is affected by unemployment rate.
Chowdhury (2012)	Australia	ARDL Test	It was determined that government expenditures affect real exchange rate.
Berke (2012)	Turkey	Engle Granger Causality Test	There is a negative relationship between foreign exchange rate and BIST 100 index.
Kia (2013)	Canada	Regression	The change in interest rate, the growth of money supply and the US debt per GDP have a negative impact on the growth of the real exchange rate.
De Grauwe and Markiewicz (2013)	USA, UK and Germany	Regression	It was analyzed that the exchange rate behaves as a random walk.
Rossi (2013)	20 different countries	VECM	The success of exchange rate prediction depends on the time.
Altıntaş (2013)	Turkey	ARDL Test	Increase in oil prices leads to rise in foreign exchange rate for oil-importing countries.
Gabaix and Maggiori (2014)	USA	Regression	There is no relationship between exchange rates and inflation rate.
Kaplan and Yapraklı (2014)	Turkey	Panel Data Analysis	Current account deficit, public debt amount and reserves are important indicators of foreign currency rate.
Ferraro et. al. (2015)	USA	Regression	It was identified that commodity prices can predict exchange rates at a daily frequency.
Brdys et. al. (2016)	Poland	Monte Carlo	A non-parametric prediction technique was created.
Chaudhury et. al. (2016)	India	GARCH	They created a model in order to predict the value of the Indian rupee.

Devereux (1997) tried to analyze real exchange rates in Canada by using regression analysis. As a result of this analysis, it was concluded that macroeconomic factors such as GDP growth and inflation rate affect real exchange rate. Berument (2002), Candelon and others (2007) and Morales-Zumaquero (2006) reached the same conclusion by using different VAR analysis. Similar to these studies, Gül and Ekinci (2006) identified that high inflation rates are the main cause of exchange rate depreciation in Turkey. Nevertheless, Gabaix and Maggiori (2014) concluded that there is no relationship between exchange rates and inflation rate.

In addition to them, there are also some studies that analyzed the relationship between interest rate and exchange rates. MacDonald (1998) made a study about the exchange rate values in G7 countries and determined that real interest rate is the significant determinant of real exchange rate. Dilbaz Alacahan (2011) and Kia (2013) made similar conclusions in their studies with the help of different methods. On the other hand, Bilgin (2004) identified that there is a strong relationship between foreign exchange rate and unemployment.

Additionally, some studies in the literature also focused on the relationship between exchange rate volatility and investment decisions. Campa (1993) tried to analyze this relationship in the USA. According to the results of tobit analysis, it was concluded that there is negative correlation between exchange rate volatility and with the number of foreign investors. Similar to this study, Gagnon (1993) also determined that exchange rate variability has a negative effect on the level of trade. Moreover, Darby and others (1999) defined the situations in which exchange rate uncertainty affect the level of investment or not for different countries.

Furthermore, it was also seen that some studies in the literature focused on the prediction of the currency exchange rate. De Grauwe and Markiewicz (2013) created a model for USA, UK and Germany in order to estimate future values of exchange rate. Rossi (2013) also made similar studies for 20 different countries by using vector error correction method. Additionally, Ferraro et. al. (2015) used regression analysis so as to predict exchange rate in USA. Parallel to these studies, Chaudhury and others (2016) also focused on the prediction of the value of the Indian rupee.

RESEARCH AND APPLICATION

Data and Variables

In this study, quarterly data for the period between 1988:1 and 2016:2 was used. The data was provided from the internet pages of World Bank, Borsa İstanbul, Turkish Statistical Institute and Central Bank of America. In addition to the data, Eviews8 program was used for unit root test. Moreover, MARS 2.0 program of Salford Company was used in MARS method.

The aim of this study is to determine the leading indicators of US Dollar/Turkish Lira currency exchange rate. Therefore, this rate was used as a dependent variable. Additionally, by analyzing similar studies in the literature, 10 different explanatory variables that may affect the value of exchange rate were defined. The details of these variables were emphasized in Table 2.

GDP growth rate is the first independent variable in this study. The effect of economic growth on exchange rate depends on the source of the growth. If the main source of GDP growth is household consumption, this will increase import and local currency will depreciate. On the other hand, if GDP growth is mainly provided by exports and investments, then local currency will appreciate (Candelon et.

Table 2. The details of independent variables

Variable	References
GDP Growth Rate	Şimşek (2004), Kia (2013), Mark (2009), Devereux (1997), Candelon et. al. (2007), Edwards (1988), Hamori and Hamori (2011), MacDonald (1998), Juhn and Mauro (2002)
Foreign Capital Inflows	Şimşek (2004), Chaudhury et. al. (2016), Edwards (1988), MacDonald (1998), Juhn and Mauro (2002)
Current Account Deficit	Şimşek (2004), Bilgin (2004), Kaplan and Yapraklı (2014), Chaudhury et. al. (2016), Chowdhury (2012), Edwards (1988), Morales-Zumaquero (2006), Juhn and Mauro (2002)
Inflation	Şimşek (2004), Gül and Ekinci (2006), Berument (2002), Savaş and Can (2011), Chaudhury et. al. (2016), Gabaix and Maggiori (2014), Rossi (2013), De Grauwe and Markiewicz (2013), Mark (2009), Devereux (1997), Cayen et. al. (2010), Hamori and Hamori (2011), MacDonald (1998), Morales-Zumaquero (2006), Juhn and Mauro (2002)
Reserves	Kaplan and Yapraklı (2014), Chaudhury et. al. (2016), Juhn and Mauro (2002)
Interest Rate	Dilbaz Alacahan (2011), Chaudhury et. al. (2016), Gabaix and Maggiori (2014), Rossi (2013), De Grauwe and Markiewicz (2013), Kia (2013), Mark (2009), Cayen et. al. (2010), Chowdhury (2012), MacDonald (1998)
External Debt	Şimşek (2004), Kaplan and Yapraklı (2014), Kia (2013), Cayen et. al. (2010), Chowdhury (2012)
Unemployment	Bilgin (2004), Acar Balaylar (2011), Mark (2009)
BIST 100 Index	Savaş and Can (2011), Berke (2012)
Oil Price	Altıntaş (2013), Chaudhury et. al. (2016), Ferraro et. al. (2015), MacDonald (1998)

al., 2007). Similar to this situation, it can also be said that there is a positive correlation between foreign direct investment and the reserves with the value of local currency (Edwards, 1988).

Additionally, when there is current account deficit in a country, international reserves of this country will decrease and this situation will decrease the value of local currency (Morales-Zumaquero, 2006). Parallel to this aspect, there is also negative relationship between the foreign debt and the value of local currency (Chowdhury, 2012). Furthermore, higher inflation rate also decreases the value of local currency (Devereux, 1997). The main reason behind this issue is that the goods of this country become more expensive in comparison with import goods. Owing to this situation, higher demand on import goods leads to decrease in the value of local currency. Because of the same reason, there should also be negative relationship between oil price and local currency value (Ferraro et. al., 2015).

Moreover, higher interest rate causes the demand of local currency to increase. As a result of this situation, US Dollar/Turkish Lira currency exchange rate is expected to decrease (Rossi, 2013). In addition to this aspect, unemployment rate is also another determinant of the value of exchange rate. Because unemployment rate is a significant indicator of the economy, the relationship between unemployment rate and US Dollar/Turkish Lira currency exchange rate should be positive (Mark, 2009). Due to the same reason, when there is an increase in BIST 100 index, the value of this exchange rate should decrease (Berke, 2012).

MARS Method

Multivariate Adaptive Regression Splines (MARS) method was firstly introduced by Jerome Friedman in 1991. Mainly, it was used in order to determine the relationship between dependent variable and independent variables. The equation of MARS method is given below.

$$Y = B_0 + \sum_{n=1}^{K} a_n B_n(X_t) + \varepsilon \tag{1}$$

In the equation above, "Y" shows dependent variable while "X" refers to the independent variable. Moreover, "B_0" gives information about the constant term. Additionally, "a_n" shows the coefficient of the basis function. Furthermore, "ε" explains error term of the equation whereas "K" demonstrates the number of basis functions.

There are many advantageous of MARS method by comparison with other regression methods. In this method, smoothing splines are used instead of simple regression line. Owing to this situation, it will be possible to have more accurate results by using this method. In addition to this issue, there is no multicollinearity problem that demonstrates the relationship among explanatory variables in MARS method. Because of this aspect, high number of independent variables can be used in the analysis. The final advantage of this model is that explanatory variables can take part more than once in equation with different coefficients. Hence, results of this analysis will be more explanatory in comparison with other methods (Friedman, 1991).

With respect to the model creation process, there are two different stages. First of all, system produces all possible basis functions by using different combination of independent variables. After achieving the most complex model which has maximum number of basis functions, system starts to eliminate some basis functions from this complex model. In this process, the basis functions which have the highest error value (GCV-generalized cross validation) will be removed from this model. As a result of this process, the most ideal model, which has the highest R2 and lowest GCV values, can be achieved (Friedman, 1991).

MARS is a very new model, so there are few numbers of studies in which this model was used. In addition to this aspect, this model was rarely used in finance and economics area. Sephton (2001) tried to identify the determinants of the recession in USA and concluded that MARS method gives more accurate results than probit method. Tunay (2001) made a study about the velocity of circulation of money and identified that it is not stable in Turkey. Moreover, Bolder and Rubin (2007) aimed to determine the best lending strategy of USA and defined that MARS method is the most efficient method with respect to determining the best lending strategy.

Also, Muzır (2011) measured the credit risk of the banks in Turkey and concluded that MARS method measures credit risk better than logit and artificial neural networks. Additionally, Tunay (2011) determined that MARS method is very successful in order to predict recession. Moreover, Oktar and Yüksel (2015) explained the leading indicators of Turkish banking crisis by using MARS method. Yüksel (2016a) also identified the determinants of current account deficit by using this method.

Analysis Results and Findings

In order to understand the relationship between dependent variable and independent variables by using MARS method, first of all, stationary analysis of these variables should be made. For this purpose, Augmented Dickey Fuller (ADF) and Philips Peron (PP) tests were used. The results of these tests were given in Table 3.

As it can be seen from Table 3, level values of two independent variables (Growth Rate and Current Account Balance) are less than 0.05 according to the results of both two tests. This situation shows that only these two variables are stationary at their level values. Because level values of other 8 variables are more than 0.05, their first differences were used in the analysis. After stationary analysis, MARS method gave us 8 different models which were explained in Table 4.

Table 3. Unit root test results of independent variables

Variable	Augmented Dickey Fuller (ADF) Test		Philips Peron Test	
	Level Value (Probability)	First Difference Value (Probability)	Level Value (Probability)	First Difference Value (Probability)
Growth Rate	0.0000	-	0.0000	-
Foreign Direct Investment	0.4313	0.0125	0.3927	0.0419
Current Account Balance	0.0097	-	0.0040	-
Inflation Rate	0.6563	0.0000	0.3677	0.0000
Reserve	0.4313	0.0000	0.6118	0.0000
Interest Rate	0.4040	0.0000	0.0953	0.0000
Government Debt	0.9309	0.0295	0.8366	0.0000
Unemployment Rate	0.6302	0.0000	0.6035	0.0000
BIST 100 Index	0.3104	0.0000	0.4391	0.0000
Oil Prices	0.6533	0.0000	0.1440	0.0000

Table 4. All models created by MARS method

Number of Basis Functions	Number of Variables	GCV	GCV R²
8	3	0.373	0.502
7	3	0.356	0.525
6	2	0.345	0.540
5	2	0.336	0.552
4	2	0.334	0.555
**3	2	0.333	0.556
2	2	0.341	0.546
1	1	0.449	0.401

As it can be understood from Table 4, each row represents different model. The undermost line shows us the starting model that has only one variable and basis function. In the analysis, the system added some basis functions to this starting model. This process went on until the system reaches the most complex model. The first row in Table 4 represents the most complex function in the analysis. It has 8 basis functions and 3 different explanatory variables. After that, the system eliminated some unnecessary basis functions from the most complex model. As a result of this process, the system achieved the best model. In Table 4, the model, which has the sign of "**", explains the best model. It has 3 basis functions and 2 independent variables. On the other hand, it can also be seen that the best model has the lowest GCV value and highest GCV R2 value. The details of the best model were given on Table 5.

As it can be seen from Table 5, the p values of all basis functions in the best model are less than 0.05. This means that all of the functions are statistically significant. In addition to this situation, the probability value of F test (0.000) is also less than 0.05. This aspect shows that the model is also meaningful as a whole. Moreover, the value of adjusted R2 (0.597) indicates that independent variables can

Table 5. Statistical information about the best model

Variable	Coefficient	p Value
Constant	1.755	0.000
Basis Function 3	0.253	0.008
Basis Function 7	-0.085	0.000
Basis Function 9	-0.281	0.000
F Test 56.717 [0.000] **p Value** 0.000 R^2 0.607 **Adj. R^2** 0.597		

explain 59.7% of the dependent variable. Furthermore, the details of the basis functions in the model were explained on Table 6.

From Table 6, it can be understood that two independent variables affect US Dollar/Turkish Lira currency exchange rate. The variable of current account balance was stated in both basis function 3 and 9. The coefficients of these functions are 0.253 and -0.281. Because the absolute value of negative coefficient is higher, this means that there is a negative relationship between the current account balance and US Dollar/Turkish Lira currency exchange rate. In other words, when there is a current account deficit, the value of US Dollar/Turkish Lira currency exchange rate will be higher. The main reason behind this situation is that international reserves of this country will decrease and foreign debt will increase in case of current account deficit. As a result of this issue, value of local currency will decrease. This conclusion is similar to many studies in the literature (Chowdhury, 2012), (Edwards, 1988), (Morales-Zumaquero, 2006), (Juhn and Mauro, 2002).

Another significant variable according to the analysis is the economic growth. This variable was stated in basis function 7 in the best model. On the other side, the coefficient of this variable is -0.085. That is to say, there is a negative relationship between GDP growth rate and US Dollar/Turkish Lira. This situation shows us that when there is an economic growth in a country, Turkish Lira gains more value in comparison with the US Dollar. The reason for this aspect is that when GDP growth is mainly provided by exports and investments, then local currency will appreciate in that country. Devereux (1997), Candelon et. al. (2007), Edwards (1988), Hamori and Hamori (2011), MacDonald (1998) and Juhn and Mauro (2002) also reached the same conclusion. The importance levels of these variables were given on Table 7.

As a result of the analysis, the best model in our analysis was formed as following.

Y = 1.755 + 0.253 * BF3 - 0.085 * BF7 - 0.281 * BF9

Table 6. Details of the basis functions in the model

Basis Functions	Details	Coefficient
Basis Function 3	max (0, Current Account Balance + 0.110)	0.253
Basis Function 7	max (0, GDP Growth – 1.000)	-0.085
Basis Function 9	max (0, Current Account Balance + 4.610)	-0.281

Table 7. Variable importance in the model

Variable	Cost of Omission	Importance (%)
Current Account Balance	0.592	100.00
GDP Growth	0.381	42.845

FUTURE RESEARCH DIRECTIONS

In this study, determinants of US Dollar/Turkish Lira currency exchange rate were tried to be analyzed. As it can be understood from this aspect, volatility of the exchange rate for only one country was evaluated. Because this subject is very significant for the countries, another research for this issue which includes many different countries will be very beneficial for the economies to make strategic decisions. While making this kind of analysis, it will be possible to consider different situations in order to understand the volatility of the exchange rates.

CONCLUSION

It was aimed to analyze the determinants of US Dollar/Turkish Lira currency exchange rate in this study. Within this context, 10 independent variables were taken into the consideration. In addition to this situation, quarterly data of these variables for the period between 1988:1 and 2016:2 was used in this study. Furthermore, Multivariate Adaptive Regression Splines (MARS) method was used so as to achieve this objective.

First of all, unit root test was made for the independent variables to understand whether they stationary or not. Within this scope, Augmented Dickey Fuller (ADF) and Phillps Perron (PP) tests were used. As a result of this analysis, it was understood that only two independent variables (Growth Rate and Current Account Balance) are stationary on their level values. Because other 8 independent variables are not stationary on their level values, the first difference of these variables were used in the analysis.

After stationary analysis, the influencing factors of US Dollar/Turkish Lira currency exchange rate were determined by using MARS method. MARS model provided 8 different models to us. Out of them, one model was chosen as the best model by the system. This model has 3 basis functions and two different independent variables. Moreover, it has the lowest GCV value and highest GCV R2 value.

According to the results of the analysis, it was determined that two independent variables affect US Dollar/Turkish Lira currency exchange rate. The first significant variable in the analysis is current account balance which was stated in basis function 3 and 9. While considering the value of the coefficients, it was identified that there is a negative relationship between the current account balance and US Dollar/Turkish Lira currency exchange rate. This means that the value of US Dollar/Turkish Lira currency exchange rate will be higher in case of current account deficit. When there is a current account deficit, there will be decrease in the amount of the reserves and the demand for US Dollar will increase. Therefore, the value of Turkish Lira will decrease in comparison to US Dollar.

In addition to this situation, it was also concluded that economic growth is also another important indicator of US Dollar/Turkish Lira currency exchange rate. This variable was stated in basis function 7 and the coefficient of this variable is -0.085. Since the coefficient is negative, it can be understood that there is an inverse relationship between economic growth and US Dollar/Turkish Lira currency exchange rate. In other words, when GDP growth is mainly provided by exports and investments, the value Turkish Lira will increase by comparison with US Dollar.

The value of exchange rate affects many important factors in the economy such as export, economic growth, and foreign direct investments. Owing to this situation, it can be said that the value of the exchange rate plays a very important role for the economies. Hence, countries try to determine the way of providing a stable exchange rate in order to prevent volatility in the market. According to the results of this analysis, the reasons of the volatile US Dollar/Turkish Lira currency exchange rate were determined. Therefore, it can be recommended that Turkey has to decrease current account deficit and should focus on higher economic growth in order to prevent the depreciation of Turkish Lira. Thus, volatility in Turkish economy will be minimized. In addition to this situation, these conclusions will be also helpful for investor so as to make strategic investment decision.

REFERENCES

Acar Balaylar, N. (2011). Reel Döviz Kuru Istihdam Iliskisi: Türkiye Imalat Sanayi Örnegi. *Sosyoekonomi*, (2), 137-160.

Altıntaş, H. (2013). Türkiye'de petrol fiyatları, ihracat ve reel döviz kuru ilişkisi: ARDL sınır testi yaklaşımı ve dinamik nedensellik analizi. *Uluslararası Yönetim İktisat ve İşletme Dergisi*, 9(19), 1–30.

Bacchetta, P., & Van Wincoop, E. (2000). Does exchange-rate stability increase trade and welfare? *The American Economic Review*, 90(5), 1093–1109. doi:10.1257/aer.90.5.1093

Berke, B. (2012). Döviz Kuru ve İMKB100 Endeksi İlişkisi: Yeni Bir Test. *Maliye Dergisi*, 163, 243–257.

Berument, H. (2002). Döviz Kuru Hareketleri ve Enflasyon Dinamiği: Türkiye Örneği. *Bilkent Üniversitesi Yayınları*, 1-15.

Bilgin, M. H. (2004). Döviz Kuru İşsizlik İlişkisi: Türkiye Üzerine Bir İnceleme. *Kocaeli Üniversitesi Sosyal Bilimler Enstitüsü Dergisi*, 8, 80–94.

Bolder, D. J., &Rubin, T. (2007). *Optimization in a simulation setting: Use of function approximation in debt strategy analysis*. Available at SSRN 1082840

Brdyś, M. A., Brdyś, M. T., & Maciejewski, S. M. (2016). Adaptive predictions of the euro/złoty currency exchange rate using state space wavelet networks and forecast combinations. *International Journal of Applied Mathematics and Computer Science*, 26(1), 161–173. doi:10.1515/amcs-2016-0011

Campa, J. M. (1993). Entry by foreign firms in the United States under exchange rate uncertainty. *The Review of Economics and Statistics*, 75(4), 614–622. doi:10.2307/2110014

Candelon, B., Kool, C., Raabe, K., & van Veen, T. (2007). Long-run real exchange rate determinants: Evidence from eight new EU member states, 1993–2003. *Journal of Comparative Economics, 35*(1), 87–107. doi:10.1016/j.jce.2006.10.003

Cayen, J. P., Coletti, D., Lalonde, R., & Maier, P. (2010). What drives exchange rates? new evidence from a panel of US dollar bilateral exchange rates. *Document de travail*, (2010-5).

Chaudhuri, T. D., & Ghosh, I. (2016). *Artificial Neural Network and Time Series Modeling Based Approach to Forecasting the Exchange Rate in a Multivariate Framework.* arXiv preprint arXiv:1607.02093

Chowdhury, K. (2012). Modelling the dynamics, structural breaks and the determinants of the real exchange rate of Australia. *Journal of International Financial Markets, Institutions and Money, 22*(2), 343–358. doi:10.1016/j.intfin.2011.10.004

Corsetti, G., Pesenti, P., & Roubini, N. (1999). Paper tigers?: A model of the Asian crisis. *European Economic Review, 43*(7), 1211–1236. doi:10.1016/S0014-2921(99)00017-3

Darby, J., Hallett, A. H., Ireland, J., & Piscitelli, L. (1999). The impact of exchange rate uncertainty on the level of investment. *The Economic Journal, 109*(454), 55–67. doi:10.1111/1468-0297.00416

De Grauwe, P., & Markiewicz, A. (2013). Learning to forecast the exchange rate: Two competing approaches. *Journal of International Money and Finance, 32*, 42–76. doi:10.1016/j.jimonfin.2012.03.001

Devereux, M. B. (1997). Real exchange rates and macroeconomics: Evidence and theory. *The Canadian Journal of Economics. Revue Canadienne dEconomique, 30*(4a), 773–808. doi:10.2307/136269

Dilbaz Alacahan, N. (2011). Enflasyon, Döviz Kuru İlişkisi ve Yansıma: Türkiye. *Sosyal Bilimler Dergisi, 1*, 49–56.

Dunning, J. H. (2002). *Regions, globalization, and the knowledge-based economy.* Oxford University Press. doi:10.1093/0199250014.001.0001

Edwards, S. (1988). Real and monetary determinants of real exchange rate behavior: Theory and evidence from developing countries. *Journal of Development Economics, 29*(3), 311–341. doi:10.1016/0304-3878(88)90048-X

Ferraro, D., Rogoff, K., & Rossi, B. (2015). Can oil prices forecast exchange rates? An empirical analysis of the relationship between commodity prices and exchange rates. *Journal of International Money and Finance, 54*, 116–141. doi:10.1016/j.jimonfin.2015.03.001

Friedman, J. H. (1991). Multivariate adaptive regression splines. *Annals of Statistics, 19*(1), 1–67. doi:10.1214/aos/1176347963

Gabaix, X., & Maggiori, M. (2014). *International liquidity and exchange rate dynamics (No. w19854).* National Bureau of Economic Research. doi:10.3386/w19854

Gagnon, J. E. (1993). Exchange rate variability and the level of international trade. *Journal of International Economics, 34*(3-4), 269–287. doi:10.1016/0022-1996(93)90050-8

Gül, E., & Ekinci, A. (2006). Türkiye'de Enflasyon ve Döviz Kuru Arasındaki Nedensellik İlişkisi: 1984-2003. *Sosyal Bilimler Dergisi, 1*, 91–106.

Hamori, S., & Hamori, N. (2011). An empirical analysis of real exchange rate movements in the euro. *Applied Economics, 43*(10), 1187–1191. doi:10.1080/00036840802600319

Juhn, G., & Mauro, P. (2002). *Long-Run Determinants of Exchange Rate Regimes A Simple Sensitivity Analysis*. IMF Working Paper.

Kaplan, F., & Yapraklı, S. (2014). Ekonomik Kırılganlık Endeksi Göstergelerinin Döviz Kuru Üzerindeki Etkileri: Kırılgan 12 Ülke Üzerine Panel Veri Analizi. *Uluslararası Alanya İşletme Fakültesi Dergisi, 6*(3), 111–121.

Kia, A. (2013). Determinants of the real exchange rate in a small open economy: Evidence from Canada. *Journal of International Financial Markets, Institutions and Money, 23*, 163–178. doi:10.1016/j.intfin.2012.09.001

MacDonald, R. (1998). What determines real exchange rates?: The long and the short of it. *Journal of International Financial Markets, Institutions and Money, 8*(2), 117–153. doi:10.1016/S1042-4431(98)00028-6

Mark, N. C. (2009). Changing monetary policy rules, learning, and real exchange rate dynamics. *Journal of Money, Credit and Banking, 41*(6), 1047–1070. doi:10.1111/j.1538-4616.2009.00246.x

Morales-Zumaquero, A. (2006). Explaining real exchange rate fluctuations. *Journal of Applied Econometrics, 9*(2), 345–381.

Muzır, E. (2011). *Basel II Düzenlemeleri Doğrultusunda Kredi Riski Analizi ve Ölçümü: Geleneksel Ekonometrik Modellerin Yapay Sinir Ağları ve MARS Modelleriyle Karşılaştırılmasına Yönelik Ampirik Bir Çalışma*. İstanbul Üniversitesi Sosyal Bilimler Enstitüsü, Yayınlanmamış Doktora Tezi.

Oktar, S., & Yüksel, S. (2015). Bankacılık Krizlerinin Erken Uyarı Sinyalleri [İlker Parasız Özel Eki]. *Türkiye Üzerine Bir Uygulama, İstanbul Ticaret Üniversitesi Sosyal Bilimler Dergisi, 14*(28), 37–53.

Rossi, B. (2013). Exchange rate predictability. *Journal of Economic Literature, 51*(4), 1063–1119. doi:10.1257/jel.51.4.1063

Savaş, İ., & Can, İ. (2011). Euro-Dolar Paritesi ve Reel Döviz Kuru'nun İMKB 100 Endeksi'ne Etkisi. *Eskişehir Osmangazi Üniversitesi İİBF Dergisi, 6*(1), 323–339.

Sephton, P. (2001). Forecasting recessions: Can we do better on MARS? *Review - Federal Reserve Bank of St. Louis, 83*(2), 39–49.

Şimşek, M. (2004). Türkiye'de Reel Döviz Kurunu Belirleyen Uzun Dönemli Etkenler. *Cumhuriyet Üniversitesi İktisadi ve İdari Bilimler Fakültesi Dergisi, 5*(2), 1–24.

Tunay, K. B. (2001). Türkiye'de paranın gelir dolaşım hızlarının MARS yöntemiyle tahmini. *ODTÜ Gelişme Dergisi, 28*(3-4).

Tunay, K. B. (2011). Türkiye'de Durgunlukların MARS Yöntemi ile Tahmini ve Kestirimi, *Marmara Üniversitesi İ.İ.B.F. Dergisi, 30*(1), 71–91.

Yüksel, S. (2016a). Türkiye'de Cari İşlemler Açığının Belirleyicileri: Mars Yöntemi ile Bir İnceleme. *Bankacılar Dergisi, 96*, 102–121.

Yüksel, S. (2016b). *Bankacılık Krizlerinin Erken Uyarı Sinyalleri: Türkiye ÜZerine Bir Uygulama.* Akademisyen Kitabevi.

Yuksel, S., Dincer, H., & Hacioglu, U. (2015). CAMELS-based Determinants for the Credit Rating of Turkish Deposit Banks. *International Journal of Finance & Banking Studies, 4*(4), 1–17.

KEY TERMS AND DEFINITIONS

Currency Exchange Rate: It shows the ratio of local currency of a country to a foreign currency.
Foreign Direct Investment (FDI): Investment made by a company in another country.
Global Economy: The economies of the whole countries, considered as a single economic system.
Strategic Decision: Action of a company that affects key factors and long run performance.
Vector Autoregression (VAR): An econometric method used to understand the interdependencies among multiple time series.

ENDNOTES

[1]   M2 Money supply includes cash, deposits, money market securities, mutual funds and other time deposits.

Chapter 14
Economic Partnership Agreement Mexico–Japan and Its Impact on Foreign Direct Investment:
A Strategic Analysis

José G. Vargas-Hernández
University of Guadalajara, Mexico

ABSTRACT

This chapter is intended to analyze the advantages to associate with a developing country like México from the perspective of the theories of the Agency, Institutional, Resource-based Theory and the Theory of Transaction Costs. Generally, FDI contributes to capital formation, expansion and diversification of exports, increasing competition, provide access to top technology and improving management systems. Mexico is of the largest FDI recipients within the developing countries. Japan, on the other hand, is one of the largest sources of FDI worldwide, and is gaining a larger share in the Mexican FDI context since the onset of the Economic Partnership Agreement. In this paper, factors that might lead to the depletion of productive spillovers from Japanese manufacturing companies are reviewed from a qualitative perspective. The analysis suggests that inefficiencies in endogenous companies; and Japanese companies being part of firm networks (keiretsu), might lead to productive spillovers depletion.

INTRODUCTION

For decades Mexico has have a good relationship with Japan. The leaders of both countries have struggled to maintain a relationship of friendly cooperation to benefit the development of both countries. Mexico, being a source of coarse natural resources has always been in the crosshairs of industries of several countries and in recent years has improved its trade relationship with Japan to complement the lack of resources of the Asian country.

DOI: 10.4018/978-1-5225-2673-5.ch014

Japan as an island has limits in the scope of resources, especially agricultural. It is a country that imports 60% of its population consumes in food. This is why it is a sourcing seeking country to resolve its situation in scarcity of resources. Mexico and Japan have economic characteristics that make them complementary to each other, mainly in the food sector, where Mexico could position itself as a leading supplier of agricultural and livestock products. This complementarity should contribute to economic development in both countries through trade and investment.

The commercial relationship between Mexico and the countries of North America and Europe has grown over the decades due to the incursions of several free trade agreements such as NAFTA and the TLCUE. On the other hand Japan's participation in the country's imports is down from 6.1% in 1994 to 4.8% in 2001, while the share of Mexico's total exports fell from 1.6% in 1994 to $ 0.3% in 2001. As regards the Japanese FDI, Mexico received between 1994 – 2001only 3.3% of equity (Secretaría de Economía, 2015).

In 2005 entered into force the Economic Partnership Agreement between Mexico and Japan, a marketing agreement between the two countries would promote cooperation and boost the economy of them. But will it be to an emerging economy booming, why he chose Mexico for free trade? The answer can be seen through the theories: Theory of transaction costs, agency theory, theory based on resources and institutional theory. It begins by giving a brief overview of the relationship between Mexico and Japan, then a review of the theories that are to be used for reference and end explaining the importance of Mexico as a trading partner.

PURPOSE OF THE STUDY

The aim of this study is to determine the impact of Japanese FDI in manufacturing in Mexico in terms of technological spills that occur in the sector. In addition, to establish whether there are flaws that do not allow technological spillovers generated, if any, are older.

JUSTIFICATION

Mexico, like other countries invested in measures to attract foreign direct investment to their territories. Trade liberalization becomes stronger in the eighties, significantly reducing import tariffs on average that passed during the course of a period of three years from 23.5% to 11.8%. The base of products with low tariffs was from 92% to 25.4% during the same period 1985-1987. Additionally, the mid-nineties initiated reductions to barriers on investment from abroad, privatization of public enterprises, among others (Hanson and Harrison, 1999).

It was decided to revise the Japanese FDI due to the significant growth experienced in recent years, and the weight it has gained in the total FDI that has received Mexico. Particularly Japanese FDI in manufacturing, given that, as presented above, is the category to which most of Japanese FDI goes. Additionally, the manufacturing sector generates great interest in inter-industry and intra-industry connections that may arise.

BACKGROUND

After the problems of commercial banks from the 80's, due to the difficulty of attracting capital to develop projects, many countries eased restrictions on the entry of foreign direct investment (FDI). For this, developing countries resorted to various measures to attract FDI. Governments in developing countries see on FDI the possibility of accelerating the economic growth of their countries through economic spills and knowledge transfers (Carkovic, and Levine, 2002). These economic spills can occur within the same industry or inter-industrial way.

Mexico receives around 20% of FDI coming to the region. This situation is a result of changes in the policies that led the country out from the economic crises of the seventies and eighties. Policies focused on liberalization, promotion of trade, privatization, among others (Jordaan, 2009). FDI coming to Mexico has as its main source, the United States, as it is possible to foresee, given the geographic proximity. The strong bilateral trade and free trade that brought down tariff barriers between them countries, with 53% on average between 1999 and 2010 followed by Spain, the Netherlands and Canada (Guzman, 2014).

At the end of 2014 it was expected that FDI flows into Mexico reached 24,000 million dollars and for 2015 is expected to exceed 28,000 million according to the economic expectations of specialists. Mexico as a country occupying the tenth largest FDI recipient worldwide, receiving 2.6% of world flows in 2013, surpassing the 12-position obtained in 2013 (Ministry of Economy, 2014). Mexico has played an active role in the search for new treaties and opportunities to enable their companies to access new markets. This work is reflected in the ten free trade agreements with forty-five countries that permit thirty bilateral agreements on investment promotion, and nine limited (Promexico, 2014). Within these agreements signed, the agreement is found the Mexico-Japan Economic Partnership Agreement (EPA) in 2005.

The Ministry of Economy of Mexico (2002), in its final report states that the agreement of Economic Partnership Association (EPA) represents a great opportunity for both countries to exploit complementarities between them, which will result in social and economic benefits for both countries. Both countries have large markets, more than one hundred million people in Mexico, over 120 million people in the Japanese market. In addition they are two of the 15 largest economies in the world. Additionally, there are complementarities in resource endowments of both countries, Mexico with labor, land and natural resources, while Japan has economic resources and knowledge.

Therefore, from the point of view of Japan, it was keen to exploit the competitive advantages that Mexico could offer to this country, including the possibility of directly accessing the US and Canadian market without tariff barriers. This is evident in the case of manufacturing industries, especially the automotive and electronics through the use of NAFTA. Additionally, localized in Mexico, Japanese companies would have the same facilities as companies in other countries with which Mexico has signed agreements to place their products in the Mexican market. Add to the above Carrillo (2014) that for Mexico signing the EPA would give preference to 99% of exports to Japan, many of these products in the agricultural sector. Being Japan a country that imports 60% of food consumed, it is a business of great economic importance.

Japan is itself one of the largest underwriters of FDI in the world, ranking among the five countries with higher outward FDI between 2008 and 2009, according to the Report on Investment in the World, 2010, despite the international financial crisis. For Mexico, Japan ranks ninth in FDI source as averages between 1999 and 2010, reaching 1% of this. However, it is observed a tendency for these flows continue to grow, allowing FDI from Japan to achieve greater weight in the total investments (Carrillo and Okabe, 2014). Despite the above, and the belief that FDI generates positive externalities in the host country through productive spills, Hanson (2001) states that there is empirical evidence for and against assertion, especially as regards the welfare of the country receiver, where there is conflicting evidence.

In this article it seeks to analyze qualitatively and from a perspective of spillovers, FDI from Japan, mainly in the manufacturing sector, in order to study the generated productive spills by this industry, so intra-industry mainly to below. Also, to review if indeed the Japanese FDI is presenting productive spills, and analyze what factors might diminish. For this, it is reviewed some aspects related with the efficiency of Mexican suppliers and institutional aspects of Japanese companies.

RECENT LITERATURE REVIEW

An analysis of the emergence of the Economic Partnership Agreement Mexico – Japan by manger (2005) asserts that it has the character of a defensive reaction initiative triggered by the impact of the North American Free Trade Agreement, giving the opportunities to Japanese companies to invest in México in the automobile, electronics and auto parts industries, among others. Not only Mexico is the market but also is a platform to export products made by Japanese firms. The Japanese approach to use a framework of bilateral trade agreements, as it is the case with Mexico, is analyzed by Sutton (2015).

A more recent analysis on "Economic Partnership Agreement Mexico - Japan: Analysis of Trade Creation and Trade Diversion 1999-2013" conducted by Lugo Sánchez (2016), she does not find any evidence that the Economic Partnership Agreement between Mexico and Japan (EPAMJ) has contributed to increase Mexico and Japan's trade with 23 countries from 1999. Other study by Guzman-Anaya (2016) found increase in foreign direct investment flows from Japan to Mexico and determines the main factors that affect local suppliers of Japanese Automobile multinational firms doing business in Western México under the framework of Economic Partnership Agreement (EPA).

Other analysis conducted by Carrillo Regalado (2016) concluded that the foreign trade between Japan and Mexico does not support the hypothesis that the Economic Partnership Agreement has a significant stimulus over the volume of bilateral trade. On the other hand, González Bravo (2016) studies the exports of manufacturing firms located in the State of Jalisco to Japan finding that the number of companies doing business with Japan had increased 60% after the agreement.

MEXICO-JAPAN RELATIONSHIP

Mexico is the world's ninth largest economy and represents a market of about 100 million people (Secretaría de economía, 2015). It is a country with abundant flora and fauna, with young and dynamic labor at low cost and in constant training work. Japan is the second largest economy and has an active market of 126 million people, is a country with high capital, purchasing power and leading edge technology. The boundary with North America returns to Mexico an attractive country to invest in it, produce and market goods to the American market, taking advantage of NAFTA and other treaties and agreements that Mexico has with more than 45 countries, so that countries like Japan are seeking to collaborate through economic agreements to reap the benefits in access to resources, as well as trade relations.

On the other hand, Japan has a growing economy. It is an important potential source of foreign direct investment and has a market for Mexican goods that could be very productive. In addition, besides this would generate the economic spill that should consider the benefit of the bilateral agreement, as the transfer of technology and knowledge, which is contributing to the creation of jobs and an increased competitiveness of human resources. By diversifying the export market, Mexico decrease its economic dependence on the United States, its main trading partner and which directs most of its exports.

Based on a friendly relationship led for decades between Japan and Mexico, it was consolidated with the signing of AAEMJ in the year 2005. The agreement was in negotiation for two years. A study group was formed for the realization comprised of government officials, businessmen and academics from both countries. On September 17, 2004 it was signed, during the government of Vicente Fox Quezada, coming into force on April 1, 2005 (Secretaría de Economía, 2015).

For Japan this treaty represented the first large-scale free trade agreement with Latin American country. To Mexico, it represents a market of potential consumers on a large scale. The main objective of the agreement is to promote trade liberalization and investment between Mexico and Japan, through tariff reduction and the facilitation of customs and immigration procedures. Expectations for Mexico's AAEMJ focused on expanding FDI from Japan, to increase and diversify Mexican exports and the promotion of the development of productive chains, led by quality inputs related to the commissary of Japanese companies by Mexican companies (Garcia De Leon, 2010).

ON FOREIGN DIRECT INVESTMENT

However, FDI is not distributed equitably among countries. The location of FDI and industry is a relevant concern that has been investigated since Marshall (1890) in his book Principles of Economics. He identified some factors, mainly physical, such as climate, soil, mineral resources, among others. Thereafter, the location of industry and its determinants, more recently, the study of the location of FDI, has been studied in the economy, leading to the identification of new factors beyond the purely physical aspects. Jordaan (2009) identifies four general factors recurring in literature. These are the potential demand which can be estimated by per capita income, GDP, population density, among others.

Companies seek to anticipate the potential market that would have on the region and others that could access their products easily. Another general aspect is the regional production costs, costs related to labor, access to resources markets, and intermediate goods that require companies. It is possible to sense that companies prefer to settle in regions where these costs are lower, and have higher returns. But some studies have shown that there is a positive relationship between wage levels and FDI, a situation that can be explained in the case of wages efficiency (Head et al, 1999).

Other factors identified by Jordaan (2009) are the public policies that encourage the arrival of foreign companies and FDI. Within regional policy strongly related FDI inflows are those related to corporate taxes, benefits to job creation, tax exemptions, among others. Finally, the presence of agglomeration economies is a key location for FDI. The importance of agglomeration lies in different aspects such as the flow of knowledge, human capital, and ease of access to suppliers and distributors, among others.

CONCEPTUAL AND THEORETICAL FRAMEWORK

Several theories are used for the study of the relationship between Mexico and Japan under the Economic Partnership Agreement signed in 2004 and implemented in 2005. The benefits of the bilateral treaty are analyzed under the agency theory, resources and capabilities theory and theory of transaction costs.

The research strategy in emerging countries has gained importance in recent years. Emerging countries have gained weight internationally, politically and economically context speaking. This has led some of the attention to these countries. Xu and Meyer (2012) decided to make a literature review on the development of research in emerging markets, checking that has obviously increased the number of articles on developing economies. Institutional theory is the mainstream of theoretical approach in the field; however, new perspectives appear as learning relationships, real options, spillovers, among others.

Spillover is the way that technology and human capital spills and is transmitted to local companies or endogenous, from FDI. Four channels for the transmission of spills from product of FDI are identified:

1. Effects of demonstration and Imitation, local businesses learn by imitating and observing foreign companies.
2. Effects of competition, through competitive firms increase production and become more competitive.
3. Effects of connection with foreign companies, through linking companies, foreign ones transmit knowledge to endogenous.
4. Training effects. Local companies hire people who were previously trained by multinationals as a means of transmitting knowledge or technology (Kinoshita, 2001).

Importantly, the absorption capacity of the company and the effort made in learning, are critical factors for spills to become effective (Kinoshita, 2001). Glaeser et al. (1992) believes that spills related to knowledge are the "engine of growth" of economies and has three models of how knowledge spills occur.

1. Externalities Marshall-Arrow-Romer type, which are between firms in the same industry. He states that the concentration of firms in the same industry in a city helps spills between companies generated, allowing businesses to grow equally to the city. This can happen in different ways, such as the spy, imitation, and ease of movement of human capital, among others.
2. The second approach, proposed by Porter (1990), goes in the same direction as the Marshall-Arrow-Romer. It believes that knowledge spillovers also generate positive effects on the industry and the region. However, it believes that it is through local competition that companies are encouraged to innovate and quickly adopt the advances that occur in the sector. Companies should strive to remain on the market or disappear against new coming firms.
3. Finally the third, where Jacobs (1969) believes that the greatest advances and innovations are developed outside the industry, so more than the agglomeration of firms in the same sector. It is necessary inter-industrial agglomeration is generated.

There are also critical positions on FDI and technological spillovers generated. Some authors believe that foreign investment does not necessarily produce technological spillovers and increased productivity. Blomström and Kokko (2003) argue that an increase in FDI does not necessarily imply an increase in national welfare. Since the arrival of investment by foreign companies, it is not immediately in an increase in productivity on the part of local businesses through spills. By contrast, local companies should be keen to learn and absorb knowledge.

Similarly, Cheol-Sung, Nielson and Alderson (2007) consider, based on the theory of dependency, that when countries are dependent on FDI, this could have a negative impact on economic growth. Depending entirely on foreign companies might not allow local businesses to grow, destroying local businesses and affect the country's development.

Agency Theory

Agency theory arises from the need for organizations to delegate and make decisions. When the owners or principals at top management positions begin to delegate decision-making to other individuals or agents in a process that involves monitoring, control and error correction begins. The agency theory studies the existing problems between the main positions based on its goal of study. The first is the positivist who mainly focuses on the relationship of firm owners and managers of the organization. The second line is more general and focuses on the relationship that can be found in many situations where there is this dual relationship of the owner and the agent (Vargas-Hernandez, Guerra Garcia Bojorquez Gutierrez Gutierrez Bojorquez, 2014).

productivo, Tambta importante y posee un mercado para bienes mexicanos que podrCANproductivo, Tambta importante y posee un mercado para bienes mexicanos que podrCAN

The owners of the company are the people who provide the economic capital and own the firm. Patterns, according to Peng (2010) are classified into three:

1. The concentrated ownership is made up of the founders and as it expands will be involving more shareholders becoming a diverse ownership.
2. Family property, which is comprised of members of a family whose objectives are common although sometimes members are unqualified for the tasks.
3. State ownership where the state is the main owner and often lacks adequate incentives for people working in these companies.

There is another theory called Reconsidered Agency Theory which indicates that not all agents are equal and some executives are doing more to be effective managers in creating a sustainable corporation. Apart from these statements in Mexican companies have the same classification of property owners, most companies start out as family businesses that continue growing, evolving and entering international markets so the companies that manage to internationalize have overcome major barriers as lack of incentives, low skills, and little knowledge. As the company grows it will need more staff and shareholders to invest and controls the actions of subordinates. There are also state-owned enterprises that sell services to Japanese companies located in the country to improve trade cooperation.

In conducting the activities in the agency theory of delegating functions and decision-making firms incur in various restructuring costs, monitoring and binding contracts between agents. The AAEMJ aims to facilitate the paperwork for the Japanese companies to import their trained human resources to management positions to improve management activities and reduce the quotas for the free access of human resources. The principal agent theoretical model may not apply to Japanese concentrated ownership structures (Ojo, 2013). However, an empirical research on the principal-agent theoretical model shows that it is week in the Japanese context of firms. Buchanan, Heesang Chai, & Deakin (2013) use the theoretical model of agency to explain corporate governance of the Japanese firms and found that shareholders do not behave as principals.

For Mexican companies, the agency theory explains that opportunism taking place in business is due to the reason that agents seek their own benefits. So employees fall into corrupt processes and the mismanagement of resources. The AAEMJ seeks to implement that better relations between the two countries, to facilitate customs and import resources procedures is to eliminate corruption in the marketing channels, which benefits SMEs in the country who wish to seek a new market policies.

Apart from the agreement there are other government measures to take action by state governments to improve internationalization experience, this through courses, seminars, etc. that show how to perform the export process and give advice with customs formalities, transport and denomination of origin.

Theory Based on Resources and Capabilities

The industry is analyzed by companies to make tools that allow them to understand the preferences of consumers in relation to their product or service offered and the position of competing companies in consumer preference. Porter designed the model of the five forces that shape the vision of industry-based strategy. These five forces are:

1. **Intensity of Rivalry Between Competitors:** Here are six different situations
   a. The number of competitors is crucial.
   b. The size of the competitor influence on competition.
   c. Set the domain can be difficult.
   d. The new capabilities increase the rivalry.
   e. The decrement or deterioration of the company makes desperate measures.
   f. The large exit costs are reflected in loses.
2. **Threat of Potential Entries:** Established firms are concerned to keep out of the market potential adversaries' incoming companies and create a brand identity and product and loyalty to their firm customers.
3. **Bargaining Power of Suppliers:** Four conditions or possible situations to negotiate with suppliers arise:
   a. That the industry has few suppliers and they have the power to decide the price or vice versa.
   b. The supplier provides unique and different products.
   c. The firm is not an important client.
   d. The supplier is able to enter the focal industry.
4. **Bargaining Power of Buyers:** Here come four conditions:
   a. The group of buyers is small.
   b. Products produced no savings or benefit to the quality and life of the consumer.
   c. Purchase standard products and raw materials without preferred brands.
   d. Enter the focal industry through backward integration.
5. **Threat of Substitutes:** A substitute, being a product that satisfies a consumer need that usually meets other product or service is subject to the price at which supply products. Its main threat is a price decrease of the focal firm.

For the company, resources and products can be two sides of the same coin, but many products require multiple resources and most resources can be used in various products. The resources of a firm at a given time can be defined as those (tangible and intangible) assets that are semi-permanently attached to the firm and used to take their production process and realize their product. A barrier to entry without a barrier resource positioning leaves the company vulnerable to diversify inputs. A technological advantage allows the firm to have higher incomes and to allow further develop more ideas than its competitors (Vargas-Hernandez, Guerra Garcia Bojorquez Gutierrez Gutierrez Bojorquez, 2014).

Companies need to find the resources to maintain their position in the barrier of resources but nobody have yet, and therefore allow them to be among the few who succeeded in creating these resources. Resources should be combined well with those who have currently and that competes with few to acquire it. And to develop and build the capacity of its human resources to enable them to compete with the competition and conduct the production process effectively and efficiently.

Product design and the introduction of organizational capabilities aimed to cut time and cost in the automobile industry enable Japanese firms to develop new products (Clark and Fujimoto 1991; Nobeoka and Cusumano 1997). Lieberman, & Dhawan (2005) measure the linkages between resources and capabilities with performance to demonstrate the efficiency of a Japanese automobile industry in scale economies and manufacturing. The economic growth of Japan increased very fast during the eighties of the last century based on innovation, reverse engineering technology and benchmarking capabilities, despite the scarce resources (Dahlman, 2007).

Being able to access resources and difficult access to power generating and developing competitive skills in their employees, companies create a competitive advantage over other competitors in their sector, which can determine their permanence in the market. Speaking of Mexican companies when negotiating with national products and resources that do not exist in another continent or have a cost of excessive production, have since their foray into the Japanese market a competitive advantage that if they know it to handle can achieve significant growth business based on exports made. The main products exported to Japan are derived from agricultural activities but major Japanese companies coming to invest in the country are manufacturing. So, both countries benefit from AAEMJ to commercialize goods that are difficult to produce in their commercial counterparts.

Japanese companies established in Mexico have been attracted by the potential both domestically and by the nearby economies: the United States and some Latin American countries. The critical masses of companies that have shaped clusters (cluster) have been another reason to be interested in Mexico. The clusters have been established not only in traditional Border States such as Baja California or Nuevo Leon, but in the Mexican Lowers (Bajio), in states like Aguascalientes, Queretaro and Guanajuato (Falck Reyes, De la Vega Shiota, 2014).

Mexican natural resources that are exported in consumable supplies like salt grain, avocado, beef, tuna, to name a few, have abundance in the country and allow Mexican companies embrace a new market and not only compete in the local market, which is already saturated with similar companies. Mexican crafts also have great momentum abroad, favoring those sectors that were disappearing in the country. On the other hand FDI by Japanese companies in different states of Mexico contribute to the development of the area where they are located, to create jobs, use local products and train human personnel and favors the Japanese company with cheap labor and easy access to natural resources that abound in the country.

Theory of Transaction Costs

Transaction costs are the costs incurred by the company or provider to get their goods or services to consumers. The agenda of the organizations is the value that is given to the decisions made in terms of getting information that the company needs (Vargas-Hernandez, Guerra García, Bojórquez Gutiérrez, Bojórquez Gutierrez, 2014). It should be understood that there is a direct relationship between employers and employees and that this relationship is direct and uses the capabilities of both to achieve the objectives of the company. The agency incurs various costs to conduct activities such as restructuring costs, monitoring and binding of a series of contracts between agents with conflicting interests. The agency theory assumes that agents tend to be opportunists who will seek their own benefit.

Asymmetric information provides the basis for opportunism. Opportunism is selfish advantage seeking an individual over others. Is when an individual uses deception or skills for the greater good or service at a price equal to or lower than other consumers (Vargas-Hernandez, Guerra Garcia Bojorquez Gutierrez Gutierrez Bojorquez, 2014).

Companies to achieve lower transaction costs can create a significant competitive advantage, improve their production, and achieve to reduce the cost of their product at low prices to compete or attain a greater margin of profits maintaining its market price. The AAEMJ to facilitate procedures and reduce tariffs enables companies of both countries and promotes the consumption of the products offered by its trading partner.

According to the AMIA between 2003 and 2013, 140 Japanese companies announced investment projects in the country, some of these companies are: Nissan, Toyota Motor, Mitsui & Co. and Mitsubishi Corporation, Honda, Bridgestone, Kyocera, Sharp, Sumimoto and Mazda. This group of companies contributed 67% of the announced investment. The states with the biggest Japanese investment flows are Aguascalientes, (27% of the investment), Guanajuato (18%), Nuevo Leon (8%), Baja California (7%) and Morelos (5.2%) (Falck Reyes, De la Vega Shiota, 2014). On the other hand, Mexican companies that export have also benefited from reduced transaction costs to market their products to Japan. The following (table 1) shows the increase in exports in recent years.

Institutional Theory

The institutions based view claims that the conditions of the business and industry should consider the impact of state and society when framing its strategy. The laws, regulations and rules are the regulatory pillar of the behavior of individuals and businesses. The fundamental changes to the formal and informal rules that affect organizations and players are defined as institutional transaction.

On the other hand, from the industrial perspective, Porter (1990) lists four factors affecting industries:

1. Firm strategy, structure and rivalry.
2. Factor endowments.
3. Related and supporting industries.
4. Domestic demand.

The theory of the industry based view defines two proposals on the importance of institutions, which are summarized below.

Table 1. Mexican exports to Japan in millions of dollars Mexican exports to Japan

Year	Investments
2005	1,470.0
2006	1,594.0
2007	1,912.6
2008	2,046.0
2009	1,600.6
2010	1,925.6
2011	2,252.3
2012	2,610.7
2013	2,244.1
2014	2,609.20

* Value in Million
Source: Based on data from the Ministry of Economy (May, 2015).

1. As managers and companies make strategic decisions in a rational way, depending on interests and constraints.
2. As the restrictions relating to the management of the company. Taking into account the culture of the company which has been the know-how of the institution.

Abroad it can be taken two forms of ethics to combine with the country's culture, ethical relativism that is adapted to the customs of the country in which is or ethical imperialism that is the belief in one universal ethics. Ethics is a principle that helps to fight corruption, so you should inculcate in citizens from an early age. By introducing the company in a new country must make three decisions for action:

1. It is important to have an understanding of the formal and informal institutions.
2. Strengthen intercultural awareness information by expanding knowledge.
3. Integrate ethical decision-making as part of the strategic process.

Property rights are social institutions that define or delimit the range of privileges granted by individuals to specific assets. Property rights can be moral, exclusive, unlimited or perpetual right. Institutional theory explains how the firm adapts to the environment that surrounds the speculations, expectations and environmental regulations and rules or sanctions that affect it.

In recent decades, multinational companies have taken advantage to the organization of production of advances in information technology, declining trends in transportation costs and the proliferation of free trade agreements, regional and bilateral, fragmenting the production processes (Falck Reyes and de la Vega Shiota, 2014).

The EPA (AAE) has been particularly beneficial for the promotion of Mexican exports with low value added. This situation is even more problematic to the extent that the provisions of the Agreement provide for exports of Mexican products in bulk, thus limiting the increase in the value added by its preparation to get ready for final consumption (Ramirez Bonilla, 2014). Apart from the benefits it gives the AAEMJ for Mexican companies; it has a significant government support in terms of advice and assistance to exporters. One example is the YOEXPORTO (I export) program, from the government of Jalisco, which is a course that will guide step by step from market selection, packaging, transportation, port procedures, etc., to optimize experience and facilitate trade to Japan or to another country through agreements or free trade agreements

METHODS

This paper presents a theoretical and literature review on foreign direct investment inflows from Japan into Mexico in manufacturing revision. From the qualitative and quantitative results obtained by different authors to determine the impact of FDI in terms of technological spillovers generated.

BARRIERS IN THE PRODUCTION OF JAPANESE FDI SPILL IN THE MANUFACTURING SECTOR OF MEXICO ANALYSIS FROM THE LITERATURE REVIEW

FDI and Spillovers

Several international studies have been conducted to try to determine the magnitude of the impact of FDI in host countries and the nature of this. With this, it is been trying to understand how FDI is impacting local economies, and how FDI should have major positive impacts to leave. Therefore, it is important to understand how multinational companies with domestic enterprises are related, and thus able to focus efforts to attract FDI to sectors where it leaves greater benefits. In Indonesia, Blomström and Sjöholm (1998) study the impact of FDI and productivity of domestic firms from technological spillovers that may arise. Through an econometric analysis of data obtained through the 1991 industry survey, conclude that local businesses benefit from technology spillovers.

However, there is no significant evidence that requires multinational partnerships with local companies, generate greater technological spillovers, so it does not have a significant impact on productivity. Fauzel, Seetanah and Sannasee (2015) study the relationship between flows of FDI in the manufacturing industry and the effects on productivity. In that sector in Mauritius, a country located in the Southern Indian Ocean. The results collected during 1980 and 2010 show that FDI if it has had an impact on factor productivity and labor productivity. This has gone hand in hand with government efforts to encourage FDI. Importantly, the results measured in the short term, are not very significant. But in the long-term outcomes are more favorable to FDI spills, at the point of having local investment also impacted favorably.

China remains one of the largest recipients of FDI globally. Hu and Jefferson (2002, 1075) performed a study based on census data from the National Bureau of Statistics country. Through the econometric analysis, the authors determine the impact of FDI for the electronics and textiles sectors at industry level. For the electronics industry, the authors find a statistically significant negative spill-level industry. Spills are positive for the company receiving the investment, but the other companies in the industry lost market and the effects are negative in the short term. Otherwise, it is in the case of the textile industry. In the long term, the advantage gained by the company receiving FDI seems to disappear.

Pritish and Sakiru examine productive spills of FDI in the manufacturing sector in India during the period 2000-2009. Econometric studies indicate that there is a positive impact on FDI and business productivity. Both, the company receiving investment flows and the sector in general, which runs counter to that found in other studies. Also identify policies taken by the government and the general change of attitude to the impacts of FDI that have led to improvements in manufacturing productivity.

SOLUTIONS AND RECOMMENDATIONS

In order to verify the impact and understand how spillovers generated by FDI in Mexico, Guzman (2013) studied the Japanese and US FDI in the country focusing on vertical spillovers generated within the same industry work. His first conclusion suggests that there are differences in productivity spills in the investment coming from both countries. In the case of Japanese FDI, there is a positive effect related to the production of the related industries with backward vertical (suppliers). For US FDI, a negative effect was observed. In the case of vertical spills up, there was a positive impact on the presence of Japanese investment, but no significant effect for investment from the United States.

However, FDI inflows to an industry is not sufficient reason to generate productive spills, companies must be able to absorb these spills. The existence of a technological gap increases the benefits of technological spillovers, however if the gap is very large, local companies will not be able to absorb spills. In turn, through a frame of awareness-motivation- capabilities Meyer and Sinani (2009: 1089) express the benefits of technological spillovers have a curvilinear relationship with the level of economic development. Promptly with issues such as income, human capital and institutions and concluding that the poorest and the richest countries are those that benefit most from FDI inflows. Meyer and Sinani (2009) argue that institutions and human capital are essential if companies create the motivation and skills they need to absorb technological spillovers.

For poor countries, spills occur through demonstration effects channel through competition effect, whereas in developed countries spills occur. Companies in developed countries prepare for the arrival of foreign companies and define strategies to cope and stay in the market. Through the Survey of Japanese Companies in western Mexico, Guzman Carrillo and Okabe (2014) can identify certain characteristics that reveal inefficiencies in supplier Mexican companies of Japanese companies. This would indicate that there could be problems for endogenous companies could absorb production spills. The survey was conducted in companies of the states of Guanajuato, Queretaro, San Luis Potosi, Aguascalientes and Jalisco, of which more than 70% of surveyed companies are engaged in manufacturing. Some of the characteristics obtained by the author from the survey are:

Japanese companies used more to foreign suppliers to Mexican suppliers. Importantly, Japanese companies prefer to hire foreign suppliers with high-tech aspects, technical and technological assistance, among others. While the endogenous suppliers related to training, purchase of computer equipment and low value-added activities related to cleaning, security and transport (Guzman Carrillo and Okabe, 2014) is preferred activities

In addition to the above, the Japanese companies surveyed believe that endogenous providers in general have not met the conditions required quality, with more than 60% of companies indicating this situation. In a second step, the Japanese companies identified that the lack of endogenous production capacity of suppliers is an obstacle to the link between endogenous suppliers and Japanese multinationals. The third reason that hinders linking is the fact that Mexican suppliers do not produce inputs that Japanese companies need. (Guzman Carrillo and Okabe, 2014).

Finally, it is important to consider that Japanese multinationals consider that there are significant differences between endogenous suppliers and foreign suppliers. While they consider that over 60% of foreign suppliers have good quality, only 12% of endogenous qualified suppliers are positive. Most domestic suppliers started regularly and bad. Regarding time delivery of the requested products or services, over 50% of endogenous suppliers were rated as poor and 30% as a regular (Guzman Carrillo and Okabe, 2014).

For foreign suppliers, none was rated as bad, more than 50% as fair, and 30% were rated as good. Similarly, with regard to sufficient supply, about 90% of endogenous suppliers were rated as fair or poor. While for foreign suppliers, more than 80% was rated fair or good, in relation to the offer. Mexican suppliers receive a better score in relation to costs, where approximately 80% of the companies were rated as good or fair, while foreign suppliers for more than 70% is rated as fair or poor (Guzman Carrillo and Okabe, 2014).

On the side of Japanese multinationals in Mexico, it is worth highlighting the impact that could have on keiretsu technological spillovers to endogenous suppliers. The keiretsu are networks of companies that are interrelated among them. Many of these networks come from before the Second World War. Networks may be of two types, horizontal or vertical. Horizontal networks are between companies from different industries, while the vertical can be up (with distributors or buyers) or down (with suppliers). Businesses take advantage of the keiretsu reductions in risk and uncertainty in their relations with companies belonging to the same keiretsu, mutual assistance, reducing information asymmetries, among others.

Moreover, it may involve over investment costs because it can lead to lower performance and increase information asymmetries between member companies and those outside the keiretsu (McGuire & Dow, 2009). Based on the Survey of Japanese Companies in Western Mexico, Guzman Carrillo and Okabe (2014) identify aspects that might indicate the involvement of multinational Japanese companies to a keiretsu. In a first step, the fact that Japanese companies must import most of the inputs used in their production. Over 80% of Japanese companies manufacturing imports inputs from Japan. To a lesser extent, the United States with 60% of companies importing inputs from this country, taking advantage of the proximity and the elimination of tariff barriers product of the Treaty of the North Atlantic Free Trade Agreement (NAFTA).

The fact that Japanese companies have obtained information for localization in Mexico of other Japanese companies, can give signs that belong to these networks. Trying to agglomerate near other Japanese companies would be within their own production chain. However, it is important to note that Japanese multinationals showed interest in the survey work in the future with Mexican suppliers, 70% of companies surveyed (Guzman Carrillo and Okabe, 2014).

The possible membership of Japanese multinational companies to any keiretsu could have negative implications for technological spillover that is expected to happen between multinational and endogenous companies. Japanese companies likely will prefer to continue working with companies from their keiretsu or companies which already has worked before, since Japanese companies know the quality of their product and way of working. This situation is difficult to endogenous providers being able to establish links with Japanese companies.

This situation would be affected more by the possible dissatisfaction of Japanese multinationals with endogenous suppliers. Domestic suppliers should in turn improve the quality of their products, improve delivery times and increase the supply of their products in order to be more closely linked to multinationals, and power in a medium or long term in activities linked to higher value added and of more technology.

Finally, under the framework of Economic Partnership Agreement, where technical cooperation between Mexico and Japan is highlighted, it is important to find ways to strengthen the effects channel connection between the companies, such as transmission channel of technological spillovers from FDI. Thus, both endogenous suppliers as Japanese multinationals could benefit from technology transfers and human capital. The willingness of Japanese multinationals to link to Mexican suppliers is proof that it can be possible to work in this regard.

FUTURE RESEARCH DIRECTIONS

Challenges to Mexico's export and foreign direct investment position in the Japanese market under the Economic Partnership Agreement Mexico – Japan are likely to continue and to benefit after United States withdrawal from the Trans-pacific agreement. This is one important issue to conduct research on the impact of basic structural features of both partners, Mexico and Japan, and to analyze the interdependency of business cycles and industries in relevant sectors such as the Japanese automobile industry and electronics, etc., investments in Mexico, after the imminent withdrawal of United States plants from Mexico.

CONCLUSION

If a developing country does not have financial institutions that allow saving on traditional sectors to be used in order to finance new areas, then the growth of new industries will be restricted by the ability of companies to get benefits now. Low initial benefits will be obstacle to investment, despite the high long-term benefits that can be obtained (Krugman, Paul.R, Obstfeld, Maurice, Melitz, Marc J, 2012, p.266). Mexico is endowed with many natural resources, land, and labor and comparatively skilled and productive, while Japan has a high capital and technology. Producers and consumers of Mexico and Japan may benefit from bilateral trade in sectors where each country has a comparative advantage, thereby strengthening the economic relationship.

Japan imports 60% of its food consumption, but Mexico's share in total imports of food products from Japan is negligible. Therefore, the potential impact of the elimination of tariffs on agricultural products from Mexico would not constitute any threat to Japanese agriculture. However, it is recognized the need to create a product-by-product analysis to arrive at specific recommendations on the most appropriate measures to ensure preferential treatment for agricultural products that Mexico is already exporting and those with export potential to Japan, modalities to prevent any distortion in the Japanese agricultural sector (Ministry of Economy, 2015).

THE AARMJ would be similar to many other international treaties that Mexico has, however what makes it remarkable is the clear provision of economic cooperation in SMEs. Through bilateral cooperation it could be expected that Mexican companies will develop, especially small and medium that are the foundation of the Mexican economy (Okabe, 2004).

Both countries are net importers of cereals, fodder, oilseeds, dairy products and meat, using third country imports to meet domestic demand. Mexico considers that complementary areas are located in areas such as tropical products, fruit and vegetables, beef, chicken and pork, fruit juices and other drinks, as well as processed products. There is a need to focus on areas of complementarity and economic potential to achieve a mutually satisfactory trading, as both Japan and Mexico can complement its domestic production of food products through imports of products from its trading partner.

In order to have a continuous flow of goods and investment between Mexico and Japan, both countries should cooperate to improve the business environment and work on several projects for the promotion of trade and investment. Some examples which are exported to Japan are shown in table 2 below.

With the implementation of AAEMJ Japan seeks greater autonomy from the US economy, reorient its trade policy and enhance its industrial policy of encouraging free trade and improve its economy benefits granted by the agreement on investment, exports and imports. Mexico sought, meanwhile, to reduce dependence on the United States, which is its main trading partner, increase participation in the Japanese market, preferential treatment of export products, comparative advantages (González García, 2014). Apart from AAEMJ Mexican imports and exports, it has been affected by changes in tariff measures, trade policy and support for Mexican SMEs.

According to data provided by the Ministry of Economy (Secretaria de Economía) since 2005, year in which enters into force on AAEMJ treaty can be seen, although exports have increased over the benefits of the agreement, imports have increased to a greater extent, so the aim of the agreement is to promote the economic development of Mexican companies to the extent it has been provided.

Imports of Mexican origin belonging to groups 0: Food and live animals and 2: inedible raw materials were the main beneficiaries of the EPA; in 2004, the first year of operation of the Agreement, the import value of the two groups was 52,000 million yen and 32,000 million yen, respectively (22.03% and 12.96% of the value of total imports from Mexico) ; in 2013, it was 89, 000 million yen and 48,000 million yen (20.27% and 11.04% of the value of total imports of Mexican origin). The main advantages of the products of Mexican origin were recorded in 003 sectors: meat and meat preparations, 011: Fruits and vegetables, 213: Fertilizers and minerals, 215 metal ores and scrap (Secretaría de Economía, 2015).

Japanese exports of both groups had minimal values: in 2004, 127 million yen and 471 million yen; in 2013, 310 million yen and 1,998 million yen. In September 2011, on the occasion of the signing of the Protocol Amending the Agreement for the Strengthening of the Economic Partnership, the participants emphasize Mexican agencies, thanks to the Agreement, Mexico had become: leading supplier of mangoes, avocados, melons, asparagus, beans, sardines and sesame oil; Second provider: frozen orange juice, squash, stout, tuna and pectin; third largest supplier of tomatoes, jojoba oil, broccoli and rambutan: fourth provider: meat (pork, beef, horse), papayas, sea urchins, and squid and cuttlefish (Ramirez Bonilla, 2014).

The EPA has been particularly beneficial for the promotion of Mexican exports with low value added; the modifying agreements were aimed at greater inclusion of Mexican products to the Japanese market and promote FDI and bilateral cooperation of both countries. As mentioned Juan Jose Ramirez (2014),

Table 2. Products exported to Japan: Main products that Mexico currently exports to Japan

Crude Oils	Aguacate	Salt Commonly Used	Bluefin Tuna in the Atlantic and Pacific
Copper minerals	Silver minerals	Animal casings (except fish)	Bladders (except fish)
Stomachs of animals (other than fish)	Tequila	Stout	Adapters
Transmitters	Photographic plates	Cylinders	Photovoltaic cells

Source: Based on data from Secretaría de Economía (Mayo, 2015)

the Mexico-Japan bilateral relationship has been exceeded and to re-nationalize the EPA now must be taken into account regional integration processes where economic and political actors involved from both countries to interact, there with their counterparts.

Without this update AEE any future evaluation will continue calling with "regular, low or stagnant" performance. There are theories related to the inability of Mexican firms to act as agents for suppliers for Japanese companies to create systems that allow to produce supplies of imported for the purpose of increasing the volume of added value of national content and domestic products and exploit a niche constant and necessary for Japanese companies market. It has been speculated that it is the lack of commitment of Mexican businessmen, culture and ingrained habits such as lack of punctuality.

On the other hand it is possible that Mexican companies do not have enough motivation to want to venture into the production of goods for suppliers for Japanese and modify their plants and production methods, so the market has not been exploited as it should. Like the other treaties and free trade agreements as Mexico has celebrated, the AAEMJ has applications that have not yet been exploited by Mexican entrepreneurs; it may be due to lack of motivation, lack thereof, lack of government support or export complicated processes. Furthermore, the agreement improved the economic situation of the states where Japanese FDI is concentrated, creating jobs and providing goods and services to families of Japanese businessmen who come to the region.

It has also managed to improve the development of Mexican companies that have decided to enter the Japanese market and provide some of the products that Japan demand. So even though the results have not matched expectations cannot be denied that the AAEMJ is important to achieve development tool Mexican SMEs and should promote their use, as well as that of other FTAs and EPAs that has the benefiting the country and foreign trade.

REFERENCES

Blomström, M., & Kokko, A. (2003). *The Economics of Foreign Direct Investment Incentives.* National Bureau of Economic Research. Working Paper No. 9489.

Blomström, M., & Sjöholm, F. (1998). *Technological Transfer And Spillovers: Does Local Participation With Multinationals Matter?* National Bureau of Economic Research. Working Paper No. 6816.

Buchanan, J., Heesang Chai, D., & Deakin, S. (2013). *Agency theory in practice: a qualitative study of hedge fund activism in japan.* Centre for Business Research, University of Cambridge. Working Paper No. 448. CBR, University of Cambridge.

Carkovic, M., & Levine, R. (2002). Capitulo 8, Does Foreign Direct Investment Accelerate Economic Growth? In Does Foreign Direct Investment Promote Development?. Peterson Institute for International Economics.

Carrillo, S., & Okabe, T. (Ed.). (2014). Relaciones México-Japón en el Contexto del Acuerdo de Asociación Económica. Universidad de Guadalajara.

Carrillo Regalado, S. (2016). The impact on trade of the Mexico-Japan. Economic Partnership Agreement (MJEPA). In Economic impact of Economic Partnership Agreement Mexico – Japan – theoretical and empirical aspects, (pp. 17-42). The Institute for Economic Studies. Seijo University.

Cheol-Sung, L., Nielsen, L., & Alderson, A. (2007). Income Inequality, Global Economy, and the State. *Social Forces*, (86), 77–111.

Clark, K., & Fujimoto, T. (1991). *Product Development Performance: Strategy, Organization and Management in the World Auto Industry*. Boston: HBS Press.

Dahlman, C. (2007). *Technology, globalization and international competitiveness: Challenges for developing Countries*. Industrial development for the 21st century, Department of economic and social affairs of United Nations.

Dunning, J. (1993). *The Globalization of Business*. London: Routledge.

Falck Reyes, M., & De la Vega Shiota, V. (2014). La inversión japonesa en México en el marco del Acuerdo para el Fortalecimiento de la Asociación Económica entre Méxicoy Japón. El caso del sector de equipode transporte. *Comercio Exterior*, *64*(6).

Fauzel, S., Seetanah, B., & Sannasee, R. (2015). Productivity Spillovers Of Fdi In The Manufacturing Sector Of Mauritius. Evidence From A Dynamic Framework. *Journal of Developing Areas*, *49*(2), 295–316. doi:10.1353/jda.2015.0026

García De León, P. G. (2010). México y Japón: comercio bilateral en el marco del Acuerdo de Asociación Económica. *Comercio Exterior, 60*(2).

Glaeser, E., Kallal, H., Scheinkman, J., & Shleifer, A. (1992). Growth in Cities. *Journal of Political Economy*, *100*(6), 1126–1153. doi:10.1086/261856

González Bravo, R. (2016). Advantages of the Mexico – Japan Economic Partnership Agreement for Mexican manufacturing exports companies located in Jalisco state. In Economic impact of Economic Partnership Agreement Mexico – Japan – theoretical and empirical aspects, (pp. 43-58). The Institute for Economic Studies. Seijo University.

González García, J. (2014). El Acuerdo de Asociación Económica México-Japón:¿es posible un relanzamiento? *Comercio Exterior, 64*(6).

Guzmán, L. (2013). *Are productivity spillovers from Japanese FDI larger than from U.S. FDI? Interindustry evidence from Mexico*. Universidad de Guadalajara.

Guzman-Anaya, L. (2016). Japanese Automotive FDI Linkages with Local Suppliers – Evidence from Survey data in Mexico's Western Region. In *Economic impact of Economic Partnership Agreement Mexico – Japan – theoretical and empirical aspects*. The Institute for Economic Studies. Seijo University.

Hanson, G. (2001). *Should countries promote Foreign Direct Investment?* G24 Discussion Paper Series. No. 9. United Nations.

Hanson, G., & Harrison, A. (1999). Trade Liberalization and Wage Inequality in Mexico. *Industrial and Labor Relations Review*, *52*(2), 271 – 288.

Hu, A. G. Z., & Jefferson, G. H. (2002, August). FDI Impact and Spillover: Evidence from Chinas Electronic and Textile Industries. *World Economy*, *25*(8), 1063–1076. doi:10.1111/1467-9701.00481

Jacobs, J. (1969). *The Economy of Cities*. New York: Vintage.

Jordaan, J. (2009). *Foreign Direct Investment Agglomeration and Externalities. In Capítulo 3: Agglomeration and FDI Location in Mexican Regions.* Ashgate.

Kinoshita, Y. (2001). *R&D and Technology Spillovers via FDI: Innovation and Absorptive Capacity.* Working Paper 349a. CERGE-EI, WDI, University of Michigan and CEPR. Retrieved from http://citeseerx.ist.psu.edu/viewdoc/download?doi=10.1.1.200.1078&rep=rep1&type=pdf

Krugman, P. R., Obstfeld, M., & Melitz, M. J. (2012). Economía Internacional. *Pearson Educación, Madrid, 2012,* 266.

Lieberman, M. B., & Dhawan, R. (2005, July). Assessing the Resource Base of Japanese and U.S. Auto Producers: A Stochastic Frontier Production Function Approach. *Management Science, 51*(7), 1060–1075. doi:10.1287/mnsc.1050.0416

Lugo Sánchez, M. G. (2016). Economic Partnership Agreement Mexico - Japan: Analysis of Trade Creation and Trade Diversion 1999-2013. In Economic impact of Economic Partnership Agreement Mexico – Japan – theoretical and empirical aspects (pp. 1-16). The Institute for Economic Studies. Seijo University.

Manger, M. S. (2005). Competition and bilateralism in trade policy: The case of Japans free trade agreements. *Review of International Political Economy, 12*(5), 804–828. doi:10.1080/09692290500339800

Marshall, A. (1890). *Principios de Economía.* London: Ingletarra.

McGuire, J., & Dow, S. (2009, June). Japanese keiretsu: Past, present, future. *Asia Pacific Journal of Management, 26*(2), 333–351. doi:10.1007/s10490-008-9104-5

Meyer, K., & Sinani, E. (2009) When and Where Does Direct Investment Generate Positive Spillovers? A Meta- Analysis. *Journal of International Business Studies, 40*(7), 1075-1094.

Nobeoka, K., & Cusumano, M. A. (1997). Multiproject Strategy and Sales Growth: The Benefits of Rapid Design Transfer in New Product Development. *Strategic Management Journal, 18*(3), 169–186. doi:10.1002/(SICI)1097-0266(199703)18:3<169::AID-SMJ863>3.0.CO;2-K

Ojo, M. (2013). *Why the traditional principal agent theory may no longer apply to concentrated ownership systems and structures.* MPRA Paper No. 50832. Covenant University. Online at http://mpra.ub.uni-muenchen.de/50832/

Okabe, T. (2004). Sinopsis del acuerdo de asociación económica entre México y Japón. *México y la Cuenca del Pacífico, 7*(23).

Peng, M. (2010). *Estrategia global. In Governing the corporation around the world* (2nd ed.). CENAGE Learning.

Peng, M. W. (2005). From China strategy to global strategy. *Asia Pacific Journal of Management, 22*(2), 123–141. doi:10.1007/s10490-005-1251-3

Porter, M. (1990). *The Competitive Advantage of Nations.* New York: Free Press. doi:10.1007/978-1-349-11336-1

Porter, M. E. (1990). *The competitive advantage of Nations.* New York: Frer Press. doi:10.1007/978-1-349-11336-1

Pritish, K., & Sakiru, A. (2013, April). Foreign Shareholding and Productivity Spillover: A Firm-Level Analysis of Indian Manufacturing. *IUP Journal of Applied Economics, 12*(2), 7–24.

Promexico. (n.d.). *México y sus tratados de libre comercio.* Retrieved from http://www.promexico.gob.mx/comercio/mexico-y-sus-tratados-de-libre-comercio-con-otros-paises.html

Ramírez Bonilla, J. J. (2014). La relación comercial México-Japón, diez años después de la firma del Acuerdo parael Fortalecimiento de Asociación Económica. *Comercio Exterior, 64*(6).

Secretaría de Economía. (2015). *Consulta en línea: Abril 2015.* Retrieved from http://www.economia.gob.mx/comunidad-negocios/comercio-exterior/tlcacuerdos/asia-pacifico

Secretaría de Economía de México. (2002). *Grupo de Estudio México-Japón sobre el Fortalecimiento de las Relaciones Económicas Bilaterales, Informe Final.* Retrieved from http://www.economia.gob.mx/files/japon_completo.pdf

Sutton, M. (2005). Japanese Trade Policy and 'Economic Partnership Agreements':A New Conventional Wisdom. *Ritsumeikan Annual Review of International Studies, 4,* 113-135.

UNCTAD. (2010). *Informe sobre las Inversiones en el Mundo 2010. Panorama General, Invertir en una economía de bajo carbono.* United Nations Publication. Retrieved from http://unctad.org/es/Docs/wir2010overview_sp.pdf

UNCTAD. (2014). *Foreign direct investment shows uneven growth in Latin America and the Caribbean, says UNCTAD Report. Informe de prensa.* United Nations Publication. Retrieved from http://unctad.org/en/pages/PressRelease.aspx?OriginalVersionID=187

Vargas-Hernandez, J. G., Guerra García, E., Bojórquez Gutiérrez, A., & Bojórquez Gutierrez., F. (2014). *Gestión Estratégica de Organizaciones.* Ediciones Insumisos Latinoamericanos.

Xu, D. & Meyer, K. (2012). Linking Theory and Context: Strategy Research in Emerging Economies. *Journal of Management Studies.*

KEY TERMS AND DEFINITIONS

ALADI: Latin American Integration Association.

AMIA: Mexican Association of the Automotive Industry.

APPRIs: Arrangements for the Promotion and Reciprocal Protection of Investments.

Capital Formation: The increase in fixed assets, inventories of materials, supplies, finished products and goods during a given period in industries and power producers, which together account for stocks calls.

Economic Development: The ability to produce and obtain wealth, both at the level of personal development as applied to countries or regions, linked to livelihood and economic expansion so as to ensure the welfare, prosperity is maintained and meets the personal or social needs and thereby human dignity.

EPA: Economic Partnership Agreement.

FDI: Foreign Direct Investment.

Foreign Direct Investment: Bets performing companies that want to internationalize by expanding the market for their products or services outside their national territory.

FTA: Free Trade Agreement.

Japan: Insular country located in East Asia between the Pacific Ocean and the Sea of Japan.

JEL: Journal of Economic Literature.

Mexico: Mexico, officially United Mexican States, is a country that belongs to the American continent. It is located in the southern part of North America and is made then by 32 states to hold congress and own constitution.

NAFTA: North American Free Trade Agreement.

OECD: Organization for Economic Cooperation and Development.

Spillovers: are the overflows, economies of scale or synergies generated as externalities in terms of benefits, services, opportunities, etc. that favor local economies, district or cluster formed by companies.

Strategy: is a managerial and entrepreneurial activity that aligns internal resources of firms to promote change in a complex and uncertain business and organizational environment to obtain advantages and benefits.

TLCUE: Free Trade Agreement Mexico-European Union.

WTO: World Trade Organization.

Chapter 15
A Profile of Foreign Nationals in a Globalising Second-Tier City, Suzhou, China

Hyung Min Kim
The University of Melbourne, Australia

ABSTRACT

The recent development of Chinese cities has witnessed an increasing number of foreign nationals working in China. Foreign nationals tied up with MNEs are one of the powerful drivers for urban transformation in the post-reform era. However, little attention has been paid to their socio-economics characteristics. This chapter, therefore, is to analyse characteristics of foreign nationals in socio-economic, demographic and spatial aspects. This chapter focuses on a globalising Chinese second tier-city, Suzhou as a case study.

INTRODUCTION

The recent development of Chinese cities has witnessed an increasing number of foreign nationals working in China due to a wide range of driving forces including multinational enterprises (MNEs). Approximately 3 million foreign nationals came to China for employment purpose in 2007 (Skeldon, 2011). Firms seek out economic opportunities in Chinese cities in favour of low-cost production sites and/or in search of access to China's growing markets. A strategy to control business operation at distance is to dispatch expatriate managers to the host city. In addition to dispatched managers by the firms, language teachers, academic staff, retailers and traders have sought out opportunities in China. Incoming foreign nationals are one of the major sources for urban transformation associated with emerging territorial and social inequality because foreign nationals are generally highly paid due to their professional skills, international experiences and knowledge sets.

As seen in the global city literature, large Chinese cities are globalising by housing MNEs and international immigrants (Chubarov & Brooker, 2013; Kang & Shouzhen, 2003; Zhang, 2014). Despite the increasing number of foreign nationals as one of the powerful drivers for urban transformation, little attention has been paid to socio-economic status of foreign nationals in China. How their social status is

DOI: 10.4018/978-1-5225-2673-5.ch015

different from the locals? What differences can be found in different origins and industrial types? This research pays attention to these research questions to better understand the role of foreign firms and foreign nationals in China's urban transformation, using a globalising second-tier city, Suzhou as a case study. Suzhou has been rapidly urbanising and globalising by virtue of FDI-oriented growth strategies.

BACKGROUND

Two Key Players in Emerging Global Cities: MNEs and International Immigrants

Global cities are referred as globally significant cities with economic, political, and cultural dominance in a world system. High-level command-and-control functions tend to be concentrated geographically in global cities or world cities (Friedmann, 1986; Friedmann & Wolff, 1982). Global cities play a crucial role as an international node in building international production and transport networks (Keeling, 1995). Harris (1997) pointed out that the new global economy facilitated massive flows of products (trading), people (international migration), capital (e.g., FDI), and information along with 'time-space compression' process (Harvey, 1990). Typical examples of global cities are New York, London and Tokyo (Sakia Sassen, 2001). Emerging globalising cities have at least the two fundamental players: MNEs and international immigrants.

Firstly, the global city literature has emphasised the significance of capital accumulation in evolving into global cities (Sakia Sassen, 1999, 2001; Saskia Sassen, 1995). Massive presence of Foreign Direct Investment (FDI) channelled via MNEs has been observed in global cities. Firms' strategic approaches to cross-border business operations have been implemented in search of low-production sites with respect to affordable land prices and cheap labour costs and access to global markets (Dunning, 1998; Hodos, 2002). While advanced producer services are becoming a crucial element in FDI flows, manufacturing production has been relocated to periphery of city-regions and regional areas where labour-intensive and land-intensive industries can reduce their production costs (Glickman & Woodward, 1988; Harris, 1997). Recently, East Asian economies, such as China, Korea, and Taiwan, have evolved with growth in FDI in technology-oriented manufacturing sectors (Chien & Zhao, 2008; Kim & Han, 2014; Yang & Hsia, 2007). The impacts of FDI inflows are not limited simply to capital accumulation, but also associated with spill-over effects. FDI is involved with 'a package of assets' that include money capital, management and organisational expertise, technology, entrepreneurship and access to global markets (Dunning, 1993). Inflows of FDI are, accordingly, tied up with foreign nationals to manage business operations at distance (Kim & Han, 2014).

Secondly, there has been evident presence of foreign nationals in global cities. These international immigrants appeared in high-income countries as international migrants have sought out better economic opportunities and liveable environments (Hugo, 2004). Diasporic networks, such as through family networks and shared ethnicity, have facilitated international migration (Hugo, 2005; Sakia Sassen, 2005). Due to a variety of immigrants, global cities have witnessed cosmopolitan culture as obviously seen in London, New York and Sydney (Friedmann, 1995). In newly emerging global cities international immigration was strengthened by massive inflows of FDI as MNEs have dispatched their managers. While high income countries accommodate both highly-paid professionals and low-skilled labourers, it is rare for less skilful labourers to immigrate into emerging global cities, in particular Chinese cities, due to abundant labourers within the country. Rural-to-urban migrants, in general, provide labour force for

Chinese large cities (Fan, 2008). Spatial and socio-economic polarisation has appeared in global cities associated with economic restructuring and globalisation process (Sakia Sassen, 2001). Co-location of high-level professionals and low-waged jobs (or bifurcation of the labour market) has stimulated inequality in global cities. Highly globalised service sectors have offered professional jobs mostly in global cities. By virtue of the nature of international service businesses, global links and international experiences are critical for these business operations. Representative examples are advanced producer services such as financial services, insurance services, advertisement, accounting services, law firms, and real estate investment and management (Beaverstock, Smith, & Taylor, 1999; Taylor, 2004). Due to large-scale economic agglomerations associated with urbanisation and localisation economies, global cities better provide opportunities for immigrants. Native labour force in high income countries is unwilling to work for, so called, 3D occupations (i.e, dirty, dangerous, and difficult) (Hugo, 2004). As manufacturing industries are fading away from post-industrial cities, middle-income class has been shrunken triggering socio-economic polarisation.

High concentrations of global activities are found in small part of global cities. For instance, Chinese migrants have formed ethnic communities in declining industrial sites of Seoul (Lee, 2014). The global CBD was established spatially separated from national and local CBDs in Mumbai and Accra (Grant & Nijman, 2002). Despite the debate on different levels of polarisation in global cities especially in 'developmental states' such as Tokyo, Seoul, Taipei, and Hong Kong (Chiu & Lui, 2004; Hill & Kim, 2000; Wang, 2003), cities are evolving under the process of globalisation associated with increasing inequality and spatial polarisation (Rhein, 1998; Walks, 2001). Growing inequality does not necessarily represent how globalised the cities are, but the globalising labour market has led to more unequal patterns. Although many Chinese cities are not yet considered as globally significant cities equipped with high-level command-and-control functions, they are also on this process toward increasing socio-economic and spatial polarisation (Z. Li & Wu, 2006; Ren, 2013: Ch. 5; Wu, 2006).

Globalising Chinese Cities

When China was under the socialist regime, flows into Chinese cities were regulated. However, Deng Xiaoping's reform and opening up policy brought fundamental changes to Chinese cities. Since 1978 the Chinese government has employed a pro-growth regime embracing the triple processes of marketization, decentralisation and globalisation (Y. D. Wei, Yuan, & Liao, 2013; Y. H. D. Wei, Lu, & Chen, 2009; Y. H. D. Wei, Luo, & Zhou, 2010). The Chinese economy has made use of market mechanisms for resource allocation. Not only products, but land and housing have been also commoditised to the extent to establish land and housing markets (Wu, 2001). There has been a shift of fiscal and planning power from the central government to local governments, which is called decentralisation (Y. Li & Wu, 2012). Local governments, therefore, are active in raising revenue and keen to economic growth (Ren, 2013: ch. 2). One of the strategic approaches is to take advantage of global forces that are foci of this research. Chinese cities were eager to attract inward FDI in favour of technology transfer and capital investment in the reform era (Sun, Tong, & Yu, 2002). A wide range of manufacturing firms established production plants transforming China from the 'state factory' to the 'world factory' (L. J. C. Ma & Wu, 2005). The amount of inward FDI increased markedly in China. In the mid-1990s, China became the second largest recipient of inward FDI after the U.S.A. (Sun et al., 2002). In addition to manufacturing industries, China has attracted FDI in service sectors, too (He & Yeung, 2011). The massive inflows of global capital have brought local impacts to Chinese cities. For instance, the growth of inward FDI has been in parallel with GDP growth; newly created plants provided jobs for both the locals and rural-to-urban migrants; and foreign national numbers are on the increase alongside the growth in inward FDI (Kim, 2015).

As seen in the Global Cities Index, Chinese cities have grown into emerging global cities (ATkearney, 2012). Beijing was ranked at 14th; Shanghai was at the 21st in 2012. By the Globalisation and World City (GaWC) Research Network, Shanghai and Beijing were listed as alpha+ world cities along with Hong Kong, Paris, Singapore, Tokyo, Sydney and Dubai after the two alpha++ cities, London and New York in 2012. In mainland China, in addition to these two top-tier cities, Guangzhou (beta+), Shenzhen (beta-), Tianjin (gamma-), Chengdu, Qingdao, Hangzhou, Nanjing, Chongqing (high sufficiency), Dalian, Xiamen, and Xian (sufficiency) were identified as key globalising cities (Globalization and World Cities Research Network).

As Chinese cities are urbanising and globalising (Gu, Kesteloot, & Cook, 2015), nationwide uneven development has been observed. Most economically developed cities are located in the coastal region such as Pearl River Delta (PRD), Yangtze River Delta (YRD), and Bohai Rim Region (BRR). In 2004 these three regions produced more than half of the national GDP; accounted for 79% of trading volumes; and accounted for 85% of the total realised FDI (Zhao & Zhang, 2007). Spatial polarisation also appeared within the Chinese city, including informal settlements mostly for regional migrants (L. J. Ma, 2004; Ren, 2013: ch. 3; Wu, Zhang, & Webster, 2013), gated communities (L. J. C. Ma & Wu, 2005), exotic residential areas (Shen & Wu, 2012) and ethnic communities revolving around foreign nationals (Kim, 2015).

Despite increasingly growing numbers of MNEs and foreign nationals in Chinese large cities, little attention has been paid to socio-economic status of foreign nationals working in China. In particular, second-tier Chinese cities have been under-researched in this aspect in spite of noticeable numbers of local and foreign populations. The purpose of this research, therefore, is to explore foreign nationals in terms of socio-economic and spatial characteristics. The investigation of foreign nationals has significance at least in the following three aspects. First, massive presence of foreign nationals appeared only after the reform policy. Thus, a mix of ethnicity other than Chinese minority groups is new to Chinese cities. Although China has relatively short history of international immigration, the process of urbanisation and globalisation shows trends in polarising patterns and cosmopolitan culture as found in highly globalised cities. As the Chinese socialist regime had a great emphasis on socio-economic and spatial equity, the emergence of inequality, associated with international immigrants, is against the socialist ideal. Second, foreign nationals, as professional workers, are expected to have higher consumption power than the locals. They may be attracted to Chinese cities after rigorous risk-return analysis at an individual and household level in multiple aspects including career, income, family considerations and living environments. Foreign nationals have at least equivalent income levels to their home city. China is still ranked as a 'less developed region' by the U.N. and a 'lower-middle' income country in terms of GNP per capita (Stephens, 2010). Thus, foreigners' higher income levels and consumption patterns are expected to stimulate the transforming of Chinese urban space although the detail has not been fully addressed in the literature, which can justify this research. Third, spatial expression of foreign nationals is distinctive as foreign nationals tend to form ethnic communities. The impact of foreign nationals is strengthened through residential location choice. Due to 'disadvantages of alien status (Caves, 1971)', location choice of firms is conservative to well-known places and residential choice is geographically limited to small areas within the cities (Grant & Nijman, 2002; Kim, Han, & O'Connor, 2015). The spatial concentration is found to share language-specific facilities and stick to other foreign national groups.

MAIN FOCUS OF THE CHAPTER

Data Collection

For this research survey questionnaires were conducted with foreign nationals living in Suzhou for more than six months for the purpose of working in 2014. The author stayed in Suzhou for two years in the period 2013 – 2015 and an auxiliary visit was made in 2016. In this research foreign nationals refer to people with non-Chinese nationality. International students and short-term visitors were excluded. Survey questionnaires included a set of questions about socio-economic status including occupations, duration of stay in Suzhou, family composition, income levels and residential location. The questionnaires were made in three language versions (i.e., English, Korean and Japanese) after preliminary findings about major population groups in Suzhou. This research recruited participants through on and offline expat communities and street survey in the public space. The online link for the survey questionnaire was sent to foreign nationals via expatriate communities and international schools. On street survey was used to secure the participants who were possibly inactive in expat communities. This survey included 508 foreign nationals staying long-term. High numbers of respondents at 508 provide solid research findings. This survey referred to student enrolment numbers in international schools and nationwide statistics about foreign nationals as benchmarks. The size of samples from each origin is generally proportional to the benchmarks.

The collected information was tabulated, graphed and mapped for analysis. The analysis in this research is not inferential but descriptive. The findings outline 'who' they are, 'what' they do and 'where' they live in the city, which is a basic step for further rigorous research. The geographical focus of this research is upon urban districts in Suzhou.

FDI-Oriented Urban Growth in Suzhou

Suzhou is a fast urbanising and globalising second-tier Chinese city with an emphasis on global production links (see the location map in Figure 1). The Suzhou Industrial Park (SIP) was planned and implemented by the collaboration between the China and the Singapore governments with a focus on a FDI-oriented development strategy (Fook, 2014; Kim & Cocks, 2017; Pereira, 2004; Y. D. Wei et al., 2013). Wei et al. (2013; 2009) have claimed that global-local production networks were weak in Suzhou while FDI firms formed a spatially-mismatched satellite district from local Chinese firms. Kim (2015) has also described the growth of foreign nationals in conjunction with FDI inflows in Suzhou, in particular, in the SIP. As a result of large-scale investment in the SIP and surrounding city-regions, Suzhou has achieved rapid economic growth, ranked at the 6th largest China's economic agglomeration in terms of the GDP. In the Suzhou urban districts, the SIP had lion's share in terms of FDI inflows, accounting for 50.2% of the aggregated inward FDI in the period 2003 – 2012 (Suzhou Statistical Yearly Book). Suzhou is a leading city within Jiangsu Province, accounting for 22.2% of the total provincial GDP in 2012 (Jiangsu Province Statistical Yearly Book).

Another platform for the inflows of foreign nationals is internationalising universities in which international academic staff and English teachers play an active role in tertiary education. In the education town of the SIP, there were 28 universities and more than 190 R&D institutions that provided positions for international staff members in 2013 (*Dushu* Lake Higher Education Exhibition Centre). Due to

Figure 1. Map of Suzhou
Note: Regions with grey colour are county-level municipalities

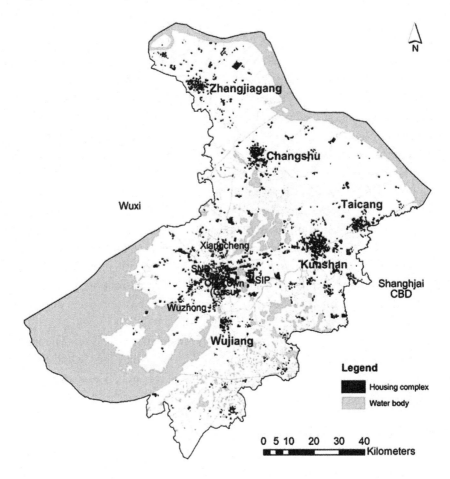

business expansion tied up with global production networks, and internationalising education services, foreign nationals accounted for 2.1% of the total population in the SIP in 2011 (SIP website).

Profiles of Foreign Nationals

This section provides an overview of foreign nationals in Suzhou. The vast majority of foreign nationals have stayed in Suzhou for the short-term from the result of survey questionnaires. 61.2% of the respondents replied that their stay in Suzhou was less than three years. Approximately one-third of foreign nationals have lived for 3-10 years. Only 4.5% have stayed in Suzhou for more than 10 years. On the one hand, since the development of the SIP and the Suzhou New District (SND) began in the late 1990s, long-term staying foreign nationals were limited. The result confirms that the inflows of foreign nationals are very recent. On the other hand, foreign nationals stay in a host city for the short-term. MNEs have a policy on the human resource management of expatriate employees. After the pre-determined terms in Suzhou, MNEs send back their managers to another office; after substantial work experience in Suzhou, foreign nationals may relocate to another place voluntarily. The average stay was 3.5 years estimated by the mid-values in Table 1.

Official statistics were unavailable for the origins of foreign nationals in Suzhou. Nationwide statistics reported that Koreans (20.3%), Americans (12.0%) and the Japanese (11.1%) were the top three origins in 2013 (Kim, 2015). Kim (2015) displayed international students' enrolment in Suzhou Singapore International School, showing the top five origins were Korea (33%) followed by Taiwan (11%), the U.S.A. (8%), Germany (7%) and Malaysia (4.5%) in 2014. Another international school had similar composition of students' enrolment with the highest number of Korean students (approximately 30%) followed by American students (approximately 10%) according to a phone interview with the admission officer. The survey respondents in this research were composed of a wide range of origins; the top origin countries were Korea (48.2%), USA (12.0%), and Japan (10.6%), representing a similar origin composition in international schools.

China, Japan and Korea are located in Far East Asia and these countries have long historical interactions sharing Asian values such as Confucianism although modern society has transformed the Asian value in different ways. Moreover, Japan and Korea have advanced industries in Information and Communication Technology (ICT). Most FDI in Suzhou made by Japanese, Korean and Taiwanese firms was ICT-oriented manufacturing such as Liquid Crystal Displays (LCD), semiconductors and laptops (Chien & Zhao, 2008; Fook, 2014; Y. H. D. Wei, Liefner, & Miao, 2011). ICT-oriented manufacturing was manifested in occupations of foreign nationals (Table 3). Due to the increases in a production cost, these firms chose offshore production sites. The Suzhou region provided favourable environments for these industries by virtue of proximity to Shanghai, quality infrastructure emphasised via development zones and industrial parks, improved administrative services trained by the Singapore government (Fook, 2014; Pereira, 2004), affordable land partially subsidised by the local governments, and cheap labour force associated with rural-to-urban migrants. MNEs played a leading role in inflows of foreign nationals as they dispatched their managers and engineers for offshore production management. Not only single MNEs, but inter-related suppliers followed MNEs in search of new business opportunities to the extent that the entire supply chain and production networks were established (Kim, 2015). Moreover, quality living environments were encouraged in building the SIP, which has played an important role in attracting or retaining foreign nationals.

The category of developed regions in Table 2 included high income nations such as the U.S.A. (12.0%), France (5.7%), the U.K. (4.9%), Germany (2.0%) and Australia (2.0%). Proportion of Americans

Table 1. Duration of stay of foreign nationals in Suzhou

Duration of Stay in Suzhou	Frequency	%
Less than one year	115	22.6%
1-3 years	196	38.6%
3-5 years	92	18.1%
5-10 years	81	15.9%
10 years or more	23	4.5%
N.A.	1	0.2%
Total	508	100%

Table 2. Origins of foreign nationals in Suzhou

Origins	Frequency	%
Korea	245	48.2%
Japan	54	10.6%
Developed regions	146	28.7%
Other European countries	31	6.1%
Developing Asian regions	20	3.9%
Developing regions other than Asia	5	1.0%
Others	7	1.4%
Total	508	100.0%

Table 3. Occupations of foreign nationals in Suzhou

	Occupations	Frequency	%
1	IT related manufacturing (e.g., semi-conductor, LCD panel, and computer)	126	24.8%
2	Other manufacturing	80	15.7%
3	Education (including kindergarten, schools, colleges, language teaching etc.)	67	13.2%
4	Car manufacturing	41	8.1%
5	Electronics manufacturing	36	7.1%
6	Higher Education or research (including academic jobs)	35	6.9%
7	Precise machine	34	6.7%
9	Business service (e.g. consulting)	23	4.5%
10	Trading	14	2.8%
11	Financial service (e.g., bank)	8	1.6%
	Others	33	6.5%
	N.A.	11	2.2%
	Total	508	100.0%

is noteworthy same as the Chinese national level. Language teachers from English speaking countries have added significant layers to the expatriate communities, which will be further discussed. Immigrants from other European countries and developing regions were rare. The composition of foreign nationals in Suzhou was different from highly globalised cities where there is evident presence of international immigrants from developing regions (Hugo, 2004; Sakia Sassen, 2005).

The majority of foreign nationals were in their 30s (34.1%) and 40s (40.4%), accounting for 74.4%. 14.0% were in their 50s while 8.5%, in 20s. The most economically active age groups were observed. 202 out of the 508 respondents or 39.8% had school-aged kid(s). More than half of the expatriate parents (52.5%) sent their kid(s) to international schools where only foreign nationals can attend. In spite of expensive tuition fees for these international schools ranging US $22,000 to US $32,000 annually (Suzhou Singapore International School, n.d.; Dulwich International School, 2015; and Eton International

School, n.d.), firms provided education subsidies for expatriate children. 59.4% of the children enrolled in the international school received education subsidies more than 80% of the tuition fees in addition to regular salary. Only 4.7% received no education subsidy. The rest of expatriate parents received partial support for children's education. In addition to the international schools, ethnic-specific schools (26.7%) and foreign language schools (19.8%) were dominant. Ethnic-specific schools meant Korean schools and Japanese schools in the Suzhou region. Due to the increasing number of Koreans and the Japanese, these governments established own schools with the similar curriculums to their home country. Foreign language schools teach in Chinese mostly for international students and the Chinese can attend. Only 10 expatriate parents or 5.0% had kid(s) in a local Chinese school.

The major occupations of expatriates were manufacturing. Dominant manufacturing sectors were knowledge-intensive manufacturing such as IT-related manufacturing (24.8%), car manufacturing (8.1%), electronics (7.1%) and precise machine (6.7%). Massive presence of knowledge-intensive manufacturing implies the hierarchy of Suzhou as a second-tier city among Chinese cities. Labour-intensive manufacturing has already faded away into even cheaper production sites such as inland Chinese regions while high-value added manufacturing has become dominant in Suzhou (Zhou, 2013). Presence of producer services in Suzhou was not as evident as in Shanghai (Han & Qin, 2009). While education (13.2%) and tertiary education/research (6.9%) sectors had relatively higher numbers of foreign nationals, producer services showed less significance as seen in the number of foreign nationals working for business services (4.5%) and financial services (1.6%). However, although the absolute number of foreign nationals in producer services was much lower than the one in knowledge-intensive manufacturing, the result displayed the evidence about emerging producer services. Due to the non-labour-intensiveness of producer services, the small number of professionals can manage their business operations.

Most expatriate professionals were middle (25.6%) or senior-level (37.4%) managers while junior-level managers were rare at 3.9%. Other than these managers, the rest were minor such as teachers (6.9%), self-employed (6.1%), and academic staff/researchers (5.7%).

This section provided a brief about foreign nationals working in Suzhou. Their duration of stay was short-term and ICT-related manufacturing was dominant for their occupations. There was a wide range of mixture of ethnicity, but the two neighbouring countries and high income nations played a key role as origin countries. Foreign nationals were likely to be high-level managers. The focus of the next section turns into detailed analysis about income levels that can describe socio-economic status in comparison with the locals.

Income Distributions of Foreign Nationals

The literature has reported increasing inequality of income distribution among the Chinese as seen in the stark increase in the *Gini* coefficient from 0.16 in 1978 to 0.45 in 2001 (Stephens, 2010). Remarkable differences in income levels between foreign nationals and the locals were observed according to the official statistics and the survey results. While the average monthly household income of the Chinese was RMB 12,000, the one of foreign nationals reached at 39,000 RMB per month showing more than a 3.3-times difference (Table 4). The difference between foreign nationals and the locals was more obvious in higher income groups, implying very high income groups were one of the primary sources to inequality in Chinese cities. While the low income household had a 1.8-times gap, the high income household had a 4.5-times difference. The top 20% Chinese household had income as low as the second

Table 4. Household income levels of the locals and foreign nationals in Suzhou

Households	Locals* (2013) (A)	Foreign Nationals (2014) (B)	(B) / (A)
High income (20%)	20,597	92,102	4.5
Upper middle income (20%)	13,305	40,000	3.0
Middle income (20%)	10,471	29,355	2.8
Lower middle income (20%)	8,274	19,839	2.4
Low income (20%)	6,604	11,702	1.8
Average	11,837	38,559	3.3
Gini coefficient	0.37 – 0.42 (China)	0.40 (Surveyed in Suzhou)	

Source: * Urban household average monthly income estimated from Suzhou Statistical Yearly Book

lowest 20% foreign nationals. The highest 20% income group among foreign nationals reached at almost RMB 92,000 per month (app. USD 15,000).

In addition, income inequality was found among foreign nationals. The *Gini* coefficient given the categorical income information among the surveyed foreign nationals reached 0.40. This inequality level was very similar to overall China's nationwide *Gini* coefficient, 0.42 in 2010 and 0.37 in 2011. (For China's *Gini* coefficient see the World Bank, http://data.worldbank.org/indicator/SI.POV.GINI. As the income data used here were from the survey with foreign nationals. The calculation of the *Gini* coefficient was based upon income bands instead of precise household income, which included a limitation. However, the *Gini* coefficient calculated with rent that had precise amounts showed a similar result, at 0.35).

Dissimilarity was observed among foreign nationals by occupation (Table 5). Although the absolute number of professionals in producer services was low, their income levels were the highest. As pointed out in the global city literature, the growth of producer services stimulated to widen income gaps (Sakia Sassen, 2001), which was also observed in Suzhou. However, income levels in manufacturing sectors were also high. As expatriates worked with professional skills as a manager or engineer in these industries, their jobs were not routinized but specialised at management or engineering having high income levels. As Daniels and Bryson (2002) have claimed that distinction between manufacturing and services was becoming unclear, manufacturing jobs as professionals were highly paid. In addition to the regular salary, substantial amounts of housing allowance were provided ranging 10% to 20% of the income.

Table 5. Characteristics of foreign nationals by occupation in Suzhou

	Income (RMB/Month)	Housing Subsidy (RMB/Month)	Duration of Stay (Years)	Ratio of Singles (Marriage Status)	Average age
Producer services	49,828	7,341	3.0	19.4%	43.3
ICT manufacturing	41,644	8,456	3.0	11.4%	42.1
Other manufacturing	43,286	8,492	3.8	13.9%	44.6
Higher education/research	33,281	3,798	2.7	51.4%	41.3
Education	17,344	3,191	2.3	59.1%	36.3

Expatriates in producer services and manufacturing were mostly dispatched by the headquarters office. Firms provide at least the same salary levels and offer for allowances to secure stable living and working environments. Often higher salaries were offered to attract qualified employees. This is particularly the case when the host cities are less well-known. Firms try to provide housing allowances to the extent that expatriates can stay, at least, in the same quality housing with their hometowns.

Income levels in universities and education sectors were relatively low (Table 5). Especially education sectors, such as English teachers, had the lowest income levels. Expatriates in the education sector were likely singles at relatively younger age staying in Suzhou for the short-term. Respondents in the education sector had stayed in Suzhou for 2.3 years on average. Expatriates in higher education/research and education tended to choose Suzhou voluntarily while the other groups were sent by the firm. So, instead of large-size family, singles and small-size family were dominant as they were, in general, more globally mobile. One possible explanation of the short-term stay is the recent establishment of the university town in the SIP. While MNEs have been encouraged to be in Suzhou since the 1990s when the SIP and the SND were built, a number of universities were established in the southern SIP in the 2000s. Hence, most expatriates in education sectors relocated after the establishments of these universities.

Three major origins were identified in the previous section. Table 6 reports the differences between these three origins. For Koreans and the Japanese, expatriates worked for manufacturing predominantly while education sectors were very limited. However, developed countries had diverse occupations. The highest number of expatriates worked for the education sector (31.5%) followed by knowledge-intensive manufacturing (20.5%), other manufacturing (19.2%) and higher education/research (15.8%). Possibly due to high demand for English education and tertiary education in the English speaking environments, English native speakers from Anglophone countries, such as the U.S.A., the U.K., Canada and Australia, were attracted to Suzhou. In addition, growing numbers of foreign nationals created new demand for education for their children such as international schools, ethnic-specific schools and international kindergartens.

Demographic characteristics of these three groups were noteworthy. Most Korean expats were married and had children. They tended to stay slightly longer than the other two groups. Koreans and the Japanese were more homogenous than the expats from developed countries as observed in the low Coefficient of Variation (CV) of Korean and Japanese expatriates in age and income information. Expatriates from developed countries had a wider mixture of income groups, occupations, and demographic structure. Higher income levels of Korean expatriates than the Japanese might present the emphasis of Korean knowledge-intensive manufacturing on production in China. The stark difference in income levels between Koreans and the Japanese was unexpected. Only 37.0% of the Japanese expats have brought their whole family to Suzhou while vast majority of the Korean expats accompanied their entire family (81.2%). Interviews with expats confirmed that Japanese firms provided dual salaries in both Chinese currency and Japanese currency. In this survey, Japanese respondents revealed only their Chinese income, not disclosing their Japanese income in their home country.

This section investigated income distribution of foreign nationals in a range of aspects, displaying high income levels. Dissimilarity has been found in different occupations and origins. While Koreans and partially the Japanese accompanied dependent children, singles at younger age were more dominant among expats from developed countries. Homogenous demographic and socio-economic structure was identified among Koreans and the Japanese. The next section will address spatial distribution of these groups.

Table 6. Characteristics of foreign nationals by major origins in Suzhou

			Korea	Japan	Developed Countries
Occupational characteristics	Producer services		5.3%	7.4%	5.5%
	Knowledge-intensive manufacturing		66.1%	51.9%	20.5%
	Manufacturing		10.6%	29.6%	19.2%
	Higher Education/Research		0.4%	0.0%	15.8%
	Education		4.1%	3.7%	31.5%
	Others		13.5%	7.4%	7.5%
	Total		100.0%	100.0%	100.0%
Demographic characteristics	Num. of children (persons)		2.4	1.9	0.6
	Family information	Singles	4.1%	13.0%	48.6%
		Entire family relocation (the married)	81.2%	37.0%	28.8%
		Only expat's relocation	3.3%	44.4%	11.0%
		Part of family relocation	11.4%	5.6%	11.0%
		N.A.	0%	0%	0.7%
		Sub-total	100.0%	100.0%	100.0%
	Age	Average	43.0	42.8	39.3
		STD	7.2	9.5	11.0
		CV	0.17	0.22	0.28
	Average duration of stay		3.9	3.0	3.0
Economic characteristics	Income	Average	44,515	18,542	36,455
		STD	33,019	12,026	32,501
		CV	0.74	0.65	0.89
	Housing subsidy	Average	8605	4783	6697
		STD	5110	2457	6050
		CV	0.59	0.51	0.90

Intra-Urban Spatial Specification

Ethnic communities were observed from the survey result. The residential location choice of foreign nationals was highly concentrated around the *Jinji* Lake in the SIP (Figure 2). The observed ethnic communities were the core to the SIP, co-developed by the Singapore government and the Chinese government. The lakeside location offered for good views and access to waterfront leisure and entertainment areas. In fact, the waterfront area of the *Jinji* Lake has been designed to provide high-quality cultural activities such as the Suzhou Culture and Arts Centre, high-end restaurants, and public parks. The northern *Jinji* Lake was between two major new business centres in which large-scale landmark mixed-use buildings are under construction at the time of writing. Moreover, the first Suzhou subway was constructed to connect these places, implying that ethnic communities were formed in the most active, well-designed areas of newly developed Suzhou.

In spite of overall co-location of foreign nationals, spatial specialisation was observed by different origins. Figure 2 represents residential locations of three distinctive ethnic groups. Koreans were the most dominant in the northern *Jinji* Lake with a highly concentrated spatial pattern. As the most dominant group among foreign nationals in Suzhou, Koreans have formed well-established ethnic communities (Kim, 2015). Their homogenous characteristics were also observed in their residential choice. At least the following five reasons can explain their spatial concentration. First, there is a language barrier as non-English speaking, non-Chinese speaking backgrounds. While employed expats are working, their family members stick to this Korean community for social interactions and access to local information. Due to relatively short duration of stay in Suzhou (3.9 years on average as seen in Table 6), Chinese language skills could be limited to interact with the Chinese. Their English ability is likely limited to interact with English-speaking foreign nationals. In this area Korean-written magazines including local information, Korean social activities and advertisement were readily available from retail shops. In addition, massive co-location can have Korean-speaking services such as medical services, dental clinics, Korean kindergartens, and religious services. These Korean-based services have been facilitated by large-scale inflows of Korean expats and their concentration. Some service providers were relocated from Korea in search of new business opportunities; others were the Chinese with Korean language skills. The Korean-Chinese or *Chosunjok* are typical examples (Kim et al., 2015). Second, firms want their expatriates to stay together in favour of efficient human resource management. As an industrial park, production sites are geographically distant from residential areas. Firms generally operate shuttle buses or vehicles for easy commuting. Agglomeration helps efficient management for commuting. Thus, Korean firms have dormitories for singles in the ethnic communities and encourage married staff to locate in the same community. Third, foreign nationals have a concern about safety in China. Agglomeration in a gated community offers for safer environments. Most housing complexes in expats' communities in Suzhou are gated with a number of security guards. From the sample in this research, the highest number of Koreans was found in the housing complex named, Bayside Garden or *Linglongwan* (see the largest red circle in Figure 2). To access this high-rise apartment complex, several steps were required with access key cards such as access to the block (a group of apartment buildings), the building, the elevator and each house. Also, Koreans might perceive safe psychologically when they stay together. Fourth, as noted in demographic characteristics of Koreans (Table 6), majority of them have brought family members to Suzhou. Thus, they have family considerations. Above all, education for children is one of the most critical challenges among expat families. Due to lack of available land for international schools nearby the ethnic communities, international schools are located across the Suzhou region. However, their locations could be easily connected through school buses operated by the international schools. Korean-speaking kindergartens were located in the ethnic community. In addition, it was easy to find private tutoring here for languages and general subjects which are common in Korea (Kim & Han, 2012). Fifth, Korean lifestyles are available in the Korean communities (Kim, 2015). There were Korean grocery stores, Korean restaurants, and Korean clothing shops. Delivery of these goods could be easily arranged due to short distance. Housing was equipped with Korean-style floor heating that was unusual in Suzhou.

While Koreans were dominant in the SIP, Japanese communities were observed in the SND due to massive presence of Japanese firms in the SND. There was a Japanese street where Japanese shops and restaurants were highly concentrated; there was a Japanese school in the SND. However, Japanese residential areas were not as obvious as Koreans due to the limited number partially associated with

Figure 2. Residential location distribution of surveyed expatriate families
Note: The districts marked in brown are Suzhou urban districts while the rest are county-level municipalities.

less involvement in family relocation as seen in Table 6. Moreover, their income levels in Chinese RMB were not as high as other foreign nationals. Thus, their consumption power in Suzhou was likely lower.

Expats from developed regions were relatively dispersed possibly due to diverse socio-economic and occupational backgrounds in Suzhou. The largest ethnic communities were Bayside Garden, where the highest number of Koreans was found, *Huzuoan* and Marina Cove. Both *Huzuoan* and Marina Cove were located in the western *Jinji* Lake. However, these two neighbouring residential complexes targeted different groups. While *Huzuoan* accommodated middle-income households recognised by the average income in this complex at 23,000 RMB per month, Marina Cove housed high income household offering luxurious housing options. There were six respondents living in Marina Cove; five were from developed regions. The average monthly income in Marina Cove was 47,500 RMB with an average rent at 20,000 RMB of which over 90% was paid by the firm, according to the interview with the real estate agency working for foreign nationals in Suzhou. It had membership-only indoor gyms and indoor and outdoor swimming pools, comprised of villas, town houses, and high-rise apartments, that were rarely available in Suzhou housing.

SOLUTIONS AND RECOMMENDATIONS

Inflows of affluent foreign nationals highly paid by MNEs will play a significant role in boosting the local economy. By providing quality living environments, the host city may be able to attract or retain foreign nationals who are likely global talent in the Chinese context. However, economic benefits from their influx tend to be limited within a small geographical area as discussed in this chapter. Infrastructure development in less globalised areas are required to mitigate growing concerns of spatial-economic inequality in globalising cities. This will be a critical task by local and provincial level governments.

FUTURE RESEARCH DIRECTIONS

This research provides evidence to display the trend of globalising Chinese territory. Although the development trajectory of Suzhou was different from the global cities at the mature stage, growing inequality associated with inflows of high-income professionals has appeared in conjunction with spatial specialisation in selected small geographical areas due to socio-economic, demographic distinctiveness. The presence of foreign nationals was primarily led by corporate strategies at the beginning of Suzhou urban growth. Also, this research displayed partial evidence of immigration at individual levels such as teachers and self-employed businessmen. Suzhou may enter into more mature globalised stages if a more diverse group of foreign nationals immigrate for the longer term, which will result in more complicated urban structure. This result also provides implications to globalising and restructuring developing countries with respect to socio-economic and spatial polarisation. As most manufacturing firms are seeking out cross-border production sites, the host city-regions would face with growing concerns about equity among the locals, between the locals and foreign nationals, and among foreign nationals, which needs further policy attentions.

CONCLUSION

This research investigated socio-economic and spatial status of foreign nationals in Suzhou which is emerging into a global city-region associated with massive inflows of MNEs. Global city formation has been a research focus primarily in the first-tier Chinese cities. However, the research findings displayed the similar process taking place in the second-tier Chinese city, Suzhou. This research sheds light on the following findings. First, foreign nationals drive growing income and spatial inequality in China. Their average income was 3.3 times higher than the locals and the gap was wider in higher foreign national income groups.

Second, due to the emphasis on industrial development, ICT-oriented manufacturers have played a proactive role in attracting foreign nationals into Suzhou. Intensive influences from Japan and Korea, as leading countries in this industry, were found in Suzhou, particularly in the two newly developed industrial parks. The influx of relatively homogeneous industrial types in FDI firms has resulted in the growth of Suzhou benefiting from localisation economies. In addition to the two neighbouring evident countries, foreign nationals from developed regions were noteworthy while there were limited foreign nationals from developing countries. The composition of international immigrants was significantly different from global cities in high income nations that have long history of immigration. While a number of less skilful labourers have permanently migrated to high income nations at an individual level in search of better economic opportunities (Hugo, 2004), Suzhou has had temporary immigrants with professional, international skills facilitated by corporate business strategies. (It is reported that there are increasing numbers of irregular workers from Vietnam and other Southeast Asian countries into southern China (Skeldon, 2011), but this did not happen in Suzhou).

Third, inequality was observed among foreign nationals possibly due to occupational backgrounds. The income gap between the lowest 20% income group and the highest 20% group reached almost eight times. The *Gini* coefficient was 0.40, showing significant unequal income distributions. Fourth, differences were found by origin groups in terms of occupations, residential choice, and demographic characteristics. Koreans and the Japanese were homogeneous in their occupation mostly on manufacturing, but foreign nationals from developed regions were more diverse possibly due to high demand for English education in China. Although foreign nationals chose core areas with quality public facilities and better security, minor inter-urban differences were observed in their residential choice as manifested in Korean and Japanese communities in the SIP and the SND, respectively.

ACKNOWLEDGMENT

This work was supported by the Academy of Korean Studies Grant (AKS-2016-R00) and 2014 Jiangsu University Natural Science Research Programme (Reference number: 14KJB170020). I appreciate Miss. Ting Wang and Miss. Jessica Wong who provided assistance for this chapter.

REFERENCES

Beaverstock, J. V., Smith, R. G., & Taylor, P. J. (1999). A roster of world cities. *Cities (London, England)*, *16*(6), 445–458. doi:10.1016/S0264-2751(99)00042-6

Caves, R. E. (1971). International corporations: The industrial economics of foreign investment. *Economica*, *38*(149), 1–27. doi:10.2307/2551748

Chien, S.-S., & Zhao, L. (2008). The Kunshan Model: Learning from Taiwanese Investors. *Built Environment*, *34*(4), 427–443. doi:10.2148/benv.34.4.427

Chiu, S. W. K., & Lui, T.-l. (2004). Testing the global city-social polarisation thesis: Hong Kong since the 1990s. *Urban studies, 41*(10), 1863-1888.

Chubarov, I., & Brooker, D. (2013). Multiple pathways to global city formation: A functional approach and review of recent evidence in China. *Cities (London, England)*, *35*, 181–189. doi:10.1016/j.cities.2013.05.008

Daniels, P. W., & Bryson, J. R. (2002). Manufacturing services and servicing manufacturing: Knowledge-based cities and changing forms of production. *Urban Studies (Edinburgh, Scotland)*, *39*(5-6), 977–991. doi:10.1080/00420980220128408

Dulwich International School. (2015). Retrieved October 13, 2015, from www.dulwich-suzhou.cn

Dunning, J. H. (1993). *Multinational enterprises and the global economy*. Wokingham, UK: Addison-Wesley.

Dunning, J. H. (1998). Globalization and the New Geography of Foreign Direct Investment. *Oxford Development Studies, 26*(1), 47-69. Retrieved from http://www.tandf.co.uk/journals/titles/13600818.asp

Eton International School. (n.d.). Retrieved October 13, 2015, from www.etonhouse-sz.com

Fan, C. C. (2008). *China on the Move: Migration, the State, and the Household*. Abingdon, UK: Routledge.

Fook, L. L. (2014). Suzhou Industrial Park: Going Beyong a Commercial Project. In S. Swee-Hock & J. Wong (Eds.), *Advancing Singapore-China Economic Relations* (pp. 62–93). Singapore: Institute of Southeast Asian Studies.

Friedmann, J. (1986). The world city hypothesis. *Development and Change, 17*(1), 69–83. doi:10.1111/j.1467-7660.1986.tb00231.x

Friedmann, J. (Ed.). (1995). *Where we stand: a decade of world city research*. Cambridge, UK: Cambridge UP.

Friedmann, J., & Wolff, G. (1982). World city formation: An agenda for research and action. *International Journal of Urban and Regional Research, 6*(3), 309–344. doi:10.1111/j.1468-2427.1982.tb00384.x

Glickman, N. J., & Woodward, D. P. (1988). The Location of Foreign Direct Investment in the United States: Patterns and Determinants. *International Regional Science Review, 11*(2), 137–154. doi:10.1177/016001768801100203

Globalization and World Cities Research Network. (2014). Retrieved September 1, 2014, from http://www.lboro.ac.uk/gawc/world2012t.html

Grant, R., & Nijman, J. (2002). Globalization and the corporate geography of cities in the less-developed world. *Annals of the Association of American Geographers, 92*(2), 320–340. doi:10.1111/1467-8306.00293

Gu, C., Kesteloot, C., & Cook, I. G. (2015). Theorising Chinese urbanisation: A multi-layered perspective. *Urban Studies (Edinburgh, Scotland), 52*(14), 2564–2580. doi:10.1177/0042098014550457

Han, S. S., & Qin, B. (2009). The spatial distribution of producer services in Shanghai. *Urban Studies (Edinburgh, Scotland), 46*(4), 877–896. doi:10.1177/0042098009102133

Harris, N. (1997). Cities in a Global Economy: Structural Change and Policy Reactions. *Urban Studies (Edinburgh, Scotland), 34*(10), 1693–1703. doi:10.1080/0042098975402

Harvey, D. (1990). *The condition of postmodernity*. Oxford, UK: Blackwell Publishers.

He, C., & Yeung, G. (2011). The Locational Distribution of Foreign Banks in China: A Disaggregated Analysis. *Regional Studies, 45*(6), 733–754. doi:10.1080/00343401003614282

Hill, R. C., & Kim, J. W. (2000). Global cities and developmental state: New York, Tokyo and Seoul. *Urban Studies (Edinburgh, Scotland), 37*(12), 2167–2195. doi:10.1080/00420980020002760

Hodos, J. I. (2002). Globalization, regionalism, and urban restructuring: The case of Philadelphia. *Urban Affairs Review, 37*(3), 358–379. doi:10.1177/10780870222185379

Hugo, G. (2004). A new global migration regime. *Around the Globe, 1*(3), 18-23.

Hugo, G. (2005). The new international migration in Asia. *Asian Population Studies, 1*(1), 93–120. doi:10.1080/17441730500125953

Kang, X., & Shouzhen, W. (2003). *Economic Globalization and Foreign Direct Investment in Shanghai.* Paper presented at the The 15th Annual Conference of the Association for Chinese Economics Studies Australia (ACESA), Melbourne, Australia.

Keeling, D. J. (Ed.). (1995). *Transport and the world city paradigm.* Cambridge, UK: Cambridge UP. doi:10.1017/CBO9780511522192.008

Kim, H. M. (2015). The role of foreign firms in China's urban transformation: a case study of Suzhou. In T.-C. Wong, S. S. Han, & H. Zhang (Eds.), *Population Mobility, Urban Planning and Management in China* (pp. 127–143). London: Springer. doi:10.1007/978-3-319-15257-8_8

Kim, H. M., & Cocks, M. (2017). The role of Quality of Place factors in expatriate international relocation decisions: A case study of Suzhou, a globally-focused Chinese city. *Geoforum, 81*, 1–10. doi:10.1016/j.geoforum.2017.01.018

Kim, H. M., & Han, S. S. (2012). City profile: Seoul. *Cities (London, England), 29*(2), 142–154. doi:10.1016/j.cities.2011.02.003

Kim, H. M., & Han, S. S. (2014). Inward foreign direct investment in Korea: Location patterns and local impacts. *Habitat International, 44*, 146–157. doi:10.1016/j.habitatint.2014.05.011

Kim, H. M., Han, S. S., & OConnor, K. B. (2015). Foreign housing investment in Seoul: Origin of investors and location of investment. *Cities (London, England), 42*, 212–223. doi:10.1016/j.cities.2014.07.006

Lee, W. (2014). Development of Chinese enclaves in the Seoul-Incheon metropolitan area, South Korea. *International Development Planning Review, 36*(3), 293–311. doi:10.3828/idpr.2014.17

Li, Y., & Wu, F. (2012). The transformation of regional governance in China: The rescaling of statehood. *Progress in Planning, 78*(2), 55–99. doi:10.1016/j.progress.2012.03.001

Li, Z., & Wu, F. (2006). Socioeconomic transformations in Shanghai (19902000): Policy impacts in global-national-local contexts. *Cities (London, England), 23*(4), 250–268. doi:10.1016/j.cities.2006.01.002

Ma, L. J. (2004). Economic reforms, urban spatial restructuring, and planning in China. *Progress in Planning, 61*(3), 237–260. doi:10.1016/j.progress.2003.10.005

Ma, L. J. C., & Wu, F. (2005). Restructuring the Chinese city. In L. J. C. Ma & F. Wu (Eds.), *Restructuring the Chinese city: changing society, economy and space* (pp. 1–18). London: Routledge. doi:10.4324/9780203414460_chapter_1

Pereira, A. A. (2004). The Suzhou Industrial Park Experiment: The case of China-Singapore governmental collaboration. *Journal of Contemporary China, 13*(38), 173–193. doi:10.1080/1067056032000151391

Ren, X. (2013). *Urban China.* Cambridge, UK: Polity.

Rhein, C. (1998). Globalisation, social change and minorities in metropolitan Paris: The emergence of new class patterns. *Urban Studies (Edinburgh, Scotland)*, *35*(3), 429–447. doi:10.1080/0042098984844

Sassen, S. (Ed.). (1995). *On concentration and centrality in the global city*. Cambridge, UK: Cambridge UP. doi:10.1017/CBO9780511522192.005

Sassen, S. (1999). Global financial centers. *Foreign Affairs*, *45*(1), 75–87. doi:10.2307/20020240

Sassen, S. (2001). The global city: New York, London, Tokyo (2nd ed.). Princeton, NJ: Princeton University Press, 2nd.

Sassen, S. (Ed.). (2005). Global cities and diasporic networks: Vol. 1. *Overviews and Topics*. New York: Springer.

Shen, J., & Wu, F. (2012). The development of master-planned communities in Chinese suburbs: A case study of Shanghas Thames town. *Urban Geography*, *33*(2), 183–203. doi:10.2747/0272-3638.33.2.183

SIP Website. (2010). Retrieved November 15, 2014, from http://www.sipac.gov.cn/english

Skeldon, R. (2011). *China: An Emerging Destination for Economic Migration*. Retrieved from http://www.migrationpolicy.org/article/china-emerging-destination-economic-migration/

Stephens, M. (2010). Locating Chinese Urban Housing Policy in an International Context. *Urban Studies (Edinburgh, Scotland)*, *47*(14), 2965–2982. doi:10.1177/0042098009360219 PMID:21114090

Sun, Q., Tong, W., & Yu, Q. (2002). Determinants of Foreign Direct Investment across China. *Journal of International Money and Finance*, *21*(1), 79-113. Retrieved from http://www.elsevier.com/wps/find/journaldescription.cws_home/30443/description#description

Suzhou Singapore International School. (n.d.). Retrieved October 13, 2015, from www.ssis-suzhou.net

Taylor, P. J. (2004). *World city network: A global urban analysis*. London: Routledge.

Tkearney. (2012). *2012 Global Cities Index and Emerging Cities Outlook*. Retrieved from https://www.atkearney.com/research-studies/global-cities-index

Walks, R. A. (2001). The social ecology of the post-fordist/global city? Economic restructuring and socio-spatial polarisation in the Toronto urban region. *Urban Studies (Edinburgh, Scotland)*, *38*(3), 407–447. doi:10.1080/00420980120027438

Wang, C.-H. (2003). Taipei as a global city: A theoretical and empirical examination. *Urban Studies (Edinburgh, Scotland)*, *40*(2), 309–334. doi:10.1080/00420980220080291

Wei, Y. D., Yuan, F., & Liao, H. (2013). Spatial Mismatch and Determinants of Foreign and Domestic Information and Communication Technology firms in Urban China. *The Professional Geographer*, *65*(2), 247–264. doi:10.1080/00330124.2012.679443

Wei, Y. H. D., Liefner, I., & Miao, C.-H. (2011). Network configurations and R&D activities of the ICT industry in Suzhou. *Geoforum*, *42*(4), 484–495. doi:10.1016/j.geoforum.2011.03.005

Wei, Y. H. D., Lu, Y., & Chen, W. (2009). Globalizing regional development in Sunan, China: Does Suzhou Industrial Park fit a neo-Marshallian district model? *Regional Science*, *43*(3), 409–427.

Wei, Y. H. D., Luo, J., & Zhou, Q. (2010). Location decisions and network configurations of foreign investment in urban China. *The Professional Geographer*, 62(2), 264–283. doi:10.1080/00330120903546684

Wu, F. (2001). Chinas recent urban development in the process of land and housing marketisation and economic globalisation. *Habitat International*, 25(3), 273–289. doi:10.1016/S0197-3975(00)00034-5

Wu, F. (Ed.). (2006). *Globalization and China's new urbanism*. Oxon, UK: Routledge.

Wu, F., Zhang, F., & Webster, C. (2013). Informality and the Development and Demolition of Urban Villages in the Chinese Peri-urban Area. *Urban Studies (Edinburgh, Scotland)*, 50(10), 1919–1934. doi:10.1177/0042098012466600

Yang, Y. R., & Hsia, C. J. (2007). Spatial clustering and organizational dynamics of transborder production networks: A case study of Taiwanese information-technology companies in the Greater Suzhou Area, China. *Environment & Planning A*, 39(6), 1346–1363. doi:10.1068/a38156

Zhang, L.-Y. (2014). Dynamics and Constraints of State-led Global City Formation in Emerging Economies: The Case of Shanghai. *Urban Studies (Edinburgh, Scotland)*, 51(6), 1162–1178. doi:10.1177/0042098013495577

Zhao, S. X. B., & Zhang, L. (2007). Foreign direct investment and the formation of global city-regions in China. *Regional Studies*, 41(7), 979–994. doi:10.1080/00343400701281634

Zhou, Y. (2013). Time and spaces of China's ICT industry. In P. Cooke, G. Searle, & K. O'Connor (Eds.), *The economic geography of the IT industry in the Asia Pacific region* (pp. 68–85). Oxon, UK: Routledge.

KEY TERMS AND DEFINITIONS

Expatriates: People living outside their home country mostly for working purpose. Expatriates are often dispatched by firms to manage business operation.

Foreign Direct Investment (FDI): Investment made by a firm located outside the country. FDI is involved directly with flows of capital for production and indirectly with flows of people, technology and managerial skills.

Global City: Cities with economic, political and/or cultural significance in a world system. Global cities are command-and-control centres where globally significant decisions/activities are made.

International Migration: Cross-border human movement. Presence of evident pull and push factors increases the volume of international migration.

Knowledge-Intensive Manufacturing: Manufacturing products that involve high technology. A typical example of knowledge-intensive manufacturing is to produce semi-conductors, computers, mobile phones, and aircrafts.

Multinational Enterprises (MNEs): Firms operational in two or more countries over the national boundaries. MNEs seek out global markets, low production sites, natural resources and human resources that might not be available in their origin country.

Spatial Inequality: Heterogeneity in human activities in different places. Typical measurements of spatial inequality are income, wealth, property prices, and ethnic concentration. Often these are systematically associated. Unequal spatial distribution of one or more of these activities is called spatial inequality.

Chapter 16
Cooperation and Competition Among Regions:
The Umbrella Brand as a Tool for Tourism Competitiveness

Arminda Almeida Santana
Universidad de Las Palmas de Gran Canaria, Spain

Sergio Moreno Gil
Universidad de Las Palmas de Gran Canaria, Spain

ABSTRACT

Many brands exist within the tourism industry. Territorial brands exist at local, regional, national, and supranational level where they overlap and are interrelated. Therefore, it is necessary that tourist destinations develop and manage their brands to obtain a strong differentiated position in the competitive market. This study analyzed relationships between destinations in the new global scenario. It aimed to improve brand architecture and increase tourist loyalty. A comprehensive analysis considering 6,964 tourists from 17 countries was applied. The study offered recommendations to destinations in order to expand the design of marketing activities, improve coopetition strategies, and advance competitiveness. The results confirmed that the destinations must adapt their promotional strategies to the new global landscape of interconnected business. In addition, they need to develop strategies for horizontal loyalty between destinations.

INTRODUCTION

Geopolitics is becoming increasingly complex. In order to achieve a mutual benefit between regions, it is necessary to develop an analytical and strategic management perspective. This chapter will focus on the tourism industry. Tourism is one of the most important worldwide economic activities, representing 9.8% of world global gross domestic product (world GDP), as well as 1 out 11 jobs for the global economy in 2015 (World Travel & Tourism Council, 2015). In the case of Spain, where the present case

DOI: 10.4018/978-1-5225-2673-5.ch016

study is located, the total contribution of Travel & Tourism to GDP was 16.0% in 2015, furthermore, the industry supported 19.2% of total employment (World Travel & Tourism Council, 2015). The main purpose of this chapter will be to focus on relationships that collaborators and competitors face in the new global scenario. Thus, the promotional strategies of tourism destinations must evolve in the global interconnected business landscape.

Tourist destinations aim to manage a "brand architecture," which establishes a valuable relationship between the portfolio of different brands (Harish, 2010). Brand architecture is a crucial issue for tourist destinations as they work to optimize portfolio of brands and the relationships between the brands (Datzira-Masip & Poluzzi, 2014). Strategic organization of the brands helps to avoid internal competition, it also adds value to the brands by achieving synergy and a multiplier effect (Harish, 2010).

On the other hand, growing competition between tourist destinations is an increasingly important trend (Mariani & Baggio, 2012). Table 1 shows a greater dispersion of tourists among "new" destinations with a significant increase in promotional investment and competition between these destinations to capture outbound markets. The current tourism trends show an increased number of holidays per tourist. Yet, the length of the holidays is shorter. Both the unstoppable growth of tourism and the increased number of destinations in the market (UNWTO, 2014) make necessary for destinations to develop strategies for obtaining a competitive advantage. Literature highlights collaboration and cooperation between tourist destinations as one relevant strategy (Fyall, Garrod, & Wang, 2012). In this example, the development of loyalty plays a key role in collaboration (Weaver & Lawton, 2011).

The fact that tourists share their holiday time between several destinations supports a collaborative and cooperative approach. It opens a discussion on the desirability of integrating various brands under

Table 1. Evolution Top 15 incoming countries

Rank	1950		1970		1980		1990		2007	
1	EEUU	71%	Italy	43%	France	40%	France	39%	France	32%
2	Canada		Canada		EEUU		EEUU		Spain	
3	Italy		France		Spain		Spain		EEUU	
4	France		Spain		Italy		Italy		China	
5	Switzerland		EEUU		Austria		Austria		Italy	
6	Ireland	17%	Austria	22%	Mexico	20%	Mexico	18%	UK	13%
7	Austria		Germany		Canada		Germany		Germany	
8	Spain		Switzerland		UK		UK		Ukraine	
9	Germany		Yugoslavia		Germany		Canada		Turkey	
10	UK		UK		Belgium		China		Mexico	
11	Norway	9%	Hungary	10%	Switzerland	10%	Greece	9%	Malaysia	11%
12	Argentina		Czechoslovakia		Yugoslavia		Portugal		Austria	
13	Mexico		Belgium		Poland		Switzerland		Russian	
14	Holland		Bulgaria		Czechoslovakia		Yugoslavia		Canada	
15	Denmark		Romania		Grecia		Malaysia		Greece	
	Others	3%	Others	25%	Others	30%	Others	34%	Others	44%
Total	25 millions		166 millions		276 millions		436 millions		903 millions	

Source: WTO (2012)

one umbrella to promote consistent quality among destination partners and differentiate them from their competitors (Aaker, 2004; Keller, 2003). While destinations could increase profits through the efficient use of their brands, in the context of tourist destinations the concept of branding is relatively new (Blain, Levy, & Ritchie, 2005). Tourist literature has ignored the relationship between tourists to multiple destinations at the same time. Thus, this study aims to:

Explore the relationship between tourists and the different regions they visit within a set of competing destinations. Thus, it provides guidance on which regions to compete with in the brand architecture, with which to cooperate and how to guide the creation of an umbrella brand.

In order to accomplish the proposed goal, the consideration set was the Canary Islands (Spain). The justification of this selection is that the Canary Islands is a leading European destination (Gil, 2003), with more than 14 million international tourists a year, and it is a very well-known and popular destination in Europe. The Canary Islands consist of seven islands: Tenerife, Gran Canaria, Lanzarote, Fuerteventura, La Palma, La Gomera, and El Hierro, with a complex ecosystem (García-Rodríguez, García-Rodríguez & Castilla-Gutiérrez, 2016), showing an interesting complementary relationship between them (Promotur, 2012). Promotur is a destination marketing organization that manages the umbrella brand (Canary Islands) and it has to deals with the coexistence of seven islands-brands. Furthermore, the analysis of this complementarity has been noted for other authors, claiming for further research applied to destinations geographically close (Shih, 2006). Thus, this study has taken into consideration a set of competitive destinations—the seven islands (destinations) within the Canary Islands. In order to reach the set goal, a wide survey with 6,964 questionnaires was developed, considering tourists from 17 European countries.

This chapter will analyze products (destinations) competing within an umbrella brand. It will look at whether these products should cooperate, as well as consider an effective methodology and analysis to meet this need. Thus the implications of this study are valuable for other similar regions that compete and cooperate under a common umbrella brand. It can be islands destinations (e.g., Hawaii: 8 main destinations; Maldives: several islands), but also to mainland destinations promoted under a country, region or sub-region brand.

BACKGROUND

Coopetition

During the 20th century, the study of competitiveness was a dominant paradigm in the tourism industry (Kylänen & Rusko, 2011). Competitiveness in tourism has been defined as a destination's ability to attract potential tourists to their region while meeting their needs and desires (Enrigth & Newton, 2004). According to Dawes, Romaniuk, and Mansfield (2009), tourist destinations compete for an individual's allocated travel time or for being a traveler's destination choice on consecutive trips.

According to Mariani, Buhalis, Longhi, and Vitouladiti (2014), in a highly-competitive tourist industry, pure competition is one of many tools used by destinations to achieve sustainable competitive advantage. However, cooperation plays a key role for tourism destination (Beritelli, 2011). Collaboration and cooperation among destinations is a relevant strategy for a destination to achieve a competitive advantage in the longer run (Fyall et al., 2012).

In the field of management, marketing, and tourism studies, these two leading paradigms (competition and cooperation) have recently been juxtaposed to a novel situation referred to as coopetition

(Mariani et al., 2014). Thus, the term "coopetition" is understood as the simultaneous cooperation and competition between companies and destinations (Luo, 2007). This cooperative approach, introduced during the last few decades (Kylänen & Rusko, 2011), will continue to change the dominant economic landscape (Fyall & Garrod, 2005; Jorde & Teece, 1990). Coopetition strategy has important policy and management implications influencing tourist destination marketing activities and presenting positive stakeholder benefits. Furthermore, it is also important to highlight the key role of consumer loyalty as a valuable tool to improve the competitiveness of tourism destinations (Weaver & Lawton, 2011). The resulting question is, to what extent coopetition strategy can be applied to brand management and loyalty?

Defining Loyalty and Explaining Its Importance

Customer loyalty has become an important marketing strategy due to the benefits associated with keeping existing tourists (McMullan & Gilmore, 2008). Financial and marketing-related benefits of tourists revisiting a destination justifies the destination's efforts to keep their tourists (Darnell & Johnson, 2001). According to literature, loyalty has two dimensions: (1) behavioral and (2) attitudinal (Baloglu, 2002). From a behavioral point of view, loyalty can be understood as a "revisit" to a holiday destination. The "attitudinal" approach represents personal attitudes and emotions involved with an individual's loyalty to a destination. The intent to revisit a destination is a manifestation of the latter. Although there is significant research on loyalty and its relationship to marketing strategies (Sivadas & Baker-Prewitt, 2000), few studies examine loyalty to tourist destinations (Moore, Rodger, & Taplin, 2015).

Horizontal Loyalty

Previous literature on loyalty shows that customers can be loyal to more than one brand (Cunningham, 1956; Dowling & Uncles, 1997; Felix, 2014; Jacoby & Kyner, 1973; Olson & Jacoby, 1974; Sharp & Sharp, 1997; Yim & Kannan, 1999). Thus destination can cooperate and compete at the same time, sharing tourists that travel to multiple destinations in different trips. These relationships have been empirically demonstrated in different sectors, such as the cigarette industry (Dawes, 2014) and mobile phone sectors (Quoquab, Yasin, & Abu, 2014). Outside of the tourist context, loyalty to multiple brands has been conceptualized and described in different ways. However, an individual's loyalty to several destinations at the same time (referred to in literature as "horizontal loyalty") has not been thoroughly studied within the tourist sector (McKercher, Denizci-Guillet, & Ng, 2012).

In the tourism sector, according to Dawes et al., (2009), a person may book multiple trips, either separately or at the same time, which makes it possible to purchase different brands or repeat a purchase. Seeking a new experience is innate in travelers (Bowen & Shoemaker, 1998). Therefore, they may find themselves as being loyal to more than one destination (Alegre & Juaneda, 2006; Jang & Feng, 2007).

According to McKercher et al., (2012), studies on loyalty in the tourism context traditionally consider a single unit of analysis (e.g., a single destination). They have not yet considered the complex interrelationships between multiple units of analysis at the same time within the tourism system. McKercher et al., (2012) suggest carrying out studies on loyalty from the perspective of the consumer. They propose a horizontal loyalty approach to demonstrate that tourists may show loyalty to different providers at the same level within the tourism system (e.g., a tourist can show a loyal behavior to two destinations at once) (McKercher et al., 2012). Therefore, destinations must understand that tourists share their journeys between different destinations; loyal behavior can be divided among several destinations at the same time (Dawes et al., 2009). The modern traveler can choose from an unlimited range of destinations that offer similar attractions and facilities (Bianchi & Pike, 2011).

In addition, a shared loyalty behavior is motivated by the fact that many of the goods and services within the tourism sector are similar in quality and the provided experience (Baloglu, 2002; Campó & Yague, 2007; Darnell & Johnson, 2001). This behavior is supported by the novelty-seeking perspective, considered by some authors as innate to travelers (Bowen & Shoemaker, 1998). This can inhibit loyalty toward a single destination (Alegre & Juaneda, 2006; Jang & Feng, 2007). This fact supports the coopetition approach among destinations and it is a challenge for tourist destinations which must be able to manage their brands with the aim to achieve a strong position in the competitive market.

Brand Architecture

Brand architecture has been defined as an organized structure of a portfolio of brands specifying brand roles, as well as the nature of their relationships (Aaker & Joachimsthaler, 2000; Carballo, Araña, León & Moreno-Gil, 2015). Limited research has been conducted on the study of brand architecture (Dooley & Bowie, 2005; Harish, 2010). There are few cases where brand architecture has been meticulously planned so it is difficult to find examples of models for managing brand portfolios (Datzira-Masip & Poluzzi, 2014). According to Harish (2010), there are only a few studies covering both brand architecture and brand destination. It shows the need to explore the implementation of brand architecture to the destination brand since limited studies have analyzed different forms of brand architecture (Carballo, Araña, León, González & Moreno, 2011).

An umbrella brand serves as a quality guarantee among brand partners (Laforet & Saunders, 1994). Through the creation of the umbrella brand of a destination, marketers can achieve economies of scale and consistency of message in the promotion of the destination (Iversen & Hem, 2008). Moving from many local brands to a single umbrella brand also provides substantial savings in communication costs (Schuiling & Kapferer, 2004). In any case, the debate about the best way to integrate local brands with regional or national brands, as well as with other brands that are geographically close, or far, but with similar characteristics (d'Hauteserre & Funck, 2016) remains open. What should be the union of regions that are integrated into an umbrella brand? The brand architecture design should be adapted to the patterns of tourists' behavior (Jackson & Murphy, 2006).

Thus, the research hypothesis is the following:

The brand architecture design considering tourist horizontal loyalty, and a coopetition relationship between regions under one umbrella brand, could benefit all the regions which participate in.

METHODOLOGY

In order to reach the set goals, a structured loyalty questionnaire was used which included socio-demographic and geographic variables. The questionnaire combined open and closed questions. The study used Likert scales from 1 to 7, with 1 being the minimum and 7 being the maximum. The questionnaire was designed based on literature review and took into account the specific nature of the analyzed destination (Canary Islands, Spain).

Population

Representing more than half of the international arrivals each year, Europe remains the largest traveling region in the world (UNWTO, 2015). The population used for this study consisted of potential tourists:

- More than 16 years of age
- Either male or female
- From one of the main outgoing tourism 17 European countries, traveling to the destination being researched: Germany, Austria, Belgium, Denmark, Spain, Finland, France, Holland, Ireland, Italy, Norway, Poland, Portugal, Russia, Sweden, Switzerland, and the United Kingdom

Sampling Selection

An internet survey (CAWI) was used to conduct the research using a panel sampling from the 17 countries mentioned in the "Population" section. In order to guarantee the sample's representativeness within each country, a random selection took into account the stratification variables of the geographic location and province, as well as the gender and age. The initial sample consisted of 8,500 tourists (500 per country). The real final sample consisted of 6,964 tourists, including between 400 and 459 tourists per country. The selected sample was sent a personalized email inviting them to participate in the study, finding in the mail itself a personalized link that led them to the online survey (Table 2).

Quality Control and Data Analysis

The questionnaire was pre-tested to consider the corresponding language of the potential tourists who were analyzed. Corrections were made after tourists found questions that were difficult to understand. Next, the survey was launched. After being programmed, the online system revised the interviews and monitored the time spent by participants in answering the survey. Surveys answered in less than three were deleted as "invalid." Once the field work was completed, and after having applied the corresponding quality controls, the researchers performed a frequency analysis and binomial logit analysis using the latest version of SPSS statistical software. In this case, the logit model based on random use theory was chosen. The fit of the logit model was assessed by two log likelihood (LL) ratios and their associated chi-square.

Tourists were asked whether they had ever visited the Canary Islands before (no time frames were used). Only those tourists who had visited one of the Canary Island destinations were selected (2,067 tourists). And then, they were asked which islands they had visited. Tourists who had visited the consideration set (Canary Islands) twice or more were considered loyal tourists. Canary Islands is an archipelago in the Atlantic Ocean that forms 1 of the 17 autonomous communities of Spain. This offshore region is two and a half hours flying time from the capital (Madrid) and approximately four hours from central Europe. It is geographically located near the African coast (see Figure 1). A leading European destination, it receives more than 13 million tourists a year. It consists of seven islands: (1) Gran Canaria, (2)

Table 2. Sample description

		Frequency	Percentage
Nationality	Germany	423	6.07
	Austria	403	5.80
	Belgium	404	5.80
	Denmark	405	5.82
	Spain	406	5.83
	Finland	411	5.90
	France	402	5.77
	Holland	403	5.79
	Ireland	403	5.79
	Italy	402	5.80
	Norway	400	5.70
	Poland	402	5.80
	Portugal	459	6.59
	Russia	405	5.82
	Sweden	431	6.19
	Switzerland	400	5.74
	United Kingdom	405	5.82
Gender	Man	3453	49.58
	Woman	3508	50.40
Age	from 16 to 24	1368	19.60
	from 25 to 34	1395	20.03
	from 35 to 44	1375	19.70
	from 45 to 54	1406	20.19
	from 55 to 64	1023	14.70
	more than 64	396	5.69

Fuerteventura, (3) Lanzarote, (4) Tenerife, (5) La Gomera, (6) La Palma, and (7) El Hierro. The four larger islands (Tenerife, Gran Canaria, Lanzarote, and Fuerteventura) receive a greater flow of international tourists annually. This adds up to 93% of total tourists (see Table 3). For that reason, the present study focuses on the four larger islands.

A joint promotion of the islands under the umbrella brand "Canary Islands" is developed by the regional destination marketing organization (Promotur). Each island also develops promotional material as independent destinations. Thus, eight brands exist: one per island plus the regional umbrella brand (see Figure 2). Each brand attempts to communicate a distinct message through differing promotional claims. In addition, in many promotions, the Canary Islands are promoted under the brand Spain, as part of the country. Finally, in some products (cruises, nautical tourism, etc.) it is promoted in a network with other islands of the Macaronesian Archipelago, promoting itself as a tourist experience (Carballo et al., 2015).

Figure 1. Geographic location of Canary Islands

Table 3. Tourist arrivals (Canary Islands, 2015)

Islands	Tourists
Lanzarote	2.740.126
Fuerteventura	2.202.974
Gran Canaria	3.681.217
Tenerife	4.945.285
La Gomera	438.867
La Palma	377.183
El Hierro	29.906
Canary Islands	14.415.558

Source: Istac

MAIN RESULTS AND IMPLICATIONS

The main analysis related to loyalty and the relationship that tourists establish with the brands are developed in the next paragraphs. Table 4 shows that 17.82% of the tourist sample are loyal to the Canary Islands (1,241 tourists). This group has visited the Canary Islands destination at least twice. The horizontal loyalty tourists (14.3% or 996 tourists) have visited different island destinations under the Canary Islands umbrella brand. The horizontal loyalty tourists represent 80.25% of loyal tourists. Of these tourists, the following are loyal to specific islands: 6.7% to Gran Canaria; 5.9% to Tenerife; 2.7% to Lanzarote; 1.1% to Fuerteventura; 0.8% to La Palma; 0.3% to La Gomera; and 0.1% to El Hierro.

Focusing on the horizontal loyalty tourists, and with the aim of obtaining a greater understanding of this specific sample, Table 5 shows the number of horizontal loyalty tourists who have visited each of the Canary Islands. As shown in Table 4: 78.2% of horizontal loyalty tourists visited Tenerife; 75.2% visited Gran Canaria; 56.8% visited Lanzarote; and 32.5% visited Fuerteventura. The four most frequented

Figure 2. The Canary Islands brand architecture and promotional claims

Brand	Claim
Canary Islands	Latitude of life
Gran Canaria	Great Destination
Tenerife	100% Life
Lanzarote	Lanzarote, a unique island
Fuerteventura	The beach of Canary Islands
La Palma	The beautiful island
La Gomera	Nature and magic

Table 4. Horizontal loyal behavior

Island	Number of Tourists	Percentage
Loyal tourists to Canary Islands	1,241	17.82%
Loyal tourists to Tenerife	414	5.9%
Loyal tourists to Gran Canaria	467	6.7%
Loyal tourists to Lanzarote	185	2.7%
Loyal tourists to Fuerteventura	77	1.1%
Loyal tourists to La Palma	56	0.8%
Loyal tourists to La Gomera	19	0.3%
Loyal tourists to El Hierro	8	0.1%

Table 5. Islands visited by horizontal loyalty tourists

Island	Number of Tourists	Percentage
Tenerife	779	78.2
Gran Canaria	749	75.2
Lanzarote	566	56.8
Fuerteventura	324	32.5
La Palma	206	20.7
La Gomera	132	13.3
El Hierro	32	3.2

islands by horizontal loyalty tourists are the most visited islands within the umbrella brand. This result shows that a joint and horizontal promotion could attract visitors to the smaller islands. Additional research is required prior to making decisions surrounding marketing and design of the destination brand architecture. It is necessary to determine whether there are islands whose promotional strategies must link more closely to the other islands in order to increase visits to a specific island destination, as well as improve loyalty to the umbrella brand.

It is necessary to study tourist behavior patterns in order to improve the design of the destination brand architecture. For instance, 49.2% of horizontal loyalty tourists who visited Tenerife were traveling on their first visit to the Canary Islands. As shown in Table 6, a higher percentage of tourists visited the islands of Tenerife and Gran Canaria during their first visit to the Canary Islands. The islands of Lanzarote, Fuerteventura, La Palma, and La Gomera are usually chosen for a second visit. Additionally, the island of El Hierro is usually visited on the fifth trip to the destination.

Table 7 shows the number of islands visited by horizontal loyalty tourists. It is observed that: 50.9% of horizontal loyalty tourists visited two of the Canary Islands; 29.8% visited three; and 12.2% visited four. These results confirm the destination's need to manage and improve brand architecture related to horizontal loyalty tourists. It is necessary to know if there are islands whose promotion strategies must be more closely linked.

Table 8 illustrates the combination of islands visited by horizontal loyalty tourists. For example, 58.3% of horizontal loyalty tourists visited at least the islands of Gran Canaria and Tenerife; 42.5% visited

Table 6. The order in which horizontal loyalty tourists visited the Canary Islands

	TF	GC	LZ	FV	LP	LG	EH
First	49.2	49.9	22.4	16.0	23.8	7.6	3.1
Second	38.5	35.6	40.6	33.3	26.2	27.3	3.1
Third	9.8	11.6	29.9	23.1	19.9	26.5	18.8
Fourth	1.9	1.7	6.0	20.7	17.5	17.4	12.5
Fifth	0.5	0.7	0.7	4.6	10.7	8.3	28.1
Sixth	0.1	0.3	0	1.9	1.0	10.6	9.4
Seventh	0	0.1	0.4	0.3	1.0	2.3	25.0
Total	100	100	100	100	100	100	100

Table 7. Number of islands visited by horizontal loyalty tourists

N° of Islands Visited	Number of Tourists	Percentage
Two	507	50.9
Three	297	29.8
Four	122	12.2
Five	42	4.2
Six	11	1.1
Seven	17	1.7
Total	996	100

Table 8. Combination of islands (two-by-two) visited by horizontal loyalty tourists

	TF	GC	LZ	FV	LP	LG	EH
TF		58.3%	42.5%	21.7%	15.3%	12.1%	2.9%
GC	58.3%		40.0%	22.8%	15.7%	8.9%	2.5%
LZ	42.5%	40.0%		23.5%	9.7%	7.5%	2.4%
FV	21.7%	22.8%	23.5%		6.4%	5.0%	1.8%
LP	15.3%	59.5%	9.7%	6.4%		4.2%	2.6%
LG	12.1%	8.9%	7.5%	5.0%	4.2%		2.5%
EH	2.9%	2.5%	2.4%	1.8%	2.6%	2.5%	

Lanzarote and Tenerife; and 40% visited Gran Canaria and Lanzarote. The percentages highlight the need for a common brand strategy between those islands. This result reveals the existence of a relationship between the islands to consider in the marketing decision making and especially for the correct design of the destination's brand architecture, which requires more analysis in this regard.

With the aim of acquiring further knowledge related to the behavior of horizontal loyalty tourists, Table 9 shows their most common patterns (order and sequence) when visiting different islands (see the extended table 12 in Appendix 1). The most common patterns are visits to: Gran Canaria followed by Tenerife; Tenerife followed by Gran Canaria; and Tenerife followed by Lanzarote. However, a deeper analysis is required to determine whether the visit to one island influenced a visit to another island.

To achieve the goals, it was necessary to estimate four logit binomial models exploring the relationship between visits to different destinations. For example, the first model attempts to explain if the visit to Gran Canaria is influenced by a prior visit to another island. The same is explored in the case of Tenerife, Lanzarote, and Fuerteventura. In addition, the models included other sociodemographic variables to explain the visit to a destination. These include: gender, educational level, and income (see Table 10).

Table 11. summarizes the estimation results of the four proposed models. It is observed that a higher level of education shows that a tourist is less likely to visit Gran Canaria. Instead, this tourist is likely to visit Tenerife. In addition, there is a positive relationship between income level and visits to the islands of Gran Canaria, Tenerife, and Fuerteventura. An analysis of greater importance is the cooperation and/or competition relationship between different destinations. The above table shows the values of the coefficients of the variables so called of coopetition.

Table 9. Behavior patterns to visit the destination

	Number of Tourists	Percentage
GC TF	105	10.5
TF GC	88	8.8
TF LZ	56	5.6
GC TF LZ	37	3.7
GC LZ	35	3.5
TF GC LZ	30	3.0
LZ GC	25	2.5
TF FV	21	2.1
GC FV	20	2.0
LZ TF	20	2.0
TF LZ GC	20	2.0
LZ FV	19	1.9
GC LZ TF	18	1.8
GC TF LZ FV	17	1.7
LZ TF GC	17	1.7
FV LZ	16	1.6
LP GC	13	1.3
LP TF	13	1.3
GC LZ FV	12	1.2
TF GC LZ FV	12	1.2
FV GC	10	1.0
TF LZ FV	10	1.0
Otros	382	38.2
Total	996	100

Table 10. Variables included in the models

	Variables	Definition
Sociodemographic	Gender	Dichotomous variable
	Educational level	Number of years
	Incomes	Annual income in thousands of euros
Coopetition	Previous visit to Tenerife, Previous visit to Gran Canaria, Previous visit to Lanzarote, Previous visit to Fuerteventura, Previous visit to La Palma, Previous visit to La Gomera and Previous visit to El Hierro	Dichotomous variable
Endogenous	Visit to Tenerife, visit to Gran Canaria, visit to Lanzarote, visit to Fuerteventura	Dichotomous variable

Table 11. Logit binomial models

	Gran Canaria		Tenerife		Lanzarote		Fuerteventura	
	β	ε	β	ε	β	ε	β	ε
Gender	-	-	-	-	-	-	-	-
Education	-.043***	.013	.029**	.013	-	-	-	-
Incomes	.011***	.002	.005*	.002	-	-	.010***	.003
Visit TF	-.763***	.103	-	-	.294***	.111	-.260*	.134
Visit GC	-	-	-.764***	.103	-	-	-	-
Visit LZ	-	-	.289**	.112	-	-	1.255***	.130
Visit FV	-	-	-.274**	.135	1.256***	.130	-	-
Visit LP	-	-	-	-	-	-		-
Visit LG	.637**	.233	2.076***	.349	.737***	.229	.446*	.259
Visit EH	1.083**	.503	1.382*	.785	.961*	.497	1.098**	.454
Constant	.876***	.192	-.007	.195	-.980***	.210	-2.224***	.256
-2 Log likelihood	2271.4		2236.3		2061.0		1545.7	
n	2067		2067		2067		2067	

A strong inverse relationship was observed between visits to the islands of Gran Canaria and Tenerife. This means that the more times a tourist visited Tenerife, the less likely it would be that the tourist would visit Gran Canaria (and the same occurs the other way around). Moreover, it is important to highlight the strong direct relationship between visits to the islands of Lanzarote and Fuerteventura and between Tenerife and La Gomera. A higher number of visits to Lanzarote increases the probability to visit Fuerteventura (and vice versa). The same applies to the islands of Tenerife and La Gomera.

Models differentiated by country of origin were performed in an attempt to be more specific in the analysis of coopetition between different destinations depending on the specific target market under research (Figure 3). These results show that cultural background (nationality) must be analyzed in detail to understand the complementary relationship between destinations. It is important to highlight the strong direct relationship between visits to Tenerife and Gran Canaria in different markets. This means that those islands have a strong complementarity relationship. In the case of the UK, this complementary relationship was observed between Tenerife and Gran Canaria, Fuerteventura and Tenerife, Fuerteventura and Gran Canaria, Tenerife and Lanzarote, Gran Canaria and Lanzarote, Lanzarote and Fuerteventura, and Lanzarote and La Palma.

FUTURE RESEARCH DIRECTIONS

To better understand relationships between destinations, future studies on geographic distance must be considered. Short-haul vs. long-haul destinations may require a different focus. Connectivity (transportation) is crucial considering the different means of transportation, as well as its cost and comfort. Moreover, culture and country of origin must be considered. Future work should also replicate the study analyzing different market segments. It should study destinations and tourists from other geographic areas,

Cooperation and Competition Among Regions

Figure 3. Complementarity of the different islands of the Canary Islands by nationality

	TENERIFE	GRAN CANARIA	FUERTEVENTURA	LANZAROTE
TENERIFE		0.971, 1.251, 2.105, 2.328, 4.280, 21.203, 2.808, 2.178, 1.981, 2.224, 0.904, 1.403, 1.365, 1.504, 1.561	2.666, 1.517, 1.124	2.306, 2.754, 2.409, 1.019, 1.911, 1.299, 1.528, 3.140, 1.771, 2.761, 1.778, 1.135, 2.848, 1.379
GRAN CANARIA	2.150, 2.361, 2.082, 3.437, 2.189, 2.003, 1.322, 1.158, 0.914, 1.416, 1.419, 1.275, 1.802, 5.833		1.358, 1.393, 1.323, 1.147, 1.816, 1.090, 1.023	1.852, 2.072, 1.337, 0.939, 1.329, 0.967, 1.245, 1.057, 1.754
FUERTEVENTURA	2.542, 0.912, 3.612, 0.995, 1.421	1.041, 1.139, 0.918, 4.640, 2.734, 1.087, 1.533		4.108, 3.321, 2.062, 2.666, 1.986, 2.418, 2.649, 1.738, 2.689, 2.252, 2.995, 1.799
LANZAROTE	1.709, 2.449, 1.359, 1.563, 2.629, 1.969, 1.322, 1.911, 1.153, 1.549, 3.312, 2.113, 2.503, 2.070, 1.117	1.514, 2.132, 1.350, 1.452, 25.567, 1.229, 0.992, 2.417, 1.180	3.680, 2.274, 2.228, 2.785, 1.849, 2.588, 2.826, 2.218, 3.394, 2.120, 3.023, 1.976	
LA PALMA	2.542, 1.726, 2.542, 1.857	1.398, 2.238, 1.905, 3.113, 2.226, 1.348	1.677, 1.223	0.747, 2.122
LA GOMERA	2.802, 3.995	2.342, -1.365, 0.278		3.846, 2.763, 5.984
EL HIERRO				

as well as consider alternative demographic variables. Furthermore, it should consider the differences between loyal behavior toward the umbrella brand compared to attitudinal loyalty. Finally, development a longitudinal analysis could also be considered. In addition to a further in depth qualitative research to provide new insights to this topic.

SOLUTIONS AND RECOMMENDATIONS

This study contributes to destination marketing literature. Given the lack of current research, this study contributes to destination branding with an emphasis on brand architecture design and its influence on

328

the development of destination loyalty. Furthermore, these results are useful to continue work on the analysis of brand architecture and co-branded marketing between complementary destinations that may not be geographically close but are linked around experiential loyalty.

This methodology allows destinations to find out what are the other destinations to compete or cooperate with, depending on the final target market. Thus umbrella brands could develop a similar analysis in any region and make policies according to the results. Thus there is a possibility of generalization of the study. Destinations where there is a strong direct relationship between visits (e.g., Lanzarote and Fuerteventura in our study), requires a specific consideration within the umbrella brand. For instance, the physical location of the destinations (representatives and stands) within a tourism trade fair, the display and location of the destinations within the common communication content (web site, brochures, etc.). The same applies when destinations are competing, as they might need a major differentiation within the umbrella brand, developing a brand architecture with clear differentiated destinations sets. Subsequently, there is a need to enforce differentiation within destinations that are competing, and enhance bundling options when trading the brand among destinations that show complementarity.

CONCLUSION

In today's evolving world, global managers face serious geopolitical issues. Within the tourism industry, these challenges mean that brand architecture and country of origin are topics that need further analysis. Traditionally, destinations have designed their marketing strategies without considering other destinations to compete or cooperate with. They have not paid attention to the relationship of the tourist with multiple destinations at the same time. This study shows that cooperation between tourist destinations could be a strategy in which all destinations under the umbrella brand obtain benefits and improve performance. Thus, destination managers can get a better understanding related to destinations to compete or cooperate with.

REFERENCES

Aaker, D. A. (2004). Leveraging the corporate brand. *California Management Review*, 46(3), 6–18. doi:10.2307/41166218

Aaker, D. A., & Joachimsthaler, E. (2000). The brand relationship spectrum: The key to the brand architecture challenge. *California Management Review*, 42(4), 8–23. doi:10.2307/41166051

Alegre, J., & Juaneda, C. (2006). Destination loyalty: Consumers economic behavior. *Annals of Tourism Research*, 33(3), 684–706. doi:10.1016/j.annals.2006.03.014

Baloglu, S. (2002). Dimensions of customer loyalty: Separating friends from well wishers. *The Cornell Hotel and Restaurant Administration Quarterly*, 43(1), 47–59. doi:10.1016/S0010-8804(02)80008-8

Beritelli, P. (2011). Cooperation among prominent actors in a tourist destination. *Annals of Tourism Research*, 38(2), 607–629. doi:10.1016/j.annals.2010.11.015

Bianchi, C., & Pike, S. (2011). Antecedents of destination brand loyalty for a long-haul market: Australias destination loyalty among chilean travelers. *Journal of Travel & Tourism Marketing, 28*(7), 736–750. do i:10.1080/10548408.2011.611742

Blain, C., Levy, S. E., & Ritchie, J. B. (2005). Destination branding: Insights and practices from destination management organizations. *Journal of Travel Research, 43*(4), 328–338. doi:10.1177/0047287505274646

Bowen, J. T., & Shoemaker, S. (1998). Loyalty: A strategic commitment. *The Cornell Hotel and Restaurant Administration Quarterly, 39*(1), 12–25. doi:10.1177/001088049803900104

Campo, S., & Yagüe, M. J. (2007). The formation of the tourists loyalty to the tourism distribution channel: How does it affect price discounts? *International Journal of Tourism Research, 9*(6), 453–464. doi:10.1002/jtr.617

Carballo, M., Araña, J., León, C., González, M., & Moreno, S. (2011). «Valoración Económica de la Imagen de un Destino», *Pasos. Revista de Turismo y Patrimonio Cultural, 9*(1), 1–14.

Carballo, M. M., Araña, J. E., León, C. J., & Moreno-Gil, S. (2015). Economic valuation of tourism destination image. *Tourism Economics, 21*(4), 741–759. doi:10.5367/te.2014.0381

Cunningham, R. M. (1956). Brand loyalty-what, where, how much. *Harvard Business Review, 34*(1), 116–128.

d'Hauteserre, A. M., & Funck, C. (2016). Innovation in island ecotourism in different contexts: Yakushima (Japan) and Tahiti and its Islands. *Island Studies Journal, 11*(1), 227–244.

Darnell, A. C., & Johnson, P. S. (2001). Repeat visits to attractions: A preliminary economic analysis. *Tourism Management, 22*(2), 119–126. doi:10.1016/S0261-5177(00)00036-4

Datzira-Masip, J., & Poluzzi, A. (2014). Brand architecture management: The case of four tourist destinations in Catalonia. *Journal of Destination Marketing & Management, 3*(1), 48–58. doi:10.1016/j.jdmm.2013.12.006

Dawes, J. (2014). Cigarette brand loyalty and purchase patterns: An examination using US consumer panel data. *Journal of Business Research, 67*(9), 1933–1943. doi:10.1016/j.jbusres.2013.11.014

Dawes, J., Romaniuk, J., & Mansfield, A. (2009). Generalized pattern in competition among tourism destinations. *International Journal of Culture. Tourism and Hospitality Research, 3*(1), 33–53. doi:10.1108/17506180910940333

Dooley, G., & Bowie, D. (2005). Place brand architecture: Strategic management of the brand portfolio. *Place Branding and Public Diplomacy, 1*(4), 402–419. doi:10.1057/palgrave.pb.5990037

Dowling, G., & Uncles, M. (1997). Do customer loyalty programs really work? *Sloan Management Review, 38*(4), 71–71.

Enright, M. J., & Newton, J. (2004). Tourism destination competitiveness: A quantitative approach. *Tourism Management, 25*(6), 777–788. doi:10.1016/j.tourman.2004.06.008

Felix, R. (2014). Multi-brand loyalty: When one brand is not enough. *Qualitative Market Research: An International Journal, 17*(4), 464–480. doi:10.1108/QMR-11-2012-0053

Fyall, A., & Garrod, B. (2005). *Tourism marketing: A collaborative approach* (Vol. 18). Channel View Publications.

Fyall, A., Garrod, B., & Wang, Y. (2012). Destination collaboration: A critical review of theoretical approaches to a multi-dimensional phenomenon. *Journal of Destination Marketing & Management*, *1*(1), 10–26. doi:10.1016/j.jdmm.2012.10.002

García-Rodríguez, J. L., García-Rodríguez, F. J., & Castilla-Gutiérrez, C. (2016). Human heritage and sustainable development on arid islands: The case of the Eastern Canary Islands. *Island Studies Journal*, *11*(1), 113–130.

Gil, S. M. (2003). Tourism development in the Canary Islands. *Annals of Tourism Research*, *30*(3), 744–747. doi:10.1016/S0160-7383(03)00050-1

Harish, R. (2010). Brand architecture in tourism branding: The way forward for India. *Journal of Indian Business Research*, *2*(3), 153–165. doi:10.1108/17554191011069442

Iversen, N. M., & Hem, L. E. (2008). Provenance associations as core values of place umbrella brands: A framework of characteristics. *European Journal of Marketing*, *42*(5/6), 603–626. doi:10.1108/03090560810862534

Jackson, J., & Murphy, P. (2006). Clusters in regional tourism An Australian case. *Annals of Tourism Research*, *33*(4), 1018–1035. doi:10.1016/j.annals.2006.04.005

Jacoby, J., & Kyner, D. B. (1973). Brand loyalty vs. repeat purchasing behavior. *JMR, Journal of Marketing Research*, *10*(1), 1–9. doi:10.2307/3149402

Jang, S. S., & Feng, R. (2007). Temporal destination revisit intention: The effects of novelty seeking and satisfaction. *Tourism Management*, *28*(2), 580–590. doi:10.1016/j.tourman.2006.04.024

Jorde, T. M., & Teece, D. J. (1990). Innovation and cooperation: Implications for competition and antitrust. *The Journal of Economic Perspectives*, *4*(3), 75–96. doi:10.1257/jep.4.3.75

Keller, K. L. (2003). Understanding brands, branding and brand equity. *Interactive Marketing*, *5*(1), 7–20. doi:10.1057/palgrave.im.4340213

Kylänen, M., & Rusko, R. (2011). Unintentional coopetition in the service industries: The case of pyhä-luosto tourism destination in the finish Lapland. *European Management Journal*, *29*(3), 193–205. doi:10.1016/j.emj.2010.10.006

Laforet, S., & Saunders, J. (1994). Managing brand portfolios: How the leaders do it. *Journal of Advertising Research*, *34*(5), 64–77.

Luo, Y. (2007). A coopetition perspective of global competition. *Journal of World Business*, *42*(2), 129–144. doi:10.1016/j.jwb.2006.08.007

Mariani, M. M., & Baggio, R. (2012). Special issue: Managing tourism in a changing world: Issues and cases. *Anatolia*, *23*(1), 1–3. doi:10.1080/13032917.2011.653636

Mariani, M. M., Buhalis, D., Longhi, C., & Vitouladiti, O. (2014). Managing change in tourism destinations: Key issues and current trends. *Journal of Destination Marketing & Management, 2*(4), 269–272. doi:10.1016/j.jdmm.2013.11.003

McKercher, B., Denizci-Guillet, B., & Ng, E. (2012). Rethinking loyalty. *Annals of Tourism Research, 39*(2), 708–734. doi:10.1016/j.annals.2011.08.005

McMullan, R., & Gilmore, A. (2008). Customer loyalty: An empirical study. *European Journal of Marketing, 42*(9/10), 1084–1094. doi:10.1108/03090560810891154

Moore, S. A., Rodger, K., & Taplin, R. (2015). Moving beyond visitor satisfaction to loyalty in nature-based tourism: A review and research agenda. *Current Issues in Tourism, 18*(7), 667–683. doi:10.1080/13683500.2013.790346

Olson, J. C., & Jacoby, J. (1974). Measuring multi-brand loyalty. *Advances in Consumer Research. Association for Consumer Research (U. S.), 1*(1), 447–448.

Quoquab, F., Mohd. Yasin, N., & Abu Dardak, R. (2014). A qualitative inquiry of multi-brand loyalty: Some propositions and implications for mobile phone service providers. *Asia Pacific Journal of Marketing and Logistics, 26*(2), 250–271. doi:10.1108/APJML-02-2013-0023

Schuiling, I., & Kapferer, J. N. (2004). Executive insights: real differences between local and international brands: strategic implications for international marketers. *Journal of International Marketing, 12*(4), 97–112. doi:10.1509/jimk.12.4.97.53217

Sharp, B., & Sharp, A. (1997). Loyalty programs and their impact on repeat-purchase loyalty patterns. *International Journal of Research in Marketing, 14*(5), 473–486. doi:10.1016/S0167-8116(97)00022-0

Shih, H. Y. (2006). Network characteristics of drive tourism destinations: An application of network analysis in tourism. *Tourism Management, 27*(5), 1029–1039. doi:10.1016/j.tourman.2005.08.002

Sivadas, E., & Baker-Prewitt, J. L. (2000). An examination of the relationship between service quality, customer satisfaction, and store loyalty. *International Journal of Retail & Distribution Management, 28*(2), 73–82. doi:10.1108/09590550010315223

UNWTO. (2015). *Tourism Highlights.* Retrieved from http://www.eunwto.org.bibproxy.ulpgc.es/doi/book/10.18111/9789284416899

Weaver, D. B., & Lawton, L. J. (2011). Visitor loyalty at a private South Carolina protected area. *Journal of Travel Research, 50*(3), 335–346. doi:10.1177/0047287510362920

World Tourism Organization (2014). *Panorama OMT del turismo internacional.* Author.

World Travel & Tourism Council. (2015). *Economic Impact Analysis.* Retrieved from http://www.wttc.org/research/economic-research/economic-impact-analysis/

Yim, C. K., & Kannan, P. (1999). Consumer behavioral loyalty. *Journal of Business Research, 44*(2), 75–92. doi:10.1016/S0148-2963(97)00243-9

ADDITIONAL READING

Baldacchino, G. (2016). *Archipelago tourism: policies and practices*. Routledge.

KEY TERMS AND DEFINITIONS

Destination Branding: Activities aimed at identifying and differentiating a tourist destinations.

Brand Architecture: A valuable relationship between structuration and organization of portfolio of brands.

Competitiveness: A destination's ability to attract potential tourists to their region, as well as meet their needs and desires.

Consumer Loyalty: A commitment to rebuy or repatronize a preferred product or service despite situational influences and marketing efforts to switch behavior.

Coopetition: The simultaneous cooperation and competition between companies.

Horizontal Loyalty: Loyalty to different providers at the same level within the tourism system.

Umbrella Brand: The use of a single brand name for the marketing of two or more related regions.

APPENDIX

Table 12. Behavior patterns to visit the destination (completed table)

	Number of Tourists	Percentage
GC TF	105	10.5
TF GC	88	8.8
TF LZ	56	5.6
GC TF LZ	37	3.7
GC LZ	35	3.5
TF GC LZ	30	3
LZ GC	25	2.5
TF FV	21	2.1
GC FV	20	2
LZ TF	20	2
TF LZ GC	20	2
GC LP	19	1.9
LZ FV	19	1.9
GC LZ TF	18	1.8
GC TF LZ FV	17	1.7
LZ TF GC	17	1.7
FV LZ	16	1.6
TF LG	16	1.6
GC TF LG	13	1.3
LP GC	13	1.3
LP TF	13	1.3
GC LZ FV	12	1.2
TF GC LZ FV	12	1.2
TF LP	11	1.1
FV GC	10	1
GC TF LP	10	1
TF GC LP	10	1
TF LZ FV	10	1
LZ GC TF	9	0.9
GC LZ TF FV	7	0.7
GC TF FV	7	0.7
LP GC TF	7	0.7
TF GC FV	7	0.7
TF LZ GC FV	7	0.7

continued in next column

Table 12. Continued

	Number of Tourists	Percentage
GC FV LZ	6	0.6
GC TF LZ LP	6	0.6
LZ TF FV	6	0.6
FV LZ GC	5	0.5
TF FV GC	5	0.5
GC LP TF	4	0.4
GC TF FV LZ	4	0.4
GC TF LZ LG	4	0.4
LG TF	4	0.4
TF FV LZ	4	0.4
TF GC LZ FV LP	4	0.4
TF GC LZ LP	4	0.4
TF LG GC	4	0.4
FV TF	3	0.3
GC FV TF	3	0.3
GC LZ FV TF	3	0.3
LP GC LZ	3	0.3
LZ FV GC	3	0.3
TF GC FV LZ	3	0.3
TF GC LG	3	0.3
TF GC LZ LG FV	3	0.3
TF LZ FV GC	3	0.3
TF LZ LG	3	0.3
FV LP	2	0.2
FV LZ TF	2	0.2
FV TF LZ	2	0.2
GC FV LP	2	0.2
GC FV LP LZ	2	0.2
GC FV LZ TF	2	0.2
GC LG	2	0.2
GC TF LG LP	2	0.2
GC TF LG LZ	2	0.2
GC TF LZ FV LP LG	2	0.2
LG LZ	2	0.2
LP LZ	2	0.2
LP TF LZ	2	0.2

continued on next page

Table 12. Continued

Table 12. Continued

	Number of Tourists	Percentage
LZ FV TF	2	0.2
LZ TF GC FV	2	0.2
TF FV GC LZ	2	0.2
TF FV LZ GC	2	0.2
TF GC LG LP	2	0.2
TF GC LZ FV LG	2	0.2
TF GC LZ FV LP LG	2	0.2
TF LG LP LZ	2	0.2
TF LG LZ	2	0.2
TF LP GC	2	0.2
TF LP LZ	2	0.2
TF LP LZ GC FV	2	0.2
TF LZ FV GC LP	2	0.2
TF LZ GC LG FV	2	0.2
TF LZ GC LP	2	0.2
TF LZ LP	2	0.2
EH LP	1	0.1
FV GC LZ	1	0.1
FV GC TF	1	0.1
FV GC TF LZ	1	0.1
FV LP TF	1	0.1
FV LZ GC LP	1	0.1
FV LZ GC TF	1	0.1
FV LZ LG	1	0.1
FV LZ TF GC	1	0.1
FV LZ TF GC LP	1	0.1
FV LZ TF LG	1	0.1
FV TF GC	1	0.1
FV TF LG	1	0.1
GC FV LG LZ TF	1	0.1
GC FV LZ LG TF	1	0.1
GC FV TF LZ	1	0.1
GC LG TF	1	0.1
GC LG TF FV LP	1	0.1
GC LP FV	1	0.1
GC LP FV TF LZ	1	0.1
GC LP LZ TF	1	0.1

continued in next column

	Number of Tourists	Percentage
GC LP TF LZ FV LG	1	0.1
GC LZ EH TF	1	0.1
GC LZ FV LP	1	0.1
GC LZ FV LP TF	1	0.1
GC LZ LP TF LG FV	1	0.1
GC LZ TF LG FV	1	0.1
GC LZ TF LP	1	0.1
GC LZ TF LP EH	1	0.1
GC TF FV LP	1	0.1
GC TF FV LZ LG	1	0.1
GC TF FV LZ LP	1	0.1
GC TF LP FV LZ	1	0.1
GC TF LP LG EH FV LZ	1	0.1
GC TF LP LZ	1	0.1
GC TF LP LZ LG EH	1	0.1
GC TF LZ FV LG	1	0.1
GC TF LZ LG EH	1	0.1
GC TF LZ LG FV	1	0.1
GC TF LZ LP FV	1	0.1
GC TF LZ LP FV EH LG	1	0.1
GC TF LZ LP LG FV	1	0.1
LG EH	1	0.1
LG GC	1	0.1
LG GC FV	1	0.1
LG TF LP	1	0.1
LP FV	1	0.1
LP FV LZ	1	0.1
LP GC LZ TF	1	0.1
LP GC TF FV EH	1	0.1
LP LG LZ EH	1	0.1
LP LZ GC	1	0.1
LP LZ TF	1	0.1
LP TF EH	1	0.1
LP TF LG	1	0.1
LZ FV GC LP LG TF	1	0.1
LZ FV GC LP TF	1	0.1

continued on next page

Table 12. Continued

	Number of Tourists	Percentage
LZ FV LG GC	1	0.1
LZ FV LP	1	0.1
LZ FV TF GC	1	0.1
LZ FV TF LG	1	0.1
LZ FV TF LG LP GC	1	0.1
LZ GC FV LP	1	0.1
LZ GC FV TF	1	0.1
LZ GC LG TF	1	0.1
LZ GC LP TF FV	1	0.1
LZ GC TF FV	1	0.1
LZ GC TF FV EH LG LP	1	0.1
LZ GC TF LG	1	0.1
LZ GC TF LP	1	0.1
LZ LG	1	0.1
LZ LG TF	1	0.1
LZ LP GC	1	0.1
LZ LP GC TF	1	0.1
LZ LP TF	1	0.1
LZ TF EH LG LP FV GC	1	0.1
LZ TF FV LP	1	0.1
LZ TF LG	1	0.1
LZ TF LG FV	1	0.1
TF FV GC LG	1	0.1
TF FV GC LZ LP LG EH	1	0.1
TF FV LZ LG GC LP EH	1	0.1
TF GC EH	1	0.1
TF GC FV LP LZ	1	0.1
TF GC FV LZ EH LG LP	1	0.1

continued in next column

Table 12. Continued

	Number of Tourists	Percentage
TF GC FV LZ EH LP LG	1	0.1
TF GC FV LZ LG	1	0.1
TF GC FV LZ LP	1	0.1
TF GC FV LZ LP LG	1	0.1
TF GC FV LZ LP LG EH	1	0.1
TF GC LP FV LZ	1	0.1
TF GC LP LZ	1	0.1
TF GC LZ FV LP LG EH	1	0.1
TF GC LZ LG	1	0.1
TF GC LZ LP FV EH LG	1	0.1
TF GC LZ LP FV LG EH	1	0.1
TF GC LZ LP LG FV EH	1	0.1
TF LG EH	1	0.1
TF LG EH LP GC FV LZ	1	0.1
TF LG GC LZ	1	0.1
TF LG GC LZ FV	1	0.1
TF LG LP EH	1	0.1
TF LG LZ LP GC	1	0.1
TF LP GC EH	1	0.1
TF LP LG LZ GC	1	0.1
TF LP LZ EH LG	1	0.1
TF LZ FV LP GC	1	0.1
TF LZ GC FV LP	1	0.1
TF LZ GC FV LP LG	1	0.1
TF LZ GC FV LP LG EH	1	0.1
TF LZ LP LG EH GC	1	0.1
Total	996	100

Compilation of References

(1988). Critical success factors in effective project implementation. InCleland, D. I., & King, W. R. (Eds.), *Project management handbook* (2nd ed., pp. 479–512). New York: Van Nostrand Reinhold.

Aaker, D. A. (2004). Leveraging the corporate brand. *California Management Review, 46*(3), 6–18. doi:10.2307/41166218

Aaker, D. A., & Joachimsthaler, E. (2000). The brand relationship spectrum: The key to the brand architecture challenge. *California Management Review, 42*(4), 8–23. doi:10.2307/41166051

Abratt, R., Nel, D., & Higgs, N. S. (1992). An examination of the ethical beliefs of managers using selected scenarios in a cross-cultural environment. *Journal of Business Ethics, 11*(1), 29–35. doi:10.1007/BF00871989

Acar Balaylar, N. (2011). Reel Döviz Kuru Istihdam Iliskisi: Türkiye Imalat Sanayi Örnegi. *Sosyoekonomi,* (2), 137-160.

Acs, Z. J., Audretsch, D. B., Braunerhjelm, P., & Carlsson, B. (2004). *The missing link: The knowledge filter, entrepreneurship and endogenous growth.* Discussion Paper, No. 4783, December. London, UK: Center for Economic Policy Research.

Acs, Z. J., & Amoros, J. E. (2008). Entrepreneurship and competitiveness dynamics in Latin America. *Small Business Economics, 31*(3), 305–322. doi:10.1007/s11187-008-9133-y

Acs, Z., & Szerb, L. (2007). Entrepreneurship, economic growth and public policy. *Small Business Economics, 28*(2/3), 109–122. doi:10.1007/s11187-006-9012-3

Adger, W. N. (2000). Social and ecological resilience: Are they related? *Progress in Human Geography, 24*(3), 347–364. doi:10.1191/030913200701540465

Adler, N. J., & Gundersen, A. (2008). *International dimensions of organizational behavior* (5th ed.). Mason, OH: Thomson Higher Education.

Adler, P. S., & Cole, R. E. (1995). Designed for learning: A tale of two auto plants. In I. McLoughlin, D. Preece, & P. Dawson (Eds.), *Technology, organizations and innovation: Critical perspectives in business and management* (pp. 1230–1245). London: Routledge.

Affairs, F., & the Trade and Development Canada. (2017). *Canada-United States Free Trade Agreement (FTA).* Retrieved February, 13, 2017, from http://www.international.gc.ca/trade-agreements-accords-commerciaux/agr-acc/us-eu.aspx?lang=eng

Ahlstrom, D., & Bruton, G. (2002). An institutional perspective on the role of culture in shaping strategic actions by technology-focused entrepreneurial firms in China. *Entrepreneurship Theory and Practice, 26*(4), 53–70.

Aidis, R. (2005). Institutional Barriers to Small- and Medium-Sized Enterprise Operations in Transition Countries. *Small Business Economics, 25*(4), 305–318. doi:10.1007/s11187-003-6463-7

Aidis, R., Estrin, S., & Mickiewicz, T. (2008). Institutions and entrepreneurship development in Russia: A comparative perspective. *Journal of Business Venturing*, *23*(6), 656–672. doi:10.1016/j.jbusvent.2008.01.005

Aidis, R., & van Praag, M. (2007). Illegal entrepreneurship experience: Does it make a difference for business performance and motivation? *Journal of Business Venturing*, *22*(2), 283–310. doi:10.1016/j.jbusvent.2006.02.002

Akmaliah, P. P., Afsaneh, B., & Soaib, A. (2014). School Leadership and Innovative Principals: Implications for Enhancing Principals' Leadership Knowledge and Practice. *Proceedings of the European Conference on Management, Leadership & Governance*, 162-167.

Alas, R., Gao, J., & Carneiro, J. (2015). Connections between ethics and cultural dimensions. *Engineering Economics*, *21*(3).

Alderson, A., & Nielsen, F. (2002). Globalization and the great u-turn: Income inequality trends in 16 oecd countries. *American Journal of Sociology*, *107*(5), 1244–1299. doi:10.1086/341329

Aldrich, H. E., & Fiol, C. M. (1994). Fools rush in? The institutional context of new industry creation. *Academy of Management Review*, *19*, 645–670.

Alegre, J., & Juaneda, C. (2006). Destination loyalty: Consumers economic behavior. *Annals of Tourism Research*, *33*(3), 684–706. doi:10.1016/j.annals.2006.03.014

Alesina, A., & Perotti, R. (1996). Income distribution, political instability, and investment. *European Economic Review*, *40*(6), 1203–1228. doi:10.1016/0014-2921(95)00030-5

Alesina, A., & Rodrik, D. (1994). Distributive politics and economic-growth. *The Quarterly Journal of Economics*, *109*(2), 465–490. doi:10.2307/2118470

Alesi, P. (2008). Building enterprise-wide resilience by integrating business continuity capability into day-to-day business culture and technology. *Journal of Business Continuity & Emergency Planning*, *2*(3), 214–220. PMID:21339108

Allen, R. E. (1991). *The concise Oxford dictionary of current English* (8th ed.). New York, NY: Oxford University Press.

Alphabetti spaghetti: Are regional trade agreements a good idea? (1998). *The Economist*. Retrieved February, 12, 2017, from http://www.economist.com/node/605199

Altheide, D. L. (1994). An ecology of communication: Toward a mapping of the effective environment. *The Sociological Quarterly*, *35*(4), 665–683. doi:10.1111/j.1533-8525.1994.tb00422.x

Altıntaş, H. (2013). Türkiye'de petrol fiyatları, ihracat ve reel döviz kuru ilişkisi: ARDL sınır testi yaklaşımı ve dinamik nedensellik analizi. *Uluslararası Yönetim İktisat ve İşletme Dergisi*, *9*(19), 1–30.

Altuna, N., Contri, A. M., DellEra, C., Frattini, F., & Maccarrone, P. (2015). Managing social innovation in for-profit organizations: The case of Intesa Sanpaolo. *European Journal of Innovation Management*, *18*(2), 258–280. doi:10.1108/EJIM-06-2014-0058

Alvaredo, F., Atkinson, A. B., Piketty, T., & Saez, E. (2013). The top 1 percent in international and historical perspective. *The Journal of Economic Perspectives*, *27*(3), 3–20. doi:10.1257/jep.27.3.3

Alvord, S. H., Brown, D. L., & Letts, C. W. (2004). Social entrepreneurship and social transformation: An exploratory study. *The Journal of Applied Behavioral Science*, *40*(3), 260–283. doi:10.1177/0021886304266847

Alwitt, L. F. (1995). Marketing and the poor. *The American Behavioral Scientist*, *38*(4), 564–577. doi:10.1177/0002764295038004007

Amit, R., & Zott, C. (2001). Value creation in e-business. *Strategic Management Journal, 22*(6-7), 493–520. doi:10.1002/smj.187

Anderson, B., & Fagenhaug, T. (2000). *RCA: Simplified tool and techniques.* Milwaukee, WI: ASQ Quality Press.

Anderson, E., & Gatignon, H. (1986). Modes of foreign entry: A transaction cost analysis and propositions. *Journal of International Business Studies, 17*(3), 1–26. doi:10.1057/palgrave.jibs.8490432

Anderson, T. (2008). Teaching in an online learning context. In T. Anderson (Ed.), *Theory and practice of online learning* (2nd ed.; pp. 343–365). Edmonton, AB: AU Press.

Andrade, J. (2004). Brazil's Piracy, a Cultural Challenge. *Brazzil.* Retrieved from http://www.brazzil.com/2004/html/articles/aug04/p141aug04.htm

Andreano, K. (2008). Knowledge Management 2.0? The Relationship between Web 2.0 Technologies and KM Theory. In *Knowledge about knowledge: Knowledge Management in Organizations* (pp. 15-22). Rutgers University. Retrieved May 6, 2016, from http://eclipse.rutgers.edu/wp-content/uploads/sites/30/2014/04/Knowledge.pdf#page=17

Andrés, A. R. (2006). Software piracy and income inequality. *Applied Economics Letters, 13*(2), 101–105. doi:10.1080/13504850500390374

Andrews, R. N. (2012). History of environmental leadership. In D. R. Gallagher (Ed.), *Environmental leadership: A reference handbook* (Vol. 1, pp. 17–28). Los Angeles, CA: SAGE Publications. doi:10.4135/9781452218601.n3

Ansoff, H. I. (1991). Critique of Henry Mintzbergs. The design school: Reconsidering the basic premises of strategic management. *Strategic Management Journal, 12*(6), 449–462. doi:10.1002/smj.4250120605

Arasa, R., & K'obonyo, P. (2012). The relationship between strategic planning and firm performance. *International Journal of Humanities and Social Science, 2*(22), 201–213.

Archibald, R. D. (2004). *Project Management: la gestione di progetti e programmi complessi.* Milano, Italy: Franco Angeli.

Ardichvili, A., Cardozo, R., & Ray, S. (2003). A theory of entrepreneurial opportunity identification and development. *Journal of Business Venturing, 18*(1), 105–123. doi:10.1016/S0883-9026(01)00068-4

Arenius, P., & Minniti, M. (2005). Perceptual Variables and Nascent Entrepreneurship. *Small Business Economics, 24*(3), 233–247. doi:10.1007/s11187-005-1984-x

Armstrong, R. W., Stening, B. W., Ryans, J. K., Marks, L., & Mayo, M. (1990). International Marketing Ethics: Problems Encountered by Australian Firms. *Asia Pacific Journal of International Marketing, 2*(2), 6–15.

Arslan, M. (2001). The work ethic values of protestant British, Catholic Irish and Muslim Turkish managers. *Journal of Business Ethics, 31*(4), 321–339. doi:10.1023/A:1010787528465

Atkinson, A. B. (1975). *The Economics of Inequality.* Oxford, UK: Clarendon Press.

Audretsch, D., Keilbach, M., & Lehman, E. (2006). *Entrepreneurship and economic growth.* Oxford, UK: Oxford University Press. doi:10.1093/acprof:oso/9780195183511.001.0001

Austin, J., Stevenson, H., & Wei-Skillern, J. (2006). Social and commercial entrepreneurship: Same, different, or both? *Entrepreneurship Theory and Practice, 30*(1), 1–22. doi:10.1111/j.1540-6520.2006.00107.x

Autio, E., Sapienza, H. J., & Almeida, J. G. (2000). Effects of age at entry, knowledge intensity, and imitability on international growth. *Academy of Management Journal, 43*(5), 909–924. doi:10.2307/1556419

Averch, H., & Johnson, L. (1962). Behavior of the Firm Under Regulatory Constraint. *The American Economic Review*, *52*(5), 1052–1069.

Baccarini, D. (1996). The concept of project complexity – a review. *International Journal of Project Management*, *14*(4), 201–204. doi:10.1016/0263-7863(95)00093-3

Bacchetta, P., & Van Wincoop, E. (2000). Does exchange-rate stability increase trade and welfare? *The American Economic Review*, *90*(5), 1093–1109. doi:10.1257/aer.90.5.1093

Bagwell, K., & Staiger, R. W. (1998). Will Preferential Agreements Undermine the Multilateral Trading System. *The Economic Journal*, *108*(July), 1162–1182. doi:10.1111/1468-0297.00336

Baier, S. L., & Bergstrand, J. H. (2007). Do Free Trade Agreements Actually Increase Members International Trade? *Journal of International Economics*, *71*(1), 72–95. doi:10.1016/j.jinteco.2006.02.005

Baldwin, R. (1993). *A Domino Theory of Regionalism*. National Bureau of Economic Research Working Paper Series, 4665. Retrieved September, 9, 2013 from http://www.nber.org/papers/w4465.pdf

Baloglu, S. (2002). Dimensions of customer loyalty: Separating friends from well wishers. *The Cornell Hotel and Restaurant Administration Quarterly*, *43*(1), 47–59. doi:10.1016/S0010-8804(02)80008-8

Banca Prossima. (2017). *Information about Banca Prossima*. Retrieved January 13, 2017, from www.bancaprossima.it

Bandura, A. (1997). *Self-efficacy: The Exercise of Control*. New York: WH Freeman.

Baporikar, N. (2013). CSF Approach for IT Strategic Planning. *International Journal of Strategic Information Technology and Applications*, *4*(2), 35–47. doi:10.4018/jsita.2013040103

Baporikar, N. (2014a). Effective E-Learning Strategies for a Borderless World. In J. Pelet (Ed.), *E-Learning 2.0 Technologies and Web Applications in Higher Education* (pp. 22–44). Hershey, PA: Information Science Reference. doi:10.4018/978-1-4666-4876-0.ch002

Baporikar, N. (2014b). Information Strategy as Enabler of Competitive Advantage. *International Journal of Strategic Information Technology and Applications*, *5*(1), 30–41. doi:10.4018/ijsita.2014010103

Baporikar, N. (2014c). Organizational Barriers and Facilitators in Embedding Knowledge Strategy. In M. Chilton & J. Bloodgood (Eds.), *Knowledge Management and Competitive Advantage: Issues and Potential Solutions* (pp. 149–173). Hershey, PA: Information Science Reference. doi:10.4018/978-1-4666-4679-7.ch009

Baporikar, N. (2014d). Innovation in the 21st Century Organization. In B. Christiansen, S. Yildiz, & E. Yildiz (Eds.), *Transcultural Marketing for Incremental and Radical Innovation* (pp. 339–365). Hershey, PA. doi:10.4018/978-1-4666-4749-7.ch016

Baporikar, N. (2015). *Innovation Knowledge Management Nexus. Innovation Management* (pp. 85–110). Berlin: De Gruyter.

Baporikar, N. (2016a). Talent Management Integrated Approach for Organizational Development. In A. Casademunt (Ed.), *Strategic Labor Relations Management in Modern Organizations* (pp. 22–48). Hershey, PA: Business Science Reference. doi:10.4018/978-1-5225-0356-9.ch002

Baporikar, N. (2016b). Strategies for Enhancing the Competitiveness of MNEs. In M. Khan (Ed.), *Multinational Enterprise Management Strategies in Developing Countries* (pp. 50–71). Hershey, PA: Business Science Reference. doi:10.4018/978-1-5225-0276-0.ch003

Baporikar, N. (2017a). Corporate Leadership and Sustainability. In Z. Fields (Ed.), *Collective Creativity for Responsible and Sustainable Business Practice* (pp. 160–179). Hershey, PA: IGI Global; doi:10.4018/978-1-5225-1823-5.ch009

Baporikar, N. (2017b). Imperatives in Leading Institutions of Higher Learning: Focus B-School. *International Journal of Technology and Educational Marketing, 7*(1), 38–51. doi:10.4018/IJTEM.2017010104

Barkema, H., Bell, J. H. J., & Pennings, J. M. (1996). Foreign entry, cultural barriers, and learning. *Strategic Management Journal, 17*(2), 151–166. doi:10.1002/(SICI)1097-0266(199602)17:2<151::AID-SMJ799>3.0.CO;2-Z

Barkema, H., & Drogendijk, R. (2007). Internationalising in small, incremental or larger steps? *Journal of International Business Studies, 38*(7), 1132–1148. doi:10.1057/palgrave.jibs.8400315

Baron, R. (2000). Psychological Perspectives on Entrepreneurship: Cognitive and Social Factors in Entrepreneurs Success. *Current Directions in Psychological Science, 9*(1), 15–19. doi:10.1111/1467-8721.00050

Barros, R., Mendonca, R., & Velazco, T. (1994). Is poverty the main cause for child work in Brazil? Rio de Janeiro: Ipea.

Barry, D., & Elmes, M. (1997). Strategy retold Toward a narrative view of strategic discourse. *Academy of Management Review, 22*(2), 429–452.

Bass, B. M., & Steidlmeier, P. (1999). Ethics, character, and authentic transformational leadership behavior. *The Leadership Quarterly, 10*(2), 181–217. doi:10.1016/S1048-9843(99)00016-8

Bassi, A. (Ed.). (2007). *Gestire l'innovazione nelle PMI. Il project management come competenza manageriale.* Milano, Italy: Franco Angeli.

Basu, P., & Guariglia, A. (2007). Foreign direct investment, inequality, and growth. *Journal of Macroeconomics, 29*(4), 824–839. doi:10.1016/j.jmacro.2006.02.004

Baumol, W. J. (1990). Entrepreneurship: Productive, unproductive, and destructive. *Journal of Political Economy, 98*(5), 893–921. doi:10.1086/261712

Beauchamp, T. L., & Bowie, N. E. (2001). *Ethical Theory and Business.* Upper Saddle River, NJ: Prentice-Hall.

Beaverstock, J. V., Smith, R. G., & Taylor, P. J. (1999). A roster of world cities. *Cities (London, England), 16*(6), 445–458. doi:10.1016/S0264-2751(99)00042-6

Begley, T., & Boyd, D. (1987). Psychological Characteristics Associated with Performance in Entrepreneurial Firms and Small Businesses. *Journal of Business Venturing, 2*(1), 79–93. doi:10.1016/0883-9026(87)90020-6

Belderbos, R., & Zou, J. L. (2009). Real options and foreign affiliate divestments: A portfolio perspective. *Journal of International Business Studies, 40*(4), 600–620. doi:10.1057/jibs.2008.108

Bentham, J. (1789). *The principles of moral and legislation.* Cambridge, MA: Oxford University.

Bergsten, F. (2005). Rescuing the Doha Round. *Foreign Affairs.* Retrieved October, 23, 2016, from http://s06.middlebury.edu/ECON0340A/Rescuing%20the%20Doha%20Round.pdf

Beritelli, P. (2011). Cooperation among prominent actors in a tourist destination. *Annals of Tourism Research, 38*(2), 607–629. doi:10.1016/j.annals.2010.11.015

Berke, B. (2012). Döviz Kuru ve İMKB100 Endeksi İlişkisi: Yeni Bir Test. *Maliye Dergisi, 163,* 243–257.

Berument, H. (2002). Döviz Kuru Hareketleri ve Enflasyon Dinamiği: Türkiye Örneği. *Bilkent Üniversitesi Yayınları,* 1-15.

Bhagwati, J. (1992). Regionalism versus Multilateralism. *World Economy, 15*(5), 535–556. doi:10.1111/j.1467-9701.1992.tb00536.x

Bianchi, C., & Pike, S. (2011). Antecedents of destination brand loyalty for a long-haul market: Australias destination loyalty among chilean travelers. *Journal of Travel & Tourism Marketing*, *28*(7), 736–750. doi:10.1080/10548408.2011.611742

Bilgin, M. H. (2004). Döviz Kuru İşsizlik İlişkisi: Türkiye Üzerine Bir İnceleme. *Kocaeli Üniversitesi Sosyal Bilimler Enstitüsü Dergisi*, *8*, 80–94.

Biloshapka, V., Osiyevskyy, O., & Meyer, M. H. (2016). The value matrix: A tool for assessing the future of a business model. *Strategy and Leadership*, *44*(4), 41–48. doi:10.1108/SL-04-2016-0026

Binder, J. (2016). *Global Project Management. Communication, Collaboration and Management Across Boarders*. New York: Routledge.

Bishop, P., Hines, A., & Collins, T. (2007). The Current State of Scenario Development: An Overview of Techniques. *Foresight*, *9*(1), 5–25. doi:10.1108/14636680710727516

Black, J. S. (1987). Japanese/American negotiations: The Japanese perspective. *Business and Economic Review*, *6*(1), 27–30.

Black, J. S., & Mendenhall, M. (1990). Cross-Cultural Training Effectiveness: A Review and a Theoretical Framework for Future. *Academy of Management Review*, *15*(1), 113–136.

Blain, C., Levy, S. E., & Ritchie, J. B. (2005). Destination branding: Insights and practices from destination management organizations. *Journal of Travel Research*, *43*(4), 328–338. doi:10.1177/0047287505274646

Blanchard, A. (2004). The effects of dispersed virtual communities on face-to-face social capital. In M. Huysman & V. Wulf (Eds.), *Social capital and information technology* (pp. 53–73). Cambridge, MA: MIT Press.

Blanchard, A., & Horan, T. (2000). Virtual communities and social capital. In E. L. Lesser (Ed.), *Knowledge and social capital: Foundations and applications* (pp. 159–178). Woburn, MA: Butterworth-Heinemann. doi:10.1016/B978-0-7506-7222-1.50010-6

Blanchflower, D. G. (2004). *Self-Employment: More May Not Be Better*. NBER Working Paper No. 10286.

Blomström, M., & Kokko, A. (2003). *The Economics of Foreign Direct Investment Incentives*. National Bureau of Economic Research. Working Paper No. 9489.

Blomström, M., & Sjöholm, F. (1998). *Technological Transfer And Spillovers: Does Local Participation With Multinationals Matter?* National Bureau of Economic Research. Working Paper No. 6816.

Boddewyn, J. J. (1994). International-business political-behavior: New theoretical directions. *Academy of Management Review*, *19*(1), 119–143.

Boje, D. M. (1991). The storytelling organization: A study of story performance in an Office-supply firm. *Admistrative Science Quarterly*, 106-126.

Bolder, D. J., &Rubin, T. (2007). *Optimization in a simulation setting: Use of function approximation in debt strategy analysis*. Available at SSRN 1082840

Bolisani, E., & Scarso, E. (1999). Information technology management: A knowledge-based perspective. *Technovation*, *19*(4), 209–217. doi:10.1016/S0166-4972(98)00109-6

Bonardi, J. P., Holburn, G. L. F., & Bergh, R. G. V. (2006). Nonmarket strategy performance: Evidence from US electric utilities. *Academy of Management Journal*, *49*(6), 1209–1228. doi:10.5465/AMJ.2006.23478676

Borodzicz, E. P. (2005). *Risk, Crisis and Security Management*. Chichester, UK: John Wiley & Sons.

Bourdieu, P. (1985). The forms of capital. In J.G. Richardson (Ed.), Handbook for Theory and Research for the Sociology of Education (pp. 241–258). Academic Press.

Bourdieu, P. (1977). *Outline of a theory of practice* (Vol. 16). Cambridge University Press. doi:10.1017/CBO9780511812507

Bourdieu, P. (1983). Forms of social capital. In J. C. Richards (Ed.), *Handbook of theory and research for sociology of education* (pp. 241–258). New York, NY: Greenwood Press.

Bowen, J. T., & Shoemaker, S. (1998). Loyalty: A strategic commitment. *The Cornell Hotel and Restaurant Administration Quarterly, 39*(1), 12–25. doi:10.1177/001088049803900104

Boynton, A. C., & Zmud, R. W. (1984). An Assessment of Critical Success Factors. *Sloan Management Review, 25*, 17–27.

Branger, N., & Schlag, C. (2004). *Model Risk: A Conceptual Framework for Risk Measurement and Hedging*. Retrieved October, 15, 2016, from https://www.wiwi.uni-muenster.de/fcm/downloads /forschen/2004_Model_Risk.pdf

Brdyś, M. A., Brdyś, M. T., & Maciejewski, S. M. (2016). Adaptive predictions of the euro/złoty currency exchange rate using state space wavelet networks and forecast combinations. *International Journal of Applied Mathematics and Computer Science, 26*(1), 161–173. doi:10.1515/amcs-2016-0011

Brews, J., & Tucci, C. L. (2004). Exploring the Structural Effects of Internetworking. *Strategic Management Journal, 25*(5), 429–452. doi:10.1002/smj.386

Broni, J. V. G. (2010). Ethical dimensions in the conduct of business: Business ethics, corporate social responsibility and the law. The" ethics in business" as a sense of business ethics. In *International Conference On Applied Economics–ICOAE* (p. 795).

Brouthers, K. D. (2002). Institutional, cultural and transaction cost influences on entry mode choice and performance. *Journal of International Business Studies, 33*(2), 203–221. doi:10.1057/palgrave.jibs.8491013

Brouthers, K. D., & Brouthers, L. E. (2001). Explaining the national cultural distance paradox. *Journal of International Business Studies, 32*(1), 177–189. doi:10.1057/palgrave.jibs.8490944

Brown, J. S., & Duguid, P. (1991). Organizational learning and communities-of-practice: Toward a unified view of working, learning, and innovation. *Organization Science, 2*(1), 40–57. doi:10.1287/orsc.2.1.40

Brush, C. G. (1992). Research on Women Business Owners: Past Trends, a New Perspective and Future Directions. *Entrepreneurship Theory and Practice, 16*, 5–30.

Bruton, G. D., Ireland, R. D., & Ketchen, D. J. Jr. (2012). Toward a Research Agenda on the Informal Economy. *The Academy of Management Perspectives, 26*(3), 1–11. doi:10.5465/amp.2012.0079

Bruton, G., Ahlstrom, D., & Li, H. (2010). Institutional Theory and Entrepreneurship: Where Are We Now and Where Do We Need to Move in the Future? *Entrepreneurship Theory and Practice, 34*(3), 421–440. doi:10.1111/j.1540-6520.2010.00390.x

Buchanan, J., Heesang Chai, D., & Deakin, S. (2013). *Agency theory in practice: a qualitative study of hedge fund activism in japan*. Centre for Business Research, University of Cambridge. Working Paper No. 448. CBR, University of Cambridge.

Buckley, P. J., Devinney, T. M., & Louviere, J. J. (2007). Do managers behave the way theory suggests? A choice-theoretic examination of foreign direct investment location decision-making. *Journal of International Business Studies, 38*(7), 1069–1094. doi:10.1057/palgrave.jibs.8400311

Buckley, P., & Casson, M. (1976). *The Future of Multinational Enterprise.* London: Macmillan. doi:10.1007/978-1-349-02899-3

Building blocks: Regional deals are the only game in town for supporters of free trade. Are they any good? (2012). *The Economist.* Retrieved August, 12, 2016, from http://www.economist.com/news/finance-and-economics/21568717-regional-deals-are-only-game-town-supporters-free-trade-are-they-any

Bullen, C. V. (1995). Productivity CSFs for knowledge workers. *Information Strategy: The Executive's Journal, 12*(1), 14–20.

Bullen, C. V., & Rockart, J. F. (1981). *A Primer on Critical Success Factors.* Center for Information Systems Research, Sloan School of Management, Massachusetts Institute of Technology.

Buono, A. F., Bowditsch, J. L., & Lewis, J. (1989). When cultures collide. The Anatomy of a Merger. *Human Relations, 38*(5), 477–500. doi:10.1177/001872678503800506

Burritt, R., & Christ, K. (2014). *Taking Water Into Account.* Retrieved January 15, 2017, from: http://www.accaglobal.com/vn/en/technical-activities/technical-resources-search/2014/september/taking-water-into-account.html

Burritt, R., & Christ, K. (2014). *Water Accounting: A Short-Term Drought?* Retrieved January 15, 2017, from: https://www.charteredaccountantsanz.com/en/Site-Content/Business-Trends-Insights/Acuity/December-2014/Water-accounting-a-short-term-drought.aspx#.Vs9c2vl97IU

Burt, R. S. (2000). The network structure of social capital. Re-print for a chapter. In B. M. Staw & R. I. Sutton (Eds.), *Research in Organizational Behavior* (Vol. 22). Greenwich, CT: JAI Press.

Busenitz, L. W. (1996). Research on entrepreneurial alertness. *Journal of Small Business Management, 34*(4), 35–44.

Bygrave, W., Brush, C., Davidsson, P., Fiet, F., Greene, P., Harrison, R., & Zacharackis, A. et al. (1997). *Frontiers of Entrepreneurship Research.* Wellesley, MA: Babson College Press.

Bygrave, W., & Minniti, M. (2000). The social dynamics of entrepreneurship. *Entrepreneurship Theory & Practice, 24,* 25–36.

Camillus, J. C. (1986). *Strategic Planning and Management Control: Systems for Survival and Success.* Lexington, MA: Lexington Books.

Camillus, J. C. (1996). Reinventing Strategic Planning. *Strategy and Leadership, 24*(3), 6–12. doi:10.1108/eb054552

Campa, J. M. (1993). Entry by foreign firms in the United States under exchange rate uncertainty. *The Review of Economics and Statistics, 75*(4), 614–622. doi:10.2307/2110014

Campo, S., & Yagüe, M. J. (2007). The formation of the tourists loyalty to the tourism distribution channel: How does it affect price discounts? *International Journal of Tourism Research, 9*(6), 453–464. doi:10.1002/jtr.617

Candelon, B., Kool, C., Raabe, K., & van Veen, T. (2007). Long-run real exchange rate determinants: Evidence from eight new EU member states, 1993–2003. *Journal of Comparative Economics, 35*(1), 87–107. doi:10.1016/j.jce.2006.10.003

Canestrino, R. (2007, May). *Business Ethics and Firms' internationalization processes. The impact of culture on "moral gap".* Paper presented at the IACCM Annual Conference "Cross-cultural Life of Social Values", Rotterdam, The Netherlands.

Canestrino, R., & Calvelli, A. (2010, September). *Culture and Business Ethics: the impact on firms' management of value chain activities.* Paper presented at the EBEN annual conference, Which values for which organizations? Trento, Italy.

Canestrino, R., & Magliocca, P. (2016). Transferring Knowledge through Cross-border Communities of Practice. In *Organizational Knowledge Facilitation through Communities of Practice in Emerging Markets* (vol. 1, pp. 1-30). Academic Press. DOI: 10.4018/978-1-5225-0013-1.ch004

Canestrino, R., Magliocca, P., & Guarino, A. (2015). Environmental sustainability in the Italian organic wine industry: preliminary results. In Contemporary Trends and Perspectives in Wine and Agri-food Management. Academic Press.

Canestrino, R., Magliocca, P., & Nigro, C. (2015). Drivers and implications of medical tourism: a neo-institutional perspective. *Sinergie Italian Journal of Management*, 271-290.

Canestrino, R. (2008). La dissonanza etica nei processi di internazionalizzazione delle imprese. In A. Calvelli (Ed.), *Cross Cultural Management* (pp. 167–240). Naples: Enzo Albano Editore.

Canestrino, R., Magliocca, P., & Nigro, C. (2016). Understanding medical tourism within the field of neo-institutionalism: An ethical insight. *International Journal of Environment and Health*, 8(1), 76-99. doi:10.1504/IJENVH.2016.077659

Cantwell, J., & Mudambi, R. (2005). Mne competence-creating subsidiary mandates. *Strategic Management Journal*, 26(12), 1109–1128. doi:10.1002/smj.497

Cap and Trade. (n.d.). Retrieved January 26, 2017, from: http://12.000.scripts.mit.edu/mission2017/solutions/economic-solutions/cap-and-trade-2/

Capaldo, A., Della Piana, B., Monteleone, M., & Sergi, B. (2012). *Cross-Cultural Management: A Mosaic of Words and Concepts*. Milano, Italy: McGrawHill.

Capaldo, A., Della Piana, B., & Vecchi, A. (2012). Managing across cultures in a globalized world. Findings from a systematic literature review. In *The Global Community* (Vol. 1, pp. 7–40). New York: Oxford University Press.

Carballo, M. M., Araña, J. E., León, C. J., & Moreno-Gil, S. (2015). Economic valuation of tourism destination image. *Tourism Economics*, 21(4), 741–759. doi:10.5367/te.2014.0381

Carballo, M., Araña, J., León, C., González, M., & Moreno, S. (2011). «Valoración Económica de la Imagen de un Destino», *Pasos. Revista de Turismo y Patrimonio Cultural*, 9(1), 1–14.

Cardone, R., & Fonseca, C. (2003). *Financing and Cost Recovery. Thematic Overview Paper*. Retrieved January 15, 2017, from: http://www.unep.or.jp/ietc/kms/data/1972.pdf

Carkovic, M., & Levine, R. (2002). Capitulo 8, Does Foreign Direct Investment Accelerate Economic Growth? In Does Foreign Direct Investment Promote Development?. Peterson Institute for International Economics.

Carrillo Regalado, S. (2016). The impact on trade of the Mexico-Japan. Economic Partnership Agreement (MJEPA). In Economic impact of Economic Partnership Agreement Mexico – Japan – theoretical and empirical aspects, (pp. 17-42). The Institute for Economic Studies. Seijo University.

Carrillo, S., & Okabe, T. (Ed.). (2014). Relaciones México-Japón en el Contexto del Acuerdo de Asociación Económica. Universidad de Guadalajara.

Carroll, A. B. (1991). The pyramid of corporate social responsibility: Toward the moral management of organizational stakeholders. *Business Horizons*, 34(4), 39–48. doi:10.1016/0007-6813(91)90005-G

Carter, C., Clegg, S., & Kornberger, M. (2008). Critical strategy: Revising strategy as practice. *Strategic Organization*, 6(1), 83–99. doi:10.1177/1476127007087154

Casero, J. C. D., González, M. A., Escobedo, M. C. S., Martínez, A. C., & Mogollón, R. H. (2013). Institutional variables, entrepreneurial activity and economic development. *Management Decision*, 51(2), 281–305. doi:10.1108/00251741311301821

Caves, R. E. (1971). International corporations: The industrial economics of foreign investment. *Economica, 38*(149), 1–27. doi:10.2307/2551748

Cayen, J. P., Coletti, D., Lalonde, R., & Maier, P. (2010). What drives exchange rates? new evidence from a panel of US dollar bilateral exchange rates. *Document de travail,* (2010-5).

Certo, S. T., & Miller, T. (2008). Social entrepreneurship: Key issues and concepts. *Business Horizons, 51*(4), 267–271. doi:10.1016/j.bushor.2008.02.009

Chang, S. J. (1995). International expansion strategy of Japanese firms - capability building through sequential entry. *Academy of Management Journal, 38*(2), 383–407. doi:10.2307/256685

Chaudhuri, T. D., & Ghosh, I. (2016). *Artificial Neural Network and Time Series Modeling Based Approach to Forecasting the Exchange Rate in a Multivariate Framework.* arXiv preprint arXiv:1607.02093

Cheol-Sung, L., Nielsen, L., & Alderson, A. (2007). Income Inequality, Global Economy, and the State. *Social Forces,* (86), 77–111.

Chesbrough, H. W. (2003). *Open Innovation: The New Imperative for Creating and Profiting from Technology.* Boston: Harvard Business School Press.

Chia, R., & MacKay, B. (2007). Post-processual challenges for the emerging strategy-as-practice perspective: Discovering strategy in the logic of practice. *Human Relations, 60*(1), 217–242. doi:10.1177/0018726707075291

Chien, S.-S., & Zhao, L. (2008). The Kunshan Model: Learning from Taiwanese Investors. *Built Environment, 34*(4), 427–443. doi:10.2148/benv.34.4.427

China Water Risk. (2010). *Water: The New Business Risk Part II,* 1-13. Retrieved from: http://chinawaterrisk.org/wp-content/uploads/2011/06/Water-The-New-Business-Risk-Part-2.pdf

Chiu, S. W. K., & Lui, T.-l. (2004). Testing the global city-social polarisation thesis: Hong Kong since the 1990s. *Urban studies, 41*(10), 1863-1888.

Chowdhury, K. (2012). Modelling the dynamics, structural breaks and the determinants of the real exchange rate of Australia. *Journal of International Financial Markets, Institutions and Money, 22*(2), 343–358. doi:10.1016/j.intfin.2011.10.004

Chow, W. S. (2000). Success factors for IS disaster recovery planning in Hong Kong. *Information Management & Computer Security, 8*(2), 80–87. doi:10.1108/09685220010321326

Christian-Smith, J., Gleick, P. H., & Cooley, H. (2011). *US Water Policy Reform, Pacific Institute, World's Water series along with select content from the newest release.* Retrieved January 15, 2017, from: http://ceowatermandate.org/accounting/about/preface/

Christie, M. J., & Honig, B. (2006). Social entrepreneurship: New research findings. *Journal of World Business, 41*(1), 1–5. doi:10.1016/j.jwb.2005.10.003

Chubarov, I., & Brooker, D. (2013). Multiple pathways to global city formation: A functional approach and review of recent evidence in China. *Cities (London, England), 35,* 181–189. doi:10.1016/j.cities.2013.05.008

Chu, D., Strand, R., & Fjelland, R. (2003). Theories of complexity – Common denominators of complex systems. *Essays & Commentaries. Complexity, 8*(3), 19–30. doi:10.1002/cplx.10059

Chung, K. H. (1987). *Management: Critical success factors.* Newton, MA: Allyn and Bacon, Inc.

Cicmil, S., Williams, T., Thomas, J., & Hodgson, D. (2006). Rethinking Project Management: Researching the actuality of projects. *International Journal of Project Management, 24*(8), 675–686. doi:10.1016/j.ijproman.2006.08.006

Clark, K., & Fujimoto, T. (1991). *Product Development Performance: Strategy, Organization and Management in the World Auto Industry.* Boston: HBS Press.

Clegg, S. R., Carter, C., Kornberger, M., & Schweitzer, J. (2011). Strategy: Theory and Practice. *Sage (Atlanta, Ga.)*.

Clegg, S., Carter, C., & Kornberger, M. (2004). Get up, I feel like being a strategy machine. *European Management Review, 1*(1), 21–28. doi:10.1057/palgrave.emr.1500011

Coase, R. H. (1937). The nature of the firm. *Economica-New Series, 4*(16), 386–405. doi:10.1111/j.1468-0335.1937.tb00002.x

Cobb, J. A. (2016). How firms shape income inequality: Stakeholder power, executive decision making, and the structuring of employment relationships. *Academy of Management Review, 41*(2), 324–348. doi:10.5465/amr.2013.0451

Cohen, D., & Prusak, L. (2001). *In good company: How social capital makes organizations work.* Boston, MA: Harvard Business School Press.

Cohen, J. R., Pant, L. W., & Sharp, D. J. (1996). A methodological note on cross-cultural accounting ethics research. *The International Journal of Accounting, 31*(1), 55–66. doi:10.1016/S0020-7063(96)90013-8

Coleman, J. S. (1988). Social capital in the creation of human capital. *American Journal of Sociology, 94*, 95–120. doi:10.1086/228943

Collier, J., & Esteban, R. (2007). Corporate social responsibility and employee commitment. *Business Ethics (Oxford, England), 16*(1), 19–33. doi:10.1111/j.1467-8608.2006.00466.x

Collins, J. C., & Porras, J. I. (1996). Building your company's vision. *Harvard Business Review, 74*(5), 65–77.

Committee of Sponsoring Organization (CoSo). (2004). *Enterprise Risk Management – Integrated Framework.* New York: COSO.

Compeau, D. R., & Higgins, C. A. (1995). Computer self-efficacy: Development of a measure and initial test. *Management Information Systems Quarterly, 19*(2), 189–211. doi:10.2307/249688

Cooper, R. G., & Kleinschmidt, E. J. (1996). Winning businesses in product development: The critical success factors. *Research-Technology Management, 39*(4), 18–29.

Corsetti, G., Pesenti, P., & Roubini, N. (1999). Paper tigers?: A model of the Asian crisis. *European Economic Review, 43*(7), 1211–1236. doi:10.1016/S0014-2921(99)00017-3

Crane, A. (2000). Corporate greening as amoralization. *Organization Studies, 21*(4), 673–696. doi:10.1177/0170840600214001

Cressy, R. (2006). Why do most firms die young? *Small Business Economics, 26*(2), 103–116. doi:10.1007/s11187-004-7813-9

Crtistoph, A. J., & Konrad, S. (2014). Project Complexity as an Influence Factor on the Balance of Costs and Benefits in Project Management Maturity Modeling. *Procedia: Social and Behavioral Sciences, 119*(March), 162–171. doi:10.1016/j.sbspro.2014.03.020

Cuervo-Cazurra, A. (2006). Who cares about corruption? *Journal of International Business Studies, 37*(6), 807–822. doi:10.1057/palgrave.jibs.8400223

Cummings, J. N., Butler, B., & Kraut, R. (2002). The quality of online social relationships. *Communications of the ACM*, *45*(7), 103–108. doi:10.1145/514236.514242

Cuñat, A., & Melitz, M. J. (2012). Volatility, labor market flexibility, and the pattern of comparative advantage. *Journal of the European Economic Association*, *10*(2), 225–254. doi:10.1111/j.1542-4774.2011.01038.x

Cunningham, R. M. (1956). Brand loyalty-what, where, how much. *Harvard Business Review*, *34*(1), 116–128.

Cyert, R. M., & March, J. G. (1963). *A Behavioral Theory of the Firm*. Malden, MA: Blackwell.

d'Hauteserre, A. M., & Funck, C. (2016). Innovation in island ecotourism in different contexts: Yakushima (Japan) and Tahiti and its Islands. *Island Studies Journal*, *11*(1), 227–244.

Dacin, T. M., Dacin, P. A., & Tracey, P. (2011). Social entrepreneurship: A critique and future directions. *Organization Science*, *22*(5), 1203–1213. doi:10.1287/orsc.1100.0620

Dahlman, C. (2007). *Technology, globalization and international competitiveness: Challenges for developing Countries*. Industrial development for the 21st century, Department of economic and social affairs of United Nations.

Dai, L., Eden, L., & Beamish, P. W. (2013). Place, space, and geographical exposure: Foreign subsidiary survival in conflict zones. *Journal of International Business Studies*, *44*(6), 554–578. doi:10.1057/jibs.2013.12

Daniel, B., Schwier, R. A., & McCalla, G. (2003). Social capital in virtual learning communities and distributed communities of practice. *SANDBOX-Canadian Journal of Learning and Technology/La Revue Canadienne de l'apprentissage et de la Technologie, 29*(3).

Daniels, P. W., & Bryson, J. R. (2002). Manufacturing services and servicing manufacturing: Knowledge-based cities and changing forms of production. *Urban Studies (Edinburgh, Scotland)*, *39*(5-6), 977–991. doi:10.1080/00420980220128408

Darby, J., Hallett, A. H., Ireland, J., & Piscitelli, L. (1999). The impact of exchange rate uncertainty on the level of investment. *The Economic Journal*, *109*(454), 55–67. doi:10.1111/1468-0297.00416

Darnell, A. C., & Johnson, P. S. (2001). Repeat visits to attractions: A preliminary economic analysis. *Tourism Management*, *22*(2), 119–126. doi:10.1016/S0261-5177(00)00036-4

Das, B., Fernandez, C. F., Van der Gaag, N., McIntyre, P., & Rychlewski, M. (2016). *Water Integrity Global Outlook*. Retrieved January 15, 2017, from: http://www.womenforwater.org/uploads/7/7/5/1/77516286/water_integrity_global_outlook__book_2016_full__1_.pdf

Dasgupta, S. (2003). Structural and behavioural characteristics of informal service employment: Evidence from a survey in New Delhi. *The Journal of Development Studies*, *39*(3), 51–80. doi:10.1080/00220380412331322821

Datzira-Masip, J., & Poluzzi, A. (2014). Brand architecture management: The case of four tourist destinations in Catalonia. *Journal of Destination Marketing & Management*, *3*(1), 48–58. doi:10.1016/j.jdmm.2013.12.006

Davenport, T. H. (1997). Ten principles of knowledge management and four case studies. *Knowledge and Process Management*, *4*(3), 187–208. doi:10.1002/(SICI)1099-1441(199709)4:3<187::AID-KPM99>3.0.CO;2-A

Davidson, W. H. (1980). The location of foreign direct investment activity: Country characteristics and experience effects. *Journal of International Business Studies*, *11*(2), 9–22. doi:10.1057/palgrave.jibs.8490602

Dawes, J. (2014). Cigarette brand loyalty and purchase patterns: An examination using US consumer panel data. *Journal of Business Research*, *67*(9), 1933–1943. doi:10.1016/j.jbusres.2013.11.014

Dawes, J., Romaniuk, J., & Mansfield, A. (2009). Generalized pattern in competition among tourism destinations. *International Journal of Culture. Tourism and Hospitality Research, 3*(1), 33–53. doi:10.1108/17506180910940333

Dawes, T. (2004). Crisis planning. *British Journal of Administrative Management, 42*(Aug/Sep), 26–27.

De George, R. T. (1993). *Competing with Integrity in International Business*. Oxford, UK: Oxford University Press.

De Grauwe, P., & Markiewicz, A. (2013). Learning to forecast the exchange rate: Two competing approaches. *Journal of International Money and Finance, 32*, 42–76. doi:10.1016/j.jimonfin.2012.03.001

de Soto, H. (2000). *The Mystery of Capital: Why Capitalism Triumphs in the West and Fails Everywhere Else*. New York: Basic Books.

De Vita, L., Mari, M., & Poggesi, S. (2014). Women entrepreneurs in and from developing countries: Evidences from the literature. *European Management Journal, 32*(3), 451–460. doi:10.1016/j.emj.2013.07.009

Dees, G. J. (2001). *The meaning of social entrepreneurship*. Available at: www.caseatduke.org/documents/dees_sedef.pdf

Dees, G. J. (2012). A tale two cultures: Charity, problem solving, and the future of social entrepreneurship. *Journal of Business Ethics, 111*(3), 321–334. doi:10.1007/s10551-012-1412-5

Defourny, J., & Nyssens, M. (2010). Conceptions of social enterprise and social entrepreneurship in Europe and the United States: Convergences and Divergences. *Journal of Social Entrepreneurship, 1*(1), 120–132. doi:10.1080/19420670903442053

Delios, A., & Henisz, W. J. (2003). Political hazards, experience, and sequential entry strategies: The international expansion of Japanese firms, 19801998. *Strategic Management Journal, 24*(11), 1153–1164. doi:10.1002/smj.355

Della Piana, B., & Testa, M. (2009). L'efficacia dei processi di negoziazione crosscultural nei business internazionali. *Sviluppo & Organizzazione, 235*(1), 2–21.

Deng, W. S., & Lin, Y. C. (2013). Parameter heterogeneity in the foreign direct investment-income inequality relationship: A semiparametric regression analysis. *Empirical Economics, 45*(2), 845–872.

Deshpande, M., & Baporikar, N. (2014). Excellence in a Borderless World: Evidence from Pune Auto-Components SMEs. *Journal of Shinawatra University, 1*(2), 182–196.

Devereux, M. B. (1997). Real exchange rates and macroeconomics: Evidence and theory. *The Canadian Journal of Economics. Revue Canadienne dEconomique, 30*(4a), 773–808. doi:10.2307/136269

Dilbaz Alacahan, N. (2011). Enflasyon, Döviz Kuru İlişkisi ve Yansıma: Türkiye. *Sosyal Bilimler Dergisi, 1*, 49–56.

DiMaggio, P. J., & Powell, W. W. (1983). The iron cage revisited: Institutional isomorphism and collective rationality in organizational fields. *American Sociological Review, 48*(2), 147–160. doi:10.2307/2095101

DiMaggio, P., Hargittai, E., Neuman, W. R., & Robinson, J. P. (2001). Social implications of the Internet. *Annual Review of Sociology, 27*(1), 307–336. doi:10.1146/annurev.soc.27.1.307

Djankov, S., Miguel, E., Qian, Y., Roland, G., & Zhuravskaya, E. (2005). Who are Russias Entrepreneurs? *Journal of the European Economic Association, 3*(2/3), 587–597. doi:10.1162/jeea.2005.3.2-3.587

Djankov, S., Qian, Y., Roland, G., & Zhuravskaya, E. (2006). Who Are Chinas Entrepreneurs? *The American Economic Review, 96*(2), 348–352. doi:10.1257/000282806777212387

Dodgson, M. (1993). Learning, trust, and technological collaboration. *Human Relations, 46*(1), 77–94. doi:10.1177/001872679304600106

Doherty, B., Haugh, H., & Lyon, F. (2014). Social Enterprises as Hybrid Organizations: A Review and Research Agenda. *International Journal of Management Reviews, 16*(4), 417–439. doi:10.1111/ijmr.12028

Donaldson, L. (2001). The contingency theory of organizations. *Sage (Atlanta, Ga.)*.

Donaldson, T. (1996). Values in tension: Ethics away from home. *Harvard Business Review, 74*(5), 48.

Donaldson, T., & Dunfee, T. W. (1994). Toward a unified conception of business ethics: Integrative social contracts theory. *Academy of Management Review, 19*(2), 252–284.

Donaldson, T., & Dunfee, T. W. (1999). When ethics travel: The promise and peril of global business ethics. *California Management Review, 41*(4), 45–63. doi:10.2307/41166009

Dooley, G., & Bowie, D. (2005). Place brand architecture: Strategic management of the brand portfolio. *Place Branding and Public Diplomacy, 1*(4), 402–419. doi:10.1057/palgrave.pb.5990037

Douglas, M., & Wildavsky, A. (1982). *Risk and culture*. Berkeley, CA: University of California Press.

Dowling, G., & Uncles, M. (1997). Do customer loyalty programs really work? *Sloan Management Review, 38*(4), 71–71.

Down, J. (2014). *What is Strategy-As-Practice and why is it important?* Retrieved from http://drjasondowns.com/what-is-strategy-as-practice-and-why-is-it-important/

Drucker, P. F. (1967). *The Effective Executive*. Harper Business.

Dubinsky, A. J., & Loken, B. (1989). Analyzing ethical decision making in marketing. *Journal of Business Research, 19*(2), 83–107. doi:10.1016/0148-2963(89)90001-5

Dugan, J. P., & Komives, S. R. (2010). Influence on college students capacities for socially responsible leadership. *Journal of College Student Development, 51*(5), 525–549. doi:10.1353/csd.2010.0009

Du, H. S., & Wagner, C. (2006). Weblog success: Exploring the role of technology. *International Journal of Human-Computer Studies, 64*(9), 789–798. doi:10.1016/j.ijhcs.2006.04.002

Dulwich International School. (2015). Retrieved October 13, 2015, from www.dulwich-suzhou.cn

Dunning, J. H. (1998). Globalization and the New Geography of Foreign Direct Investment. *Oxford Development Studies, 26*(1), 47-69. Retrieved from http://www.tandf.co.uk/journals/titles/13600818.asp

Dunning, J. (1993). *The Globalization of Business*. London: Routledge.

Dunning, J. H. (1988). The eclectic paradigm of international production: A restatement and some possible extensions. *Journal of International Business Studies, 19*(1), 1–31. doi:10.1057/palgrave.jibs.8490372

Dunning, J. H. (1993). *Multinational enterprises and the global economy*. Wokingham, UK: Addison-Wesley.

Dunning, J. H. (1993). *Multinational Enterprises and the Global Economy*. Workingham, UK: Addison Wesley.

Dunning, J. H. (2000). The eclectic paradigm as an envelope for economic and business theories of mne activity. *International Business Review, 9*(2), 163–190. doi:10.1016/S0969-5931(99)00035-9

Dunning, J. H. (2002). *Regions, globalization, and the knowledge-based economy*. Oxford University Press. doi:10.1093/0199250014.001.0001

Dunning, J. H. (2012). *International Production and the Multinational Enterprise (RLE International Business)* (Vol. 12). Routledge.

Dyer, J. H. (1996a). Does governance matter? Keiretsu alliances and asset specificity as sources of Japanese competitive advantage. *Organization Science, 7*(6), 649–666. doi:10.1287/orsc.7.6.649

Dyer, J. H. (1996b). Specialized supplier networks as a source of competitive advantage: Evidence from the auto industry. *Strategic Management Journal, 17*(4), 271–292. doi:10.1002/(SICI)1097-0266(199604)17:4<271::AID-SMJ807>3.0.CO;2-Y

Dyer, J. H., & Nobeoka, K. (2000). Creating and managing a high-performance knowledge-sharing network: The Toyota case. *Strategic Management Journal, 21*(3), 345–367. doi:10.1002/(SICI)1097-0266(200003)21:3<345::AID-SMJ96>3.0.CO;2-N

Easterly, W., Ritze, J., & Woolcock, M. (2006). Social cohesion, institutions and growth. *Economics and Politics, 18*(2), 103–120. doi:10.1111/j.1468-0343.2006.00165.x

Economist. (2015). Why trade unions are declining. *The Economist.*

Edwards, S. (1988). Real and monetary determinants of real exchange rate behavior: Theory and evidence from developing countries. *Journal of Development Economics, 29*(3), 311–341. doi:10.1016/0304-3878(88)90048-X

Eisenhardt, K. M., & Brown, S. L. (1998). Patching. Restitching business portfolios in dynamic markets. *Harvard Business Review, 77*(3), 72–82. PMID:10387579

Elliot, D., Swartz, E., & Herbane, B. (2010). *Business Continuity Management: A Crisis Management Approach* (2nd ed.). London, UK: Rutledge.

Ellison, N. B., Steinfield, C., & Lampe, C. (2007). The benefits of Facebook friends: Social capital and college students use of online social network sites. *Journal of Computer-Mediated Communication, 12*(4), 1143–1168. doi:10.1111/j.1083-6101.2007.00367.x

Energy Regulators Regional Association (ERRA). (2009). *Determination of RAB after Asset Revaluation. (ERRA).* Retrieved January 15, 2017, from: http://www.erranet.org/wp-content/uploads/2016/03/ERRA_Regulatory_Asset_Base_final_report_STC.pdf

Enright, M. J., & Newton, J. (2004). Tourism destination competitiveness: A quantitative approach. *Tourism Management, 25*(6), 777–788. doi:10.1016/j.tourman.2004.06.008

Eriksson, K., Johanson, J., Majkgard, A., & Sharma, D. D. (1997). Experiential knowledge and cost in the internationalization process. *Journal of International Business Studies, 28*(2), 337–360. doi:10.1057/palgrave.jibs.8490104

Ethier, W. J. (1998). The New Regionalism. *The Economic Journal, 108*(July), 1149–1161. doi:10.1111/1468-0297.00335

Eton International School. (n.d.). Retrieved October 13, 2015, from www.etonhouse-sz.com

Etzioni, A. (1961). *A Comparative Analysis of Complex Organizations.* New York: Free Press.

Etzioni, A. (1987). Entrepreneurship, adaptation and legitimation. *Journal of Economic Behavior, 8*(2), 175–189. doi:10.1016/0167-2681(87)90002-3

EU Water Framework Directive WFD. (2000). Official Journal of EU, L 327, 22 December. *Article, 9,* 29.

European Commission. (2012). *Antitrust: Commission opens proceedings against companies in French water sector.* Retrieved January 15, 2017, from: http://europa.eu/rapid/press-release_IP-12-26_en.htm

European Environment Agency. (2013). *Assessment of Cost Recovery Through Water Pricing* (Technical Report No 16). Retrieved from: www.eea.europa.eu/publications/assessment-of-full-cost-recovery/download

European Union and The Young Foundation. (2010). *Study of Social Innovation, A paper presented by the Social Innovation Exchange (SIX) and the Young Foundation for the Bureau of European Policy Advisors.* London: Young Foundation.

European Union Enlargement. Keeping up with the Croats. (2013). *The Economist.* Retrieved February, 1, 2017, from http://www.economist.com/news/leaders/21580145-after-croatias-accession-europe-should-be-ready-admit-more-new-members-keeping-up

European Union. (2017a). *The history of the European union.* Retrieved February, 4, 2017, from http://europa.eu/about-eu/eu-history/index_en.htm

European Union. (2017b). *How the EU Works: Countries.* Retrieved February, 4, 2017, from http://europa.eu/about-eu/countries/index_en.htm

European Union. (2017c). *How the EU Works: EU Institutions and other bodies* Retrieved February, 4, 2017, from http://europa.eu/about-eu/institutions-bodies/index_en.htm

European Union. (2017d). *How the EU Works: European Economic and Social Committee.* Retrieved February, 4, 2017, from http://europa.eu/about-eu/institutions-bodies/ecosoc/index_en.htm

Fahey, L. (1981). On Strategic Management Decision Proces. *Strategic Management Journal, 2*(1), 43–60. doi:10.1002/smj.4250020105

Falck Reyes, M., & De la Vega Shiota, V. (2014). La inversión japonesa en México en el marco del Acuerdo para el Fortalecimiento de la Asociación Económica entre Méxicoy Japón. El caso del sector de equipode transporte. *Comercio Exterior, 64*(6).

Falkenberg, L., & Osiyevskyy, O. (2014). Managing conflicting stakeholder expectations in the publishing industry. In J. Bishop (Ed.), *Gamification for Human Factors Integration: Social, Educational, and Psychological Issues* (pp. 52–79). IGI Global. doi:10.4018/978-1-4666-5071-8.ch004

Fan, C. C. (2008). *China on the Move: Migration, the State, and the Household.* Abingdon, UK: Routledge.

Fankhauser, S., & Tepic, S. (2007). Can Poor Consumers Pay For Energy And Water? An Affordability Analysis for Transition Countries. *Energy Policy, 35*(2), 1038–1049. doi:10.1016/j.enpol.2006.02.003

Fauzel, S., Seetanah, B., & Sannasee, R. (2015). Productivity Spillovers Of Fdi In The Manufacturing Sector Of Mauritius. Evidence From A Dynamic Framework. *Journal of Developing Areas, 49*(2), 295–316. doi:10.1353/jda.2015.0026

Feldstein, M. (1997). *The political economy of the Europe economic and monetary union: Political sources of an economic liability.* National Bureau of Economic Research. Retrieved February, 12, 2017, from http://www.nber.org/papers/w6150.pdf

Felix, R. (2014). Multi-brand loyalty: When one brand is not enough. *Qualitative Market Research: An International Journal, 17*(4), 464–480. doi:10.1108/QMR-11-2012-0053

Fenton, C., & Langley, A. (2011). Strategy as practice and the narrative turn. *Organization Studies, 32*(9), 1171–1196. doi:10.1177/0170840611410838

Fernández, R., & Jonathan Portes, J. (1998). Returns to Regionalism: An Analysis of Nontraditional Gains from Regional Trade Agreements. *The World Bank Economic Review, 12*(2), 197–220. doi:10.1093/wber/12.2.197

Ferraro, D., Rogoff, K., & Rossi, B. (2015). Can oil prices forecast exchange rates? An empirical analysis of the relationship between commodity prices and exchange rates. *Journal of International Money and Finance, 54*, 116–141. doi:10.1016/j.jimonfin.2015.03.001

Ferrell, O. C., & Fraedrich, J. (1997). *Business Ethics* (3rd ed.). Boston: Houghton Mifflin Co.

Ferrell, O. C., & Fraedrich, J. (2015). *Business ethics: Ethical decision making & cases.* Nelson Education.

Ferrell, O. C., & Gresham, L. G. (1985). A contingency framework for understanding ethical decision making in marketing. *Journal of Marketing, 49*(3), 87–96. doi:10.2307/1251618

Ferrer Paccess, F. M. (1974). *I sistemi d'impresa.* Bologna, Italy: Il Mulino.

Fisher, C. M., & Lovell, A. (2009). *Business Ethics and values: Individual, corporate and international perspectives.* Pearson Education.

Flores, R. G., & Aguilera, R. V. (2007). Globalization and location choice: An analysis of US multinational firms in 1980 and 2000. *Journal of International Business Studies, 38*(7), 1187–1210. doi:10.1057/palgrave.jibs.8400307

Follett, A. (2016, March 17). Venezuela Shuts Down for a Week due to Water, Power Crisis. *The Daily Caller.* Retrieved from: http://dailycaller.com

Fondazione Fits 2014. (2017). *Information about Fondazione Fits 2014.* Retrieved January 13, 2017, from Retrieved January 13, 2017, from www.fondazionefits2014.com

Fook, L. L. (2014). Suzhou Industrial Park: Going Beyong a Commercial Project. In S. Swee-Hock & J. Wong (Eds.), *Advancing Singapore-China Economic Relations* (pp. 62–93). Singapore: Institute of Southeast Asian Studies.

Formisano, V., Fedele, M., & Antonucci, E. (2016). Innovation in Financial Services: A Challenge for Start-Ups Growth. *International Journal of Business and Management, 11*(3), 149–162. doi:10.5539/ijbm.v11n3p149

Formisano, V., & Russo, G. (2011). Service Logic, Value Co-Creation And Networks in the Banking services. Giannini Editore.

Förster, J. (2014). Water use in industry. *Statistics in Focus, 14.* Retrieved from: http://ec.europa.eu/eurostat/statistics-explained/index.php/Water_use_in_industry

Foster, S. P., & Karen, D. (2005). Building continuity into strategy. *Journal of Corporate Real Estate, 7*(2), 105–119. doi:10.1108/14630010510812530

Fountain, J. E. (1998). Social capital: Its relationship to innovation in science and technology. *Science & Public Policy, 25*(2), 103–107.

Fowles, R., & Merva, M. (1996). Wage inequality and criminal activity: An extreme bounds analysis for the United States, 19751990. *Criminology, 34*(2), 163–182. doi:10.1111/j.1745-9125.1996.tb01201.x

Franzen, A. (2003). Social capital and the new communication technologies. In J. E. Katz (Ed.), Machines that become us: The social context of personal communication technology (pp. 105-116). New Brunswick, NJ: Transaction Publishers.

Frederick, W. C., Davis, K., & Post, J. E. (1988). *Business and society: Corporate strategy, public policy, ethics* (6th ed.). New York: McGraw-Hill.

Freeman, R. E. (1984). The politics of stakeholder theory. *Business Ethics Quarterly, 4*(4), 409–421. doi:10.2307/3857340

Freeman, R. E., & Evan, W. M. (1990). Corporate Governance: A Stakeholder Interpretation. *The Journal of Behavioral Economics, 19*(4), 337–359. doi:10.1016/0090-5720(90)90022-Y

Freeman, R. E., & Gilbert, D. R. (1988). *Corporate strategy and the search for ethics (No. 1).* Englewood Cliffs, NJ: Prentice Hall.

French, P. A. (1979). The corporation as a moral person. *American Philosophical Quarterly, 16*(3), 207–215.

Friedman, J. H. (1991). Multivariate adaptive regression splines. *Annals of Statistics, 19*(1), 1–67. doi:10.1214/aos/1176347963

Friedmann, J. (1986). The world city hypothesis. *Development and Change, 17*(1), 69–83. doi:10.1111/j.1467-7660.1986.tb00231.x

Friedmann, J. (Ed.). (1995). *Where we stand: a decade of world city research.* Cambridge, UK: Cambridge UP.

Friedmann, J., & Wolff, G. (1982). World city formation: An agenda for research and action. *International Journal of Urban and Regional Research, 6*(3), 309–344. doi:10.1111/j.1468-2427.1982.tb00384.x

Furrer, O., Thomas, H., & Goussevskaia, A. (2008). The structure and evolution of the strategic management field: A content analysis of 26 years of strategic management research. *International Journal of Management Reviews, 10*(1), 1–23. doi:10.1111/j.1468-2370.2007.00217.x

Fyall, A., & Garrod, B. (2005). *Tourism marketing: A collaborative approach* (Vol. 18). Channel View Publications.

Fyall, A., Garrod, B., & Wang, Y. (2012). Destination collaboration: A critical review of theoretical approaches to a multi-dimensional phenomenon. *Journal of Destination Marketing & Management, 1*(1), 10–26. doi:10.1016/j.jdmm.2012.10.002

Gabaix, X., & Maggiori, M. (2014). *International liquidity and exchange rate dynamics (No. w19854).* National Bureau of Economic Research. doi:10.3386/w19854

Gaglio, C. M., & Katz, J. A. (2001). The psychological basis of opportunity identification: Entrepreneurial alertness. *Small Business Economics, 16*(2), 95–111. doi:10.1023/A:1011132102464

Gagnon, J. E. (1993). Exchange rate variability and the level of international trade. *Journal of International Economics, 34*(3-4), 269–287. doi:10.1016/0022-1996(93)90050-8

Gallagher, M. (2003). *Business Continuity Management: How to protect your company from danger.* London, UK: Financial Times Management.

Gallagher, D. R. (2012). Why environmental leadership? In D. R. Gallagher (Ed.), *Environmental leadership: A reference handbook* (Vol. 1, pp. 3–10). Los Angeles, CA: SAGE Publications. doi:10.4135/9781452218601.n1

García De León, P. G. (2010). México y Japón: comercio bilateral en el marco del Acuerdo de Asociación Económica. *Comercio Exterior, 60*(2).

García-Rodríguez, J. L., García-Rodríguez, F. J., & Castilla-Gutiérrez, C. (2016). Human heritage and sustainable development on arid islands: The case of the Eastern Canary Islands. *Island Studies Journal, 11*(1), 113–130.

Gatti, M., Della Piana, B., & Testa, M. (2008). Cross-cultural practices in international negotiation process. The Alenia Aeronautica case. *EIASM Proceedings on 5th Workshop on International strategy and cross-cultural management.* Instanbul, Turkey: KOC University.

Gaudenzi, B. (2006). Nuovi approcci di gestione dei rischi d'impresa: Verso l'integrazione tra imprenditore e management. *Sinergie: Italian Journal of Management, 71*(Sep), 221–243.

Geller, N. (1985). Tracking the Critical Success Factors for Hotel Companies. *The Cornell Hotel and Restaurant Administration Quarterly, 25*(4), 76–81. doi:10.1177/001088048502500414

George, G., & Bock, A. J. (2011). The business model in practice and its implications for entrepreneurship research. *Entrepreneurship Theory and Practice, 35*(1), 83–111. doi:10.1111/j.1540-6520.2010.00424.x

Gibb, F., & Buchanan, S. (2006). A framework for business continuity management. *International Journal of Information Management, 26*(2), 128–141. doi:10.1016/j.ijinfomgt.2005.11.008

Gil, S. M. (2003). Tourism development in the Canary Islands. *Annals of Tourism Research, 30*(3), 744–747. doi:10.1016/S0160-7383(03)00050-1

Gilsing, B. N. V., & Nooteboom, B. (2004). Density and strength of ties in innovation networks: a competence and governance view. *CentER Discussion Paper, 2005*(40). Retrieved May 17, 2016, from https://pure.uvt.nl/ws/files/773647/40.pdf

Gjølberg, M. (2009). Measuring the immeasurable?: Constructing an index of CSR practices and CSR performance in 20 countries. *Scandinavian Journal of Management, 25*(1), 10–22. doi:10.1016/j.scaman.2008.10.003

Gjølberg, M. (2011). Explaining regulatory preferences: CSR, soft law, or hard law? Insights from a survey of Nordic pioneers in CSR. *Business and Politics, 13*(2), 1–31. doi:10.2202/1469-3569.1351

Glaeser, E., Kallal, H., Scheinkman, J., & Shleifer, A. (1992). Growth in Cities. *Journal of Political Economy, 100*(6), 1126–1153. doi:10.1086/261856

Glaister, K., & Falshaw, R. (1999). Strategic planning: Still going strong? *Long Range Planning, 32*(1), 107–116. doi:10.1016/S0024-6301(98)00131-9

Glickman, N. J., & Woodward, D. P. (1988). The Location of Foreign Direct Investment in the United States: Patterns and Determinants. *International Regional Science Review, 11*(2), 137–154. doi:10.1177/016001768801100203

Globalization and World Cities Research Network. (2014). Retrieved September 1, 2014, from http://www.lboro.ac.uk/gawc/world2012t.html

González Bravo, R. (2016). Advantages of the Mexico – Japan Economic Partnership Agreement for Mexican manufacturing exports companies located in Jalisco state. In Economic impact of Economic Partnership Agreement Mexico – Japan – theoretical and empirical aspects, (pp. 43-58). The Institute for Economic Studies. Seijo University.

González García, J. (2014). El Acuerdo de Asociación Económica México-Japón:¿es posible un relanzamiento? *Comercio Exterior, 64*(6).

Goodin, R., & Dryzek, J. (1980). Rational participation: The politics of relative power. *British Journal of Political Science, 10*(Jul), 273–292. doi:10.1017/S0007123400002209

Goold, M. (1992). Design, learning and planning: A further observations on the design school debate. *Strategic Management Journal, 13*(2), 169–170. doi:10.1002/smj.4250130208

Goold, M., & Quinn, J. J. (1993). *Strategic Control: Establishing Milestones for Long-term Performance.* Reading, MA: Addison-Wesley.

Gopal, R. D., & Sanders, G. L. (2000). Global software piracy: You cant get blood out of a turnip. *Communications of the ACM, 43*(9), 82–89. doi:10.1145/348941.349002

Graf, N. S. (2008). Industry critical success factors and their importance in strategy. In Olsen & Zhao (Eds.), Handbook of Hospitality Strategic Management. Elsevier. doi:10.1016/B978-0-08-045079-7.00004-1

Graham, J. (1985). The influence of culture on the process of business negotiations, an exploratory study. *Journal of International Business Studies, 16*(1), 81–96. doi:10.1057/palgrave.jibs.8490443

Graham, J. L., Mintu, A. T., & Rodgers, W. (1994). Explorations of Negotiation Behaviors in Ten Foreign Cultures Using a Model Developed in the United States. *Management Science, 40*(1), 72–95. doi:10.1287/mnsc.40.1.72

Graham, J., & Kaye, D. (2006). *A Risk Management Approach to Business Continuity: Aligning Business Continuity with Corporate Governance*. Rothstein Associates Inc.

Granovetter, M. (1973). The strength of weak ties. *American Journal of Sociology*, 78(6), 1360–1380. doi:10.1086/225469

Grant, R. M. (1996). Toward a knowledge-based theory of the firm. *Strategic Management Journal*, 17(S2), 109–122. doi:10.1002/smj.4250171110

Grant, R. M. (2003). Strategic Planning in a Turbolent Environment: Evidence from the Oil Majors. *Strategic Management Journal*, 24(6), 491–517. doi:10.1002/smj.314

Grant, R., & Nijman, J. (2002). Globalization and the corporate geography of cities in the less-developed world. *Annals of the Association of American Geographers*, 92(2), 320–340. doi:10.1111/1467-8306.00293

Griesse, M. (2006). The geographic, political, and economic context for corporate social responsibility in Brazil. *Journal of Business Ethics*, 73(1), 21–37. doi:10.1007/s10551-006-9194-2

Grigsby, R. K. (2015). Enhancing the Behavioral Science Knowledge and Skills of 21st-Century Leaders in Academic Medicine and Science. *Journal of Organizational Behavior Management*, 35(1/2), 123–134. doi:10.1080/01608061.2015.1031428

Grøgaard, B., & Verbeke, A. (2012). Twenty key hypotheses that make internalization theory the general theory of international strategic management. Handbook of Research in International Strategic Management, 7-30.

Grøgaard, B., Verbeke, A., & Zargarzadeh, M. A. (2011). Entrepreneurial Deficits in the Global Firm. *Entrepreneurship in the Global Firm*, 6, 117–137. doi:10.1108/S1745-8862(2011)0000006009

Gross, D. M., & Ryan, M. (2008). FDI location and size: Does employment protection legislation matter? *Regional Science and Urban Economics*, 38(6), 590–605. doi:10.1016/j.regsciurbeco.2008.05.012

Grossman, G. M., & Helpman, E. (1995). The Politics of Free Trade Agreements. *The American Economic Review*, 85, 667–690.

Gu, C., Kesteloot, C., & Cook, I. G. (2015). Theorising Chinese urbanisation: A multi-layered perspective. *Urban Studies (Edinburgh, Scotland)*, 52(14), 2564–2580. doi:10.1177/0042098014550457

Gulati, R. (1998). Alliances and networks. *Strategic Management Journal*, 19(4), 293–317. doi:10.1002/(SICI)1097-0266(199804)19:4<293::AID-SMJ982>3.0.CO;2-M

Gül, E., & Ekinci, A. (2006). Türkiye'de Enflasyon ve Döviz Kuru Arasındaki Nedensellik İlişkisi: 1984-2003. *Sosyal Bilimler Dergisi*, 1, 91–106.

Guzman-Anaya, L. (2016). Japanese Automotive FDI Linkages with Local Suppliers – Evidence from Survey data in Mexico's Western Region. In *Economic impact of Economic Partnership Agreement Mexico – Japan – theoretical and empirical aspects*. The Institute for Economic Studies. Seijo University.

Guzmán, L. (2013). *Are productivity spillovers from Japanese FDI larger than from U.S. FDI? Inter-industry evidence from Mexico*. Universidad de Guadalajara.

Habib, M., & Zurawicki, L. (2002). Corruption and foreign direct investment. *Journal of International Business Studies*, 33(2), 291–307. doi:10.1057/palgrave.jibs.8491017

Hakkala, K. N., Norback, P. J., & Svaleryd, H. (2008). Asymmetric effects of corruption on FDI: Evidence from Swedish multinational firms. *The Review of Economics and Statistics*, 90(4), 627–642. doi:10.1162/rest.90.4.627

Hall, D., & Lobina, E. (2012a). *The Birth, Growth and Decline of Multinational Water.* University of Greenwich. Retrieved from: http://www.right2water.eu/sites/water/files/the%20birth,%20growth%20and%20decline%20of%20water%20MNCs%20-D.%20Hall%20May%202012.pdf

Hall, D., & Lobina, E. (2012b). *Water Companies and Trends in Europe.* University of Greenwich. Retrieved from: http://www.epsu.org/sites/default/files/article/files/2012_Water_companies-EWCS.pdf

Hall, J., Matos, S., & Langford, C. (2008). Social exclusion and transgenic technology: The case of Brazilian agriculture. *Journal of Business Ethics, 77*(1), 45–63. doi:10.1007/s10551-006-9293-0

Hall, J., Matos, S., Silvestre, B., & Martin, M. (2011). Managing the Technological, Commercial, Organizational and Social Uncertainties of Industrial Evolution: The Case of Brazilian Energy and Agriculture. *Technological Forecasting and Social Change, 78,* 1147–1157. doi:10.1016/j.techfore.2011.02.005

Halme, M., Roome, N., & Dobers, P. (2009). Corporate responsibility: Reflections on context and consequences. *Scandinavian Journal of Management, 25*(1), 1–9. doi:10.1016/j.scaman.2008.12.001

Hamori, S., & Hamori, N. (2011). An empirical analysis of real exchange rate movements in the euro. *Applied Economics, 43*(10), 1187–1191. doi:10.1080/00036840802600319

Hampton, K., & Wellman, B. (2003). Neighboring in Netville: How the Internet supports community and social capital in a wired suburb. *City & Community, 2*(4), 277–311. doi:10.1046/j.1535-6841.2003.00057.x

Hanifan, L. J. (1916). The rural school community centre. *The Annals of the American Academy of Political and Social Science, 67*(1), 130–138. doi:10.1177/000271621606700118

Han, S. S., & Qin, B. (2009). The spatial distribution of producer services in Shanghai. *Urban Studies (Edinburgh, Scotland), 46*(4), 877–896. doi:10.1177/0042098009102133

Hansen, M. T., & Nohria, N. (2004). How to Build Collaborative Advantage, *MIT. Sloan Management Review, 46*(1), 22–31.

Hanson, G. (2001). *Should countries promote Foreign Direct Investment?* G24 Discussion Paper Series. No. 9. United Nations.

Hanson, G., & Harrison, A. (1999). Trade Liberalization and Wage Inequality in Mexico. *Industrial and Labor Relations Review, 52*(2), 271 – 288.

Hardcastle, J. (2015, August 26). Water Scarcity Puts Revenue At Risk. *Environmental Leader.* Retrieved from http://www.environmentalleader.com

Harish, R. (2010). Brand architecture in tourism branding: The way forward for India. *Journal of Indian Business Research, 2*(3), 153–165. doi:10.1108/17554191011069442

Harmon, G. (1984). Is there a single true morality? In *Krausz, M. (1989), Relativism: Interpretation and Confrontation.* Notre Dame, IN: University of Notre Dame Press.

Harris, N. (1997). Cities in a Global Economy: Structural Change and Policy Reactions. *Urban Studies (Edinburgh, Scotland), 34*(10), 1693–1703. doi:10.1080/0042098975402

Harris, P. R., & Moran, R. T. (1999). *Managing Cultural Differences: Leadership Strategies for a New World of Business* (5th ed.). Burlington, MA: Gulf Professional Publishing.

Hart, S. L., & Milstein, M. B. (2003). Creating sustainable value. *The Academy of Management Executive, 17*(2), 56–67. doi:10.5465/AME.2003.10025194

Harvey, D. (1990). *The condition of postmodernity*. Oxford, UK: Blackwell Publishers.

Haugh, H. (2007). New Strategies for a Sustainable Society: The growing contribution of Social Entrepreneurship. *Business Ethics Quarterly*, *17*(4), 743–749. doi:10.5840/beq20071747

Hawley, A. (1968). Human Ecology. In D. L. Sills (Ed.), *International Encyclopedia of the Social Sciences*. New York, NY: Macmillan.

Haynie, M. J., Shepherd, D., Mosakowski, E., & Earley, C. (2008). A situated metacognitive model of the entrepreneurial mindset. *Journal of Business Venturing*, *25*(2), 217–229. doi:10.1016/j.jbusvent.2008.10.001

Heath, J., Moriarty, J., & Norman, W. (2010). Business ethics and (or as) political philosophy. *Business Ethics Quarterly*, *20*(03), 427–452. doi:10.5840/beq201020329

He, C., & Yeung, G. (2011). The Locational Distribution of Foreign Banks in China: A Disaggregated Analysis. *Regional Studies*, *45*(6), 733–754. doi:10.1080/00343401003614282

Hechanova-Alampay, R., Beehr, T. A., Christiansen, N. D., & Van Horn, R. K. (2002). Adjustment and Strain among Domestic and International Student Sojourners. A Longitudinal Study. *School Psychology International*, *23*(4), 458–474. doi:10.1177/0143034302234007

Hedstrom, G., Poltorzycki, S., & Strob, P. (1998). *Sustainable develop- ment: the next generation of business opportunity*. Available at: http://www.resourcesaver.com/file/toolmanager/O16F4954.pdf

Heidenreich, M. (2012). The social embeddedness of multinational companies: A literature review. *Socio-economic Review*, *10*(3), 549–579. doi:10.1093/ser/mws010

Hellier, J., & Chusseau, N. (2010). Globalization and the inequality-unemployment tradeoff. *Review of International Economics*, *18*(5), 1028–1043. doi:10.1111/j.1467-9396.2010.00924.x

Helmer, R. (1997). Water Demand and Supply. In *Proceeding of the IAEA, Symposium, Tajeon, Republic of Korea* (pp. 15–24). Vienna, Austria: IAEA

Hendry, J. (2000). Strategic decision making, discourse, and strategy as social practice. *Journal of Management Studies*, *37*(7), 955–977. doi:10.1111/1467-6486.00212

Henisz, W. J. (2000). The institutional environment for multinational investment. *Journal of Law Economics and Organization*, *16*(2), 334–364. doi:10.1093/jleo/16.2.334

Henisz, W. J., & Williamson, O. E. (1999). Comparative economic organization: Within and between countries. *Business and Politics*, *1*(3), 261–277. doi:10.1515/bap.1999.1.3.261

Henisz, W. J., & Zelner, B. (2004). Explicating political hazards and safeguards: A transaction cost politics approach. *Industrial and Corporate Change*, *13*(6), 901–915. doi:10.1093/icc/dth036

Hennart, J. F. (1982). *A Theory of Multinational Enterprise*. Ann Arbor, MI: University of Michigan Press.

Hennart, J. F. (1991). The transaction costs theory of joint ventures: An empirical study of Japanese subsidiaries in the United States. *Management Science*, *37*(4), 483–497. doi:10.1287/mnsc.37.4.483

Hennart, J. F. (2014). The accidental internationalists: A theory of born globals. *Entrepreneurship Theory and Practice*, *38*(1), 117–135. doi:10.1111/etap.12076

Herbane, B., Elliott, D., & Swartz, E. (2004). Business Continuity Management: Time for a Strategic Role? *Long Range Planning*, *37*(5), 435–457. doi:10.1016/j.lrp.2004.07.011

Herreros, F. (2004). *The Problem of Forming Social Capital: Why Trust?* New York: Palgrave/Macmillan. doi:10.1057/9781403978806

Higgins, A., Power, C., & Kohlberg, L. (1984). The relationship of moral atmosphere to judgments of responsibility. *Morality, moral behavior, and moral development*, 74-106.

Hiles, A. (2004). *Business Continuity Management: Global Best Practices* (4th ed.). Rothstein Publishing.

Hill, R. C., & Kim, J. W. (2000). Global cities and developmental state: New York, Tokyo and Seoul. *Urban Studies (Edinburgh, Scotland)*, *37*(12), 2167–2195. doi:10.1080/00420980020002760

Hills, G. E., Lumpkin, G. T., & Singh, R. P. (1997). *Opportunity recognition: perceptions and behaviors of entrepreneurs. In Frontiers of Entrepreneurship Research*. Wellesley, MA: Babson College Press.

Hillson, D. (2003). *Effective Opportunity Management for Projects Exploiting Positive Risk*. New York: Marcel Dekker Inc. doi:10.1201/9780203913246

Hinds, P. J., & Pfeffer, J. (2003). Why organizations don't "know what they know": Cognitive and motivational factors affecting the transfer of expertise. In M. S. Ackerman, V. Pipek, & V. Wulf (Eds.), *Sharing expertise: Beyond knowledge management* (pp. 3–26). Cambridge, MA: The MIT Press.

Hirsch, P. M., & Levin, D. Z. (1999). Umbrella advocates versus validity police: A life-cycle model. *Organization Science*, *10*(1), 199–212. doi:10.1287/orsc.10.2.199

Hockerts, K. (2006). Entrepreneurial opportunity in social purpose business ventures. In J. Mair, J. Robinson, & K. Hockerts (Eds.), *Social Entrepreneurship* (pp. 142–154). New York: Palgrave Macmillan. doi:10.1057/9780230625655_10

Hodgson, D., & Cicmil, S. (Eds.). (2006). *Making projects critical*. New York: Palgrave McMillan Publishing. doi:10.1007/978-0-230-20929-9

Hodos, J. I. (2002). Globalization, regionalism, and urban restructuring: The case of Philadelphia. *Urban Affairs Review*, *37*(3), 358–379. doi:10.1177/10780870222185379

Hofstede, G. (1984). *Culture's consequences: International differences in work-related values* (Vol. 5). Los Angeles, CA: Sage Publication.

Hofstede, G. (1994). The business of international business is culture. *International Business Review*, *3*(1), 1–14. doi:10.1016/0969-5931(94)90011-6

Hofstede, G., Hofstede, G. J., & Minkov, M. (1991). *Cultures and organizations: Software of the mind* (Vol. 2). London: McGraw-Hill.

Hofstede, G., Hofstede, G. J., & Minkov, M. (2010). *Cultures and Organizations: Software of the Mind* (3rd ed.). New York: McGraw-Hill.

Holburn, G. L. F., & Zelner, B. A. (2010). Political capabilities, policy risk, and international investment strategy: Evidence from the global electric power generation industry. *Strategic Management Journal*, *31*(12), 1290–1315. doi:10.1002/smj.860

Hooker, J. N. (2008). *Corruption from a Cross-Cultural Perspective*. Retrieved from http://ethisphere.com/a-cross-cultural-view-of-corruption

Howaldt, J., & Schwarz, M. (2010). *Social Innovation: Concepts, research fields and international trends*. Dortmund: Sozialforschungsstelle Dortmund.

Hu, A. G. Z., & Jefferson, G. H. (2002, August). FDI Impact and Spillover: Evidence from Chinas Electronic and Textile Industries. *World Economy*, *25*(8), 1063–1076. doi:10.1111/1467-9701.00481

Hugo, G. (2004). A new global migration regime. *Around the Globe*, *1*(3), 18-23.

Hugo, G. (2005). The new international migration in Asia. *Asian Population Studies*, *1*(1), 93–120. doi:10.1080/17441730500125953

Hulett, D. T. (1995). Project Schedule Risk Assessment. *Journal of Project Management*, *26*(1), 21–31.

Hunt, J. G. (1999). Transformational/charismatic leaderships transformation of the field: An historical essay. *The Leadership Quarterly*, *10*(2), 129–144. doi:10.1016/S1048-9843(99)00015-6

Hunt, S. D., & Vitell, S. (1986). A general theory of marketing ethics. *Journal of Macromarketing*, *6*(1), 5–16. doi:10.1177/027614678600600103

Hurley-Hanson, A. E. (2006). Organizational responses and adaptations after 9-11. *Management Research News*, *29*(8), 480–494. doi:10.1108/01409170610692806

Husted, B. W. (2000). *Toward a model of cross-cultural business ethics: The impact of individualism and collectivism on the ethical decision-making process*. Academy of Management Proceedings.

Hutchinson, J. W. (1983). Expertise and the structure of free recall. In R. P. Bagozzi & A. M. Tybout (Eds.), *Advances in consumer research* (Vol. 10, pp. 585–589). Ann Arbor, MI: Association for Consumer Research.

Hutzschenreuter, T., Pedersen, T., & Volberda, H. W. (2007). The role of path dependency and managerial intentionality: A perspective on international business research. *Journal of International Business Studies*, *38*(7), 1055–1068. doi:10.1057/palgrave.jibs.8400326

Huysman, M., & Wulf, V. (2006). IT to support knowledge sharing in communities: Towards a social capital analysis. *Journal of Information Technology*, *21*(1), 40–51. doi:10.1057/palgrave.jit.2000053

IBGE. (2010). Instituto Brasileiro de Geografia e Estatística. Sintese de Indicadores Sociais. *Uma analise das condicoes de vida da populacao Brasileira*. Governo do Brasil. Rio de Janeiro. Retrieved from http://www.ibge.gov.br/home/estatistica/populacao/condicaodevida/indicadoresminimos/sinteseindicsociais2010/SIS_2010.pdf

IBNet Tariff Database. (n.d.). *Tariff list*. Retrieved from https://tariffs.ib-net.org/TariffTable?countryId=0

International Accounting Standard Board. (2011). *IFRS No 13 Fair Value Measurement*. Author.

Intesa Sanpaolo. (2017). *Information about Intesa Sanpaolo*. Retrieved January 13, 2017, from www.intesasanpaolo.it

Iversen, N. M., & Hem, L. E. (2008). Provenance associations as core values of place umbrella brands: A framework of characteristics. *European Journal of Marketing*, *42*(5/6), 603–626. doi:10.1108/03090560810862534

Izraeli, D. (1988). Ethical beliefs and behavior among managers: A cross-cultural perspective. *Journal of Business Ethics*, *7*(4), 263–271. doi:10.1007/BF00381831

Jackson, J., & Murphy, P. (2006). Clusters in regional tourism An Australian case. *Annals of Tourism Research*, *33*(4), 1018–1035. doi:10.1016/j.annals.2006.04.005

Jacobs, J. (1965). *The death and life of great American cities*. Penguin Books.

Jacobs, J. (1969). *The Economy of Cities*. New York: Vintage.

Jacoby, J., & Kyner, D. B. (1973). Brand loyalty vs. repeat purchasing behavior. *JMR, Journal of Marketing Research,* *10*(1), 1–9. doi:10.2307/3149402

Jang, S. S., & Feng, R. (2007). Temporal destination revisit intention: The effects of novelty seeking and satisfaction. *Tourism Management, 28*(2), 580–590. doi:10.1016/j.tourman.2006.04.024

Jarzabkowski, P. (2003). Strategic practices: An activity theory perspective on continuity and change. *Journal of Management Studies, 40*(1), 23–55. doi:10.1111/1467-6486.t01-1-00003

Jarzabkowski, P. (2004). Strategy as practice: Recursive, adaptive and practices-in-use. *Organization Studies, 25*(4), 529–560. doi:10.1177/0170840604040675

Jarzabkowski, P., Balogun, J., & Seidl, D. (2007). Strategizing: The challenges of a practice perspective. *Human Relations, 60*(1), 5–27. doi:10.1177/0018726707075703

Jarzabkowski, P., & Fenton, E. (2006). Strategizing and organizing in pluralistic contexts. *Long Range Planning, 39*(6), 631–648. doi:10.1016/j.lrp.2006.11.002

Jarzabkowski, P., & Paul Spee, A. (2009). Strategy as practice: A review and future directions for the field. *International Journal of Management Reviews, 11*(1), 69–95. doi:10.1111/j.1468-2370.2008.00250.x

Jarzabkowski, P., Paul Spee, A., & Smets, M. (2013). Material artifacts: Practices for doing strategy with 'stuff. *European Management Journal, 31*(1), 41–54. doi:10.1016/j.emj.2012.09.001

Jarzabkowski, P., & Seidl, D. (2008). The role of meetings in the social practice of strategy. *Organization Studies, 29*(11), 1391–1426. doi:10.1177/0170840608096388

Jarzabkowski, P., & Whittington, R. (2008). A strategy-as-practice approach to strategy research and education. *Journal of Management Inquiry, 17*(4), 282–286. doi:10.1177/1056492608318150

Jarzabkowski, P., & Wilson, D. C. (2002). Top teams and strategy in a UK university. *Journal of Management Studies, 39*(3), 355–387. doi:10.1111/1467-6486.00296

Jelenc, L., & Raguž, I. V. (2016). Past and Future: NeoStrategic Management. In I. V. Raguž, N. Podrug, & L. Jelenc (Eds.), *Neostrategic Management* (pp. 1–13). Springer International Publishing. doi:10.1007/978-3-319-18185-1_1

Jenkins, H. (2006). Small business champions for corporate social responsibility. *Journal of Business Ethics, 67*(3), 241–256. doi:10.1007/s10551-006-9182-6

Jennings, P. L., & Velasquez, M. (2015). Towards an Ethical Wealth of Nations: An Institutional Perspective on the Relation between Ethical Values and National Economic Prosperity. *Business Ethics Quarterly, 25*(04), 461–488. doi:10.1017/beq.2015.42

Jensen, N. M. (2006). *Nation-states and the Multinational Corporation: A Political Economy of Foreign Direct Investment.* Princeton, NJ: Princeton University Press.

Jensen, N. M., & Rosas, G. (2007). Foreign direct investment and income inequality in Mexico, 19902000. *International Organization, 61*(3), 467–487. doi:10.1017/S0020818307070178

Jiang, G. L. F., Holburn, G. L. F., & Beamish, P. W. (2014). The impact of vicarious experience on foreign location strategy. *Journal of International Management, 20*(3), 345–358. doi:10.1016/j.intman.2013.10.005

Jiao, H. (2011). A conceptual model for social entrepreneurship directed toward social impact on society. *Social Enterprise Journal, 7*(2), 130–149. doi:10.1108/17508611111156600

Johanson, J., & Vahlne, J. (1977). The internationalization process of the firm: A model of knowledge development and increasing foreign market commitments. *Journal of International Business Studies, 8*(1), 23–32. doi:10.1057/palgrave.jibs.8490676

Johnson, S., Kaufmann, D., & Zoido, P. (1999). *Corruption, Public Finance, and the Unofficial Economy.* World Bank Policy Research Working Paper No. 2169. Available at SSRN: http://ssrn.com/abstract=192569

Johnson, G., Langley, A., Melin, L., & Whittington, R. (2007). *Strategy as Practice: Research Directions and Resources.* Cambridge, UK: Cambridge University Press. doi:10.1017/CBO9780511618925

Johnson, G., Melin, L., & Whittington, R. (2003). Guest editors" introduction: Micro strategy and strategizing: towards an activity-based view. *Journal of Management Studies, 40*(1), 3–22. doi:10.1111/1467-6486.t01-2-00002

Johnson, S., Kaufmann, D., Shleifer, A., Goldman, M. I., & Weitzman, M. L. (1997). The unofficial economy in transition. *Brookings Papers on Economic Activity, 2*(2), 159–240. doi:10.2307/2534688

Johnson, S., McMillan, J., & Woodruff, C. (2000). Entrepreneurs and the Ordering of Institutional Reform: Poland, Slovakia, Romania, Russia and Ukraine Compared. *Economics of Transition, 8*(1), 1–36. doi:10.1111/1468-0351.00034

Jones, T. M. (1991). Ethical decision making by individuals in organizations: An issue-contingent model. *Academy of Management Review, 16*(2), 366–395.

Jordaan, J. (2009). *Foreign Direct Investment Agglomeration and Externalities. In Capítulo 3: Agglomeration and FDI Location in Mexican Regions.* Ashgate.

Jorde, T. M., & Teece, D. J. (1990). Innovation and cooperation: Implications for competition and antitrust. *The Journal of Economic Perspectives, 4*(3), 75–96. doi:10.1257/jep.4.3.75

Juhn, G., & Mauro, P. (2002). *Long-Run Determinants of Exchange Rate Regimes A Simple Sensitivity Analysis.* IMF Working Paper.

Kahneman, D., & Lovallo, D. (1993). Timid choices and bold forecasts: A cognitive perspective on risk-taking. *Management Science, 39*(1), 17–31. doi:10.1287/mnsc.39.1.17

Kaish, S., & Gilad, B. (1991). Characteristics of Opportunities Search of Entrepreneurs vs Executives: Sources, interests, and general alertness. *Journal of Business Venturing, 6*(1), 45–61. doi:10.1016/0883-9026(91)90005-X

Kang, X., & Shouzhen, W. (2003). *Economic Globalization and Foreign Direct Investment in Shanghai.* Paper presented at the The 15th Annual Conference of the Association for Chinese Economics Studies Australia (ACESA), Melbourne, Australia.

Kant, I. (1785). Groundwork for the Metaphysics of Morals. Academic Press.

Kaplan, A. M., & Haenlein, M. (2010). Users of the world, unite! The challenges and opportunities of Social Media. *Business Horizons, 53*(1), 59–68. doi:10.1016/j.bushor.2009.09.003

Kaplan, F., & Yapraklı, S. (2014). Ekonomik Kırılganlık Endeksi Göstergelerinin Döviz Kuru Üzerindeki Etkileri: Kırılgan 12 Ülke Üzerine Panel Veri Analizi. *Uluslararası Alanya İşletme Fakültesi Dergisi, 6*(3), 111–121.

Kash, T. J., & Darling, J. R. (1998). Crisis management: Prevention, diagnosis and intervention. *Leadership and Organization Development Journal, 19*(4), 179–186. doi:10.1108/01437739810217151

Kasurova, V. (2010). *Modeli i Pokazateli za Analiz na Finansovata Ustoiychivost na Kompaniyata* [Models and Indicators for Analysis of Financial Stability of the Company]. Unpublished manuscript, New Bulgarian University, Sofia, Bulgaria. Retrieved from: http://eprints.nbu.bg/637/1/FU_1_FINAL.pdf

Katz, J. P., Swanson, D. L., & Nelson, L. K. (2001). Culture-based expectations of corporate citizenship: A propositional framework and comparison of four cultures. *The International Journal of Organizational Analysis, 9*(2), 149–171. doi:10.1108/eb028931

Kavanaugh, A. L., Reese, D. D., Carroll, J. M., & Rosson, M. B. (2005). Weak ties in networked communities. *The Information Society, 21*(2), 119–131. doi:10.1080/01972240590925320

Kawachi, I., Kennedy, B. P., & Wilkinson, R. G. (1999). Crime: Social disorganization and relative deprivation. *Social Science & Medicine, 48*(6), 719–731. doi:10.1016/S0277-9536(98)00400-6 PMID:10190635

Keefer, P., & Knack, S. (2002). Polarization, politics and property rights: Links between inequality and growth. *Public Choice, 111*(1-2), 127–154. doi:10.1023/A:1015168000336

Keeling, D. J. (Ed.). (1995). *Transport and the world city paradigm.* Cambridge, UK: Cambridge UP. doi:10.1017/CBO9780511522192.008

Keller, K. L. (2003). Understanding brands, branding and brand equity. *Interactive Marketing, 5*(1), 7–20. doi:10.1057/palgrave.im.4340213

Kelly, A. (1983). Case Study -- Italian Tax Mores. In *Ethical Issues in Business: A Philosophical Approach* (2nd ed.). Englewood Cliffs, NJ: Prentice Hall Inc.

Kendrick, T. (2015). *Identifying and Managing Project Risks: essential tools for failure-proofing your project* (3rd ed.). Amacon.

Kenis, P., & Knoke, D. (2002). How organizational field networks shape interorganizational tie-formation rates. *Academy of Management Review, 27*(2), 275–293.

Kerzner, H. (2009). *Project Management* (10th ed.). Hoboken, NJ: John Wiley & Sons, Inc.

Kia, A. (2013). Determinants of the real exchange rate in a small open economy: Evidence from Canada. *Journal of International Financial Markets, Institutions and Money, 23*, 163–178. doi:10.1016/j.intfin.2012.09.001

Kieser, A. (1989). Organizational, institutional, and societal evolution: Medieval craft guilds and the genesis of formal organizations. *Administrative Science Quarterly, 34*(4), 540–564. doi:10.2307/2393566

Kihlstrom, R., & Laffont, J. (1979). A General Equilibrium Entrepreneurial Theory of Firm Formation Based on Risk Aversion. *Journal of Political Economy, 87*(4), 719–740. doi:10.1086/260790

Kim, H. M. (2015). The role of foreign firms in China's urban transformation: a case study of Suzhou. In T.-C. Wong, S. S. Han, & H. Zhang (Eds.), *Population Mobility, Urban Planning and Management in China* (pp. 127–143). London: Springer. doi:10.1007/978-3-319-15257-8_8

Kim, H. M., & Cocks, M. (2017). The role of Quality of Place factors in expatriate international relocation decisions: A case study of Suzhou, a globally-focused Chinese city. *Geoforum, 81*, 1–10. doi:10.1016/j.geoforum.2017.01.018

Kim, H. M., & Han, S. S. (2012). City profile: Seoul. *Cities (London, England), 29*(2), 142–154. doi:10.1016/j.cities.2011.02.003

Kim, H. M., & Han, S. S. (2014). Inward foreign direct investment in Korea: Location patterns and local impacts. *Habitat International, 44*, 146–157. doi:10.1016/j.habitatint.2014.05.011

Kim, H. M., Han, S. S., & OConnor, K. B. (2015). Foreign housing investment in Seoul: Origin of investors and location of investment. *Cities (London, England), 42*, 212–223. doi:10.1016/j.cities.2014.07.006

Kinoshita, Y. (2001). *R&D and Technology Spillovers via FDI: Innovation and Absorptive Capacity.* Working Paper 349a. CERGE-EI, WDI, University of Michigan and CEPR. Retrieved from http://citeseerx.ist.psu.edu/viewdoc/downl oad?doi=10.1.1.200.1078&rep=rep1&type=pdf

Kippenberger, T. (1999). Reducing the Impact of the Unexpected. *Management Research, 4*(3), 28–31.

Kirzner, I. M. (1973). *Competition and Entrepreneurship.* Chicago, IL: University of Chicago Press.

Kirzner, I. M. (1979). *Perception, Opportunity, and Profit.* Chicago, IL: University of Chicago Press.

Klaiber, H., Smith, V., Kaminsky, M., & Strong, A. (2010). *Estimating the Price Elasticity of Demand for Water with Quasi Experimental Methods.* Paper presented at 2010 Annual Meeting of Agricultural and Applied Economics Association, Denver, CO. Retrieved from: http://ageconsearch.umn.edu/bitstream/61039/2/010260.pdf

Knack, S., & Keefer, P. (1997). Does inequality harm growth only in democracies? A replication and extension. *American Journal of Political Science, 41*(1), 323–332. doi:10.2307/2111719

Knight, F. (1964). *Risk, Uncertainly and Profit.* Retrieved from: https://mises.org/sites/default/files/Risk,%20Uncertainty,%20and%20Profit_4.pdf

Knight, F. (1921). *Risk, Uncertainty, and Profit.* Boston, MA: Hart, Schaffner and Marx, Houghton Mifflin.

Knight, P. (2001). *Small-Scale Research: Pragmatic Inquiry in Social Science and the Caring Professions.* London, UK: SAGE Publications.

Knights, D., & Morgan, G. (1995). Strategy Under the Microscope: Strategic Management and It in Financial Services. *Journal of Management Studies, 32*(2), 191–214. doi:10.1111/j.1467-6486.1995.tb00340.x

Kodama, M. (2005). New knowledge creation through leadership-based strategic community – a case of new product development in IT and multimedia business fields. *Technovation, 25*(8), 895–908. doi:10.1016/j.technovation.2004.02.016

Kohlberg, L. (1976). Moral stages and moralization: The cognitive-developmental approach. *Moral development and behavior: Theory, research, and social issues,* 31-53.

Kohlberg, L. (1969). Stage and sequence: the cognitive-developmental approach to socializa- tion. In D. A. Goslin (Ed.), *Handbook of socialisation theory and research* (pp. 347–480). Chicago: Rand McNally.

Koivu, T., Nummelin, J., Tukiainen, S., Tainio, R., & Atkin, B. (2004). *Institutional complexity affecting the outcomes of global projects.* Working Papers 14. VTT.

Kolvereid, L. (1992). Growth aspirations among Norwegian entrepreneurs. *Journal of Business Venturing, 5*(3), 209–222. doi:10.1016/0883-9026(92)90027-O

Kothari, C. R. (2004). *Research methodology: methods and techniques.* New Delhi, India: Age International.

Krugman, P. R., Obstfeld, M., & Melitz, M. J. (2012). Economía Internacional. *Pearson Educación, Madrid, 2012,* 266.

Ksenia, Z. (2014). Leadership in organizational practice: Closing the knowing-doing gap. *Strategic HR Review, 13*(2), 69–74. doi:10.1108/SHR-10-2013-0093

Kumar, L. V. (2008). Urban infrastructure and water resources. *Water and Energy International, 65*(3), 77–80.

Kuznets, S. (1955). Economic growth and income inequality. *The American Economic Review, 45*(1), 1–28.

Kylänen, M., & Rusko, R. (2011). Unintentional coopetition in the service industries: The case of pyhä-luosto tourism destination in the finish Lapland. *European Management Journal, 29*(3), 193–205. doi:10.1016/j.emj.2010.10.006

Ladyshewsky, R. K., & Flavell, H. (2012). Transfer of Training in an Academic leadership Development Program for Program Coordinators. *Educational Management Administration & Leadership, 40*(1), 127–147. doi:10.1177/1741143211420615

Lafontaine, F., & Sivadasan, J. (2009). Do labor market rigidities have microeconomic effects? Evidence from within the firm. *American Economic Journal. Applied Economics, 1*(2), 88–127. doi:10.1257/app.1.2.88

Laforet, S., & Saunders, J. (1994). Managing brand portfolios: How the leaders do it. *Journal of Advertising Research, 34*(5), 64–77.

Lallana, C. (2003). *Water Prices* [Fact Sheet]. Retrieved from: http://www.eea.europa.eu/data-and-maps/indicators/water-prices/water-prices

Lan, L., Qing-hua, H., & Long-long, S. (2015). Identifying the Project Complexity Factors of Complex Construction Projects. *Proceedings of International Conference on Management Science & Engineering (22ᵗʰ)* (pp. 1697-1702). Retrieved October 07, 2016 from http://icmse.hit.edu.cn/icmsecn/ch/reader/create_pdf.aspx?file_no=L2015090226&flag=2

Langowitz, N., & Minniti, M. (2007). The entrepreneurial propensity of women. *Entrepreneurship Theory and Practice, 31*(3), 341–364. doi:10.1111/j.1540-6520.2007.00177.x

Larrison, T. (1998). Ethics and international development. *Business Ethics (Oxford, England), 7*(1), 63–67. doi:10.1111/1467-8608.00089

Larson, M. S. (1979). The rise of professionalism. *SA. Sociological Analysis, 233*. PMID:489184

Laszlo, E. (1994). The evolutionary project manager. In D. I. Cleland & R. Gareis (Eds.), *Global project management handbook* (International Editions). New York: McGraw-Hill.

Lave, J., & Wenger, E. (1991). *Situated learning: Legitimate peripheral participation.* Cambridge University Press. doi:10.1017/CBO9780511815355

Lawrence, T. B., Hardy, C., & Phillips, N. (2002). Institutional effects of interorganizational collaboration: The emergence of proto-institutions. *Academy of Management Journal, 45*(1), 281–290. doi:10.2307/3069297

Le Bas, C., & Sierra, C. (2002). Location versus home country advantages in R&D activities: Some further results on multinationals locational strategies. *Research Policy, 31*(4), 589–609. doi:10.1016/S0048-7333(01)00128-7

Leadbeater, C. (2007). *Social enterprises and social innovation: strategies for the next ten years. A social enterprise think piece for the Office of the Third Sector.* Cabinet Office. Retrieved from http://www.sagepub.com/sites/default/files/upm-binaries/66035_Cnaan_Chapter_2.pdf

Lebreton, P. P. (1957). The Case Study Method and the Establishment of Standards of Efficiency. Academy of Management Proceedings, 103.

Lee, W. (2014). Development of Chinese enclaves in the Seoul-Incheon metropolitan area, South Korea. *International Development Planning Review, 36*(3), 293–311. doi:10.3828/idpr.2014.17

Lehmacher, W. (2016). *Don't blame china for taking u.S. Jobs.* Fortune.

Leibenstein, H. (1968). Entrepreneurship and development. *The American Economic Review, 58*(2), 72–83.

Leidecker, J. K., & Bruno, A. V. (1984). Identifying and using critical success factors. *Long Range Planning, 17*(1), 23–32. doi:10.1016/0024-6301(84)90163-8

Lei, H. S., & Chen, Y. S. (2011). The right tree for the right bird: Location choice decision of Taiwanese firms FDI in China and Vietnam. *International Business Review, 20*(3), 338–352. doi:10.1016/j.ibusrev.2010.10.002

Lesser, E. L., & Storck, J. (2001). Communities of practice and organizational performance. *IBM Systems Journal*, *40*(4), 831–841. doi:10.1147/sj.404.0831

Lesser, E., & Prusak, L. (2000). Communities of practice, social capital, and organizational knowledge. In J. A. Woods & J. Cortada (Eds.), *The knowledge management yearbook 2000-2001* (pp. 251–259). Amsterdam: Elsevier. doi:10.1016/B978-0-7506-7293-1.50011-1

Levie, J., & Hunt, S. (2005). *Culture, Institutions and New Business Activity: Evidence from Global Entrepreneurship Monitor*. Babson College. Retrieved from http://fusionmx.babson.edu/entrep/fer/fer_2004/web-content/Section%20XIX/P2/XIX-P2_Text.html

Levie, J., & Autio, E. (2008). A theoretical grounding and test of the GEM model. *Small Business Economics*, *31*(3), 235–263. doi:10.1007/s11187-008-9136-8

Levin, G., & Ward, J. L. (2011). *Project Management Complexity. A Competency Model*. Taylor & Francis Group.

Levitt, B., & March, J. G. (1988). Organizational learning. *Annual Review of Sociology*, *14*(1), 319–340. doi:10.1146/annurev.so.14.080188.001535

Liao, J., & Welsch, H. (2003). Social capital and entrepreneurial growth aspiration: A comparison of technology- and non-technology-based nascent entrepreneurs. *The Journal of High Technology Management Research*, *14*(1), 149–170. doi:10.1016/S1047-8310(03)00009-9

Lieberman, M. B., & Dhawan, R. (2005, July). Assessing the Resource Base of Japanese and U.S. Auto Producers: A Stochastic Frontier Production Function Approach. *Management Science*, *51*(7), 1060–1075. doi:10.1287/mnsc.1050.0416

Lin, N. (1982). Social resources and instrumental action. In M. Peter & N. Lin (Eds.), *Social Structure and Network Analysis* (pp. 131–145). Beverly Hills, CA: Sage.

Lin, N. (1999). Social networks and status attainment. *Annual Review of Sociology*, *25*(1), 467–488. doi:10.1146/annurev.soc.25.1.467

Lin, S. C., Kim, D. H., & Wu, Y. C. (2013). Foreign direct investment and income inequality: Human capital matters. *Journal of Regional Science*, *53*(5), 874–896. doi:10.1111/jors.12077

Li, Y., & Wu, F. (2012). The transformation of regional governance in China: The rescaling of statehood. *Progress in Planning*, *78*(2), 55–99. doi:10.1016/j.progress.2012.03.001

Li, Z., & Wu, F. (2006). Socioeconomic transformations in Shanghai (19902000): Policy impacts in global-national-local contexts. *Cities (London, England)*, *23*(4), 250–268. doi:10.1016/j.cities.2006.01.002

Locke, J. (1924). *An essay concerning human understanding*. Academic Press.

Lokman, D., & Sitki, C. (2014). The Relationship between Servant Leadership Behaviors and Leader-Member Exchange: A research on a State University. *Suleyman Demirel University Journal of Faculty of Economics & Administrative Sciences*, *19*(4), 287–310.

Lommerud, K. E., Meland, F., & Sorgard, L. (2003). Unionised oligopoly, trade liberalisation and location choice. *The Economic Journal*, *113*(490), 782–800. doi:10.1111/1468-0297.t01-1-00154

Loosemore, M., Raftery, J., Reilly, C., & Higgon, D. (2006). *Risk Management in Projects*. New York: Taylor & Francis.

Lopez Gonzalez, J., Kowalski, P., & Achard, P. (2015). Trade, global value chains and wage-income inequality. *OECD Trade Policy Papers*, (182).

Lopez-Perez, M. V., Perez-Lopez, M. C., & Rodriguez-Ariza, L. (2009). Corporate Social Responsibility and Innovation in European Companies. An empirical research. *Corporate Ownership & Control, 7*(1), 274–285. doi:10.22495/cocv7i1c2p3

Lorange, P., & Vancil, R. F. (1995). How to design a strategic planning system. In P. Lorange (Ed.), *Strategic Planning and Control: Issues in the Strategy Process*. Cambridge, MA: Blackwell.

Low, S. P., Liu, J., & Sio, S. (2010). Business continuity management in large construction companies in Singapore. *Disaster Prevention and Management, 19*(2), 219–232. doi:10.1108/09653561011038011

Lucifora, A., Bianco, F., & Vagliasindi, G. M. (2015). *Environmental crime and corporate and corporate mis-compliance: A case study on the ILVA steel plant in Italy. In Study in the framework of the EFFACE research project*. Catania: University of Catania.

Lugo Sánchez, M. G. (2016). Economic Partnership Agreement Mexico - Japan: Analysis of Trade Creation and Trade Diversion 1999-2013. In Economic impact of Economic Partnership Agreement Mexico – Japan – theoretical and empirical aspects (pp. 1-16). The Institute for Economic Studies. Seijo University.

Luo, Y. (2007). A coopetition perspective of global competition. *Journal of World Business, 42*(2), 129–144. doi:10.1016/j.jwb.2006.08.007

Lu, X. (2001). Ethical issues in the globalization of the knowledge economy. *Business Ethics (Oxford, England), 10*(2), 113–119. doi:10.1111/1467-8608.00221

Lynch, R. (2009). Strategic Management (5th ed.). Pearson Education Limited.

MacDonald, R. (1998). What determines real exchange rates?: The long and the short of it. *Journal of International Financial Markets, Institutions and Money, 8*(2), 117–153. doi:10.1016/S1042-4431(98)00028-6

Macher, J. T., & Richman, B. (2008). Transaction cost economics: An assessment of empirical research in the social sciences. *Business and Politics, 10*(1), 1–63. doi:10.2202/1469-3569.1210

Madhok, A. (1997). Cost, value and foreign market entry mode: The transaction and the firm. *Strategic Management Journal, 18*(1), 39–61. doi:10.1002/(SICI)1097-0266(199701)18:1<39::AID-SMJ841>3.0.CO;2-J

Mah, J. S. (2012). Foreign direct investment, labour unionization and income inequality of Korea. *Applied Economics Letters, 19*(15), 1521–1524. doi:10.1080/13504851.2011.637888

Mahler, V. A., Jesuit, D. K., & Roscoe, D. D. (1999). Exploring the impact of trade and investment on income inequality: A cross-national sectoral analysis of the developed countries. *Comparative Political Studies, 32*(3), 363–395. doi:10.1177/0010414099032003004

Ma, L. J. (2004). Economic reforms, urban spatial restructuring, and planning in China. *Progress in Planning, 61*(3), 237–260. doi:10.1016/j.progress.2003.10.005

Ma, L. J. C., & Wu, F. (2005). Restructuring the Chinese city. In L. J. C. Ma & F. Wu (Eds.), *Restructuring the Chinese city: changing society, economy and space* (pp. 1–18). London: Routledge. doi:10.4324/9780203414460_chapter_1

Malone, S. (1989). Selected correlates of business continuity planning in the family business. *Family Business Review, 2*(4), 341–353. doi:10.1111/j.1741-6248.1989.tb00003.x

Manger, M. S. (2005). Competition and bilateralism in trade policy: The case of Japans free trade agreements. *Review of International Political Economy, 12*(5), 804–828. doi:10.1080/09692290500339800

Mann, T. (2016, Nov. 14). GA appliance workers reject contract offer from Chinese owner. *Wall Street Journal*.

Manolova, T. S., Eunni, R. V., & Gyoshev, B. S. (2008). Institutional Environments for Entrepreneurship: Evidence from Emerging Economies in Eastern Europe. *Entrepreneurship Theory & Practice*, *32*(1), 203–218. doi:10.1111/j.1540-6520.2007.00222.x

Mariani, M. M., & Baggio, R. (2012). Special issue: Managing tourism in a changing world: Issues and cases. *Anatolia*, *23*(1), 1–3. doi:10.1080/13032917.2011.653636

Mariani, M. M., Buhalis, D., Longhi, C., & Vitouladiti, O. (2014). Managing change in tourism destinations: Key issues and current trends. *Journal of Destination Marketing & Management*, *2*(4), 269–272. doi:10.1016/j.jdmm.2013.11.003

Mark, N. C. (2009). Changing monetary policy rules, learning, and real exchange rate dynamics. *Journal of Money, Credit and Banking*, *41*(6), 1047–1070. doi:10.1111/j.1538-4616.2009.00246.x

Marron, D. B., & Steel, D. G. (2000). Which countries protect intellectual property? The case of software piracy. *Economic Inquiry*, *38*(2), 159–174. doi:10.1111/j.1465-7295.2000.tb00011.x

Marshall, A. (1890). *Principios de Economía*. London: Ingletarra.

Marsick, V. J., & Watkins, K. E. (1999). *Facilitating learning organizations*. Gower.

Martin, L. (2009). Reproductive tourism in the age of globalization. *Globalizations*, *6*(2), 249–263. doi:10.1080/14747730802500398

Martin, R. L., & Osberg, S. (2007). Social entrepreneurship: The case for definition. *Stanford Social Innovation Review*, *5*(2), 29–39.

Marx, K. (1965). *Capital: a critical analysis of capitalistic production* (Vol. 3). Progress Publishers.

Marx, K. (1973). *Grundrisse: Foundation of the critique of political economy* (M. Nicolaus, Trans.). Harmondsworth, UK: Penguin.

Marx, K. (1978). *Wage Labour and Capital*. Peking: Foreign Language Press.

Marx, K. (2012). *Economic and philosophic manuscripts of 1844*. Courier Corporation.

Mathieu, J. E., Kukenberger, M. R., DInnocenzo, L., & Reilly, G. (2015). Modeling reciprocal team cohesion–performance relationships, as impacted by shared leadership and members competence. *The Journal of Applied Psychology*, *100*(3), 713–734. doi:10.1037/a0038898 PMID:25751749

Matten, D., & Moon, J. (2004). Corporate social responsibility education in Europe. *Journal of Business Ethics*, *54*(4), 323–337. doi:10.1007/s10551-004-1822-0

Matten, D., & Moon, J. (2008). Implicit and explicit CSR: A conceptual framework for a comparative understanding of corporate social responsibility. *Academy of Management Review*, *33*(2), 404–424. doi:10.5465/AMR.2008.31193458

Mayerhofer, H., Hartmann, L. S., Michelitsch-Riedl, G., & Kollinger, I. (2004). Expatriate Assignments: A Neglected Issue in Global Staffing. *International Journal of Human Resource Management*, *15*(8), 1371–1389. doi:10.1080/0958519042000257986

McAfee, A. P. (2006). Enterprise 2.0: The dawn of emergent collaboration. *MIT Sloan Management Review*, *47*(3), 21–28.

McGuire, J., & Dow, S. (2009, June). Japanese keiretsu: Past, present, future. *Asia Pacific Journal of Management*, *26*(2), 333–351. doi:10.1007/s10490-008-9104-5

McKercher, B., Denizci-Guillet, B., & Ng, E. (2012). Rethinking loyalty. *Annals of Tourism Research*, *39*(2), 708–734. doi:10.1016/j.annals.2011.08.005

McMillan, J., & Woodruff, C. (1999). Interfirm Relationships and Informal Credit in Vietnam. *The Quarterly Journal of Economics*, *114*(4), 1285–1320. doi:10.1162/003355399556278

McMillan, J., & Woodruff, C. (2002). The Central Role of Entrepreneurs in Transition Economies. *The Journal of Economic Perspectives*, *16*(3), 153–170. doi:10.1257/089533002760278767

McMullan, R., & Gilmore, A. (2008). Customer loyalty: An empirical study. *European Journal of Marketing*, *42*(9/10), 1084–1094. doi:10.1108/03090560810891154

Mehanna, R. A., & Shamsub, H. (2002). Who is benefitting the most from NAFTA? An intervention time series analysis. *Journal of Economic Development*, *27*(2), 69–79.

Mendenhall, M. E., & Stahl, G. K. (2000). Expatriate training and development: Where do we go from here? *Human Resource Management*, *39*(2), 251–265. doi:10.1002/1099-050X(200022/23)39:2/3<251::AID-HRM13>3.0.CO;2-I

Mendenhall, M., & Oddou, G. (1986). Acculturation profiles of expatriate managers: Implications for cross-cultural training programs. *The Columbia Journal of World Business*, *21*(4), 73–79.

Menz, M. (2012). Functional Top Management Team Members: A Review, Synthesis, and Research Agenda. *Journal of Management*, *38*(1), 45–80. doi:10.1177/0149206311421830

Metcalf, L. E., Bird, A., Shankarmahesh, M., Aycan, Z., Larimo, J., & Valdelamar, D. D. (2006). Cultural tendencies in negotiation: A comparison of Finland, India, Mexico, Turkey, and the United States. *Journal of World Business*, *41*(4), 382–294. doi:10.1016/j.jwb.2006.08.004

Meyer, K., & Sinani, E. (2009) When and Where Does Direct Investment Generate Positive Spillovers? A Meta- Analysis. *Journal of International Business Studies*, *40*(7), 1075-1094.

Meyer, M. H., & Crane, F. G. (2014). *New Venture Creation*. SAGE Publications.

Millen, D. R., & Patterson, J. F. (2003). Identity disclosure and the creation of social capital. CHI'03 extended abstracts on Human factors in computing systems, 720-721. doi:10.1145/765891.765950

Mill, J. S. (1910). *Utilitarianism, Liberty, Representative Government*. London: Dent.

Minniti, M. (2004). Entrepreneurial alertness and asymmetric information in a spin-glass model. *Journal of Business Venturing*, *19*(5), 637–658. doi:10.1016/j.jbusvent.2003.09.003

Mintzberg, H., Ahlstrand, B., & Lampel, J. (1998). *Strategy Safari: A guided tour through the wilds of strategic management*. Free Press.

Mintzberg, H. (1973). Strategy making in three modes. *Management Review*, *16*(2), 44–53.

Mintzberg, H. (1973). *The Nature of Managerial Work*. New York: Harper & Row.

Mintzberg, H. (1975). The Manager's Job: Folklore and Fact. *Harvard Business Review*, 56–62.

Mintzberg, H. (1980). Structure in 5's: A Synthesis of the Research on Organization Design. *Management Science*, *26*(3), 322–341. doi:10.1287/mnsc.26.3.322

Mintzberg, H. (1994a). *The Rise and Fall of Strategic Management*. Hemel Hempstead, UK: Prentice-Hall.

Mintzberg, H. (1994b). The Rise and Fall of Strategic Management. *Harvard Business Review*, *72*(1), 107–114.

Mintzberg, H., & Waters, J. A. (1978). Patterns in strategy formation. *Management science, 24*(9), 934948. Mintzberg H & Waters J (1985). Of Strategies, Deliberate and Emergent. *Strategic Management Journal, 6*(3), 257–272. doi:10.1002/smj.4250060306

Mirvis, P. H. (1996). Historical foundations of organization learning. *Journal of Organizational Change Management, 9*(1), 13–31. doi:10.1108/09534819610107295

Molden, D. (Ed.). (2007). *Water for Food, Water for Life: A Comprehensive Assessment of Water.* Routledge.

Moon, J., Crane, A., & Matten, D. (2005). Can corporations be citizens? Corporate citizenship as a metaphor for business participation in society. *Business Ethics Quarterly, 15*(03), 429–453. doi:10.5840/beq200515329

Moore, S. A., Rodger, K., & Taplin, R. (2015). Moving beyond visitor satisfaction to loyalty in nature-based tourism: A review and research agenda. *Current Issues in Tourism, 18*(7), 667–683. doi:10.1080/13683500.2013.790346

Moores, T. T. (2003). The effect of national culture and economic wealth on global software piracy rates. *Communications of the ACM, 46*(9), 207–215. doi:10.1145/903893.903939

Moorman, C., & Miner, A. S. (1998). Organizational improvisation and organizational memory. *Academy of Management Review, 23*(4), 698–723.

Morais, M.N. (2006). Uma análise da relação entre o Estado e o tráfico de drogas: O mito do Poder Paralelo. *Revista Ciências Sociais em Perspectiva,* 117-136.

Morales-Zumaquero, A. (2006). Explaining real exchange rate fluctuations. *Journal of Applied Econometrics, 9*(2), 345–381.

Morgan, G. (1997). *Images of organization.* London: Sage Publications.

Morgan, N., Jones, G., & Hodges, A. (2012). *Social media.* The Complete Guide to Social Media From The Social Media Guys.

Morris, M., Schindehutte, M., & Allen, J. (2005). The entrepreneurs business model: Toward a unified perspective. *Journal of Business Research, 58*(6), 726–735. doi:10.1016/j.jbusres.2003.11.001

Morris, M., & Western, B. (1999). Inequality in earnings at the close of the twentieth century. *Annual Review of Sociology, 25*(1), 623–657. doi:10.1146/annurev.soc.25.1.623

Mort, G. S., Weerawardena, J., & Carnegie, K. (2003). Social entrepreneurship: Towards conceptualization. *International Journal of Nonprofit and Voluntary Sector Marketing, 8*(1), 76–88. doi:10.1002/nvsm.202

Motet, G. (2009). Les cahiers de la sécurité industrielle. *La Norme ISO, 31000,* 10.

Mugenda, O. M., & Mugenda, A. G. (2008). *Research methods.* Nairobi, Kenya: Nairobi Press.

Mullany, G. (2017, January 16). World's 8 richest have as much a wealth as bottom half, Oxfam says. *New York Times.*

Muzır, E. (2011). *Basel II Düzenlemeleri Doğrultusunda Kredi Riski Analizi ve Ölçümü: Geleneksel Ekonometrik Modellerin Yapay Sinir Ağları ve MARS Modelleriyle Karşılaştırılmasına Yönelik Ampirik Bir Çalışma.* İstanbul Üniversitesi Sosyal Bilimler Enstitüsü, Yayınlanmamış Doktora Tezi.

Naffziger, D., Hornsby, J. S., & Kuratko, D. F. (1994). A proposed research model of entrepreneurial motivation. *Entrepreneurship Theory and Practice, 18*(3), 29–39.

NAFTA Secretariat. (1994). *North American Free Trade Agreement.* Retrieved January, 30, 2017, from http://www.nafta-sec-alena.org/en/view.aspx?conID=590&mtpiID=ALL

Nahapiet, J., & Ghoshal, S. (1998). Social capital, intellectual capital, and the organizational advantage. *Academy of Management Review*, *23*(2), 242–266.

Neckerman, K. M., & Torche, F. (2007). Inequality: Causes and consequences. *Annual Review of Sociology*, *33*(1), 335–357. doi:10.1146/annurev.soc.33.040406.131755

Nelson, R. R., & Winter, S. G. (1982). *An Evolutionary Theory of Economic Change*. Cambridge, UK: Belknap.

Neri, M. (2009). Income Policies, Income Distribution, and the Distribution of Opportunities in Brazil. In L. Brainard & L. Martinez-Diaz (Eds.), *Brazil as an Economic Superpower?: Understanding Brazil's Changing Role in the Global Economy*. Washington, DC: Brookings Institution Press.

Neuman, W. L. (2010). *Social Research Methods: Qualitative and Quantitative Approaches* (4th ed.). Pearson Education.

Nicholls, A. (2006). Playing the field: A new approach to the meaning of social entrepreneurship. *Social Enterprise Journal*, *2*(1), 1–5.

Nielsen, B., Asmussen, C., & Weatherall, C. (2017). The location choice of foreign direct investments: Empirical evidence and methodological challenges. *Journal of World Business*, *52*(1), 62–82. doi:10.1016/j.jwb.2016.10.006

Nobeoka, K., & Cusumano, M. A. (1997). Multiproject Strategy and Sales Growth: The Benefits of Rapid Design Transfer in New Product Development. *Strategic Management Journal*, *18*(3), 169–186. doi:10.1002/(SICI)1097-0266(199703)18:3<169::AID-SMJ863>3.0.CO;2-K

Nokes, S., & Kelly, S. (2008). *Il project management. Tecniche e processi*. Milano, Italy: FT Prentice Hall.

Nonaka, I. (1991). The knowledge-creating company. *Harvard Business Review*, *69*(6), 96–104.

Nonaka, I. (1994). A dynamic theory of organizational knowledge creation. *Organization Science*, *5*(1), 14–37. doi:10.1287/orsc.5.1.14

Nonaka, I., & Teece, D. J. (Eds.). (2001). *Managing industrial knowledge: Creation, transfer and utilization*. Sage Publications.

Nooteboom, B. (2004). *Inter-firm collaboration, learning and networks: An integrated approach*. London: Routledge.

Norris, P. (2002). The bridging and bonding role of online communities. *The Harvard International Journal of Press/Politics*, *7*(3), 3–13. doi:10.1177/1081180X0200700301

North, D. C. (1990). *Institutions, Institutional Change and Economic Performance*. Cambridge, UK: Cambridge University Press. doi:10.1017/CBO9780511808678

O'Brien, B. (2010). *Water licenses valued at A$2.8 billion traded in Australia's emerging water markets*. Retrieved January 26, 2017, from: http://voxeu.org/article/price-precious-commodity-water-trading-australia

ODell, C., & Grayson, C. J. (1998). If only we knew what we know: Identification and transfer of internal best practice. *California Management Review*, *40*(3), 154–174. doi:10.2307/41165948

OECD. (2010). *Pricing Water Resources and Water and Sanitation Services*. OECD. doi:10.1787/9789264083608-en

OECD. (2012). *OECD Environmental Outlook to 2050: The Consequences of Inaction*. Retrieved from: https://www.oecd.org/env/indicators-modelling-outlooks/49846090.pdf

OECD. (2015). *In it together: Why Less Inequality Benefits All*. doi:10.1787/9789264235120-en

Ojo, M. (2013). *Why the traditional principal agent theory may no longer apply to concentrated ownership systems and structures.* MPRA Paper No. 50832. Covenant University. Online at http://mpra.ub.uni-muenchen.de/50832/

Okabe, T. (2004). Sinopsis del acuerdo de asociación económica entre México y Japón. *México y la Cuenca del Pacífico, 7*(23).

Oktar, S., & Yüksel, S. (2015). Bankacılık Krizlerinin Erken Uyarı Sinyalleri [İlker Parasız Özel Eki]. *Türkiye Üzerine Bir Uygulama, İstanbul Ticaret Üniversitesi Sosyal Bilimler Dergisi, 14*(28), 37–53.

Olson, J. C., & Jacoby, J. (1974). Measuring multi-brand loyalty. *Advances in Consumer Research. Association for Consumer Research (U. S.), 1*(1), 447–448.

Ong'ayo, E. (2012). *Employee perception of the influence of strategic planning on organization performance at the ministry of Foreign affairs, Kenya* (Unpublished MBA thesis). University of Nairobi, Nairobi, Kenya.

Orden, D. (1996). *Agricultural Interest Group Bargaining over the North American Free Trade Agreement.* The Political Economy of Trade Protection.

O'Reilly, C. A., & Tushman, M. L. (2004). The Ambidextrous Organization. *Harvard Business Review, 82*(4), 74–82. PMID:15077368

Ornelas, E. (2005). Endogenous Free Trade Agreements and the Multilateral Trading System. *Journal of International Economics, 67*(2), 471–497. doi:10.1016/j.jinteco.2004.11.004

Orr, J. E. (1996). *Talking about machines: An ethnography of a modern job.* Ithaca, NY: Cornell University Press.

Osiyevskyy, O. (2014). *Established Firms' Strategic Decision Making when Faced with Low-End Disruptive Innovation* (Doctoral dissertation). University of Calgary. Available from: http://theses.ucalgary.ca/jspui/handle/11023/1412

Osiyevskyy, O., & Dewald, J. (2015a). Explorative versus exploitative business model change: The cognitive antecedents of firm-level responses to disruptive innovation. *Strategic Entrepreneurship Journal, 9*(1), 58–78. doi:10.1002/sej.1192

Osiyevskyy, O., & Dewald, J. (2015b). Inducements, impediments, and immediacy: Exploring the cognitive drivers of small business managers intentions to adopt business model change. *Journal of Small Business Management, 53*(4), 1011–1032. doi:10.1111/jsbm.12113

Osiyevskyy, O., & Zargarzadeh, M. A. (2015). Business model design and innovation in the process of expansion and growth of global enterprises. In A. A. Camillo (Ed.), *Global Enterprise Management: New Perspectives on Challenges and Future Development* (Vol. 1, pp. 115–133). New York, NY: Palgrave McMillan. doi:10.1057/9781137429599.0011

Osterwalder, A., & Pigneur, Y. (2010). *Business Model Generation: A Handbook for Visionaries, Game Changers, and Challengers.* John Wiley & Sons.

Oxley, J. E. (1999). Institutional environment and the mechanisms of governance: The impact of intellectual property protection on the structure of inter-firm alliances. *Journal of Economic Behavior & Organization, 38*(3), 283–309. doi:10.1016/S0167-2681(99)00011-6

Parente, S. (2003). O mercado financeiro e a população de baixa renda. *Comissão Econômica para América Latina e o Caribe – CEPAL.*

Parker, D. B. (1998). *Fighting Computer Crime–A New Framework for Protecting Information.* Wiley Computer Publishing.

Parker, M., & Welch, E. W. (2013). Professional networks, science ability and gender determinants of three types of leadership in academic science and engineering. *The Leadership Quarterly, 24*(2), 332–348. doi:10.1016/j.leaqua.2013.01.001

Patterson, E. (2010). What's Wrong with the WTO: Rethinking the Institutional Design. *Global Policy Journal.* Retrieved February, 3, 2017, from http://www.globalpolicyjournal.com/articles/world-economy-trade-and-finance/what%C3%A2%E2%82%AC%E2%84%A2s-wrong-wto-rethinking-institutional-design

Patton, M. Q. (2002). *Qualitative research.* London, UK: John Wiley and Sons Limited.

Payne, J. W., Bettman, J. R., & Johnson, E. J. (1992). Behavioral decision research: A constructive processing perspective. *Annual Review of Psychology, 43*(1), 87–131. doi:10.1146/annurev.ps.43.020192.000511

Pellicano, M., Perano, M., & Casali, G. L. (2016). The Enterprise Relational View (ERV): Exploring future in Strategic Management. In *Book of Abstract of fourth B.S. Lab International Symposium on Governing Business Systems, Theories and Challenges for Systems Thinking in Practice* (pp. 105-109). Vilnius, Lithuania: Mykolas Romeris University, B.S. Lab.

Peluffo, A. (2015). Foreign direct investment, productivity, demand for skilled labour and wage inequality: An analysis of Uruguay. *World Economy, 38*(6), 962–983. doi:10.1111/twec.12180

Peng, M. (2010). *Estrategia global. In Governing the corporation around the world* (2nd ed.). CENAGE Learning.

Peng, M. W. (2005). From China strategy to global strategy. *Asia Pacific Journal of Management, 22*(2), 123–141. doi:10.1007/s10490-005-1251-3

Peng, M. W., & Heath, P. S. (1996). The growth of the firm in planned economies in transformation: Institutions, organizations and strategic choice. *Academy of Management Review, 21*, 492–528.

Peng, M., & Zhou, J. (2005). How network strategies and institutional transitions evolve in Asia. *Asia Pacific Journal of Management, 22*(4), 321–336. doi:10.1007/s10490-005-4113-0

Peng, Y., Dashdeleg, A., & Chih, H. L. (2014). National Culture and Firm's CSR Engagement: A Cross-Nation Study. *Journal of Marketing and Management, 5*(1), 38–49.

Perano, M. (2010). Il Project Management. In M. Pellicano & M. V. Ciasullo (Eds.), *La visione strategica dell'impresa* (pp. 321–355). Torino, Italy: Giappichelli Editore.

Pereira, A. A. (2004). The Suzhou Industrial Park Experiment: The case of China-Singapore governmental collaboration. *Journal of Contemporary China, 13*(38), 173–193. doi:10.1080/1067056032000151391

Perkmann, M., & Spicer, A. (2010). What are business models? Developing a theory of performative representations. *Research in the Sociology of Organizations, 29*, 269–279. doi:10.1108/S0733-558X(2010)0000029020

Phills, J., Deiglmeier, K., & Miller, D. (2008). Rediscovering Social Innovation. *Social Innovation Review, 6*(4), 1–11.

Pickett, K. E., & Wilkinson, R. G. (2007). Child wellbeing and income inequality in rich societies: Ecological cross sectional study. *British Medical Journal, 335*(7629), 1080–1085. doi:10.1136/bmj.39377.580162.55 PMID:18024483

Pickett, K. E., & Wilkinson, R. G. (2015). Income inequality and health: A causal review. *Social Science & Medicine, 128*, 316–326. doi:10.1016/j.socscimed.2014.12.031 PMID:25577953

Pigg, K. E., & Crank, L. D. (2004). Building community social capital: The potential and promise of information and communications technologies. *The Journal of Community Informatics, 1*(1), 58–73.

Pinto, J. K., & Prescott, J. E. (1988). Variations in critical success factors over the stages in the project life cycle. *Journal of Management, 14*(1), 5–18. doi:10.1177/014920638801400102

Pinto, J. K., & Slevin, D. P. (1988). Critical success factors across the project life cycle. *Project Management Journal, 19*(3), 67–75.

Pisano, G. (1989). Using equity participation to support exchange: Evidence from the biotechnology industry. *Journal of Law Economics and Organization, 6*(1), 109–126.

Pitt, M., & Goyal, S. (2004). Business continuity planning as a facilities management tool. *Facilities, 22*(3/4), 87–99. doi:10.1108/02632770410527824

PMI (Project Management Institute). (2009). *Practice Standard for Project Risk Management*. Philadelphia: PMI.

Pol, E., & Ville, S. (2009). Social innovation: Buzz word or enduring term? *Journal of Socio-Economics, 38*(6), 878–885. doi:10.1016/j.socec.2009.02.011

Popchev, I. (2016). *Shest Temi po Upravlenie na Riska* [Six Themes on Risk Management]. Bulgarian Academy of Science. Retrieved from: http://is.iinf.bas.bg/I_Popchev/6_themes_on_Risk_Management.pdf

Porter, M. (1987). The State of Strategic Thinking. *Economist*, (May): 23.

Porter, M. (1990). *The Competitive Advantage of Nations*. New York: Free Press. doi:10.1007/978-1-349-11336-1

Porter, M. E. (1980). *Competitive Strategy*. New York: Free Press.

Portes, A. (1998). Social capital: Its origins and applications in modern sociology. *Annual Review of Sociology, 24*(1), 1–24. doi:10.1146/annurev.soc.24.1.1

Potter, P. (2014). *Building a Stronger, More Strategic BCM Program*. Retrieved March 10, 2016, from https://www.continuityinsights.com/article/2014/02/building-stronger-more-strategic-bcm-program

Prahalad, C. K., & Hart, S. L. (2002). The fortune at the bottom of the pyramid. *Strategy+Business, 26*(First Quarter), 2-14.

Prahalad, C. K. (2005). *The Fortune at the Bottom of the Pyramid*. Upper Saddle River, NJ: Wharton School Pub.

Preble, J. (1997). Integrating the Crisis Management Perspective into the Strategic Management Process. *Journal of Management Studies, 34*(5), 769–791. doi:10.1111/1467-6486.00071

Preece, J. (2002). Supporting community and building social capital. *Communications of the ACM, 45*(4), 37–39. doi:10.1145/505248.505269

PricewaterhouseCoopers. (2009). *Navigation: Managing commodity risk through market uncertainty* (in-depth discussion). Retrieved from: https://www.pwc.com/gx/en/metals/pdf/managing-commodity-risk.pdf

Pritish, K., & Sakiru, A. (2013, April). Foreign Shareholding and Productivity Spillover: A Firm-Level Analysis of Indian Manufacturing. *IUP Journal of Applied Economics, 12*(2), 7–24.

Proctor, T. (1997). Establishing a strategic direction: A review. *Management Decision, 35*(2), 143–154. doi:10.1108/00251749710160304

Promexico. (n.d.). *México y sus tratados de libre comercio*. Retrieved from http://www.promexico.gob.mx/comercio/mexico-y-sus-tratados-de-libre-comercio-con-otros-paises.html

Protiviti. (2013). *Guide to Business Continuity Management* (3rd ed.). Retrieved April 15, 2016, from https://www.protiviti.com/en-US/Documents/Resource-Guides/Guide-to-BCM-Third-Edition-Protiviti.pdf

Putnam, R. (1995). Bowling alone: Americas declining social capital. *Journal of Democracy, 6*(1), 65–78. doi:10.1353/jod.1995.0002

Putnam, R. (2000). *Bowling alone: The collapse and revival of American community*. New York, NY: Simon Schuster. doi:10.1145/358916.361990

Qizilbash, M. (1997). Needs, incommensurability and well-being. *Review of Political Economy*, *9*(3), 261–276. doi:10.1080/751245295

Quan-Haase, A., & Wellman, B. (2004). How does the Internet affect social capital. *Social Capital and Information Technology*, *113*, 135–113.

Quoquab, F., Mohd. Yasin, N., & Abu Dardak, R. (2014). A qualitative inquiry of multi-brand loyalty: Some propositions and implications for mobile phone service providers. *Asia Pacific Journal of Marketing and Logistics*, *26*(2), 250–271. doi:10.1108/APJML-02-2013-0023

Raber, D., & Budd, J. M. (2003). Information as sign: Semiotics and information science. *The Journal of Documentation*, *59*(5), 507–522. doi:10.1108/00220410310499564

Rai, A., Borah, S., & Ramaprasad, A. (1996). Critical success factors for strategic alliances in the information technology industry: An empirical study. *Decision Sciences*, *7*(1), 141–155. doi:10.1111/j.1540-5915.1996.tb00848.x

Ramírez Bonilla, J. J. (2014). La relación comercial México-Japón, diez años después de la firma del Acuerdo parael Fortalecimiento de Asociación Económica. *Comercio Exterior*, *64*(6).

Rausch, A., Lindquist, T., & Steckel, M. (2014). A Test of US versus Germanic European Ethical Decision-Making and Perceptions of Moral Intensity: Could Ethics Differ within Western Culture? *Journal of Managerial Issues*, *26*(3), 259.

Rayner, S. (1990). *Risk in cultural perspective: Acting under uncertainty*. Norwell, MA: Klewer. doi:10.1007/978-94-015-7873-8_7

Reficco, E., & Marquez, P. (2009). Inclusive networks for building BOP markets. *Business & Society*, *48*, 140–172.

Regner, P. (2003). Strategy creation in the periphery: Inductive versus deductive strategy making. *Journal of Management Studies*, *40*(1), 57–82. doi:10.1111/1467-6486.t01-1-00004

Reis, T., & Clohesy, S. (1999). *Unleashing New Resources and Entrepreneurship for the Common Good: A Scan, Synthesis and Scenario for Action*. Battle Creek, MI: WK Kellogg Foundation.

Renn, O., & Rohrmann, B. (2000). Cross-cultural risk perception: State and challenges. In O. Renn et al. (Eds.), *Cross-Cultural Risk Perception. A survey on empirical studies*. Dordrecht, The Netherlands: Kluwer. doi:10.1007/978-1-4757-4891-8_6

Ren, X. (2013). *Urban China*. Cambridge, UK: Polity.

Report, C. P. (2011). *Best Buy Children's Foundation Youth Grants*. Academic Press.

Resick, C. J., Martin, G. S., Keating, M. A., Dickson, M. W., Kwan, H. K., & Peng, C. (2011). What ethical leadership means to me: Asian, American, and European perspectives. *Journal of Business Ethics*, *101*(3), 435–457. doi:10.1007/s10551-010-0730-8

Resnick, P. (2001). Beyond bowling together: Sociotechnical capital. *HCI in the New Millennium*, *77*, 247–272.

Rest, J. R. (1986). *Moral development: Advances in research and theory*. New York: Praeger publishers.

Reynolds, P., Bosma, N., Autio, E., Hunt, S., De Bono, N., Servais, I., & Chin, N. et al. (2005). Global Entrepreneurship Monitor: Data collection design and implementation 1998–2003. *Small Business Economics*, *24*(3), 205–231. doi:10.1007/s11187-005-1980-1

Rhein, C. (1998). Globalisation, social change and minorities in metropolitan Paris: The emergence of new class patterns. *Urban Studies (Edinburgh, Scotland)*, *35*(3), 429–447. doi:10.1080/0042098984844

Richards, M. D. (1986). *Setting Strategic Goals and Objectives* (2nd ed.). St. Paul, MN: West Publishing.

Ritchie, B. W. (2004). Chaos, Crises and Disasters: A strategic Approach to Crisis Management in the Tourism Industry. *Tourism Management, 25*(6), 669–683. doi:10.1016/j.tourman.2003.09.004

Roberts, D., & Woods, C. (2005). Changing the world on a shoestring: The concept of social entrepreneurship. *University of Auckland Business Review, 19*(1), 45–51.

Robertson, D. C. (2002). Business ethics across cultures. In The Blackwell handbook of cross-cultural management, (pp. 361-392). Blackwell Business.

Roberts, P. W. F., & Stephens, M. (2009). Implementing Business Continuity Management in a Distributed Organisation. *The Business Continuity Journal, 3*(4), 16–26.

Robinson, D. T. (2003). Strategic alliances and the boundaries of the firm. *Review of Financial Studies, 21*(2), 649–681. doi:10.1093/rfs/hhm084

Robinson, J. A., Mair, J., & Hockerts, K. (Eds.). (2009). *International Perspectives of Social Entrepreneurship*. London: Palgrave.

Rockart, J. F. (1979). Chief executives define their own data needs. *Harvard Business Review, 57*(2), 81–93. PMID:10297607

Rodrigues, C. A. (1997). Developing expatriates cross-cultural sensitivity: Cultures where your cultures OK is really not OK. *Journal of Management Development, 16*(9), 690–702. doi:10.1108/02621719710190211

Rodrik, D. (1999). Where did all the growth go? External shocks, social conflict, and growth collapses. *Journal of Economic Growth, 4*(4), 385–412. doi:10.1023/A:1009863208706

Ronald, D. D. (1961). Management Information Crisis. *Harvard Business Review, 39*(5), 111–121.

Rosenberg, J. M. (1983). Dictionary of Business and Management (2nd ed.). A Wiley-Inderscience Publication.

Rossi, B. (2013). Exchange rate predictability. *Journal of Economic Literature, 51*(4), 1063–1119. doi:10.1257/jel.51.4.1063

Rost, J. C. (1997). Moving from individual to relationship: A post-industrial paradigm of leadership. *The Journal of Leadership Studies, 4*(4), 3–16. doi:10.1177/107179199700400402

Rowat, C. (2003). LRN supply-chain risk and vulnerability workshop. *Logistics & Transports Focus, 5*(2), 68–69.

Roxas, M. L., & Stoneback, J. Y. (2004). The importance of gender across cultures in ethical decision-making. *Journal of Business Ethics, 50*(2), 149–165. doi:10.1023/B:BUSI.0000022127.51047.ef

Rüede, D., & Lurtz, K. (2012). *Mapping the Various Meanings of Social Innovation: Towards a Differentiated Understanding of an Emerging Concept*. EBS University.

Ruefli, T. W., Collins, J. M., & Lacugna, J. R. (1999). Risk measures in strategic management research: Auld lang syne? *Strategic Management Journal, 20*(2), 167–194. doi:10.1002/(SICI)1097-0266(199902)20:2<167::AID-SMJ9>3.0.CO;2-Q

Ruggles, R. (1998). The state of the notion: Knowledge management in practice. *California Management Review, 40*(3), 80–89. doi:10.2307/41165944

Rugman, A. M., & Almodovar, P. (2011). The born global illusion and the regional nature of international business. The future of foreign direct investment and the multinational enterprise (pp. 251-269). London: Emerald Group Publishing.

Rugman, A. M. (1981). *Inside the Multinationals: The Economics of Internal Markets*. New York: Columbia University Press.

Rugman, A. M., & Verbeke, A. (1992). A note on the transnational solution and the transaction cost theory of multinational strategic management. *Journal of International Business Studies, 23*(4), 761–771. doi:10.1057/palgrave.jibs.8490287

Rugman, A. M., & Verbeke, A. (2005). Towards a theory of regional multinationals: A transaction cost approach. *Management International Review, 45*(S1), 5–17.

Saint-Onge, H., & Wallace, D. (2012). *Leveraging communities of practice for strategic advantage.* Butterworth-Heinemann.

Saka-Helmhout, A., Deeg, R., & Greenwood, R. (2016). The MNE as a challenge to institutional theory: Key concepts, recent developments and empirical evidence. *Journal of Management Studies, 53*(1), 1–11. doi:10.1111/joms.12172

Salacuse, J. W. (1998). Ten ways that culture affects negotiating style: Some survey results. *Negotiation Journal, 14*(3), 221–240. doi:10.1111/j.1571-9979.1998.tb00162.x

Sambharya, R., & Musteen, M. (2014). Institutional environment and entrepreneurship: An empirical study across countries. *Journal of International Entrepreneurship, 12*(4), 314–330. doi:10.1007/s10843-014-0137-1

Sampson, R. C. (2004). The cost of misaligned governance in R&D alliances. *Journal of Law Economics and Organization, 20*(2), 484–526. doi:10.1093/jleo/ewh043

Santos, F. M. (2012). A Positive Theory of Social Entrepreneurship. *Journal of Business Ethics, 111*(3), 335–351. doi:10.1007/s10551-012-1413-4

Santos, J., Doz, Y., & Williamson, P. (2004). Is your innovation process global? *Sloan Management Review, 45*(4), 31–37.

Sassen, S. (2001). The global city: New York, London, Tokyo (2nd ed.). Princeton, NJ: Princeton University Press, 2nd.

Sassen, S. (1999). Global financial centers. *Foreign Affairs, 45*(1), 75–87. doi:10.2307/20020240

Sassen, S. (Ed.). (1995). *On concentration and centrality in the global city.* Cambridge, UK: Cambridge UP. doi:10.1017/CBO9780511522192.005

Sassen, S. (Ed.). (2005). Global cities and diasporic networks: Vol. 1. *Overviews and Topics.* New York: Springer.

Saunders, M., Lewis, P., & Thornhill, A. (2015). *Research Methods for Business Students* (7th ed.). Essex, UK: Pearson.

Sautet, F. (2013). Local and Systemic Entrepreneurship: Solving the Puzzle of Entrepreneurship an Economic Development. *Entrepreneurship Theory and Practice, 37*(2), 387–402. doi:10.1111/j.1540-6520.2011.00469.x

Savage, M. (2002). Business continuity planning. *Work Study, 51*(5), 254–261. doi:10.1108/00438020210437277

Savaş, İ., & Can, İ. (2011). Euro-Dolar Paritesi ve Reel Döviz Kuru'nun İMKB 100 Endeksi'ne Etkisi. *Eskişehir Osmangazi Üniversitesi İİBF Dergisi, 6*(1), 323–339.

Schein, E. H. (1981). Improving face-to-face relationships. *Sloan Management Review, 22*(2), 43–52. PMID:10250386

Schein, E. H. (2004). *Organizational culture and leadership* (3rd ed.). San Francisco: Jossey-Bass.

Schoenhoff, D. M. (1993). The barefoot expert. Westport, CT: Greenwood Press.

Schollhammer, H. (1973). Strategies and Methodologies in International Business and Comparative Management Research. *Management International Review, 13*(6), 17–31.

Schott, J., & Hufbauer, G. (2007). NAFTA Revisited. *Policy Options.* Retrieved February, 17, 2017, from http://archive.irpp.org.ezproxy.library.dal.ca/po/archive/oct07/schott.pdf

Schraeder, M., Tears, R., & Jordan, M. (2005). Organizational Culture in Public Sector Organization: Promoting Change through Training and Leading by Example. *Leadership and Organization Development Journal*, *26*(6), 492–502. doi:10.1108/01437730510617681

Schuiling, I., & Kapferer, J. N. (2004). Executive insights: real differences between local and international brands: strategic implications for international marketers. *Journal of International Marketing*, *12*(4), 97–112. doi:10.1509/jimk.12.4.97.53217

Schumpeter, J. (1934). *The Theory of Economic Development*. Harvard University Press.

Schumpeter, J. (1942). *Capitalism, Socialism and Democracy*. New York: Harper and Row.

Schwalbe, K. (2007). *Information Technology Project Management* (5th ed.). Boston, MA: Thomson Course Technology.

Schwartz, M. A. (1998). NAFTA and the Fragmentation of Canada. *The American Review of Canadian Studies*, *28*(1-2), 1–2, 11–28. doi:10.1080/02722019809481561

Schwartzman, S., & Brock, C. (Eds.). (2005). *Os desafios da educação no Brasil*. Rio de Janeiro: Nova Fronteira.

Schwarz, M., & Thompson, M. (1990). *Divided we stand: Redefining politics, technology, and social choice*. Philadelphia: University of Pennsylvania Press.

Scott, W. R. (1995). *Institutions and organizations*. Newbury Park, CA: Sage.

Secretaría de Economía de México. (2002). *Grupo de Estudio México-Japón sobre el Fortalecimiento de las Relaciones Económicas Bilaterales, Informe Final*. Retrieved from http://www.economia.gob.mx/files/japon_completo.pdf

Secretaría de Economía. (2015). *Consulta en línea: Abril 2015*. Retrieved from http://www.economia.gob.mx/comunidad-negocios/comercio-exterior/tlcacuerdos/asia-pacifico

Seelos, C., & Mair, J. (2007). Profitable business models and market creation in the context of deep poverty: A strategic view. *The Academy of Management Perspectives*, *21*(4), 49–63. doi:10.5465/AMP.2007.27895339

Selden, S., & Perks, S. (2007). How a structured BIA aligned business continuity management with Gallaher's strategic objectives. *Journal of Business Continuity & Emergency Planning*, *1*(4), 348–355.

Self, D. R., Armenakis, A. A., & Schraeder, M. (2007). Organizational change content, process, and context: A simultaneous analysis of employee reactions. *Journal of Change Management*, *7*(2), 211–229. doi:10.1080/14697010701461129

Senge, P. M. (1993). Transforming the practice of management. *Human Resource Development Quarterly*, *4*(1), 5–32. doi:10.1002/hrdq.3920040103

Senor, D., & Singer, S. (2009). *Start-up nation: The story of Israel's economic miracle*. McClelland & Stewart.

Sephton, P. (2001). Forecasting recessions: Can we do better on MARS? *Review - Federal Reserve Bank of St. Louis*, *83*(2), 39–49.

Sexton, D. W., Lemak, C. H., & Wainio, J. A. (2014). Career inflection points of women who successfully achieved the hospital CEO position. *Journal of Healthcare Management*, *59*(5), 367–383. PMID:25647957

Shah, S. T. H., Jamil, R. A., Shah, T. A., & Kazmi, A. (2015). Critical Exploration of Prescriptive and Emergent approaches to Strategic management: A review paper. *International Journal of Information. Business and Management*, *7*(3), 91.

Shane, S., Locke, E., & Collins, C. J. (2003). Entrepreneurial motivation. *Human Resource Management Review*, *13*(2), 257–279. doi:10.1016/S1053-4822(03)00017-2

Shapiro, J. M., Ozanne, J. L., & Saatcioglu, B. (2008). An interpretive examination of the development of cultural sensitivity in international business. *Journal of International Business Studies*, *39*(1), 71–87. doi:10.1057/palgrave.jibs.8400327

Sharp, B., & Sharp, A. (1997). Loyalty programs and their impact on repeat-purchase loyalty patterns. *International Journal of Research in Marketing*, *14*(5), 473–486. doi:10.1016/S0167-8116(97)00022-0

Sheaffer, Z., & Mano-Negrin, R. (2003). Executives Orientations as Indicators of Crisis Management Policies and Practices. *Journal of Management Studies*, *40*(2), 573–606. doi:10.1111/1467-6486.00351

Shen, J., & Wu, F. (2012). The development of master-planned communities in Chinese suburbs: A case study of Shanghas Thames town. *Urban Geography*, *33*(2), 183–203. doi:10.2747/0272-3638.33.2.183

Shenkar, O., & Zeira, Y. (1992). Role Conflict and Role Ambiguity of Chief Executive Officers in International Joint Ventures. *Journal of International Business Studies*, *23*(1), 55–75. doi:10.1057/palgrave.jibs.8490259

Shepard, M. (2012). *Il nuovo standard internazionale di project management: ISO 21500. Il Project Manager, 11.*

Sherriff, L. (2006, October 26). *Intel to close Cambridge research centre*. Retrieved October 3, 2016, from http://www.theregister.co.uk/2006/10/26/intel_closing_cambridge/

Shih, H. Y. (2006). Network characteristics of drive tourism destinations: An application of network analysis in tourism. *Tourism Management*, *27*(5), 1029–1039. doi:10.1016/j.tourman.2005.08.002

Shin, S. K., Gopal, R. D., Sanders, G. L., & Whinston, A. B. (2004). Global software piracy revisited. *Communications of the ACM*, *47*(1), 103–107. doi:10.1145/962081.962088

Shlamao, B., & Karsten, J. (2012). Ethical Leadership: Lessons from Moses. *Journal of Management Development*, *31*(9), 962–973. doi:10.1108/02621711211259901

Short, J. C., Moss, T. W., & Lumpkin, G. T. (2009). Research in social entrepreneurship: Past contributions and future opportunities. *Strategic Entrepreneurship Journal*, *3*(2), 161–194. doi:10.1002/sej.69

Sider, S. (2007). *Handbook to life in Renaissance Europe*. New York, NY: Oxford University Press.

Siegel, J. (2007). Contingent political capital and international alliances: Evidence from South Korea. *Administrative Science Quarterly*, *52*(4), 621–666. doi:10.2189/asqu.52.4.621

Siggelkow, N. (2007). Persuasion with case studies. *Academy of Management Journal*, *50*(1), 20–24. doi:10.5465/AMJ.2007.24160882

Simpson, K. (2013). *Embedding Culture Into BCM*. Retrieved April 10, 2016, from: http://www.continuityinsights.com/arti cles/2013/03/embedding-culture-bcm

Şimşek, M. (2004). Türkiye'de Reel Döviz Kurunu Belirleyen Uzun Dönemli Etkenler. *Cumhuriyet Üniversitesi İktisadi ve İdari Bilimler Fakültesi Dergisi*, *5*(2), 1–24.

Sine, W. D., Haveman, H. A., & Tolbert, P. S. (2005). Risky Business? Entrepreneurship in the New Independent-Power Sector. *Administrative Science Quarterly*, *50*(2), 200–232. doi:10.2189/asqu.2005.50.2.200

Singhapakdi, A., & Marta, J. K. (2005). Comparing marketing students with practitioners on some key variables of ethical decisions. *Marketing Education Review*, *15*(3), 13–25. doi:10.1080/10528008.2005.11488918

SIP Website. (2010). Retrieved November 15, 2014, from http://www.sipac.gov.cn/english

Sirkin, H. L. (2012). Nafta: After 20 Years, We're Not There Yet. *Bloomberg BusinessWeek*. Retrieved February, 14, 2017, from http://www.businessweek.com/articles/2012-08-01/nafta-20-years-and-not-there-yet

Sithole, K. (2011). *A Strategy-as-Practice perspective: A case study of a business unit within a multinational engineering organization* (Unpublished Doctoral Dissertation). Stellenbosch University.

Sivadas, E., & Baker-Prewitt, J. L. (2000). An examination of the relationship between service quality, customer satisfaction, and store loyalty. *International Journal of Retail & Distribution Management, 28*(2), 73–82. doi:10.1108/09590550010315223

Skeldon, R. (2011). *China: An Emerging Destination for Economic Migration.* Retrieved from http://www.migrationpolicy.org/article/china-emerging-destination-economic-migration/

Smallbone, D., & Welter, D. (2001). The distinctiveness of entrepreneurship in transition economies. *Small Business Economics, 16*(4), 249–263. doi:10.1023/A:1011159216578

Smeeding, T. M. (2005). Public policy, economic inequality, and poverty: The United States in comparative perspective. *Social Science Quarterly, 86*(5), 955–983. doi:10.1111/j.0038-4941.2005.00331.x

Smith, A. (1759). The Theory of Moral Sentiments. Cambridge, UK: Cambridge University Press.

Smith, D. J. (2002). *Business Continuity Management: Good Practices Guidelines.* London, UK: The Business Continuity Institute.

Smith, D. J. (2013). Organisational Resilience and BCM. *Institute of Business Continuity Management,* 1-33. Retrieved April 03, 2016, from: https://www.continuitycentral.com/organisational resilienceandBCM.pdf

Solomon, R. C. (1991). Business ethics, literacy, and the education of the emotions. *The Ruffin Series in Business Ethics,* 188-211.

Solt, F. (2008). Economic inequality and democratic political engagement. *American Journal of Political Science, 52*(1), 48–60. doi:10.1111/j.1540-5907.2007.00298.x

Solt, F. (2009). Standardizing the world income inequality database. *Social Science Quarterly, 90*(2), 231–242. doi:10.1111/j.1540-6237.2009.00614.x

Spencer, L. M. (1955). 10 problems that worry presidents. Harvard Business Review, 33(6), 75-83.

Spilimbergo, A., Londono, J. L., & Szekely, M. (1999). Income distribution, factor endowments, and trade openness. *Journal of Development Economics, 59*(1), 77–101. doi:10.1016/S0304-3878(99)00006-1

Squire, K., & Johnson, C. (2000). Supporting distributed communities of practice with interactive television. *Educational Technology Research and Development, 48*(1), 23–43. doi:10.1007/BF02313484

Starr, R., Newfrock, J., & Delurey, M. (2003). Enterprise Resilience: Managing Risk in the Networked Economy. *Booz & Company, 30.* Retrieved April 07, 2016, from: http://www.strategy-business.com/article/8375?gko=1c92d

Steinberg, R. H. (1997). Trade-Environment Negotiations in the EU, NAFTA, and WTO: Regional Trajectories of Rule Development. *The American Journal of International Law, 91*(2), 231–267. doi:10.2307/2954211

Stephen, A., Stumpf, P. E., & Chaudhry, L. P. (2011). Fake: Can business stanch the flow of counterfeit products? *The Journal of Business Strategy, 32*(2), 4–12. doi:10.1108/02756661111109725

Stephens, M. (2010). Locating Chinese Urban Housing Policy in an International Context. *Urban Studies (Edinburgh, Scotland), 47*(14), 2965–2982. doi:10.1177/0042098009360219 PMID:21114090

Steven, J. (2001). *Emergence: The Connected Lives of Ants, Brains, Cities and software.* New York: Scribner.

Stinchcombe, A. L. (1965). Organizations and social structure. In J. G. March (Ed.), *Handbook of Organizations*. Chicago: Rand-McNally.

Storey, D. (1994). *Understanding the Small Business Sector*. London: Routledge.

Suchman, L. (1987). *Plans and situated actions: The problem of human-machine communication*. New York, NY: Cambridge University Press.

Suchman, M. C. (1995). Managing legitimacy: Strategic and institutional approaches. *Academy of Management Review, 20*, 571–610.

Sun, Q., Tong, W., & Yu, Q. (2002). Determinants of Foreign Direct Investment across China. *Journal of International Money and Finance, 21*(1), 79-113. Retrieved from http://www.elsevier.com/wps/find/journaldescription.cws_home/30443/description#description

Sustainability Accounting Standards Board. (2016). *Climate Risk* (Technical Bulletin TB001-10182016). Retrieved from: http://using.sasb.org/wp-content/uploads/2016/10/Climate-Risk-Technical-Bulletin-101816.pdf

Sutton, M. (2005). Japanese Trade Policy and 'Economic Partnership Agreements': A New Conventional Wisdom. *Ritsumeikan Annual Review of International Studies, 4*, 113-135.

Suzhou Singapore International School. (n.d.). Retrieved October 13, 2015, from www.ssis-suzhou.net

Swati, M., & Lochan, D. R. (2015). Transformational leadership and employee creativity. *Management Decision, 53*(5), 894–910. doi:10.1108/MD-07-2014-0464

Swinyard, W. R., Rinne, H., & Kau, A. K. (2013). The Morality of Software Piracy: A Cross-Cultural Analysis. In *Citation Classics from the Journal of Business Ethics* (pp. 565–578). Springer Netherlands. doi:10.1007/978-94-007-4126-3_29

Tallman, S., & Chacar, A. S. (2011). Knowledge accumulation and dissemination in MNEs: A practice-based framework. *Journal of Management Studies, 48*(2), 278–304.

Tang, J., Kacmar, K. M., & Busenitz, L. (2012). Entrepreneurial alertness in the pursuit of new opportunities. *Journal of Business Venturing, 27*(1), 77–94. doi:10.1016/j.jbusvent.2010.07.001

Taylor, P. J. (2004). *World city network: A global urban analysis*. London: Routledge.

Taylor, S. E. (1975). On inferring ones attitudes from ones behavior: Some delimiting conditions. *Journal of Personality and Social Psychology, 31*(1), 126–131. doi:10.1037/h0076246

Tharp, B. M. (2009). *Defining "Culture" and "Organizational Culture": From Anthropology to the Office*. Haworth. Retrieved from: http://www.haworth.com/en-us/knowledge/workplace-library/documents/defining-culture-and-organizationa-culture_5.pd

Thayer, C., Bruno, J., & Remorenko, M. (2013). Using data analytics to identify revenue at risk. *Healthcare Financial Management Magazine, 67*(9), 72-80. Retrieved from: https://www2.deloitte.com/content/dam/Deloitte/us/Documents/life-sciences-health-care/us-lshc-hfm.pdf

The deal is done. (1999). *The Economist*. Retrieved February, 7, 2017, from http://www.economist.com/node/8765752?zid=307&ah=5e80419d1bc9821ebe173f4f0f060a07

The Dublin Statement on Water and Sustainable Development. (1992). *Principle No.1*. Retrieved from: http://www.un-documents.net/h2o-dub.htm

Thomas, J. (2000). Making sense of project management. In R. Lundin, F. Hartman, & C. Navarre (Eds.), *Projects as business constitutents and guiding motives*. London, UK: Elsevier Academic. doi:10.1007/978-1-4615-4505-7_3

Thompson, J. (2008). Social enterprise and social entrepreneurship: where have we reached?: a summary of issues and discussion points. *Social Enterprise Journal, 4*(2), 149–161. doi:10.1108/17508610810902039

Thompson, J. D., & MacMillan, I. C. (2010). Business models: Creating new markets and societal wealth. *Long Range Planning, 43*(2), 291–307. doi:10.1016/j.lrp.2009.11.002

Tkearney. (2012). *2012 Global Cities Index and Emerging Cities Outlook*. Retrieved from https://www.atkearney.com/research-studies/global-cities-index

Tominc, P., & Rebernik, M. (2007). Growth aspirations and cultural support for entrepreneurship: A comparison of post-socialist countries. *Small Business Economics, 28*(2-3), 239–255. doi:10.1007/s11187-006-9018-x

Tomohara, A., & Yokota, K. (2011). Foreign direct investment and wage inequality: Is skill upgrading the culprit? *Applied Economics Letters, 18*(8), 773–781. doi:10.1080/13504851.2010.491448

Tonchia, S. (2007). *Il Project Management*. Milano, Italy: Il Sole24Ore.

Tonchia, S., & Nonino, F. (2007). *Il Project Management*. Milano, Italy: Il Sole24Ore

Trevino, L. K. (1986). Ethical decision making in organizations: A person-situation interactionist model. *Academy of Management Review, 11*(3), 601–617.

Trevino, L. K., & Nelson, A. K. (2011). *Managing business ethics: Straight talk about how to do it right*. Hoboken, NJ: Wiley.

Tsai, P. L. (1995). Foreign direct-investment and income inequality: Further evidence. *World Development, 23*(3), 469–483. doi:10.1016/0305-750X(95)00136-Z

Tsalikis, J., & Nwachukwu, O. (1988). Cross-cultural business ethics: Ethical beliefs difference between blacks and whites. *Journal of Business Ethics, 7*(10), 745–754. doi:10.1007/BF00411021

Tsui, A. S., Nifadkar, S. S., & Ou, A. Y.Amy Yi Ou. (2007). Cros-snational, cross-cultural organizational behavior research: Advances, gaps, and recommendations. *Journal of Management, 33*(3), 426–478. doi:10.1177/0149206307300818

Tunay, K. B. (2001). Türkiye'de paranın gelir dolaşım hızlarının MARS yöntemiyle tahmini. *ODTÜ Gelişme Dergisi, 28*(3-4).

Tunay, K. B. (2011). Türkiye'de Durgunlukların MARS Yöntemi ile Tahmini ve Kestirimi, *Marmara Üniversitesi İ.İ.B.F. Dergisi, 30*(1), 71–91.

Tung, R. L. (1984). *Business negotiations with the Japanese*. Lexington, MA: Lexington Books.

Tversky, A., & Kahneman, D. (1974). Judgment under uncertainty: Heuristics and biases. *Science, 185*(4157), 1124–1131. doi:10.1126/science.185.4157.1124 PMID:17835457

UNCTAD. (2010). *Informe sobre las Inversiones en el Mundo 2010. Panorama General, Invertir en una economía de bajo carbono*. United Nations Publication. Retrieved from http://unctad.org/es/Docs/wir2010overview_sp.pdf

UNCTAD. (2014). *Foreign direct investment shows uneven growth in Latin America and the Caribbean, says UNCTAD Report. Informe de prensa*. United Nations Publication. Retrieved from http://unctad.org/en/pages/PressRelease.aspx?OriginalVersionID=187

UNWTO. (2015). *Tourism Highlights*. Retrieved from http://www.eunwto.org.bibproxy.ulpgc.es/doi/book/10.18111/9789284416899

UrbanWater Consortium. (2014). *The European Water Market Analysis* (Deliverable 1.1). Retrieved from http://urbanwater-ict.eu/wp-content/uploads/2014/08/URBANWATER-D1.1-The-European-Water-Market-Analysis.pdf

Uslaner, E. M. (1998). Social capital, TV and the Mean World: Trust, optimism, and civic participation. *Political Psychology*, *19*(3), 441–467. doi:10.1111/0162-895X.00113

Uslaner, E. M. (2008). *Corruption, Inequality, and the Rule of Law: The Bulging Pocket Makes the Easy Life*. New York, NY: Cambridge University Press. doi:10.1017/CBO9780511510410

Uslaner, E. M., & Brown, M. (2005). Inequality, trust, and civic engagement. *American Politics Research*, *33*(6), 868–894. doi:10.1177/1532673X04271903

Vaara, E., & Whittington, R. (2012). Strategy-as-practice: Taking social practices seriously. *The Academy of Management Annals*, *6*(1), 285–336. doi:10.1080/19416520.2012.672039

Valliere, D. (2013). Towards a schematic theory of entrepreneurial alertness. *Journal of Business Venturing*, *28*(3), 430–442. doi:10.1016/j.jbusvent.2011.08.004

Van den Berg, C. (2015). Pricing Municipal Water and Wastewater Services in Developing Countries: Are Utilities Making Progress Toward Sustainability? In A. Dinar, V. Pochat, & J. Albiac-Murillo (Eds.), *Pricing Experiences and Innovations* (pp. 443–462). doi:10.1007/978-3-319-16465-6_23

Van Reenen, J. (2011). Wage inequality, technology and trade: 21st century evidence. *Labour Economics*, *18*(6), 730–741. doi:10.1016/j.labeco.2011.05.006

VanDeusen, J. (1996). Honing an effective tool for community improvement. *Journal for Quality and Participation*, *19*(5), 54–63.

Varela-Ortega, C., Sumpi, J. M., Garrido, A., Blanco, M., & Iglesias, E. (1998). Water pricing policies, public decision making and farmers response: Implication for water policy. *Agricultural Economics*, *19*(1-2), 193–202. doi:10.1016/S0169-5150(98)00048-6

Vargas-Hernandez, J. G., Guerra García, E., Bojórquez Gutiérrez, A., & Bojórquez Gutierrez., F. (2014). *Gestión Estratégica de Organizaciones*. Ediciones Insumisos Latinoamericanos.

Varyani, M. E., & Khammar, M. (2010). *A Review of Strategy-as-Practice and the Role of Consultants and Middle Managers* (Unpublished Master's Thesis). Chalmers University of Technology, Göteborg, Sweden.

Velásquez, T. A. (2012). The science of corporate social responsibility (CSR): Contamination and conflict in a mining project in the southern Ecuadorian Andes. *Resources Policy*, *37*(2), 233–240. doi:10.1016/j.resourpol.2011.10.002

Veolia Water. (2014a). *Finding the Blue Path for a Sustainable Economy* (White Paper). Retrieved from: http://www.veolianorthamerica.com/sites/g/files/dvc596/f/assets/documents/2014/10/19979IFPRI-White-Paper.pdf

Veolia Water. (2014b). *The True Cost of Water. An Economic Evaluation of Risks and Benefits Related to Water Use* [Brochure]. Retrieved from: http://www.veoliawatertechnologies.com/sites/g/files/dvc471/f/assets/documents/2014/10/32794True-Cost-of-Water-2014-LR_0.pdf

Verbeke, A. (2013). *International Business Strategy*. Cambridge University Press. doi:10.1017/CBO9781139227162

Verbeke, A., & Yuan, W. (2010). A strategic management analysis of ownership advantages in the eclectic paradigm. *Multinational Business Review*, *18*(2), 89–108. doi:10.1108/1525383X201000012

Verbeke, A., Zargarzadeh, A., & Osiyevskyy, O. (2014). Internationalization theory, entrepreneurship and international new ventures. *Multinational Business Review, 22*(3), 246–269. doi:10.1108/MBR-06-2014-0023

Vermeulen, F., & Barkema, H. (2001). Learning through acquisitions. *Academy of Management Journal, 44*(3), 457–476. doi:10.2307/3069364

Vidal, L.-A., & Marle, F. (2008). Understanding project complexity: Implications on project management. *Kybernetes, 37*(8), 1094–1110. doi:10.1108/03684920810884928

Viswanathan, M. (2007). Understanding Product and Market Interactions in Subsistence marketplaces: A study in Southern India. *Advances in International Management, 20*, 21–57. doi:10.1016/S1571-5027(07)20002-6

Viswanathan, M., Sridharan, S., & Ritchie, R. (2010). Understanding consumption and entrepreneurship in subsistence marketplaces. *Journal of Business Research, 63*(6), 570–581. doi:10.1016/j.jbusres.2009.02.023

Vitell, S. J., Nwachukwu, S. L., & Barnes, J. H. (2013). The effects of culture on ethical decision-making: an application of Hofstede's typology. In *Citation Classics from the Journal of Business Ethics* (pp. 119–129). Springer Netherlands. doi:10.1007/978-94-007-4126-3_6

Vodniy Codex Rossiiskoy Federaciy (Water Code of the Russian Federation). (2006). Retrieved on January 27, 2017, from: http://pravo.gov.ru/proxy/ips/?docbody=&nd=102107048

Vossen, G. (2009). Web 2.0: A buzzword, a serious development, just fun, or what?. *SECRYPT*, 33-40.

Walbank, F. W., Astin, A. E., Fredriksen, M. W., & Ogilvie, R. M. (1989). *The Cambridge ancient history VII. 2: The rise of Rome to 220 BC*. Retrieved from http://www.jstor.org/stable/41655564

Walks, R. A. (2001). The social ecology of the post-fordist/global city? Economic restructuring and socio-spatial polarisation in the Toronto urban region. *Urban Studies (Edinburgh, Scotland), 38*(3), 407–447. doi:10.1080/00420980120027438

Wallace, D., & Saint-Onge, H. (2003, May). Leveraging communities of practice. *Intranets: Enterprise Strategies and Solutions*, 1-5.

Walsh, J. J., & Kanter, J. (1988). Toward more successful project management. *Journal of Systems Management,* 16–21.

Wang, C.-H. (2003). Taipei as a global city: A theoretical and empirical examination. *Urban Studies (Edinburgh, Scotland), 40*(2), 309–334. doi:10.1080/00420980220080291

Wang, L., Fang, L., & Hipel, K. (2008). Basin-wide cooperative water resources allocation. *European Journal for Operational Researches, 190*(3), 798–817. doi:10.1016/j.ejor.2007.06.045

Warford, J. (1997). Marginal Opportunity Cost Pricing for Municipal Water Supply (Special Paper). Ottawa, Canada: International Development Research Centre. Retrieved from https://idl-bnc.idrc.ca/dspace/bitstream/10625/32032/7/118129.pdf

Warner, J., Butterworth, J., Wegerich, K., Mora Vallejo, A., Martinez, G., Gouet, C., & Visscher, J. T. (2009). *Corruption Risks in Water Licensing with Case Studies from Chile and Kazakhstan* (SWH Report No. 27). Retrieved from: http://www.swedishwaterhouse.se/wp-content/uploads/1259084220867Corruption-Risks-in-Water-Licensing.pdf

Water Accounting Standards Board. (2012). *Preparation and Presentation of General Purpose Water Accounting Reports* (Australian Water Accounting Standard 1). Retrieved from: http://www.bom.gov.au/water/standards/documents/awas1_v1.0.pdf

Water as a Financial Risk. (n.d.). Retrieved January 27, 2017, from: http://www.swedishwaterhouse.se/en/cluster-groups/water-financial-risk/

Weaver, D. B., & Lawton, L. J. (2011). Visitor loyalty at a private South Carolina protected area. *Journal of Travel Research, 50*(3), 335–346. doi:10.1177/0047287510362920

Weaver, G. R. (1998). The Process of Reentry. In G. R. Weaver (Ed.), *Culture, Communication, and Conflict: Readings in Intercultural Relations* (2nd ed.; pp. 230–238). Simon & Schuster Publishing.

Webb, J., Tihanyi, L., Ireland, D., & Sirmon, D. (2009). You say illegal, I say legitimate: Entrepreneurship in the informal economy. *Academy of Management Review, 34*(3), 492–510. doi:10.5465/AMR.2009.40632826

Weick, K. E. (1987). Organizational Culture as a Source of High Reliability. *California Management Review, 29*(2), 112–127. doi:10.2307/41165243

Wei, Y. D., Yuan, F., & Liao, H. (2013). Spatial Mismatch and Determinants of Foreign and Domestic Information and Communication Technology firms in Urban China. *The Professional Geographer, 65*(2), 247–264. doi:10.1080/00330 124.2012.679443

Wei, Y. H. D., Liefner, I., & Miao, C.-H. (2011). Network configurations and R&D activities of the ICT industry in Suzhou. *Geoforum, 42*(4), 484–495. doi:10.1016/j.geoforum.2011.03.005

Wei, Y. H. D., Luo, J., & Zhou, Q. (2010). Location decisions and network configurations of foreign investment in urban China. *The Professional Geographer, 62*(2), 264–283. doi:10.1080/00330120903546684

Wei, Y. H. D., Lu, Y., & Chen, W. (2009). Globalizing regional development in Sunan, China: Does Suzhou Industrial Park fit a neo-Marshallian district model? *Regional Science, 43*(3), 409–427.

Wellman, B. (1982). Studying personal communities. In P. Marsden & N. Lin (Eds.), *Social structure and network analysis*. Beverly Hills, CA: Sage Publications.

Wellman, B. (1997). An electronic group is virtually a social network. In S. Kiesler (Ed.), *Culture of the Internet* (pp. 179–205). Mahwah, NJ: Lawrence Erlbaum.

Wellman, B., Hasse, A., Witte, J., & Hampton, K. (2001). Does the Internet increase, decrease, or supplement social capital? Social networks, participation, and community commitment. *The American Behavioral Scientist, 45*(3), 436–459. doi:10.1177/00027640121957286

Wenger, E. (1998). *Communities of practice: Learning, meaning, and identity*. Cambridge University Press. doi:10.1017/CBO9780511803932

Wenger, E., McDermott, R. A., & Snyder, W. (2002). *Cultivating communities of practice: A guide to managing knowledge*. Harvard Business Press.

Werner, B., & Collins, R. (2012). *Towards efficient use of water resources in Europe*. Retrieved January 15, 2017, from: http://www.enorasis.eu/uploads/files/Water%20Governance/2.EEAreport.pdf

Werner, S. (2002). Recent developments in international management research: A review of 20 top management journals. *Journal of Management, 28*(3), 277–305. doi:10.1177/014920630202800303

Westley, F. R. (1990). Middle managers and strategy: Micro-dynamics of inclusion. *Strategic Management Journal, 11*(5), 337–351. doi:10.1002/smj.4250110502

Whalley, J. (1998). *Why Do Countries Seek Regional Trade Agreements?* National Bureau of Economic Research. Retrieved February, 14, 2017, from Google Scholar http://www.nber.org/chapters/c7820

White, A. (2009). *From comfort zone to performance management*. White & MacLean Publishing.

White, D., & Fortune, J. (2002). Current practice in project management – an empirical study. *International Journal of Project Management, 20*(1), 1–11. doi:10.1016/S0263-7863(00)00029-6

Whittington, R. (2001). Learning to strategise: problems of practice. *SKOPE Research Paper, 20*.

Whittington, R. (1996). Strategy as Practice. *Long Range Planning, 29*(5), 731–735. doi:10.1016/0024-6301(96)00068-4

Whittington, R. (2003). The work of strategizing and organizing: For a practice perspective. *Strategic Organization, 1*(1), 119–127. doi:10.1177/14761270030011001221

Whittington, R. (2004). Strategy after Modernism: Recovering Practice. *European Management Review, 1*(1), 62–68. doi:10.1057/palgrave.emr.1500006

Whittington, R. (2006a). Completing the practice turn in strategy research. *Organization Studies, 27*(5), 613–634. doi:10.1177/0170840606064101

Whittington, R., Jarzabkowski, P., Mayer, M., Mounoud, E., Nahapiet, J., & Rouleau, L. (2003). Taking strategy seriously: Responsibility and reform for an important social practice. *Journal of Management Inquiry, 12*(4), 396–409. doi:10.1177/1056492603258968

Williams, C. C., & Youssef, Y. (2013). Evaluating the Gender Variations in Informal Sector Entrepreneurship: Some Lessons From Brazil. *Journal of Developmental Entrepreneurship, 18*(1), 16p. doi:10.1142/S1084946713500040

Williamson, O. E. (1979). Transaction-cost economics: The governance of contractual relations. *The Journal of Law & Economics, 22*(2), 233–261. doi:10.1086/466942

Williamson, O. E. (1981). The economics of organization the transaction cost approach. *American Journal of Sociology, 87*(3), 548–577. doi:10.1086/227496

Williamson, O. E. (1985). *The Economic Institutions of Capitalism: Firms, Markets, Relational Contracting*. New York, NY: Free Press.

Williams, T. M. (1999). The need for new paradigms for complex projects. *International Journal of Project Management, 17*(5), 269–273. doi:10.1016/S0263-7863(98)00047-7

Wilson, D., & Purushothaman, R. (2003). *Dreaming with BRICs: the path to 2050. Global Economics Paper 99*. Goldman Sachs.

Wines, W. A., & Napier, N. K. (1992). Toward an understanding of cross-cultural ethics: A tentative model. *Journal of Business Ethics, 11*(11), 831–841. doi:10.1007/BF00872361

Wirick, D. W. (2009). *Public-Sector Project Management*. Hoboken, NJ: Wiley. doi:10.1002/9780470549131

Wiseman, R., & Gomez-Mejia, L. R. (1998). A behavioral agency model of risk taking. *Academy of Management Review, 23*(1), 133–153.

Wojcik, J. (2002). Continuity Management Requires Commitment. *Business Insurance, 36*(17), 18.

Wolff, E. N. (2015). Inequality and rising profitability in the United States, 19472012. *International Review of Applied Economics, 29*(6), 741–769. doi:10.1080/02692171.2014.956704

Wong, W. (2009). The Strategic Skills of Business Continuity Manager: Putting Business Continuity Management into Corporate Long-term Planning. *Journal of Business Continuity & Emergency Planning, 4*(1), 62–68. PMID:20378494

Woodman, P. (2008, March). Business Continuity Management. Chartered Management Institute, 1-17.

Woolcock, M. (1998). Social capital and economic development: Toward a theoretical synthesis and policy framework. *Theory and Society, 27*(2), 151–208. doi:10.1023/A:1006884930135

Woolcock, M. (2001). Microenterprise and social capital: A framework for theory, research, and policy. *Journal of Socio-Economics, 30*(2), 193–198. doi:10.1016/S1053-5357(00)00106-2

Woolcock, M., & Narayan, D. (2001). Social capital: Implications for development theory, research and policy. *The World Bank Research Observer, 15*(2), 225–249. doi:10.1093/wbro/15.2.225

World Tourism Organization (2014). *Panorama OMT del turismo internacional.* Author.

World Trade Organization. (2013a) *Key developments in 2011 a snapshot Table 1.1 [Excel spreadsheet].* Retrieved October, 30, 2017, from http://www.wto.org/english/res_e/statis_e/its2012_e/its12_world_trade_dev_e.htm

World Trade Organization. (2013b). *Merchandise trade by a selected group of economies 2001-2011 Table A4* [Excel spreadsheet]. Retrieved October, 30, 2017, from http://www.wto.org/english/res_e/statis_e/its2012_e/its12_appendix_e.htm

World Trade Organization. (2013c). *Regional Trade Agreements-RTA Database.* Retrieved October, 30, 2017, from http://rtais.wto.org/UI/PublicAllRTAList.aspx

World Trade Organization. (2017a). *Understanding the WTO: Basics The GATT years: from Havana to Marrakesh.* Retrieved February, 2, 2017, from http://www.wto.org/english/thewto_e/whatis_e/tif_e/fact4_e.htm

World Trade Organization. (2017b). *10 benefits of the WTO trading system.* Retrieved February, 2, 2017 from http://www.wto.org/english/thewto_e/whatis_e/10ben_e/10b00_e.htm

World Trade Organization. (2017c). *Understanding the WTO: Members and Observers.* Retrieved February, 2, 2017, from http://www.wto.org/english/thewto_e/whatis_e/tif_e/org6_e.htm

World Trade Organization. (2017d). *Regional Trade Agreements.* Retrieved February, 2, 2017, from http://www.wto.org/english/tratop_e/region_e/region_e.htm

World Trade Organization. (2017e). *RTA Database Free Trade Agreements* [Excel Spreadsheet]. Retrieved February, 2, 2017, from http://rtais.wto.org/UI/PublicSearchByCrResult.aspx

World Trade Organization. (2017f). *Doha Round: What are they negotiating?* Retrieved February, 7, 2017, from http://www.wto.org/english/tratop_e/dda_e/update_e.htm

World Trade Organization. (2017g). *Understanding the WTO: Who we are.* Retrieved February, 2, 2017, from http://www.wto.org/english/thewto_e/whatis_e/who_we_are_e.htm

World Trade Organization. (2017h). *World Trade Organization...In Brief.* Retrieved February, 2, 2017, from http://www.wto.org/english/res_e/doload_e/inbr_e.pdf

World Trade Organization. (2017i). *Understanding the WTO.* Retrieved February, 2. 2017, from http://www.wto.org/english/thewto_e/whatis_e/tif_e/understanding_e.pdf

World Trade Organization. (2017m). *Statistics Database: Trade Profiles.* Retrieved February, 2, 2017, from http://stat.wto.org/CountryProfile/WSDBCountryPFReporter.aspx?Language=E

World Travel & Tourism Council. (2015). *Economic Impact Analysis.* Retrieved from http://www.wttc.org/research/economic-research/economic-impact-analysis/

Wu, F. (2001). Chinas recent urban development in the process of land and housing marketisation and economic globalisation. *Habitat International, 25*(3), 273–289. doi:10.1016/S0197-3975(00)00034-5

Wu, F. (Ed.). (2006). *Globalization and China's new urbanism*. Oxon, UK: Routledge.

Wu, F., Zhang, F., & Webster, C. (2013). Informality and the Development and Demolition of Urban Villages in the Chinese Peri-urban Area. *Urban Studies (Edinburgh, Scotland)*, *50*(10), 1919–1934. doi:10.1177/0042098012466600

Wu, J. Y., & Hsu, C. C. (2012). Foreign direct investment and income inequality: Does the relationship vary with absorptive capacity? *Economic Modelling*, *29*(6), 2183–2189. doi:10.1016/j.econmod.2012.06.013

Wurbs, R. A. (2005). Modeling river/reservoir system management, water allocation, and supply reliability. *Journal of Hydrology (Amsterdam)*, *300*(1-4), 100–113. doi:10.1016/j.jhydrol.2004.06.003

Xu, D. & Meyer, K. (2012). Linking Theory and Context: Strategy Research in Emerging Economies. *Journal of Management Studies*.

Yang, D. L., & Sonmez, M. (2007). Economic and Cultural Impact on Intellectual Property Violations: A Study of Software Piracy. *Journal of World Trade*, *41*, 731–750.

Yang, Y. R., & Hsia, C. J. (2007). Spatial clustering and organizational dynamics of transborder production networks: A case study of Taiwanese information-technology companies in the Greater Suzhou Area, China. *Environment & Planning A*, *39*(6), 1346–1363. doi:10.1068/a38156

Yeh, Y. C., Huang, L. Y., & Yeh, Y. L. (2011). Knowledge management in blended learning: Effects on professional development in creativity instruction. *Computers & Education*, *56*(1), 146–156. doi:10.1016/j.compedu.2010.08.011

Yim, C. K., & Kannan, P. (1999). Consumer behavioral loyalty. *Journal of Business Research*, *44*(2), 75–92. doi:10.1016/S0148-2963(97)00243-9

Yip, G. S., Loewe, P. M., & Yoshino, M. Y. (1988). How to take your company to the global market. *The Columbia Journal of World Business*, *23*(4), 37–48.

Yoo, C. W., Sanders, G. L., Rhee, C., & Choe, Y. C. (2014). The effect of deterrence policy in software piracy cross-cultural analysis between Korea and Vietnam. *Information Development*, *30*(4), 342–357. doi:10.1177/0266666912465974

Yuan, Y. C., Zhao, X., Liao, Q., & Chi, C. (2013). The use of different information and communication technologies to support knowledge sharing in organizations: From e-mail to micro-blogging. *Journal of the American Society for Information Science and Technology*, *64*(8), 1659–1670. doi:10.1002/asi.22863

Yüksel, S. (2016a). Türkiye'de Cari İşlemler Açığının Belirleyicileri: Mars Yöntemi ile Bir İnceleme. *Bankacılar Dergisi*, *96*, 102–121.

Yüksel, S. (2016b). *Bankacılık Krizlerinin Erken Uyarı Sinyalleri: Türkiye Üzerine Bir Uygulama*. Akademisyen Kitabevi.

Yuksel, S., Dincer, H., & Hacioglu, U. (2015). CAMELS-based Determinants for the Credit Rating of Turkish Deposit Banks. *International Journal of Finance & Banking Studies*, *4*(4), 1–17.

Zafaroni, E.R. (1997). *Manual de Direito Penal Brasileiro: Parte Geral*. São Paulo: RT.

Zahedi, F. (1987). Reliability of information systems based on the critical success factors—Formulation. *Management Information Systems Quarterly*, *11*(2), 187–203. doi:10.2307/249362

Zaheer, A., McEvily, B., & Perrone, V. (1998). Does trust matter? Exploring the effects of interorganizational and interpersonal trust on performance. *Organization Science*, *9*(2), 141–159. doi:10.1287/orsc.9.2.141

Zahra, S. A. (1989). Executive values and the ethics of company politics: Some preliminary findings. *Journal of Business Ethics*, *8*(1), 15–29. doi:10.1007/BF00382013

Zahra, S. A. (2005). A theory of international new ventures: A decade of research. *Journal of International Business Studies*, *36*(1), 20–28. doi:10.1057/palgrave.jibs.8400118

Zahra, S. A., Gedajlovic, E., Neubaum, D. O., & Shulman, J. M. (2009). A typology of social entrepreneurs: Motives, search processes and ethical challenges. *Journal of Business Venturing, 24*(5), 519–532. doi:10.1016/j.jbusvent.2008.04.007

Zahra, S. A., Rawhouser, H. N., Bhawe, N., Neubaum, D. O., & Hayton, J. C. (2008). Globalization of social entrepreneurship opportunities. *Strategic Entrepreneurship Journal*, *2*(2), 117–131. doi:10.1002/sej.43

Zetland, D. (2011). Global Water Tariffs Continue Upward Trend. *Global Water Intelligence, 12*(9), 35-40. Retrieved from: https://www.globalwaterintel.com/global-water-intelligence-magazine/12/9/market-profile/global-water-tariffs-continue-upward-trend

Zhang, L.-Y. (2014). Dynamics and Constraints of State-led Global City Formation in Emerging Economies: The Case of Shanghai. *Urban Studies (Edinburgh, Scotland)*, *51*(6), 1162–1178. doi:10.1177/0042098013495577

Zhao, H. X., Luo, Y. D., & Suh, T. (2004). Transaction cost determinants and ownership-based entry mode choice: A meta-analytical review. *Journal of International Business Studies*, *35*(6), 524–544. doi:10.1057/palgrave.jibs.8400106

Zhao, S. X. B., & Zhang, L. (2007). Foreign direct investment and the formation of global city-regions in China. *Regional Studies*, *41*(7), 979–994. doi:10.1080/00343400701281634

Zhou, Y. (2013). Time and spaces of China's ICT industry. In P. Cooke, G. Searle, & K. O'Connor (Eds.), *The economic geography of the IT industry in the Asia Pacific region* (pp. 68–85). Oxon, UK: Routledge.

Zietlow, J. T. (2002). Releasing a new wave of social entrepreneurship. *Nonprofit Management & Leadership, 13*(1), 85–90. doi:10.1002/nml.13107

Zott, C., & Amit, R. (2010). Business model design: An activity system perspective. *Long Range Planning, 43*(2), 216–226. doi:10.1016/j.lrp.2009.07.004

Zott, C., & Amit, R. (2013). The business model: A theoretically anchored robust construct for strategic analysis. *Strategic Organization, 11*(4), 403–411. doi:10.1177/1476127013510466

Zott, C., Amit, R., & Massa, L. (2011). The business model: Recent developments and future research. *Journal of Management, 37*(4), 1019–1042. doi:10.1177/0149206311406265

About the Contributors

Angelo Presenza is Assistant Professor in Management at University of Molise (Italy). He has a PhD in Business Management. He has been Visiting in several International Universities such as University of Calgary, Dalhousie University, Huelva University, Universitad de Gran Canarie. He teaches themes mainly related to tourism management and tourism destination governance. He has several previous experiences in European projects as coordinator of local unit ("Strategic support on establishment and development of sustainable structures on quality assurance, international relations and student support services at the newly founded Public University Haxhi Zeka in Kosova" - acronym: SD@UHZ) or member of local units ("Modernizing the 3rd cycle at the University of Prishtina and Developing a PhD Program at the Faculty of Economics"- acronym: MODPhD; "Network for Post Graduate Masters in Cultural Heritage and Tourism Management in Balkan Countries" - acronym: CHTMBAL). In the same topics, he did presentations in National and International Conferences and more recently on smart tourism. He has around 50 publications most of them focused on tourism and related issues.

Lorn Sheehan is Professor of Strategy and Area Coordinator of Strategy for the Rowe School of Business in the Faculty of Management at Dalhousie University. He is also cross appointed to the School of Resource and Environmental Studies and holds a faculty appointment at the University Bayreuth in Germany. Dr. Sheehan has a PhD in Strategy, an MBA in Finance, a Masters Degree in Environmental Design specializing in Planning, and a Bachelor's degree in Science. He teaches in the areas of strategic management and tourism management. His research is related to tourism destination management, stakeholder management, and entrepreneurship.

* * *

Tindara Abbate is Assistant Professor of Business Economics and Management at the University of Messina (Italy). She received Ph.D. in Business Economics and Management of the University of Messina (Italy). She is involved, as presenter and member of scientific committee, in several national and international conferences. She participates to different research projects, as member and scientific coordinator. Her research interests refer to open innovation and open innovation intermediaries; social innovation; market orientation; territorial brand and destination marketing.

Arminda Almeida-Santana is part of the research staff at the University of Las Palmas de Gran Canaria since 2013. She is part of the Institute of Tourism Studies and Economic and Sustainable Development (Tides). Her research interests focus on Loyalty, Branding, Brand Management, Consumer Behavior, Hospitality Marketing, Destination Marketing and Management, Customer Experience and Satisfaction, Social Media and Digital Destinations.

Vernon Bachor (Ph.D. 2008 University of Calgary's Haskayne School of Business) is an Associate Professor for Innovation and Entrepreneurship in the College of Business at Winona State University and a business consultant on research based technology and innovation. He has professional designations as a Project Management Professional (PMP), an Information Systems Professional (ISP), and an Information Technology Certified Professional (ITCP). Vern's research is an interdisciplinary approach to understanding the interrelations of strategy, technology & innovation management, sustainability, technical knowledge diffusion, entrepreneurship, international business, project/program management, and MIS. He has most recently published in California Management Review, Technovation, and Research-Technology Management. He is the Managing Editor for the Journal of Engineering and Technology Management, an international scholarly-refereed research journal that aims to promote the theory and practice of technology, innovation, and engineering management. Vern is also an editorial board member for the International Journal of Knowledge Management and the International Journal of Information Technology Project Management.

Yongjian Bao is an Associate Professor at the Faculty of Management, University of Lethbridge. He earned a PhD in Knowledge Management in 2000 from the University of Southern California, Los Angeles, U.S.A. His research focuses on Trust, Ethics, and Power in TMT Decision Making; Cognitive dimension of organization; Organizational Learning and Tacit Knowledge Acquisition; Organizational Changes and Innovation.

Neeta Baporikar is currently Director/Professor (Business Management) at Harold Pupkewitz Graduate School of Business (HP-GSB), Namibia University of Science and Technology, Namibia. Prior to this she was Head-Scientific Research, with Ministry of Higher Education CAS-Salalah, Sultanate of Oman, Professor (Strategic Management and Entrepreneurship) at IIIT Pune and BITS India. With more than a decade of experience in industry, consultancy and training, she made a lateral switch to research and academics in 1995. Dr. Baporikar holds D.Sc. (Management Studies) USA, PhD in Management, University of Pune INDIA with MBA (Distinction) and Law (Hons.) degrees. Apart from this, she is also an External Reviewer, Oman Academic Accreditation Authority, Accredited Management Teacher, Qualified Trainer, Doctoral Guide and Board Member of Academics and Advisory Committee in accredited B-Schools. Reviewer for international journals, she has to her credit 5 conferred doctorates, several refereed research papers, and authored books in the area of Entrepreneurship, Strategy, Management and Higher Education.

Mario Calabrese, PhD, is an Adjunct Professor of Management at Sapienza University of Rome. His main interests are about strategy, entrepreneurship, innovation and change process in new organisation and Government and Innovation Management: 'Management of Corporate Development Process' (strategy implementation, acquisitions management, financial strategies and valuation). He is a financial, economic and corporate consultant whit a peculiar interest in company strategy. He takes part in research, development and planning of business company studies.

Rossella Canestrino is Assistant Professor at "Parthenope" University of Naples (Italy), where She teaches Firms' Networks and Alliances; Business Ethics and CSR and Quality Management. She is reviewer for the "Journal of Business Ethics"; the "Journal of Sustainable Entrepreneurship and Corporate Social Responsibility" and "Sinergie, Italian Journal of Management". She has been visiting researcher at ESADE Business School (Barcelona) and member of the GRACO research group, actively participating in the studies of knowledge-in-context, of practice-based learning, of knowledge transfer and the use of narratives and rhetoric in economics and management sciences. From 2015 she has been selected as a Track Organizer for IFKAD the International Forum for Knowledge Management. Her research topics are focused on Knowledge Management, Cross-Cultural Management, International networks, and Business Ethics. Among the underlined research fields, Her research activity focus on the way both cultural diversities and collaborative arrangements may foster, or limit cross-border knowledge transfer. She also investigates the role of culture in shaping firms' propensity to social responsibility and to adopt sustainable practices. Accepted visiting researcher at Cracow University of Economics (Poland) She is actually involved in international collaborations and research projects about Social Entrepreneurship and Social Innovation.

Gian Luca Casali has more than ten years' experience in the Hospitality and Tourism industry as a small business owner. This has given him a deep understanding of the issues that industry professionals are facing every day. Fifteen years' experience in the NFP and charity industry by fulfilling different roles (board member, board advisor, club president, young professional's coordinator). His research interests cover Business ethics (Corporate social responsibility ethical Managerial decision making in healthcare industry), Entrepreneurship & Innovation (innovation in the public sector, nascent firms' business ideas, and SMEs business venture), Strategic management and Teaching & Learning (university first years students' expectation, learning and satisfaction of completing higher degree students, study ethics in higher degree, AACSB accreditation and AOL goals). Luca was given two Vice chancellor performance awards, one on excellence in team teaching and the other on in community engagement.

Bice Della Piana holds a PhD in Public Management. She is currently an Assistant Professor at University of Salerno in Italy. Her main research interests are focused on the cultural differences, family business group and institutional perspective on innovation. Her current lines of research include the impact of cultural variables on the firm's governance mechanisms, FBG's governance mechanisms considering the network development research and the influence of family values on the family firms' resilience from a cross-cultural perspective. In addition, she is also working on a research line devoted to multi-cultural team management and dynamics. She has previously published several papers in international journals. She teaches Cross Cultural Management and Strategic Management at undergraduate, graduate and PhD level and she also participates in the X-Culture Project as an instructor. She has also been a visiting scholar at University of Burgos (Spain), at International Business School at Vilnius University (Lithuania) and at Institute for Cross Cultural Management at Florida Institute of Technology (US) where she is also Research Fellow. She is project reviewer for the Italian Ministry of Education, University and Research.

Hasan Dincer is an Associate Professor of finance at Istanbul Medipol University, Faculty of Economics and Administrative Sciences, Istanbul-Turkey. Dr. Dincer has BAs in Financial Markets and Investment Management at Marmara University. He received PhD in Finance and Banking with his thesis entitled "The Effect of Changes on the Competitive Strategies of New Service Development in the Banking Sector". He has work experience in the finance sector as a portfolio specialist and hismajor academic studies focusing on financial instruments, performance evaluation, and economics.He is the executive editor of the International Journal of Finance and Banking Studies (IJFBS) and the founder member of the Society for the Study of Business and Finance (SSBF).

Sinem Ergun studied Beyoğlu Anatolian High School. She graduated from Marmara University, Faculty of Economics and Administrative Sciences, department of Business Administration. She received Master's Degree from Middlesex University. She completed her Ph.D in Management and Organization (in English) at Marmara University, Social Sciences Institute in 2006. Since 2001, she has been member of Marmara University, Faculty of Business Administration, Business Administration (in English) department. Her research and teaching areas include entrepreneurship, strategic management, small business management and research methods in social sciences.

Luis Fernando Escobar is Assistant Professor of International Management and Policy & Strategy at the Faculty of Management, University of Lethbridge, Canada. He completed his PhD at the University of Calgary, Canada. Luis Fernando current research interests are at the intersection of strategy, social factors and multinational companies. Prior to his academic career, he worked in the oil and gas industry in South America.

Gulruh Gurbuz studied at English High School for Girls. She graduated from Marmara University, Faculty of Economics and Administrative Sciences, Department of Business Administration (in English). She received her Master's and PhD degree from Marmara University Social Sciences Institute. Still, she has been a faculty member of Business Administration and Director of Marmara University Social Sciences Institute, member of Marmara University Senate, Head of Management and Organization (in English) Department and supervisor for several MA and PhD programs.

Serkan Gürsoy is assistant professor of business and management science at Beykoz University in Istanbul. He is also currently the director of the R&D and Innovation Center of the same institution. He has a Ph.D. in Science and Technology Policy Studies from Middle East Technical University. Besides his academic and entrepreneurial engagements, he has received grants from various institutions and participated in multinational research projects involving innovation strategies, smart city applications and supply chain networks. His main research fields cover knowledge strategies, innovation literacy and organizational development. His recent work is aimed at combining academic and entrepreneurial endeavors by focusing on the dynamic complexities among ICT, knowledge society, big data analysis and online communities.

Umit Hacioglu is an Associate Professor of finance at Istanbul Medipol University, Faculty of Economics and Administrative Sciences, Istanbul-Turkey. Dr. Hacioglu has BAs in Business and International Business from Beykent University. He received his MBA from Beykent University and his PhD in Finance and Banking from KadirHas University. He has published extensively in major academic journal focusing on financial markets, behavioral finance, performance evaluation, and economics of markets. He edits and serves on several journals related to his core research areas—behavioral finance and financial decision making.

Jeremy Hall (D.Phil., University of Sussex, MBA and B.Sc., Dalhousie University) is the Director of the International Centre for Corporate Social Responsibility (ICCSR) and Chaired Professor of Corporate Social Responsibility/ Sustainable Business at Nottingham University Business School, University of Nottingham. He is also Editor-in-Chief of the Journal of Engineering and Technology Management.

Xhimi Hysa is Assistant Professor of Management, Leadership & Organizational Behavior at Epoka University. He is also the Head of Business Administration Department at the same university. Dr. Hysa has a Bachelor, a Master of Science, and a PhD from Sapienza University of Rome in which he has previously worked as research and teaching assistant. Actually, Dr. Hysa is teaching also as a part time staff at the Department of Management of University of Tirana. His research interests include: service science, systems thinking applied to management, leadership, social business and sustainability, group cohesiveness and conformity.

Guoliang F. Jiang (Ph.D., The University of Western Ontario) is an Associate Professor of International Business at the Sprott School of Business at Carleton University in Canada. His research interests include firm internationalization strategy, international management and corporate social responsibilities. His research has appeared in the Journal of International Management, the Journal of Management Studies, and the Journal of World Business, among others. He serves on the editorial boards of the Journal of International Management and the Canadian Journal of Administrative Sciences. Prior to his academic career, he worked at General Electric and Kao in China.

Hyung Min Kim is a Lecturer in Faculty of Architecture, Building and Planning, The University of Melbourne, Australia. After he received his PhD from the University of Melbourne, he worked for Xian Jiaotong-Liverpool University in Suzhou, China (2013 – 2015) and RMIT University, Melbourne, Australia (2015 - 2016). His research interest is upon economic and spatial dynamics of the Asia-Pacific cities. He has published his research outcomes to international journals such as Cities, Progress in Planning, and Habitat International.

Nathaniel C. Lupton (Ph.D., The University of Western Ontario) is an Assistant Professor of International Management at the University of Lethbridge. His research focuses on internationalization processes of knowledge transfer, location choice, non-market strategy and investment modes. His research has appeared in Academy of Management Perspectives, Journal of World Business, Journal of Knowledge Management, among others. Prior to his academic career, he worked in the telecommunications and information technology industries.

Pierpaolo Magliocca is Assistant Professor at University of Foggia (Italy), where He teaches Operation Management, Marketing and Tourism Management. He is reviewer for "Sinergie, Italian Journal of Management" and member of the Register of auditors for the evaluation of ministerial research programs in the following areas: Competitiveness, Innovation, Research and Development, Marketing, Organization Studies. From 2015 He has been selected as a Track Organizer for IFKAD the International Forum for Knowledge Management. His research interests are focused on Firms Governance, Process Management and International Business. Within the field of Knowledge Management and firms' internationalization process, He focused his attention on the conditions upon which intra-organizational knowledge transfer may occur and corporate learning process may be fostered. With reference to firms' internationalization He also analyzes both risks and opportunities managers face when go abroad. The research activities of Pierpaolo Magliocca are reinforced by his involvement in several academic research projects. Actually he is the scientific coordinator for the Project "Medical Tourism: managerial and legal dynamics", selected for funding by the University of Foggia. He is also business consultant and his professional activity belong to firms' re-organization and process re-engineering.

Stelvia Matos received her PhD in Civil Engineering from the University of Paulo, Brazil. Her research is primarily focused on understanding the complex interactions among social, environmental and economic factors, and specifically how they affect, and/or are affected by innovation dynamics, entrepreneurial behavior and policy development. A large part of Dr. Matos' research concerns the difficult process of responding to technological and social change through innovation, which can be conceptualized as a panacea and paradox - a main driver of social improvement but also the cause of many problems faced by society. Her areas include technological, commercial, organizational and social uncertainties of innovation, life cycle assessment, technical-economic cost modeling and sustainable development innovation. It involves the agriculture, chemical, energy, forestry, and tourism sectors, with field studies performed in Brazil, Bosnia, Canada, China, Italy, the Netherlands, the UK, and the US.

Carolan McLarney is a Full Professor who joined the faculty at Dalhousie as an Assistant Professor of International and Strategic Management in July 1999. She came to Dalhousie from Illinois State University where she taught International and Strategic Management since 1996. She teaches the undergraduate and graduate International Business and Strategic Management courses as well as in the MBA (Financial Services) Program. Her research interests include the interface between small businesses and international business strategy, and the use of strategic alliances. She has published over three-dozen articles in a number of journals, including the Journal of Global Business, Journal of Organizational Change Management, International Journal of Social Economics, Women in Management, The Learning Organization, Journal of Management Education and the New England Journal of Entrepreneurship.

Sergio Moreno Gil is Director of Institutional Relations UNESCO Chair of Tourism Planning and Sustainable Development. ULPGC. Director of marketing and destination development at TIDES Tourism and Sustainable Development Institute. University of Las Palmas de Gran Canaria. In the past, he has worked for Hilton Hotels in Germany; TUI Group Spain, in the quality department; and as a visiting researcher at World Tourism Research Centre (U of Calgary – Canada). He has written more than 20 books and book chapters, 25 international papers (Annals of Tourism Research, Tourism Management, Journal of Travel Research, International Journal of Tourism Research, Tourism Economics, Journal of Vacation Marketing, International Journal of Hospitality and Leisure Marketing, etc.).

James P. Murphy is the Director, Wealth Planning at BMO Nesbitt Burns. He provides high net worth and ultra-high net worth tax and financial advice to advisors and clients. He holds a Bachelor of Commerce from the University of Toronto and a Masters of Business Administration from Dalhousie University. He also holds the following designations:CFP, CIM, FCS, and CIWM.

Ninel Nesheva-Kiosseva received her Master Degree and PhD in University of National and World Economy, Sofia, Bulgaria. Her habilitation is held at the Higher Attestation Commission to the Council of Ministers of Bulgaria. She has published books in finance, environmental and social accounting, economic theory and history. Teaches at the New Bulgarian University, Sofia.

Oleksiy Osiyevskyy is an Assistant Professor of Entrepreneurship & Innovation at the Haskayne School of Business, University of Calgary. His research focuses on the process of development and growth of innovative new ventures and corporate spin-offs, analyzed from the perspectives of entrepreneurship and strategy literature (evolutionary economics, entrepreneurial cognition, Schumpeterian competition). Dr. Osiyevskyy has 13 articles published in academic journals, as well as two book chapters. His academic works have been recognized with the Killam Memorial Scholarship, and by the United States Association for Small Business and Entrepreneurship, and featured in the business press. Dr. Osiyevskyy earned a PhD in Strategic Management from the University of Calgary, Canada, in 2014.

Mirko Perano, Ph.D., is Vice Rector and Director of Department of Management at Reald University of Vlore (ASAR), Albania. In the same institution he is Professor in Management, Dean of "MAT-TOUR", an international Research Group on Management, Technology and Tourism, and Director of "Reald Summer School on Methodology Research". He was Adjunct Professor in Management and Strategic Management at University of Salerno (Italy). He holds a double PhD, one at University of Rome 'La Sapienza' (IT), and one at University of Huelva (ES). He is a member of international research groups in the tourism field at University of Huelva (España) – GEIDETUR (Research Group on Tourism) – and University of Leiria (Portugal) – GITUR (Tourism Research Group). He is editorial board member of the following journal: "Enlightening Tourism: A Pathmaking Journal" (ISSN: 2174-548X) and "International Journal of Markets and Business Systems" (ISSN: 2056-4112). He is co-author of a book in Strategic Management and of several book chapters, journal papers and proceedings in the field of strategic management, tourism, innovation, ethical decision making and value co-creation.

Bruno Silvestre is currently an Associate Professor in the Department of Supply Chain Management, Asper School of Business, University of Manitoba. Previously, he was an Associate Professor and the Chancellor's Research Chair in Sustainable Supply Chain & Innovation Management in the Faculty of Business and Economics, University of Winnipeg. Prior to that, Dr. Silvestre worked as a Research Associate at the Beedie School of Business, Simon Fraser University and a Visiting Research Scholar at SPRU, University of Sussex, UK. Dr. Silvestre's research mainly focuses on two interconnected streams. The first research stream is related to sustainable supply chain management, and more specifically why and how supply chains incorporate sustainability aspects (including environmental and social aspects) into their business practices. The second stream is related to the management of innovation, and how innovation dynamics affect organizations, businesses, industries, operations and supply chains. Dr. Silvestre's research includes articles published in top tier business journals. His research has appeared in journals such as Long Range Planning, Energy Policy, International Journal of Production Economics, International Journal of Production Research, Journal of Management Studies, Journal of Cleaner Production, Business Horizons, Technological Forecasting & Social Change, Production Planning & Control, Technovation, and others. In addition to his academic work, Dr. Silvestre has 13 years of industry experience. His experience has been in manufacturing/operations/supply chain management, business development and project management in the energy, mining, manufacturing and high-tech industries. This 'real world' experience has provided him with powerful insights, industry contacts and interpersonal skills that he has since used in the classroom, consulting projects and in research activities.

Begum Teraman studied at Gelibolu Anatolian High School. She graduated from Istanbul Kultur University, department of International Relations (in English) with an honour degree. She received MBA (in English) degree from Yasar University Institute of Social Sciences in 2011. She worked for Okan University as a part-time lecturer and worked for Istanbul Aydın University as a Research Assistant. Then, she worked for FMV Isik University as a research assistant in the department of Business Administration.

José G. Vargas-Hernández has a Ph.D. in Public Administration and a Ph.D. in Organizational Economics. He has undertaken studies in Organisational Behaviour and has a Master of Business Administration, published four books and more than 200 papers in international journals and reviews (some translated to English, French, German, Portuguese, Farsi, Chinese, etc.) and more than 300 essays in national journals and reviews. He has obtained several international Awards and recognition.

Murat Yücelen, PhD, is assistant professor of management, organization and strategy at Yeditepe University Faculty of Commerce, where he is also chair of the Tourism and Hotel Management Department. Dr. Yücelen has traveled extensively for international conferences and multipartner EU funded projects, also spending one semester as visiting professor at University of Molise in Termoli (IT). He was previously a team member during the establishment of two higher education institutions, where he led vocational and executive MBA programs, while also designing and delivering e-learning courses. His teaching duties involve the areas of strategic management, organization theory, behavioral sciences, tourism and corporate governance. His research interests include knowledge management, organizational learning, governance and ethics, workplace behavior and relevant industrial implementations of these fields of study.

Serhat Yüksel is an assistant professor at Istanbul Medipol University, School of Business and Management Sciences, Istanbul, Turkey.

Index

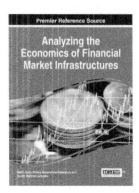

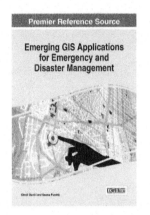 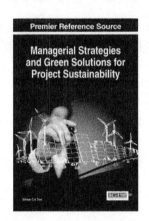